Frommer's®
Paris 2011

by Darwin Porter & Danforth Prince

Wiley Publishing, Inc.

Published by:
WILEY PUBLISHING, INC.
111 River St.
Hoboken, NJ 07030-5774

ISBN 978-0-470-61441-9 (paper); 978-0-470-87716-6 (paper); 978-0-470-90126-7 (ebk); 978-0-470-92903-2 (ebk)

Editors: Elizabeth Heath and Jennifer Polland
Production Editor: Jonathan Scott
Cartographer: Elizabeth Puhl
Photo Editors: Cherie Cincilla and Alden Gewirtz
Cover Photo Editor: Richard Fox
Production by Wiley Indianapolis Composition Services
Front cover photo: Cafe table in Montmartre, Paris ©Kevin George / Alamy Images.
Back cover photo: *Left:* Cakes at Angelina Tea Room, Paris ©Will Salter / Lonely Planet Images / Alamy Images. *Middle:* Crowds sitting on the steps in front of Basilique du Sacre Coeur, Montmartre, Paris ©Manfred Gottschalk / Lonely Planet Images. *Right:* Notre Dame North Rose Window 13th century stained glass window depicting the Virgin Mary encircled by figures, Paris ©Cosmo Condina Western Europe / Alamy Images.

For information on our other products and services or to obtain technical support, please contact our Customer Care Department within the U.S. at 877/762-2974, outside the U.S. at 317/572-3993 or fax 317/572-4002.

Wiley also publishes its books in a variety of electronic formats. Some content that appears in print may not be available in electronic formats.

Manufactured in the United States of America

5 4 3 2 1

CONTENTS

List of Maps vi

1 THE BEST OF PARIS 1

The Most Unforgettable Travel Experiences 2

The Best Splurge Hotels 5

The Best Moderately Priced Hotels 7

The Most Unforgettable Dining Experiences 9

The Best Things to Do for Free (or Almost) 12

The Best Museums 15

The Best Neighborhoods for Getting Lost 17

2 PARIS IN DEPTH 20

Paris Today 21

Looking Back at Paris 24

DATELINE 24

Art & Architecture 35

Paris in Popular Culture: Books, Films & Music 42

Eating & Drinking in Paris 49

3 PLANNING YOUR TRIP TO PARIS 54

When to Go 55

PARIS CALENDAR OF EVENTS 56

Entry Requirements 60

Getting There & Getting Around Paris 62

UNDER THE CHANNEL 64

DISCOUNT TRANSIT PASSES 67

Money & Costs 68

Staying Healthy 72

Crime & Safety 72

Specialized Travel Resources 74

Responsible Tourism 76

Special-Interest Trips & Escorted General-Interest Tours 77

GENERAL RESOURCES FOR RESPONSIBLE TRAVEL 77

Staying Connected 79

4 SUGGESTED PARIS ITINERARIES 82

Arrondissements in Brief 83

The Best of Paris in 1 Day 89

The Best of Paris in 2 Days 94

The Best of Paris in 3 Days 97

5 WHERE TO STAY 102

Best Hotel Bets 105
On the Right Bank 107
FAMILY-FRIENDLY HOTELS 117

On the Left Bank 132
Near the Airports 149

6 WHERE TO DINE 151

Best Dining Bets 152
Food for Thought 153
DINING SAVOIR-FAIRE 155
Restaurants by Cuisine 156
On the Right Bank 158
A PARISIAN PIQUE-NIQUE 170

FAMILY-FRIENDLY RESTAURANTS 186
On the Left Bank 190
IN PURSUIT OF THE PERFECT PARISIAN PASTRY 206
The Top Cafes 209

7 EXPLORING PARIS 213

Attractions by Arrondissement 214
The Top Attractions: Arc de Triomphe to the Tour Eiffel 216
TIME OUT AT THE TOWER 239
The Major Museums 241
Specialty Museums 250
The Major Churches 258
Architectural & Historic Highlights 263

Literary Landmarks 268
Parks & Gardens 270
Cemeteries 274
Paris Underground 278
Sports & Recreation 279
Neighborhood Highlights 282
Especially for Kids 289
Organized Tours 292

8 STROLLING AROUND PARIS 296

Walking Tour 1: Montmartre 297
Walking Tour 2: The Latin Quarter 303

Walking Tour 3: The Marais 308

9 SHOPPING IN PARIS 317

The Shopping Scene 318
Shopping A to Z 321

FOOD MARKETS 333
THE SCENT OF A PARISIAN 339

10 PARIS AFTER DARK 343

The Performing Arts 344

The Club & Music Scene 348

*AFTER-DARK DIVERSIONS:
DIVES, DRAG & MORE* 355

Bars, Pubs & Clubs 356

Gay & Lesbian Bars & Clubs 362

Literary Haunts 363

11 SIDE TRIPS FROM PARIS 365

Versailles 366

A RETURN TO FADED GLORY 372

The Forest & Chateau of
Rambouillet 375

The Cathedral at Chartres 377

Giverny 381

Disneyland Paris 384

*FOR THOSE WITH ANOTHER DAY:
WALT DISNEY STUDIOS* 386

Fontainebleau 389

12 FAST FACTS 395

Fast Facts: Paris 395

Airline Websites 399

13 USEFUL TERMS & PHRASES 401

French Language Terms 401

Basic Menu Terms 411

Index 413

Accommodations Index 420

Restaurant Index 421

LIST OF MAPS

The Best of Paris in One Day   91

The Best of Paris in Two Days   95

The Best of Paris in Three Days   99

Where to Stay on the Right Bank (1–4, 9, 11–12 & 18e)   108

Where to Stay on the Right Bank (8 & 16–17e)   126

Where to Stay on the Left Bank (5–6 & 13–14e)   134

Where to Stay on the Left Bank (7 & 15e)   147

Where to Dine on the Right Bank (1–4, 9–12 & 18–19e)   160

Where to Dine on the Right Bank (8 & 16–17e)   178

Where to Dine on the Left Bank (5–6 & 13–14e)   192

Where to Dine on the Left Bank (7 & 15e)   203

Top Paris Attractions   218

Attractions in the 1st Arrondissement   220

Attractions in the 3rd–4th Arrondissements   221

Attractions in the 5th–6th Arrondissements   222

Attractions in the 7th Arrondissement   224

Attractions in the 8th Arrondissement   225

Attractions in the 16th Arrondissement   226

Attractions in the 18th Arrondissement   228

Notre-Dame de Paris   230

The Louvre   235

Cimetière du Père-Lachaise   275

Walking Tour 1: Montmartre   299

Walking Tour 2: The Latin Quarter   305

Walking Tour 3: The Marais   309

Ile-de-France   367

Versailles   369

Notre-Dame de Chartres   379

Fontainebleau   391

ABOUT THE AUTHORS

As a team of veteran travel writers, **Darwin Porter** and **Danforth Prince** have produced numerous titles for Frommer's which have included Italy, France, the Caribbean, Spain, and Germany. Porter wrote the first-ever Frommer's guide to Paris and the first-ever Frommer's guide to France. A Francophile, he has lived and worked in Paris on and off for many years. He was joined by Danforth Prince in 1982. Prince was previously employed by the Paris bureau of the *New York Times* and is the president of Blood Moon Productions and other media-related firms. Porter is also a film critic, columnist, broadcaster, and Hollywood biographer.

HOW TO CONTACT US

In researching this book, we discovered many wonderful places—hotels, restaurants, shops, and more. We're sure you'll find others. Please tell us about them, so we can share the information with your fellow travelers in upcoming editions. If you were disappointed with a recommendation, we'd love to know that, too. Please write to:

Frommer's Paris 2011
Wiley Publishing, Inc. • 111 River St. • Hoboken, NJ 07030-5774
frommersfeedback@wiley.com

AN ADDITIONAL NOTE

Please be advised that travel information is subject to change at any time—and this is especially true of prices. We therefore suggest that you write or call ahead for confirmation when making your travel plans. The authors, editors, and publisher cannot be held responsible for the experiences of readers while traveling. Your safety is important to us, however, so we encourage you to stay alert and be aware of your surroundings. Keep a close eye on cameras, purses, and wallets, all favorite targets of thieves and pickpockets.

FROMMER'S STAR RATINGS, ICONS & ABBREVIATIONS

Every hotel, restaurant, and attraction listing in this guide has been ranked for quality, value, service, amenities, and special features using a **star-rating system.** In country, state, and regional guides, we also rate towns and regions to help you narrow down your choices and budget your time accordingly. Hotels and restaurants are rated on a scale of zero (recommended) to three stars (exceptional). Attractions, shopping, nightlife, towns, and regions are rated according to the following scale: zero stars (recommended), one star (highly recommended), two stars (very highly recommended), and three stars (must-see).

In addition to the star-rating system, we also use **eight feature icons** that point you to the great deals, in-the-know advice, and unique experiences that separate travelers from tourists. Throughout the book, look for:

Special finds—those places only insiders know about

Fun facts—details that make travelers more informed and their trips more fun

Kids—best bets for kids and advice for the whole family

Special moments—those experiences that memories are made of

Overrated—places or experiences not worth your time or money

Insider tips—great ways to save time and money

Great values—where to get the best deals

Warning—traveler's advisories are usually in effect

The following **abbreviations** are used for credit cards:

AE	American Express	**DISC**	Discover	**V**	Visa
DC	Diners Club	**MC**	MasterCard		

TRAVEL RESOURCES AT FROMMERS.COM

Frommer's travel resources don't end with this guide. Frommer's website, **www.frommers.com**, has travel information on more than 4,000 destinations. We update features regularly, giving you access to the most current trip-planning information and the best airfare, lodging, and car-rental bargains. You can also listen to podcasts, connect with other Frommers.com members through our active-reader forums, share your travel photos, read blogs from guidebook editors and fellow travelers, and much more.

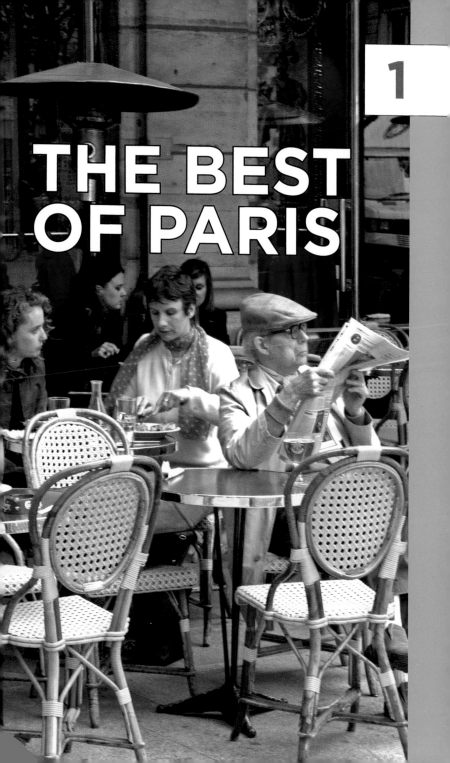

1

THE BEST OF PARIS

Discovering the City of Light and making it your own has always been the most compelling reason to visit Paris. If you're a first-timer, everything, of course, will be new to you. If you've been away for awhile, expect changes: Taxi drivers may no longer correct your fractured French, but address you in English—tantamount to a revolution. More Parisians have a rudimentary knowledge of the language, and France, at least at first glance, seems less xenophobic than in past years. Paris, aware of its role within a united Europe, is an international city. Parisians are attracted to foreign music, videos, and films, especially those from America.

Though Paris is in flux culturally and socially, it lures travelers for the same reasons as always. You'll still find such classic sights as the Tour Eiffel, Notre-Dame, the Arc de Triomphe, Sacré-Coeur, and all those atmospheric cafes, as well as daringly futuristic projects such as the Grande Arche de La Défense, the Cité des Sciences et de l'Industrie, the Cité de la Musique, and the Bibliothèque François-Mitterrand. Don't forget the parks, gardens, and squares; the Champs-Elysées and other grand boulevards; and the river Seine and its quays. Paris's beauty is still overwhelming, especially at night, when it truly is the City of Light.

THE most unforgettable
TRAVEL EXPERIENCES

o **Whiling Away an Afternoon in a Parisian Cafe:** The cafes are where passionate meetings of writers, artists, philosophers, thinkers, and revolutionaries once took place—and perhaps still do. Parisians stop by their favorite cafes to meet lovers and friends, to make new ones, or to sit in solitude with a newspaper or book. For our recommendations, see "The Top Cafes," in chapter 6, "Where to Dine."

o **Taking Afternoon Tea à la Française:** Drinking tea in London has its charm, but the Parisian *salon de thé* is unique. Skip the cucumber-and-watercress sandwiches and delve into a luscious dessert such as the Mont Blanc, a creamy purée of sweetened chestnuts and meringue. The grandest Parisian tea salon is **Angélina,** 226 rue de Rivoli, 1er (*©* **01-42-60-82-00;** Métro: Tuileries or Concorde; p. 165).

o **Strolling Along the Seine:** Such painters as Sisley, Turner, and Monet have fallen under the Seine's spell. On its banks, lovers still walk hand in hand, anglers cast their lines, and *bouquinistes* (secondhand-book dealers) peddle

PREVIOUS PAGE: **A typical scene at one of Paris's many cafes.**

Strolling the picturesque quays of the Seine.

their mix of postcards, 100-year-old pornography, and tattered histories of Indochina. For more details on the sights and moments of Paris, see chapter 7, "Exploring Paris."

o **Spending a Day at the Races:** Paris boasts eight tracks for horse racing. The most famous and the classiest is **Hippodrome de Longchamp,** in the Bois de Boulogne, the site of the Prix de l'Arc de Triomphe and Grand Prix (p. 280). These and other top races are major social events, so you'll have to dress up (buy your outfit on rue du Faubourg St-Honoré). Take the Métro to Porte d'Auteuil and then a bus from there to the track. The racing newspaper *Paris Turf* and weekly entertainment magazines have details about race times.

o **Calling on the Dead:** You don't have to be a ghoul to be thrilled by a visit to Europe's most famous cemetery, **Père-Lachaise** (p. 276). You can pay your respects to the resting places of Gertrude Stein and her longtime companion, Alice B. Toklas; Oscar Wilde; Yves Montand and Simone Signoret; Edith Piaf; Isadora Duncan; Abélard and Héloïse; Frédéric Chopin; Marcel Proust; Eugène Delacroix; Jim Morrison; and others. The tomb designs are intriguing and often eerie. Laid out in 1803 on a hill in Ménilmontant, the cemetery offers surprises with its bizarre monuments, unexpected views, and ornate sculpture.

o **Window-Shopping in the Faubourg St-Honoré:** In the 1700s, the wealthiest Parisians resided in the Faubourg St-Honoré; today, the quarter is home to stores catering to the rich, particularly on rue du Faubourg St-Honoré and avenue Montaigne. Even if you don't buy anything, it's great to window-shop big names such as Hermès, Dior, Laroche, Courrèges, Cardin, and Saint Laurent. If you want to browse in the stores, be sure to dress the part. See chapter 9, "Shopping in Paris," for the lowdown on these boutiques.

o **Exploring Ile de la Cité's Flower Market:** A fine finish to any day (Mon–Sat) spent meandering along the Seine is a stroll through the **Marché aux Fleurs,** place Louis-Lépine (p. 337). You can buy rare flowers, the gems of the French Riviera—bouquets that have inspired artists throughout the centuries. Even the most basic hotel room will feel like a luxury suite after you fill it with bunches of carnations, lavender, roses, and tulips. On Sundays, the area is transformed into the **Marché aux Oiseaux,** where you can admire rare birds from around the world.

o **Going Gourmet at Fauchon:** An exotic world of food, **Fauchon** (p. 207) offers more than 20,000 products from around the globe. Everything you never knew you were missing is in aisle after aisle of coffees, spices, pastries, fruits, vegetables, rare Armagnacs, and much more. Take your pick: Tonganese mangoes, Scottish smoked salmon, preserved cocks' combs, Romanian rose-petal jelly, blue-red Indian pomegranates, golden Tunisian dates, larks stuffed with foie gras, dark morels from France's rich soil, Finnish reindeer's tongue, century-old eggs from China, and a creole punch from Martinique, reputed to be the best anywhere.

o **Attending a Ballet or an Opera:** In 1989, the **Opéra Bastille** (p. 345) was inaugurated to compete with the grande dame of the music scene, the **Opéra Garnier** (p. 346), which then was used solely for dance and soon closed for renovations. The Opéra Garnier reopened a few years ago, and opera has joined dance in the rococo splendor created by Charles Garnier, beneath a controversial ceiling by Chagall. The modern Opéra Bastille, France's largest opera house, with curtains by designer Issey Miyake, has opera and symphony performances in four concert halls (its main hall seats 2,700). Whether for a performance of Bizet or Tharp, dress with pomp and circumstance.

o **Sipping Cocktails at Willi's:** Back in the early 1970s, the first-timer to Paris might have arrived with a copy of Hemingway's *A Moveable Feast* and, taking the author's endorsement to heart, headed for Harry's Bar at "Sank roo doe Noo." Harry's is still around but now draws an older, more conservative clientele. Today's chic younger expats head for **Willi's Wine Bar,** 13 rue des Petits-Champs, 1er (© **01-42-61-05-09; www.williswinebar.com;** Métro: Bourse, Palais Royal, or Pyramides; p. 358). Here, the long-haired young bartenders are mostly English, as are the waitresses, who are dressed in Laura Ashley garb. The place is like an informal club for Brits, Australians, and Yanks, especially in the afternoon. Some 300 wines await your selection.

Enjoying cocktails at Willi's Wine Bar.

Shopping along rue Montorgueil.

- **Checking Out the Marchés:** A daily Parisian ritual is ambling through one of the open-air markets to buy fresh food—perhaps a properly creamy Camembert or a pumpkin-gold cantaloupe—to be eaten before sundown. Our favorite market is on rue Montorgueil, beginning at rue Rambuteau, 1er (Métro: Les Halles). During mornings at this grubby little cluster of food stalls, we've spotted some of France's finest chefs stocking up for the day. For more details, see the box "Food Markets" in chapter 9.

THE best SPLURGE HOTELS

- **Hôtel Ritz** (15 place Vendôme, 1er; ✆ **800/223-6800** or 01-43-16-30-30; www.ritzparis.com): This hotel, which gave the world the word "ritzy," meaning posh, occupies a magnificent palace overlooking the octagonal borders of one of the most perfect squares in the world. The decor is pure opulence. Marcel Proust wrote parts of *Remembrance of Things Past* here, and the world's greatest chef, Georges-Auguste Escoffier, perfected many of his recipes in the Ritz kitchens. See p. 111.
- **Four Seasons Hotel George V** (31 av. George V, 8e; ✆ **800/332-3442** or 01-49-52-70-00; www.fourseasons.com): Humorist Art Buchwald once wrote, "Paris without the George V would be Cleveland." The swanky address has long been a favorite of celebrities in every field, including Duke Ellington, who once wrote in his memoirs that his suite was so big that he couldn't find the way out. Its public and private rooms are decorated with a vast array of antiques and Louis XIV tapestries worth millions. See p. 124.

- **Hôtel Meurice** (228 rue de Rivoli, 1er; © **01-44-58-10-10;** www.meurice hotel.com) has been restored to its former glory. It reigned as the queen-bee hotel of Paris in the 19th century and has made a comeback to preside over post-millennium Paris as well. From its Winter Garden to its sumptuous bedrooms that sheltered kings, this one is a winner. See p. 110.

- **Plaza Athénée** (25 av. Montaigne, 8e; © **866/732-1106** or 01-53-67-66-65; www.plaza-athenee-paris.com) is still the favorite lunchtime hangout for Parisian couturiers. It's also a lot more than that, providing luxurious accommodations for the likes of the Rockefellers and super-wealthy Brazilians. This swanky citadel is graced with potted palms, crystal chandeliers, and elegant furnishings—you name it: Louis XV, Louis XVI, Regency, whatever. Its ivy-covered courtyard is a slice of heaven. See p. 125.

- **Hôtel d'Aubusson** (33 rue Dauphine, 6e; © **01-43-29-43-43;** www. hoteldaubusson.com) lies in the heart of St-Germain-des-Prés and is our favorite boutique hotel in Paris. It takes its name from the original Aubusson tapestries gracing its elegant public rooms. Antiques and luxurious accessories make a stay here evocative of a visit to a classy private home, filled with tasteful, beautifully decorated bedrooms and intimate public salons with baronial furnishings recalling the era of Louis XV. You can sleep under a ceiling with exposed beams in a canopied bed. See p. 138.

- **L'Hôtel** (13 rue des Beaux-Arts, 6e; © **01-44-41-99-00;** www.l-hotel.com) is precious—just precious—the Left Bank's most charming little town-house hotel. And, yes, this former fleabag was where the great Oscar Wilde died, disgraced and penniless. That was Glenn Close or Robert De Niro you saw

A suite at the Four Seasons Hotel George V.

The Windsor Suite at Hôtel Ritz.

walking through the lobby, but not Elizabeth Taylor, because the rooms were too small for her luggage. The hotel is a triumph of Directoire architecture, and the ambience is oh, so seductive. See p. 138.

THE best MODERATELY PRICED HOTELS

- **The Five Hotel** (5 rue Flatters, 5e; ℃ 01-43-31-74-21; www.thefivehotel. com): In the Left Bank's Latin Quarter, this boutique hotel is installed in a 19th-century town house. Okay, the rooms may be a bit small, but the place is a charmer, attracting fashionistas to its individually designed bedrooms in bold colors such as blood red. There's Chinese lacquer galore. See p. 133.

- **Hôtel St-Jacques** (35 rue des Ecoles, 5e; ℃ 01-44-07-45-45; www.paris-hotel-stjacques.com): Cary Grant and Audrey Hepburn, who made *Charade* here, have long ago checked out, but this longtime favorite with its Belle Epoque atmosphere still has its allure. With furnishings that evoke France's Second Empire, it's the cliché of Left Bank charm. Its well-furnished and attractive bedrooms have each been restored. See p. 136.

- **Hôtel Duo** (11 rue du Temple, 4e; ℃ 01-42-72-72-22; www.duoparis.com) is a winner in the increasingly fashionable Marais district, convenient to the Centre Pompidou. Parisian fashionistas have made this a favorite nesting place. The old architecture, including time-worn stones and exposed beams, has been respected; otherwise, the place is as up-to-date as tomorrow. A member of the staff jokingly suggested to us that this sophisticated rendez-vous is "not for virgins." See p. 116.

o **Hôtel des Deux-Iles** (59 rue St-Louis-en-l'Ile, 4e; 🕿 **01-43-26-13-35;** www.deuxiles-paris-hotel.com): There exists no more platinum real estate, at least in our view, than the Ile St-Louis, Paris's most beautiful isle in the Seine. For a charming, yet unpretentious hotel on this island, we'd choose this restored 18th-century town house. We like the abundance of fresh flowers and the fireplace in the cellar bar. The rooms are a bit small, but this is one of the city's greatest locations for a hotel, and that should count for something. See p. 117.

o **Hôtel Saint-Louis** (75 rue St-Louis-en-l'Ile, 4e; 🕿 **01-46-34-04-80;** www.saintlouisenlisle.com): As with Hôtel des Deux-Iles, this cozy nest, a restored 17th-century town house, occupies a "world apart" on a tiny island in the middle of the Seine. The rooms may be *petit,* but the charm of the place compensates, with its exposed ceiling beams, wooden Louis XIII furnishings, and modern bathrooms. Opt for a fifth-floor bedroom for a panoramic view over the rooftops of Paris. See p. 118.

o **Galileo Hôtel** (54 rue Galilee, 8e; 🕿 **01-47-20-66-06;** www.galileo-paris-hotel.com): In the super-expensive 8th arrondissement, site of the Champs-Elysées and France's most expensive street, avenue Montaigne, this is a holdout because it's actually affordable to many visitors. In the epicenter of Paris, this restored town house is imbued with Parisian elegance and charm. Though understated, the bedrooms are tastefully furnished and most comfortable, and a few choice ones have glass-covered verandas. See p. 129.

A stylish room at the Five Hotel.

A guest room at fashionable Hôtel Duo.

- **Hôtel de l'Abbaye Saint-Germain** (10 rue Cassette, 6e; ✆ **01-45-44-38-11;** www.hotel-abbaye.com): For those who'd like to stay in the heart of the Quartier Latin in the 5th arrondissement, this charming boutique hotel, originally a convent in the 1700s, has been restored with a certain grace and sophisticated flair. Brightly painted rooms with traditional French furnishings are inviting and comfortable, and the maintenance is first-rate. Grace notes include a courtyard with a fountain, along with flowerbeds and climbing ivy. Try for the upper-floor room with a terrace overlooking Paris. See p. 139.

THE most unforgettable DINING EXPERIENCES

- **Le Grand Véfour** (17 rue de Beaujolais, 1er; ✆ **01-42-96-56-27;** www.grand-vefour.com): Seductively and appropriately timeworn, this dining room is where Napoleon wooed Joséphine. Its Louis XVI–Directoire interior is a protected historic monument. With its haute cuisine, it has been the haunt of celebrities since 1760. The cuisine is even better than ever, because it insists on hiring only the world's leading chefs. This monument to the past still tantalizes 21st-century palates. See p. 159.

- **Mélac** (42 rue Léon-Frot, 11e; ✆ **01-43-70-59-27;** www.melac.fr): When it was established in 1938, 2 years before France's involvement in the war, Mélac looked like something out of the 1880s, with a zinc bar that became famous. That bar is still there, and it's one of the most time-honored old cafes in Paris. Naturally, you have to walk through the kitchen to get to the dining room to feast on such delights from the Auvergne as veal tripe "bundles" or pig's liver. Here, old Paris lives on. See p. 175.

- **Aux Lyonnais** (32 rue St-Marc, 2e; ✆ **01-42-96-65-04;** www.auxlyonnais.com): Paris's bistro of bistros has been taken over by Alain Ducasse, the six-star Michelin chef and self-proclaimed "greatest in the world." In spite of that takeover, Aux Lyonnais remains the quintessential Parisian dining choice for Lyonnais specialties. As any city dweller of Lyon will tell you, that city is the gastronomic capital of France. The market-fresh produce is as new as the 1890s bistro is old, with its backdrop of potted palms, etched glass, and globe lamps in the best of the Belle Epoque style. See p. 166.

- **Au Pied de Cochon** (6 rue Coquillière, 1er; ✆ **01-40-13-77-00;** www.pieddecochon.com): For years, it's been a Paris tradition to stop off at this

Serving the cheese course at Le Grand Véfour.

joint in Les Halles for the famous onion soup at 3 o'clock in the morning after a night of revelry. The true Parisian also orders the restaurant's namesake—grilled pigs' feet with béarnaise sauce. You can also do as your grandpa did and wash down a dozen different varieties of oysters at the time-mellowed bar—along with champagne, of course. See p. 162.

o **Taillevent** (15 rue Lamennais, 8e; © **01-44-95-15-01**; www.taillevent. com): Forget about sending the kids to college and instead enjoy one of the most memorable meals of your life at what is consistently hailed as Paris's temple of haute cuisine. Named after a 14th-century chef to the king and the author of the first French cookbook, this restaurant comes as close to perfection as any in the world. In all our years of dining here, the chef has never had a bad day. This is a true temple of grand cuisine with one of the world's top 10 wine lists. Although we've enjoyed much of the innovative cuisine of Alain Solivères, we are also grateful that he's kept that airy, sausage-shaped lobster soufflé on the menu. See p. 180.

o **Carré des Feuillants** (14 rue de Castiglione, 1er; © **01-42-86-82-82**; www.carredesfeuillants.fr): Chef Alain Dutournier presides over this temple of haute gastronomy, thrilling diners with his take on new French cuisine. As always, deluxe ingredients are prepared with one of the most finely honed techniques in all of Paris. This chef knows the value of simplicity touched with inspiration. See p. 158.

o **Lasserre** (17 av. Franklin D. Roosevelt, 8e; © **01-43-59-02-13**; www. restaurant-lasserre.com): Each new generation discovered this elegant bastion of chic for itself. A tradition since the late 1930s, Lasserre has seen the faces of the Golden Age (everyone from Marlene Dietrich to

Audrey Hepburn) but also welcomes the stars of today, tempting them with sublime cuisine both modern and traditional. See p. 176.

○ **Crémerie-Restaurant Polidor** (41 rue Monsieur-le-Prince, 6e; ℂ **01-43-26-95-34;** www.polidor.com.): A longtime favorite of students, artists, and the literati such as James Joyce and Jack Kerouac, this bistro in St-Germain-des-Prés has been around since 1845. We've been such regulars that our favorite waitress used to store our linen napkins in a wooden drawer for use on our next visit. One habitué we met here claimed he'd been dining at Polidor 2 or 3 nights a week for half a century. The pumpkin soup, the boeuf bourguignon, the *blanquette de veau*—yes, the same recipes that delighted Hemingway—are still served here. See p. 199.

○ **L'Ami Louis** (32 rue du Vertbois, 3e; ℂ **01-48-87-77-48**): Even Bill Clinton gets roughed up here ("So, you were the president—but no more!"). Even so, he returns every time he's in town. Against a backdrop of a brown gravy patina, this is the most famous brasserie in Paris from the 1930s. We don't have to tell you that its cuisine is traditional French, and we're talking grilled veal kidneys, duckling confit, and foie gras. See p. 166.

○ **La Petite Chaise** (36 rue de Grenelle, 7e; ℂ **01-42-22-13-35;** www.al apetitechaise.fr): Even on the most rushed of visits to Paris, we always drop in here for one of the best prix-fixe menus at the more affordable restaurants in Paris. "The Little Chair" (its English name) first opened as an inn in 1680, when it was used for both food and its bedrooms upstairs, where discretion for afternoon dalliances was virtually assured. The time-honored cuisine is as French as Charles de Gaulle—and that is as it should be. See p. 205.

The wine cellar at Taillevent.

Aux Lyonnais.

THE best THINGS TO DO FOR FREE (OR ALMOST)

o **Meeting the Natives:** There is no page number to which you can turn for guidance here. You're on your own. But meeting Parisians, and experiencing their cynical metropolitanism, is one of the adventures of traveling to Paris—and it's free. Tolerance, gentleness, and patience are not their strongest points; they don't suffer fools gladly, but adore eccentrics. Visitors often find Parisians brusque to the point of rudeness and preoccupied with their own affairs. However, this hardened crust often protects a soft center. Compliment a surly bistro owner on her cuisine, and—9 times out of 10—she'll melt before your eyes. Admire a Parisian's dog or praise a window display and you'll find a loquaciously knowledgeable companion for the next 5 minutes. Ask about the correct pronunciation of a French word (before you mispronounce it), and a Parisian may become your language teacher. Try to meet a Parisian halfway with some kind of personalized contact. Only then do you learn their best qualities: their famed charm, their savoir-faire—and, yes, believe it or not, the delightful courtesy that marks their social life.

o **Trailing les Américains:** At 35 rue de Picpus, a few blocks from the place de la Nation, is a spot over which the Stars and Stripes have flown for more than a century and a half. It lies in a small secluded cemetery, marking **the grave of the Marquis de Lafayette**—the man who, during the American Revolution, forged the bond that has linked the two countries ever since. Col. Charles E. Stanton came here to utter the famous words, *Lafayette, nous voila!* ("Lafayette, we are here!") to announce the arrival of the World War I doughboys on French soil. At the Pont de Grenelle, at Passy, you'll find the original model of the **Statue of Liberty** that France presented to the people of the United States. One of the most impressive paintings in the **Musée de l'Armée** (p. 230) shows the Battle of Yorktown, which—however you learned it in school—was a combined Franco-American victory. Throughout the city, you'll keep coming across statues, monuments, streets, squares, and plaques commemorating George Washington, Benjamin Franklin, presidents Wilson and Roosevelt, generals Pershing and Eisenhower, and scores of lesser Yankee names.

Lovely place des Vosges.

o **Attending a Free Concert:** Summer brings a Paris joy: free concerts in parks and churches all over the city. Pick up an

Checking out one of the Latin Quarter's modern art galleries.

entertainment weekly for details. Some of the best concerts are held at the **American Church in Paris,** 65 quai d'Orsay, 7e (🕿 **01-40-62-05-00;** Métro: Invalides or Alma-Marceau; p. 346), which sponsors free concerts from September to June on Sunday at 5pm. You can also attend free concerts at **Eglise St-Merry,** 78 rue St-Martin, 4e (🕿 **01-42-71-93-93;** Métro: Hôtel-de-Ville; p. 346). These performances are staged based on the availability of the performers, from September to July on Saturday at 9pm and again on Sunday at 4pm.

- **Hanging Out at Place des Vosges:** Deep in the Marais, place des Vosges is more an enchanted island than a city square. This serenely lovely oasis is the oldest square in Paris and the most entrancing. Laid out in 1605 by order of Henri IV, it was the scene of innumerable cavaliers' duels. In the middle is a tiny park where you can sit and sun, listen to the splashing waters of the fountains, or watch the kids at play. On three sides is an encircling arcaded walk, supported by arches and paved with ancient, worn flagstones. Sit sipping an espresso as the day passes you by. It's our all-time favorite spot in Paris for people-watching. See p. 310.

- **Viewing Avant-Garde Art:** Space is too tight to document the dozens of art galleries that abound in Paris, but the true devotee will find that not all great art in Paris is displayed in a museum. There is a tendency, however, for owners to open galleries around major museums, hoping to lure the art lovers in. This is especially true around the Centre Pompidou, in the Marais. Our favorite gallery in the Marais is **La Maison Rouge,** the red house at 10 bd. de la Bastille, 12e (🕿 **01-40-01-08-81;** www.lamaisonrouge.org; Métro: Quai de la Rapée). It displays an ever-changing array of the "hottest" work and the most avant-garde of Parisian artists. The more traditional galleries are found in St-Germain-des-Prés, with **Galerie Adrien Maeght,** 42 rue du Bac, 7e (℡ **01-45-48-45-15;** www.maeght.com) being the market leader.

o **Strolling the World's Grandest Promenade:** Pointing from place de la Concorde like a broad, straight arrow to the Arc de Triomphe at the far end, the **Champs-Elysées** (the main street of Paris) presents its grandest spectacle at night. Guidebook writers to Paris grow tired of repeating "the most in the world," but, of course, the Champs-Elysées is the world's most famous promenade. For the first third of the stroll from place de la Concorde, the avenue is hedged by chestnut trees. Then it changes into a double row of palatial hotels and shops, movie houses, office buildings, and block after block of sidewalk cafes. The automobile showrooms and gift stores have marred the Belle Epoque elegance of this stretch, but it's still the greatest vantage point from which to watch Paris roll by.

o **Cooling Off in the Jardin des Tuileries:** Right-Bank Parisians head to the Tuileries Gardens to cool off on a hot summer day. The park stretches on the Right Bank of the Seine from the place de la Concorde to the doorstep of the Louvre. This exquisitely formal garden was laid out as a royal pleasure ground in 1564, but was thrown open to the public by the French Revolution. Filled with statues, fountains, and mathematically trimmed hedges, it's a bit too formal for English gardeners who like their green spaces a little wilder. Its nicest feature is a series of round ponds on which kids sail armadas of model boats.

Playing with the rental sailboats in the Tuileries.

Seeing Paris by city bus.

Stand on the elevated terrace by the Seine, enjoying panoramic views over Paris, including the Arc de Triomphe and the Cour Napoléon of the Louvre. The sculptures by Rodin aren't bad either. Food stands and cafes with refreshing drinks await you.

○ **Seeing Paris from a Bus:** Most tours of Paris are expensive, but for only 1.30€ you can ride one of the city's public buses traversing some of the most scenic streets. Our favorite is no. 29, which begins at historic Gare St-Lazare (Métro: St-Lazare), subject of Monet's painting *La Gare St-Lazare* at Musée d'Orsay and featured in Zola's novel *La Bête Humainee.* Aboard no. 29, you pass the famous Opéra Garnier (home of the Phantom) and proceed into the Marais district, passing by Paris's most beautiful square, place des Vosges. You end up at the Bastille district, home of the new opera. What we like about this bus is that it takes you along the side streets of Paris and not the major boulevards. It's a close encounter with backstreet Paris and a cheap way to see the city without a tour guide's commentary.

THE best MUSEUMS

○ **Musée du Louvre** (34–36 quai du Louvre, 1er; ℰ **01-40-20-53-17;** www. louvre.fr): The Louvre's exterior is a triumph of French architecture, and its interior shelters an embarrassment of art, one of the greatest treasure-troves known to Western civilization. Of the Louvre's more than 300,000 paintings, only a small percentage can be displayed at one time. The museum maintains its staid dignity and timelessness even though thousands of visitors traipse daily through its corridors, looking for the *Mona Lisa* or the *Venus de Milo.*

I. M. Pei's controversial Great Pyramid nearly offsets the grandeur of the Cour Carrée, but it has a real functional purpose, as you will soon see. See p. 234.

o **Musée d'Orsay** (1 rue de Bellechasse, 7e; ℂ **01-40-49-48-14;** www. musee-orsay.fr): The spidery glass-and-iron canopies of a former railway station frame one of Europe's greatest museums of art. Devoted mainly to paintings of the 19th century, d'Orsay contains some of the most celebrated masterpieces of the French Impressionists, along with sculptures and decorative objects whose designs forever changed the way European artists interpreted line, movement, and color. In case you didn't know, d'Orsay is also where *Whistler's Mother* sits in her rocker. See p. 232.

o **Centre Pompidou** (place Georges-Pompidou, 4e; ℂ **01-44-78-12-33;** www. centrepompidou.fr): "The most avant-garde building in the world," or so it is known, is a citadel of modern art, with exhibitions drawn from more than 40,000 works. Everything seemingly is here—from Calder's 1928 *Josephine Baker* (one of his earliest versions of the mobile) to a re-creation of Brancusi's Jazz Age studio. See p. 241.

o **Musée Jacquemart-André** (158 bd. Haussmann, 8e; ℂ **01-45-62-11-59;** www.musee-jacquemart-andre.com): The 19th-century town house, with its gilt salons and elegant winding staircase, contains the best small collection of 18th-century decorative art in Paris. The building and its contents were a bequest to the Institut de France by the late Mme Nélie Jacquemart-André, herself an artist of note. To her amazing collection of rare French decorative art, she added a rich trove of painting and sculpture from the Dutch and Flemish schools, as well as paintings and objets d'art from the Italian Renaissance. See p. 246.

o **Musée National du Moyen Age/ Thermes de Cluny** (in the Hôtel de Cluny, 6 place Paul-Painlevé, 5e; ℂ **01-53-73-78-00;** www. musee-moyenage.fr): This is an enchantress of a museum, housing some of the most beautiful medieval art still in existence. The museum occupies one of the two Gothic private residences left from Paris in the 15th century. Dark, rough-walled, and evocative, the Cluny is devoted to the church art and castle crafts of the Middle Ages. It is more celebrated for its

Winged Victory of Samothrace at the Louvre.

The *Lady and the Unicorn* tapestry at the Musée National du Moyen Age/Thermes de Cluny.

tapestries—among them the world-famed series of *The Lady and the Unicorn,* gracefully displayed in a circular room on the second floor. Downstairs you can visit the ruins of Roman baths, dating from around A.D. 200. See p. 248.

o **Musée Marmottan Monet** (2 rue Louis-Boilly, 16e; ℂ **01-44-96-50-33;** www.marmottan.com): On the edge of the Bois de Boulogne, this once rarely visited museum is now one of the most frequented in Paris. It was rescued from obscurity on February 5, 1966, when the museum fell heir to more than 130 paintings, watercolors, pastels, and drawings of Claude Monet, the "father of Impressionism." A gift of Monet's son Michel, the bequest is one of the greatest art acquisitions in France. Had an old widow in Brooklyn suddenly inherited the fortune of a J. P. Morgan, the event would not have been more startling. Exhibited here is the painting, *Impression, Sunrise,* which named the artistic movement. See p. 247.

o **Musée Rodin** (in the Hotel Biron, 77 rue de Varenne, 7e; ℂ **01-44-18-61-10;** www.musee-rodin.fr): Auguste Rodin, the man credited with freeing French sculpture from classicism, once lived at and had his studio in this charming 18th-century mansion across from Napoleon's tomb. Today, the house and its garden are filled with his works, a soul-satisfying feast for the Rodin enthusiast. In the cobbled Court of Honor, within the walls as you enter, you'll see *The Thinker* crouched on his pedestal. The *Burghers of Calais* are grouped off to the left; and, to the far left, the writhing *Gates of Hell* can be seen, atop which another *Thinker* once more meditates. In the almost-too-packed rooms, men and angels emerge from blocks of marble, their hands twisted in supplication, and the nude torso of Balzac rises from a tree. See p. 249.

THE best NEIGHBORHOODS FOR GETTING LOST

o **Montmartre:** Striding a hill atop Paris, Montmartre used to be a village of artists, glorified by masters such as Utrillo, and painted, sketched, sculpted, and photographed by 10,000 lesser talents. Today, it's overrun by tourists, building speculators, and nightclub entrepreneurs who moved in as the artists moved out. However, a few still linger and so does much of the villagelike charm. Of all the places for wandering the cobbled streets of old Paris, Montmartre, especially in its back streets and alleyways, gets our vote. The center point is the place du Tertre, where you can head out on your journey of exploration. Gleaming through the trees from here is the Basilica of Sacré-Coeur, built in an oddly Oriental neo-Byzantine style. Behind the church and clinging to the hillside below are steep and crooked little streets that seem—almost—to have survived the relentless march of progress. Rue des Saules still has Montmartre's last vineyard. The rue Lepic still looks—almost—the way Renoir, Toulouse-Lautrec, and the melancholic Van Gogh saw it. See p. 297.

o **Quartier Latin:** Over the Seine on the Left Bank, the Latin Quarter lies in the 5th arrondissement and consists of streets winding around the Paris University, of which the Sorbonne is only a part. The logical starting point is place Saint-Michel, right on the river, with its impressive fountain. From here you can wander at leisure, getting lost as you discover the doglegged cluster of alleys adjoining the river—rue de la Huchette, rue de la Harpe, rue St-Séverin. Each generation makes discoveries of its own, and everything is new again. End up by strolling along boulevard St-Germain, lined with sophisticated cafes and some of the most avant-garde fashion shops in Paris. See p. 303.

Boulevard Montmartre by Camille Pissarro.

A quiet Latin Quarter street.

○ **Le Marais:** Very few cities on earth boast an entire district that can be labeled a sight. Paris has several, including the vaguely defined maze of streets north of place de la Bastille, known as Le Marais, or "the Marsh." During the 17th century, this was a region of aristocratic mansions, which lost their elegance when the fashionable set moved elsewhere. The houses lost status, but they remain standing and restored today, as the once-decaying Marais has been gentrified. Today, it's one of the most fashionable districts in Paris, home to funky shops, offbeat hotels, dozens of bistros, hot bars, and "gay Paree." See p. 308.

○ **Ile St-Louis:** A footbridge behind Notre-Dame leads to another enchanting island on the Seine, a world of tree-shaded quays, town houses with courtyards, and antiques shops. This smaller and more tranquil of the Seine islands has remained much as it was in the 17th century. Over the years, many illustrious French have called St-Louis home—none more famous than Voltaire. Sober patrician houses stand along the four quays, and the feverish beat of Paris seems 100 miles away. This is our favorite real estate for wandering in the whole city. See p. 284.

○ **Ile de la Cité:** "The cradle of Paris," where the city was born, is actually an island shaped like a great ship in the middle of the Seine. Home to France's greatest cathedral, Notre-Dame, it invites exploration and wandering. Home to French kings until the 14th century, Cité still has a curiously medieval air, with massive gray walls rising up all around you, relieved by tiny patches of parkland. The island is home to Sainte-Chapelle and the Conciergerie. After these stellar attractions, save time for wandering about and discovering Cité's secrets, such as the square du Vert Galant. See p. 282.

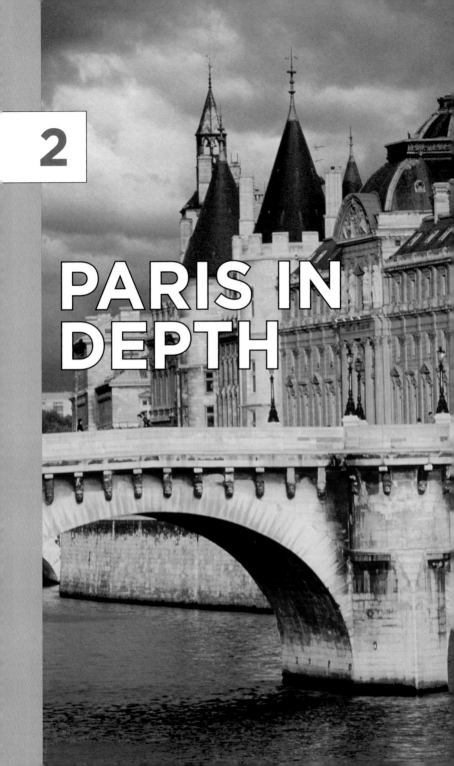

2

PARIS IN DEPTH

E rnest Hemingway called the many splendors of Paris a "moveable feast" and wrote, "There is never any ending to Paris, and the memory of each person who has lived in it differs from that of any other." It's this aura of personal discovery that has always been the most compelling reason to come to Paris. Perhaps that's why France has been called *le deuxième pays de tout le monde* (everybody's second country).

The Seine not only divides Paris into the Right Bank and the Left Bank, but also seems to split the city into two vastly different sections and ways of life. Depending on your time, interest, and budget, you may quickly decide which section of Paris suits you best.

The old clichés about the Left Bank being for poor, struggling artists and the Right Bank being for the well-heeled were broken down long ago. The very heart of the Left Bank, including the areas around Odéon and St-Germain-des-Prés, is as chic as anything on the Right Bank—and just as expensive.

The history of Paris repeats itself. In the old days, Montmartre was the artists' quarter until prices and tourism drove these "bohemians" to less-expensive *quartiers* such as Montparnasse. But Montparnasse long ago became gold-plated real estate.

So where does the struggling artist go today? Not to the central core of the Right or Left Bank, but farther afield. First, it was the Marais, until that district, too, saw rents spiral and the average visitor carried an American Express gold card. Now it's farther east, into the 11th arrondissement, a blue-collar neighborhood between the Marais, Ménilmontant, and République. The heartbeat of this area is rue Oberkampf.

PARIS TODAY

Paris has been celebrated in so many songs, poems, stories, books, paintings, and movies that for millions of people it is an abstraction rather than a city. To French people living in the provinces, Paris is the center of the universe, the place where laws and careers are made and broken. To North American tourists, it is still "gay Paree" inviting you for a fling, the hub of everything "European," and the epitome of that nebulous attribute known as "chic." Say "Paris" and you produce an instant image of sidewalk cafes and strolling lovers beneath the Eiffel Tower.

Paris is by day a stone mosaic of delicate gray and green, by night a stunning, unforgettable sea of lights—white, red, and orange. Broad, tree-lined boulevards open before you; mansions loom tall, ornate, and graceful. Everywhere you look are trees, squares, and monuments. Whether you see it for the first or fiftieth time, the discovery of the city, and making it your own, is and always has been the most compelling reason for coming to Paris.

FACING PAGE: **Pont Neuf with the Conciergerie in the background.**

The New Parisians

The entire world continues to arrive on the city's doorstep. Some come to visit and leave money behind. (Parisians like that kind of visitor.) Friction, however, has accompanied another kind of visitor: the kind who comes to find a new life. A sizable number of Parisians have balked at the perceived drain on their resources brought about by immigration. Others are more welcoming, in the same way they were to black artists such as Josephine Baker in the 1920s or author James Baldwin in the 1950s, both of whom came to Paris to find an audience, acceptance, and honor.

Many Parisians view the immigrant population as a group that has diversified French society and has had an important impact on the country's culture. The impact is evident in the vast array of new restaurants opening in Paris, with cuisine as diverse as Vietnamese, Senegalese, and Martinique creole. The immigrants have also changed Paris's nightlife; anything Cuban is en vogue, and you can find just as fine a salsa band in Paris today as you can in Havana.

African cuisine remains all the rage, and restaurants specializing in Senegalese fare are heavily patronized, even though you'll have to go to the less touristy arrondissements to find them.

Perhaps no one symbolizes the changing face of France more than Zinedine Zidane, who scored the goals that won France the World Cup in 1998. French kids voted this soccer hero, the son of Algerian immigrants, the most popular man in France, and French women found him sexier than Brad Pitt or Johnny Depp. After France won the World Cup, anti-immigration fever cooled perceptibly, and the country experienced a feeling of generosity and goodwill unlike anything it had known since the liberation of World War II. No soccer fan, then-President Chirac pinned Legion of Honor ribbons on Zidane and his teammates. But to expect Zidane to lead France into its multicultural future was a bit much to ask, even for a World Cup hero. So far, no towering figure like Zidane has emerged post-millennium. Anti-immigrant fever still remains a major social problem, not only in Paris, but throughout France.

The government may be shaky, the economy of 2010 a disaster, the natives restless, but Paris has more *joie de vivre* in the new millennium than it did throughout the 1970s and 1980s. No one is proclaiming it to be the most happening city in Europe: London, temporarily at least, has staked out that claim. But Paris is still queen of the Continent. It's got more museums, more nighttime diversions, better hotels, more amusements, better shops, and the greatest brigade of talented chefs, both young and old, than it's ever had in its history.

Neighborhoods such as Montmartre and Montparnasse, St-Germain and Le Marais, are waiting to be explored for the first time, or to be rediscovered by a returning visitor. In some ways, they remain the same, as if etched in stone, but after a second look it's obvious that they have changed. Everything is new and different—not always better, but always fresh and exciting.

The Seine has always flowed through Paris's culture and history, an inspiration for painters and lovers, sheltering in its gentle S-shaped curve that pair of islands, Ile de la Cité and Ile St-Louis, upon which the city was born.

All *quartiers* (quarters) are different, and because your experiences will likely be formed by where you choose to stay, so will your memory of Paris. Do

I.M. Pei's glass pyramid at the Louvre.

you prefer a hotel deep in the heart of St-Germain, sleeping in a room where Jean-Paul Sartre and Simone de Beauvoir might have spent the night? Or do you identify with the Rive Droite, preferring to sleep in sumptuous quarters at the Crillon Hotel? Do you prefer looking for that special curio in a dusty shop on the Left Bank's rue Jacob, or inspecting the latest haute couture of Karl Lagerfeld, Jean Patou, or Guy Laroche in a Right Bank boutique along the avenue Montaigne?

Paris today, at least at first glance, seems less hysterically xenophobic than in past years. Taxi drivers may no longer correct your fractured French, but address you in English—and that's tantamount to a revolution. Additionally, more Parisians have a rudimentary knowledge of English. Part of this derives from Parisians' interest in music, videos, and films from foreign countries, and part from France's growing awareness of its role within a united Europe.

Yet France has never been more concerned about the loss of its unique identity within a landscape that has attracted an increasing number of immigrants from its former colonies. Many have expressed the legitimate concern that France will continue to lose the battle to keep its language strong, distinct, and unadulterated by foreign slang or catchwords. But as the country moves deeper into the second decade of the millennium, foreign tourists spending much-needed cash are no longer perceived as foes or antagonists. *Au contraire:* The rancor of France's collective xenophobia has been increasingly redirected toward the many immigrants seeking better lives in Paris, where the infrastructure has nearly been stretched to its limits.

Though Paris is clearly a city in flux culturally and socially, it still lures travelers for all the same reasons. Grand indestructible sights such as the Tower Eiffel are still here, as is the spruced-up Champs-Elysées—both are as crowded as ever. The beauty of Paris is still overwhelming, especially in the illumination of night. The City of Light, one of the premier tourist destinations in the world, always provides a memorable performance.

LOOKING BACK AT PARIS

In the Beginning

Paris emerged at the crossroads of three major traffic arteries on the muddy island in the Seine that today is known as Ile de la Cité.

By around 2000 B.C., the island served as the fortified headquarters of the Parisii tribe, who called it Lutétia. The two wooden bridges connecting the island to the river's left and right banks were among the region's most strategically important, and the settlement attracted the attention of the Roman Empire. In his *Commentaries*, Julius Caesar described his conquest of Lutétia, recounting how its bridges were burned during the Gallic War of 52 B.C. and how the town on the island was pillaged, sacked, and transformed into a Roman-controlled stronghold.

Within a century, Lutétia became a full-fledged Roman town, and some of the inhabitants abandoned the frequently flooded island in favor of higher ground on what is today the Left Bank. By A.D. 200, barbarian invasions threatened the stability of Roman Gaul, and the populace from the surrounding hills flocked to the island's fortified safety. During the next 50 years, a Christian community gained a foothold there. According to legend, St. Denis served as the city's first bishop (around 250). By this time the Roman Empire's political power had begun to wane in the region, and the cultural and religious attachment of the community to the Christian bishops of Rome grew even stronger.

During the 400s, with the decline of the Roman armies, Germanic tribes from the east (the Salian Franks) were able to invade the island, founding a Frankish dynasty and prompting a Frankish-Latin fusion in the burgeoning town. The first of these Frankish kings, Clovis (466–511), founder of the Merovingian dynasty, embraced Christianity as his tribe's religion and spearheaded an explicit

DATELINE

2000 B.C. Lutétia thrives along a strategic crossing of the Seine, the headquarters of the Parisii tribe.	**350** Paris's Christianization begins.
52 B.C. Julius Caesar conquers Lutétia during the Gallic Wars.	**400s** The Franks invade Paris, with social transformation from the Roman to the Gallo-Roman culture.
A.D. 150 Lutétia flourishes as a Roman colony, expanding to the Left Bank.	**466** Clovis, founder of the Merovingian dynasty and first non-Roman ruler of Paris since the Parisii, is born.
200 Barbarian Gauls force the Romans to retreat to the fortifications on Ile de la Cité.	**800** Charlemagne, founder of the Carolingian dynasty, is crowned Holy Roman Emperor and rules from Aachen in modern Germany.
300 Lutétia is renamed Paris; Roman power weakens in northern France.	

rejection of Roman cultural imperialism by encouraging the adoption of Parisii place names such as "Paris," which came into common usage during this time.

The Merovingians were replaced by the Carolingians, whose heyday began with Charlemagne's coronation in 800. The Carolingian Empire sprawled over western Germany and eastern France, but Paris was never its capital. The city remained a commercial and religious center, sacred to the memory of St. Geneviève, who reputedly protected Paris when the Huns attacked it in the final days of the Roman Empire. The Carolingians came to an end in 987, when the empire fragmented because of the growing regional, political, and linguistic divisions between what would become modern France and modern Germany. Paris became the seat of a new dynasty, the Capetians, whose kings ruled France throughout the Middle Ages. Hugh Capet (938–96), the first of this line, ruled as comte de Paris and duc de France from 987 to 996.

The Middle Ages

Around 1100, Paris began to emerge as a great city, boasting on its Left Bank a university that attracted scholars from all over Europe. Meanwhile, kings and bishops began building the towering Gothic cathedrals of France, one of the greatest of which became Paris's Notre-Dame, a monument rising from the beating heart of the city. Paris's population increased greatly, as did the city's mercantile activity. During the 1200s, a frenzy of building transformed the skyline with convents and churches (including the jewel-like Sainte-Chapelle, completed in 1248). During the next century, the increasingly powerful French kings added dozens of monuments of their own.

As time passed, Paris's fortunes became closely linked to the power struggles between the French monarchs in Paris and the various highly competitive feudal lords of the provinces. Because of this tug of war, Paris was dogged by civil unrest, takeovers by one warring faction after another, and a dangerous alliance between the English and the powerful rulers of Burgundy during the Hundred Years' War. Around the same time, the city suffered a series of plagues, including

987 Hugh Capet, founder of France's foremost early medieval dynasty, rises to power; his family rules from Paris.

1100 The Université de Paris attracts scholars from throughout Europe.

1200s Paris's population and power grow, though it is often unsettled by plagues and feudal battles.

1422 England invades Paris during the Hundred Years' War.

1429 Joan of Arc tries to regain Paris for the French; the Burgundians later capture and sell her to the English, who burn her at the stake in Rouen.

1500s François I, first of the French Renaissance kings, embellishes Paris but chooses to maintain his court in the Loire Valley.

1549 Henri II rules from Paris; construction of public and private residences begins, many in the Marais.

1564 Construction begins on Catherine de Médici's Palais des Tuileries; building facades in Paris move from half-timbered to more durable chiseled stonework.

continues

the Black Death. To the humiliation of the French monarchs, the English army invaded the city in 1422. Joan of Arc (ca. 1412–31) tried unsuccessfully to reconquer Paris in 1429, and 2 years later the English, supported by a tribunal of French ecclesiastics, burned her at the stake in Rouen. Paris was reduced to poverty and economic stagnation, and its embittered and greatly reduced population turned to banditry and street crime to survive.

Despite Joan's tragic end, the revolution she inspired continued until Paris was finally taken back from the English in 1436. During the following several decades, the English retreated to the port of Calais, abandoning their once-mighty French territories. France, under the leadership of Louis XI (1423–83), witnessed an accelerating rate of change that included the transformation of a feudal and medieval social system into the nascent structure of a modern state.

The Renaissance & the Reformation

The first of the Renaissance monarchs, François I (1494–1547), began an enlargement of Paris's Louvre (which had begun as a warehouse storing the archives of Philippe Auguste before being transformed into a Gothic fortress by Louis IX in the 1100s) to make it suitable as a royal residence. Despite the building's embellishment and the designation of Paris as the French capital, he spent much of his time at other châteaux amid the hunting grounds of the Loire Valley. Many future monarchs came to share his opinion that Paris's narrow streets and teeming commercialism were unhealthy and chose to reside elsewhere.

In 1549, however, Henri II (1519–59) triumphantly established his court in Paris and successfully ruled France from within its borders, solidifying the city's role as the nation's undisputed capital. Following their ruler's lead, fashionable aristocrats quickly began to build *hôtels particuliers* (private residences) on the Right Bank, in a marshy low-lying area known as Le Marais (the Marsh).

It was during this period that the Paris we know today came into existence. The expansion of the Louvre continued, and Catherine de Médici (1518–89) began building her Palais des Tuileries in 1564. From the shelter of dozens of

---

DATELINE continued

1572 The Wars of Religion reach their climax with the St. Bartholomew's Day massacre of Protestants.

1598 Henri IV, the most eccentric and enlightened monarch of his era, endorses the Edict of Nantes, granting tolerance to Protestants; a crazed monk fatally stabs him 12 years later.

1615 Construction begins on the Palais du Luxembourg for Henri IV's widow, Marie de Médici.

1636 The Palais Royal is launched by Cardinal Richelieu; soon two

marshy islands in the Seine are interconnected and filled in to create Ile St-Louis.

1643 Louis XIV, the "Sun King," one of the most powerful rulers since the Caesars, rises to power; he moves his court to the newly built Versailles.

1776 The American Declaration of Independence strikes a revolutionary chord in France.

1789 The French Revolution begins.

1793 Louis XVI and his Austrian-born queen, Marie Antoinette, are publicly guillotined.

elegant urban residences, France's aristocracy imbued Paris with its sense of architectural and social style, as well as the Renaissance's mores and manners. Stone quays were added to the Seine's banks, defining their limits and preventing future flood damage, and royal decrees established a series of building codes. To an increasing degree, Paris adopted the planned perspectives and visual grace worthy of the residence of a monarch.

During the late 1500s and 1600s, the French kings persecuted Protestants. The bloodletting reached a high point under Henri III (1551–89) during the St. Bartholomew's Day massacre of 1572. Henri III's tragic and eccentric successor, Henri IV (1553–1610), ended the Wars of Religion in 1598 by endorsing the Edict of Nantes, offering religious freedom to the Protestants of France. Henri IV also laid out the lines for one of Paris's memorable squares: place des Vosges. A deranged monk infuriated by the king's support of religious tolerance stabbed him to death in 1610.

After Henri IV's death, his second wife, Marie de Médici (1573–1642), acting as regent, planned the Palais du Luxembourg (1615), whose gardens have functioned ever since as a rendezvous point for Parisians. In 1636, Cardinal Richelieu (1585–1642), who virtually ruled France during the minority of Louis XIII, built the sprawling premises of the Palais Royal. Under Louis XIII (1601–43), two uninhabited islands in the Seine were joined with landfill, connected to Ile de la Cité and to the mainland with bridges, and renamed Ile St-Louis. Also laid out was the Jardin des Plantes, whose flowers and medicinal herbs were arranged according to their scientific and medical categories.

The Sun King & the French Revolution

Louis XIV (1638–1715) was crowned king of France when he was only 9 years old. Cardinal Mazarin (1602–61), Louis's Sicilian-born chief minister, dominated the government in Paris during the Sun King's minority. This era marked the emergence of the French kings as absolute monarchs. As if to concretize their power, they embellished Paris with many of the monuments that still serve as

1799 Napoleon Bonaparte crowns himself Master of France and embellishes Paris further with neoclassical splendor.

1803 Napoleon abandons French overseas expansion and sells Louisiana to America.

1812 Napoleon is defeated in the Russian winter campaign.

1814 Aided by a coalition of France's enemies, especially England, the Bourbon monarchy under Louis XVIII is restored.

1821 Napoleon Bonaparte dies.

1824 Louis XVIII dies, and Charles X succeeds him.

1830 Charles X is deposed, and the more liberal Louis-Philippe is elected king; Paris prospers as it industrializes.

1848 A violent working-class revolution deposes Louis-Philippe, who's replaced by autocratic Napoleon III.

continues

symbols of the city. These included new alterations to the Louvre and the construction of the Pont Royal, quai Peletier, place des Victoires, place Vendôme, Champs-Elysées, and Hôtel des Invalides. Meanwhile, Louis XIV absented himself from the city, constructing, at a staggering expense, the Château de Versailles, 21km (13 miles) to the southwest. Today, the palace stands as the single most visible monument to the most flamboyant era of French history.

Meanwhile, the rising power of England, particularly its navy, represented a serious threat to France, otherwise the world's most powerful nation. One of the many theaters of the Anglo-French conflict was the American Revolution, during which the French kings supported the Americans in their struggle against the Crown. Ironically, within 15 years, the revolutionary fervor the monarchs had nurtured crossed the Atlantic and destroyed them. The spark that kindled the fire came from Paris itself. For years before the outbreak of hostilities between the Americans and the British, the

Portrait of Louis XVI by Antoine-François Callet.

Enlightenment and its philosophers had fostered a new generation of thinkers who opposed absolutism, religious fanaticism, and superstition. Revolution had been brewing for almost 50 years, and after the French Revolution's explosive events, Europe was completely changed.

Though it began with moderate aims, the Revolution had soon turned the radical Jacobins into overlords, led by Robespierre (1758–94). On August 10,

---

DATELINE continued

1853–70 On Napoleon III's orders, Baron Haussmann redesigns Paris's landscapes and creates the Grands Boulevards.

1860s The Impressionist style of painting emerges.

1870 The Franco-Prussian War ends in the defeat of France; Paris is threatened by Prussian cannons placed on the outskirts of the city; a revolution in the aftermath of this defeat destroys the Palais des Tuileries and overthrows the government; the Third Republic rises with its elected president, Marshal MacMahon.

1878–1937 Several international expositions add monuments to the Paris skyline, including the Tour Eiffel and Sacré-Coeur.

1895 Capt. Alfred Dreyfus, a Jew, is wrongfully charged with treason and sentenced to life on Devil's Island. The incident will lead to one of the major French political scandals of the 19th century.

1898 Emile Zola publishes "J'Accuse" in defense of Dreyfus and flees into exile in England.

1906 Dreyfus is finally exonerated, and his rank is restored.

1792, troops from Marseilles, aided by a Parisian mob, threw Louis XVI (1754–93) and his Austrian-born queen, Marie Antoinette (1755–93), into prison. Several months later, after countless humiliations and a bogus trial, they were guillotined at place de la Révolution (later renamed place de la Concorde) on January 21, 1793. The Reign of Terror continued for another 18 months, with Parisians of all political persuasions fearing for their lives.

The Rise of Napoleon

It required the militaristic fervor of Napoleon Bonaparte (1769–1821) to unite France once again. Considered then and today a strategic genius with almost limitless ambition, he restored to Paris and France a national pride that had diminished during the Revolution's horror. After many impressive political and military victories, he entered Paris in 1799, at the age of 30, and crowned himself "First Consul and Master of France." In 1804, he named himself emperor of France.

A brilliant politician, Napoleon moderated the atheistic rigidity of the early adherents of the Revolution by establishing peace with the Vatican. Soon thereafter, the legendary love of Parisians for their amusements began to revive; boulevard des Italiens became the rendezvous point of the fashionable, while boulevard du Temple, which housed many of the capital's theaters, became the favorite watering hole of the working class. In his self-appointed role as a French Caesar, Napoleon continued to alter Paris's face with the construction of the neoclassical arcades of rue de Rivoli (1801), the Arc du Carrousel, and Arc de Triomphe, and the neoclassical grandeur of La Madeleine. On a less grandiose scale, the city's slaughterhouses and cemeteries were sanitized and moved away from the center of town, and new industries began to crowd workers from the countryside into the cramped slums of a newly industrialized Paris.

Napoleon's victories had made him the envy of Europe, but his infamous retreat from Moscow during the winter of 1812 reduced his formerly invincible army to tatters as 400,000 Frenchmen lost their lives. After a complicated series

1914–18 World War I rips apart Europe.

1940 German troops invade Paris; the French government, under Marshal Pétain, evacuates to Vichy, while the French Resistance under Gen. Charles de Gaulle maintains symbolic headquarters in London.

1944 U.S. troops liberate Paris; de Gaulle returns in triumph.

1948 The revolt in the French colony of Madagascar costs 80,000 French lives; France's empire continues to collapse in Southeast Asia and equatorial Africa.

1954–62 War begins in Algeria and is eventually lost; refugees flood Paris, and the nation becomes divided over its North African policies.

1958 France's Fourth Republic collapses; General de Gaulle is called out of retirement to head the Fifth Republic.

1968 Paris's students and factory workers engage in a general revolt; the French government is overhauled in the aftermath.

continues

of events that included his return from exile, Napoleon was defeated at Waterloo by the armies of the English, the Dutch, and the Prussians. Exiled to the British-held island of St. Helena in the remote South Atlantic, he died in 1821, possibly the victim of an unknown poisoner. Sometime later, his body was returned to Paris and interred in a massive porphyry sarcophagus in the Hôtel des Invalides, Louis XIV's monument to the ailing and fallen warriors of France.

In the power vacuum that followed Napoleon's expulsion and death, Paris became the scene of intense lobbying over France's future. The Bourbon monarchy was soon reestablished, but with reduced powers. In 1830, the regime was overthrown. Louis-Philippe (1773–1850), duc d'Orléans and the son of a duke who had voted in 1793 for the death of Louis XVI, was elected king under a liberalized constitution. His prosperous reign lasted for 18 years, during which England and France more or less collaborated on matters of foreign policy.

Paris reveled in its prosperity, grateful for the money and glamour that had elevated it to one of the world's top cultural and commercial centers. Paris opened its first railway line in 1837 and erected its first gas-fed streetlights shortly after. It was a time of wealth, grace, culture, and expansion, though the industrialization of certain working-class districts produced great poverty. The era also witnessed the development of French cuisine to the high form that still prevails, while a newly empowered bourgeoisie reveled in its attempts to create the good life.

The Second Empire

In 1848, a series of revolutions spread from one European capital to the next. The violent upheaval in Paris revealed the dissatisfaction of members of the working class. Fueled by a financial crash and scandals in the government, the revolt forced Louis-Philippe out. That year, Emperor Napoleon's nephew, Napoleon III (1808–73), was elected president by moderate and conservative elements. Appealing to the property-owning instinct of a nation that hadn't forgotten the violent Revolution of less than a century before, he established a right-wing government and assumed complete power as emperor in 1851.

DATELINE continued

1981 François Mitterrand is elected France's first Socialist president since the 1940s; he's reelected in 1988.

1989 Paris celebrates the bicentennial of the French Revolution.

1992 Euro Disney opens on the outskirts of Paris.

1994 François Mitterrand and Queen Elizabeth II ride under the English Channel in the new Chunnel.

1995 Jacques Chirac is elected over Mitterrand, who dies the following year; Paris is crippled by a

general strike; terrorists bomb the subway.

1997 Authorities enforce strict immigration laws, causing strife for African and Arab immigrants and dividing the country; French voters elect Socialist Lionel Jospin as Chirac's new prime minister.

1998 Socialists triumph in local elections across France.

1999 The euro is introduced; on Christmas Day a violent storm assaults Paris and the Île de France, dam-

In 1853, Napoleon III undertook Europe's largest urban redevelopment project by commissioning Baron Eugène-Georges Haussmann (1809–91) to redesign Paris. Haussmann created a vast network of boulevards interconnected with a series of squares that cut across old neighborhoods. Although this reorganization gave the capital the look for which it's now famous, screams of outrage sounded throughout the neighborhoods split apart by construction. By 1866, the entrepreneurs of an increasingly industrialized Paris began to regard the Second Empire as a hindrance. In 1870, during the Franco-Prussian War, the Prussians defeated Napoleon III at Sedan and held him prisoner, along with 100,000 of his soldiers. Paris was threatened with bombardments from German cannons, by far the most advanced of their age, set up on the city's eastern periphery.

Although agitated diplomacy gained a Prussian withdrawal, international humiliation and perceived military incompetence sparked a revolt in Paris. One of the immediate effects was the burning of one of Paris's historic landmarks, the Palais des Tuileries. Today, only the gardens of this once-great palace remain. The events of 1870 ushered in the Third Republic and its elected president, Marshal Marie Edme Patrice Maurice de MacMahon (1808–93), in 1873.

Under the Third Republic, peace and prosperity gradually returned, and Paris regained its glamour. Universal expositions held in 1878, 1889, 1900, and 1937 were catalysts for the construction of such enduring monuments as the Trocadéro, the Palais de Chaillot, the Tour Eiffel, the Grand Palais and the Petit Palais, and the neo-Byzantine Sacré-Coeur. The *réseau métropolitain* (the Métro) was constructed, providing a model for subway systems throughout Europe.

World War I

International rivalries and conflicting alliances led to World War I, which, after decisive German victories for 2 years, degenerated into the mud-slogged horror of trench warfare. Industrialization during and after the war transformed Paris and its environs into one of the largest metropolitan areas in Europe, undisputed even today as the center of France's intellectual and commercial life.

aging buildings and toppling thousands of trees.

2002 France replaces its national currency, the franc, and switches to the euro, the new European currency.

2003 Attacks on French Jews mark the rise of anti-Semitism, the worst since World War II.

2005 Mostly French Arab rioters attack Paris suburbs, as violence spreads to French cities.

2006 Massive demonstrations against a new labor law are held in Paris

and other cities. Jacques Chirac revokes the law.

2007 Pro-American Nicholas Sarkozy becomes president of France, sparking riots.

2008 France bans smoking in public places.

2010 Economic woes and a battered euro plague France.

Immediately after the Allied victory, grave economic problems, coupled with a populace demoralized from years of fighting, encouraged the rise of Socialism and the formation of a Communist party, both movements centered in Paris. Also from Paris, the French government, led by the vindictive Georges Clemenceau (1841–1929), occupied Germany's Ruhr Valley—then and now one of that country's most profitable and industrialized regions—and demanded every centime of reparations it could wring from its humiliated neighbor, a policy that contributed to the outbreak of World War II.

The 1920s: Americans in Paris

The so-called Lost Generation, led by American expatriates Gertrude Stein and Alice B. Toklas, topped the list of celebrities who "occupied" Paris after World War I, ushering in one of its most glamorous eras. The living was cheap in Paris. Two people could manage for about a year on a $1,000 scholarship, provided they could scrape up another $500 or so in extra earnings. Paris attracted the *littérateur, bon viveur,* and drifter. Such writers as Henry Miller, Ernest Hemingway, and F. Scott Fitzgerald all lived here. Even Cole Porter came, living first at the Ritz and then at 13 rue de Monsieur. James Joyce, half blind and led around by Ezra Pound, arrived in Paris and went to the salon of Natalie Barney. She became famous for pulling off such stunts as inviting Mata Hari to perform a Javanese dance completely nude at one of her parties, labeled "for women only, a lesbian orgy." Novelist Colette

Sylvia Beach and James Joyce in the 1920s.

was barred from attending, though she begged her husband to let her go.

With the collapse of Wall Street, many Americans returned home, except hard-core artists such as Henry Miller, who wandered around smoking Gauloises and writing *Tropic of Cancer,* which was banned in America. "I have no money, no resources, no hopes. I am the happiest man alive," Miller said. Eventually, he met diarist Anaïs Nin, and they began to live a life that gave both of them material for their prose. But even such die-hards as Miller and Nin eventually realized that 1930s Paris was collapsing as war clouds loomed. Gertrude and Alice remained in France as other American expats fled to safer shores.

The Winds of War

Thanks to an array of alliances, when Germany invaded Poland in 1939, France had no choice but to declare war. Within a few months, on June 14, 1940, Nazi armies marched down the Champs-Elysées and passed beneath the Arc de

Triomphe. Newsreel cameras recorded the French openly weeping at the sight. The city suffered little from the war materially, but for 4 years it survived in a kind of half-life—cold, dull, and drab—fostering scattered pockets of fighters who resisted sometimes passively and sometimes with active sabotage.

During the Nazi occupation of Paris, the French government, under Marshal Henri Pétain (1856–1951), moved to the isolated resort of Vichy and cooperated (or collaborated, depending on your point of view) with the Nazis. Tremendous internal dissension, the memory of which still simmers today, pitted many factions against one another. The Free French Resistance fled for its own safety to London, where it was headed by Charles de Gaulle (1880–1970). On September 9, 1945, a government of national unity was formed under de Gaulle's presidency. A constituent National Assembly was then elected. De Gaulle's disagreement with the National Assembly led in January 1946 to the tendering of his resignation.

Postwar Paris

Despite gains in prestige and prosperity after the end of World War II, Paris was rocked many times by internal dissent as domestic and international events embroiled the government in controversy. In 1951, Paris celebrated the 2,000th anniversary of the city's founding and poured much energy into rebuilding its image as a center of fashion, lifestyle, and glamour. Paris became internationally recognized as both a staple in the travel diets of many North Americans and a beacon for art and artists.

The War of Algerian Independence (1954–58), in which Algeria sought to change from being a French *département* (an integral extension of the French nation) to being an independent country, was an anguishing event, more devastating than the earlier loss of France's colonies. The population of France (Paris in particular) ballooned as French citizens fled Algeria and returned with few possessions and much bitterness. In 1958, as a result of the enormous loss of lives, money, and prestige in the Algerian affair, France's Fourth Republic collapsed, and de Gaulle was called out of retirement to form a new government, the Fifth Republic. In 1962, the Algerian War ended with victory for Algeria, as France's colonies in central and equatorial Africa became independent one by one. The sun had finally set on the French Empire.

In 1968, a general revolt by Parisian students, whose activism mirrored that of their counterparts in the United States, turned the capital into an armed camp, causing a near collapse of the national government and the very real possibility of total civil war. Though the

Celebrating the Allied victory, August 25, 1944.

crisis was averted, for several weeks it seemed as if French society were on the brink of anarchy.

Contemporary Paris

In 1981, François Mitterrand (1916–96) was elected the first Socialist president of France since before World War II by a very close vote. Massive amounts of capital were taken out of the country, and though the drain slowed after initial jitters, many wealthy Parisians still prefer to invest their money elsewhere.

Paris today still struggles with social unrest in Corsica and with Muslim fundamentalists both inside and outside France. In the mid-1990s, racial tensions continued to nag at France as the debate over immigration raged. Many right-wing political parties have created a racial backlash against North Africans and against "corruptive foreign influences" in general.

On his third try, Jacques Chirac (b. 1932), a longtime mayor of Paris, won the presidency of France in 1995 with 52% of the vote. Mitterrand turned over the reins on May 17 and died shortly thereafter. France embarked on a new era, but Chirac's popularity faded in the wake of unrest caused by an 11.5% unemployment rate. In the spring of 1998, France ousted its Conservative parties in an endorsement of Prime Minister Lionel Jospin (b. 1937) and his Socialist-led government. The triumph of Jospin and his Communist and Green Party allies represented a disavowal of the center-right Conservatives. This was a stunning blow to Chirac's neo-Gaullists and the center-right parties led by François Leotard, and to Jean-Marie Le Pen's often-fanatical National Front.

By putting the Left back in charge, the French had voted against all the new ideas proposed for pushing their country into competitiveness and out of its economic doldrums. But Jospin's popularity gradually diminished, and in the elections of 2002, he was voted out of office and announced his retirement from politics. Jacques Chirac came back into power and became one of the most powerful leaders opposing the United States' war in Iraq.

In 1999, France joined 11 other European Union countries in adopting the euro as its standard of currency, though the French franc remained in circulation until March 2002.

In February 2005, President George W. Bush flew to Europe to mend fences with some of his worst critics, notably French President Chirac. The two political foes, who will never be great friends, found common ground on such issues as Syria and Lebanon. Iraq remained a thorny problem. Chirac, a self-styled expert on cows after serving as a former agriculture minister, was not invited to Bush's Texas ranch. When asked why not, Bush enigmatically said, "I'm looking for a good cowboy."

Late in 2005, decades of pent-up resentment felt by the children of African immigrants exploded into an orgy of violence and vandalism. Riots began in the suburbs of Paris and spread around the country. Throughout France, gangs of youths battled the French police, torched schools, cars, and businesses, and even attacked commuter trains. Rioting followed in such cities as Dijon, Marseilles, and Rouen. Most of the rioters were the sons of Arab and black African immigrants; Muslims living in a mostly Catholic country. The reason for the protests? Leaders of the riots claimed they live "like second-class citizens," even though they are French citizens. Unemployment is 30% higher in the ethnic ghettos of France.

In the spring of 2006, Jacques Chirac signed a law that made it easier for employers to fire workers, which set off massive demonstrations across France. Some one million protesters staged marches and strikes against the law, which was rescinded on April 10, 2006.

In June of 2007, Nicolas Sarkozy, the combative son of a Hungarian immigrant, was elected president of France. He promised to reinvigorate ties with France's traditional ally, the United States. His election was followed with scattered violence throughout the country from anti-Sarkozy protesters. In 2005 he'd called rioters in Paris's immigrant heavy suburbs "scum," which was blamed for inciting the country's worst violence in 4 decades. Sarkozy has promised to be president of "all the French" during his administration.

In all this muddle, Sarkozy found time to divorce a wife and take a beautiful new bride. A glamorous model turned singer, the sexy Carla Bruni is the new first lady of France. "The Carla effect," as it's called in Paris, has decreased Sarkozy's popularity—that and his failure to revive France's ailing economy. The tabloids have had a field day with the First Lady, revealing former lovers such as Mick Jagger, Eric Clapton, and Donald Trump, even Laurent Fabius (a former French prime minister).

A Frenchman's taste for rich, dark, tobacco is the stuff of legend. Imagine the shock when the time-honored tradition of smoking in public was banned according to a law passed in 2008. About one-fourth of France's population of 60 million are smokers, and one in two regular smokers dies of smoking-related illnesses. Gone from the Paris cafe and nightlife scene is the scent of Gauloises, which for years was associated with a French sense of rebellion, the intelligentsia, and the Gallic sense of *joie de vivre.*

Many of the French became uncertain of their future as a European Union member in 2010. The financial instability in Greece, and the continuing woes of debt-ridden Italy, Spain, and Portugal contributed to the drop in the euro's value.

ART & ARCHITECTURE

Paris is one of the artistic capitals of Europe. For centuries the city has produced, and been home to, countless artists and artistic movements. This section helps you find the best examples of each period in the city's museums and architecture.

Art

GOTHIC (1100–1400)

Almost all artistic expression in medieval France was church-related. Paris retains almost no art from the classical or Romanesque eras, but much remains from the medieval Gothic era, when artists created sculpture and stained glass for churches.

Outstanding examples include: the **Cathédrale de Chartres** (1194–1220), which is a day trip from Paris and boasts magnificent sculpture and some of the best stained glass in Europe; the **Cathédrale de Notre-Dame** (1163–1250), whose Gothic high points are the sculpture on the facade, an interior choir screen lined with deep-relief carvings, and three rose windows filled with stained glass; and the tiny chapel of **Sainte-Chapelle** (1246–48), adorned with the finest stained glass in the world.

THE RENAISSANCE (1400–1600)

Humanist thinkers rediscovered the wisdom of the ancients, while artists strove for greater naturalism, using newly developed techniques such as linear perspective to achieve new heights of realism.

Aside from collecting Italian art, the French had little to do with the Renaissance, which started in Italy and was quickly picked up in Germany and the Low Countries. France owes many of its early Renaissance treasures to **François I,** who imported art (by Raphael and Titian, and da Vinci). Henri II's Florentine wife, **Catherine de Médici,** also collected 16th-century Italian masterpieces.

THE BAROQUE (1600–1800)

At first reaffirming Renaissance spirituality, the true baroque later exploded into dynamic fury, movement, color, and figures—that are well-balanced but in such cluttered abundance as to appear untamed. **Rococo** is this later baroque art gone awry, frothy, and chaotic.

Significant practitioners of the baroque with examples in the **Louvre** include: **Nicolas Poussin** (1594–1665), the most classical French painter, who created mythological scenes; **Antoine Watteau** (1684–1721), who indulged in the wild, untamed complexity of the rococo; **François Boucher** (1703–70), Louis XV's rococo court painter; and **Jean-Honoré Fragonard** (1732–1806), Boucher's student and the master of rococo.

NEOCLASSICAL & ROMANTIC (1770–1890)

As the baroque got excessive, the rococo got cute, and the somber Counter-Reformation got serious about the limits on religious art, several artists looked for

The intricate stained glass of Sainte-Chapelle.

The Continence of Scipio by Nicolas Poussin.

relief to the ancients. This gave rise to a **neoclassical** artistic style that empha-sized symmetry, austerity, clean lines, and classical themes.

The **romantics,** on the other hand, felt that both the ancients and the Renaissance had gotten it wrong and that the Middle Ages was the place to be. They idealized romantic tales of chivalry and the nobility of peasantry.

Some great artists and movements of the era, all with examples in the **Lou-vre,** include: **Jean Ingres** (1780–1867), who became a defender of the neoclas-sicists and the Royal French Academy and opposed the romantics; **Theodore Géricault** (1791–1824), one of the great early romantics, who painted *The Raft of the Medusa* (1819), which served as a model for the movement; and **Eugène Delacroix** (1798–1863), whose *Liberty Leading the People* (1830) was painted in the romantic style.

IMPRESSIONISM (1870–1920)

Seeking to capture the *impression* light made as it reflected off objects, the Impressionists adopted a free, open style; deceptively loose compositions; swift, visible brushwork; and often light colors. For subject matter, they turned to land-scapes and scenes of modern life. You'll find some of the best examples of their works in the **Musée d'Orsay.**

Impressionist greats include: **Edouard Manet** (1832–83), whose ground-breaking *Picnic on the Grass* (1863) and *Olympia* (1863) helped inspire the movement with their harsh realism, visible brushstrokes, and thick outlines; **Claude Monet** (1840–1926), who launched the movement officially in an 1874 exhibition in which he exhibited his Turner-inspired *Impression, Sunrise* (1874), now in the **Musée Marmottan; Pierre-Auguste Renoir** (1841–1919), known for his figures' ivory skin and chubby pink cheeks; **Edgar Degas** (1834–1917), an accomplished painter, sculptor, and draftsman—his pastels of dancers and bathers are particularly memorable; and **Auguste Rodin** (1840–1917), the greatest Impressionist-era sculptor, who crafted remarkably expressive bronzes. The **Musée Rodin,** his former Paris studio, contains, among other works, his *Burghers of Calais* (1886), *The Kiss* (1886–98), and *The Thinker* (1880).

POST-IMPRESSIONISM (1880–1930)

The smaller movements or styles of Impressionism are usually lumped together as "post-Impressionism." Again, you'll find the best examples of their works at the **Musée d'Orsay,** though you'll find pieces by Matisse, Chagall, and the cubists, including Picasso, in the **Centre Pompidou.**

Important post-Impressionists include: Paul Cézanne (1839–1906), who adopted the short brushstrokes, love of landscape, and light color palette of his Impressionist friends; Paul Gauguin (1848–1903), who developed

The Musée de Cluny combines magnificent gothic and renaissance elements in its facade.

synthetism (black outlines around solid colors); Henri de Toulouse-Lautrec (1864–1901), who created paintings and posters of wispy, fluid lines anticipating Art Nouveau and often depicting the bohemian life of Paris's dance halls and cafes; Vincent Van Gogh (1853–90), who combined divisionism, synthetism, and a touch of Japanese influence, and painted with thick, short strokes; Henri Matisse (1869–1954), who created fauvism (a critic described those who used the style as fauves, meaning "wild beasts"); and Pablo Picasso (1881–1973), a Málaga-born artist who painted objects from all points of view at once, rather than using such optical tricks as perspective to fool viewers into seeing three dimensions. The fractured result was cubism. You can see art from all of his periods at the Musée Picasso in the Marais.

Architecture

It's worth pointing out that very few buildings (especially churches) were built in one particular architectural style. These massive, expensive structures often took centuries to complete, during which time tastes would change and plans would be altered.

ANCIENT ROMAN (125 B.C.–A.D. 450)

France was Rome's first transalpine conquest, and the legions of Julius Caesar quickly subdued the Celtic tribes across France, converting it into Roman Gaul and importing Roman building concepts. Except for the **Parvis Archaeological Excavations** of the Romanized village of Lutétia (later renamed after its native Parisii tribe of Celtic Gauls), very little remains in Paris. These excavations are under place du Parvis in front of Notre-Dame. **Musée de Cluny,** a medieval monastery, was built on top of a **Roman baths complex,** remnants of which are still visible on the grounds outside and in the huge preserved *frigidarium* (the cold-water bath), which is now a room of the museum.

> Impressions
>
> *I am the man who accompanied Jacqueline Kennedy to Paris, and I have enjoyed it.*
> —John F. Kennedy, 1961

ROMANESQUE (800–1100)

The Romanesque style took its inspiration from ancient Rome (hence the name). Early Christians in Italy had adapted the basilica (ancient Roman law-court buildings) to become churches. Few examples of the Romanesque style remain in Paris, however, with most churches having been rebuilt in later eras.

The best remaining example of this style is on the Left Bank at the church of **St-Germain-des-Prés.** The overall building is Romanesque, including the fine sculpted column capitals near the entrance of the left aisle; only the far left corner is original, the others are copies.

The Gothic exterior of Sainte-Chapelle.

GOTHIC (1100–1500)

By the 12th century, engineering developments freed church architecture from the heavy, thick walls of Romanesque structures and allowed ceilings to soar, walls to thin, and windows to proliferate. Gothic interiors enticed churchgoers' gazes upward to high ceilings filled with light. Graceful buttresses and spires soared above town centers.

The best examples in and around Paris of the Gothic are: **Basilique St-Denis** (1140–44), the world's first Gothic cathedral in a Paris suburb; **Cathédrale de Chartres** (1194–1220), a Gothic masterpiece with some 150 glorious stained-glass windows; and, of course, **Cathédrale de Notre-Dame** (1163–1250), which possesses pinnacled flying buttresses, a trio of France's best rose windows, good portal carvings, a choir screen of deeply carved reliefs, and spiffy gargoyles.

Typical Haussmann-style boulevards and buildings.

RENAISSANCE (1500–1630)

In architecture, the Renaissance style stressed proportion, order, classical inspiration, and precision to create unified, balanced structures.

The best examples are: **Hôtel Carnavalet** (1544), a Renaissance mansion, the only 16th-century hotel left in Paris; and **Place des Vosges** (1605), a square lined by Renaissance mansions rising above a lovely arcaded corridor that wraps all the way around.

CLASSICISM & ROCOCO (1630–1800)

During the reign of Louis XIV, art and architecture were subservient to political ends. Buildings were grandiose and severely ordered on the Versailles model. Opulence was saved for interior decoration, which increasingly (especially 1715–50, after the death of Louis XIV) became an excessively detailed and self-indulgent **rococo** (*rocaille* in French).

Rococo tastes didn't last long, though, and soon a **neoclassical** movement was raising structures, such as Paris's **Panthéon** (1758), which were even more strictly based on ancient models.

The best examples include: **Palais du Louvre** (1650–70), a collaborative classical masterpiece, designed as a palace with **Le Vau** (1612–70) as its chief architect, along with collaborators such as **François Mansart** (1598–1666); **Versailles** (1669–85), Europe's grandest palace, the Divine Monarchy writ as a statement of fussily decorative, politically charged classical architecture, though the interior was redecorated in more flamboyant styles; and the **Panthéon** (1758), a Left Bank perfect example of the strict neoclassical style.

THE 19TH CENTURY

Architectural styles in 19th-century Paris were eclectic, beginning in a severe classical mode and ending with an identity crisis torn between Industrial Age technology and Art Nouveau organic.

Identifiable styles include the neoclassical **First Empire** with its strong lines often accented with a simple curve—the rage during Napoleon's reign; and **Second Empire,** which occurred during Napoleon III's reign, a reinterpretation of classicism in an ornate mood. During this period Paris became a city of wide boulevards, courtesy of **Baron Georges-Eugène Haussmann** (1809–91), commissioned by Napoleon III in 1852 to redesign the city. Haussmann lined the boulevards with simple, six-story apartment blocks, such as elongated 18th-century town houses with continuous balconies wrapping around the third and sixth floors and mansard roofs with dormer windows.

The **Third Republic** expositions in 1878, 1889, and 1900 used the engineering prowess of the Industrial Revolution to produce such Parisian monuments as the Tour Eiffel and Sacré-Coeur.

Art Nouveau architects and decorators rebelled against the Third Republic era of mass production by creating asymmetrical, curvaceous designs based on organic inspiration (plants and flowers) in such mediums as wrought iron, stained glass, and tile.

The best examples are the **Tour Eiffel** (1889), which **Gustave Eiffel** (1832–1923) slapped together to form the world's tallest structure at 320m (1,050 ft.); and **Métro station entrances.**

An original Art Nouveau Métro stop.

Centre Pompidou escalator.

THE 20TH CENTURY

France commissioned some ambitious architectural projects in the last century, most of them the *grand projets* of the late François Mitterrand. The majority were considered controversial or even offensive when completed.

At **Centre Pompidou** (1977), Britisher Richard Rogers (b. 1933) and Italian Renzo Piano (b. 1937) turned architecture inside out—literally—to craft Paris's eye-popping modern-art museum, with exposed pipes, steel supports, and plastic-tube escalators wrapping around the exterior; **Louvre's glass pyramids** (1989) were created by Chinese-American architect I. M. Pei (b. 1917); and **Opéra Bastille** (1989) is a curvaceous, dark glass mound of space designed by Canadian Carlos Ott.

PARIS IN POPULAR CULTURE: BOOKS, FILMS & MUSIC

Books

There are numerous books on all aspects of French history and society—ranging from the very general, such as the section on France in the *Encyclopedia Americana,* International Edition (Grolier, 1989), which presents an excellent, illustrated overview of the French people and their way of life, to the very specific, such as Judi Culbertson and Tom Randall's *Permanent Parisians: An Illustrated Guide to the Cemeteries of Paris* (Chelsea Green, 1986), which depicts the lives of the famous buried in Paris.

HISTORY In addition to the encyclopedia reference above, a broad overview of French history can be found in other encyclopedias and general history books. One very good one is *History of France* by Guillaume de Bertier de Savigny and David H. Pinkney, a comprehensive history with illustrations and plenty of obscure but interesting facts.

Two books that present French life and society in the 17th century are Warren Lewis's *The Splendid Century* (Waveland, 1997) and Madame de Sévigne's *Selected Letters* (Penguin, 1955), edited by Leonard W. Tancock, which contains imaginative and witty letters written to her daughter during the reign of Louis XIV.

Simon Schama's *Citizens* (Vintage, 1990) is "a magnificent and electrifyingly new history of the French Revolution"—long, but enjoyable.

Moving into the 20th century, *Pleasure of the Belle Epoque: Entertainment and Festivity in Turn-of-the-Century France* (Yale, 1988), by Charles Rearick, depicts public diversions in the changing and troubled times of the Third Republic. *Paris Was Yesterday, 1925–1939* (Virago, 2003) is a fascinating collection of excerpts from Janet Flanner's "Letters from Paris" column of the *New Yorker*. Larry Collins and Dominique Lapierre have written a popular history of the liberation of Paris in 1944 called *Is Paris Burning?* (BookSales, 2000).

TRAVEL Since 1323 some 10,000 books have been devoted to exploring Paris. One of the best is *Paris: Capital of the World* (Belknap, 2005) by Patrice Higonnet. This book takes a fresh, social, cultural, and political look at this City of Light. Higonnet even explores Paris as "the capital of sex," and in contrast the "capital of art." The gang's all here from Balzac to Zola.

Showing a greater fondness for gossip is Alistair Horne in his *Seven Ages of Paris* (Knopf, 2002). From the Roman founding up to the student riots of 1968, this is one of the most amusing books on Paris we've ever read. Horne is not a timid writer. He calls the Palais de Chaillot fascistic and hideous, the Pompidou Center a horror. We even learn that a woman once jumped off the Eiffel Tower, bounced off the roof of a parked car, and survived. In *The Flâneur, A Stroll Through the Paradoxes of Paris* (Bloomsbury USA, 2008), Edmund White wants the reader to experience Paris as Parisians do. Hard to translate exactly, a *flâneur* is someone who strolls, loafs, or idles. With White, you can circumnavigate Paris as whim dictates.

BIOGRAPHY You can get a more intimate look at history through biographies of historical figures. The best book yet on the architect who changed the face of Paris is *Haussmann: His Life and Times and the Making of Modern Paris* (Ivan R. Dee, 2002) by Patrick Camiller.

Representing a very different era are *A Moveable Feast* (Scribner, 1996), Ernest Hemingway's recollections of Paris during the 1920s, and Morley Callaghan's *That Summer in Paris: Memories of Tangled Friendships with Hemingway, Fitzgerald and Some Others* (Coward McCann, 1963), an anecdotal account of the same period. Another great read is *The Autobiography of Alice B. Toklas* (Vintage, 1990), by Gertrude Stein. It's not only the account of 30 years in Paris, but also the autobiography of Gertrude Stein.

THE ARTS Much of France's beauty can be found in its art. Three books that approach France from this perspective are *The History of Impressionism* (Abrams, 1990), by John Rewald, which is a collection of writings about and quotations from the artists, illuminating this period in art; *The French through Their Films* (Ungar, 1988), by Robin Buss, an exploration of more than 100 widely circulated films; and *The Studios of Paris: The Capital of Art in the Late Nineteenth Century* (Yale, 1990), by John Milner. In the last, Milner presents the dynamic forces that made Paris one of the most complex centers of the art world in the early modern era.

FICTION The *Chanson de Roland* (Editions Gallimard, 1991), edited by F. Whitehead, written between the 11th and 14th centuries, is the earliest and most celebrated of the "songs of heroic exploits." *The Misanthrope* and *Tartuffe* are two masterful satires on the frivolity of the 17th century by the great comic dramatist Molière. François-Marie Arouet Voltaire's *Candide* (Dover, 1991) is a classic satire attacking the philosophy of optimism and the abuses of the ancient regime.

A few of the masterpieces of the 19th century are *Madame Bovary* (Oxford, 2005), by Gustave Flaubert, in which the carefully wrought characters, setting, and plot attest to Flaubert's genius in presenting the tragedy of Emma Bovary; Victor Hugo's *Les Misérables* (Everyman's Library, 1998), a classic tale of social oppression and human courage set in the era of Napoleon I; and *Selected Stories of Guy de Maupassant* (Boomer Books, 2007) by the master of short stories himself.

Honoré de Balzac's *La Comédie Humaine* (Book Jungle, 2007) depicts life in France from the fall of Napoleon to 1848. Henry James's *The Ambassadors* (Penguin, 2008) and *The American* (Norton, 1978) both take place in Paris. *The Vagabond,* by Colette, evokes the life of a French music-hall performer.

Tropic of Cancer (Grove Press, 1994) is the semiautobiographical story of Henry Miller's years in Paris. One of France's leading thinkers, Jean-Paul Sartre, shows individuals struggling against their freedom in *No Exit and Three Other Plays* (Vintage, 1988).

For more recent reads you might pick up a tattered copy of *The Da Vinci Code* (Anchor, 2006) if you haven't already read it, or David Sedaris's *Me Talk Pretty One Day* (Little, Brown and Company, 2000), revealing the viewpoint of an American tourist as he tries to absorb French culture.

Films

Although Americans understood—and very quickly, too—the commercial wealth to be made from films, the French are credited with the scientific and technical inventions that made them possible. French physicists had laid the groundwork for a movie camera as early as the mid-1880s, and the world's first movie was shown in Paris on December 28, 1895. Its makers were the Lumière brothers, who considered filmmaking a scientific oddity and stubbornly confined its use to the production of international newsreels. Later, a vaudevillian actor and illusionist, Georges Méliés, used film to convey plot and drama.

Charles Pathé and Léon Gaumont were the first to exploit filmmaking on a grand scale. Beginning in 1896, they produced and distributed their own films, building their company into a giant before World War I. When Gaumont made his first film, he enlisted his secretary, Alice Guy-Blanché, to create the plot, design the scenery, and direct it. She proved so successful that she was eventually promoted to the head of Paris's largest studio and became the world's first female director.

Before World War I, the many talented actors arriving *en scène* included Max Linder, a popular French comic, whose style influenced Charlie Chaplin and helped him develop his keen sense of timing. After World War I a flood of film imports from the United States and an economic depression slowed down the growth of French filmmaking.

By the 1920s the French began to view filmmaking as an art form, and infused it with surreal and Dada themes. These were eventually named avant-garde and included experiments viewed (sometimes skeptically, sometimes encouragingly) in Hollywood and around the world. Examples include Man Ray's *Le retour à la raison* (1923), Fernand Léger's *Le ballet mécanique* (1924), and Jean Cocteau's *Le sang d'un poète* (1930).

The golden age of the silent screen on both sides of the Atlantic was from 1927 to 1929. Actors were directed with more sophistication, and technical abilities reached an all-time high. One of our favorite films—despite its mind-numbing length—is Abel Gance's sweepingly evocative masterpiece *Napoléon* (1927); its grisly battle scenes are easily as chilling as any war film made today. Other highlights from this era include René Clair's *Un chapeau de paille d'Italie* (*An Italian Straw Hat;* 1927), Carl Dreyer's *La passion de Jeanne d'Arc* (1928), and an adaptation of Emile Zola's *Thérèse Raquin* (1928) by Jacques Feyder.

Experiments with the early productions of "talkies" were less successful. One popular film director, Pagnol, declared outright that the role of films was to publicize to the masses the benefits of the theatrical stage. During this period, many of the counterculture's most gifted directors either left France altogether (as did René Clair, who immigrated to England in 1934) or died (Jean Vigo, *Zéro de Conduite*).

In 1936 the Cinémathèque Française was established to find and preserve old (usually silent) French films. By that time, French cinematographers had divorced themselves completely from the value system of the stage and had found a style of their own. An average of 130 films a year were made in France, by (among others) Jean Renoir, Charles Spaak, and Marcel Carne. This was also the era that brought such French luminaries as Claudette Colbert and Maurice Chevalier to Hollywood.

Scene from *Breathless* (1960).

During World War II, the best known (to Americans) of the French directors fled to Hollywood. Those who remained were heavily censored by the Vichy government. Despite that, more than 350 French films, many relating to long past (and therefore uncontroversial) events were produced. Exceptions were Carne's *Les enfants du paradis* (*Children of Paradise;* 1945).

In 1946 France slapped a heavy quota system onto the importation of foreign (especially American) films. A semigovernmental film authority (le Centre national du Cinéma Français) financed independent French film companies and encouraged liaisons between the French and Italian film industries. Many directors who had supported the Vichy government's Nazi collaboration were soon accepted back into the cinematic community.

Two strong traditions—film noir and a return to literary traditions—grew strong. Film noir included such existentially inspired nihilistic themes as André Cayatte's *Nous sommes tous des assassins* (*We Are All Assassins;* 1952) and Yves Allegret's *Dedée d'Anvers* (1948). Examples of the literary tradition include Bresson's *Journal d'un curé de campagne* (*Diary of a Country Priest;* 1951) and a film rendition of Stendahl's *Le rouge et le noir* (*The Red and the Black;* 1954) by Autant-Lara. By the 1950s comedy adopted a new kind of genre with Jacques Tati's *Les vacances du Monsieur Hulot* (*Mr. Hulot's Holiday;* 1953). By the mid-1950s French filmmaking ushered in the era of enormous budgets, a la Hollywood, and the creation of such frothy potboilers as *And God Created Woman,* which helped make Brigitte Bardot a penthouse name around the world, contributing greatly to the image in America of France as a kingdom of sexual liberation.

By the late 1950s François Truffaut, widely publicizing his auteur theories, rebelled with a series of short films (the most famous of which was *The 400 Blows,* 1959), which was partly financed by government funds, partly by wealthy benefactors. With Jean-Luc Godard (*A bout de soufflé,* or *Breathless,* 1960) and Claude Chabrol (*Le beau Serge;* 1959), they pioneered one of the most publicized movements in 20th-century French art, *la nouvelle vogue.* In the early 1960s, dozens of new directors joined the movement, furiously making films, some of which are considered classics, others of which have been thrown into the dustbin of forgotten artistic endeavors. Enthusiastically endorsed by the counterculture on both sides of the Atlantic, these directors included Renais (*Muriel*), Roger Vadim, Agnès Varda (*Le Bonheur*), Jacques Demy (*Les parapluies de Cherbourg*), Godard (*Pierrot-le-Fou*), Louis Malle, Chris Marker, and Marguerite Duras (*Detruire, dit-elle*).

After a switch to political themes (Costa Gavras's Z) during the 1968 rebellions (and a politically motivated abandonment of the film festival at Cannes by at least a dozen prominent French directors), French cinema turned to comedy in the early 1970s. Examples include Buñuel's *Le charme discret de la bourgeoisie* (1972) and Yanne's *Tout le monde il est beau, tout le monde il est gentil* (1972).

Many American films—still shown rather frequently on TV—were filmed in Paris (or else used sets to simulate Paris). Notable ones have included the classic *An American in Paris,* starring Gene Kelly, and *Moulin Rouge,* starring José Ferrer as Toulouse-Lautrec. Truffaut's *The Last Metro* and Clément's *Is Paris Burning?* gained worldwide audiences, as did *The Sun Also Rises,* an adaptation of Hemingway's celebrated novel, with Ava Gardner and Tyrone Power. *Last Tango in Paris,* with Marlon Brando, was one of the most controversial films set in Paris, and the always-provocative Roman Polanski used Paris as a setting for his *Frantic.*

La Belle Noiseuse, in French, with English subtitles, is a 4-hour film that opened in New York in 1991. Director Jacques Rivette tells the story of a once-celebrated painter, Edouard Frenhofer, who attempts to transform a beautiful young woman into his crowning masterpiece.

In 1992, Michael Bene directed *Le ciel de Paris,* about emotional isolation. The film, which opened in New York, starred Sandrine Bonnaire and Marc Fourastier. It was Mr. Bene's first and last feature film, as he died of AIDS before its release.

Betty Blue, the stylish Jean-Jacques Beineix film about a torrid summertime love affair, was released in English in 1992. It was first shown in France in 1986 when it was that country's nominee for the Oscar as best foreign film.

One French film that continues to enjoy good DVD sales is a flick called *Amélie* by Jean-Pierre Jeunet, which tugs at the heartstrings. You'll fall in love with those scenes shot in Montmartre. You can also rent *Le Placard* by Francis Veber, starring Gérard Depardieu and dealing with gay life in French society.

The most recent French film to achieve world renown is *La Vie en Rose,* which won its star Marion Cotillard an Oscar in 2008 for her performance as "The Little Sparrow," Edith Piaf. This film documenting Piaf's tragic life is an astonishing immersion of one performer (Cotillard) into the body and soul of another (Piaf).

Today the transatlantic movie deal is a relatively common occurrence, and movie executives from California, New York, and Paris regularly collaborate and compete on films suitable for both cultures.

Music

You might not immediately think of music when you think of France, but music and France have gone together since the monks in the 12th century sang Gregorian chants in Notre-Dame. Troubadours with their ballads went all over France in the Middle Ages. In the Renaissance era, **Josquin des Prez** (ca. 1440–1521) was the first master of the High Renaissance style of polyphonic vocal music. He became the greatest composer of his age, a magnificent virtuoso. **Jean-Baptiste Lully** (1632–87) entertained the decadent court of Versailles with his operas. During the reign of Robespierre, **Claude-Joseph Rouget de Lisle** (1760–1836) immortalized himself in 1792 when he wrote *La Marseillaise,* the French national anthem. Regrettably, he died in poverty.

The rise of the middle class in the 1800s gave birth to both grand opera and *opéra comique.* Both styles merged into a kind of lyric opera, mixing soaring arias and tragedy in such widely popular hits as Bizet's **Carmen** in 1875 and St-Saën's *Samson et Dalila* in 1877.

During the romantic period of the 19th century, foreign composers moving to Paris often dominated the musical scene. **Frédéric Chopin** (1810–49) was half-French, half-Polish. He became the most influential composer for piano and even invented new musical forms such as the *ballade.* **Félix Mendelssohn** (1809–47) had to fight against anti-Semitism to establish himself with his symphonies, *concerti,* and chamber music.

Franz Liszt (1811–86), a composer, pianist, and conductor, emerging from Hungary, became the greatest virtuoso pianist of his day.

At the dawn of the 20th century, music became more Impressionistic,

Josephine Baker costumed for her Danse Banane. She rose to fame in the mid-1920s as a singer and dancer.

Paris brims with musical acts.

as evoked by **Claude Debussy** (1862–1918). In many ways, he helped launch modernist music. His *Prélude à L'Après-midi d'un Faune* in 1894 and *La Mer* in 1905 were performed all over Europe. From Russia came **Igor Stravinsky** (1882–1971), who made *Time* magazine's list of the 100 most influential people of the 20th century. He achieved fame as a pianist, conductor, and composer. His *Le sacre du printemps (The Rite of Spring)* provoked a riot in Paris when it was first performed in 1913, with its pagan rituals.

A revolutionary artist, **Yves Klein** (1928–62) was called a "neo-Dada." His 1960 "The Monotone Symphony" with three naked models became a notorious performance. For 20 minutes he conducted an orchestra on one note. Dying of a heart attack at the age of 34, Klein is considered today an enigmatic post-Modernist. **Pierre Boulez** (b. 1925) developed a technique known as integral serialism using a 12-tone system pioneered in the 1920s. As director of the IRCAM institute at the Centre Pompidou, he has influenced young musicians around the world.

France took to American jazz like no other country. Louis Armstrong practically became a national hero to Parisians in the 1930s. **Stephane y Grappelli** (1908–97), a French jazz violinist, founded the Quintette du Hot Club de France, the most famous of all-string jazz bands. **Django Reinhardt** (1910–53) became one of the most prominent jazz musicians of Europe, known for such works as "Belleville" and "My Sweet." In 1949 Paris welcomed the arrival of **Miles Davis** (1926–91), the American jazz artist and trumpeter.

Some French singers went on to achieve world renown, notably **Edith Piaf** (1915–63), "The Little Sparrow" and France's greatest pop singer. Wherever you go in France, you will hear her "La Vie en Rose," which she first recorded in 1946. Even though he was born in 1924, **Charles Aznavour** remains an eternal favorite. He's known for his unique tenor voice with its gravely and soulful low notes. **Jacques Brel** (1929–78), a singer-songwriter, has seen his songs interpreted by everybody from Frank Sinatra to David Bowie. A popular *chanson* singer, **Juliette Greco** (b. 1927) became known as "The High Priestess of Existentialism" on Paris's Left Bank and was beloved by Jean-Paul Sartre. She dressed all in black and let her long, black hair hang free before coming to Hollywood and becoming the mistress of mogul Darryl Zanuck.

Among rock stars, the French consider **Johnny Halladay** (b. 1943) their equivalent of Elvis Presley. He has scored 18 platinum albums, selling more than 100 million records. Another pop icon is **Serge Gainsbourg** (1928–91). He was a master of everything from rock to jazz to reggae. Upon his death, then French President François Mitterand called him "our Baudelaire, our Apollinaire."

Artists with immigrant backgrounds often are the major names in the vibrant French music scene of today, with influences from French Africa, the French Caribbean, and the Middle East. Along with rap and hip-hop, these sounds rule the nights in the *boîtes* of France's biggest cities. **Khaled** (b. 1960) from Algeria has become known as the "king of Raï." The most loved French rapper today is **MC Solaar** (b. 1969), a francophone hip-hop and rap artist, and the most influential of the French rappers. Born in Senegal, he explores racism and ethnic identity in his wordplays based on dance rhythms.

EATING & DRINKING IN PARIS

There is really no such thing as Parisian cuisine, unless you include a platter of entrecôte with *pommes frites*. The capital of France borrows from all provinces, each of which has a distinctive cuisine. Even if you don't venture outside the city limits, you can get an amazing sampling of the diversified regional cuisine of France. All the kitchens from the Jura to Bordeaux, from Brittany and Normandy to Provence and the Auvergne, are represented by the restaurants of Paris.

The most promising trend for those who don't want to sell the family homestead is to patronize one of the *neo-bistrots*. Some of the top chefs of Paris, even Guy Martin of Grand Véfour, have opened these more simplified bistros where haute cuisine isn't

A chocolate dessert at Le Grand Véfour.

served, just good-tasting and often regionally inspired dishes. Chefs have fun creating these more affordable menus, perhaps borrowing dishes that their *grande-mères* taught them. We feature a number of these bistros in this guide, including those run by the country's most famous chef, Alain Ducasse.

Volumes have been written about French gastronomy—our comments are meant to be a brief introduction only. First, as any French person will tell you, French food is the best in the world. That's as true today as it was in the days of the great Escoffier. More than ever, young *chefs du cuisine* are making creative statements in the kitchen, and never in the history of the country has there been such an emphasis on super-fresh ingredients. One chef we know in Paris has been

Baking bread at Poilâne.

known to shut down his restaurant for the day if he doesn't find exactly what he wants in the marketplace that morning.

Of course, you may want to ask, "What will it cost?" Paris has gained a reputation as a damnably expensive place in the food department. True, its star-studded, internationally famous establishments—such as Taillevent—are very expensive indeed. In such culinary cathedrals, you pay not only for superb decor and regal service but also for the art of celebrated chefs on ministerial salaries.

There is also a vast array of expensive restaurants in Paris that exist almost exclusively for the tourist trade. Their food may be indifferent or downright bad, but they'll also have ice water and ketchup to anesthetize your tastebuds, trilingual waiters, and quadrilingual menus. Luckily, there are others—hundreds of others. Paris, which is said to have more restaurants than any other city on earth, has many good, reasonably priced ones. And they aren't hard to find. We've counted 18 of them on a single, narrow Left Bank street.

MEALS & DINING CUSTOMS   In many of the less expensive places described in this guide, the menu will be handwritten, in French only. Don't let that intimidate you. Nor should you be timid about ordering dishes without knowing precisely what they are. You'll get some delightful surprises. We know a woman who wouldn't have dreamed of asking for escargots if she'd realized they were snails cooked in garlic sauce. As it was, she ate this appetizer in a spirit of thrift rather than adventure—and has been addicted to it ever since. As for vegetables, the French regard them as a separate course and eat them apart from the meat or poultry dishes. But we wouldn't advise you to order them especially unless you're an exceptionally hearty eater. Most main courses come with a small helping, or *garni*, of vegetables anyway.

You'll find a large number of specific dishes explained in the glossary of menu terms in "Useful Terms & Phrases" on p. 401 as well as in the restaurant descriptions themselves. No one, however, can explain the subtle nuances of flavor that distinguish them. Those you have to taste for yourself.

As a rule, it's better to order an aperitif—often the house will have a specialty—rather than a heavy drink such as a martini before a classic French dinner. Vodka or scotch can assault your palate, destroying your tastebuds for the festive repast to come.

Allow plenty of time for a gourmet dinner. Orders are often prepared individually, and it takes time to absorb the wine and the flavors. Sometimes sorbet (a sherbet) is served midway in your meal to cleanse the palate.

Making reservations is important, and please try to show up on time. Too many Americans make reservations and then become a no-show, which creates ill will, especially because many nine-table restaurants must be filled completely every night to make a profit. If you're window-shopping for a restaurant, you'll find the menu most often displayed outside. Parisians read it like a book. It's there for you to study and ponder—so read it in anticipation. Most French people have their main meal during the day; you, too, may want to follow that custom, dining more lightly in the evening.

Most meals consist of several small courses. You can begin, for example, with hors d'oeuvres or a light *potage* (soup). The classic restaurant used to serve a small order of fish after the appetizer, and then the meat or poultry course, but nowadays it's likely to be either fish or meat. A salad follows the main course, then a selection of cheese (there are 365 registered French cheeses) and dessert (often a fruit concoction or a sorbet). In this book, prices are given for fixed-price or a la carte main courses.

If you find the food too rich, with too many sauces, that may be because you've been overdoing it. Elaborately prepared gourmet banquets should not be consumed for both lunch and dinner, or even every day. Sometimes an omelet or a roast chicken can make a delightful light meal, and you can save up for your big dining experience.

THE CUISINE   The revolution against Escoffier has been raging for so long that many of the early rebels are now returning to the old style of cookery, as exemplified by the boeuf bourguignon, the *blanquette de veau,* and the *pot-au-feu.*

Cuisine moderne is here to stay, and some restaurants feature both traditional and contemporary. The new cooking is often based on the classic principles of French cookery, but with a big difference. Rich sauces, for example, are eliminated. Cooking times that can destroy the best of fresh ingredients are considerably shortened. The aim is to release the natural flavor of food without covering it with heavy layers of butter and cream. New flavor combinations in this widely expanding repertoire are often inspired.

WINE   French cookery achieves palate perfection only when lubricated by wine, which is not considered a luxury or even an addition, but rather an integral part of every meal. Certain rules about wine drinking have been long established in France, but no one except traditionalists seems to follow them anymore. "Rules" would dictate that if you're having a roast, steak, or game, a good burgundy should be your choice. If it's chicken, lamb, or veal, you would choose a red from the Bordeaux country, certainly a full-bodied red with cheese such as Camembert, and a blanc-de-blanc with oysters. A light rosé can go with almost anything, especially if enjoyed on a summer terrace overlooking the Seine.

Let your own good taste—and sometimes almost as important, your pocketbook—determine your choice of wine. Most wine stewards, called sommeliers, are there to help you in your choice, and only in the most dishonest of restaurants will they push you toward the most expensive selections. Of course, if you prefer only bottled water, or perhaps a beer, then be firm and order either without embarrassment. In fact, bottled water might be a good idea at lunch if you're planning to drive later. Some restaurants include a beverage in their menu rates *(boisson compris)*, but that's only in the cheaper places. Nevertheless, some of the most satisfying wines we've drunk in Paris came from unlabeled house bottles or carafes, called a *vin de la maison*. In general, unless you're a real connoisseur, don't worry about labels and vintages.

When in doubt, you can rarely go wrong with a good burgundy or bordeaux, but you may want to be more adventurous than that. That's when the sommelier can help you, particularly if you tell him or her your taste in wine (semidry or very dry, for example). State frankly how much you're willing to pay and what you plan to order for your meal. If you're dining with others, you may want to order two or three bottles with an entire dinner, selecting a wine to suit each course. However, Parisians at informal meals—and especially if there are only two persons dining—select only one wine to go with all their platters, from hors d'oeuvres to cheese. As a rule of thumb, expect to spend about one-third of the restaurant tab for wine.

WINE LABELS   Since the latter part of the 19th century, French wines sold in France (and sometimes elsewhere) have been labeled. The general label is known as *appellations contrôlées*. These controls, for the most part, are by regions such as Bordeaux and the Loire. These are the simple, honest wines of the district. They can be blended from grapes grown at any place in the region. Some are composed of the vintages of different years.

In most cases, the more specific the label, the better the wine. For example, instead of a bordeaux, the wine might be labeled "Médoc" (pronounced *May*-doc), which is the name of a triangle of land extending some 50 miles north from Bordeaux. Wine labels can be narrowed down to a particular vine-growing property, such as a Château Haut-Brion, one of the most famous and greatest of red wines of Bordeaux. (This château produces only about 10,000 cases a year.)

On some burgundies, you are likely to see the word *clos* (pronounced clō). Originally, that meant a walled or otherwise enclosed vineyard, as in Clos-de-Bèze, which is a celebrated Burgundian vineyard producing a superb red wine. *Cru* (pronounced croo, and meaning "growth") suggests a wine of superior quality when it appears on a label as a *vin-de-cru*. Wines and vineyards are often divided into crus. A grand cru or premier cru should, by implication, be an even superior wine.

Labels are only part of the story. It's the vintage that counts. Essentially, vintage is the annual grape harvest and the wine made from those

Classic French wine label.

grapes. Therefore, any wine can be a vintage wine unless it is a blend. But there are good vintages and bad vintages. The variation between wine produced in a "good year" and wine produced in a "bad year" can be great, and even noted by the neophyte.

Finally, champagne is the only wine that can be correctly served through all courses of a meal—but only to those who can afford its astronomical cost.

PLANNING YOUR TRIP TO PARIS

3

Flying into France, if your documents are in order, is one of the most effortless undertakings in global travel. There are no shots to get, no particular safety precautions, no unusual aspects of planning a trip. With your passport, airline ticket, and enough money, you just go. In general, if you're not bringing any illegal items into France, Customs officials are courteous and will speed you on your way into their country.

Of course, before you lift off the ground in your native country, you can do some advance preparation as will be detailed in this chapter and in "Fast Facts" on p. 395. That could mean checking to see if your passport is up to date (or obtaining one if you don't already possess one), or taking care of health needs before you go, including medication. In the case of Paris, you might want to make reservations at some highly acclaimed restaurants or even buy tickets in advance to certain performances.

In the pages that follow, you find everything you need to know about the practicalities of planning your trip in advance: finding the best airfare, deciding when to go, figuring out the euro, and more.

For additional help in planning your trip and for more on-the-ground resources in Paris, please turn to "Fast Facts," on p. 395.

WHEN TO GO

The best time to visit Paris is in the spring (Apr–June) or fall (Sept–Nov), when things are easier to come by—from Métro seats to good-tempered waiters. The weather is temperate year-round. July and August are the worst for crowds. Parisians desert their city then, leaving it to the tourists.

Hotels used to charge off-season rates during the cold, rainy period from November through February; now, they're often packed with business travelers, trade fairs, and winter tour groups, and hoteliers have less incentive to offer discounts. Airfares are still cheaper during these months, and more promotions are available. They rise in the spring and fall, peaking in the summer, when tickets cost the most.

In even-numbered years, don't come to Paris during the first 2 weeks of October without a confirmed hotel room. The weather's fine, but the city is jammed for the auto show.

Paris's Average Daytime Temperatures & Rainfall

	JAN	FEB	MAR	APR	MAY	JUNE	JULY	AUG	SEPT	OCT	NOV	DEC
TEMP. °F	38	39	46	51	58	64	66	66	61	53	45	40
TEMP. °C	3	4	8	11	14	18	19	19	16	12	7	4
RAINFALL (IN.)	3.2	2.9	2.4	2.7	3.2	3.5	3.3	3.7	3.3	3.0	3.5	3.1

FACING PAGE: **Reading along the Seine.**

Holidays in France are known as *jours fériés*. Shops and banks are closed, as well as many (but not all) restaurants and museums. For a list of major holidays, see "Fast Facts," p. 395.

Paris Calendar of Events

Check the Paris Tourist Office website at **www.parisinfo.com** (✆ **08-92-68-30-00**; .34€ per minute) for up-to-the-minute details on these and other events. For an exhaustive list of events beyond those listed here, check http://events.frommers.com, where you'll find a searchable up-to-the-minute roster of what's happening in cities all over the world, including Paris.

FEBRUARY

Special Exhibitions, Special Concerts. During Paris's grayest month, look for a splash of expositions and concerts designed to perk up the city. Concerts and theaters spring up at such diverse sites as the **Cité de la Musique,** 221 av. Jean-Jaurès, 19e (✆ **01-44-84-45-00;** www.cite-musique.fr; Métro: Porte-de-Pantin); the **Théâtre des Champs-Elysées,** 15 av. Montaigne, 8e (✆ **01-49-52-50-50;** www.theatre champselysees.fr; Métro: Alma-Marceau); and the **Maison de Radio-France,** 116 av. du Président-Kennedy, 16e (✆ **01-56-40-15-16;** www.radiofrance.fr; Métro: Passy-Ranelagh). Also look for openings of new operas at the **Opéra Bastille,** 2 place de la Bastille, 4e (✆ **08-92-89-90-90;** www.operadeparis.fr; Métro: Bastille); operas and dance at the **Opéra Garnier,** place de l'Opéra, 9e (✆ **01-40-01-25-14;** Métro: Opéra); and concerts at the **Auditorium du Louvre,** 1er (✆ **01-40-20-50-50;** www.louvre.fr; Métro: Musée du Louvre), and the **Salle Cortot,** 78 rue Cardinet, 17e (✆ **01-47-63-80-16;** Métro: Malesherbes). A copy of *Pariscope* or *L'Officiel des Spectacles,* available at most newsstands, is the best info source.

MARCH

International Ready-to-Wear Fashion Shows (Salon International de Prêt-à-Porter), Parc des Expositions (Hall no. 7), 15e. Hundreds of designers, from the giants to the unknown, unveil their visions (hallucinations?) of what you will be wearing in 6 months. The event in the Porte de Versailles convention facilities is geared to wholesalers, retailers, buyers, journalists, and industry professionals, but for the merely fashion-conscious, the rules are usually bent. Much more exclusive are the *défilés* (fashion shows) at the headquarters of houses such as Lagerfeld, Lanvin, Courrèges, and Valentino. For details, call ✆ **01-44-94-70-00;** www.pretparis.com. Early March.

Foire du Trône, Bois de Vincennes, 12e. A mammoth amusement park that its fans call France's largest country fair, the Foire du Trône originated in A.D. 957, when merchants met with farmers to exchange grain and wine. This high-tech continuation of that tradition, held on the lawns of the Pelouse de Reuilly, has a Ferris wheel, carousels, acrobats, fire eaters, and diversions that seem like a Gallic Coney Island. It's open daily from 2pm to midnight. Call ✆ **01-46-27-52-29;** www.foiredutrone.com. End of March to end of May.

APRIL

International Marathon of Paris. Beginning on the Champs-Elysées at 9am, runners take over Paris's boulevards in a race that draws competitors from around the world. Depending on their speed and endurance, participants arrive at the finishing point on avenue Foch, 16e, starting about 2½ hours later. For details, call ✆ **01-41-33-14-00;** www.paris marathon.com. Early April.

Les Grandes Eaux Musicales, Versailles. These musical events are intended to re-create the atmosphere of the ancient regime. The fountains around the palace are turned on, with special emphasis on the Neptune Fountain, which sits squarely in front of the best view of the château. You can promenade in the garden and listen to the music of French composers (Couperin, Charpentier, and Lully) and others (Mozart or Haydn) whose careers thrived during the years of the palace's construction. The music is recorded, but the vistas are monumental, and the music, the fountains, and the architectural vistas of the world's grandest château all operate in unison. The events occur every Saturday and Sunday from 11:15am till noon and 2:30pm till 5pm between April and early September. For details, call ☎ **01-30-83-78-89;** www.chateauversailles-spectacles.fr.

MAY

VE Day (in French: *Jour de l'Armistice*), citywide. The celebration commemorating the capitulation of the Nazis on May 7, 1945, lasts 4 days in Paris, with a parade along the Champs-Elysées and additional ceremonies in Reims. Pro-American sentiments are probably higher during this festival than at any other time of year. May 5 to 8.

Grand Steeplechase de Paris, Auteuil and Longchamp racetracks, Bois de Boulogne. In this equestrian event, obstacle courses at both Auteuil and Longchamp racetracks are laid out to incorporate hurdles and crossings over streams. The result is a rougher, more rustic counterpoint to the flatbed races conducted at Chantilly (see below). For details, call ☎ **01-49-10-20-30;** www.france-galop.com. Mid-May.

French Open Tennis Championship, Stade Roland-Garros, 16e. The Open features 10 days of Grand Slam men's and women's tennis, with European and South American players traditionally dominating on the hot, dusty red courts. For details, call ☎ **01-47-43-48-00;** www.fft.fr. Late May to early June.

Fête de St-Denis, St-Denis. This series presents a month of artfully contrived music in the burial place of the French kings, a grim, early Gothic monument in this industrialized northern suburb. For details, call ☎ **01-48-13-06-07;** www.festival-saint-denis.com. Early June to July.

Prix du Jockey Club & Prix Diane-Hermès, Hippodrome de Chantilly. Thoroughbreds from as far away as Kentucky and Brunei, as well as mounts sponsored by Europe's old and new fortunes, compete in a very civil competition broadcast around France and talked about in horse circles around the world. On race days, as many as 30 trains depart from Paris's Gare du Nord for Chantilly, where they're met by free shuttle buses to the track. For details on this and all other equine events in this calendar, call ☎ **01-49-10-20-30;** www.france-galop.com. First week of June (Jockey Club) and second week of June (Prix Diane-Hermès).

Paris Air Show, Le Bourget. This is where France's military-industrial complex shows off enough high-tech hardware to make anyone think twice about invading La Patrie. Fans, competitors, and industrial spies mob the airport's exhibition halls for a taste of what Gallic technocrats have wrought. For details, call ☎ **01-53-23-33-16;** www.paris-air-show.com. Mid-June.

Fête de la Musique, citywide. This celebration at the summer solstice is the only day that noise laws don't apply in Paris. Musicians and wannabes pour into the streets, where you can make music with anything, even if it means banging two garbage cans together or driving around blowing your car horn (illegal otherwise). You might hear anything from Russians playing balalaikas to Cubans playing mambo rhythms. Musical parties pop up in virtually all the open

3

spaces, with more organized concerts at place de la Bastille and place de la République, and in La Villette and the Latin Quarter. For details, call ☎ **01-40-03-94-70;** www.fetedelamusique. culture.fr. Third week of June.

Festival Musique en l'Ile. A series of concerts, most including dignified masses composed from the 17th to the late–19th centuries, is presented at the Church St-Louis-en-l'Ile and the Church St-Germain-des-Prés. For more information, call La Toison d'Art at ☎ **01-44-62-00-55;** www.latoisondart.com. Late June to late August.

La Course des Garçons de Café, throughout the city. Although it has diminished somewhat in importance in Paris since the postwar years, when it was much more visible, there's no more amusing race in Paris. Balancing heavy trays, the *garçons* (both waiters and waitresses) line up in front of the Hôtel de Ville in the 4th arrondissement and then race for 8km (5 miles) through the streets, ending back at the Hôtel de Ville. Some, obviously, don't make it. A Sunday in the last week of June or first week of July.

Gay Pride Parade, place de la République to place de la Bastille. A week of expositions and parties climaxes in a parade patterned after those in New York and San Francisco. It's followed by a dance at the Palais de Bercy, a convention hall/sports arena. For more information about gay pride and any other aspect of gay, lesbian, and transgendered life in and around Paris, contact Lesbian and Gay Pride, Ile de France, 3 rue Keller, BP 255, 75524 Paris Cedex 11. For information about the parade, call or fax ☎ **01-72-70-39-22;** www.inter-lgbt. org. Late June.

Tour de France. This is Europe's most visible, highly contested, and overabundantly televised bicycle race. Crews of

wind tunnel–tested athletes speed along an itinerary tracing the six sides of the French "hexagon," detouring deep into the Massif Central and across the Swiss Alps. The race is decided at a finish line drawn across the Champs-Elysées. For details, call ☎ **01-41-33-14-00;** www. letour.fr. First 3 weeks of July.

Bastille Day, citywide. This celebration of the 1789 storming of the Bastille is the birth date of modern France, and festivities reach their peak in Paris with street fairs, pageants, fireworks, and feasts. The day begins with a parade down the Champs-Elysées and ends with fireworks in Montmartre. Wherever you are, before the end of the day, you'll hear Piaf warbling "La Foule" ("The Crowd"), the song that celebrated her passion for the stranger she met and later lost in a crowd on Bastille Day, and lots of people singing "La Marseillaise." July 14.

Paris Quartier d'Eté, Latin Quarter. For 4 weeks, the Arènes de Lutèce or the Sorbonne's Cour d'Honneur host pop orchestral concerts. The dozen or so concerts are grander than the outdoor setting would imply and include performances by the Orchestre de Paris, Orchestre National de France, and Baroque Orchestra of the European Union. On the fringes, you can find plays, jazz, and parades in the Tuileries Gardens. For details, call ☎ **01-44-94-98-00;** www.quartierdete.com. Mid-July to mid-August.

International Ready-to-Wear Fashion Shows (Salon International de Prêt-à-Porter), Parc des Expositions, 15e. More of what took place at the fashion shows in March (see above), with an emphasis on what *le beau monde* (the rich and the beautiful) will be wearing next spring. For details, call ☎ **01-44-94-70-00;** www.pretparis.com. Early September.

La Villette Jazz Festival, La Villette. This homage to the art of jazz incorporates

50 concerts in churches, auditoriums, and concert halls in all neighborhoods of this Paris suburb. Past festivals have welcomed Herbie Hancock, Shirley Horn, Michel Portal, and other artists from around the world. For details, call ℂ **01-40-03-75-75;** www.cite-musique. fr. Early September.

Fête d'Automne (Autumn Festival), citywide. Paris welcomes the return of its residents from their August holidays with an ongoing and eclectic festival of modern music, ballet, theater, and art. Venues include art galleries, churches, concert halls, auditoriums, and parks citywide. There's an emphasis on experimental works, which the festival's promoters scatter judiciously among more traditional productions. Depending on the event, tickets cost from 15€ to 95€. For details, contact the **Fête d'Automne,** 156 rue de Rivoli, 75001 Paris. Or call ℂ **01-53-45-17-17;** www.festival-automne.com. Mid-September to late December.

Biennale des Antiquaires, Carrousel du Louvre, 99 rue de Rivoli, 1er. Antiques dealers and lovers from all over gather at this gilded event in even-numbered years. Precious furnishings and objets d'art are displayed in the underground exhibit halls linked to the Louvre, or perhaps in the Grand Palais after it's restored. For details, call ℂ **01-44-51-74-74;** www.bdafrance.eu. Usually third week in September. Next event: 2012.

OCTOBER

Prix de l'Arc de Triomphe, Hippodrome de Longchamp, 16e. France's answer to England's Ascot is the country's most prestigious horse race, culminating the equine season in Europe. For details, call ℂ **01-49-10-20-30;** www.france-galop. com. Early October.

Paris Auto Show, Parc des Expositions, 15e. Glitzy attendees and lots of hype

attend this showcase for European car design. The show takes place in even-numbered years near the Porte de Versailles. In addition, a permanent exhibit on French auto design at the Cité des Sciences et de l'Industrie is upgraded and enriched during October. For details, call ℂ **01-56-88-22-40;** www.mondial-automobile.com. Two weeks in October (dates vary).

NOVEMBER

Armistice Day, citywide. The signing of the controversial document that ended World War I is celebrated with a military parade from the Arc de Triomphe to the Hôtel des Invalides. November 11.

Release of the Beaujolais Nouveau, citywide. Parisians eagerly await the yearly release of the first new Beaujolais, that fruity wine from Burgundy. Signs are posted in bistros, wine bars, and cafes—these places report their heaviest patronage of the year during this celebration of the grape. Third Thursday in November.

DECEMBER

Le Salon Nautique de Paris (Boat Fair), Parc des Expositions, 15e. This is Europe's most visible exposition of what's afloat and of interest to wholesalers, retailers, boat owners (or wannabes), and anyone involved in the business of waterborne holidaymaking. For details, call ℂ **01-47-56-50-00,** or check on the Web at www.salon nautiqueparis.com. Ten days in early December.

Fête de St-Sylvestre (New Year's Eve), citywide. It's most boisterously celebrated in the Latin Quarter around the Sorbonne. At midnight, the city explodes. Strangers kiss strangers, and boulevard St-Michel and the Champs-Elysées become virtual pedestrian malls. December 31.

ENTRY REQUIREMENTS

Passports

Citizens of such countries as New Zealand, Australia, Canada, and the United States need only a valid passport to enter France. The passport is valid for a stay of 90 days in France.

For information on how to get a passport, go to "Passports" on p. 398—the websites listed provide downloadable passport applications as well as the current fees for processing passport applications.

To prevent international child abduction, E.U. governments have initiated procedures at entry and exit points. These often (but not always) include requiring documentary evidence of relationship and permission for the child's travel from the parent or legal guardian not present. Having such documentation on hand, even if not required, facilitates entries and exits. All children must have their own passports.

Customs

WHAT YOU CAN BRING INTO FRANCE:

NON-E.U. NATIONALS   Non-E.U. nationals can bring in 200 cigarettes, 100 cigarillos, 50 cigars, or 250 grams of smoking tobacco, duty-free. This amount is doubled if you live outside Europe. You can also bring in 2 liters of wine and 1 liter of alcohol of more than 22%, or 2 liters of wine 22% or less. In addition, you can bring in 60cc of perfume, or a quarter liter of eau de toilette. Visitors ages 15 and older can bring in other goods totaling 175€; for those younger than 15, the limit is 90€. Customs officials tend to be lenient about general merchandise as the limits are very low.

E.U. NATIONALS   Citizens of E.U. countries can bring in any amount of goods as long as the goods are intended for their personal use and not for resale.

WHAT YOU CAN TAKE HOME FROM FRANCE:

U.S. CITIZENS   Returning U.S. citizens who have been away for 48 hours or more are allowed to bring back, once every 30 days, $800 worth of merchandise duty-free. You're charged a flat rate of duty on the next $1,000 worth of purchases, and any dollar amount beyond that is subject to duty at whatever rates apply. On mailed gifts, the duty-free limit is $200. Have your receipts or purchases handy to expedite the declaration process. **Note:** If you owe duty, you are required to pay on your arrival into the United States, using cash, personal check, government or traveler's check, or money order; some locations also accept Visa or MasterCard.

To avoid having to pay duty on foreign-made personal items you owned before your trip, bring along a bill of sale, insurance policy, jeweler's appraisal, or receipt of purchase. Or you can register items that can be readily identified by a permanently affixed serial number or marking—think laptop computers, cameras, and CD players—with Customs before you leave. Take the items to the nearest Customs office, or register them with Customs at the airport from which you're departing. You'll receive, at no cost, a Certificate of Registration, which allows duty-free entry for the life of the item.

You cannot bring fresh foodstuffs into the U.S.; canned foods are allowed. For specifics on what you can bring back and the corresponding fees, download the invaluable free pamphlet *Know Before You Go* online at **www.cbp.gov**. (Click "Travel," and then click "Know Before You Go.") Or, contact the **U.S. Customs & Border Protection (CBP),** 1300 Pennsylvania Ave., NW, Washington, DC 20229 (✆ **877/287-8667**), and request the pamphlet.

CANADIAN CITIZENS Canada allows its citizens a C$750 exemption, and you're allowed to bring back duty-free one carton of cigarettes, one can of tobacco, 40 imperial ounces of liquor, and 50 cigars. In addition, you're allowed to mail gifts to Canada from abroad valued at less than C$60 a day, provided they're unsolicited and don't contain alcohol or tobacco (write on the package "Unsolicited gift, under C$60 value"). All valuables, including serial numbers of valuables you already own, such as expensive foreign cameras, should be declared on the Y-38 form before departure from Canada. *Note:* The C$750 exemption can be used only once a year and only after an absence of 7 days.

For a clear summary of Canadian rules, write for the booklet *I Declare,* issued by the **Canada Border Services Agency** (✆ **800/461-9999** in Canada, or 204/983-3500; www.cbsa-asfc.gc.ca).

U.K. CITIZENS Citizens of the U.K. returning from an E.U. country such as France go through a Customs exit (called the "Blue Exit") especially for E.U. travelers. In essence, there is no limit on what you can bring back from an E.U. country, as long as the items are for personal use (this includes gifts) and you have already paid the duty and tax. However, Customs law sets out guidance levels. If you bring in more than these levels, you may be asked to prove that the goods are for your own use. Guidance levels on goods bought in the E.U. for your own use are 3,200 cigarettes, 200 cigars, 400 cigarillos, 3 kilograms of smoking tobacco, 10 liters of spirits, 90 liters of wine, 20 liters of fortified wine (such as port or sherry), and 110 liters of beer.

For information, contact **HM Revenue Customs** at ✆ **0845/010-9000** (from outside the U.K., 02920/501-261), or consult their website at www.hmrc.gov.uk.

AUSTRALIAN CITIZENS The duty-free allowance in Australia is A$900 or, for those 17 or younger, A$450. Citizens can bring in 250 cigarettes or 250 grams of loose tobacco, and 2.25 liters of alcohol. If you're returning with valuables you already own, such as foreign-made cameras, you should file form B263.

A helpful brochure available from Australian consulates or Customs offices is *Know Before You Go.* For more information, call the **Australian Customs Service** at ✆ **1300/363-263,** or log on to www.customs.gov.au.

NEW ZEALAND CITIZENS The duty-free allowance for **New Zealand** is NZ$700. Citizens 17 and older can bring in 200 cigarettes, 50 cigars, or 250 grams of tobacco (or a mixture of all three if the combined weight doesn't exceed 250g), plus 4.5 liters of wine and beer, or 1.125 liters of liquor. New Zealand currency does not carry import or export restrictions. Fill out a certificate of export, listing the valuables you are taking out of the country; that way, you can bring them back without paying duty.

Most questions are answered in a free pamphlet available at New Zealand consulates and Customs offices: *New Zealand Customs Guide for Travellers, Notice no. 4.* For more information, contact **New Zealand Customs Service,** The Customhouse, 17–21 Whitmore St., P.O. Box 2218, Wellington (*©* **04/473-6099** or 0800/428-786; www.customs.govt.nz).

Medical Requirements

Unless you are arriving from an area of the world known to be suffering from an epidemic, especially cholera or yellow fever, inoculations or vaccinations are not required for entry in France.

GETTING THERE & GETTING AROUND PARIS

BY PLANE

Paris has two international airports: **Aéroport d'Orly,** 14km (8⅔ miles) south of the city, and **Aéroport Roissy–Charles de Gaulle,** 22km (14 miles) northeast. A shuttle (16€) makes the 50- to 75-minute journey between the two airports about every 30 minutes.

CHARLES DE GAULLE AIRPORT (ROISSY)   At Charles de Gaulle (*©* **01-48-62-12-12** or 39-50 from France only; www.paris-cdg.com), foreign carriers use Aérogare 1, while Air France uses Aérogare 2. From Aérogare 1, you take a moving walkway to the passport checkpoint and the Customs area. A *navette* (shuttle bus) links the two terminals.

The free shuttle buses also transport you to the **Roissy rail station,** from which fast RER (Réseau Express Régional; www.ratp.fr) trains leave every 10 minutes between 5am and midnight for Métro stations including Gare du Nord, Châtelet, Luxembourg, Port-Royal, and Denfert-Rochereau. A typical fare from Roissy to any point in central Paris is 9.05€ per adult, 4.50€ for children 4 to 10. Travel time from the airport to central Paris is around 35 to 40 minutes.

You can also take an **Air France shuttle bus** (*©* **08-92-35-08-20** or 01-48-64-14-24; www.cars-airfrance.com) to central Paris for 15€ one-way; children 2 to 11 pay 7.50€. It stops at the Palais des Congrès (Port Maillot) and continues to place Charles de Gaulle–Etoile, where subway lines can carry you to any point in Paris. That ride, depending on traffic, takes 45 to 55 minutes. The shuttle departs about every 20 minutes between 5:40am and 11pm.

The **Roissybus** (*©* **01-58-76-16-16**), operated by the RATP, departs from the airport daily from 6am to 11:45pm and costs 8.60€ for the 45- to 50-minute ride. Departures are about every 15 minutes, and the bus leaves you near the corner of rue Scribe and place de l'Opéra in the heart of Paris.

A **taxi** from Roissy into the city will cost about 65€ to 95€; from 8pm to 7am the fare is 40% higher. Long, orderly lines for taxis form outside each of the airport's terminals.

ORLY AIRPORT   Orly (*©* **01-49-75-52-52** or 39-50 from France only) has two terminals—Orly Sud (south) for international flights and Orly Ouest (west) for domestic flights. A free shuttle bus connects them in 3 minutes.

Air France buses leave from exit E of Orly Sud and from exit F of Orly Ouest every 12 minutes between 6am and 11:30pm for Gare des Invalides; the fare is 12€ one-way, 19€ round-trip, and 5.50€ for children ages 2 to 11. Returning to the airport (about 30 min.), buses leave both the Montparnasse and the Invalides terminal for Orly Sud or Orly Ouest every 15 minutes.

The Paris Airport Shuttle

The **Paris Airport Shuttle** (✆ **01-53-39-18-18;** fax 01-53-39-13-13; www.parishuttle.com) is the best option for airport transit. It charges 20€ for one person or 18€ per person for parties of two or more going to or from Charles de Gaulle or Orly. Both shuttles accept American Express, Visa, and MasterCard, with 1-day advance reservations required.

There are no direct trains from Orly to the center of Paris; however, you can take the Monorail ("Orly Val"), but you have to change at the RER station "Anthony" for continued RER services into the center. Combined travel time is about 45 to 55 minutes. To return to the airport, you can take the RER from points throughout central Paris to the station at Point-de-Rungis/Aéroport d'Orly. Either going into Paris or returning, the one-way fare is 12€. Once at Pont-de-Rungis, take the free shuttle bus that departs every 15 minutes to both of Orly's terminals.

A **taxi** from Orly to central Paris costs about 55€ to 85€, more at night. Don't take a meterless taxi from Orly—it's much safer (and usually cheaper) to hire one of the metered cabs, which are under the scrutiny of a police officer.

BY TRAIN

Paris has six major stations: **Gare d'Austerlitz,** 55 quai d'Austerlitz, 13e (serving the southwest, with trains to and from the Loire Valley, Bordeaux, the Pyrénées, and Spain); **Gare de l'Est,** place du 11-Novembre-1918, 10e (serving the east, with trains to and from Strasbourg, Reims, and beyond, to Zurich and Austria); **Gare de Lyon,** 20 bd. Diderot, 12e (serving the southeast, with trains to and from the Côte d'Azur [Nice, Cannes, St-Tropez], Provence, and beyond, to Geneva and Italy); **Gare Montparnasse,** 17 bd. Vaugirard, 15e (serving the west, with trains to and from Brittany); **Gare du Nord,** 18 rue de Dunkerque, 15e (serving the north, with trains to and from London, Holland, Denmark, and northern Germany); and **Gare St-Lazare,** 13 rue d'Amsterdam, 8e (serving the northwest, with trains to and from Normandy). Buses operate between the stations, and each station has a Métro stop. For train information and to make reservations, call ✆ **08-92-35-35-35** from abroad, or 36-35 from France, between 8am and 8pm daily. From Paris, one-way rail passage to Tours costs 30€ to 51€; one-way to Strasbourg 55€ or 80€, depending on the routing.

Warning: The stations and surrounding areas are usually seedy and frequented by pickpockets, hustlers, hookers, and addicts. Be alert, especially at night.

BY BUS

Most buses arrive at the **Eurolines France** station, 28 av. du Général-de-Gaulle, Bagnolet (✆ **08-92-89-90-91;** toll call .34€ per minute; www.eurolines.fr; Métro: Gallieni).

UNDER THE channel

Queen Elizabeth II and the late French president François Mitterrand opened the Channel Tunnel in 1994, and the *Eurostar Express* has daily passenger service from London to Paris and Brussels. The $15-billion tunnel, one of the great engineering feats of our time, is the first link between Britain and the Continent since the Ice Age. The 50km (31-mile) journey takes 35 minutes, with actual time spent in the Chunnel 19 minutes.

Eurostar tickets are available through **Rail Europe** (🕾 888/382-7245; www.raileurope.com). In London, make reservations for Eurostar (or any other train in Europe) at 🕾 **0870/518-6186.** In Paris, call 🕾 **01-70-70-60-88,** and in the United States, call 🕾 **800/EUROSTAR** [387-6782]; www.eurostar.com. Chunnel train traffic is competitive with air travel, if you calculate door-to-door travel time. Trains leave from London's St. Pancras Station and arrive in Paris at Gare du Nord.

Fares are complicated and depend on a number of factors. The cheapest fare is Leisure RT, requiring a purchase at least 14 business days before the date of travel and a minimum 2-night stay. A return ticket must be booked to receive this discounted fare.

The Chunnel accommodates not only trains but also cars, buses, taxis, and motorcycles. **Eurotunnel,** a train carrying vehicles under the Channel (🕾 **0870/535-3535** in the U.K.; www.eurotunnel.com), connects Calais, France, with Folkestone, England. It operates 24 hours a day, 365 days a year, running every 15 minutes during peak travel times and at least once an hour at night.

Before boarding Eurotunnel, you stop at a toll booth to pay, and then pass through Immigration for both countries at one time. During the ride, you travel in air-conditioned carriages, remaining in your car or stepping outside to stretch your legs. An hour later, you simply drive off.

Eurostar Chunnel one-way tickets cost from 79€ when booking in England to go to France. A car with passenger going through the Eurotunnel costs from 200€.

BY CAR

Driving in Paris is *not* recommended. Parking is difficult and traffic dense. If you drive, remember that Paris is encircled by a ring road, the *périphérique*. Always obtain detailed directions to your destination, including the name of the exit on the *périphérique* (exits aren't numbered). Avoid rush hours.

The major highways into Paris are A1 from the north; A13 from Rouen, Normandy, and other points northwest; A10 from Spain and the southwest; A6 and A7 from the French Alps, the Riviera, and Italy; and A4 from eastern France.

BY FERRY FROM ENGLAND

Ferry travel between England and France appears to be in its waning days, since more and more travelers are opting for a much speedier Chunnel passage. Two leading operators of ferries across the Channel are **P&O Ferries** (🕾 0871/664-5645 in the U.K.; www.poferries.com) and **Britanny Ferries** 🕾 0871/2440744 in the UK; www.britanny-ferries.com). Prices and routes are in flux, so call or check websites for specific times, prices, and points of departure/arrival.

Getting Around

CITY LAYOUT

Paris is surprisingly compact. Occupying 2,723 sq. km (1,051 sq. miles), its urban area is home to more than 11 million people. The river Seine divides Paris into the **Rive Droite (Right Bank)** to the north and the **Rive Gauche (Left Bank)** to the south. These designations make sense when you stand on a bridge and face downstream (west)—to your right is the north bank, to your left the south. A total of 32 bridges link the Right Bank and the Left Bank. Some provide access to the two islands at the heart of the city—**Ile de la Cité,** the city's birthplace and site of Notre-Dame; and **Ile St-Louis,** a moat-guarded oasis of 17th-century mansions.

The main street on the Right Bank is **avenue des Champs-Elysées,** beginning at the Arc de Triomphe and running to place de la Concorde. Avenue des Champs-Elysées and 11 other avenues radiate like the arms of an asterisk from the Arc de Triomphe, giving it its original name, place de l'Etoile (*étoile* means "star"). It was renamed place Charles de Gaulle following the general's death; today, it's often referred to as place Charles de Gaulle–Etoile.

FINDING AN ADDRESS

Paris is divided into 20 municipal wards called **arrondissements,** each with its own city hall, police station, and post office; some have remnants of market squares. Arrondissements spiral out clockwise from the 1st, in the geographical center of the city. The 2nd through the 8th form a ring around the 1st, and the 9th through the 17th form an outer ring around the inner ring. The 18th, 19th, and 20th are at the far northern and eastern reaches of the Right Bank. Arrondissements 5, 6, 7, 13, 14, and 15 are on the Left Bank.

Most city maps are divided by arrondissement, and addresses include the arrondissement number (in Roman or Arabic numerals and followed by "er" or "e"). Paris also has its own version of a zip code. The mailing address for a hotel is written as, for example, "Paris 75014." The last two digits, 14, indicate that the address is in the 14th arrondissement—in this case, Montparnasse.

Numbers on buildings running parallel to the Seine usually follow the course of the river—east to west. On perpendicular streets, building numbers begin low closer to the river.

MAPS

If you're staying more than 2 or 3 days, purchase an inexpensive pocket-size book called *Paris par arrondissement,* available at newsstands and bookshops; prices start at 6.50€. This guide provides you with a Métro map, a foldout map of the city, and maps of each arrondissement, with all streets listed and keyed.

BY MÉTRO (SUBWAY)

The Métro (✆ **08-92-69-32-46** from abroad, or 32-46 from France; www.ratp. fr) is the most efficient and fastest way to get around Paris. All lines are numbered, and the final destination of each line is clearly marked on subway maps, in the system's underground passageways, and on the train cars. The Métro runs daily from 5:30am to 1:15am (last departure at 2am on Sat). It's reasonably safe at any hour, but beware of pickpockets.

To familiarize yourself with the Métro, check out the color map on the inside back cover of this book. Most stations display a map of the Métro at the entrance. To locate your correct train on a map, find your destination, follow the line to the end of its route, and note the name of the final stop, which is that line's direction. In the station, follow the signs for your direction in the passageways until you see the label on a train. Many larger stations have maps with push-button indicators that light up your route when you press the button for your destination.

Transfer stations are *correspondances*—some require long walks; Châtelet is the most difficult—but most trips require only one transfer. When transferring, follow the orange CORRESPONDANCE signs to the proper platform. Don't follow a SORTIE (exit) sign, or you'll have to pay again to get back on the train.

On the urban lines, one ticket for 1.60€ lets you travel to any point. On the Sceaux, Boissy-St-Léger, and St-Germain-en-Laye lines to the suburbs, fares are based on distance. A *carnet* is the best buy—10 tickets for about 11€.

At the turnstile entrances to the station, insert your ticket and pass through. At some exits, tickets are also checked, so hold onto yours. There are occasional ticket checks on trains and platforms and in passageways, too.

RER TRAINS

A suburban train system, RER (Réseau Express Regional), passes through the heart of Paris, traveling faster than the Métro and running daily from 5:30am to 1am. This system works like the Métro and requires the same tickets. The major stops within central Paris, linking the RER to the Métro, are Nation, Gare de Lyon, Charles-de-Gaulle–Etoile, Gare-Etoile, and Gare du Nord as well as Châtelet-Les-Halles. All these stops are on the Right Bank. On the Left Bank, RER stops include Denfert-Rochereau and St-Michel. The five RER lines are marked A through E. Different branches are labeled by a number, the C5 Line serving Versailles-Rive Gauche, for example. Electric signboards next to each track outline all the possible stops along the way. Make sure that the little square next to your intended stop is lit.

BY BUS

Buses are much slower than the Métro. The majority run from 6:30am to 9:30pm (a few operate until 12:30am, and 10 operate during early morning hours). Service is limited on Sundays and holidays. Bus and Métro fares are the same; you can use the same tickets on both. Most bus rides require one ticket, but some destinations require two (never more than two within the city limits).

At certain stops, signs list destinations and bus numbers serving that point. Destinations are usually listed north to south and east to west. Most stops are also posted on the sides of the buses. During rush hours, you may have to take a ticket from a dispensing machine, indicating your position in the line at the stop.

If you intend to use the buses a lot, pick up a RATP bus map at the office on place de la Madeleine, 8e, or at the tourist offices at RATP headquarters, 54 Quai de La Rapée, 12e. For detailed recorded information (in English) on bus and Métro routes, call ✆ **01-58-76-16-16;** www.ratp.fr (or 32-46 in France), open Monday to Friday 7am to 9pm.

The RATP also operates the **Balabus,** big-windowed, orange-and-white motorcoaches that run only during limited hours: Sundays and national holidays from noon to 8:30pm, from April 15 to the end of September. Itineraries run in both directions between Gare de Lyon and the Grande Arche de La Défense, encompassing some of the city's most beautiful vistas. It's a great deal—three

discount **TRANSIT PASSES**

For those jetting in and out of Paris on quick trips, two discount passes are economical if you plan to limit your visit to the heart of Paris and its immediate environs. **Carte Orange** is sold at large Métro stations. This pass is sold only Monday to Wednesday, and you'll have to submit a passport size photo. In first or second class, the pass costs from 17€ to 38€.

For even shorter visits, you can purchase the **Carte Mobilis,** allowing unlimited travel on bus, underground, or RER lines for 1 day. You can buy it at any Métro station from 5.80€ to 16€.

The most luxurious discount pass of all, with many extras, is the **Paris Pass** (www.parispass.com), valid for 2, 4, or 6 days. Passes can be purchased at RAPT offices, tourist offices, and Métro stations. For 2 days, the pass costs 97€ for adults, 54€ for teens (13–19), and 29€ for children; for 4 days, 139€ for adults, 74€

for teens, and 38€ for children; for 6 days, 169€ for adults, 84€ for teens, and 48€ for children.

This pass not only grants you unlimited rides on public transport, including the Métro, city buses, the funicular to Montmartre and the RER trains, but also entrance to 55 museums, including the Louvre. That's not all—a Seine river cruise, a bus tour, and discounts at certain shops and restaurants are also offered.

Métro tickets for 1.60€ each, will carry you the entire route. You'll recognize the bus and the route it follows by the *Bb* symbol emblazoned on each bus's side and on signs posted beside the route it follows.

BY TAXI

It's virtually impossible to get a taxi at rush hour, so don't even try. Taxi drivers are organized into a lobby that limits their number to 15,000.

Watch out for common rip-offs: Always check the meter to make sure you're not paying the previous passenger's fare; beware of cabs without meters, which often wait outside nightclubs for tipsy patrons; and settle the tab in advance.

You can hail regular cabs on the street when their signs read LIBRE. Taxis are easier to find at the many stands near Métro stations. The flag drops at 2.20€, and from 10am to 5pm you pay .80€ per kilometer; minimum fare is 6€ from 5pm to 10am, and you pay .89€ to 1.38€ per kilometer. On airport trips, you're not required to pay for the driver's empty return ride.

You're allowed several pieces of luggage free if they're transported inside and are less than 5 kilograms (11 lb.). Heavier suitcases carried in the trunk cost 1€ to 2€ apiece. Tip 12% to 15%—the latter usually elicits a *merci*. For radio cabs, call **Les Taxis Bleus** (© **08-25-16-10-10**) or **Taxi G7** (© **01-47-39-47-39**)—but note that you'll be charged from the point where the taxi begins the drive to pick you up.

BY BOAT

The **Batobus** (© **08-25-05-01-01**; toll call .15€/min.; www.batobus.com) is a 150-passenger ferry with big windows. Every day between April and December, the boats operate along the Seine, stopping at such points of interest as the

Eiffel Tower, Musée d'Orsay, the **Louvre, Notre-Dame,** and the **Hôtel de Ville.** Unlike the Bateaux-Mouche (see chapter 7), the Batobus does not provide recorded commentary. The only fare option available is a day pass valid for either 1, 2, or 5 days, each allowing as many entrances and exits as you want. A 1-day pass costs 12€ for adults, 6€ for children 15 and under; a 2-day pass costs 16€ for adults, 8€ for children 15 and under; a 5-day pass costs 19€ for adults, 9€ for children 15 and under. Boats operate daily (closed most of Jan) every 15 to 30 minutes, starting between 10 and 10:30am and ending between 4:30 and 10:30pm, depending on the season of the year.

BY BICYCLE

Riding a bike through the traffic-congested center of Paris is recommended only to battle-hardened veterans. Bike riding in Paris is not for the faint of heart, and can be dangerous to inexperienced city bikers. For a bike-riding interlude, you can visit either the Bois de Vincennes or the Bois de Boulogne, where you'll find safe bike paths, often shaded. In arranging your rental, ask for a helmet, even though it is not legally required. Bikes can be taken aboard all RER trains except during rush hours Monday to Friday 6:30 to 9am and 4:30 to 7pm.

Bike or scooter rentals are available at such locations as Paris-Vélo, 2 rue de Fer-à-Moulin 5e (✆ **08-1-43-37-59-22;** Métro: Cenmsier-Daubenton; Mon–Sat 10am–7pm, Sun 10am–2pm and 5–7pm). Rentals cost from 15€ per day. Another outfitter is Paris à vélo, c'est sympa!, 22 rue Alphonse Baudin (✆ **01-48-87-60-01;** www.partsvelosympa.com; Métro: St-Richard Lenoir). Rentals cost from 16€ but require a 150€ deposit on a credit card. Hours are 9am to 1pm and 2 to 6pm daily.

ON FOOT

Of all the cities of Europe, Paris, rivaled only by Rome and London, is a city made for walking. In fact, it is the only real way to explore the city in any depth. Stroll the streets and absorb the sights and smells. On almost every block you will find something of interest—a Belle Epoque shopping mall, a little curiosity shop, a Renaissance square, a medieval rampart. After your long walk through an arrondissement, there is always a cafe for catching your breath, having a coffee, and people watching. If you'd like more guidance instead of an aimless stroll, you can always refer to chapter 8, "Strolling Around Paris."

MONEY & COSTS

THE VALUE OF THE EURO VS. OTHER POPULAR CURRENCIES

Euro (€)	US$	C$	UK£	A$	NZ$
1	1.35	1.35	0.88	1.44	1.88

Frommer's lists exact prices in the local currency. The currency conversions quoted above were correct at press time. However, rates fluctuate, so before departing consult a currency exchange website such as **www.oanda.com/convert/classic** to check up-to-the-minute rates.

	€
Taxi from Charles de Gaulle Airport to the city center	65.00
Taxi from Orly Airport to the city center	55.00
Public Transportation for a trip within the city	1.60
Double room at the Ritz (very expensive)	770.00
Double room at the Lord Byron (moderate)	140.00
Double room at the Hotel Bellevue & du Chariot d'Or (inexpensive)	72.00
Lunch for one, without wine, at Au Pied de Cochon (moderate)	35.00
Lunch for one, without wine, at Crémerie-Restaurant Polidor (inexpensive)	22.00
Dinner for one, without wine, at Le Grand Véfour (very expensive)	268.00
Dinner for one, without wine, at Brasserie Balzar (moderate)	36.00
Dinner for one, without wine, at Le Béarn (inexpensive)	17.00
Glass of wine in a cafe	4.00
Glass of soda in a cafe	3.00
Cup of espresso	3.50
Admission to the Louvre	9.00
Theater ticket (at Comédie-Française)	28.00

For decades Paris was known as one of the most expensive cities on earth. It still is a pricey destination, but London has not only caught up with Paris in prices but surpassed it. Because of the lower dollar value, New York appears to be a bargain to some visiting Parisians. Paris is not as expensive as Tokyo or Oslo, but even an average hotel can cost 140€ or more—in many cases, much, much more.

It's always advisable to bring money in a variety of forms on a vacation: a mix of cash, credit cards, and traveler's checks. You should also exchange enough petty cash to cover airport incidentals, tipping, and transportation to your hotel before you leave home, or withdraw money upon arrival at an airport ATM.

In many international destinations, ATMs offer the best exchange rates. Avoid exchanging money at commercial exchange bureaus and hotels, which often have the highest transaction fees.

Not just Paris, but all of France is a very expensive destination. Part of the cost is the value-added tax (VAT in English, TVA in French), which adds between 6% and 33% to everything. To compensate, you can often find top-value food and lodging.

Rental cars (and fuel) are expensive, and flying within France costs more than within the U.S. Train travel is relatively inexpensive, especially with a rail pass. Prices in Paris are higher than in the provinces.

Currency

France's old currency, the French franc, disappeared into history on March 1, 2002, replaced by the **euro,** which is officially abbreviated "EUR" or €. Exchange rates of participating countries are locked into a common currency fluctuating against the dollar, and the difference could affect the relative costs of your trip. For up-to-the-minute currency conversions, go to **www.xe.com/ucc**.

Most banks in Paris are open Monday to Friday from 9am to 4:30pm, and a few are open Saturday; ask at your hotel for the location of the one nearest you. Most post offices will convert currency, and exchanges are also available at Paris airports and train stations and along most of the major boulevards. They charge a small commission. Some exchange places charge favorable rates to lure you into their stores. For example, **Paris Vision,** 214 rue de Rivoli, 1er (*℡* **01-42-60-31-25;** Métro: Tuileries), maintains a minibank in the back of a travel agency, open daily from 7am to 9pm. Its rates are only a fraction less favorable than those offered for large blocks of money as listed by the Paris stock exchange.

ATMs

The easiest and best way to get cash away from home is from an ATM, sometimes referred to as a "cash machine," or a "cashpoint." The **Cirrus** (*℡* **800/424-7787;** www.mastercard.com) and **PLUS** (www.visa.com) networks span the globe; look at the back of your bank card to see which network you're on, then call or check online for ATM locations at your destination. Be sure you know your personal identification number (PIN) and daily withdrawal limit before you depart.

ATMs are widely available in France, certainly in all cities and bigger towns, and even at a bank or two in smaller places. But don't always count on it. If you're venturing into rural France, it's always good to have cash in your pocket.

There are problems involved in the use of ATMs. For example, if you make a mistake and punch your secret code wrong into the machine three times, that machine will swallow your card on the assumption that it is being fraudulently used.

Users with alphabetical rather than numerical PINs may be thrown off by the lack of letters on French cash machines. If your PIN is longer than four digits, check with your bank to see if you can use the first four digits or will have to get a new number for use in France.

To get a cash advance by using a credit card at an ATM, ask for a PIN from your credit card company such as Visa before leaving your home country.

Note: Remember that many banks impose a fee every time you use a card at another bank's ATM, and that fee can be higher for international transactions than for domestic ones. In addition, the bank from which you withdraw cash may charge its own fee. For international withdrawal fees, ask your bank.

Credit Cards

Credit cards are another safe way to carry money, but their use has become more difficult, especially in France (see below). They also provide a convenient record of all your expenses, and they generally offer relatively good exchange rates. You can usually withdraw cash advances from your credit cards at banks or ATMs, provided you know your PIN. Keep in mind that you'll pay interest from the moment of your withdrawal, even if you pay your monthly bills on time. Also, note that many banks now assess a 1% to 3% "transaction fee" on **all** charges you incur abroad (whether you're using the local currency or your native currency).

There is almost no difference in the acceptance of a debit or a standard credit card.

Major Change in Credit Cards

In the interim between traditional swipe credit cards and those with an embedded computer chip, here's what you can do to protect yourself:

- Get a 4-digit PIN from your credit card's issuing bank before leaving home.

- Call the number on the back of each card and ask for a 4-digit PIN.

- Keep an eye out for the right logo displayed in a retailer's window. You want Visa or MasterCard, not Maestro, Visa Electron, or Carte Bleue.

- Know that your Amex card will work where an Amex logo is displayed (but the card is not as widely accepted as Visa and MasterCard).

- As a last resort, make sure you have enough cash to cover your purchase.

Chip and PIN represents a change in the way that credit and debit cards are used. The program is designed to cut down on the fraudulent use of credit cards. More and more banks are issuing customers Chip and PIN versions of their debit or credit cards. In the future, more and more vendors will be asking for a four-digit personal identification or PIN, which will be entered into a keypad near the cash register. In some cases, a waiter will bring a hand-held model to your table to verify your credit card.

Warning: Some establishments in France might not accept your credit card unless you have a computer chip imbedded in it. The reason? To cut down on credit card fraud. Places in France are moving away from the magnetic strip credit card to the new system of Chip and PIN. In the changeover in technology, some retailers have falsely concluded that they can no longer take swipe cards or signature cards that don't have PINs. For the time being, both the new and old cards are used in shops, hotels, and restaurants, regardless of whether they have the old credit and debit card machines or the new Chip and PIN machines installed. Expect a lot of confusion.

Traveler's Checks

You can buy traveler's checks at most banks, and they are widely accepted in France, although frankly, merchants prefer cash. Because of difficulties with credit cards (see above) or ATMs that can reject your card for no apparent reason, travelers are once again buying traveler's checks for security in case something goes wrong with their plastic. They are offered in denominations of $20, $50, $100, $500, and sometimes $1,000. Generally, you'll pay a service charge ranging from 1% to 4%.

The most popular traveler's checks are offered by **American Express** (© **800/528-4800,** or 800/221-7282; www.americanexpress.com for cardholders—this number accepts collect calls, offers service in several foreign languages, and exempts Amex gold and platinum cardholders from the 1% fee); **Visa** (© **800/732-1322;** www.visa.com)—AAA members can obtain Visa checks for a $9.95 fee (for checks up to $1,500) at most AAA offices or by calling © **866/339-3378;** and **MasterCard** (© **800/223-9920;** www.mastercard.com).

American Express, Thomas Cook, Visa, and **MasterCard** offer **foreign currency traveler's checks,** which are useful if you're traveling to one country or to the euro zone; they're accepted at locations where dollar checks may not be.

If you carry traveler's checks, keep a record of their serial numbers separate from your checks in the event that they are stolen or lost—you'll get your refund faster.

STAYING HEALTHY

In general, Paris is a "safe" destination, although problems can and do occur anywhere. You don't need shots, most foodstuffs are safe, and the water in Paris is potable. If you're concerned, order bottled water. It is easy to get a prescription filled in Paris, and nearly all hospitals have English-speaking doctors with well-trained medical staffs. It's also easy to get over-the-counter medicine in Paris. In other words, France is part of the civilized world.

Contact the **International Association for Medical Assistance to Travelers** (**IAMAT**; ✆ **716/754-4883** in the U.S. or, in Canada, 416/652-0137; www.iamat.org) for tips on travel and health concerns in the countries you're visiting, and for lists of local, English-speaking doctors. The United States **Centers for Disease Control and Prevention** (✆ **800/232-4636;** www.cdc.gov) provides up-to-date information on health hazards by region or country and offers tips on food safety. **Travel Health Online** (www.tripprep.com), sponsored by a consortium of travel medicine practitioners, may also offer helpful advice on traveling abroad. You can find listings of reliable medical clinics overseas at the **International Society of Travel Medicine** (www.istm.org).

If You Get Sick

For travel abroad, you may have to pay all medical costs upfront and be reimbursed later. Medicare and Medicaid do not provide coverage for medical costs outside the U.S. Before leaving home, find out what medical services your health insurance covers. To protect yourself, consider buying medical travel insurance.

U.K. nationals will need a **European Health Insurance Card** (**EHIC;** ✆ **0845/605-0707;** www.ehic.org.uk) to receive free or reduced-cost health benefits during a visit to a European Economic Area (EEA) country (European Union countries plus Iceland, Liechtenstein, and Norway) or Switzerland.

We list **hospitals** and **emergency numbers** in "Fast Facts" on p. 396.

If you suffer from a chronic illness, consult your doctor before your departure. Pack **prescription medications** in your carry-on luggage and carry them in their original containers, with pharmacy labels—otherwise they won't make it through airport security. Carry the generic name of prescription medicines, in case a local pharmacist is unfamiliar with the brand name.

We list additional **emergency numbers** in "Fast Facts", p. 396.

CRIME & SAFETY

The most common menace in Paris is the plague of pickpockets and roving gangs of Gypsy children who surround you, distract you, and steal your purse or wallet. They prey on tourists around attractions such as the Louvre, Eiffel Tower, and Notre-Dame, and they can often strike in the Métro, sometimes blocking a victim from the escalator. A band of these young thieves can clean your pockets even while you try to fend them off. Their method is to get very close to a target, ask for a handout (sometimes), and deftly help themselves to your money or passport.

Never leave valuables in a car, and never travel with your car unlocked. A U.S. Department of State travel advisory warns that every car (whether parked, stopped at a traffic light, or moving) can be a potential target for armed robbery. In these uncertain times, it is prudent to check the U.S. Department of State's travel advisories at **http://travel.state.gov**.

The government of France maintains a national antiterrorism plan; in times of heightened security concerns, the government mobilizes police and armed forces, and installs them at airports; train and Métro stations; and high-profile locations such as schools, embassies, and government installations.

In recent years, Paris has experienced political assassinations and random bombings. One U.S. citizen was injured in these attacks, but none have been killed. All passengers on subways and trains are urged to be aware of their surroundings and to report any unattended baggage to the nearest authority.

Student demonstrations, labor protests, or other demonstrations have turned into violent confrontations between demonstrators and police. Americans are advised to avoid street demonstrations.

Gangs of thieves operate on the rail link from Charles de Gaulle Airport to downtown Paris by preying on jet-lagged, luggage-burdened tourists. Often, one thief distracts the tourist with a question about directions while an accomplice takes a momentarily unguarded backpack, briefcase, or purse. Thieves also time their thefts to coincide with train stops so that they may quickly exit the car. Travelers may wish to consider traveling from the airport to the city by bus or taxi.

Although public safety is not as much a problem in Paris as it is in some large American cities, concerns are growing. Robbery at gunpoint or knifepoint is uncommon, but not unknown. Be careful, especially late at night. There have been a number of violent armed robberies, including knife attacks, in the vicinity of the Eiffel Tower late at night.

Thieves on motorcycles have been known to reach into moving cars by opening the car door or reaching through an open window to steal purses and other bags visible inside. Those traveling by car in Paris should remember to keep windows closed and doors locked.

The no. 1 subway line, which runs by many major tourist attractions (including the Grand Arch at La Défense, Arc de Triomphe, Champs-Elysées, Concorde, Louvre, and Bastille), is the site of many thefts. Pickpockets are especially active on this Métro line during the summer months.

Gare du Nord train station, where the express trains from the airport arrive in Paris, is also a high-risk area for pickpocketing and theft.

Many thefts occur at the major department stores (Galeries Lafayette, Printemps, and La Samaritaine), where tourists often leave wallets, passports, and credit cards on cashier counters during transactions.

In hotels, thieves frequent lobbies and breakfast rooms, and take advantage of a minute of inattention to snatch jackets, purses, and backpacks. Also, although many hotels do have safety latches that allow guests to secure their rooms while they are inside, this feature is not as universal as it is in the United States. If no chain or latch is present, a chair placed up against the door is usually an effective obstacle to surreptitious entry during the night.

In restaurants, many Americans have reported that women's purses placed on the floor under the table at the feet of the diner are stolen during the meal.

Dealing with Discrimination

Discrimination against West and North African immigrants to France—a population estimated to number more than a million—does exist. Anyone who might be taken for an immigrant (often illegal) from Africa is subject to verbal abuse. Racism is more prevalent in the southeast of France than Paris. So far, there has been almost no harassment of African-American tourists to Paris or France itself. Many expatriate Americans, in fact, including such cultural figures as Josephine Baker and author James Baldwin, fled to Paris in decades past to escape the racism of America. **S.O.S. Racisme,** 51 av. de Flandre, 19e (© **01-40-35-36-55;** www.sos-racisme.org), offers legal advice to victims of prejudice and will even intervene to help with the police.

SPECIALIZED TRAVEL RESOURCES

In addition to the destination-specific resources listed below, please visit Frommers.com for other specialized travel resources.

LGBT Travelers

France is one of the world's most tolerant countries toward gays and lesbians. "Gay Paree" boasts a large gay population, with many clubs, restaurants, organizations, and services.

Purple Roofs (www.purpleroofs.com) offers a directory of LGBT-friendly or -owned accommodations worldwide, ranging from inexpensive guesthouses to elegant boutique hotels.

Lesbian or bisexual women can also pick up a copy of *Lesbia.* This publication and others are available at Paris's largest, best-stocked gay bookstore, **Les Mots à la Bouche,** 6 rue Ste-Croix-de-la-Bretonnerie, 4e (© **01-42-78-88-30;** www.motsbouche.com; Métro: Hôtel-de-Ville), which carries publications in both French and English.

Many agencies offer tours and travel itineraries specifically for gay and lesbian travelers. **Above and Beyond Tours** (© **800/397-2681;** www.abovebeyondtours.com) are gay Australia tour specialists. San Francisco–based **Now, Voyager** (© **800/255-6951;** www.nowvoyager.com) offers worldwide trips and cruises, and **Olivia** (© **800/631-6277;** www.olivia.com) offers lesbian cruises and resort vacations.

The following travel guides are available at many bookstores, or you can order them from any online bookseller: *Spartacus International Gay Guide* (Bruno Gmünder Verlag; www.spartacusworld.com/gayguide) and the *Damron* guides (www.damron.com), with separate, annual books for gay men and lesbians. For more gay and lesbian travel resources, visit Frommers.com.

Travelers with Disabilities

Most disabilities shouldn't stop anyone from traveling. There are more options and resources out there than ever before.

Facilities for travelers in Paris and nearly all modern hotels provide accessible rooms. Older hotels (unless they've been renovated) may not provide elevators, special toilet facilities, or wheelchair ramps.

The TGVs (high-speed trains) are wheelchair accessible; older trains have compartments for wheelchair boarding. On the Paris Métro, passengers with disabilities are able to sit in wider seats. Guide dogs ride free. However, some stations don't have escalators or elevators.

Knowing which hotels, restaurants, and attractions are accessible can save you a lot of frustration. **Association des Paralysés de France,** 17 bd. Auguste-Blanqui, Paris 75013 (✆ **01-40-78-69-66;** www.apf.asso.fr), provides documentation, moral support, and travel ideas for individuals who use wheelchairs. In addition to the Paris office, it maintains an office in each of the 90 *départements* ("ministates" into which France is divided) and can help find hotels, transportation, sightseeing, house rentals, and (in some cases) companionship for paralyzed or partially paralyzed travelers. It's not, however, a travel agency.

Family Travel

To locate accommodations, restaurants, and attractions that are particularly kid-friendly, refer to the "Kids" icon throughout this guide.

Although much of the world thinks of Paris as a place for adult amusement, it is also filled with children's activities. Sold at most newsstands, *Pariscope* lists dozens of children's activities in the *enfants* section. From boat rides on the Siene to visits to Parc Zoologique in the Bois de Vincennes, there are many attractions that will interest the entire family, especially the Eiffel Tower.

Women Travelers

A good local source of information of concern to women is *Bibliotheque Marguerita Duras*, 79 rue Nationale, 13e (✆ **01-45-70-80-30;** Métro: Nationale), open only Tuesday to Saturday 2 to 6pm. Women walking in the streets of Paris will face no particular problems that they would not find in such cities as New York or London.

Check out the award-winning website **Journeywoman** (www.journeywoman.com), a "real life" women's travel-information network where you can sign up for a free e-mail newsletter and get advice on everything from etiquette and dress to safety. For general travel resources for women, go to Frommers.com.

Multicultural Travelers

Since the days of the celebrated chanteuse Josephine Baker and, later, the author James Baldwin, Paris has welcomed African-American travelers. That welcome continues today. A good book on the subject is Tyler Stovall's *Paris Noir.* Another worthwhile resource is the website **www.cafedelasoul.com**.

Senior Travel

Many discounts are available to seniors—men and women of the "third age," as the French say (those 60 and older).

Air France offers seniors a 10% reduction on its regular non-excursion fares within France. Some restrictions apply. Discounts of around 10% are offered to passengers ages 62 and older on select Air France international flights. Be sure to ask for the discount when booking.

Many senior citizen discounts seem to apply to residents of E.U. countries. Nonetheless, it pays to announce at the ticket window to a museum or monument that you are 60 years old or more, if such is the case. You may not receive a discount, but it doesn't hurt to ask. "Senior," incidentally, is pronounced *seenyore* in France. Senior citizens do not get a discount for traveling on mass transit, however. If you're going outside of Paris, you can get discounts on long-distance trains, perhaps 25% to 50% off the ticket price. Check www.voyages-sncf.com.

Recommended publications offering travel resources and discounts for seniors include the quarterly magazine **Travel 50 & Beyond** (www.travel50and beyond.com) and the bestselling paperback **Unbelievably Good Deals and Great Adventures That You Absolutely Can't Get Unless You're Over 50** (McGraw-Hill), by Joann Rattner Heilman. Frommers.com offers more information and resources on travel for seniors.

RESPONSIBLE TOURISM

Compared with such bicycle-riding and pollution savvy cities as Amsterdam, Paris is hardly the greenest of European destinations. But as a visitor to the city, you can do your part in not adding to its already existing pollution.

Traveling green in Paris can be a simple thing, like throwing your rubbish in a trash can instead of littering the streets. At a hotel, you might request that your sheets not be changed every day, and you can be sparing in your use of fluffy towels and lots of hot water. Every little bit counts. If you can walk to your sightseeing attraction, do so instead of burning up energy getting there. For example, if you divide up your sightseeing attractions per arrondissement, you can walk to almost everything you want to see before having to take transportation to another sector of Paris.

If you haven't visited Paris in a while, you will notice more bike, pedestrian, and bus lanes than before. You'll even see billboards urging Parisians to clean up after their dogs. The streets are cleaner than ever before, and Parisians frown on visitors who drop their wrappings after consuming street or fast food.

Some visitors, mostly young, take responsible travel very seriously, even volunteering to leave Paris a better place than which they found it. Obviously, these programs appeal only to the most serious and dedicated, even idealistic, visitors. Social programs in which you can participate range from tutoring prisoners to fighting AIDS.

Many of these organizations do not require a long-term commitment. Two major international service databases that have information on such green programs are the *University of California at Irvine's International Service Database* (www.cie.uci.edu/iop/voluntee.html), or *Concordia International Volunteer*, Heversham House, 20–22 Boundary Rd., Hove BN34ET, England (© **12-73-42-22-18**).

One unusual program signs up volunteers in Paris to help restore damaged monuments, perhaps those harmed in student riots. A storehouse for information about such programs is *Archaeological Institute of America*, 656 Beacon St., Boston, MA 02215 (© **617/353-9361;** www.archaeological.org).

GENERAL RESOURCES FOR responsible travel

In addition to the resources for Paris listed above, the following websites provide valuable wide-ranging information on sustainable travel.

o **Responsible Travel** (www.responsible travel.com) is a great source of sustainable travel ideas; the site is run by a spokesperson for ethical tourism in the travel industry. **Sustainable Travel International** (www.sustainable travelinternational.org) promotes ethical tourism practices, and manages an extensive directory of sustainable properties and tour operators around the world.

o **Carbonfund** (www.carbonfund.org), **TerraPass** (www.terrapass.org), and **Cool Climate** (http://coolclimate. berkeley.edu) provide info on "carbon offsetting," or offsetting the green-house gas emitted during flights.

o **Greenhotels** (www.greenhotels.com) recommends green-rated member hotels around the world that fulfill the company's stringent environmental requirements. **Environmentally Friendly Hotels** (www.environmentally friendlyhotels.com) offers more green accommodations ratings.

o **Volunteer International** (www. volunteerinternational.org) has a list of questions to help you determine the intentions and the nature of a volunteer program. For general info on volunteer travel, visit **www. volunteerabroad.org** and **www. idealist.org**.

SPECIAL-INTEREST TRIPS & ESCORTED GENERAL-INTEREST TOURS

Special-Interest Trips

In a country as diverse and popular as France, there are numerous options.

COOKING SCHOOLS

The famous/infamous Georges-Auguste Escoffier (1846–1935) taught the Edwardians how to eat. Today the Hôtel Ritz maintains the **Ritz-Escoffier Ecole de Gastronomie Française,** 38 rue Cambon, 75001 Paris (© **01-43-16-30-50;** www.ritzparis.com), which offers demonstration classes of the master's techniques on Saturdays. These cost 135€ to 225€ each. Courses, taught in French and English, start at 1,000€ for 1 week, up to 11,400€ for 6 weeks.

   Le Cordon Bleu, 8 rue Léon-Delhomme, 75015 Paris (© **800/457-2433** in the U.S. or 01-53-68-22-50; www.cordonbleu.edu), was established in 1895 and is the most famous French cooking school—where Julia Child learned to perfect her *pâté brisée* and *mousse au chocolat.* The best-known courses last 10 weeks, after which you are awarded a certificate. Many enthusiasts prefer a less intense immersion and opt for a 4-day workshop or a 2-hour demonstration class. Enrollment in either is first-come, first-served; costs start at 50€ for a demonstration and start at 950€ for the 4-day workshop. Classes are in English.

LANGUAGE SCHOOLS

The **Alliance Française,** 101 bd. Raspail, Paris 75270 (℃ **01-42-84-90-00;** fax 01-42-84-91-01; www.alliancefr.org), a nonprofit organization with a network of 1,100 establishments in 138 countries, offers French-language courses to some 350,000 students. The school in Paris is open all year; month-long courses range from 400€ to 900€, depending on the number of hours per day. Request information and an application at least 1 month before your departure. In North America, the largest branch is the **Alliance Française,** 53 W. Jackson Blvd., Ste. 1225, Chicago, IL 60604 (℃ **312/431-1880;** www.afusa.org).

A clearinghouse for information on French-language schools is **Lingua Service Worldwide,** 42 Artillery Dr., Woodbury, CT 06798 (℃ **800/394-LEARN** [394-5981] or 203/263-6294; www.linguaserviceworldwide.com). Its programs are available in many cities throughout France. They cost $1,043 to $2,940 for 2 weeks, depending on the city, the school, and the accommodations.

MUSIC TOURS

One outfit that coordinates hotel stays in Paris with major musical events, usually in at least one (and often both) of the city's opera houses, is **Dailey-Thorp Travel,** P.O. Box 670, Big Horn, WY 82833 (℃ **800/998-4677** or 307/673-1555; fax 307/674-7474; www.daileythorp.com). Sojourns tend to last 3 to 7 days and, in many cases, tie in with performances in other cities (usually London, Berlin, or Milan). Expect accommodations in deluxe hotels such as the Hôtel du Louvre or the Hôtel Scribe, and a staff that has made arrangements for all the nuts and bolts of your arrival in, and artistic exposure to, Paris.

TENNIS TOURS

Die-hard fans around the world set their calendars by the French Open, held at Paris's Roland-Garros stadium. You can book your hotel and tickets to the event on your own, but if you're unsure about scheduling, consider a California-based company, **Advantage Tennis Tours,** 33 White Sail Dr., Ste. 100, Laguna Niguel, CA 92677 (℃ **800/341-8687** or 949/661-7331; fax 949/489-2837; www.advantagetennistours.com). They typically book packages including 5 or 6 nights of hotel accommodations in Paris, 2 or 3 days on Center Court, and the skills of a bilingual hostess; rates per person, without airfare, begin at $3,455, double occupancy, depending on your choice of hotel and the duration of your visit.

General-Interest Tours

Franceway (www.franceway.com) puts together French packages, including airfares and government-rated three-star hotels from Paris to the Riviera. **Travel in France** (www.travel-in-france.com) is not a travel agency but helps you organize your own French package trip, featuring the best airfares on Air France. It also provides information on hotels in a range of prices.

Travel packages are also listed in the travel section of your local Sunday newspaper. Or check ads in national travel magazines such as *Arthur Frommer's Budget Travel Magazine, Travel + Leisure, National Geographic Traveler,* and *Condé Nast Traveler.*

For more information on package tours and tips for booking your trip, see Frommers.com.

Escorted General-Interest Tours

Escorted tours are structured group tours, with a group leader. The price usually includes everything from airfare to hotels, meals, tours, admission costs, and local transportation.

The two largest operators conducting escorted tours of both Paris and scenic parts of France and Europe are **Globus + Cosmos Tours** (✆ 866/755-8581; www.globusandcosmos.com) and **Trafalgar** (✆ 800/854-0103; www.trafalgartours.com). Both have first-class tours that run about $300 a day and budget tours for about $100 a day. The differences are mainly in hotel location and the number of activities. There's little difference in the companies' services, so choose your tour based on the itinerary and date of departure. Brochures are available at travel agencies, and all tours must be booked through travel agents.

Tauck World Discovery, 10 Norden Place, Norwalk, CT 06855 (✆ 800/788-7885; www.tauck.com), provides first-class, escorted coach grand tours of both Paris and the countryside of France, as well as 1-week general tours of regions in France. Its 13-day tour covering the Normandy landing beaches, the Bayeux tapestry, and Mont-St-Michel begins at $4,990 per person, double occupancy (land only); an 8-day trip beginning in Nice and ending in Paris starts at $2,990 per person.

Despite the fact that escorted tours require big deposits and predetermine hotels, restaurants, and itineraries, many people derive security and peace of mind from the structure they offer. Escorted tours—whether they're navigated by bus, motorcoach, train, or boat—let travelers sit back and enjoy the trip without having to drive or worry about details. They take you to the maximum number of sights in the minimum amount of time with the least amount of hassle. They're particularly convenient for people with limited mobility, and they can be a great way to make new friends.

On the downside, you'll have little opportunity for serendipitous interactions with locals. The tours can be jampacked with activities, leaving little room for individual sightseeing, whim, or adventure—plus they often focus on the heavily touristed sites, so you miss out on many a lesser-known gem.

For more information on package-escorted, general-interest tours, including questions to ask before booking a trip, see Frommers.com.

STAYING CONNECTED
Mobile Phones

The three letters that define much of the world's wireless capabilities are **GSM** (Global System for Mobile Communications), a big, seamless network that makes for easy cross-border cellphone use throughout Europe and dozens of other countries worldwide. In the U.S., T-Mobile, AT&T Wireless, and Cingular use this quasi-universal system; in Canada, Microcell and some Rogers customers are GSM, and all Europeans and most Australians use GSM. GSM phones function with a removable plastic SIM card, encoded with your phone number and account information. If your cellphone is on a GSM system, and you have a world-capable multiband phone such as many Sony Ericsson, Motorola, or Samsung models, you can make and receive calls across civilized areas around much of the globe. Just call your wireless operator and ask for "international roaming" to be activated on your account. Unfortunately, per-minute charges can be high—usually $1 to $2 in western Europe and up to $5 in places like Russia and Indonesia.

For some, **renting** a phone can be a good idea. Although you can rent a phone from any number of overseas sites, including kiosks at airports and at car-rental agencies, we suggest renting the phone before you leave home. North Americans can rent one before leaving home from **InTouch USA** (✆ **800/872-7626;** www.intouchglobal.com) or **RoadPost** (✆ **888/290-1606** or 905/272-5665; www.roadpost.com). InTouch will also, for free, advise you on whether your existing phone will work overseas; simply call ✆ **703/222-7161** between 9am and 4pm EST, or go to **http://intouchglobal.com/travel.htm**.

Buying a phone can be economically attractive, as many nations have cheap prepaid phone systems. Once you arrive at your destination, stop by a local cellphone shop and get the cheapest package; you'll probably pay less than 75€ for a phone and a starter calling card. Local calls may be as low as 0.05€ per minute, and in many countries incoming calls are free.

Internet & E-mail

Wi-Fi is becoming common in many Parisian hotels and cafes. To find cybercafes in Paris, check **www.cybercaptive.com** and **www.cybercafe.com**. The latter lists 20 such cafes scattered throughout central Paris. The most popular in Paris seems to be **Luxembourg Micro,** 81 bd. Saint-Michel, 5e (✆ **01-46-33-27-98;** Métro: Luxembourg; www.luxembourg-micro.com). For 20 minutes, you pay 1€; for 30 minutes 1.50€, and for an hour 2.50€. It's open daily from 9am to 11pm.

Aside from formal cybercafes, most youth hostels and public libraries have Internet access. Avoid hotel business centers unless you're willing to pay exorbitant rates.

Newspapers & Magazines

English-language newspapers are available at nearly every kiosk. Published Monday to Saturday, the *International Herald-Tribune* (www.global.nytimes.com) is the most popular paper with visiting Americans and Canadians; the *Guardian* (www.guardian.co.uk) provides a British point of view. Kiosks are generally open daily from 8am to 9pm.

Telephones

Public phones are found everywhere in France. The most widely accepted method of payment is the **télécarte,** a prepaid calling card available at kiosks, post offices, and Métro stations and costs 11€ to 16€ for 50 and 120 units, respectively. A local call costs one unit, which provides you 6 to 18 minutes of conversation, depending on the rate. Avoid making calls from your hotel, which may double or triple the charges.

To call **long distance within France,** dial the 10-digit number (9 digits in some cases outside Paris) of the person or place you're calling. To reach the long-distance operator for AT&T, the direct access number is ✆ **0800-99-0011** or 0805-701-288; for Canada, dial ✆ **0800-99-00-16** or 0800-99-02-16.

If you have a **phone card,** you can recharge it anywhere, anytime, with **eKit** (www.eKit.com) via the Web. You can recharge over the phone using a self-service recharge menu. If you prefer to speak to someone, you can call eKit's 24-hour Customer Service: ℭ **888/310-4168** in the U.S., ℭ 0800-028-2402 in Britain, ℭ 800/094-747 in Australia, and ℭ 866/626-9724 in Canada. With eKit, you can save up to 70% on calls in 200 countries worldwide, including France. One of the many advantages is that family and friends can leave you messages at no cost to them.

To call Paris:

1. Dial the international access code: 011 from the U.S.; 00 from the U.K., Ireland, or New Zealand; or 0011 from Australia.

2. Dial the country code 33.

3. Dial the city code 1 and then the number.

To make international calls from Paris, first dial 00 and then the country code (U.S. or Canada 1, U.K. 44, Ireland 353, Australia 61, New Zealand 64). Next you dial the area code and number. For example, if you want to call the British Embassy in Washington, D.C., you would dial ℭ 00-1-202-588-7800.

For directory assistance: For numbers inside and outside France, dial ℭ **118-008.**

For operator assistance: With the inauguration of increasing numbers of cellphones (each of which has a different carrier), and with the decentralization of what used to be the P. T. T., local operators within France are less and less widespread. Even if you dial "0," depending on where you are within France, it might not get you a live body. Everyone automatically expects, according to the director of phone services in Paris, that dialers know the codes of the countries or regions they're trying to reach.

As for reaching an operator for the **placement of calls outside of France,** the system involves bypassing French operators, and relying on the operators based in the country you're trying to call. The prefix for accessing a foreign (specifically, non-French) operator involves dialing the access code **0800-99-00** followed by the **country code.**

Toll-free numbers: Numbers beginning with **0800** within France are toll-free, but calling a 1-800 number in the States from France costs the same as an overseas call.

4

SUGGESTED PARIS ITINERARIES

E ach of Paris's 20 arrondissements possesses a unique style and flavor. You'll want to decide which district appeals most to you and then try to find accommodations there. Later on, try to visit as many areas as you can so you get the full taste of Paris.

For a map of Paris's arrondissements, please refer to the color map titled "Neighborhoods of Paris" at the beginning of this book.

ARRONDISSEMENTS IN BRIEF

1ST ARRONDISSEMENT (MUSÉE DU LOUVRE/LES HALLES) "I never knew what a palace was until I had a glimpse of the Louvre," wrote Nathaniel Hawthorne. Perhaps the world's greatest art museum, the **Louvre,** a former royal residence, still lures visitors to the 1st arrondissement. Walk through the **Jardin des Tuileries,** Paris's most formal garden (laid out by Le Nôtre, gardener to Louis XIV). Pause to take in the classic beauty of **place Vendôme,** the opulent home of the Hôtel Ritz. Zola's "belly of Paris" (Les Halles) is no longer the food-and-meat market of Paris (traders moved to the new, more accessible suburb of Rungis); today the **Forum des Halles** is a center of shopping, entertainment, and culture.

FACING PAGE: **Arc de Triomphe from the Eiffel Tower.** ABOVE: **The Louvre from the Jardin des Tuileries.**

2ND ARRONDISSEMENT (LA BOURSE)   Home to the **Bourse** (stock exchange), this Right Bank district lies between the Grands Boulevards and rue Etienne-Marcel. From Monday to Friday, brokers play the market until it's time to break for lunch, when the movers and shakers of French capitalism channel their hysteria into the area restaurants. Much of the eastern end of the arrondissement **(Le Sentier)** is devoted to wholesale outlets of the Paris garment district, where thousands of garments are sold (usually in bulk) to buyers from clothing stores throughout Europe. "Everything that exists elsewhere exists in Paris," wrote Victor Hugo in *Les Misérables,* and this district provides ample evidence of that.

3RD ARRONDISSEMENT (LE MARAIS)   This district embraces much of Le Marais (the Marsh), one of the best-loved Right Bank neighborhoods. (It extends into the 4th as well.) After decades of decay, Le Marais recently made a comeback, though it may never again enjoy the prosperity of its 17th-century aristocratic heyday; today it contains Paris's **gay neighborhood,** with lots of gay/lesbian restaurants, bars, and stores, as well as the remains of the old Jewish quarter, centered on **rue des Rosiers.** Two of the chief attractions are the **Musée Picasso,** a kind of pirate's ransom of painting and sculpture, which the Picasso estate had to turn over to the French government in lieu of the artist's astronomical death duties, and the **Musée Carnavalet,** which brings to life the history of Paris from prehistoric times to the present.

4TH ARRONDISSEMENT (ILE DE LA CITÉ/ILE ST-LOUIS & BEAUBOURG)   It seems as if the 4th has it all: Notre-Dame on Ile de la Cité, and Ile St-Louis and its aristocratic town houses, courtyards, and antiques shops. **Ile St-Louis,** a former cow pasture and dueling ground, is home to dozens of 17th-century mansions and 6,000 lucky Louisiens, its permanent residents. Seek out **Ile de la Cité**'s two Gothic churches, **Sainte-Chapelle** and **Notre-Dame,** a majestic structure that, according to poet e e cummings, "doesn't budge an inch for all the idiocies of this world." You'll find France's finest bird and flower markets along with the nation's law courts, which Balzac described as a "cathedral of chicanery." It was here that Marie Antoinette was sentenced to death in 1793. The 4th is also home to the freshly renovated **Centre Pompidou,** one of the top-three attractions in France. After all this pomp and glory, you can retreat to **place des Vosges,** a square of perfect harmony and beauty where Victor Hugo lived from 1832 to 1848 and penned many of his famous masterpieces. (His house is now a museum—see p. 99.)

Yiddish delicatessen in the Marais.

5TH ARRONDISSEMENT (QUARTIER LATIN)   The Latin Quarter is the intellectual heart and soul of Paris. Bookstores, schools, churches, clubs, student dives, Roman ruins, publishing houses, and expensive boutiques characterize the district. Discussions of Artaud or Molière over cups of coffee may be rarer than in the past, but they aren't out of place. Beginning with the founding of the **Sorbonne** in 1253, the quarter was called Latin because students and professors spoke the language. You'll follow in the footsteps of Descartes, Verlaine, Camus, Sartre, James Thurber, Elliot Paul, and Hemingway as you explore. Changing times have brought Greek, Moroccan, and Vietnamese immigrants, among others, offering everything from couscous to fiery-hot spring rolls and souvlaki. The 5th borders the Seine, and you'll want to stroll along quai de Montebello, inspecting the inventories of the *bouquinistes* (secondhand-book dealers), who sell everything from antique Daumier prints to yellowing copies of Balzac's *Père Goriot* in the shadow of Notre-Dame. The 5th also has the **Panthéon,** built by Louis XV after he recovered from gout and wanted to do something nice for St. Geneviève, Paris's patron saint. It's the resting place of Rousseau, Gambetta, Zola, Braille, Hugo, Voltaire, and Jean Moulin, the World War II Resistance leader whom the Gestapo tortured to death.

6TH ARRONDISSEMENT (ST-GERMAIN/LUXEMBOURG)   This is the heartland of Paris publishing and, for some, the most colorful Left Bank quarter, where waves of young artists still emerge from the Ecole des Beaux-Arts. The secret of the district lies in discovering its narrow streets, hidden squares, and magnificent gardens. To be really authentic, stroll with an unwrapped loaf of sourdough bread from the wood-fired ovens of **Poilâne** at 8 rue du Cherche-Midi. Everywhere you turn, you'll encounter historic and literary associations, nowhere more so than on **rue Jacob.** At no. 7, Racine lived with his uncle as a teenager; Richard Wagner resided at no. 14 from 1841 to 1842; Ingres lived at no. 27 (now it's the office of the French publishing house Editions du Seuil); and Hemingway once occupied a tiny upstairs room at no. 44. The 6th takes in the **Jardin du Luxembourg,** a 24-hectare (59-acre) playground where Isadora Duncan went dancing in the predawn hours and a destitute Ernest Hemingway went looking for pigeons for lunch, carrying them in a baby carriage back to his humble flat for cooking.

7TH ARRONDISSEMENT (EIFFEL TOWER/MUSÉE D'ORSAY)   Paris's most famous symbol, **la Tour Eiffel,** dominates Paris and especially the 7th, a Left Bank district of residences and offices. The tower is one of the most recognizable landmarks in the world, despite the fact that many Parisians (especially its nearest neighbors) hated it when it was unveiled in 1889. Many of Paris's most imposing monuments are in the 7th, such as **Hôtel des Invalides,** which contains Napoleon's Tomb and the Musée de l'Armée, and the **Musée d'Orsay,** the world's premier showcase of 19th-century French art and culture, housed in the old Gare d'Orsay. But there's much hidden charm here as well. **Rue du Bac** was home to the swashbuckling heroes of Dumas's *The Three Musketeers* and to James McNeill Whistler, who moved to no. 110 after selling *Mother.* Auguste Rodin lived at what's now the **Musée Rodin,** 77 rue de Varenne, until his death in 1917.

8TH ARRONDISSEMENT (CHAMPS-ELYSÉES/MADELEINE) The showcase of the 8th is the **Champs-Elysées,** stretching from the **Arc de Triomphe** to the Egyptian obelisk on **place de la Concorde.** By the 1980s, the Champs-Elysées had become a garish strip, with too much traffic, too many fast-food joints, and too many panhandlers. In the 1990s, Jacques Chirac, then the Gaullist mayor, launched a cleanup, broadening the sidewalks and planting new trees. Now you'll find fashion houses, elegant hotels, restaurants, and shops. Everything in the 8th is the city's best, grandest, and most impressive. It has the best restaurant **(Taillevent),** the sexiest strip joint **(Crazy Horse Saloon),** the most splendid square **(place de la Concorde),** the grandest hotel (the **Crillon**), the most impressive arch **(Arc de Triomphe),** the most expensive residential street **(av. Montaigne),** the world's oldest subway station **(Franklin-D-Roosevelt),** and the most ancient monument (the 3,300-year-old **Obelisk of Luxor**).

9TH ARRONDISSEMENT (OPÉRA GARNIER/PIGALLE) From the Quartier de l'Opéra to the strip joints of Pigalle (the infamous "Pig Alley" of World War II GIs), the 9th endures, even if fashion prefers other addresses. Over the decades, the 9th has been celebrated in literature and song for the music halls that brought gaiety to the city. The building at 17 bd. de la Madeleine was where Marie Duplessis, who gained fame as the heroine Marguerite Gautier in Alexandre Dumas the younger's *La Dame aux Camellias,* died. (Greta Garbo played her in the film *Camille.*) **Place Pigalle** has nightclubs, but is no longer home to cafe La Nouvelle Athènes, where Degas, Pissarro, and Manet used to meet. Other attractions include the **Folies-Bergère,** where cancan dancers have been high-kicking since 1868. It is the rococo **Opéra Garnier** (home of the Phantom) that made the 9th the last hurrah of Second Empire opulence. Renoir hated it, but generations later, Chagall painted its ceilings. Pavlova danced *Swan Lake* here, and Nijinsky took the night off to go cruising.

10TH ARRONDISSEMENT (GARE DU NORD/GARE DE L'EST) The **Gare du Nord** and **Gare de l'Est,** along with porno houses and dreary commercial zones, make the 10th one of the least desirable arrondissements for living, dining, or sightseeing. We try to avoid it except for one of our longtime favorite restaurants: **Brasserie Flo** (© **01-47-70-13-59;** www.flobrasseries.com), 7 cour des Petites-Ecuries, best known for its formidable *choucroute,* a heap of sauerkraut garnished with everything.

11TH ARRONDISSEMENT (OPÉRA BASTILLE) For many years, this quarter seemed to sink lower and lower into decay, overcrowded by working-class immigrants from the far reaches of the former Empire. The opening of the **Opéra Bastille,** however, has given the 11th new hope and new life. The facility, called the "people's opera house," stands on the landmark place de la Bastille, where on July 14, 1789, 633 Parisians stormed the fortress and seized the ammunition depot, as the French Revolution swept across the city. Over the years, the prison held such luminaries as Voltaire and the Marquis de Sade. The area between the Marais, Ménilmontant, and République is now being called "blue-collar chic," as the *artistes* of Paris who've been driven from the costlier sections of the Marais can now be found walking the gritty sidewalks of rue Oberkampf. Hip Parisians in search of a more cutting-edge experience are now living and working among the decaying 19th-century apartments and the 1960s public housing with graffiti-splattered walls.

12TH ARRONDISSEMENT (BOIS DE VINCENNES/GARE DE LYON) Very few out-of-towners came here until a French chef opened a restaurant called **Au Trou Gascon** (p. 175). The 12th's major attraction remains the **Bois de Vincennes,** sprawling on the eastern periphery of Paris. This park is a long-time favorite of French families who enjoy its zoos and museums, its royal châteaux and boating lakes, and its **Parc Floral de Paris,** a celebrated flower garden boasting springtime rhododendrons and autumn dahlias. Venture into the dreary **Gare de Lyon** for **Le Train Bleu,** first floor in the Gare de Lyon, place Louis Armand (© 01-43-43-09-06; www.le-train-bleu.com), a restaurant whose ceiling frescoes and Art Nouveau decor are national artistic treasures; the food is good, too. The 12th, once a depressing urban wasteland, has been singled out for budgetary resuscitation and is beginning to sport new housing, shops, gardens, and restaurants. Many will occupy the site of the former Reuilly rail tracks.

13TH ARRONDISSEMENT (GARE D'AUSTERLITZ) Centered on the grimy **Gare d'Austerlitz,** the 13th might have its devotees, but we've yet to meet one. British snobs who flitted in and out of the train station were among the first of the district's foreign visitors and wrote the 13th off as a dreary working-class counterpart of London's East End. The 13th is also home to Paris's **Chinatown,** stretching for 13 square blocks around the Tolbiac Métro stop. It emerged out of the refugee crisis at the end of the Vietnam War, taking over a neighborhood that held mostly Arab-speaking peoples. Today, recognizing overcrowding in the district, the Paris civic authorities are imposing new, not particularly welcome, restrictions on population densities.

14TH ARRONDISSEMENT (MONTPARNASSE) The northern end of this large arrondissement is devoted to **Montparnasse,** home of the "Lost Generation" and stomping ground of Stein, Toklas, Hemingway, and other American expatriates of the 1920s. After World War II, it ceased to be the center of intellectual life, but the memory lingers in its cafes. One of the monuments that sets the tone of the neighborhood is **Rodin's statue of Balzac** at the junction of boulevards Montparnasse and Raspail. At this corner are some of the world's most famous **literary cafes,** including La Rotonde, Le Select, La Dôme, and La Coupole. Though Gertrude Stein avoided them (she loathed cafes), other American expats, including Hemingway and Fitzgerald, had no qualms about enjoying a drink here (or quite a few of them, for that matter). Stein stayed at home (27 rue de Fleurus) with Alice B. Toklas, collecting paintings, including those of Picasso, and entertaining the likes of Max Jacob, Apollinaire, T. S. Eliot, and Matisse.

15TH ARRONDISSEMENT (GARE MONTPARNASSE/INSTITUTE PASTEUR) This is a mostly residential district beginning at **Gare Montparnasse** and stretching to the Seine. In size and population, it's the largest quarter of Paris, but it draws few tourists and has few attractions except for the **Parc des Expositions,** the **Cimetière du Montparnasse,** and the **Institut Pasteur.** In the early 20th century, many artists—such as Chagall, Léger, and Modigliani—lived here in a shared atelier known as "the Beehive."

16TH ARRONDISSEMENT (TROCADÉRO/BOIS DE BOULOGNE) Originally the village of Passy, where Benjamin Franklin lived during most of his time in Paris, this district is still reminiscent of Proust's world. Highlights include the **Bois de Boulogne; the Jardin du Trocadéro; the Maison de Balzac; the Musée Guimet** (famous for its Asian collections); and the **Cimetière de Passy,** resting place of Manet, Talleyrand, Giraudoux, and Debussy. One of the largest arrondissements, it's known today for its well-heeled bourgeoisie, its upscale rents, and some rather posh residential boulevards. The arrondissement also has the best vantage point to view the Eiffel Tower: **place du Trocadéro.**

17TH ARRONDISSEMENT (PARC MONCEAU/PLACE CLICHY) Flanking the northern periphery of Paris, the 17th incorporates neighborhoods of bourgeois respectability (in its west end) and less affluent neighborhoods in its east end. It boasts two of the great restaurants of Paris, **Guy Savoy** and **Michel Rostang** (see chapter 6, "Where to Dine").

18TH ARRONDISSEMENT (MONTMARTRE) The 18th is the most famous outer quarter of Paris, containing **Montmartre,** the **Moulin Rouge, Sacré-Coeur,** and ultratouristy **place du Tertre.** Utrillo was its native son, Renoir lived here, and Toulouse-Lautrec adopted the area as his own. The most famous enclave of artists in Paris's history, the **Bateau-Lavoir** of Picasso fame, gathered here. Max Jacob, Matisse, and Braque were all frequent visitors. Today, place Blanche is known for its prostitutes, and Montmartre is filled with honky-tonks, souvenir shops, and terrible restaurants. You can still find pockets of quiet beauty, though. The city's most famous flea market, the **Marché aux Puces de Clignancourt,** is another landmark.

19TH ARRONDISSEMENT (LA VILLETTE) Today, visitors come to what was once the village of La Villette to see the angular **Cité des Sciences et de l'Industrie,** a spectacular science museum and park built on a site that for years was devoted to the city's slaughterhouses. Mostly residential and not at all upscale, the district is one of the most ethnically diverse in Paris, the home of people from all parts of the former Empire. A highlight is **Les Buttes Chaumont,** a park where kids can enjoy puppet shows and donkey rides.

20TH ARRONDISSEMENT (PÈRE-LACHAISE CEMETERY) The 20th's greatest landmark is **Père-Lachaise Cemetery,** the resting place of Edith Piaf, Marcel Proust, Oscar Wilde, Isadora Duncan, Sarah Bernhardt, Gertrude Stein and Alice B. Toklas, Colette, Jim Morrison, and many others. Otherwise, the 20th arrondissement is a dreary and sometimes volatile melting pot comprising residents from France's former colonies. Though nostalgia buffs sometimes head here to visit Piaf's former neighborhood, **Ménilmontant-Belleville,** it has been almost totally bulldozed and rebuilt since the bad old days when she grew up here.

Pont Neuf.

THE BEST OF PARIS IN 1 DAY

Because time is wasting, arise early and begin your day with some live "theater" by walking the streets around your hotel—Right Bank or Left Bank, it doesn't matter at this point. This walk can acclimate you to the sights, sounds, and smells of the City of Light faster than anything, and it gets you centered before catching a taxi or hopping aboard the Métro for a ride underground to your first attraction.

We suggest you duck into a cafe for breakfast, and it doesn't matter where. On virtually every street in Paris, there is usually more than one cafe.

Any neighborhood will provide a slice of Parisian life, so order breakfast as thousands of locals do. Sit back, enjoy, and breathe deeply before beginning your descent on Paris. **Start:** *Métro to Palais Royal-Musée du Louvre.*

1 Musée du Louvre ★★★

You know you must see the Louvre, perhaps the greatest museum of art in the world. You wouldn't dare go home without storming that citadel. Because it opens at 9am, be among the first in line.

We've been going to this repository of art for years and, on every visit, discover something we've overlooked before. This palatial treasure-trove is richly endowed, and some of its art is the most acclaimed on earth. With your clock ticking, at least call on the "great ladies of the Louvre": the *Mona Lisa* with her enigmatic smile, the sexy *Venus de Milo,* and *Winged Victory* (alas, without a head). Try to allot at least 2 hours of viewing time for some world-class masterpieces. See p. 234.

Around 11am, go for a walk along:

2 The Quays of the Seine ★★★

After leaving the Louvre, walk south toward the river and head east for a stroll along the Seine. You'll encounter the most splendid panoramic vistas that Paris has to offer. Trees shade the banks of the river, and 14 bridges span the Seine. So much of the city's fortune has depended on this river, and you'll be in the nerve center of Paris life as you stroll along.

You'll see Paris's greatest island on the Seine, the Cité, emerging before you. Cross over the:

3 Pont Neuf ★

The oldest and most evocative of the bridges of Paris, Pont Neuf (p. 283) dates from 1578 and still looks the same. From the bridge, the view down (or up) the river is perhaps the most memorable in Paris.

Walk down the steps emerging on your right along Pont Neuf to:

4 Square du Vert Galant

The steps take you behind the statue dedicated to Henri IV to the square du Vert Galant (p. 284) at the western tip of Ile de la Cité. The square takes its designation from the nickname given Henri IV, meaning "gay old spark." The square is the best vantage point for viewing Pont Neuf and the Louvre. As you stand on this square, you'll be at the "prow" of Cité if you liken the island to a giant ship.

After taking in that view, continue east, pausing at:

5 Place Dauphine

This square—perfect for a picnic—was named in honor of the Dauphin, the future Louis XIII. It faces the towering mass of La Conciergerie (p. 264), whose gloomy precincts and memories of the French Revolution you can save for another visit to Paris.

With time moving on, head east along:

6 Quai des Orfèvres

This Seine-bordering quay leads east to Notre-Dame. It was the former market of the jewelers of 17th- and 18th-century Paris. Marie Antoinette's celebrated necklace, subject of countless legends, was fashioned here.

The quay leads you to:

7 Sainte-Chapelle ★★★

This Gothic chapel (p. 237) is sublime, and entering its upper chapel is like climbing into Tiffany's most deluxe jewel box. As the colored light from the 13th-century windows shines through, you'll bathe in perhaps the most brilliantly colored "walls of glass" in the world. Taking in the deep glow of these astonishing windows is one of the great joys of a visit to the City of Light. The windows, the oldest in Paris, are known not only for their brilliant colors, but also for the vitality of their characters, including everybody from Adam and Eve to St. John the Baptist and the Virgin.

After a visit, it's time for lunch. Because first-day visitors have little time to absorb Left Bank life, here's your chance.

The Best of Paris in 1 Day

1 Musée du Louvre
2 The Quays of the Seine
3 Pont Neuf
4 Square du Vert Galant
5 Place Dauphine
6 Quai des Orfèvres
7 Sainte-Chapelle
8 Place St-Michel
🍵 Allard
9 Cathédrale de Notre-Dame
10 Place de la Concorde
11 Champs-Elysées
12 Arc de Triomphe
13 Tour Eiffel

Continue east along quai des Orfèvres until you come to the Pont St-Michel. Cross the bridge to the Left Bank of Paris, arriving at the Latin Quarter centering on:

8 Place St-Michel

One of the inner chambers of Left Bank life, this square was named in memory of the ancient chapel of St-Michel that stood here once upon a time. The square, a bustling hub of Sorbonne life, centers on a fountain from 1860 designed by Gabriel Davioud, rising 23m (75 ft.) high and stretching out to 5m (15 ft.), a "monster" spouting water. A bronze statue depicts Saint Michael fighting the dragon.

Why not do lunch in one of the most evocative of all Left Bank bistros?

🍵 Allard ★

Arm yourself with a good map to reach Allard, which is only a 5-minute walk southwest of place St-Michel. You can easily get lost in the narrow maze of Left Bank streets. Little has changed at this classic bistro with its mellow decor and traditional menu. Against a nostalgic ambience of Paris of the 1930s, you can join cosmopolitan patrons enjoying the sole meunière or canard d'olives, finishing off with that most divine pastry known to all Parisians as *tarte tatin*. And, yes, if you've never tried them before, you'll find frogs' legs on the menu. See p. 197. 41 rue St-André-des-Arts, 6e. ☎ **01-43-26-48-23.**

After lunch, walk back to place St-Michel.

Still on the Left Bank, continue east along quai St-Michel until it becomes quai de Montebello. At the "green lung" or park, square Rene Viviani, pause to take in the most dramatic view of Notre-Dame across the Seine. Then cross the bridge, Pont au Double, to visit the cathedral itself.

9 Cathédrale de Notre-Dame ★★★

In so many ways, the exterior is more exciting than the vast and hollow interior that, since its denuding during the French Revolution, is almost tomb-like. One of the supreme masterpieces of Gothic art, Notre-Dame cathedral still evokes Victor Hugo's novel *The Hunchback of Notre-Dame*. You stand in awe, taking in the majestic and perfectly balanced portals. After a walk through the somber interior, climb the towers (around to the left facing the building) for a close encounter with tons of bells and an eerie inspection of what are history's most bizarre gargoyles, some so terribly impish that they seem to be mocking you. See p. 225.

After Notre-Dame, take the Métro to the:

10 Place de la Concorde ★★★

This octagonal traffic hub, built in 1757, is dominated by an Egyptian obelisk from Luxor, the oldest manmade object in Paris, from 1300 B.C. In the Reign of Terror at the time of the French Revolution, the dreaded guillotine was erected on this spot to claim thousands of heads. For a spectacular view, look down the Champs-Elysées.

Place de la Concorde.

The grandest walk in Paris begins here, leading all the way to the Arc de Triomphe (see "Champs-Elysées" below). It's a distance of 3.2km (2 miles) and is the most popular walk in Paris.

However, because your afternoon is short, you may want to skip most of it, taking the Métro to Franklin-D-Roosevelt and continuing west from there. At least you'll see the busiest and most commercial part of the:

11 Champs-Elysées ★★★

Called "the highway of French grandeur," this boulevard was designed for promenading. It's witnessed some of the greatest moments in French history and some of its worst defeats, such as when Hitler's armies paraded

The Champs-Elysées and Arc de Triomphe at night.

down the street in 1940. Louis XIV ordered the construction of the 1.8km (1-mile) avenue in 1667. Without worrying about any particular monument, stroll along its avenue of sidewalk cafes, automobile showrooms, airline offices, cinemas, lingerie stores, and even hamburger joints. The Champs has obviously lost its *fin-de-siècle* elegance as evoked by Marcel Proust in *Remembrance of Things Past.* But then, what hasn't?

At the end of the broad boulevard, you approach:

12 Arc de Triomphe ★★★

The greatest triumphal arch in the world, the 49m (161-ft.) arch can be climbed for one of the most panoramic views of Paris. The arch marks the intersections of the 8th, 16th, and 17th arrondissements. Sculptures, including François Rude's famous *La Marseillaise,* depicting the uprising of 1792 (p. 28), are embedded in the arch.

After a visit, and with the afternoon fading, take the Métro to the Champ de Mars-Tour Eiffel for an ascent up the:

13 Tour Eiffel ★★★

It's open until 11pm or midnight, so don't worry about missing it. A close encounter with this tower, a 10,000-ton dark metal structure is more inspiring up close than when seen from afar. A source of wonder since the 1889 World Exposition, this 317m (1,040-ft.) tower was the world's tallest building until the Chrysler Building went up in New York in 1930. If the afternoon is clear, you can see for 65km (40 miles). See p. 239.

THE BEST OF PARIS IN 2 DAYS

If you've already made your way through "The Best of Paris in 1 Day," you'll find that your second full-day tour takes in other fascinating sections of Paris, including Ile St-Louis (the most beautiful island in the Seine) and Montmartre (the hill crowning Paris), along with major attractions such as the greatest works of the Impressionists in the Musée d'Orsay, Napoleon's Tomb, and other amusements. **Start:** *Pont-Marie Métro stop.*

1 Ile St-Louis ★★

The neighboring island to La Cité is Ile St-Louis (p. 284), lying to the immediate east of the larger island. Beautiful antique town houses with charming courtyards, tree-shaded quays opening onto the Seine, mansions that once housed such famous literati as Voltaire and his mistress, antiques shops, and little restaurants and cafes fill the narrow streets on this island of platinum real estate. A great way to break in your second day in Paris is by wandering the streets and quays in the early morning before the museums and attractions open. After arriving at Pont-Marie on the Right Bank, head south across the bridge, Pont-Marie, to Ile St-Louis. Cut immediately to your right and walk along quai de Bourbon. We suggest that you circle the entire Seine-bordering quays, including those south of the island, quai d'Orléans and quai de Béthune. When you reach square Barye in the far southeastern corner, take in the scenic view down river before crossing by Pont de Sully. At this point you can cut inland and walk the entire length of

A quiet street on Ile St-Louis.

Sculptures at Musée d'Orsay.

The Best of Paris in 2 Days

1. Ile St-Louis
2. Musée d'Orsay
   - Restaurant du Musée d'Orsay
3. Hôtel des Invalides/ Napoleon's Tomb
4. Bateaux-Mouche Cruises of the Seine
5. Basilique du Sacré-Coeur
6. Harry's New York Bar

rue St-Louis-en-l'Ile, which will take you along the "main street" and the most historic part of the island.

After your stroll, take the Métro to Solférino.

2 Musée d'Orsay ★★★

This splendid museum will take up the rest of your morning; at least 2 hours. It shelters the world's greatest collection of the Impressionists, including Manet, Monet, and Van Gogh. You'll even get to see the fabled painting of *Whistler's Mother*—and it's by an American. This former railway station also presents a vast array of sculptures and decorative arts, with other departments devoted to architecture, photography, and cinema. Most of the works span the period from 1848 to 1914 and the beginning of World War I. To speed you on your way, English-language information is available at the entrance. Audio guides offer analyses of more than 50 masterpieces on display. See p. 232.

Because it's time for lunch, we suggest you eat on-site.

☕ Restaurant du Musée d'Orsay

Serving first-class cuisine, this elegant restaurant should be visited if only for its setting, although the food is excellent. Gabriel Ferrier designed this Belle Epoque room with its panoramic vista of the Seine and its splendid chandeliers. If you want something cheaper, you can patronize **Café des Hauteurs,** on the fifth floor behind one of the former train station's huge iron clocks. For food on the run, patronize a self-service food stand directly above the cafe; it's open Tuesday to Sunday 10:30am to 5pm; Thursday 10:30am to 9pm. 1 rue de Bellechasse, 7e. ☎ **01-45-49-47-03.**

After lunch, take the Métro to:

3 Hôtel des Invalides/Napoleon's Tomb ★★★

Still beloved by many French people, the little megalomaniac who tried to conquer Europe lies locked away (or at least his remains are) with some of his family members in six coffins of red Finnish porphyry. After seeing the tomb in Église du Dome, you can leave at once or else take a quick look at the **Musée de l'Armée** located here. This is a gaudy celebration of French military history, but most first-timers to Paris skip it. See p. 230.

From Invalides take the Métro to the Right Bank, getting off at the Alma-Marceau stop. Here, you can embark on one of the:

4 Bateaux-Mouche Cruises of the Seine

We know of no better way to enjoy Paris than on one of these scenic boat tours from the riverbank point of view. They allow for one of the most

A Bateaux-Mouche cruise under the Pont de l'Alma.

dramatic vistas of Notre-Dame. Tours depart every 20 to 30 minutes during the day and are in English, lasting about 75 minutes. First, you sail east all the way to Ile St-Louis, and then you return west past the Eiffel Tower.

As the afternoon fades, head for "the top of Paris," the legendary Montmartre district, reached by Métro going north to the Abbesses stop.

5 Basilique du Sacré-Coeur ★★

Before heading for Sacré-Coeur, you can wander around the legendary square, **place du Tertre** (p. 300 of our walking tour of Montmartre). Dozens of young artists wait for you to give them the nod to paint your portrait. This may sound corny to sophisticated travelers, but thousands of visitors consider these portraits their most memorable souvenirs of Paris. Perhaps your portrait will be painted by tomorrow's Toulouse-Lautrec. The basilica of Sacré-Coeur, or the Church of the Sacred Heart, with its many cupolas, is a brilliant white and as much a part of the Paris skyline as the Eiffel Tower. Ascend to the dome at 80m (262 ft.) for one of the greatest panoramas in all of Europe, extending for 65km (40 miles) on a clear afternoon. After coming down from the dome, we always like to sit with dozens of other visitors on the steps of Sacré-Coeur, watching the afternoon fade and the lights go on all over Paris.

After dinner, perhaps in one of the little bistros that surround place du Tertre, head for a Paris landmark for your final toast to the City of Light. Take the Métro to Opéra or Pyramides.

6 Harry's New York Bar

This is the official headquarters of the International Bar Flies (p. 363). Such cocktails as the bloody mary, the Sidecar, and the White Lady were created here. The bar looks much as it did at the time of the Liberation, when Hemingway was one of its patrons. The main bar attracts sports fans, especially rugby rooters, but the downstairs piano bar is more attuned to a romantic conversation over a cocktail.

A final stroll through the streets of Paris before turning in will be your *adieu* to everyone's favorite city (well, almost everyone).

THE BEST OF PARIS IN 3 DAYS

Having survived 2 days in the capital of France, you are by now a veteran Parisian. Now it's time to "Hit the Road, Jack" (or Jill) and head for the single most glorious monument to pomp and pomposity that France ever erected to royal pretensions and kingly vanity. ***Start:*** *RER line C to Versailles Rive Gauche station.*

1 Château de Versailles ★★★

There is nothing in all of Paris to equal this regal wonder, former stomping ground of everyone from Madame de Pompadour, the royal mistress, to Marie Antoinette, the Austrian princess doomed to marry a French king who lost his head. The palace opens at 9am, so try to arrive at that time because it will take a minimum of 3 hours to see just some of the highlights.

A first-time visitor will want to concentrate on the **Grands Apparte-ments** ★★★, the glittering **Hall of Mirrors** ★★★, and the **Petits Appartements** ★★ where Louis XV died in 1774 of smallpox. Other "don't miss" attractions include the **Opéra** that Gabriel designed for Louis XV in 1748 and the **Royal Chapel** ★★★ that Hardouin-Mansart didn't live to complete. There's more. For your final hour, wander through Le Nôtre's "Garden of Eden"—in other words, the **Gardens of Versailles** ★★★, paying a visit to the **Grand Trianon** ★★ where Nixon once slept in the room in which Madame de Pompadour died, and the **Petit Trianon** ★★ that Louis XV used for trysts with his mistress, Madame du Barry. See p. 373.

☕ Le Potager du Roy ★

This is one of the best of the middle-bracket restaurants of Versailles. Philippe Letourneur makes it easy for you by offering one of the best, most generous and well-prepared prix-fixe menus in Versailles, although it's rather pricey. The choice of ingredients is skillful and the preparation inventive. The menu is adjusted to take advantage of the best produce of any season. 1 rue du Maréchal-Joffre. ✆ **01-39-50-35-34.** See p. 375.

Note: Should your time be too precious for a sit-down meal, you can have a fast lunch on the run and save those dwindling hours to see more of Paris itself. You can visit a deli in the morning before leaving Paris and secure the makings of a *pique-nique,* which you can enjoy by the canal in the Gardens of Versailles after touring the palace. Within various corners of the gardens, you'll also encounter snack bars discreetly tucked away. There's even a McDonald's on the walk back from the palace to the train station, which you'll need to visit anyway to take the RER back to Paris.

Once in Paris, take the Métro to Rambuteau, Hôtel-de-Ville, or Châtelet–Les Halles to visit:

2 Centre Pompidou
★★★

The exterior is controversial, called daringly innovative and avant-garde or else "the eyesore of Paris." But inside, virtually everyone agrees that this museum dominating Beaubourg is a repository of one of the world's greatest collections of modern art. Amazingly, more art lovers visit Pompidou per day than the Louvre or the Eiffel Tower. Beginning with Rousseau's *Snake Charmer* and

Centre Pompidou.

The Best of Paris in 3 Days

Petit Palais
Champs Elysées
place de la Concorde
Jardin des Tuileries
place Vendôme
r. Saint-Honoré
av. de l'Opéra
2e
10e
place de la République
r. du Faubourg du Temple
av. de la République
bd. Voltaire
11e
1er
Forum des Halles
r. du Louvre
bd. de Sébastopol
r. de Turbigo
3e
Musée du Louvre
Musée d'Orsay
Seine
2 Centre Pompidou
MARAIS
r. de Turenne
7e
bd. Saint-Germain
r. du Bac
Hôtel de Ville
4e
4
ÎLE DE LA CITÉ
r. de Rivoli
3
r. St-Antoine
pl. de la Bastille
bd. des Invalides
r. de Sèvres
bd. Raspail
r. de Rennes
6e
Palais du Luxembourg
Jardin du Luxembourg
bd. Saint-Michel
Cathédrale Notre-Dame
bd. St-Germain
ÎLE ST-LOUIS
bd. Henri IV
Opéra Bastille
Sorbonne
LATIN QUARTER
Panthéon
12e
1 Le Potager du Roy
r. de Vaugirard
bd. d'Assas
5e
15e
Tour Montparnasse
La Coupole
5
av. du Maine
Montparnasse
6
MONTPARNASSE
Gare Montparnasse
Cimetière du Montparnasse
14e

0   1/2 mi
0   0.5 km

1 Château de Versailles
🍴 Le Potager du Roy
2 Centre Pompidou
3 Place des Vosges
4 Rue des Rosiers
5 Montparnasse
🍴 La Coupole
6 Closerie des Lilas

ending with the latest acquisition from the 21st century, you can view the greatest modern artists of the 20th century: the inevitable Picassos, but also Chagall, Francis Bacon, Calder, Magritte, Matisse, Mondrian, Pollock, Kandinsky—and the beat goes on. Allow at least 2 hours. See p. 241.

Take the Métro to:

3 Place des Vosges ★★★

Having tasted the glories of such districts as Montmartre and Ile St-Louis, it's time to discover the charms of one of Paris's most enchanting neighborhoods, the Marais. Place des Vosges, one of the world's most perfectly designed and harmonious squares, is found at the very center of the Marais. For those with extra time, we've designed a complete walking tour of the Marais (p. 308). But most 3-day visitors, especially if they visit Versailles, will not have time to see the entire district.

The oldest square in Paris is flanked by 36 matching pavilions with red-and-gold, brick-and-stone facades. Architecturally, this square represents the first time in Paris that an arcade was used to link houses. Balconies were also designed for the first time—not just for decorative reasons, but to be used. The most famous resident of this square (no. 6) was the French writer Victor Hugo, who lived here from 1833 to 1848 until Napoleon III came to power and Hugo fled into voluntary exile in the Channel Islands. His home is now a museum (p. 269), which at this point may have to be saved until your next trip to Paris.

Arm yourself with a good map and spend at least an hour wandering the narrow Marais streets to the west of place des Vosges. You can make discoveries on every block as you explore trendy cafes and funky shops. At the northern tier of the place des Vosges, head west along rue des Francs Bourgeois, one of the most historic streets.

At some point, dip south to visit the parallel street:

4 Rue des Rosiers

"The Street of Rose Bushes" (its English name) remains from the heyday of the old Jewish ghetto that once flourished here. The street, deep in the heart of the Marais, is still packed with kosher butchers, bakeries, and falafel shops. Despite Nazi attempts to exterminate the Jews in World War II, their families survived and are still living in the Marais. A synagogue is at 25 rue des Rosiers. In the 1960s, the waves of North African Sephardim radically changed the street. One more famous neighborhood awaits discovery.

5 Montparnasse ★★★

Take the Métro to Montparnasse-Bienvenüe. Montparnasse was once the retreat of bohemian artists and the working class. Today, it's been as successfully gentrified with urban renewal projects as the Marais. The district teems with cafes (many of literary fame), cinemas, and nightclubs, along with artisan shops and bars. For a description of some of the highlights of the area, see coverage beginning on p. 287. For the best overview, take an elevator to the 56th floor of **Tour Montparnasse** (℃ **01-45-38-52-56**), which, when it was built, was accused of bringing Manhattan to Paris. The tower, completed in 1973, rises 206m (676 ft.) above the Parisian skyline.

After taking in the view, descend on the most famous cafe of Montparnasse.

☕ La Coupole ★

One doesn't see as many writers and publishers as before, but this is still the best viewing platform for Montparnasse life. In this citadel to the bohemian life of Paris in the 1920s and 1930s, Hemingway, Picasso, and Louis Armstrong once scribbled, sketched, or composed. Chanteuse Josephine Baker would show up accompanied by her lion cub, and Jean-Paul Sartre would dine here. Eugène Ionesco always ordered the café liegeois. Henry Miller came for his morning porridge, and the famous "Kiki of Montparnasse" picked up tricks here to service back in her hotel room. James Joyce patronized the joint, as did F. Scott Fitzgerald when he didn't have much money; when the royalty check came in, he fled to the Ritz Bar. You can order drinks here and sit back to enjoy the cafe scene in Montparnasse, perhaps not as colorful as in days gone by, but still a lively, bustling place to be at night. Join the local fauna for the memories if for no other reason. 102 bd. du Montparnasse, 14e. ℃ **01-43-20-14-20;** www.lacoupoleparis.com. See p. 211.

Enjoying a quiet afternoon at a Left Bank cafe.

For dinner on your final night, head for a restaurant that is a virtual sightseeing attraction as well as a place for food.

6 Closerie des Lilas ★

After taking the Métro Port Royal or Vavin, descend on this legend that has been wining and dining some of the most famous figures of the past 2 centuries since it opened back in 1847. It is "the Pleasure Garden of the Lilacs" (its English name), a virtual French monument. Follow the sounds of a jazz pianist and enter its hallowed precincts, heading for the *bateau* (boat) section for a champagne julep (the bartender's special). You can dine expensively in the main restaurant with formal service or else enjoy the more democratically-priced brasserie. Should you be on the strictest of budgets, you can order a coffee or beer at the bar and soak up the atmosphere, the way Hemingway did between royalty checks when he was broke and had to kill pigeons in the park for his dinner. Today, the lilacs of its namesake no longer bloom, Trotsky has long been assassinated, and Henry James is a mere skeleton of himself (if that). But young Parisians, including rising film stars, models, the pretty, and the chic, still patronize the place, giving you a close encounter with Paris after dark. And, yes, it's still going in August when the rest of the town shuts down. Have a nightcap at the bar and promise a return to Paris.

5

WHERE TO STAY

Paris boasts some 2,000 hotels—with about 80,000 rooms—spread across its 20 arrondissements. They range from the Ritz and the Crillon to dives so repellent that even George Orwell, author of *Down and Out in Paris and London,* wouldn't have considered checking in. (Of course, you won't find those in this guide!) We include deluxe places for those who can afford to live like the Sultan of Brunei, as well as a wide range of moderate and inexpensive choices for the rest of us.

Most visitors, at least those from North America, come to Paris in July and August. Many French people are on vacation, and trade fairs and conventions come to a halt, so there are usually plenty of rooms, even though these months are traditionally the peak season for European travel. In most hotels, February is as busy as April or September, due to the volume of business travelers and tourists taking advantage of off-season discounts.

Because hot weather rarely lasts long in Paris, few hotels, except the deluxe ones, provide air-conditioning. If you're trapped in a garret on a hot summer night, you'll have to sweat it out. You can open your window to get cooler air, but you also may get noise from outside. To avoid this, request a room in back when reserving. Nearly all hotels in Paris have central heating, but in some cases, you might wish the owners would turn it up a little on a cold night.

The French government grades hotels with a star system, ranging from one star for a simple inn to four stars for a deluxe hotel. Moderately priced hotels usually get two or three stars. This system is based on a complex formula of room sizes, facilities, plumbing, elevators, dining options, renovations, and so on. In one-star hotels, the bathrooms are often shared, the facilities are extremely limited (such as no elevator), the rooms may not have phones or TVs, and breakfast is often the only meal served. Two- or three-star hotels usually have elevators, and rooms will likely have baths, phones, and TVs. In four-star hotels, you'll get all the amenities plus facilities and services such as room service, 24-hour concierges, elevators, and perhaps even health clubs.

However, the system is a bit misleading. For tax reasons, a four-star hotel might elect to have a three-star rating, which, with the hotel's permission, is granted by the government. The government won't add a star where it's not merited, but will remove one at the hotel's request.

CONDOS, VILLAS, HOUSES & APARTMENTS **New York Habitat** (© 212/255-8018; fax 212/627-1416; www.nyhabitat.com) rents furnished apartments and vacation accommodations in Paris. Bookings should be done at least 3 months in advance (even farther out for the south of France) and can be arranged online or over the phone. Prices in Paris range from 450€ to 8,000€ per week.

If you want to rent an apartment in Paris, the **Barclay International Group,** 6800 Jericho Turnpike, Syosset, NY 11791 (© **800/845-6636** or

FACING PAGE: **A suite at Hôtel Balzac.**

516/364-0064; fax 516/364-4468; www.barclayweb.com), can give you access to about 3,000 apartments and villas throughout Paris (and 39 other cities in France), ranging from modest modern units to the most stylish lodgings. Units rent for 1 night to 6 months; all have TVs and kitchenettes, and many have concierge staffs and lobby-level security. The least expensive cost around $130 per night, double occupancy. Discounts are given for a stay of 1 week or longer. Rentals must be prepaid in U.S. dollars or with a U.S. credit or charge card.

Hometours International, Inc., 1108 Scottie Lane, Knoxville, TN 37919 (✆ **865/690-8484;** hometours@aol.com), offers more than 400 moderately priced apartments, apartment hotels, and villas in Paris.

Drawbridge to Europe, Inc., 98 Granite St., Ashland, OR 97520 (✆ **888/268-1148;** www.drawbridgetoeurope.com), offers everything from Paris apartments to villas scattered throughout France. Rentals are selected for their locations, interiors, and possibly historic character.

The aptly named **Home Away,** 45 St. Clair Ave. West, Ste. 1100, Toronto, Ontario, Canada M4V 1K9 (✆ **800/374-6637;** www.homeaway.com), provides private vacation villas throughout France, including apartments in Paris.

HOTEL CHAINS One good moderately priced choice is the **Mercure** chain, an organization of simple, modern hotels throughout France. Even at the peak of the tourist season, a room at a Mercure in Paris rents for as little as 99€ per night (admittedly, a rarity). For more information on Mercure hotels and its 100-page directory, call ✆ **800/221-4542** in the U.S. or visit www.mercure.com.

Which Bank Is for You?

The river dividing Paris geographically and culturally demands that you make a choice. Are you more Left Bank, wanting a room in the heart of Saint-Germain, where Jean-Paul Sartre and Simone de Beauvoir once spent their nights? Or are you more Right Bank, preferring sumptuous quarters such as those at the Crillon, where Tom Cruise once slept? Would you rather look for that special old curio in a dusty shop on the Left Bank's rue Jacob, or inspect the latest Lagerfeld or Dior couture on the Right Bank's avenue Montaigne? Each of Paris's neighborhoods has its own flavor, and your experiences and memories of the city will likely be formed by where you choose to stay.

If you desire chic surroundings, choose a Right Bank hotel. That puts you near the most elegant shops and within walking distance of major sights such as the Arc de Triomphe, place de la Concorde, the Jardin des Tuileries, the Opéra Garnier, and the Louvre. The best Right Bank hotels are near the Arc de Triomphe in the 8th arrondissement, though many first-class lodgings cluster near the Trocadéro and Bois de Boulogne in the 16th or near the Palais des Congrès in the 17th. If you'd like to be near place Vendôme, try for a hotel in the 1st. Also popular are the increasingly fashionable Marais and Bastille in the 3rd, 4th, and 11th arrondissements, and Les Halles/Beaubourg, home of the Centre Pompidou and Les Halles shopping mall, in the 1st.

If you want less formality and tiny bohemian streets, head for the Left Bank, where prices are traditionally lower. Hotels that cater to students are found in the 5th and 6th arrondissements, the 5th being known as the Latin Quarter. These areas, with their literary overtones, are home to the Sorbonne, the Panthéon, the Jardin du Luxembourg, cafe life, bookstores, and publishing houses. The 6th arrondissement provides a touch of avant-garde St-Germain.

North American and Canadian chain hotels in Paris include Marriott, Hilton, Radisson, Holiday Inn, and Four Seasons, plus Starwood (encompassing Westin and Sheraton). The French also have chain hotels or hotel associations that feature Sofitel, Mercure, Ibis, Novotel, and, in some cases, Logis de France and Relais de Silence. The latter two are mostly in the countryside.

For apartment or cottage stays of 2 weeks or more, **Idyll Untours** (© **888/868-6871;** www.untours.com) provides exceptional lodgings for a reasonable price—which includes air/ground transportation, cooking facilities, and on-call support from a local resident. Best of all: Untours—named the "Most Generous Company in America" by Newman's Own—donates most profits to provide low-interest loans to underprivileged entrepreneurs around the world (see website for details).

BEST HOTEL BETS

For full details on the following hotels, see the listings later in this chapter.

○ **Best for Families:** An affordable Left Bank choice is the **Hôtel de Fleurie,** 32–34 rue Grégoire-de-Tours, 6e (© **01-53-73-70-00**), in the heart of St-Germain-des-Prés. The accommodations are thoughtfully appointed, and many connecting rooms with two large beds are perfect for families. Children 11 or under stay free with a parent. See p. 139.

○ **Best Value:** Not far from the Champs-Elysées, the **Résidence Lord Byron,** 5 rue Chateaubriand, 8e (© **01-43-59-89-98**), is a classy little getaway that's far from opulent, but is clean and comfortable and worth every euro. See p. 130.

○ **Best Location:** Only a 2-minute walk from Paris's most historic and beautiful square, **Hôtel de la Place des Vosges,** 14 rue de Birague, 4e (© **01-42-72-60-46**), is a little charmer. In a building 350 years old, it is small and inviting, with some decorative touches that evoke the era of Louis XIII. See p. 118.

○ **Best View:** Of the 33 rooms at the **Hôtel du Quai Voltaire,** 19 quai Voltaire, 7e (© **01-42-61-50-91**), 28 open onto views of the Seine. If you stay here, you'll be following in the footsteps of Wilde, Baudelaire, and Wagner. This 17th-century abbey was transformed into a hotel back in 1856 and has been welcoming guests who appreciate its tattered charms ever since. See p. 148.

○ **Best for Nostalgia:** If you yearn for a Left Bank "literary" address, make it the **Odéon Hôtel,** 3 rue de l'Odéon (© **01-43-25-90-67**), in the heart of the 6th arrondissement, filled with the ghosts of Gide, Hemingway, Fitzgerald, Joyce, and Stein and Toklas. Evoking a Norman country inn, this charming hotel lures guests with its high, crooked ceilings, exposed beams, and memories of yesterday. See p. 141.

○ **Best-Kept Secret:** Created when a run-down five-story apartment house and a three-story parking garage were interconnected and upgraded into one coherent building, **Murano Urban Resort,** 13 bd. du Temple, 3e (© **01-42-71-20-00**), is trendsetting and aggressively minimalist. The decorative theme revolves around the transparency of Murano glass to great effect. See p. 114.

- **Best Historic Hotel:** Inaugurated by Napoleon III in 1855, the **Hôtel du Louvre,** place André-Malraux, 1er (✆ **01-44-58-38-38** in France), was once described by a French journalist as "a palace of the people, rising adjacent to the palace of kings." Today, the hotel offers luxurious accommodations and panoramic views down avenue de l'Opéra. See p. 110.

- **Most Trendy Hotel:** It's all the rage. Right off the Champs-Elysées, **Hotel Le A,** 4 rue d'Artois, 8e (✆ **01-42-56-99-99**), forsakes the traditional for a style so contemporary that it could be called avant-garde. It's as if the Paris hotel scene is reinventing itself with modern technology. See p. 128.

Alternatives to Hotels

If you want to stay somewhere more intimate (and in some cases, more restrictive) than a hotel, consider booking a room within a private home. An agency promoting upmarket B&B accommodations in Paris is **Alcôve & Agapes,** 8 bis rue Coysevox, 75018 Paris (✆ or fax **01-44-85-06-05;** www.bed-and-breakfast-in-paris.com). Reservations are made through the Internet only.

This outfit is a bridge between travelers who seek rooms in private homes and Parisians who wish to welcome visitors. Most hosts speak at least some English, range in age from 30 to 75, and have at least some points of view about entertainment and dining options within the neighborhood. Available options include individual bedrooms, usually within large, old-fashioned private apartments, as well as "unhosted" accommodations where the apartment is otherwise empty and without the benefit (or restrictions) of a live-in host.

Rates for occupancy by either one or two persons, with breakfast included, range from 65€ to 195€ per unit, depending on the apartment, the neighborhood, the setup, and the plumbing. In cases where a client occupies an unhosted apartment, the refrigerators will be stocked with sufficient breakfast supplies for the number of days you are staying (3-night minimum). The city government of Paris has launched a program seeking residents willing to rent rooms in their homes similar to a B&B. The site, **Hôtes Qualité Paris** (www.hqp.fr), encourages locals to make available their spare rooms at prices that begin around 100€ a night. It's strictly potluck; you might end up on a house barge docked between the Louvre and the place de la Concorde or else in an old-fashioned bedroom near the Bois de Boulogne with a host who happens to be a passionate history lecturer, as you'll find out at breakfast the next morning.

Coach House Rentals (www.rentals.chsparis.com) has expanded its private homes for rent to include addresses in Paris. Its website has pictures and full descriptions of the properties, with an English-speaking reservation team to handle bookings and to deal with any questions. A company representative will meet guests at their rental to show them the ropes. The company usually arranges a car to meet guests at the airport and take them to their prearranged rental.

The aptly named **Good Morning Paris,** 43 rue Lacépède, 75005 Paris (www.goodmorningparis.fr), is yet another bed-and-breakfast agency with carefully inspected rooms to rent. Prices start around 69€ for two persons with a shared bathroom or 90€ for two with private bathroom, including breakfast. A few apartments are also rented, housing two to four persons from 106€ a night. A minimum of 2 nights is required for all rentals. Arrangements are possible in apartments right off the Champs-Elysées or in more romantic sectors, including the Latin Quarter, even Montmartre.

It's a bit more risky than the previously inspected and approved recommendations, but there is a budget option for rental apartments which can be pursued by checking out the classified ads in **FUSAC** (France–USA Contacts; www.fusac.com), a free biweekly magazine that is widely distributed in bookstores, cafes, or restaurants catering to English-speaking visitors.

Using FUSAC is like taking potluck if you want an apartment. A safer bet is **Paris Attitude** at 6 rue de Sentier, 75002 Paris (✆ **01-42-96-31-46;** fax 01-42-96-27-86; www.parisattitude.com). Apartments are centrally located and are furnished and well-equipped; short- or long-term rentals are available. A studio for two people right off the Champs-Elysées might rent for 550€ per week.

Parisian Home, 12 rue Mandar, 75002 (✆ **01-45-08-03-37;** www.parisianhome.com), has a large selection of apartments available in central Paris, ranging from cramped studios to spacious, three-bedroom apartments for more luxurious and expensive living. Don't expect elegant furnishings, however, though the rentals, both short- and long-term, are well-equipped with linens, dishes, and the like. The agency's website is detailed with lots of pictures and descriptions of the services available. You deal with the agency, not the owners. The minimum stay is 1 week.

Unlike Parisian Home, **France Lodge,** 2 rue Meissonier, 75017 (✆ **01-56-33-85-85;** www.francelodge.fr), has both hosted and unhosted apartments, some 100 in all sprinkled across the central arrondissements of Paris. The agency's roster ranges from B&Bs to small studios, or even luxurious five-room apartments if you want to spread out or have a big family. The cheapest rentals, rather cramped, begin at 400€ a week, but 900€ is more average.

Parisian Home and France Lodge rent apartments that owners use only occasionally. However, **Appartement de Ville** (✆ **01-42-45-09-08;** www.appartementdeville.com) rents more upmarket apartments that owners use as their primary residences. Lodgings under this agency have more atmosphere and give you a feeling that you're living more as a Parisian, which you are, of course. Many of the apartments are owned by those in the arts, including actors and dancers who have to be away from Paris for extended periods for engagements. There are some 200 apartments, most of them quite unusual, in the agency's roster. Although most apartments are in the very heart of Paris, you can make better deals by booking into one of the unchic arrondissements, including the 10th, 11th, and 12th. Studios can range from 450€ to 840€ per week, with larger apartments costing much more, perhaps 2,000€ for a three-bedroom choice.

Finally, some good deals are possible if you'll go for an *aparthotel,* a cross between a hotel and an apartment. Short on charm, these rentals are good on convenience, each with a kitchenette. Although rates are more than short-term studios (see previously), you get more of the services of a hotel, including fresh towels and a reception desk. The best known agency renting aparthotels is **Citadines** (✆ **08-25-33-33-32;** www.citadines.com). The cheapest rentals are the studios with pull-out beds. A studio for two might range from 140€ to 250€ a night—or even more in such highly prized locations as the Louvre area or St-Germain-des-Prés on the Left Bank.

ON THE RIGHT BANK

We begin with the most centrally located arrondissements on the Right Bank and then work our way through the more outlying neighborhoods and to the area around the Arc de Triomphe.

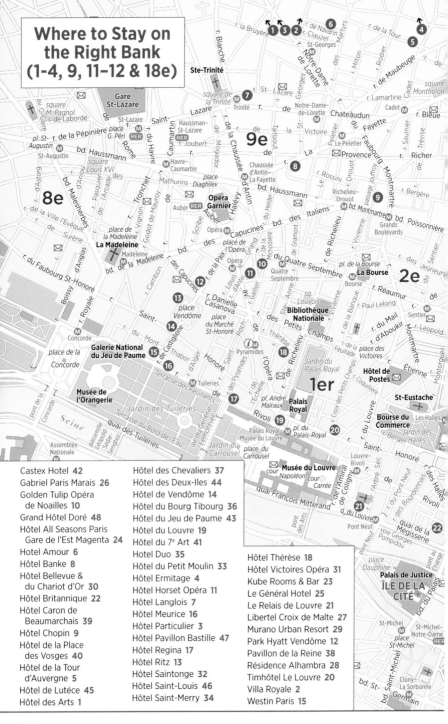

Where to Stay on the Right Bank (1-4, 9, 11–12 & 18e)

9e

8e

La Madeleine

Gare St-Lazare

Ste-Trinité

Opéra Garnier

Galerie National du Jeu de Paume

place de la Concorde

Musée de l'Orangerie

place Vendôme

Bibliothèque Nationale

La Bourse

2e

place des Victoires

Hôtel de Postes

St-Eustache

1er

Palais Royal

Bourse du Commerce

Musée du Louvre

Palais de Justice

ÎLE DE LA CITÉ

Castex Hotel **42**
Gabriel Paris Marais **26**
Golden Tulip Opéra de Noailles **10**
Grand Hôtel Doré **48**
Hôtel All Seasons Paris Gare de l'Est Magenta **24**
Hotel Amour **6**
Hôtel Banke **8**
Hôtel Bellevue & du Chariot d'Or **30**
Hôtel Britannique **22**
Hôtel Caron de Beaumarchais **39**
Hôtel Chopin **29**
Hôtel de la Place des Vosges **40**
Hôtel de la Tour d'Auvergne **5**
Hôtel de Lutéce **45**
Hôtel des Arts **1**

Hôtel des Chevaliers **37**
Hôtel des Deux-Iles **44**
Hôtel de Vendôme **14**
Hôtel du Bourg Tibourg **36**
Hôtel du Jeu de Paume **43**
Hôtel du Louvre **19**
Hôtel du 7e Art **41**
Hotel Duo **35**
Hôtel du Petit Moulin **33**
Hôtel Ermitage **4**
Hôtel Horset Opéra **11**
Hôtel Langlois **7**
Hôtel Meurice **16**
Hôtel Particulier **3**
Hôtel Pavillon Bastille **47**
Hôtel Regina **17**
Hôtel Ritz **13**
Hôtel Saintonge **32**
Hôtel Saint-Louis **46**
Hôtel Saint-Merry **34**

Hôtel Thérèse **18**
Hôtel Victoires Opéra **31**
Kube Rooms & Bar **23**
Le Général Hotel **25**
Le Relais de Louvre **21**
Libertel Croix de Malte **27**
Murano Urban Resort **29**
Park Hyatt Vendôme **12**
Pavillon de la Reine **38**
Résidence Alhambra **28**
Timhôtel Le Louvre **20**
Villa Royale **2**
Westin Paris **15**

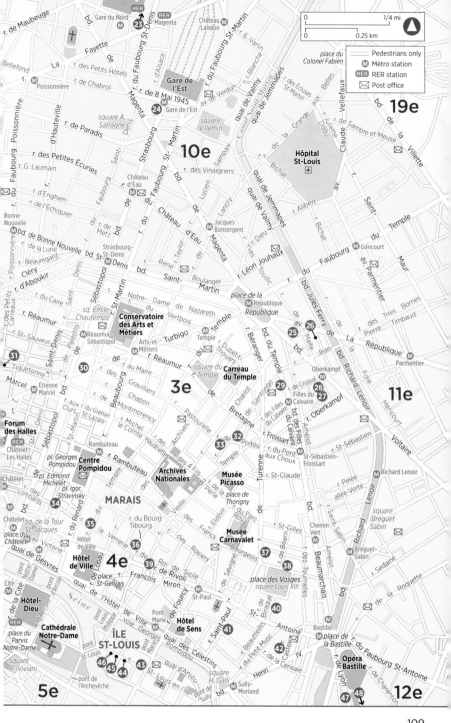

1st Arrondissement (Louvre/Les Halles)

VERY EXPENSIVE

Hôtel de Vendôme ★★   This jewel box was the embassy of Texas when that state was a nation. The hotel opened in 1998 at one of the world's most prestigious addresses. It is comparable to the Hôtel Costes but with a less-flashy clientele. Though the guest rooms are moderate in size, they're opulent and designed in classic Second Empire style, with luxurious beds and well-upholstered, hand carved furnishings. Suites have generous space and such extras as blackout draperies and quadruple-glazed windows. The security is fantastic, with TV intercoms.

1 place Vendôme, 75001 Paris. 📞 **01-55-04-55-00.** Fax 01-49-27-97-89. www.hoteldevendome. com. 29 units. High season 780€–865€ double; from 1,130€ junior suite; from 1,525€ suite; winter 550€–620€ double; from 830€ junior suite, from 970€ suite. AE, DC, MC, V. Parking 27€. Métro: Concorde or Opéra. **Amenities:** Restaurant; piano bar; babysitting; concierge; room service. *In room:* A/C, TV, hair dryer, minibar, MP3 docking station, Wi-Fi (free).

Hôtel du Louvre ★ ☺   When Napoleon III inaugurated the hotel in 1855, it was described as "a palace of the people, rising adjacent to the palace of kings." In 1897, Camille Pissarro moved into a room with a view that inspired many of his landscapes; its decor features marble, bronze, and gilt. The guest rooms are filled with souvenirs of the Belle Epoque, along with elegant fabrics, carpeting, double-glazed windows, comfortable beds, and wood furniture. Suites provide greater dimensions and better exposures, as well as such upgrades as antiques, trouser presses, and robes.

Place André-Malraux, 75001 Paris. 📞 **800/888-4747** in the U.S. and Canada, or 01-44-58-38-38. Fax 01-44-58-38-01. www.hoteldulouvre.com. 177 units. 200€–600€ double; 400€–750€ junior suite; 1,500€ suite. AE, DC, MC, V. Parking 20€. Métro: Palais-Royal–Louvre or Louvre–Rivoli. **Amenities:** Restaurant; bar; babysitting; concierge; exercise room. *In room:* A/C, TV, minibar, Wi-Fi (free).

Hôtel Meurice ★★★   This landmark lies between the place de la Concorde and the Grand Louvre, facing the Tuileries Gardens. The hotel is more media-hip, style-conscious, and better located than the George V. Since the 1800s, it has welcomed the royal, the rich, and even the radical. The mad genius Salvador Dalí made the Meurice his headquarters. The mosaic floors, plaster ceilings, hand carved moldings, and Art Nouveau glass roof atop the Winter Garden look new. Each room is individually decorated with period pieces, fine carpets, Italian and French fabrics, marble bathrooms, and modern features such as fax and Internet access. Our favorites and the least expensive are the sixth-floor rooms. Some have painted ceilings of puffy clouds and blue skies, along with canopy beds. Suites are among the most lavish in France.

228 rue de Rivoli, 75001 Paris. 📞 **01-44-58-10-10.** Fax 01-44-58-10-15. www.meuricehotel.com. 160 units. 640€–980€ double; from 1,050€ junior suite; from 1,700€ suite. AE, DC, MC, V. Parking 27€. Métro: Tuileries or Concorde. **Amenities:** 2 restaurants; bar; babysitting; concierge; health club & spa; room service. *In room:* A/C, TV, TV/DVD player, fax, hair dryer, minibar, Wi-Fi (20€ per day).

Hôtel Regina ★   Restored to its old-fashioned grandeur, Hôtel Regina is adjacent to rue de Rivoli's equestrian statue of Joan of Arc opposite the Louvre. Since 1999, the management has poured millions into a full-fledged renovation, retaining the patina of the Art Nouveau interior and making historically appropriate improvements. The guest rooms are richly decorated and spacious; those overlooking the Tuileries enjoy panoramic views as far away as the Eiffel Tower. The public areas contain every period of Louis furniture imaginable, Oriental carpets, 18th-century paintings, and bowls of flowers. This hotel has more grace notes than its closest competitor, Hôtel du Louvre.

2 place des Pyramides, 75001 Paris. ☎ **01-42-60-31-10.** Fax 01-40-15-95-16. www.regina-hotel. com. 120 units. 375€–515€ double; from 620€ junior suite; from 950€ suite. AE, DC, DISC, MC, V. Parking 20€. Métro: Pyramides or Tuileries. **Amenities:** Restaurant; bar; babysitting; concierge; room service. *In room:* A/C, TV, TV/DVD player, hair dryer, minibar, Wi-Fi (10€ for 3 hr.).

Hôtel Ritz ★★★ The Ritz is Europe's greatest hotel, an enduring symbol of elegance on one of Paris's most beautiful and historic squares. César Ritz, the "little shepherd boy from Niederwald," converted the Hôtel de Lazun into a luxury hotel in 1898. With the help of the culinary master Escoffier, he made the Ritz a miracle of luxury. In 1979, the Ritz family sold the hotel to Mohammed al Fayed, who refurbished it and added a cooking school. The hotel annexed two town houses, joined by an arcade lined with display cases representing 125 of Paris's leading boutiques. The public salons are furnished with museum-caliber antiques. Each guest room is uniquely decorated, most with Louis XIV or XV reproductions; all have fine rugs, marble fireplaces, tapestries, brass beds, and more. Ever since Edward VII got stuck in a too-narrow bathtub with his lover, the tubs at the Ritz have been deep and big.

15 place Vendôme, 75001 Paris. ☎ **800/223-6800** in the U.S. and Canada, or 01-43-16-30-30. Fax 01-43-16-31-78. www.ritzparis.com. 159 units. 770€–870€ double; from 1,020€ suite. AE, DC, MC, V. Parking 48€. Métro: Opéra, Concorde, or Madeleine. **Amenities:** Restaurant; 4 bars; babysitting; concierge; state-of-the-art health club; pool (indoor); room service. *In room:* A/C, TV, DVD player; hair dryer, minibar, Wi-Fi (25€).

EXPENSIVE

Westin Paris ★ ☺ It's location, location, location. You're 30 seconds from the Tuileries Gardens, 3 minutes from the place Vendôme, 5 minutes from the Place de la Concorde, and 7 minutes from the Louvre. Renovations have breathed new life into most of the rooms, which are a bit small for the most part but comfortably furnished and well maintained. Some patrons have written in the guest book that they found the beds "heavenly." Two connecting rooms can be blocked off for families, and family rates are available. Many of the units overlook an inner courtyard.

3 rue de Castiglione, Paris 75001. ☎ **800/454-6835** in the U.S. or 01-44-77-11-11. Fax 01-44-77-14-60. www.starwoodhotels.com. 440 units. 350€–410€ double; from 630€ suite. AE, DC, MC, V. Métro: Tuileries. **Amenities:** Restaurant; bar; babysitting; concierge; exercise room; room service. *In room:* A/C, TV, DVD player, hair dryer, minibar, Wi-Fi (25€ per day).

MODERATE

Hôtel Britannique ✦ Conservatively modern and plush, this is a much-renovated 19th-century hotel near Les Halles and Notre-Dame. The place is not only British in name, but also seems to cultivate English graciousness. The guest rooms are small, but immaculate and soundproof, with comfortable beds. A satellite receiver gets U.S. and U.K. television shows. The reading room is a cozy retreat.

Throughout the hotels in this chapter, expect the bathrooms in very expensive and expensive hotels to be a bit larger than normal, with fine toiletries, plush towels, and perhaps bathrobes. The bathrooms in moderate and inexpensive hotels tend to be cramped but still acceptable, with towels that are less plush than those at expensive places.

Be aware that some hotels offer tub/shower combinations, some offer shower stalls, and some offer a mix. If something particular is important to you, request your preference when reserving. Almost all hotels, except the inexpensive ones, include hair dryers in the bathrooms.

20 av. Victoria, 75001 Paris. ✆ **01-42-33-74-59.** Fax 01-42-33-82-65. www.hotel-britannique. com. 39 units. 190€–221€ double; from 279€ suite. AE, DC, MC, V. Métro: Châtelet. **Amenities:** Bar; room service. *In room:* A/C, TV, hair dryer, minibar, Wi-Fi (free).

Hôtel Thérèse Close to the Louvre, place Vendôme, and the Tuileries Gardens, this hotel combines French charm with English classicism. For example, the library and bar evoke a London club with wood-paneled walls and plush armchairs, but the lounge is adorned with Parisian art. It's government-rated three stars but seems more like four stars in ambience, style, and comfort. Owner Sylvia de Lattre, who likes shades of pistachio and royal blue, trolled the flea markets for paintings and prints to personalize each bedroom. The rooms are unpretentious but filled with quality furnishings, from the soft, efficient lighting by Philippe Starck to the natural wool quilts.

5–7 rue Thérèse, Paris 75001. ✆ **01-42-96-10-01.** Fax 01-42-96-15-22. www.hoteltherese.com. 43 units. 185€–320€ double. AE, MC, V. Métro: Musée du Louvre. **Amenities:** Library/bar; room service. *In room:* A/C, TV, hair dryer, Wi-Fi (free).

Le Relais du Louvre One of the neighborhood's most up-to-date hotels, Relais du Louvre overlooks the neoclassical colonnade at the eastern end of the Louvre. Between 1800 and 1941, its upper floors contained the printing presses that recorded the goings-on in Paris's House of Representatives. Its street level held the Café Momus, favored by Voltaire, Hugo, and intellectuals of the day, and where Puccini set one of the pivotal scenes of *La Bohème*. Bedrooms are outfitted in monochromatic schemes of blue, yellow, pink or soft reds, usually with copies of Directoire-style (French 1830s) furniture. Most rooms are a bit small, but some contain roomy sitting areas.

19 rue des Prêtres-St-Germain-l'Auxerrois, 75001 Paris. ✆ **01-40-41-96-42.** Fax 01-40-41-96-44. www.relaisdulouvre.com. 21 units. 145€–215€ double; 220€–435€ suite. AE, DC, MC, V. Parking 25€. Métro: Louvre or Pont Neuf. **Amenities:** Babysitting; room service. *In room:* A/C, TV, hair dryer, minibar, Wi-Fi (free).

Timhôtel Le Louvre ☺ This hotel and its sibling in the 2nd arrondissement, the Timhôtel Palais-Royal, are part of a new breed of government-rated, two-star, family friendly hotels cropping up in France. These Timhôtels share the same manager and temperament. Though the rooms at the Palais-Royal branch are a bit larger than the ones here, this branch is so close to the Louvre that it's almost irresistible. The ambience is modern, with monochromatic rooms and wall-to-wall carpeting.

5

On the Right Bank

WHERE TO STAY

4 rue Croix des Petits-Champs, 75001 Paris. ✆ **01-42-60-34-86.** Fax 01-42-60-10-39. www.
timhotel.fr. 56 units. 119€-170€ double. AE, DC, MC, V. Métro: Palais-Royal. The 46-room
Timhôtel Palais-Royal is at 3 rue de la Banque, 75002 Paris (✆ **01-42-61-53-90;** fax 01-42-60-
05-39; Métro: Bourse). **Amenities** (at both branches): Restaurant (breakfast only). *In room:* A/C,
TV, Wi-Fi (free).

2nd Arrondissement (La Bourse)

VERY EXPENSIVE

Park Hyatt Vendôme ★★★   American interior designer Ed Tuttle took five
separate Haussmann-era buildings and wove them into a seamless entity to create this citadel of 21st-century luxury living. High ceilings, colonnades, and interior courtyards speak of the buildings' former lives, but other than the facades, all
is completely modern inside—not just contemporary, but luxe modern. The third
Hyatt in Paris, this palace enjoys the greatest and most prestigious location in
"Ritz Hotel country." Graced with modern art, it is filled with elegant fabrics,
huge mirrors, walk-in closets, mahogany doors, and Jim Thompson silk. Bedrooms and bathrooms are spacious and state-of-the-art, with elegant furnishings
and glamorous bathrooms with "rain showers," plus separate tubs.

5 rue de la Paix, 75002 Paris. ✆ **800/492-8804** in the U.S. and Canada or 01-58-71-12-34. Fax
01-58-71-12-35. www.paris.vendome.hyatt.com. 168 units. 800€-910€ double; from 1,010€ suite.
AE, DC, DISC, MC, V. Métro: Tuileries or Opéra. Free parking. **Amenities:** 2 restaurants; bar; babysitting; concierge; health club & spa; room service. *In room:* A/C, TV, DVD, CD player, hair dryer,
minibar, Wi-Fi (19€ per day).

EXPENSIVE

Hôtel Victoires Opéra ★   Head to this little charmer in the fashion district if
you want a reasonably priced place convenient to Les Halles and the Pompidou
as well as to the Marais, with its shops and mix of gay and straight restaurants.
It's a classically decorated hotel, evoking the era of Louis Philippe. The rooms are
comfortable but rather small in most cases, except for the junior suites. Most of
the rooms come with tubs; the rest with showers. Skip the hotel breakfast (which
costs extra) and cross the street to Stohrer at no. 51, one of Paris's most historic
patisseries, founded in 1730 by the *pâtissier* to Louis XV.

56 rue de Montorgueil, 75002 Paris. ✆ **01-42-36-41-08.** Fax 01-45-08-08-79. www.hotel
victoiresopera.com. 24 units. 214€-275€ double; 335€ junior suite. AE, DC, MC, V. Métro: Les
Halles. **Amenities:** Concierge; access to nearby health club. *In room:* A/C, TV, TV/DVD player,
hair dryer, minibar, Wi-Fi (free).

MODERATE

Golden Tulip Opéra de Noailles   If you're looking for a choice address in the
style of Putman and Starck, this place is worth a look, in a great location. The
refined Art Deco choice offers bold colors and cutting-edge style, yet the prices
remain reasonable. The guest rooms come in various shapes and sizes, but all are
comfortable and some have small terraces and patios. A favorite is no. 601, which
has its own indoor Japanese garden.

9 rue de la Michodière, 75002 Paris. ✆ **800/344-1212** in the U.S., or 01-47-42-92-90. Fax 01-49-
24-92-71. www.paris-hotel-noailles.com. 61 units. 265€-340€ double; 495€ suite. AE, DC, MC, V.
Métro: 4 Septembre or Opéra. RER: Opéra. **Amenities:** Bar; babysitting; concierge; small health
club; room service. *In room:* A/C, TV, hair dryer, Wi-Fi (22€ per day).

Hotel Horset Opéra ★ This hotel lies in the heart of Paris, a 2-minute walk to the Opéra Garnier and only 5 to 10 minutes on foot from the Louvre. It's part of a small group of family-owned and -managed hotels, giving a warm welcome to its guests. All of its attractively decorated and comfortably furnished bedrooms have been restored in a stylish modern way. We particularly like the subtle use of color—imperial blue, raspberry red, and almond green. In honor of the opera in its name, the hotel often uses fabrics printed with musical scores. Other rooms have flowery fabrics or exotic patterns.

18 rue d'Antin, 75002 Paris. ℰ **01-44-71-87-00.** Fax 01-42-66-55-54. www.hotelhorsetopera. com. 54 units. 215€–295€ double. MC, V. Métro: Opéra. **Amenities:** Bar and breakfast salon; room service. *In room:* A/C, TV, hair dryer, minibar, Wi-Fi (free).

3rd Arrondissement (Le Marais)
EXPENSIVE
Murano Urban Resort ★ 🏨 This hotel oddity, not everyone's cup of tea but charming for some, was created when two abandoned buildings—one a run-down five-story apartment house; the other a three-story parking garage—were interconnected and upgraded into one coherent building. The result is a trend-setting, aggressively minimalist hotel with an angular sense of design. The decorative theme revolves around the transparency of Murano glass. You'll find a Murano glass chandelier in the green-toned lobby, another in a key spot on the ground floor, and very large glass-framed mirrors in some of the upper hallways. The mirrors and chandeliers are metaphors for the games that residents can play with light in their respective, and otherwise sparsely furnished, units: Up to three sets of curtains in any room filter sunlight in patterns that range from gauzy and bright to complete blackout. Additionally, individual settings switch on and off a spectrum of lights in up to six colors.

13 bd. du Temple, 75003 Paris. ℰ **01-42-71-20-00.** Fax 01-42-71-21-01. www.muranoresort.com. 52 units. 400€–650€ double; from 750€ suite. AE, DC, MC, V. Métro: Filles du Calvaire. **Amenities:** Restaurant; bar; concierge; health club & spa; room service. *In room:* A/C, TV/DVD player, hair dryer, Wi-Fi (free).

Pavillon de la Reine ★★ 🏨 This is the kind of hidden gem that Frommer's readers love, opening as it does onto the most romantic square in Paris. In days of yore the 1612 mansion was a gathering place for the likes of Racine, La Fontaine, Molière, and the Madame de Sévigné. You enter through an arcade that opens onto a small formal garden. The Louis XIII decor evokes the heyday of the square itself, and iron-banded Spanish antiques create a rustic aura. Each guest room is individually furnished in a historic or modern style—take your pick. Some units are duplexes with sleeping lofts above cozy salons.

28 place des Vosges, 75003 Paris. ℰ **01-40-29-19-19.** Fax 01-40-29-19-20. www.pavillon-de-la-reine.com. 56 units. 380€–490€ double; 610€–710€ duplex; 610€ junior suite; 710€–950€ suite. AE, MC, V. Métro: Bastille. **Amenities:** Bar; concierge; room service. *In room:* A/C, TV, minibar, Wi-Fi (free).

MODERATE
Hôtel du Petit Moulin ★ 🏨 In the heart of the Marais, this hotel, an enclave of bohemian chic, used to be a *boulangerie* where Victor Hugo came every morning to buy freshly baked baguettes. No more. Designer Christian Lacroix has

gone behind the unpretentious facade and turned it into an idiosyncratic hotel with bold, daring designs in the bedrooms, which range in price from the Comfort Rooms to the Superior or Executive Rooms. A well-heeled array of international guests meets in the trendy bar or can be seen making their way through the lounge and halls decorated with period tapestries and Flemish frescoes.

29–31 rue du Poitous, Paris 75003. ☎ **01-42-74-10-10.** www.hoteldupetitmoulin.com. 17 units. 250€–350€ double. AE, MC, V. Métro: Bastille or Filles du Calvaire. **Amenities:** Bar; room service. *In room:* TV, minibar, Wi-Fi (free).

INEXPENSIVE

Hôtel Bellevue & du Chariot d'Or   Originally built in 1860 as part of the majestic redevelopment of central Paris by Baron Haussmann, this hotel has a grand facade and inexpensive, relatively comfortable and cozy, simple bedrooms. The hotel has become more desirable because of its location in the once-neglected Arts et Métiers district north of the Pompidou Center. The second part of its name—"Chariot d'Or" (Golden Carriage)—derives from the medieval custom of placing brides-to-be (along with their dowries) in a flower-draped ceremonial carriage. During the occupation of Paris during World War II, the site was commandeered as a garrison for rank-and-file Nazi troops.

39 rue de Turbigo, 75003 Paris. ☎ **01-48-87-45-60.** Fax 01-48-87-95-04. www.hotelbellevue75. com. 59 units. 72€–75€ double; 87€ triple; 98€ quad. AE, DC, MC, V. Métro: Châtelet–Les Halles or Réaumur-Sebastopol. **Amenities:** Bar; babysitting. *In room:* TV, Wi-Fi (free).

Hôtel des Chevaliers   Half a block from the place des Vosges, this hotel occupies a corner building whose 17th-century vestiges have been elevated to high art. These include the remnants of a well in the cellar, a stone barrel vault covering the breakfast area, and Louis XIII accessories that will remind you of the hotel's origins. Each guest room is comfortable and well maintained. Units on the top floor have exposed ceiling beams. Some are larger than others, with an extra bed making them suitable for those traveling with a child or for three people on the road together.

30 rue de Turenne, Paris 75003. ☎ **01-42-72-73-47.** Fax 01-42-72-54-10. www.chevaliers-paris-hotel.com. 24 units. 94€–190€ double. AE, MC, V. Métro: Chemin Vert or St-Paul. **Amenities:** Bar. *In room:* A/C, TV, hair dryer, minibar, Wi-Fi (free).

Hôtel Saintonge ★ 📷   Its rooms are small, but there's a coziness about this hotel that you might appreciate, especially if you're attracted to beamed ceilings, patches of exposed and very old masonry, and charmingly claustrophobic upstairs hallways. It rises seven stories above a quiet neighborhood in the Marais, one of the many structures that functioned as a private house in the 17th century and was converted to a hotel or private apartment. Breakfast is served beneath the vaulted ceiling of what used to be a cellar-level storage area; the lobby boasts hand-hewn beams and a tile floor; and bedrooms have tall windows or, if they're on the building's uppermost floor, angled ceilings that evoke the feeling of an artist's studio in a garret.

16 rue Saintonge, 75003 Paris. ☎ **01-42-77-91-13.** Fax 01-48-87-76-41. www.hotel-saintonge. com. 23 units. 115€ double; 170€ suite. AE, DC, MC, V. Métro: Filles du Calvaire or République. Nearby parking 16€. **Amenities:** Babysitting; room service. *In room:* TV, hair dryer, minibar, Wi-Fi (2€ per day).

4th Arrondissement (Ile de la Cite/Ile St-Louis & Beaubourg)

EXPENSIVE

Hôtel du Bourg Tibourg ★ 🛍 Don't come here expecting large rooms with lots of elbow room: What you get is a sophisticated and supercharged color palette, a sense of high-profile design, and a deliberately cluttered venue that looks like an Edwardian town house decorated by an obsessive-compulsive individual on psychedelic drugs. It is set behind an uncomplicated, cream-colored facade in the Marais and marked only with a discreet brass plaque and a pair of carriage lamps. Its rooms have been radically overhauled by superstar decorator Jacques Garcia. Bedrooms are genuinely tiny, but rich with neo-romantic, neo-Gothic, and in some cases neo-Venetian swirls and curlicues. Each is quirky, idiosyncratic, richly upholstered, and supercharged with tassels, faux leopard skin, contrasting stripes, fringes, and lavish window treatments. Rooms facing the front get more sunlight; rooms facing the courtyard tend to be quieter.

19 rue du Bourg-Tibourg, 75004 Paris. ✆ **01-42-78-47-39.** Fax 01-40-29-07-00. www.hotel bourgtibourg.com. 30 units. 230€–260€ double; 360€ suite. AE, DC, MC, V. Métro: Hôtel-de-Ville. **Amenities:** Room service. *In room:* A/C, TV, hair dryer, minibar, Wi-Fi (free).

Hôtel du Jeu de Paume ★ This small-scale hotel encompasses a pair of 17th-century town houses accessible through a timbered passageway from the street outside. The rooms are a bit larger than those of some nearby competitors. Originally, the hotel was a clubhouse used by members of the court of Louis XIII, who amused themselves with *les jeux de paume* (an early form of tennis) nearby. Public areas are outfitted in a simple version of Art Deco. Guest rooms are freshly decorated in sleek contemporary style, with elegant materials such as oaken floors and fine craftsmanship. Some have wooden beamed ceilings. The most luxurious units are the five duplexes and two junior suites, each individually decorated and opening onto an indoor courtyard.

54 rue St-Louis-en-l'Ile, 75004 Paris. ✆ **01-43-26-14-18.** Fax 01-40-46-02-76. www.jeudepaume hotel.com. 30 units. 285€–360€ double; 450€–560€ suite. AE, DC, MC, V. Métro: Pont Marie. **Amenities:** Bar; babysitting; concierge; exercise room; room service. *In room:* TV, hair dryer, minibar, Wi-Fi (free).

Hôtel Duo ★ 🛍 Fashionistas flock to this restored hotel in the Marais, which is one of the cutting-edge places to stay in Paris. The location is convenient to the Centre Pompidou, Notre-Dame, the Louvre, and the Picasso Museum. The building has been in the family of Veronique Turmel since 1918. In 2002, she decided to completely convert the interior while retaining the facade. She hired Jean-Philippe Nuel, who kept many of the original architectural features, including exposed beams, old stones, and hardwood floors. He created a medieval look graced with Wengé-wood furnishings, white walls, and bronzed sconces—old-world charm in a tasteful and refined setting. The midsize bedrooms are completely up-to-date, with beautiful and comfortable furnishings. The so-called breakfast "cave" is a charming room with slipcovered chairs and sea-grass matting.

11 rue du Temple, 75004 Paris. ✆ **01-42-72-72-22.** Fax 01-42-72-03-53. www.parishhotelleduo. com. 58 units. 200€–340€ double; 480€ suite. AE, DC, MC, V. Métro: Hôtel-de-Ville. **Amenities:** Exercise room; room service. *In room:* A/C, TV, hair dryer, Wi-Fi (free).

FAMILY-FRIENDLY hotels

Hôtel de Fleurie (p. 139)   In the heart of St-Germain-des-Prés, this has long been a Left Bank family favorite. The hotel is known for its *chambres familiales*—two connecting rooms with a pair of large beds in each room. Children younger than 12 stay free with a parent.

Hôtel du Ministère (p. 129)   For the family on a budget that doesn't mind cramped quarters, the Ministère is one of the best bets in this expensive area near the Champs-Elysées.

Résidence Lord Byron (p. 130)   The Byron is not only a good value and a family-oriented place for the swanky 8th arrondissement, but also is only a short walk from many major monuments.

Timhôtel Le Louvre (p. 112)   This is an especially convenient choice because it offers some rooms with four beds for the price of a double. The location near the Louvre is irresistible.

MODERATE

Hôtel Caron de Beaumarchais 🔥   Built in the 18th century, this good-value choice features floors of artfully worn gray stone, antique reproductions, and elaborate fabrics based on antique patterns. Hotelier Alain Bigeard intends his primrose-colored guest rooms to evoke the taste of the French gentry in the 18th century, when the Marais was the scene of high-society dances and even duels. Most rooms retain their original ceiling beams. The smallest units overlook the courtyard, and the top-floor rooms are tiny, but have panoramic balcony views across the Right Bank.

12 rue Vieille-du-Temple, 75004 Paris. ☎ **01-42-72-34-12.** Fax 01-42-72-34-63. www.caronde beaumarchais.com. 19 units. 130€–185€ double. AE, MC, V. Métro: St-Paul or Hôtel-de-Ville. **Amenities:** Breakfast room; babysitting. *In room:* A/C, TV, hair dryer, minibar, Wi-Fi (free).

Hôtel de Lutèce   This 19th-century hotel feels like a country house in Brittany. The lounge, with its old fireplace, is furnished with antiques and contemporary paintings. Each of the guest rooms boasts antiques, adding to a refined atmosphere that attracts celebrities such as the duke and duchess of Bedford. The suites, though larger than the doubles, are often similar to doubles with extended sitting areas. Each is tastefully furnished, with an antique or two. The hotel is comparable in style and amenities to the Deux-Iles (see below), under the same ownership.

65 rue St-Louis-en-l'Ile, 75004 Paris. ☎ **01-43-26-23-52.** Fax 01-43-29-60-25. www.paris-hotel-lutece.com. 23 units. 195€ double; 230€ triple. AE, MC, V. Métro: Pont Marie or Cité. **Amenities:** Babysitting; concierge. *In room:* A/C, TV, hair dryer, Wi-Fi (free).

Hôtel des Deux-Iles ★   This is an unpretentious but charming choice in a great location. In a restored 18th-century town house, the hotel has elaborate decor, with bamboo and reed furniture and French provincial touches. The guest rooms are on the small side, but the beds are very comfortable and the bathrooms well-maintained, with tubs or shower units. A garden off the lobby leads to a basement breakfast room that has a fireplace.

59 rue St-Louis-en-l'Ile, 75004 Paris. ℭ **01-43-26-13-35.** Fax 01-43-29-60-25. www.deuxiles-paris-hotel.com. 17 units. 195€ double. AE, MC, V. Métro: Pont Marie. **Amenities:** Room service. *In room:* A/C, TV, hair dryer, Wi-Fi (free).

INEXPENSIVE

Castex Hotel 🔥   Long known to frugal travelers, the Castex lies on the fringe of both the Bastille sector and the Marais. ***Warning:*** There's no elevator and the TV is in the lounge. Bedrooms have been restored and decorated in a 17th-century style with Louis XIII furnishings along with touches of wrought iron against Toile de Jouy wallpaper. Several of the units open onto a courtyard patio that bursts into full bloom in the spring.

5 rue Castex, 75004 Paris. ℭ **01-42-72-31-52.** www.castexhotelparis.com. 30 units. 150€ double; 220€ triple. AE, MC, V. Métro: Bastille. **Amenities:** Breakfast room. *In room:* A/C, hair dryer, Wi-Fi (free).

Hôtel de la Place des Vosges ★ 🔥   Built about 350 years ago, during the same era as the majestic square for which it's named (a 2-min. walk away), this is a well-managed, small-scale property with reasonable prices and lots of charm. The structure was once used as a stable for the mules of Henri IV. Many of the small guest rooms have beamed ceilings; small TVs hanging from the ceiling; and a sense of cozy, well-ordered efficiency. The most desirable and expensive room is top-floor no. 60, overlooking the rooftops of Paris, with a luxurious private bathroom. Patches of chiseled stone in various parts of the hotel add a decorative touch.

12 rue de Birague, 75004 Paris. ℭ **01-42-72-60-46.** Fax 01-42-72-02-64. www.hotelplacedes vosges.com. 16 units. 90€–150€ double. AE, DC, MC, V. Métro: Bastille. **Amenities:** Room service. *In room:* TV, hair dryer, Wi-Fi (free).

Hôtel du 7e Art   The hotel occupies one of many 17th-century buildings classified as historic monuments in this neighborhood. Don't expect grand luxury: Rooms are cramped and outfitted with the simplest furniture, relieved by 1950s-era movie posters. Each has white walls, and some of them—including those under the sloping mansard-style roof—have exposed ceiling beams. The five-story building has a lobby bar and a breakfast room but no elevator. The "7th Art" is a reference to filmmaking.

20 rue St-Paul, 75004 Paris. ℭ **01-44-54-85-00.** Fax 01-42-77-69-10. www.paris-hotel-7art. com. 23 units. 95€–150€ double. AE, DC, MC, V. Métro: St-Paul. **Amenities:** Bar; exercise room. *In room:* A/C, TV, hair dryer.

Hôtel Saint-Louis ★ 🔥   Proprietors Guy and Andrée Record maintain a charming family atmosphere at this antiques-filled hotel in a 17th-century town house. The hotel represents an incredible value, considering its prime location on Ile St-Louis. Expect cozy, slightly cramped rooms, each with a small bathroom. With mansard roofs and old-fashioned moldings, the top-floor units sport tiny balconies that afford sweeping views. The breakfast room is in the cellar, which has 17th-century stone vaulting.

75 rue St-Louis-en-l'Ile, 75004 Paris. ℭ **01-46-34-04-80.** Fax 01-46-34-02-13. www.saintlouis enlisle.com. 19 units. 140€–220€ double. MC, V. Métro: Pont Marie or St-Michel-Notre-Dame. **Amenities:** Babysitting. *In room:* TV, hair dryer, Wi-Fi (free).

Hôtel Saint-Merry ★ 🎁 The rebirth of this once-notorious brothel as a charming, upscale hotel is an example of how this area has been gentrified. It contains only a dozen rooms, each relatively small but accented with neo-Gothic detail: exposed stone, 18th-century ceiling beams, and lots of quirky architecture. A suite, much larger than doubles, has upgraded furnishings. According to the staff, the clientele here is about 50% gay males; the other half is straight and tends to be involved in the arts scene in the surrounding neighborhood. Before it became a bordello, it was conceived as the presbytery of the nearby Church of Saint-Merry.

78 rue de la Verrerie, 75004 Paris. ✆ **01-42-78-14-15.** Fax 01-40-29-06-82. www.hotel-saint merry.com. 12 units. 110€–180€ double; from 250€ suite. AE, MC, V. Métro: Hôtel-de-Ville or Châtelet. **Amenities:** Babysitting; room service. *In room:* TV (in some), hair dryer, minibar (in some), Wi-Fi (2€ per day).

9th Arrondissement (Opera Garnier/Pigalle)

EXPENSIVE

Hotel Banke ★ In the tradition of Derby Hotels Collection, this luxurious boutique hotel is art oriented. Works of art adorn both the public rooms and the accommodations. The building dates from the Belle Epoque era and contains a majestic hall from that time, which is embellished with a great mosaic. Bedrooms are midsize to spacious and decorated with antique art and an avant-garde design. The on-site spa focuses on a self-styled "purification and regeneration of your internal ecology." Bathrooms, for the most part, are very spacious. The staff is also extremely friendly, a rarity in Paris. The terrace opens onto a panoramic view of Sacré-Coeur and the Opéra.

20 rue Lafayette, 75009 Paris. ✆ **01-55-33-22-22.** Fax 01-55-33-22-28. www.derbyhotels.com/ Banke-Hotel-Paris. 94 units. 220€–300€ double; 380€ suite. AE, DC, MC, V. Métro: Opéra. **Amenities:** 2 restaurants; bar; exercise room; room service; spa. *In room:* A/C, TV, hair dryer, minibar, Wi-Fi (free).

MODERATE

Hotel Amour This is the kind of hotel that services the needs of suburbanites looking for lodgings in the town center, or young business travelers seeking a "nouveau chic" address. One critic even claimed that thanks to the hotel bar being frequented by young European fashionistas, each flaunting his or her respective allure and neurosis, "waiting in a queue for the toilets has never been so entertaining." Each bedroom has a very comfortable mattress—they come from the same company that supplies the (much more expensive) Hôtel Ritz—and no TV or telephone (the assumption being that anyone hip enough to check in here already has a working cellphone of his or her own). The decor of each room varies widely, including some with a minimalist white-on-white decor with touches of faux baroque; others have works by graffiti artists applied directly to the walls. Overall, the place has an oddball charm.

8 rue Navarin, 75009 Paris. ✆ **01-48-78-31-80.** www.hotelamourparis.fr. 20 units. 150€–170€ double; 280€ duplex. AE, MC, V. Métro: St-Georges. **Amenities:** Restaurant; bar; room service. *In room:* A/C, minibar, no phone, Wi-Fi (free).

Hôtel de la Tour d'Auvergne Here's a good bet for those who want to be near the Opéra or the Gare du Nord. This building was erected before Baron

Haussmann reconfigured Paris's avenues around 1870. Later, Modigliani rented a room here for 6 months, and Victor Hugo and Auguste Rodin lived on this street. The interior has been modernized in a glossy international style. The guest rooms are meticulously coordinated, yet the small decorative canopies over the headboards make them feel cluttered. Though the views over the back courtyard are uninspired, some guests prefer the quiet of the rear rooms. Every year five rooms are renovated.

10 rue de la Tour d'Auvergne, 75009 Paris. ✆ **01-48-78-61-60.** Fax 01-49-95-99-00. www.hotel-tour-auvergne-opera-paris.federal-hotel.com. 24 units. 160€ double. AE, DC, MC, V. Métro: Cadet. **Amenities:** Bar; room service. *In room:* A/C, TV, hair dryer, minibar, Wi-Fi (2€ per day).

Hôtel Langlois   This hotel used to be known as Hôtel des Croises, but when it was used as a setting for the Jonathan Demme film *The Truth About Charlie,* the hotel owners changed the name to match the one used in the film. It's a well-proportioned, restored town house with a main stairwell and a spacious landing. An antique wrought-iron elevator running up the center of the building adds an old-fashioned Parisian touch. The rooms are well proportioned but not overly large; those in the front get the most light. Units in the rear are darker but quieter. Rooms, with their aura of *Ecole de Nancy* (a florid Art Nouveau style), have well-chosen antiques, tasteful rugs and fabrics, even an occasional fireplace. Bathrooms are modernized, with tub and shower. We suggest avoiding the upper floors in summer; there's no air-conditioning, and the heat is often stifling.

63 rue St-Lazare, 75009 Paris. ✆ **01-48-74-78-24.** Fax 01-49-95-04-43. www.hotel-langlois.com. 27 units. 140€–150€ double; 190€ suite. AE, DC, MC, V. Métro: Trinité. **Amenities:** Breakfast room; room service. *In room:* TV, hair dryer, minibar, Wi-Fi (free).

Villa Royale ★ 🏩   Paris can be many things to many people, and if your vision of the city involves the scarlet-toned settings once associated with the Moulin Rouge and the paintings of Toulouse-Lautrec, this designer hotel might be for you. It does a flourishing business renting small but carefully decorated rooms, each of which evokes Paris's sometimes kitschy world of glitzy and risqué night-life entertainment. Expect rooms outfitted Liberace-style, with rococo gewgaws, velvet and velour upholsteries, jewel-toned walls, and TV screens that are some-times encased in gilded frames. Each is named after someone from the world of French entertainment, including namesakes inspired by La Bardot, La Deneuve—even Claude Debussy.

2 rue Duperré, 75009 Paris. ✆ **01-55-31-78-78.** Fax 01-55-31-78-70. www.leshotelsdeparis.com. 31 units. 160€–350€ double. AE, DC, MC, V. Métro: Pigalle. Bus: 30 or 54. **Amenities:** Room service. *In room:* A/C, TV, hair dryer, Wi-Fi (10€).

INEXPENSIVE

Hôtel Chopin ✒   Enter this intimate, offbeat hotel through a passageway that includes a toy store, a bookstore, the exit from the Musée Grevin, and the architectural trappings of its original construction in 1846. Just off the Grands Boulevards, this old-fashioned hotel evokes the charm of yesteryear. In honor of its namesake, the Chopin has a piano in its reception area. The inviting lobby welcomes you behind its 1850s facade of elegant woodwork and Victorian-era glass. In the style of the Paris of long ago, the comfortably furnished bedrooms open onto a glass-topped arcade instead of the hysterically busy street, so they are rather tranquil. We prefer the bedrooms on the top floor, as they are larger and quieter, with views over the rooftops of Paris. The least expensive bedrooms lie behind the elevator bank and get less light.

10 bd. Montmartre or 46 passage Jouffroy, 75009 Paris. ☎ **01-47-70-58-10.** Fax 01-42-47-00-70. www.hotel-chopin.com. 36 units. 92€–106€ double; 125€ triple. AE, MC, V. Métro: Grands-Boulevards. **Amenities:** Wi-Fi (free). *In room:* TV, hair dryer.

10th Arrondissement (Gare de l'Est)
INEXPENSIVE

Hotel All Seasons Paris Gare de l'Est Magenta 🍃　Opposite the Gare de l'Est railway station, this hotel lives up to its name. It is truly a hotel for all seasons and a great convenience for passengers disembarking at Gare de l'Est, which has good taxi, bus, and Métro links to all of Paris. All Seasons is the budget chain link of the famous French hotel group, Accor, and, as such, it's aimed at both vacationers and business travelers who seek affordable rates. The bedroom furnishings are fairly standard, except for the bedding which emphasizes "anti-stress" quilts and pillows made with carbon threads said to channel the body's electricity. Breakfast is called "as much as you wish," and there is unlimited tea, coffee, and mineral water. Magazines and games for children are available.

87 bd. de Strasbourg, 75010 Paris. ☎ **01-42-09-12-28.** Fax 01-42-09-48-12. www.accorhotels. com. 32 units. 95€–115€ double. MC, V. Métro: Gare de l'Est. **Amenities:** Room service. *In room:* A/C, TV, hair dryer, Wi-Fi (free).

11th Arrondissement (Opera Bastille)
EXPENSIVE

Gabriel Paris Marais ★ 🎒　This boutique hotel calls itself Paris's first "detox hotel," a concept devoted to a "regeneration of your body." One example of this is that some accommodations are outfitted with "Night Cove," a system that uses sound and light to encourage natural sleeping patterns. Located in the Marais, the hotel is rated only two stars, but is most comfortable, with modern technology and comfortably furnished bedrooms that range from small to midsize. In the surrealist but harmoniously decorated "detox bar," guests can order a large choice of antioxidant drinks and teas.

25 rue du Grand-Prieure, 75011 Paris. ☎ **01-47-00-13-38.** www.hotel-gabriel-paris.com. 41 units. 240€–280€ double. AE, DC, MC, V. Métro: République. **Amenities:** Cafeteria; room service. *In room:* A/C, TV/DVD, hair dryer, minibar, MP3 docking station, Wi-Fi (free).

MODERATE

Le Général Hotel ★　As the neighborhood around place de la République and rue Oberkampf becomes increasingly tuned to Paris's sense of counterculture chic, this is a good example of that neighborhood's improving fortunes. Opened within the premises of a run-down hotel that was radically renovated and decorated by noted designer Jean-Philippe Nuel, the hotel's interior revolves around prominent rectilinear lines, spartan-looking decors, and an intelligent distribution of spaces. The result is a seven-story hotel with floors linked by two separate elevator banks and pale, monochromatic beige-and-off-white color schemes, and with furniture that is either dark (specifically, rosewood-toned) or pale (specifically, birch- or maple-toned).

5

WHERE TO STAY

On the Right Bank

5-7 rue Rampon, 75011 Paris. ✆ **01-47-00-41-57.** Fax 01-47-00-21-56. www.legeneralhotel. com. 46 units. 185€–215€ double; 275€ suite. AE, MC, V. Métro: République. **Amenities:** Bar; exercise room. *In room:* A/C, TV, hair dryer, Wi-Fi (free).

INEXPENSIVE

Libertel Croix de Malte A member of a nationwide chain of government-rated two-star hotels, this is a well-maintained lodging choice. The hotel consists of two buildings of two and three floors, one of which is accessible through a shared breakfast room. There's a landscaped courtyard in back with access to a lobby bar. The cozy guest rooms contain brightly painted modern furniture accented with vivid green, blue, and pink patterns that flash back to the 1960s.

5 rue de Malte, 75011 Paris. ✆ **01-48-05-09-36.** Fax 01-43-57-02-54. www.hotelcroixdemalte-paris.com. 29 units. 80€–97€ double. AE, DC, MC, V. Métro: Oberkampf. **Amenities:** Bar; breakfast room; babysitting; room service (breakfast). *In room:* TV, hair dryer, Wi-Fi (free).

Résidence Alhambra Named for the famous cabaret/vaudeville theater that once stood nearby, the Alhambra dates from the 1800s. A radical renovation has given the hotel its fine contemporary format. In the rear garden, where breakfast is served, its two-story chalet offers eight additional guest rooms. The small accommodations are bland but comfortable, each in a dull pastel scheme that includes white and ocher.

13 rue de Malte, 75011 Paris. ✆ **01-47-00-35-52.** Fax 01-43-57-98-75. www.hotelalhambra.fr. 58 units. 81€–90€ double; 100€–123€ triple. AE, DC, MC, V. Métro: Oberkampf. **Amenities:** Garden. *In room:* TV, Wi-Fi (free).

12th Arrondissement (Bois de Vincennes/ Gare de Lyon)

MODERATE

Hôtel Pavillon Bastille This is a bold, innovative hotel in a town house across from the Opéra Bastille, a block south of place de la Bastille. It was completely renovated in 2007 when the rooms were made soundproof. A 17th-century fountain graces the courtyard. The guest rooms have twin or double beds, partially mirrored walls, and contemporary built-in furniture.

65 rue de Lyon, 75012 Paris. ✆ **01-43-43-65-65.** Fax 01-43-43-96-52. www.paris-hotel-pavillonbastille.com. 25 units. 195€ double; 390€ suite. AE, DC, MC, V. Métro: Bastille. **Amenities:** Bar; babysitting; concierge; room service. *In room:* A/C, TV, hair dryer, minibar, Wi-Fi (free).

INEXPENSIVE

Grand Hôtel Doré Deep in the heart of the Daumesnil area, this venerated old hotel has been a Paris tradition since the early 20th century. Today it's been brought into the 21st century with a major restoration and vast improvements, so that once again it is a hotel of charm and character. Some of the past remains visible here, architecturally, but the hotel has been completely modernized. The bedrooms are small to midsize, but each is comfortably furnished and well-maintained, and the plumbing has been renewed in the bathrooms.

201 av. Daumesnil, 75012 Paris. ✆ **01-43-43-66-89.** Fax 01-43-43-65-20. www.grand-hotel-dore.com. 40 units. 115€–155€ double. AE, MC, V. Métro: Daumesnil. **Amenities:** Babysitting; concierge. *In room:* A/C, TV, minibar, Wi-Fi (free).

18th Arrondissement (Montmartre)

EXPENSIVE

Hôtel Particulier ★★★   No hotel in Paris seems quite as special as this one, lying between avenue Junot and rue Lepic and nestled in a "secret" passageway called le passage du Rocher de la Sorcière or the Witch's Rock Passage. Modern Paris meets Old Montmartre in this Directoire mansion from the 18th century, and the marriage is harmonious. Louis Bénech, one of the landscape architects who renovated the Tuileries, created the intimate gardens of the hotel. Each suite has a different personality, the work of various artists that range in decor from an erotic window by Philippe Mayaux to poems and hats by Olivier Saillard. The most unusual is the suite "Curtain of Hair," a loft created in the attic with photographs of the long hair of Natacha Lesueur, a photo artist.

23 av. Junot, 75018 Paris. ✆ **01-53-41-81-40.** Fax 01-42-58-00-87. www.hotel-particulier-montmartre.com. 5 units. 390€–590€ suite. MC, V. Métro: Blanche. **Amenities:** Breakfast room. *In room:* A/C, TV, hair dryer, Wi-Fi (free).

Kube Rooms & Bars ★ 🏨   Design-savvy clients appreciate the way the archi-tect (in-the-news Raymond Morel) made repeated use of the cube, a form that the owners refer to as "the most modern of shapes." It occupies the six-story premises of what was built in the late 1800s as the administrative headquarters of a now-defunct brewery *(Les bières de la Meuse),* which these writers remember from beer fests of yesteryear. There's a restaurant and a dance lounge on street level, where a DJ spins tunes. Bedrooms (and everything else about the place) seem to revel in the concept of the rectangular cube. Rectangular beds are lit from below and appear to float. Expect shag-covered sofas, fuzzy faux-fur slippers in tones of high-voltage yellow, and a sense of compact efficiency. On the prem-ises is the Ice Kube Bar, a deep-cooled conversational oddity whose bartop is fashioned from—you guessed it—ice.

1–5 Passage Ruelle, 75018 Paris. ✆ **01-42-05-20-00.** Fax 01-42-05-21-01. www.kubehotel.com. 41 units. 250€–400€ double; 500€–900€ suite. Parking 15€. Métro: La Chapelle. **Amenities:** Restaurant; bar; exercise room. *In room:* A/C, TV, hair dryer, Wi-Fi (free).

MODERATE

Hôtel des Arts ★   In the center of Montmartre between Place du Tertre and the Moulin Rouge, this hotel lies in a delightful quarter of Paris once made famous by poets and painters. It has a warm, welcoming atmosphere and in a former life it was a dormitory for the dancers of the Moulin Rouge. As you might expect, the rooms are small yet comfortable, with country-style curtains and bed-spreads. Opt for one of the four bedrooms on the sixth floor for a panoramic view of Paris. *Warning:* As night falls, the area around the hotel often has its share of sex workers, although the hotel itself is a fine, safe destination.

5 rue Tholozé, Paris 75018. ✆ **01-46-06-30-52.** Fax 01-46-06-10-83. www.arts-hotel-paris. com. 50 units. 140€–165€ double. AE, MC, V. Métro: Blanche. **Amenities:** Breakfast room. *In room:* TV, Wi-Fi (free).

INEXPENSIVE

Hôtel Ermitage   Built in 1870 of chiseled limestone in the Napoleon III style, this hotel's facade evokes a perfectly proportioned small villa. It's set in a calm area, a brief uphill stroll from Sacré-Coeur. Views extend over Paris, and there's a garden in the back courtyard. The small guest rooms are similar to those in a countryside *auberge* (inn), with exposed ceiling beams, flowered wallpaper, and casement windows opening onto the garden or a street seemingly airlifted from the provinces.

24 rue Lamarck, 75018 Paris. ☎ **01-42-64-79-22.** Fax 01-42-64-10-33. www.ermitagesacre coeur.fr. 12 units. 96€–100€ double; 145€ quad. Rates include breakfast. No credit cards. Métro: Lamarck-Caulaincourt. Parking 15€. **Amenities:** Babysitting; room service. *In room:* Hair dryer, Wi-Fi (free).

8th Arrondissement (Champs-Elysées/ Madeleine)

VERY EXPENSIVE

Fouquet's Barrière ★★★   This deluxe boutique hotel on the corner of the Champs-Elysées may lack the historic cachet of the neighboring George V or Plaza Athénée. It's a more contemporary brand of glitz and glamour. Standing alongside its namesake, the legendary restaurant, Fouquet's, it offers some of the most luxurious and spacious bedrooms in Paris, its decor dominated by ceiling-high padded headboards in shiny gold. The hotel contains such novel features as waterproof floating TV remotes in the bathtub, and a bedside button which, when pressed, will summon your butler. There's one butler to every eight guests, and the service is the best in Paris. That butler even arrives to unpack your luggage and serve you champagne.

46 av. George V, 75008 Paris. ☎ **01-40-69-60-00.** Fax 01-40-69-60-05. www.fouquets-barriere. com. 107 units. 730€–950€ double; from 1,000€ junior suite; from 1,190€ suite. AE, MC, V. Métro: George V. Parking 45€. **Amenities:** 2 restaurants; 2 bars; concierge; health club & spa; pool (indoor); room service. *In room:* A/C, TV, TV/DVD, hair dryer, minibar, Wi-Fi (free).

Four Seasons Hotel George V ★★★ ☺   In its latest reincarnation, with all its glitz and glamour, this hotel is one of the best in the world. The George V opened in 1928 in honor of George V of England, grandfather of Queen Elizabeth. During the liberation of Paris, it housed Dwight D. Eisenhower. The guest rooms are about as close as you'll come to residency in a well-upholstered private home where teams of decorators have lavished vast amounts of attention and money. The beds rival those at the Ritz and Meurice in comfort. The largest units are magnificent; the smallest are, in the words of a spokesperson, *"très agréable."* Security is tight—a fact appreciated by sometimes-notorious guests. The staff pampers children with bathrobes, bedtime milk and cookies, and even special menus.

31 av. George V, 75008 Paris. ☎ **800/332-3442** in the U.S. and Canada, or 01-49-52-70-00. Fax 01-49-52-70-10. www.fourseasons.com. 245 units. 750€–1,095€ double; from 1,795€ suite. Parking 40€. AE, DC, MC, V. Métro: George V. **Amenities:** 2 restaurants; 2 bars; babysitting; concierge; health club & spa; room service. *In room:* A/C, TV, TV/DVD, CD player, hair dryer, minibar, Wi-Fi (22€).

Hôtel de Crillon ★★★   The Crillon, one of Europe's grand hotels, sits across from the U.S. Embassy. Although some international CEOs and diplomats treat it as a shrine, those seeking less pomposity might prefer the Plaza Athénée or the Ritz. The 200-plus-year-old building, once the palace of the duc de Crillon, is owned by Jean Taittinger, of the champagne family. The salons boast 17th- and

18th-century tapestries, gilt-and-brocade furniture, chandeliers, fine sculpture, and Louis XVI chests and chairs. The guest rooms are luxurious. Think Madame Pompadour meets Louis XV. Some are spectacular, such as the Leonard Bernstein Suite, which has one of the maestro's pianos. The furniture, including the beds, offers grand comfort.

10 place de la Concorde, 75008 Paris. ✆ **01-44-71-15-00.** Fax 01-44-71-15-02. www.crillon.com. 147 units. 770€–950€ double; from 1,220€ junior suite; from 1,620€ suite. AE, MC, V. Free parking. **Amenities:** 2 restaurants; bar; babysitting; concierge; state-of-the-art health club; room service. *In room:* A/C, TV, TV/DVD, CD player, hair dryer, minibar, Wi-Fi (free).

Hôtel le Bristol ★★★   This palace is near the Palais d'Elysée (home of the French president), on the shopping street parallel to the Champs-Elysées. In terms of style and glamour, here's how the lineup reads in Paris: (1) Ritz, (2) Plaza Athénée, (3) Bristol, and (4) George V. The 18th-century Parisian facade has a glass-and-wrought-iron entryway, where uniformed English-speaking attendants greet you. Hippolyte Jammet founded the Bristol in 1924, installing many antiques and Louis XV and XVI furnishings. The guest rooms are opulent, with antiques or well-made reproductions, inlaid wood, bronze, crystal, Oriental carpets, and original oil paintings. Personalized old-world service is rigidly maintained here—some guests find it forbidding; others absolutely adore it.

112 rue du Faubourg St-Honoré, 75008 Paris. ✆ **01-53-43-43-00.** Fax 01-53-43-43-01. www. hotel-bristol.com. 187 units. 750€–900€ double; 1,040€–1,370€ junior suite; from 1,850€ suite. AE, DC, MC, V. Free parking. Métro: Miromesnil or Champs-Elysées. **Amenities:** Restaurant; bar; babysitting; concierge; health club & spa; pool (indoor); room service. *In room:* A/C, TV, TV/DVD; CD player; hair dryer, minibar, Wi-Fi (21€ per day).

Hôtel Pershing Hall ★★★   Set on a hyperstylish street that parallels the avenue Montaigne, this hotel was created when a late-19th-century town house was radically altered by one of France's most celebrated modern designers, Andrée Putnam. Admittedly, she had fascinating raw materials. The five-story town house was built in 1890 by the Comte de Paris—who at the time was heir apparent to the French monarchy, had it been fully restored—as a home for his mistress. During World War I, it was transformed into the Paris headquarters of American Gen. John Pershing. Today, the walls of the soaring courtyard are draped in lush tropical plants from Southeast Asia, which thrive in the microclimate of the courtyard. Inside, don't expect an homage to the imperial days of the French monarchy, as all appointments have been replaced in favor of the warm, but artfully spartan and rectilinear style favored by the woman who designed the original decor of Air France's Concorde.

49 rue Pierre Charron, 75008 Paris. ✆ **01-58-36-58-00.** Fax 01-58-36-58-01. www.pershing-hall.com. 26 units. 470€–560€ double; 780€–1,110€ suite. AE, DC, MC, V. Métro: George V. **Amenities:** Restaurant; bar; babysitting; concierge; health club & spa; room service. *In room:* A/C, TV, TV/DVD, CD player, hair dryer, minibar, Wi-Fi (free).

Plaza Athénée ★★★   The Plaza Athénée, an 1889 Art Nouveau marvel, is a landmark of discretion and style. In the 8th arrondissement, only the Bristol can compare. About half the celebrities visiting Paris have been pampered here; in the old days, Mata Hari used to frequent the place. The **Salon Gobelins** (with tapestries against rich paneling) and the **Salon Marie Antoinette,** a richly paneled and grand room, are two public rooms that add to the ambience of this lavish hotel. There's also a calm, quiet interior courtyard draped with vines and dotted

Where to Stay on the Right Bank (8 & 16–17e)

17e

❶

Palais des Congrès de Paris **❷**

❹

❸

Ⓜ Courcelles

place de la Porte Maillot

Porte Maillot

place des Ternes **❺**

place Saint-Ferdinand

Ⓜ Grande Armée

Charles de Gaulle–Étoile Ⓡ

Arc de Triomphe

place Charles de Gaulle

Charles de Gaulle–Étoile

❻ **❼**

Ⓜ Kléber

❾ **❽**

George V

Ⓜ Victor Hugo

place Victor Hugo

⓫ **❿**

Boissière Ⓜ

place des États Unis

American Cathedral in Paris

⓬

⓭

⓮

⓯

St-Didier

16e

Musée Guimet

Palais Galliera

President Wilson

Musée d'Art Moderne

Palais de Tokyo

place de l'Alma

CHAILLOT

Trocadéro

pl. de Trocadero et du 11 Novembre

Cimetière de Passy

Palais de Chaillot

Jardins du Trocadéro

place de Varsovie

Alma Marceau Ⓜ

cours Albert voie Georges

cours Albert

Seine

esplanade Habib

Pont de l'Alma Ⓡ

place de la Résistance

quai d'Orsay

Musée de Quai Branly

l'Université

7e

place de Costa Rica

Ⓜ Passy

Champ de Mars–Tour Eiffel Ⓡ

Tour Eiffel

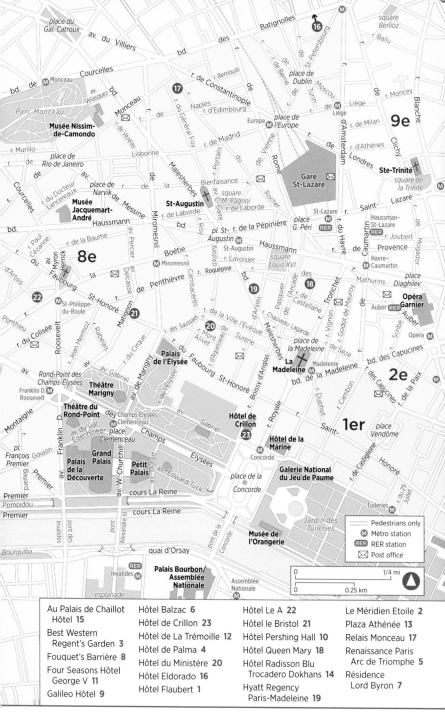

Au Palais de Chaillot
  Hôtel **15**

Best Western
  Regent's Garden **3**

Fouquet's Barrière **8**

Four Seasons Hôtel
  George V **11**

Galileo Hôtel **9**

Hôtel Balzac **6**

Hôtel de Crillon **23**

Hôtel de La Trémoille **12**

Hôtel de Palma **4**

Hôtel du Ministére **20**

Hôtel Eldorado **16**

Hôtel Flaubert **1**

Hôtel Le A **22**

Hôtel le Bristol **21**

Hôtel Pershing Hall **10**

Hôtel Queen Mary **18**

Hôtel Radisson Blu
  Trocadero Dokhans **14**

Hyatt Regency
  Paris-Madeleine **19**

Le Méridien Etoile **2**

Plaza Athénée **13**

Relais Monceau **17**

Renaissance Paris
  Arc de Triomphe **5**

Résidence
  Lord Byron **7**

with geraniums. The quietest guest rooms overlook a courtyard with awnings and parasol-shaded tables; they have ample closet space. Some rooms overlooking avenue Montaigne have views of the Eiffel Tower. The hotel is also home to **Restaurant Plaza Athénée,** where Alain Ducasse presents an award-winning menu focusing on "rare and precious ingredients." See p. 177 for complete review.

25 av. Montaigne, 75008 Paris. © **866/732-1106** in the U.S. and Canada, or 01-53-67-66-65. Fax 01-53-67-66-66. www.plaza-athenee-paris.com. 191 units. 860€–920€ double; from 1,060€ junior suite. AE, MC, V. Parking 28€. Métro: Franklin-D.-Roosevelt or Alma-Marceau. **Amenities:** 5 restaurants; bar; babysitting; concierge; state-of-the-art health club; room service. *In room:* A/C, TV, TV/DVD, CD player, hair dryer, minibar, Wi-Fi (25€ per day).

EXPENSIVE

Hôtel Balzac ★★★   Built for the director of the Paris Opéra in 1853, and once home to Balzac himself, this is a luxurious, intimate town-house hotel overlooking the Champs Elysées. Vibrant, warm colors such as plum and copper prevail throughout the elegant bedrooms furnished with tasteful modern pieces of varying styles. The hotel manages to recapture the romantic era but with a cutting modern edge. It underwent a multi-million-euro restoration to attract guests who like five-star comfort but not commercial palace hotels. For atmosphere, the hotel has lithographs depicting Balzac and scenes from his works including *La Comédie Humaine.*

6 rue Balzac, 75008 Paris. © **01-44-35-18-00.** Fax 01-44-35-18-05. www.hotelbalzac.com. 70 units. 350€–600€ double; 790€–870€ junior suite; from 870€ suite. AE, MC, V. Parking 23€. Métro: Champs Elysées. **Amenities:** Restaurant; bar; health club & spa; pool (indoor); room service. *In room:* A/C, TV, TV/DVD player, hair dryer, minibar, Wi-Fi (22€ per day).

Hôtel La Trémoille ★   In the heart of Paris and a 2-minute walk from the Champs-Elysées, this is a preferred Right Bank address for fashionistas, as it lies in the heart of the haute couture district. Built in the 19th century, the hotel opened again following a massive renovation that returned the swank address to much of its original elegance and charm. It blends modern and traditional styles. Originally a private residence, the hotel is outfitted in a Louis XV style, all in woodwork and tapestries. Rooms are cozy and comfortable, each decorated in harmonies of tawny, ocher, gray, and white, with much use of silks, synthetic furs, and mohair.

14 rue de la Trémoille, 75008 Paris. © **01-56-52-14-00.** Fax 01-40-70-01-08. www.hotel-tremoille. com. 93 units. 485€–630€ double; 700€–1,150€ suite. AE, DC, MC, V. Métro: Alma-Marceau. **Amenities:** Restaurant; bar; concierge; exercise room; room service. *In room:* A/C, TV, hair dryer, minibar, Wi-Fi (free).

Hôtel Le A ★   Lying only 2 blocks from the Champs-Elysées, this town house has been converted to an elegant enclave. It's true the rooms are a bit small—the staff refers to them as cozy—but the overall comfort may still entice your soul. Decorations in the lobby, hall, and bar were by artist Fabrice Hybert, who also painted one unique work for each guest room. The abstract paintings are both modern and figurative. A spacious lounge with a library is filled with books on art and design. Walls are painted with bold abstractions. The hotel bar, under a 19th-century glass roof, with a tasteful black-and-white decor, has become a favorite rendezvous spot with the fashionistas of the era. Rooms represent supreme comfort with adjustable lights, electronic blinds, and other modern amenities. The elevator ceiling that changes color every few seconds is a bit much, however.

4 rue d'Artois, 75008 Paris. ☎ **01-42-56-99-99.** Fax 01-42-56-99-90. www.paris-hotel-a.com. 26 units. 365€ double; 499€ junior suite. Rates include continental breakfast. AE, DC, MC, V. Parking 24€. Métro: St-Philippe-du-Roule. **Amenities:** Bar. *In room:* A/C, TV, hair dryer, minibar, Wi-Fi (free).

Hyatt Regency Paris-Madeleine ★★   In the heart of the financial district, this is Paris's latest luxury hotel and represents Hyatt's first venture into the heart of the French capital. This is our top recommendation for those visiting Paris on business, as rooms are designed not only for rest, but also for work—large writing desks, three phones, modem sockets, voice mail, individual fax machines, you name it. As you enter, the hotel evokes a noble, romantic private home with a lavish use of quality materials such as sycamore wood. Some of the units boast exceptional views over the rooftops of Paris.

24 bd. Malesherbes, 75008 Paris. ☎ **01-55-27-12-34.** Fax 01-55-27-12-35. www.paris.madeleine. hyatt.com. 86 units. 400€–600€ double; from 885€ suite. AE, DC, MC, V. Métro: Madeleine. **Amenities:** 2 restaurants; bar; babysitting; concierge; health club & spa; room service. *In room:* A/C, TV, TV/DVD, CD player, fax, hair dryer, minibar, Wi-Fi (free).

MODERATE

Hôtel Galileo ★ 🎒   This is one of the 8th's most charming hotels. Proprietors Roland and Elisabeth Buffat have won friends from all over with their Hôtel des Deux-Iles and Hôtel de Lutèce on St-Louis-en-l'Ile (see earlier in this chapter). A short walk from the Champs-Elysées, this town house is the epitome of French elegance and charm. The medium-size rooms are a study in understated taste. Within this hotel, rooms with numbers ending in 3 (specifically, 103, 203, 303, 403, and 503) are more spacious than the others. Rooms 501 and 502 have private glassed-in verandas that you can use even in winter.

54 rue Galilée, 75008 Paris. ☎ **01-47-20-66-06.** Fax 01-47-20-67-17. www.galileo-paris-hotel. com. 27 units. 185€ double. AE, DC, MC, V. Métro: Charles-de-Gaulle–Etoile or George V. *In room:* A/C, TV, hair dryer, minibar, Wi-Fi (free).

Hôtel du Ministère ★   The Ministère is a winning choice near the Champs-Elysées, though it's far from Paris's cheapest budget hotel. The guest rooms are on the small side, but they are comfortable and well maintained; many have oak beams and fine furnishings. Avoid rooms on the top floor, which are cramped. Junior suites are only slightly larger than regular doubles, but the extra space may be worth the money.

31 rue de Surène, 75008 Paris. ☎ **01-42-66-21-43.** Fax 01-42-66-96-04. www.ministerehotel. com. 28 units. 209€–249€ double. AE, MC, V. Métro: Madeleine. **Amenities:** Bar; room service. *In room:* A/C, TV, hair dryer, minibar, Wi-Fi (18€ per day).

Hôtel Queen Mary ★   Meticulously renovated inside and out, this early 1900s hotel has an iron-and-glass canopy, wrought iron, and the kind of detailing normally reserved for more expensive hotels. The public rooms have touches of greenery and reproductions of antiques; guest rooms contain upholstered headboards, comfortable beds, and mahogany furnishings, plus a carafe of sherry. Suites and triples are slightly more spacious than regular doubles and are beautifully furnished.

9 rue Greffulhe, 75008 Paris. ✆ **01-42-66-40-50.** Fax 01-42-66-94-92. www.hotelqueenmary. com. 36 units. 129€–215€ double; 209€–289€ triple. AE, DC, MC, V. Métro: Madeleine or Havre-Caumartin. **Amenities:** Bar; room service. *In room:* A/C, TV, hair dryer, Wi-Fi (free).

Relais Monceau ★ 🍴   Finding an elegant but affordable hotel in the over-priced 8th is always a challenge, but Relais Monceau is an inviting choice. A 19th-century town house with two private courtyards has been discreetly restored with a respect for the past, although all the modern amenities have been installed. A government-rated three-star hotel, it takes its name from the nearby Parc Monceau. The midsize bedrooms are furnished with elegance and taste and are spread over three floors. There are also several large public guest areas as well.

85 rue du Rocher, Paris 75008. ✆ **01-45-22-75-11.** Fax: 01-45-22-30-88. www.relais-monceau. com. 51 units. 135€–160€ double; 195€ suite. AE, MC, V. Métro: Champs-Elysées. **Amenities:** Bar. *In room:* A/C, TV, hair dryer, minibar, Wi-Fi (free).

Résidence Lord Byron ☺   Off the Champs-Elysées on a curving street of handsome buildings, the Lord Byron may not be as grand as other hotels in the neighborhood, but it's more affordable. Unassuming and a bit staid, it offers exactly what repeat guests want: a sense of luxury, solitude, and understatement. It's a fine choice for families, who often book suites for the larger living space. You can eat breakfast in the dining room or in the shaded inner garden.

5 rue Chateaubriand, 75008 Paris. ✆ **01-43-59-89-98.** Fax 01-42-89-46-04. www.escapade-paris.com. 31 units. 140€–225€ double; 205€–295€ suite. AE, DC, MC, V. Parking 20€. Métro: George V. RER: Etoile. **Amenities:** Babysitting; room service. *In room:* A/C, TV, hair dryer, minibar, Wi-Fi (free).

16th Arrondissement (Trocadero/Bois de Boulogne)

EXPENSIVE

Hôtel Radisson Blu Trocadéro Dokhan's ★★   If not for the porters walking through its public areas carrying luggage, you might suspect that this well-accessorized hotel was a private home. It's in a stately 19th-century Haussmann-styled building vaguely inspired by Palladio and contains accessories such as antique paneling, Regency-era armchairs, and chandeliers. Each guest room has a different decorative style, with antiques or good reproductions, lots of personalized touches and triple-glazed windows. Beds are often antique reproductions with maximum comfort. Suites have a larger living space and spacious bathrooms with such extras as make-up mirrors and luxe toiletries.

117 rue Lauriston, 75116 Paris. ✆ **01-53-65-66-99.** Fax 01-53-65-66-88. www.radissonblu.com 45 units. 250€–550€ double; from 590€ suite. AE, DC, MC, V. Parking 30€. Métro: Trocadéro. **Amenities:** Babysitting; champagne bar; room service. *In room:* A/C, TV, fax, hair dryer, Wi-Fi (free).

MODERATE

Au Palais de Chaillot Hôtel   When American-trained brothers Thierry and Cyrille Pien opened this hotel, budget travelers flocked here. Located between the Champs-Elysées and Trocadéro, the town house was restored from top to bottom, and the result is a contemporary yet informal variation on Parisian chic. The guest rooms come in various shapes and sizes, and are furnished with a light touch, with bright colors and wicker. Rooms 61, 62, and 63 afford partial views of the Eiffel Tower.

35 av. Raymond-Poincaré, 75016 Paris. ℂ **01-53-70-09-09.** Fax 01-53-70-09-08. www.hotel palaisdechaillot.com. 28 units. 134€–154€ double; 179€ junior suite; 20€ extra bed. AE, DC, MC, V. Métro: Victor Hugo or Trocadéro. **Amenities:** Room service. *In room:* A/C, TV, hair dryer, Wi-Fi (free).

17th Arrondissement (Parc Monceau/ Place Clichy)

EXPENSIVE

Best Western Regent's Garden ★   Near the convention center (Palais des Congrès) and the Arc de Triomphe, the Regent's Garden boasts a proud heritage: Napoleon III built this château for his physician. The interior resembles a classically decorated country house. Guest rooms have flower prints on the walls, traditional French furniture, and tall soundproof windows. A garden with ivy-covered walls and umbrella-shaded tables makes for a perfect place to meet other guests.

6 rue Pierre-Demours, 75017 Paris. ℂ **800/528-1234** in the U.S., or 01-45-74-07-30. Fax 01-40-55-01-42. www.hotel-paris-garden.com. 40 units. 289€–409€ double; from 459€ suite. AE, DC, MC, V. Parking 20€. Métro: Ternes or Charles-de-Gaulle–Etoile. **Amenities:** Babysitting. *In room:* A/C, TV, hair dryer, minibar, Wi-Fi (free).

Le Méridien Etoile   This hotel made records as the largest in Paris when it was built in 1972. Rising nine stories above a rather dull residential and commercial neighborhood at the northwestern fringe of Paris, near the exposition halls at Porte Maillot, it's the flagship of the Méridien chain. Rooms are contemporary looking, not overly large, and standardized, reflecting a bland but completely acceptable international style. Rooms on the hotel's uppermost two floors are a bit plusher than rooms on the lower floors and have a more personalized approach, including a separate breakfast and bar/lounge, separate check-in facilities, and a separate concierge. *Hint:* The enormous size of this hotel and the ongoing efforts of the sales and marketing staff to keep its occupancy levels high lead to promotional rates that can be as much as 50% less than the official rates quoted below.

81 bd. Gouvion Saint-Cyr, 75017 Paris. ℂ **01-40-68-34-34.** Fax 01-40-68-31-31. www.lemeridien etoile.com. 1,025 units. 200€–500€ double; from 600€ suite. AE, DC, MC, V. Parking 30€. Métro: Porte Maillot. **Amenities:** 2 restaurants; bar; babysitting; concierge; room service. *In room:* A/C, TV, DVD, hair dryer, minibar, Wi-Fi (20€ per day).

Renaissance Paris Arc de Triomphe ★★   On the site of the once-famous Theatre de l'Empire, this cutting-edge hotel with its intriguing modern interiors lies only steps from the Arc de Triomphe and the Champs-Elysées. The top-floor rooms and suites open onto large terraces with the panoramic views over the heart of Paris. The upscale hotel rooms and suites are spacious, tastefully decorated, and outfitted with the latest in-room technology. Its all-glass exterior has made this a distinctive landmark, even though it opened only in 2009. This is definitely a trendy and hip hotel, so probably not the best for kids. The on-site Makassar Lounge & restaurant blends French bistro flavors with authentic Indonesian dishes.

39 av. de Wagram, 75017 Paris. ☎ **01-55-37-55-37.** Fax 01-55-37-55-38. www.marriott.com. 108 units. 289€–599€ double; from 429€ suite. Parking 35€. Métro: Charles-de-Gaulle–Etoile. **Amenities:** Restaurant; bar; concierge; exercise room; room service. *In room:* A/C, TV/DVD, hair dryer, minibar, Wi-Fi (free).

MODERATE

Hôtel de Palma ★ 🎁   Although this hotel is off the beaten track for most visitors, some patrons like the quiet residential neighborhood that surrounds it, as well as its quick access by Métro to other parts of Paris. The location is only a 15-minute walk to the Air France/Roissy bus stops. Built at the beginning of the 20th century expressly as a hotel, this seven-story structure totters on the borderline between a government-rated two-star hotel and a three-star hotel, with very reasonable prices for a hostelry in that category. The lobby, with its rattan chairs and prints of animals from the savanna, has a vaguely African colonial aura. The bedrooms, with their warm, sunny colors, evoke Provence. Only the bedrooms on the sixth floor are air-conditioned.

46 rue Brunel, 75017 Paris. ☎ **01-45-74-74-51.** Fax 01-45-74-40-90. www.hotelpalma-paris.com. 37 units. 170€–200€ double; from 250€ junior suite. AE, DC, MC, V. Métro: Argentine. RER: Neuilly–Porte Maillot. **Amenities:** Bar; room service. *In room:* A/C (in some), TV, hair dryer, Wi-Fi (free).

INEXPENSIVE

Hôtel Eldorado 🖋   If you're looking for something to criticize, you might well find it here. But if you're an intrepid bargain hunter, and don't mind living in an offbeat neighborhood on the border of Montmartre, this is one of the best cheap hotels in an overpriced city. Of course, don't expect an elevator to take you to a room with a TV, phone, or air-conditioning. But the price is right. The manager, Anne Gratacos, continually decorates the hotel with flea market finds, including Buddha busts and Art Deco armoires. The most spacious and evocative units are in a separate pavilion separated from the main structure by a garden patio with a restaurant, Bistrot des Dames.

18 rue des Dames, 75017 Paris. ☎ **01-45-22-35-21.** Fax 01-43-87-25-97. www.eldoradohotel.fr. 33 units, 23 with private bathroom. 70€–80€ double with bathroom; 80€–90€ triple with bathroom. AE, MC, V. Parking 25€. Métro: Place de Clichy. **Amenities:** Restaurant. *In room:* No phone, Wi-Fi (free).

Hôtel Flaubert   For an inexpensive retreat in the 17th, this is as good as it gets. The staff long ago became accustomed to handling the problems their international guests might have. Terra-cotta tiles and bentwood furniture in the public areas make for an efficient, if not lushly comfortable, setting for breakfast. Though the climbing plants in the courtyard overshadow the guest rooms, the accommodations are appealing and, particularly those beneath the mansard's eaves, cozy. Throughout, rooms are modern, relatively small scale, and comfortable.

19 rue Rennequin, 75017 Paris. ☎ **01-46-22-44-35.** Fax 01-43-80-32-34. www.hotelflaubert. com. 41 units. 117€ double. AE, DC, MC, V. Métro: Ternes. **Amenities:** Room service. *In room:* TV, hair dryer, Wi-Fi (free).

ON THE LEFT BANK

We begin with the most centrally located arrondissements on the Left Bank and then work our way through the more outlying neighborhoods and to the area near the Eiffel Tower.

5th Arrondissement (Quartier Latin)

EXPENSIVE

Grand Hôtel Saint-Michel   Built in the 19th century, this hotel is larger and more businesslike than many town house–style inns nearby. It basks in the reflected glow of Brazilian dissident Georges Amado, whose memoirs recorded his 2-year sojourn in one of the rooms. The public areas are tasteful, with portraits and rich upholsteries. Improvements have enlarged some rooms, lowering their ceilings and adding amenities, but retained old-fashioned touches such as wrought-iron balconies (on the fifth floor). Triple rooms have an extra bed and are suitable for families, who share a private bathroom with tub and shower. Sixth-floor rooms have views over the rooftops.

19 rue Cujas, 75005 Paris. ✆ **01-46-33-33-02.** Fax 01-40-46-96-33. www.grand-hotel-st-michel.com. 47 units. 290€–350€ double; 400€ suite. AE, DC, MC, V. Métro: Cluny–La Sorbonne. RER: Luxembourg or St-Michel. **Amenities:** Bar; babysitting; exercise room; room service. *In room:* A/C, TV, hair dryer, minibar, Wi-Fi (free).

MODERATE

The Five Hotel ★ 🏨   A charmer among Left Bank boutique hotels, the Five is named for the 5th arrondissement (Latin Quarter) and lies in a restored 1800s town house on a U-shaped street off boulevard de Port-Royal. The interior design is not to everyone's taste, including a red leather paneled hall or a red-painted gas fireplace. The rooms are individually designed in various colors (blood red or Halloween orange, for example), and tiny white lights evoke a planetarium. Of course, if you want a room the color of a prune, that too is available. A Chinese lacquer artist, Isabelle Emmerique, has certainly been busy here. Some rooms are small, but all the beds are exceedingly comfortable.

3 rue Flatters, Paris 75005. ✆ **01-43-31-74-21.** Fax 01-43-31-61-96. www.thefivehotel.com. 24 units. 198€–353€ double; 392€ suite. AE, MC, V. Métro: Bastilel or Gobelins. **Amenities:** Room service. *In room:* A/C, TV, hair dryer, Wi-Fi (free).

Hôtel Agora St-Germain   One of the neighborhood's best moderately priced choices, this hotel occupies a building constructed in the early 1600s to house a group of guardsmen protecting the brother of the king at his lodgings nearby. It's in the heart of artistic/historic Paris and offers compact, soundproof guest rooms that have been sensitively renovated. All but seven of the bedrooms have tub/shower combinations; the rest have only showers.

42 rue des Bernardins, 75005 Paris. ✆ **01-46-34-13-00.** Fax 01-46-34-75-05. www.agorasaintgermain.com. 39 units. 110€–195€ double. AE, DC, MC, V. Parking 25€. Métro: Maubert-Mutualité. **Amenities:** Room service. *In room:* A/C, TV, hair dryer, minibar, Wi-Fi (free).

Hôtel des Jardins du Luxembourg   Built during Baron Haussmann's 19th-century overhaul of Paris, this hotel boasts an imposing facade of honey-colored stone accented with ornate iron balconies. Sigmund Freud stayed here in 1885. The interior is outfitted in strong, clean lines, often with groupings of Art Deco furnishings. The high-ceilinged guest rooms, some with Provençal tiles and ornate moldings, are well maintained, the sizes ranging from small to medium. Best of all, they overlook a quiet dead-end alley, ensuring relatively peaceful nights. Some have balconies overlooking the rooftops. Ongoing renovations have kept the bedrooms looking spiffy.

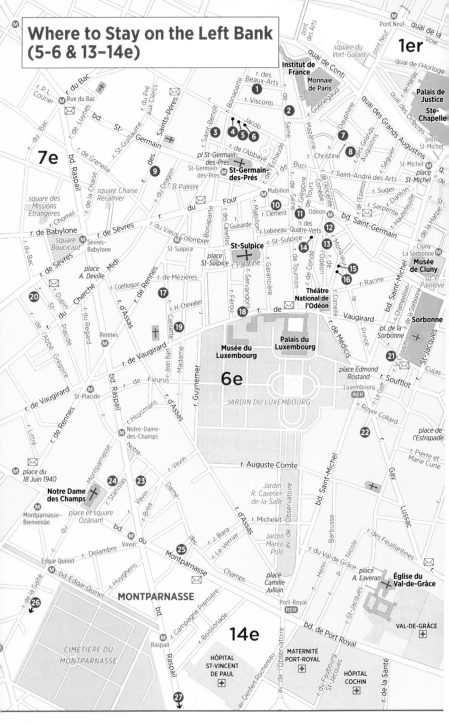

Where to Stay on the Left Bank (5-6 & 13–14e)

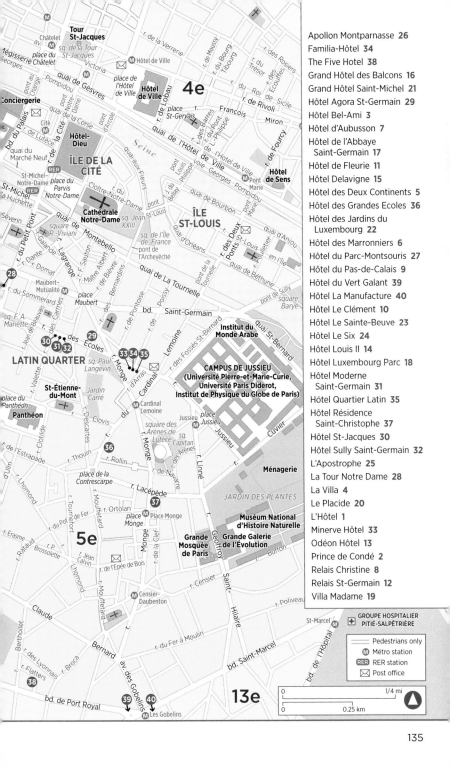

Apollon Montparnasse **26**

Familia-Hôtel **34**

The Five Hotel **38**

Grand Hôtel des Balcons **16**

Grand Hôtel Saint-Michel **21**

Hôtel Agora St-Germain **29**

Hôtel Bel-Ami **3**

Hôtel d'Aubusson **7**

Hôtel de l'Abbaye
  Saint-Germain **17**

Hôtel de Fleurie **11**

Hôtel Delavigne **15**

Hôtel des Deux Continents **5**

Hôtel des Grandes Ecoles **36**

Hôtel des Jardins du
  Luxembourg **22**

Hôtel des Marronniers **6**

Hôtel du Parc-Montsouris **27**

Hôtel du Pas-de-Calais **9**

Hôtel du Vert Galant **39**

Hôtel La Manufacture **40**

Hôtel Le Clément **10**

Hôtel Le Sainte-Beuve **23**

Hôtel Le Six **24**

Hôtel Louis II **14**

Hôtel Luxembourg Parc **18**

Hôtel Moderne
  Saint-Germain **31**

Hôtel Quartier Latin **35**

Hôtel Résidence
  Saint-Christophe **37**

Hôtel St-Jacques **30**

Hôtel Sully Saint-Germain **32**

L'Apostrophe **25**

La Tour Notre Dame **28**

La Villa **4**

Le Placide **20**

L'Hôtel **1**

Minerve Hôtel **33**

Odéon Hôtel **13**

Prince de Condé **2**

Relais Christine **8**

Relais St-Germain **12**

Villa Madame **19**

5 Impasse Royer-Collard, 75005 Paris. ✆ **01-40-46-08-88.** Fax 01-40-46-02-28. www.les-jardins-du-luxembourg.com. 26 units. 143€–153€ double. AE, DC, MC, V. Métro: Cluny–La Sorbonne. RER: Luxembourg. **Amenities:** Bar; babysitting; room service. *In room:* A/C, TV, hair dryer, minibar, Wi-Fi (10€ for 3 hr.).

Hôtel Quartier Latin   Between the Sorbonne and the Musée de Cluny, this hotel captures the flavor of the Paris literati better than any other in Paris. Its decor was conceived in 1997 by Didier Gomez, who referred to it as "contemporary with cultural references." That means walls stenciled with passages from Victor Hugo or photographs of Colette and André Gide. Even the breakfast room is stocked with bookshelves and its ceiling inscribed with quotes from Baudelaire. Bibliomania continues in the lobby, which is filled with floor-to-ceiling bookcases. Bedrooms are decorated comfortably and tastefully in blue and white, with such delicacies as linen curtains, along with fine wood furnishings, plus white-tiled bathrooms. In all, this is a "novel" hotel and ideal for bookworms.

9 rue des Ecoles, 75005 Paris. ✆ **01-44-27-06-45.** Fax 01-43-25-36-70. www.hotelquartierlatin. com. 29 units. 187€–248€ double; 242€–310€ junior suite. AE, MC, V. Métro: Cardinal Lemoine. Parking nearby 20€. **Amenities:** Babysitting; room service. *In room:* A/C, TV, hair dryer, minibar, Wi-Fi (free).

Hôtel St-Jacques ★ 🎒   Try for a room with a balcony view of Notre-Dame and the Panthéon. The Belle Epoque atmosphere of the hotel was made famous in the movie *Charade,* which starred Cary Grant and Audrey Hepburn. Jean-Paul and Martine Rousseau, the owners, welcome you to this Latin Quarter gem, filled with Second Empire overtones, including frescoes in the breakfast room and lounge, 18th-century ceiling murals in some of the bedrooms, wedding cake plasterwork, and corridors painted with *trompe l'oeil* marble. Bedrooms are generally spacious and have been attractively and comfortably restored.

35 rue des Ecoles, 75005 Paris. ✆ **01-44-07-45-45.** Fax 01-43-25-65-50. www.paris-hotel-stjacques.com. 26 units. 189€–189€ double; 176€ triple. AE, DC, MC, V. Métro: Maubert-Mutualité. **Amenities:** Babysitting. *In room:* TV, hair dryer, Wi-Fi (free).

Hôtel Sully Saint-Germain ★   With its medieval-style decoration and its numerous and beautiful antiques, this hotel is a winning choice with a bit of charm. A government-rated three-star hotel, it captures much of the spirit of the Quartier Latin in the St-Germain-des-Prés area in the heart of the Left Bank. At your doorstep are some of Paris's major attractions, including Notre-Dame, Cluny Abbey, the banks of the Seine, and even the Louvre and Orsay museums. The public rooms are not overly adorned but are furnished with taste and comfort in mind. The midsize bedrooms, with brass beds set against stone walls, are handsomely furnished and comfortable. They're not grand, but are imbued with Parisian charm.

31 rue des Ecoles, 75005 Paris. ✆ **01-43-26-56-02.** Fax 01-43-29-74-42. www.hotel-paris-sully. com. 61 units. 165€–200€ double; 240€ junior suite. AE, DC, MC, V. Métro: Maubert-Mutualité. Parking 26€. **Amenities:** Bar; exercise room; room service; sauna & steam bath. *In room:* A/C, TV, hair dryer, minibar, Wi-Fi (free).

La Tour Notre-Dame ★   In the heart of the Sorbonne district, this restored Latin Quarter hotel rises seven floors over a 17th-century vaulted cellar where breakfast is served. A hotel of Rive Gauche character, it is ideally situated for Left Bank living, lying between St-Germain-des-Prés and the cathedral of

Notre-Dame, opposite the Sorbonne and the Cluny Museum. Bedrooms, many with exposed beams, have been given a decorator's touch, and they are adorned with certain romantic accents. Liberty prints and Empire-era furniture decorate many of the bedrooms, which are beautifully maintained.

20 rue du Sommerard, 75005 Paris. ✆ **01-43-54-47-60.** Fax 01-43-26-42-34. www.la-tour-notre-dame.com. 48 units. 190€–245€ double. AE, DC, MC, V. Métro: Cluny–Sorbonne. RER: Saint-Michel or Notre-Dame. **Amenities:** Bar. *In room:* TV, hair dryer, minibar, Wi-Fi (free).

INEXPENSIVE

Familia-Hôtel   As the name implies, this hotel has been family-run for decades. Many personal touches make the place unique. Finely executed sepia-colored frescoes of Parisian scenes grace the walls of 14 rooms. Eight units have restored stone walls, and seven boast balconies with delightful views over the Latin Quarter. The dynamic owners renovate the rooms as often as needed to maintain the highest level of comfort.

11 rue des Ecoles, 75005 Paris. ✆ **01-43-54-55-27.** Fax 01-43-29-61-77. www.familiahotel.com. 30 units. 122€ double; 167€ triple; 179€ quad. Rates include breakfast. Parking 20€. AE, DC, MC, V. Métro: Jussieu or Maubert-Mutualité. **Amenities:** Breakfast room. *In room:* TV, hair dryer, minibar, Wi-Fi (free).

Hôtel des Grandes Ecoles ✦   Few hotels in the neighborhood offer so much low-key charm at such reasonable prices. It's composed of a trio of high-ceilinged buildings, interconnected via a sheltered courtyard, where in warm weather, singing birds provide a worthy substitute for the TVs deliberately missing from the rooms. Accommodations, as reflected by the price, range from snug, cozy doubles to more spacious chambers. Each room is comfortable, but with a lot of luggage, the very smallest would be cramped. The decor is old-fashioned, with feminine touches such as flowered upholsteries and ruffles. Many have views of a garden where trellises and flower beds evoke the countryside.

75 rue de Cardinal-Lemoine, 75005 Paris. ✆ **01-43-26-79-23.** Fax 01-47-47-65-48. www.hotel-grandes-ecoles.com. 51 units. 115€–140€ double. Extra bed 20€. MC, V. Parking 30€. Métro: Cardinal Lemoine, Jussieu, or Place Monge. RER: Port-Royal, Luxembourg. **Amenities:** Babysitting; room service. *In room:* Hair dryer, Wi-Fi (free).

Hôtel Moderne Saint-Germain ★   In the heart of the Latin Quarter, between the Panthéon and Saint-Michel, the Hôtel Moderne is better than ever since it ended the 20th century with a complete overhaul. Though the rooms are small, this is still one of the neighborhood's better three-star hotels. Its charming owner, Mr. Gibon, welcomes guests to his spotless accommodations. In the units fronting rue des Ecoles, double-glazed windows hush the traffic.

33 rue des Ecoles, 75005 Paris. ✆ **01-43-54-37-78.** Fax 01-43-29-91-31. www.hotel-paris-stgermain.com. 45 units. 150€ double; 180€ triple. AE, DC, MC, V. Parking 26€. Métro: Maubert-Mutualité. **Amenities:** Exercise room; room service. *In room:* A/C, TV, hair dryer, Wi-Fi (free).

Hôtel-Résidence Saint-Christophe   This hotel, in one of the Latin Quarter's undiscovered areas, offers a gracious English-speaking staff. It was created in 1987, when an older hotel was connected to a butcher shop. All the small- to medium-size rooms have Louis XV–style furniture and carpeting.

17 rue Lacépède, 75005 Paris. ✆ **01-43-31-81-54.** Fax 01-43-31-12-54. www.charm-hotel-paris.com. 31 units. 98€–138€ double. AE, DC, MC, V. Parking 24€. Métro: Place Monge. **Amenities:** Breakfast room. *In room:* TV, hair dryer, minibar, Wi-Fi (free).

Minerve Hôtel   This is a well-managed, government-rated, two-star hotel in the heart of the Latin Quarter, with good-size, comfortable rooms and a staff with a sense of humor. Bedrooms have contemporary-looking mahogany furniture and walls covered in fabric. Try for one of 10 rooms with balconies where you can look out over Notre-Dame. Depending on your room assignment, bathrooms range in dimension from cramped to midsize. If there's no space at the Minerve, a staff member will arrange an equivalent (and equivalently priced) lodging at its sibling, the Familia, next door (see description above).

13 rue des Ecoles, 75005 Paris. ℭ **01-43-26-26-04.** Fax 01-44-07-01-96. www.hotel-paris-minerve.com. 54 units. 79€–145€ double. AE, DC, MC, V. Métro: Cardinal Lemoine. Parking 20€. **Amenities:** Room service. *In room:* A/C, TV, hair dryer, Wi-Fi (free).

6th Arrondissement (St-Germain/ Luxembourg)

VERY EXPENSIVE

Hotel Bel-Ami ★ 🎁   This four-star hotel was designed expressly to appeal to fashion-conscious patrons in the heart of the Left Bank cafe district. Its name translates as "handsome (male) friend." You'll get the feeling that this is an arts-conscious hotel whose minimalist public areas were built only after months of careful design by a team of trend-following architects. Expect color schemes of lilac walls, acid-green sofas, copper-colored tiles, bleached ash, and industrial-style lighting fixtures. Bedrooms contain a palette of earth tones, such as pistachio ice cream or pumpkin pie, and an almost aggressively minimalist, even cubist, design. Bathrooms are artfully spartan.

7–11 rue St. Benoît, 75006 Paris. ℭ **01-42-61-53-53.** Fax 01-49-27-09-33. www.hotel-bel-ami. com. 112 units. 360€–530€ double; 620€–1,050€ suite. AE, DC, MC, V. Métro: St-Germain-des-Prés. **Amenities:** Bar; concierge; espresso bar; exercise room. *In room:* TV, minibar, Wi-Fi (free).

Hôtel d'Aubusson ★★★   This mansion in the heart of St-Germain-des-Prés was the site of the city's first literary salon. Fully restored, it is today one of the best luxe boutique hotels in Paris. It's graced with original Aubusson tapestries. Lying 2 blocks south of Pont Neuf and the Seine, the hotel has taken over a former private residence from the 1600s, to which is attached a 1950s building. You enter a grand hall under a beamed ceiling with a baronial fireplace and furnishings in the style of Louis XV. There are also a number of smaller, more intimate lounges. The bedrooms are midsize to large, each attractively and comfortably furnished, often in a Directoire style and sometimes with exposed ceiling beams. Antiques are often placed in front of the original stone walls. For the most traditional flair, ask for one of the rooms on the top two floors.

33 rue Dauphine, Paris 75006. ℭ **01-43-29-43-43.** Fax 01-43-29-12-62. www.hoteldaubusson. com. 49 units. 305€–535€ double. AE, DC, MC, V. Parking 25€. Métro: Odéon. **Amenities:** Bar; cafe; babysitting; room service. *In room:* A/C, TV, hair dryer, minibar, Wi-Fi (free).

L'Hôtel ★   Ranking just a notch below the Relais Christine (see the following), this is one of the Left Bank's most charming boutique hotels. It was once a 19th-century fleabag whose major distinction was that Oscar Wilde died in one of its bedrooms, but today's guests aren't anywhere near destitution. Guest rooms vary in size, style, and price; all have decorative fireplaces and fabric-covered walls. All the sumptuous beds have tasteful fabrics and crisp linens. About half the bathrooms are small, tubless nooks. Room themes reflect China, Russia, Japan,

India, or high-camp Victorian. The Cardinal room is all scarlet, the Viollet-le-Duc room is neo-Gothic, and the room where Wilde died is Victorian. One spacious room contains the furnishings (including multiple mirrors) and memorabilia of stage star Mistinguett.

13 rue des Beaux-Arts, 75006 Paris. ☎ **01-44-41-99-00.** Fax 01-43-25-64-81. www.l-hotel.com. 20 units. 280€–370€ double; 640€–740€ suite. AE, DC, MC, V. Métro: St-Germain-des-Prés. **Amenities:** Restaurant; bar (see Le Bar de L'Hôtel in chapter 10); babysitting; room service. *In room:* A/C, TV, TV/DVD, hair dryer, minibar, Wi-Fi (free).

Relais Christine ★★ This hotel welcomes you into a former 16th-century Augustinian cloister. From a cobblestone street, you enter a symmetrical courtyard and find an elegant reception area with sculpture and Renaissance antiques. Each room is uniquely decorated with wooden beams and Louis XIII–style furnishings; the rooms come in a range of styles and shapes. Some are among the Left Bank's largest, with extras such as mirrored closets, plush carpets, thermostats, and some balconies facing the courtyard. The least attractive rooms are in the interior. Bed configurations vary, but all mattresses are on the soft side, offering comfort with quality linens.

3 rue Christine, 75006 Paris. ☎ **01-40-51-60-80.** Fax 01-40-51-60-81. www.relais-christine.com. 51 units. 390€–500€ double; 580€–900€ duplex or suite. AE, DC, MC, V. Free parking. Métro: Odéon or St-Michel. **Amenities:** Honor bar; babysitting; concierge; exercise room; room service. *In room:* A/C, TV, TV/DVD, hair dryer, minibar, Wi-Fi (25€ per 48 hr.).

Relais St-Germain ★★ It's difficult to exaggerate the charm of this deeply personalized and intimate hotel created from side-by-side 17th-century town houses. You'll navigate your way through a labyrinth of narrow and winding hallways to soundproofed bedrooms that are spacious, and artfully and individually decorated in a style that evokes late-19th-century Paris at its most sensual. Two of the rooms have terraces. Come here for a discreet escape from the anonymity of larger, less personalized hotels, and for an injection of boutique-style Parisian charm. Even *Vogue* magazine referred to this place as "an oasis of Left-Bank charm." We heartily agree.

9 Carrefour de l'Odéon, 75006 Paris. ☎ **01-43-29-12-05.** Fax 01-46-33-45-30. www.hotelrsg. com. 22 units. 285€–370€ double; 395€ suite. Rates include breakfast. AE, DC, MC, V. **Amenities:** Restaurant; Wi-Fi (free). *In room:* A/C, TV, TV/DVD, hair dryer, minibar.

EXPENSIVE

Hôtel de Fleurie ★ ☺ Off the boulevard St-Germain on a colorful little street, the Fleurie is one of the best of the city's "new" old hotels; its statuary-studded facade recaptures 17th-century elegance, and the stone walls in the salon have been exposed. Many of the guest rooms have elaborate draperies and antique reproductions. Because some rooms are larger than others and contain an extra bed for one or two children, the hotel has long been a family favorite.

32–34 rue Grégoire-de-Tours, 75006 Paris. ☎ **01-53-73-70-00.** Fax 01-53-73-70-20. www.fleurie-hotel-paris.com. 29 units. 250€–320€ double; 465€ family room. Children 12 and under stay free in parent's room. AE, DC, MC, V. Métro: Odéon or Mabillon. **Amenities:** Bar; babysitting; room service; Wi-Fi (free). *In room:* A/C, TV, hair dryer, minibar.

Hôtel de l'Abbaye Saint-Germain ★ This is one of the district's most charming boutique hotels, built as a convent in the early 18th century. Its brightly colored rooms have traditional furniture, plus touches of sophisticated flair. In front is a small garden and in back is a verdant courtyard with a fountain, raised flower beds, and masses of ivy and climbing vines. If you don't mind the expense, one of the most charming rooms has a terrace overlooking the upper floors of neighboring buildings. Guest rooms are midsize to large and are continually maintained. Suites are generous in size and full of Left Bank charm, often with antique reproductions.

10 rue Cassette, 75006 Paris. ✆ **01-45-44-38-11.** Fax 01-45-48-07-86. www.hotelabbayeparis. com. 44 units. 232€–340€ double; 427€–519€ suite. Rates include breakfast. AE, MC, V. Métro: St-Sulpice. **Amenities:** Bar; room service. *In room:* A/C, TV, hair dryer, Wi-Fi (free).

Hôtel Le Six ★ 👔   This boutique hotel is a bastion of restrained charm and low-key luxury with harmonious tones and soft lighting. Its major feature is an elegant spa offering the same products as the swank Ritz Hotel. The staff promises to leave you "gorgeous." Sturdy oak furnishings and autumnal colors fill the hotel; the best accommodations are the upper suites, opening onto views of the skyline of Paris. But all the accommodations are imbued with a high comfort level, made all the more so by the soundproofing. Guests gather in the library and lounge, sheltered under a glass roof and evoking a winter garden.

14 rue Stanislas, 75006 Paris. ✆ **01-42-22-00-75.** Fax 01-42-22-00-95. www.hotel-le-six.com. 41 units. 231€–552€ double; 402€–600€ junior suite; 599€–750€ suite. AE, DC, MC, V. Métro: Notre-Dame-des-Champs or Vavin. **Amenities:** Room service; spa. *In room:* A/C, TV, minibar, Wi-Fi (free).

Hôtel Luxembourg Parc ★★   Near the Luxembourg Gardens for those lovely strolls, this elegant bastion of fine living has been called a small-scale version of the swank Hôtel de Crillon. In one of the Left Bank's most charming and historic districts, a 17th-century palace has been beautifully restored and decorated. The bedrooms are decorated in the styles of Louis XV, Louis XVI, and Napoleon III. The bar is an elegant rendezvous point and the library is relaxing. Bathrooms are generous in size, and units contain such thoughtful touches as bathrobes and plenty of hangers. The around-the-clock room service is actually takeout from nearby restaurants. The breakfast room on the ground floor overlooks the Luxembourg Gardens.

42 rue de Vaugirard, 75006 Paris. ✆ **01-53-10-36-50.** Fax 01-53-10-36-59. www.luxembourg-paris-hotel.com. 23 units. 280€–310€ double. AE, DC, MC, V. Métro: Luxembourg. **Amenities:** Bar; exercise room; room service. *In room:* A/C, TV, hair dryer, minibar, Wi-Fi (free).

L'Apostrophe ★ 👔   This Rive Gauche boutique hotel lies near the Café de Flore and Café des Deux-Magots, once the favorite literary haunts of some of France's most celebrated writers. This hotel pays homage to that tradition, becoming the first Parisian "poem hotel," an establishment devoted to the aesthetic, the beauty, and the mysteries of writing. On the ground floor is painted the story of *One Thousand and One Nights.* The first floor is devoted to the markings that pre-date writing. On the second floor are signs indicating the alphabet, calligraphy, and music. The third floor is devoted to books and posters. A stay here is like no other in Paris. Bedrooms are beautifully decorated and comfortable, though a bit small. Be aware that the shower and water basin are actually in the room—there is no separate bathroom.

3 rue de Chevreuse, 75006 Paris. ✆ **01-56-54-31-31.** www.apostrophe-hotel.com. 16 units. 162€–290€ standard double; 210€–350€ double with a Jacuzzi. Métro: Vavin. **Amenities:** Bar. *In room:* A/C, TV/DVD, CD player, hair dryer, Wi-Fi (free).

La Villa ★   This hotel's facade resembles those of many of the other buildings in the neighborhood. Inside, however, the decor is a minimalist ultramodern creation rejecting traditional French aesthetics. The public areas and guest rooms contain Bauhaus-like furniture; the lobby's angular lines are softened with bouquets of leaves and flowers. Most unusual are the tubs, with decidedly postmodern stainless steel and pink, black, or beige marble.

29 rue Jacob, 75006 Paris. ✆ **01-43-26-60-00.** Fax 01-46-34-63-63. www.villa-saintgermain.com. 31 units. 280€–370€ double; from 470€ suite. AE, DC, MC, V. Métro: St-Germain-des-Prés. **Amenities:** Bar; babysitting; room service. *In room:* A/C, TV, hair dryer, minibar, Wi-Fi (5€ per day).

Le Placide ★ ★ 🎁   Converted from a former family home in the 19th century, Le Placide has the aura of a private club. This small boutique hotel in St-Germain lies just steps from the chic Bon Marché Department Store. It was designed by a member of Philippe Starck's firm, who brought a 21st-century style of luxury and comfort to the interior, featuring white Moroccan leather, lots of glass, a bit of chrome, and a crystal pedestal table. Fresh flowers adorn each room, and rose petals are placed on your bed at night. The spacious bathrooms provide much natural light.

6 rue St-Placide, 75006 Paris. ✆ **01-42-84-34-60.** www.leplacidehotel.com. 11 units. 179€ double; 300€ suite. AE, MC, V. Métro: St-Placide. **Amenities:** Bar. *In room:* A/C, TV, TV/DVD, CD player, hair dryer, minibar, MP3 docking station, Wi-Fi (free).

Odéon Hôtel ★   Reminiscent of a modernized Norman country inn, the Odéon has such rustic touches as exposed beams, stone walls, high ceilings, and tapestries mixed with contemporary fabrics, mirrored ceilings, and black leather furnishings. Near the Théâtre de l'Odéon and boulevard St-Germain, the Odéon stands on the first street in Paris to have pavements (ca. 1779). By the 20th century, this area began attracting such writers as Gertrude Stein and her coterie. The guest rooms are small to medium in size and well furnished. The beds are excellent, with reading lamps and bedside controls.

3 rue de l'Odéon, 75006 Paris. ✆ **01-43-25-90-67.** Fax 01-43-25-55-98. www.odeonhotel.fr. 33 units. 190€–270€ double. AE, DC, MC, V. Métro: Odéon. **Amenities:** Bar; babysitting; room service. *In room:* A/C, TV, hair dryer, Wi-Fi (free).

MODERATE

Hôtel des Deux Continents   Built from three interconnected historic buildings, each between three and six stories high, this hotel is a reliable choice with a sense of Latin Quarter style. The carefully coordinated guest rooms range from small to medium size and include reproductions of antique furnishings and soundproof, upholstered walls.

25 rue Jacob, 75006 Paris. ✆ **01-43-26-72-46.** Fax 01-43-25-67-80. www.2continents-hotel. com. 41 units. 118€–185€ double; 230€ triple. MC, V. Métro: St-Germain-des-Prés. *In room:* A/C, TV, hair dryer, Wi-Fi (8€).

Hôtel des Marronniers ★ 🎁   In the heart of St-Germain-des-Prés, this is one of those hidden gems that is nestled in the back of a courtyard on a street lined with antique stores. At the rear of this "secret" address is a small garden with a veranda, where you can linger over afternoon tea. Some of the rooms open onto views of the steeple of the church of St-Germain-des-Prés. For one of the rooms, book well in advance. The midsize bedrooms are furnished with period pieces placed under exposed beams and enveloped by fabric-covered walls in rich tones.

21 rue Jacob, 75006 Paris. ✆ **01-43-25-30-60.** Fax 01-40-46-83-56. 37 units. www.paris-hotel-marroniers.com. 175€–190€ double. MC, V. Métro: St-Germain-des-Prés. *In room:* A/C, TV, hair dryer, Wi-Fi (free).

Hôtel du Pas-de-Calais   The Pas-de-Calais goes back to the 17th century. It retains its elegant facade, with wooden doors. Novelist Chateaubriand lived here from 1811 to 1814, but its most famous guest was Jean-Paul Sartre, who struggled with the play *Les Mains Sales (Dirty Hands)* in room no. 41. The hotel is a bit weak on style, but as one longtime guest confided, "We still stay here for the memories." Rooms are small; inner units surround a courtyard with two garden tables and several trellises. From January until the end of March, the hotel often grants substantial discounts.

59 rue des Sts-Pères, 75006 Paris. ✆ **01-45-48-78-74.** Fax 01-45-44-94-57. www.hotelpasde calais.com. 38 units. 185€–315€ double; 300€ suite. AE, DC, MC, V. Parking 25€. Métro: St-Germain-des-Prés or Sèvres-Babylone. **Amenities:** Bar; babysitting; room service. *In room:* A/C, TV, hair dryer, Wi-Fi (free).

Hôtel Le Sainte-Beuve ★ 🏛   Lying off the tree-lined boulevard Raspail, this Montparnasse choice is close to the "Lost Generation" cafes made famous in the pages of Ernest Hemingway's *The Sun Also Rises*. If you stay here, you're just 3 minutes from the Luxembourg Gardens. You enter a small reception area opening into a Georgian parlor with plush sofas, armchairs, columns, and even a marble fireplace for those nippy Paris nights. Bedrooms are often furnished in part with antiques, but have all the modern comforts. The cheaper rooms are small. If you can afford it, ask for one of the deluxe units that also has love seats and safes.

9 rue St-Beuve, 75006 Paris. ✆ **01-45-48-20-07.** Fax 01-45-48-67-52. www.hotel-sainte-beuve. fr. 22 units. 126€–310€ double; 256€–365€ junior suite. AE, DC, MC, V. Métro: Notre-Dame-des-Champs or Vavin. **Amenities:** Bar; babysitting; room service. *In room:* A/C, TV, hair dryer, minibar, Wi-Fi (free).

Hôtel Louis II   In an 18th-century building, this hotel offers guest rooms decorated in modern French tones. Afternoon drinks and morning coffee are served in the reception salon, where gilt-framed mirrors, fresh flowers, and antiques radiate a provincial aura, as though something out of Proust. The generally small, soundproof rooms with exposed beams and lace bedding complete the impression. Many visitors ask for the romantic attic rooms.

2 rue St-Sulpice, 75006 Paris. ✆ **01-46-33-13-80.** Fax 01-46-33-17-29. www.hotel-louis2.com. 22 units. 195€–220€ double; 310€ junior suite. AE, DC, MC, V. Métro: Odéon. **Amenities:** Bar; room service. *In room:* A/C, TV, hair dryer, minibar, Wi-Fi (free).

Prince de Condé ★   In the heart of St-Germain-des-Prés, with all its art galleries, this 18th-century building has been restored and turned into the epitome of Left Bank charm. Guests gather in the elegant lounge with its cozy ambience, carved stone walls, and arches. The wallpapered bedrooms, small to midsize, are comfortably furnished and intimate, each tidily maintained with double-glazed windows.

39 rue de Seine, 75006 Paris. ✆ **01-43-26-71-56.** Fax 01-46-34-27-95. 11 units. 195€ double; 280€ suite. AE, MC, V. Métro: St-Germain-des-Prés. *In room:* A/C, TV, hair dryer, minibar, Wi-Fi (free).

Villa Madame ★   In the heart of St-Germain-des-Prés, this hotel is a smart Left Bank address in a neighborhood of tony boutiques and fashionable hair salons, just a short walk from Jardin du Luxembourg. It reopened late in 2008 after 2 years of major renovations. The bedrooms are sleek and modern with the latest gadgets. We prefer the accommodations on the top floor, with their balconies overlooking the rooftops of Paris. There is an inside courtyard, where you can order breakfast or else drinks in the evening. The Big Salon is actually a tearoom with a fireplace.

44 rue Madame, 75006 Paris. ✆ **01-45-48-02-81.** Fax 01-45-44-85-73. www.hotelvillamadame paris.com. 28 units. 220€–320€ double; 500€ suite. AE, DC, MC. Métro: Rennes or St-Sulpice. RER: Luxembourg. *In room:* A/C, TV, minibar, Wi-Fi (free).

INEXPENSIVE

Grand Hôtel des Balcons ★ ✦   The Corroyer-André family welcome you to this restored 19th-century building, once patronized by Baudelaire and the poets Henri Michaux and Endré Ady. You enter an Art Nouveau setting with stained-glass windows and tulip-shaped molten glass lamps and chandeliers. The hotel lies behind a restored facade studded with small balconies—hence, its name. Bedrooms are not only affordable, but also harmonious in decor and big on comfort and good maintenance. Close to the gardens of Luxembourg, the rooms are not large but ample enough for big closets and full-length dressing mirrors.

3 Casimir Delavigne, 75006 Paris. ✆ **01-46-34-78-50.** Fax 01-46-34-06-27. www.balcons.com. 50 units. 125€ double; 220€ triple or quad. AE, MC, V. Métro: Odéon. RER: Luxembourg. *In room:* TV, hair dryer, Wi-Fi (5€ per day).

Hôtel Delavigne   Despite modernization, you still get a sense of the 18th-century origins of the building, which is next to the Luxembourg Gardens. The public areas reveal a rustic use of chiseled stone, some of it original. The high-ceilinged guest rooms are tasteful, sometimes with wooden furniture, often with upholstered headboards, and sometimes with Spanish-style wrought iron.

1 rue Casimir Delavigne, 75006 Paris. ✆ **01-43-29-31-50.** Fax 01-43-29-78-56. www.hotel delavigne.com. 34 units. 99€–230€ double; 130€–230€ triple. AE (accepted for Internet reservations only), MC, V. Métro: Odéon. **Amenities:** Babysitting; concierge; room service. *In room:* TV, hair dryer, Wi-Fi (free).

Hôtel Le Clément   This hotel sits on a narrow street within sight of the towers of St-Sulpice church. The building dates to the 1700s, but was renovated several years ago. Rooms are comfortably furnished but many are small.

6 rue Clément, 75006 Paris. ✆ **01-43-26-53-60.** Fax 01-44-07-06-83. www.hotelclementparis. com. 28 units. 123€–144€ double; 160€ suite. AE, DC, MC, V. Métro: Mabillon. **Amenities:** Bar; room service. *In room:* A/C, TV, fax, hair dryer, Wi-Fi (12€ for 2 hr.).

13th Arrondissement (Gare d'Austerlitz)
Moderate

Hôtel La Manufacture ★ 🎒   If you don't mind its offbeat 13th arrondissement location, this undiscovered hotel, with good rooms and decent prices, lying on a small street near place d'Italie, is a real find. It is only 10 minutes by Métro from the stations at Montparnasse and Gare de Lyon. Small to midsize bedrooms are decorated in printed fabrics and soothing pastels. The most desirable room is no. 74 because of its distant views of the Eiffel Tower. This restored 19th-century building has a wrought-iron door and is graced with iron lamps, wicker chairs, oak floors, and bright paintings. It contains a number of old-fashioned armoires called *chapeau de gendarme* (police hat).

8 rue Philippe de Champagne (av. des Gobelins), 75013 Paris. ☎ **01-45-35-45-25.** Fax 01-45-35-45-40. www.hotel-la-manufacture.com. 56 units. 145€–195€ double; 310€ triple. AE, DC, MC, V. Métro: Place d'Italie. **Amenities:** Bar; room service. *In room:* A/C, TV, hair dryer, Wi-Fi (10€ per 3 hr.).

INEXPENSIVE

Hôtel du Vert Galant   Verdant climbing plants and shrubs make this hotel feel like an *auberge* (inn) deep in the French countryside. The smallish guest rooms have tiled or carpeted floors, unfussy furniture, and (in most cases) views of the private garden or the public park across the street. One of the hotel's best aspects is the Basque restaurant next door, the Auberge Etchegorry, sharing the same management; hotel guests receive a discount.

41 rue Croulebarbe, 75013 Paris. ☎ **01-44-08-83-50.** Fax 01-44-08-83-69. www.vertgalant. com. 15 units. 95€–130€ double. AE, MC, V. Parking 15€. Métro: Corvisart or Gobelins. RER: Gare d'Austerlitz. **Amenities:** Restaurant; room service. *In room:* TV, hair dryer, minibar, Wi-Fi (free).

14th Arrondissement (Montparnasse)

INEXPENSIVE

Apollon Montparnasse   This privately owned hotel lies in Montparnasse, former home of such Left Bank residents as Gertrude Stein and Alice B. Toklas. Since opening in 1990, the hotel has established a reputation for its good rates and very comfortable bedrooms, which are midsize and furnished with flower spreads and draperies. The building was originally constructed in the 1930s as private apartments.

91 rue de l'Ouest, 75014 Paris. ☎ **01-43-95-62-00.** Fax 01-43-95-62-10. www.apollon-montparnasse.com. 33 units. 75€–132€ double. AE, DC, MC, V. Métro: Pernety. Parking 18€. **Amenities:** Room service. *In room:* A/C, TV, hair dryer, minibar, Wi-Fi (free).

Hôtel du Parc-Montsouris   The residential neighborhood is far removed from central Paris's bustle, the staff is a bit absent-minded, and the decor doesn't pretend to be stylish, but the prices are reasonable enough that this government-rated, two-star hotel attracts loyal repeat guests. They might be parents of students studying at the nearby Cité Universitaire or provincial clothiers attending fashion shows at the nearby Porte de Versailles. The guest rooms are low-key and quiet. Singles and doubles are small, but the triples are spacious, the apartments even more so. Most bathrooms contain tubs and showers, except for the seven with showers only.

4 rue du Parc de Montsouris, 75014 Paris. ☎ **01-45-89-09-72.** Fax 01-45-80-92-72. www.hotel-parc-montsouris.com. 35 units. 69€–81€ double; 79€–91€ triple; from 89€ family room. AE, DC, MC, V. Métro: Porte d'Orléans. RER: Cité-Universitaire. **Amenities:** Room service. *In room:* TV, hair dryer, Wi-Fi (free).

15th Arrondissement (Eiffel Tower)

MODERATE

Eiffel Seine ★   Rising on the banks of the Seine, this Art Nouveau–styled hotel lies only 5 minutes by foot from the Eiffel Tower. That Art Nouveau style pervades the hotel from the reception lounge to the personalized doubles and family rooms. Two ground floor rooms, opening onto an interior garden, are suited for persons with disabilities. Each room has its own special decoration, and the decor is harmonious from the tiles to the wallpaper to the mirrors and wall lamps. The famous Macintosh Rose theme recurs frequently. The quiet rooms are filled with modern technology as well as comfy beds.

3 bd. De Grenelle, 75015 Paris. ℂ **01-45-78-14-81.** Fax 01-45-79-46-95. www.paris-hotel-eiffel seine.com. 45 units. 180€–250€ double. MC, V. Métro: Bir Hakeim. **Amenities:** Exercise room. *In room:* A/C, TV, TV/DVD, room service, Wi-Fi (free).

7th Arrondissement (Eiffel Tower/ Musee d'Orsay)

VERY EXPENSIVE

Hôtel Le Bellechasse ★★ 🎁   Of all the fanciful designer hotels of Paris, this little hideaway, seconds on foot from the Musée d'Orsay, is the most daring and cutting-edge. It's the creation of couturier Christian Lacroix, who let his imagination go wild. A stay here is like wandering into a psychedelic garden. Each guest room is different in a pastiche of colors with baroque overtones. One French critic called Lacroix's designs "magpie sensibility," perhaps a reference to one room where top-hatted, frock-coated Paris dandies with butterfly wings wrap around both walls and ceilings. The helpful staff is part of the fun—that and taking a bath in a fiberglass tub.

8 rue de Bellechasse, 75007 Paris. ℂ **01-45-50-22-31.** Fax 01-45-51-52-36. www.lebellechasse. com. 34 units. 340€–390€ double. MC, V. Métro: Solferino. RER: Musée d'Orsay. **Amenities:** Dining room (breakfast). *In room:* A/C, TV, TV/DVD, CD player, hair dryer, minibar, MP3 docking station, Wi-Fi (free).

Hôtel Montalembert ★★   Unusually elegant for the Left Bank, the Montalembert dates from 1926, when it was built in the Beaux Arts style. Its beige, cream, and gold decor borrows elements of Bauhaus and postmodern design. The guest rooms are spacious except for some standard doubles that are small unless you're a very thin model. Frette linens decorate roomy beds topped with cabana-stripe duvets that crown deluxe French mattresses.

3 rue de Montalembert, 75007 Paris. ℂ **800/786-6397** in the U.S. and Canada, or 01-45-49-68-68. Fax 01-45-49-69-49. www.montalembert.com. 56 units. 410€–520€ double; 650€–900€ suite. AE, DC, MC, V. Parking 33€. Métro: Rue du Bac. **Amenities:** Restaurant; bar; concierge; access to nearby health club; room service. *In room:* A/C, TV, hair dryer, minibar, Wi-Fi (29€).

EXPENSIVE

Bourgogne & Montana   Across from the Palais Bourbon and just 2 blocks from the Seine, this boutique hotel resides in the same tony neighborhood as famous Parisian residents such as Karl Lagerfeld. It is only a short walk to the landmark place du Palais-Bourbon and the boulevard St-Germain. A six-floor hotel, the building itself dates from 1791. Two of the bedrooms open onto the Grand Palais or the Assemblée Nationale. A 1924 cage elevator takes visitors to the accommodations, which are midsize for the most part, although some are small and have no view whatsoever. Each room is individually decorated, often in Empire style or with Empire reproductions.

3 rue de Bourgogne, 75007 Paris. ℂ **01-45-51-20-22.** Fax 01-45-56-11-98. www.bourgogne montana.com. 32 units. 190€–290€ double; 360€–380€ junior suite. Rates include breakfast. AE, DC, MC, V. Métro: Invalides. **Amenities:** Bar; babysitting; room service. *In room:* A/C, TV, hair dryer, minibar, Wi-Fi (free).

Hôtel de l'Académie ★★   The exterior walls and old ceiling beams are all that remain of this 18th-century residence of the duc de Rohan's private guards. Other than its associations with the duc de Rohan, this place is locally famous for having housed poet and novelist Antonio Marchado, "the Victor Hugo of Spain," between 1909 and 1914. Guest rooms have a lush Ile-de-France decor and views over the neighborhood's 18th- and 19th-century buildings. By American standards, the rooms are small, but they're average for Paris.

32 rue des Sts-Pères, 75007 Paris. ℂ **800/246-0041** in the U.S. and Canada, or 01-45-49-80-00. Fax 01-45-44-75-24. www.academiehotel.com. 34 units. 199€–259€ double; from 299€ junior suite. AE, DC, MC, V. Parking 23€. Métro: St-Germain-des-Prés. **Amenities:** Babysitting; room service. *In room:* A/C, TV, hair dryer, minibar, Wi-Fi (free).

Hôtel de l'Université ★   Long favored by well-heeled parents facade of North American students studying in Paris, this 300-year-old, antiques-filled town house enjoys a location in a discreetly upscale neighborhood. Room no. 54 is a favorite, containing a rattan bed, period pieces, and a terrace. Another charmer is room no. 35, which has a nonworking fireplace and opens onto a courtyard with a fountain. Beds have plush comfort and discreet French styling. You'll sleep well here.

22 rue de l'Université, 75007 Paris. ℂ **01-42-61-09-39.** Fax 01-42-60-40-84. www.hoteluniversite. com. 27 units. 175€–215€ double. AE, DC, MC, V. Métro: St-Germain-des-Prés. **Amenities:** Room service; Wi-Fi (free). *In room:* A/C, TV, hair dryer, minibar, Wi-Fi (5€ per hr.).

Hôtel Le Tourville ★   This is a well-managed, personalized town house between the Eiffel Tower and Les Invalides. It originated in the 1930s as a hotel and was revitalized much later into the charmer of today. Bedrooms offer original art, antique furnishings or reproductions, and wooden furniture covered in modern, sometimes bold, upholsteries. Four of the rooms, including the suite, have private terraces. Beds are queens or twins, each of which was recently replaced. The staff is well trained, with the kinds of personalities that make you want to linger at the reception desk. Breakfast is the only meal served, but you can get a drink in the lobby.

16 av. de Tourville, 75007 Paris. ℂ **01-47-05-62-62.** Fax 01-47-05-43-90. www.hoteltourville. com. 30 units. 126€–270€ double; 245€–470€ suite. AE, MC, V. Métro: Ecole Militaire. **Amenities:** Bar; room service. *In room:* A/C, TV, hair dryer, Wi-Fi (5€ per 45 min.).

MODERATE

Derby Eiffel   This hotel faces the Ecole Militaire and contains airy public areas. Our favorite is a glass-roofed conservatory in back, filled with plants and used as a breakfast area. The soundproof and modern guest rooms employ thick fabrics and soothing neutral colors. Most front-facing rooms have views of the Eiffel Tower. In 1998, enormous sums were spent upgrading the rooms and bathrooms and improving the hotel's interior aesthetics, and renovations have been going on ever since.

5 av. Duquesne, 75007 Paris. ℂ **01-47-05-12-05.** www.hotelsderby.com. Fax 01-47-05-43-43. 43 units. 135€–155€ double; from 196€ triple. AE, DC, MC, V. Métro: Ecole Militaire. **Amenities:** Bar; babysitting; room service. *In room:* A/C, TV, hair dryer, minibar, Wi-Fi (5€).

Hôtel de Londres Eiffel   Small and charming, this independently run hotel is just a 2-minute walk from the Eiffel Tower. Completely renovated, it is "dressed" in colors of yellow and raspberry, which is far more harmonious and elegant than

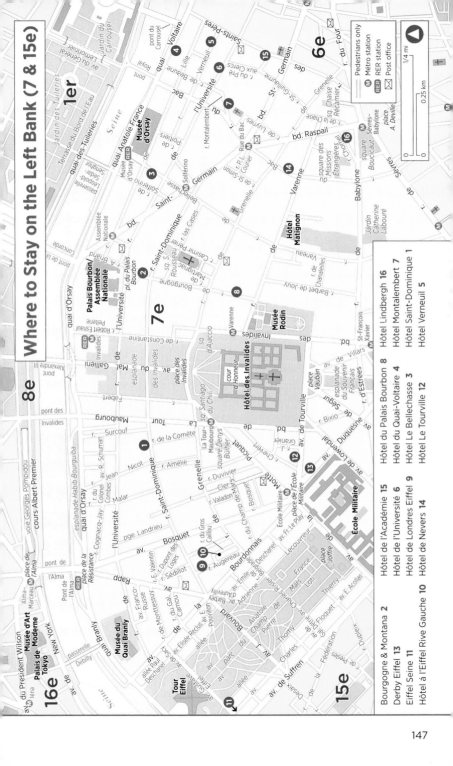

Where to Stay on the Left Bank (7e & 15e)

Bourgogne & Montana **2**
Derby Eiffel **13**
Eiffel Seine **11**
Hôtel à l'Eiffel Rive Gauche **10**

Hôtel de l'Académie **15**
Hôtel de l'Université **6**
Hôtel de Londres Eiffel **9**
Hôtel de Nevers **14**

Hôtel du Palais Bourbon **8**
Hôtel du Quai-Voltaire **4**
Hôtel Le Bellechasse **3**
Hôtel Le Tourville **12**

Hôtel Lindbergh **16**
Hôtel Montalembert **7**
Hôtel Saint-Dominique **1**
Hôtel Verneuil **5**

Pedestrians only
Ⓜ Métro station
ᴿᴱᴿ RER station
⊠ Post office

0   0.25 km
0   ¼ mi

147

the combination sounds. In a residential district (one of the best in Paris), the bedrooms are midsize and tastefully decorated, each with an individual decor. The top floors open onto views of the illuminated Eiffel Tower at night.

1 rue Augereau, 75007 Paris. ☎ **01-45-51-63-02.** Fax 01-47-05-28-96. www.londres-eiffel.com. 30 units. 185€–220€ double; 380€ suite. AE, DC, MC. Parking 34€. Métro: Ecole Militaire. *In room:* A/C, TV, hair dryer, minibar, Wi-Fi (free).

Hôtel du Quai Voltaire   Built in the 1600s as an abbey and transformed into a hotel in 1856, the Quai Voltaire is best known for such illustrious guests as Wilde, Richard Wagner, and Baudelaire, who occupied room nos. 47, 55, and 56, respectively. Camille Pissarro painted *Le Pont Royal* from the window of his fourth-floor room. Guest rooms in this modest inn were renovated in 2008; most overlook the bookstalls and boats of the Seine.

19 quai Voltaire, 75007 Paris. ☎ **01-42-61-50-91.** Fax 01-42-61-62-26. www.quaivoltaire.fr. 33 units. 150€–160€ double; 180€ triple. AE, DC, MC, V. Parking 14€. Métro: Musée d'Orsay or Rue du Bac. **Amenities:** Bar; room service. *In room:* Hair dryer, Wi-Fi (free).

Hôtel Verneuil ★ 🎒   Small-scale and personal, this hotel, in the words of a critic, "combines modernist sympathies with nostalgia for *la vieille France* old-fashioned France." Built in the 1600s as a town house, it is a creative and intimate jumble of charm and coziness inside. Expect a mixture of antique and contemporary furniture; lots of books; and, in the bedrooms, *trompe l'oeil* ceilings, antique beams, quilts, and walls covered in fabric that comes in a rainbow of colors.

8 rue de Verneuil, 75007 Paris. ☎ **01-42-60-82-14.** Fax 01-42-61-40-38. www.hotelverneuil. com. 26 units. 144€–240€ double. AE, DC, MC, V. Métro: St-Germain-des-Prés. **Amenities:** Bar; babysitting; room service. *In room:* A/C (in some), TV, hair dryer, minibar, Wi-Fi (free).

INEXPENSIVE

Hôtel à l'Eiffel Rive Gauche   The charm of this family-owned and -run, intimate hotel derives from a very small on-site team and the sense that you've entered a distinctive universe that's very closely linked to the surrounding upscale residential neighborhood. Built around 1900, the hotel retains such original touches as the black-and-white, checkerboard-patterned floor tiles from the 1930s. Bedrooms are outfitted in tones of off-white and dark bordeaux, with vaguely French Empire themes scattered with some angular furniture from the 1960s and 1970s. The hotel lies on a tranquil street in the heart of the so-called Triangle (Eiffel, Invalides, and Champs-Elysées).

6 rue du Gros Caillou, 75007 Paris. ☎ **01-45-51-51-51.** Fax 01-45-51-11-77. www.hotel-eiffel.com. 29 units. 105€–155€ double; 115€–175€ triple; 135€–205€ quad. MC, V. Métro: Ecole Militaire. *In room:* TV, fridge, hair dryer, Wi-Fi (free).

Hôtel de Nevers   This is one of the neighborhood's most historic choices—it was a convent from 1627 to 1790. Although the hotel has been renovated and upgraded through the years, the building is *classé,* meaning any restoration must respect the original architecture. That precludes an elevator, so you'll have to use the beautiful wrought-iron staircase. The cozy, pleasant guest rooms contain a mix of antique and reproduction furniture. Room nos. 10 and 11 are especially sought after for their terraces overlooking a corner of rue du Bac or a rear courtyard. About half the units have tub/shower combinations.

83 rue du Bac, 75007 Paris. ☎ **01-45-44-61-30.** Fax 01-42-22-29-47. www.hoteldenevers-saint germain.net. 11 units. 99€–139€ double. MC, V. Métro: Rue du Bac. **Amenities:** Room service. *In room:* TV, hair dryer, Wi-Fi (20€ per 5 hr.).

Hôtel du Palais Bourbon   The solid stone walls of this 18th-century building aren't as grand as those of the embassies and stately homes nearby. But don't be put off by the tight entranceway and rather dark halls: Though the guest rooms on the upper floors are larger, all the rooms are pleasantly decorated, with carefully crafted built-in furniture.

49 rue de Bourgogne, 75007 Paris. ☎ **01-44-11-30-70.** Fax 01-45-55-20-21. www.hotel-palais-bourbon.com. 29 units. 190€ double; 225€ triple; 180€–235€ quad. Rates include breakfast. MC, V. Métro: Varenne. **Amenities:** Room service. *In room:* A/C, TV, hair dryer, minibar, Wi-Fi (free).

Hôtel Lindbergh   A 5-minute walk from St-Germain-des-Prés, this hotel provides streamlined, simple guest rooms. About two-thirds of the bathrooms contain tubs as well as showers. Breakfast is the only meal served, but the staff will point out good restaurants nearby—an inexpensive bistro, Le Cigale, is quite close.

5 rue Chomel, 75007 Paris. ☎ **01-45-48-35-53.** Fax 01-45-49-31-48. www.hotellindbergh.com. 26 units. 126€–160€ double; 180€ triple. AE, DC, MC, V. Parking 26€. Métro: Sèvres-Babylone or St-Sulpice. **Amenities:** Room service. *In room:* TV, hair dryer, Internet (free).

Hôtel Saint-Dominique   Part of this place's charm derives from its division into three buildings connected through an open-air courtyard. The most visible of these is an 18th-century convent—you can still see its ceiling beams and structural timbers in the reception area. The guest rooms aren't large, but each is warm and simply decorated.

62 rue St-Dominique, 75007 Paris. ☎ **01-47-05-51-44.** Fax 01-47-05-81-28. www.hotelst dominique.com. 37 units. 101€–158€ double; 132€–178€ triple. AE, MC, V. Métro: Latour-Maubourg or Invalides. **Amenities:** Room service. *In room:* TV, hair dryer, minibar, Wi-Fi (5€ per hr.).

NEAR THE AIRPORTS
Orly
MODERATE

Hilton Paris Orly Airport ★   Boxy and bland, the Hilton at Orly is a well-maintained, especially convenient business hotel. Noise from incoming planes can't penetrate the guest rooms' sound barriers, giving you a decent shot at a night's sleep. (Unlike the 24-hr. Charles de Gaulle Airport, Orly is closed to arriving flights from midnight to 6am.) The midsize rooms are standard for a chain hotel; each has been renovated.

Aéroport Orly, 267 Orly Sud, 94544 Orly Aérogare Cedex. ☎ **800/445-8667** in the U.S. and Canada, or 01-45-12-45-12. Fax 01-45-12-45-00. www.hilton.com. 351 units. 90€–250€ double; 300€ suite. AE, DC, MC, V. Parking 14€. Transit to and from airport by complimentary shuttle bus. **Amenities:** Restaurant; bar; babysitting; concierge; exercise room; room service. *In room:* A/C, TV, TV/DVD player, hair dryer, Wi-Fi (17€ per 12 hr.).

INEXPENSIVE

Air Plus   Also boxy and contemporary-looking, and connected with Orly by frequent 10-minute complimentary shuttle-bus rides, this 1990s hotel offers standard bedrooms. Rooms are comfortable, insulated against airport noise, and a bit larger than you might expect. The location is in a leafy residential zone.

58 voie Nouvelle (near the Parc Georges Méllès), 94310 Orly. ✆ **01-41-80-75-75.** Fax 01-41-80-12-12. airplus@club-internet.fr. 72 units. 82€ double. AE, DC, MC, V. Free parking. Transit to and from airport by complimentary shuttle bus. **Amenities:** Restaurant; room service. *In room:* A/C, TV, hair dryer, Wi-Fi (free).

Charles De Gaulle

MODERATE

Hyatt Regency Paris–Charles de Gaulle ★   This property is adjacent to the Charles de Gaulle Airport. Lying only a 25-minute drive from Disneyland Paris and a half-hour from the attractions of central Paris, the Roissy property was designed by the renowned architect Helmut Jahn. He created a stunning five-story structure of sleek design and tech-smart features. Inaugurated in 1994, this is the first hotel of its size to be built in Paris since 1975, and as airport hotels go, the cutting-edge architecture puts it in a class by itself with its spectacular glass atrium overlooking the lobby. Jet-lagged passengers find ultimate comfort in the elegantly furnished and soundproof guest rooms, which meld American convenience with European style.

351 av. du Bois de la Pie, 95912 Roissy. ✆ **01-48-17-12-34.** Fax 01-48-17-17-17. www.paris.charles degaulle.hyatt.fr. 388 units. 155€–255€ double; 265€–400€ suite. AE, DC, MC, V. RER-B train to its final destination (Aéroport Charles de Gaulle-Terminal Two). From there, take the hotel's shuttle bus (departures every 20 min.) directly to the hotel. Parking 29€. Free shuttle to and from airport. **Amenities:** Restaurant; bar; babysitting; concierge; exercise room; pool (indoor); room service; 2 tennis courts. *In room:* A/C, TV, TV/DVD, hair dryer, minibar, Wi-Fi (22€).

Pullman Paris Aéroport CDG ★   Many travelers pass happily through this bustling, somewhat anonymous member of the French chain. It employs a multilingual staff accustomed to accommodating international business travelers. The conservatively furnished guest rooms are soundproof havens against the all-night roar of jets. Suites are larger and more comfortable, although they are not especially elegant and are consistent with the chain format.

Aéroport Charles de Gaulle, Zone Central, 20248, 95713 Roissy. ✆ **800/221-4542** in the U.S. and Canada, or 01-49-19-29-29. Fax 01-49-19-29-00. www.sofitel.com. 350 units. 140€–370€ double; 450€–1,100€ suite. AE, DC, MC, V. Parking 12€. Free shuttle to and from airport. **Amenities:** Restaurant; bar; concierge; exercise room; room service. *In room:* A/C, TV, hair dryer, minibar, Wi-Fi (9.90€).

INEXPENSIVE

Hôtel Campanile de Roissy   This hotel is less expensive than most other lodgings near the airport. Its cement-and-glass design is barely masked by a thin overlay of cheerful-looking and rustic artifacts. Generally, this is an efficiently decorated, but not particularly stylish, place to stay, with a well-meaning but overworked staff.

Parc de Roissy, 95700 Val-d'Oise. ✆ **01-34-29-80-40.** Fax 01-34-29-80-39. www.campanile.fr. 258 units. 91€–131€ double. AE, DC, MC, V. Free shuttle to and from airport. **Amenities:** Restaurant; bar. *In room:* TV, hair dryer, Wi-Fi (free).

WHERE TO DINE

W elcome to the city that prides itself on being the world's culinary capital. Only in Paris can you turn onto the nearest little crooked side street; enter the first nondescript bistro you see; sit down at a bare, wobbly table; order from an illegibly hand-scrawled menu; and get a wonderfully memorable meal.

See below for a list of our favorites: the best chef, the best view, the best old-fashioned bistro, and more.

BEST DINING BETS

- **Best Chef:** Proud owner of six Michelin stars, **Alain Ducasse,** at the Restaurant Plaza Athénée, 25 av. Montaigne, 8e (✆ **01-53-67-65-00;** www.alain-ducasse.com), has taken Paris by storm, dividing his time between his restaurant here and one in Monte Carlo. He combines produce from every French region in a cuisine that's contemporary but not quite new, embracing the Mediterranean without abandoning France. See p. 177.

- **Best Modern French Cuisine:** A temple of gastronomy is found at **Carré des Feuillants,** 14 rue de Castiglione, 1er (✆ **01-42-86-82-82;** www.carredesfeuillants.fr), near place Vendôme and the Tuileries. Alain Dutournier is one of the leading chefs of France, and he restored this 17th-century convent, turning it into a citadel of refined cuisine and mouthwatering specialties. See p. 158.

- **Best Provençal Cuisine:** Olympe Versini earned a Michelin star at the age of 29 and dazzled some of the most discerning palates in Paris before opening her unassuming **Casa Olympe,** 48 rue St-Georges, 9e (✆ **01-42-85-26-01;** www.casaolympe.com). Critics laud the earthiness of her cooking and her deft execution of time-honored dishes. See p. 171.

- **Best Old-Fashioned Bistro:** Established in 1931 and bouncing back from a period of decline, **Allard,** 41 rue St-André-des-Arts, 6e (✆ **01-42-63-48183**), is better than ever, from its zinc bar to its repertoire of French classics—escargot, frogs' legs, foie gras, *boeuf à la mode* (marinated beef), and cassoulet. This is a good bet for real Left Bank bistro ambience. See p. 197.

- **Best for Romance:** There is no more romantic atmosphere among restaurants than the long-established **Le Grand Véfour,** 17 rue de Beaujolais, 1er (✆ **01-42-96-56-27**). When Aristotle Onassis was wooing Jackie Kennedy, he took her here, preferring to dine with his mistress, Maria Callas, at the "more vulgar" Maxim's. Sublime dishes are served against a restaurant decor that was established during the reign of Louis XV. See p. 159.

- **Best Brasserie:** Head for the Left Bank and the **Brasserie Balzar,** 49 rue des Ecoles, 5e (✆ **01-43-54-13-67;** www.brasseriebalzar.com), which

PREVIOUS PAGE: **Tradition is alive and well among Paris's waiters.**

opened in 1898. If you dine on the familiar French food here, you'll be following in the footsteps of Sartre, Camus, and others. You can even have a complete dinner in the middle of the afternoon. See p. 190.

o **Best Seafood:** The fattest lobsters and prawns from the Rungis market emerge on platters at **Goumard,** 9 rue Duphot, 1er (© **01-42-60-36-07;** www.goumard.com), so chic that even the toilets are historic monuments. Nothing interferes with the taste of the sea: You'd have to fly to the Riviera to find a better bouillabaisse. See p. 162.

o **Best Kosher Food:** If corned beef, pastrami, herring, and dill pickles thrill you, head to **rue des Rosiers** in the 4th arrondissement (Métro: St-Paul). John Russell wrote that rue des Rosiers is the "last sanctuary of certain ways of life; what you see there in miniature is Warsaw before the ghetto was razed." North-African overtones reflect the long-ago arrival of Jews from Morocco, Tunisia, and Algeria. The best time to go is Sunday morning: You can wander the streets, eating as you go—apple strudel; Jewish rye bread; pickled lemons; smoked salmon; and *merguez,* a spicy smoked sausage from Algeria (See "Walking Tour 3: The Marais" on p. 308.)

o **Best Wine Cellar:** At the elegant **Lasserre,** 17 av. Franklin D. Roosevelt, 8e (© **01-43-59-02-13;** www.restaurant-lasserre.com), you'll find not only wonderful food, but also one of the great wine cellars of France, with some 160,000 bottles. See p. 176.

FOOD FOR THOUGHT

WHAT'S COOKING IN FRANCE   When you arrive in Paris, you'll find that the word "French," although used frequently, isn't very helpful in describing cuisine. "French" covers such a broad scope that it doesn't prepare you for the offerings of the specialty chefs. Even Parisians themselves might ask, "What *type* of French cooking?"

Sometimes a chef will include regional specialties, classic dishes, and even modern cuisine all on one menu. In that case, such a restaurant is truly "French." Other chefs prefer a more narrow focus and feature the cooking of one region or one style—classic or modern. Still others prefer to strike a middle ground between classic and modern; they're called "creative."

Regional cuisine showcases the diversity of the provinces of France, from Alsace on the German border to the Basque country at the frontier of Spain. The climate has a lot to do with these diversified offerings—olive oil, garlic, and tomatoes from Provence in the south to oysters and saltwater fish from Brittany. Every region is known for special dishes—Burgundy for its escargots plucked off the grapevines; Périgord for its truffles and foie gras; Normandy for its soft, rich cheeses, Calvados brandy, and cream sauces; and Alsace for its sauerkraut and wines. Today, one or more restaurants in Paris represent almost every region of France. You can go on a complete culinary tour of the country without leaving the city.

Few chefs today use the expression ***nouvelle cuisine,*** now called ***modern.*** This cooking style, which burst upon us in the early 1970s, is now old hat (or should we say old *toque?*). It was a rebellion against the fats, butter, and sauces of haute cuisine, and used reductions of foodstuff to create flavor, along with vegetable purées and lighter ingredients. Portions were reduced. Diners were shocked to see a piece of *boeuf* (beef) the size of an egg on their plate under a slice of fresh kiwi. Created in the name of innovation, many of these dishes were successful, while others, such as asparagus ice cream, were dismal failures.

From nouvelle cuisine grew **cuisine improvisée,** which is creative cookery based on the freshest ingredients available. Chefs make their selections at the morning market and then rush back to their kitchens to create spontaneously, often while dictating the menu of the day to an assistant who rushes it into print.

But fans of the great chef Escoffier can rest assured that modern hasn't replaced **classic cuisine**—France is still awash in béchamel and ablaze with cognac. *Haute gastronomie* is alive and thriving at restaurants not only in Paris, but also throughout France. This richly extravagant fare is often lethal in price as it makes use of expensive ingredients, including fatted ducks, lobster, truffles, and plenty of butter and cream, plus sauces that consume endless time in their preparation. Breaking from Escoffier, many chefs today have forged ahead with a **new classic cuisine,** in which they have taken classic dishes and branded them with their own distinctive style and flavor, often reducing the calories.

PARIS'S RANGE OF RESTAURANTS   Paris boasts a surplus of restaurants and cafes. Ultra-expensive **temples of gastronomy** include Alain Ducasse, L'Astor, Taillevent, Pierre Gagnaire, Lasserre, Jacques Cagna, Le Grand Véfour, and La Tour d'Argent. Savvy diners confine their trips to luxe places for special occasions. An array of other choices awaits, including simpler restaurants dispensing cuisine from every province of France and its former colonies such as Morocco and Algeria.

Paris has hundreds of restaurants serving exotic **international fare,** reflecting the changing complexion of Paris itself and the city's increasing appreciation for food from other cultures. Your most memorable meal in Paris may turn out to be Vietnamese or West African.

You'll also find hundreds of bistros, brasseries, and cafes. In modern times, their designations and roles have become almost meaningless. Traditionally, a **bistro** was a small restaurant, often with Mom at the cash register and Pop in the kitchen. Menus are most often handwritten or mimeographed, and the selection of dishes tends to be small. Menus can be chic and elegant, sometimes heavily Mediterranean, and often dispensing gutsy fare, including the *pot-au-feu* (beef simmered with vegetables) that the chef's grandmother prepared for him as a kid.

 Mystifying Menu?

If you need help distinguishing a *boeuf à la mode* from a *crème brûlée,* see "Basic Menu Terms" in chapter 13.

French for "brewery," most **brasseries** have an Alsatian connection, and that means lots of beer, although Alsatian wines are also featured. Brasseries are almost always brightly lit and open 24 hours. Both snacks and full meals are available. The Alsatian establishments serve sauerkraut with an array of pork products.

The **cafe** is a French institution and not just a place for an aperitif, a café au lait, or a croissant. Many cafes serve rib-sticking fare as well,

dining SAVOIR-FAIRE

- Most restaurants serve lunch between noon and 2:30pm and dinner from 7 to 10pm. In a cafe, if you stand at the bar for a drink, coffee, or sandwich, prices are reduced from what they would be if you were seated at a table.

- French cookery reaches perfection when accompanied by wine. The general label on bottles of national wine is known as *Appellation d'Origine Contrôllée* (abbreviated AOC). Wine labels are narrowed down to a particular vine-growing region. Of course, labels are only part of the story: It's the vintage that counts. Some of the most satisfying wines come from unlabeled house bottles or carafes, called *vin de la maison.* They're also the cheapest wines served. Some restaurants include a beverage in their fixed-price menu *(boisson compris).* French beers are cheaper than imported beers. One of the best French beers has a German sounding name. It's Kronenbourg, and it's bottled in Alsace.

- Three-star dining remains quite expensive, with appetizers sometimes priced at 60€ and dinners easily costing 185€ to 250€ per person in the top dining rooms of celebrated chefs. But you can get around that high price tag in many places by **dining at lunch** (when prices are always cheaper) or ordering a prix-fixe meal at lunch or dinner.

- The **prix-fixe (fixed-price) menu** or *le menu* is a set meal that the chef prepares that day. It is most often fresh and promptly served, and represents a greater bargain than dining a la carte. Of course, it's limited, so you'll have to like the choices provided. Sometimes there are one to three menus, beginning with the least expensive and going up for a more elaborate meal. A lot depends on your pocketbook and appetite.

- In France, **lunch** (as well as dinner) tends to be a full-course meal with meat, vegetables, salad, bread, cheese, dessert, wine, and coffee. It may be difficult to find a restaurant that serves the type of light lunch North Americans usually eat. Cafes, however, offer sandwiches, soup, and salads in a relaxed setting.

- **Coffee** in France is served after the meal and carries an extra charge. The French consider it barbaric to drink coffee during the meal. In more conscientious places, it's prepared as the traditional *café filtre,* a slow but rewarding java draw.

- In years gone by, no man would consider dining out, even at the neighborhood bistro, without a suit and tie, and no woman would be seen without a smart dress or suit. That **dress code** is more relaxed now, except in first-class and luxe establishments. Relaxed doesn't mean sloppy jeans and jogging attire, however. Parisians still value style, even when dressing informally.

- Sometimes service is added to your tab—usually 12% to 15%. If not, look for the words *service non compris* on your bill. That means that the cost of service was not added, and you'll be expected to leave a **tip.**

certainly entrecôte (rib steak) with french fries, but often classics such as *blanquette de veau* (veal in white sauce). For more cafe lore, see, "The Top Cafes," later in this chapter.

More attention in the late 1990s focused on the **wine bar,** a host of which we recommend in chapter 10, "Paris After Dark." Originally, wine bars concentrated on their lists of wines, featuring many esoteric choices and ignoring the food except for some charcuterie (cold cuts) and cheeses. Today, you're likely to be offered various daily specials, from homemade foie gras to *boeuf à la mode* (marinated beef braised with red wine and served with vegetables).

Paris prices may seem extravagant to visitors from other parts of the world, particularly those who don't live in big cities, but there has been an emergence of moderately priced **informal restaurants** here, and we recommend several.

Although not as fashionable as before, **baby bistros** are still around. At these reasonably priced spinoffs from deluxe restaurants, you can get a taste of the cuisine of famous chefs without breaking the bank. We cover the best of them.

RESTAURANTS BY CUISINE

ALGERIAN
Wally Le Saharien (**$$**, p. 171)
ALSATIAN
Bofinger ★ (**$$**, p. 169)
Brasserie Flo (**$$**, p. 172)
Chez Jenny (**$**, p. 167)
AMERICAN
Breakfast in America (**$**, p. 195)
Joe Allen ★ (**$$**, p. 163)
ASIAN
Cabaret (**$$**, p. 163)
Kambodgia (**$**, p. 187)
Le Pré Verre ★ (**$$**, p. 191)
AUVERGNAT
Chez Savy ★ (**$**, p. 184)
L'Ambassade d'Auvergne ★
 (**$**, p. 168)
BASQUE
Afaria ★ (**$**, p. 208)
Au Bascou ★ (**$**, p. 167)
Auberge Etchegorry (**$$**, p. 200)
Chez Gladines (**$**, p. 201)
Chez l'Ami Jean (**$**, p. 208)
BRETON
Chez Michel (**$$**, p. 172)
CAFES
Café Beaubourg (**$$**, p. 210)
Café de Flore ★★ (**$$$**, p. 209)
Café de la Musique (**$$**, p. 210)

Café des Deux Moulins (**$**, p. 212)
Fouquet's ★ (**$$$**, p. 210)
La Belle Hortense (**$$**, p. 210)
La Coupole ★ (**$$**, p. 211)
La Palette ★★ (**$$**, p. 211)
La Rotonde (**$$**, p. 211)
Le Procope ★★ (**$$**, p. 211)
Le Rouquet ★ (**$**, p. 212)
Les Deux Magots ★★ (**$$**, p. 212)
CAMBODIAN
Kambodgia (**$**, p. 187)
CANTONESE
Chez Vong ★ (**$$$**, p. 159)
CHINESE
Yam' 'Tcha (**$$**, p. 164)
CORSICAN
Casa Olympe ★★ (**$$**, p. 171)
FRENCH (MODERN)
Alcazar Restaurant ★ (**$$**, p. 197)
Bofinger (**$$**, p. 169)
Cabaret (**$$**, p. 163)
Café Panique ★ (**$**, p. 173)
Carré des Feuillants ★★★
 (**$$$$**, p. 158)
Citrus Etoile ★ (**$$**, p. 183)
Cristal Room ★★ (**$$$**, p. 185)
Jacques Cagna ★★★
 (**$$$$**, p. 195)

KEY TO ABBREVIATIONS:
$$$$** = Very Expensive **$$$** = Expensive **$$** = Moderate **$ = Inexpensive

L'Absinthe (**$$**, p. 163)
La Famille ★ (**$$$**, p. 176)
L'Arpège ★★★ (**$$$$**, p. 204)
Lasserre ★★★ (**$$$$**, p. 176)
L'Assiette (**$$**, p. 202)
L'Astrance ★★★ (**$$$**, p. 185)
Le Chateaubriand ★ (**$**, p. 174)
Le Dalí ★ (**$$$**, p. 162)
Le Relais du Parc ★★ (**$$$**, p. 186)
Les Ombres ★ (**$$$**, p. 204)
Le Violon d'Ingres ★★★
 (**$$$**, p. 205)
Marty ★ (**$$**, p. 194)
Michel Rostang ★★★ (**$$$$**, p. 188)
Pierre Gagnaire ★★★ (**$$$$**, p. 177)
Publicis Drugstore (**$$**, p. 184)
Restaurant de l'Astor ★ (**$$$**, p. 181)
Restaurant du Musée d'Orsay ★
 (**$$**, p. 205)
Restaurant Plaza Athénée (Alain
 Ducasse) ★★★ (**$$$$**, p. 177)
Sensing ★★ (**$$$**, p. 196)
1728 ★ (**$$$**, p. 182)
Taillevent ★★★ (**$$$$**, p. 180)
Tokyo Eat (**$$**, p. 187)
Ze Kitchen Galerie ★ (**$$**, p. 198)

FRENCH (TRADITIONAL)
Allard ★ (**$$**, p. 197)
Angélina ★★ (**$**, p. 164)
Au Petit Monsieur (**$$**, p. 173)
Au Petit Riche ★ (**$$**, p. 170)
Au Pied de Cochon ★★ (**$$**, p. 162)
Au Pied de Fouet (**$**, p. 207)
Aux Charpentiers (**$**, p. 199)
Aux Lyonnais ★ (**$$**, p. 166)
Bar des Théâtres ★ (**$**, p. 184)
Benoit ★ (**$$$**, p. 168)
Bofinger ★ (**$$**, p. 169)
Brasserie Balzar ★ (**$$**, p. 190)
Chartier (**$**, p. 171)
Chez André (**$$**, p. 182)
Chez Georges (**$$**, p. 166, 188)
Chez Gramond ★ (**$$**, p. 197)
Chez Jean ★ (**$$**, p. 171)
Chez Ramulaud ★ (**$$**, p. 173)
Closerie des Lilas ★ (**$$$**, p. 196)
Crémerie-Restaurant Polidor ★
 (**$**, p. 199)
Guy Savoy ★★★ (**$$$$**, p. 187)
Hiramatsu ★ (**$$$$**, p. 185)

Itineraire (**$**, p. 191)
Jacques Cagna ★★★ (**$$$$**, p. 195)
Jadis (**$$**, p. 208)
La Butte Chaillot ★ (**$$**, p. 187)
La Cagouille ★ (**$$**, p. 201)
La Cigale Récamier (**$$**, p. 205)
La Crèmerie (**$**, p. 199)
Ladurée ★ (**$$**, p. 183)
La Fontaine de Mars ★ (**$$$**, p. 204)
La Grille (**$$**, p. 172)
La Maison Blanche ★★
 (**$$$**, p. 180)
L'Ambassade d'Auvergne ★
 (**$**, p. 168)
L'Ambroisie ★ (**$$$$**, p. 168)
L'Ami Louis ★ (**$$$**, p. 166)
L'Angle du Faubourg ★★
 (**$$$**, p. 180)
L'Avant Comptoir ★ (**$**, p. 200)
La Petite Chaise (**$$**, p. 205)
La Poule au Pot (**$$**, p. 163)
La Régalade (**$$**, p. 202)
La Rôtisserie d'en Face ★ (**$$**, p. 198)
Lasserre ★★★ (**$$$$**, p. 176)
La Tour d'Argent (**$$$$**, p. 190)
L'Avant Comptoir (**$**, p. 200)
L'Ebauchoir ★ (**$**, p. 175)
Le Cinq ★★★ (**$$$$**, p. 177)
Le Grand Véfour ★★★
 (**$$$$**, p. 159)
Le Hide ★ (**$**, p. 189)
Le Pamphlet ★ (**$$**, p. 167)
Le Petit Marguery ★ (**$$**, p. 200)
Le Petit Pontoise ★ (**$$**, p. 191)
Le Pré Verre ★ (**$$**, p. 191)
Le Pure Café (**$**, p. 174)
Le Severo ★ (**$$**, p. 202)
Le Timbre ★ (**$$**, p. 198)
Les Papilles (**$$$**, p. 193)
Le Vaudeville (**$$**, p. 166)
Les Gourmets des Ternes (**$$**, p. 183)
Mélac (**$**, p. 175)
Michel Rostang ★★★ (**$$$$**, p. 188)
Rech ★ (**$$$**, p. 188)
Restaurant Caïus ★ (**$$**, p. 189)
Restaurant Plaza Athénée (Alain
 Ducasse) ★★★ (**$$$$**, p. 177)
Ribouldingue (**$$**, p. 194)
Taillevent ★★★ (**$$$$**, p. 180)
Yam' 'Tcha (**$$**, p. 164)

FUSION
Market ★ ($$, p. 183)

GASCONY
Au Trou Gascon ★★★ ($$$, p. 175)

INDIAN
Yugaraj ($$, p. 198)

INTERNATIONAL
Juveniles ($, p. 164)
Georges ★ ($$, p. 169)
Le Fumoir ★ ($$, p. 164)
Le Louis II ★ ($$$, p. 181)
Les Ombres ★ ($$$, p. 204)
Spoon, Food & Wine ★ ($$$, p. 182)
Ze Kitchen Galerie ★ ($$, p. 198)

ITALIAN
L'Assaggio ★ ($$, p. 164)
La Vinoteca ★ ($$$, p. 181)

JAPANESE
1728 ★ ($$$, p. 182)

LATE NIGHT
Au Pied de Cochon ★★ ($$, p. 162)
La Poule au Pot ($$, p. 163)
Le Vaudeville ($$, p. 166)

LEBANESE
Al Dar ($$, p. 190)

LOIRE VALLEY (ANJOU)
Au Petit Riche ★ ($$, p. 170)

LYONNAIS
Aux Lyonnais ★ ($$, p. 166)

MEDITERRANEAN
L'Assaggio ★ ($$, p. 164)

MOROCCAN
Mansouria ($$, p. 174)

ORGANIC
Le Grain de Folie ($, p. 176)

POITEVINE
Le Petit Marguery ($$, p. 200)

PROVENÇAL
Casa Olympe ★★ ($$, p. 171)
Chez Janou ($, p. 167)
La Bastide Odéon ★ ($, p. 199)
La Maison Blanche ★★ ($$$, p. 180)

SCOTTISH
Juveniles ($, p. 165)

SEAFOOD
Goumard ★★★ ($$$, p. 162)
La Cagouille ★ ($$, p. 201)
La Grille ($$, p. 172)
Rech ★ ($$$, p. 188)

SENEGALESE
Le Manguier ($, p. 174)

SEYCHELLE ISLANDS
Coco de Mer ★ ($, p. 195)

SOUTHWESTERN FRENCH
Chez l'Ami Jean ($, p. 208)
La Braisière ★★ ($$, p. 189)
Le Béarn ($, p. 165)
Le Pamphlet ★ ($$, p. 167)
Pinxo ★ ($$, p. 164)
Restaurant d'Hélène/Salon d'Hélène
★★★ ($$$$, p. 196)

SPANISH
L'Avant Comptoir ($, p. 200)

TEA
Angélina ★★ ($, p. 165)

THAI
Blue Elephant ★ ($$$, p. 173)

VEGETARIAN
Le Grain de Folie ($, p. 176)

VIETNAMESE
Kim Anh ($$, p. 208)

ON THE RIGHT BANK

We begin with the most centrally located arrondissements on the Right Bank and then work our way through the more outlying neighborhoods and to the area around the Arc de Triomphe.

1st Arrondissement (Louvre/Les Halles)

VERY EXPENSIVE

Carré des Feuillants ★★★ MODERN FRENCH   This is a bastion of perfection, an enclave of haute gastronomy. When chef Alain Dutournier turned this 17th-century convent between the place Vendôme and the Tuileries into a restaurant, it was an overnight success. The interior is artfully simple and even, in

No matter how long you stay in Paris, we suggest you indulge in at least one break-the-bank French meal at a fabulous restaurant. It will be a memory you'll treasure long after you've recovered from paying the tab. However, to get a table at one of these places, *you must reserve far in advance*—at least a day or two ahead, sometimes even a few weeks or months ahead! We suggest you look over these listings and call for reservations before you leave home or at least as soon as you get into town.

the eyes of some diners, spartan-looking. It has a vaguely Asian feel, shared by a series of small, monochromatic dining rooms that are mostly outfitted in tones of off-white, black, and beige, and that overlook a flowering courtyard and a glass-enclosed kitchen. You'll find a sophisticated reinterpretation of cuisine from France's southwest, using seasonal ingredients and lots of know-how. Some of the best dishes include roasted rack of milk-fed Pyrenees lamb cooked in a clay pot, or slices of John Dory with potatoes and tender cabbage lasagna. Milk-fed veal with flap mushrooms and purple artichokes is yet another specialty. For dessert, try the mango and passion fruit ravioli.

14 rue de Castiglione (near place Vendôme and the Tuileries), 1er. ⓒ **01-42-86-82-82.** Fax 01-42-86-07-71. www.carredesfeuillants.fr. Reservations required far in advance. Main courses 62€–85€; fixed-price lunch 85€–175€; fixed-price dinner 175€. AE, DC, MC, V. Mon–Fri noon–2:30pm and 7:30–10pm. Closed Aug. Métro: Tuileries, Concorde, Opéra, or Madeleine.

Le Grand Véfour ★★★ TRADITIONAL FRENCH   This is the all-time winner: a great chef, the most beautiful restaurant decor in Paris, and a history-infused citadel of classic French cuisine. This restaurant has been around since the reign of Louis XV. Napoleon, Danton, Hugo, Colette, and Cocteau dined here—as the brass plaques on the tables testify—and it's still a gastronomic experience. Guy Martin, chef for the past decade, bases many items on recipes from the French Alps. He prepares such heavenly dishes as filet of lamb with wasabi, carved into rib sections and served with the smoked essence of its own juice. Other specialties are noisettes of lamb with star anise, Breton lobster with fennel, and cabbage sorbet in dark-chocolate sauce. The desserts are often grand, such as the *gourmandises au chocolat* (medley of chocolate), served with chocolate sorbet.

17 rue de Beaujolais, 1er. ⓒ **01-42-96-56-27.** Fax 01-42-86-80-71. www.grand-vefour.com. Reservations required far in advance. Main courses 75€–125€; fixed-price lunch 88€; fixed-price dinner 268€. AE, DC, MC, V. Mon–Fri 12:30–1:45pm; Mon–Thurs 8–9:30pm. Closed July 25–Aug 23. Métro: Louvre–Palais-Royal or Pyramides.

EXPENSIVE

Chez Vong ★ CANTONESE   This is the kind of Les Halles restaurant you head for when you've had your fill of grand cuisine and pretensions. The decor is a soothing mix of greens and browns, steeped in a Chinese-colonial ambience that evokes early-1900s Shanghai. The chef's specialty is lacquered Peking duck with shrimp. Other items feature shrimp and scallops served as spicy as you like, including a super-hot version with garlic and red peppers, chicken in puff pastry with ginger, and an array of fish dishes. The whims of fashion have deemed this

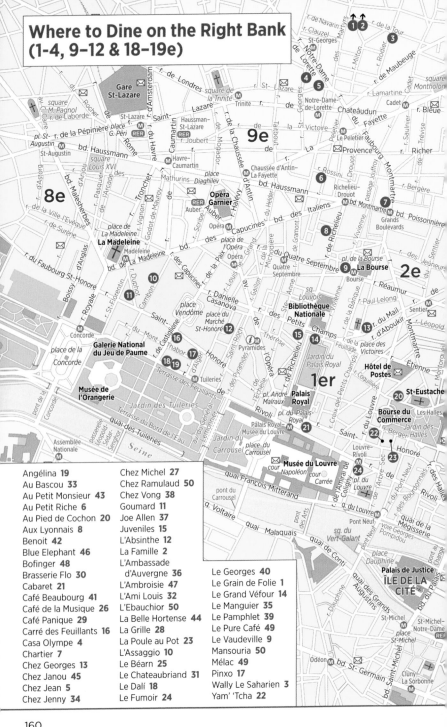

Where to Dine on the Right Bank (1–4, 9–12 & 18–19e)

Angélina **19**
Au Bascou **33**
Au Petit Monsieur **43**
Au Petit Riche **6**
Aux Lyonnais **8**
Benoit **42**
Blue Elephant **46**
Bofinger **48**
Brasserie Flo **30**
Cabaret **21**
Café Beaubourg **41**
Café de la Musique **26**
Café Panique **29**
Carré des Feuillants **16**
Casa Olympe **4**
Chartier **7**
Chez Georges **13**
Chez Janou **45**
Chez Jean **5**
Chez Jenny **34**

Chez Michel **27**
Chez Ramulaud **50**
Chez Vong **38**
Goumard **11**
Joe Allen **37**
Juveniles **15**
L'Absinthe **12**
La Famille **2**
L'Ambassade
  d'Auvergne **36**
L'Ambroisie **47**
L'Ami Louis **32**
L'Ebauchior **50**
La Belle Hortense **44**
La Grille **28**
La Poule au Pot **23**
L'Assaggio **10**
Le Béarn **25**
Le Chateaubriand **31**
Le Dalí **18**
Le Fumoir **24**

Le Georges **40**
Le Grain de Folie **1**
Le Grand Véfour **14**
Le Manguier **35**
Le Pamphlet **39**
Le Pure Café **49**
Le Vaudeville **9**
Mansouria **50**
Mélac **49**
Pinxo **17**
Wally Le Saharien **3**
Yam' 'Tcha **22**

one of the restaurants of the moment, so it's full of folks from the worlds of entertainment and the arts.

10 rue de la Grande-Truanderie, 1er. ℂ **01-40-26-09-36.** www.chez-vong.com. Reservations recommended. Main courses 25€–60€; fixed-price lunch Mon–Fri 25€. AE, DC, MC, V. Mon–Sat noon–2:30pm and 7–11:15pm. Closed 3 weeks in Aug. Métro: Etienne-Marcel or Les Halles.

Goumard ★★★ SEAFOOD   Opened in 1872, this landmark is one of Paris's leading seafood restaurants. It's so devoted to the fine art of preparing fish that other food is banned from the menu (the staff will verbally present a limited roster of meat dishes). The decor consists of a collection of Lalique crystal fish in artificial aquariums. Even more unusual are the restrooms, classified as historic monuments; the Art Nouveau master cabinetmaker Majorelle designed the commodes in the early 1900s. Much of the seafood is flown in from Brittany daily. Examples include flaky crab cakes, flash-fried scallops with black truffles, sautéed wild squid, and grilled John Dory. Nothing (no excess butter, spice, or salt) is allowed to interfere with the natural flavor of the sea.

9 rue Duphot, 1er. ℂ **01-42-60-36-07.** Fax 01-42-60-04-54. www.goumard.com. Reservations required far in advance. Main courses 19€–79€; fixed-price menu 59€. AE, DC, MC, V. Daily 11:30am–12:30am. Métro: Madeleine or Concorde.

Le Dalí ★ MODERN FRENCH   In the deluxe hotel Meurice, this informal dining room is named after the hotel's most famous guest, the mad Catalan artist, Salvador Dalí. French designer Philippe Starck and his daughter, Ara Starck, created the decor for the winter garden of the palace, with a touch of whimsy. In tribute to Dalí, you'll find feet in the form of women's shoes, a lamp with drawers, and an effigy of a lobster perched atop the phone. The cuisine of a Michelin three-star chef, Yannick Alléno, is praiseworthy. The menu is arranged in amusing divisions, going from "low fat" to "taboo." Alléno reinterprets French cooking "without excess and with 100% flavor," making it a stopover for models and others watching their waistlines. Try such favorites as carpaccio of sea scallops with fennel salad or roast sea bass with potatoes.

In the Hotel Meurice, 228 rue de Rivoli, 1er. ℂ **01-44-58-10-44.** www.lemeurice.com. Reservations recommended. Main courses 26€–50€. AE, DC, MC, V. Daily noon–3:30pm and 7–11pm. Métro: Tuileries.

MODERATE

Au Pied de Cochon ★★ LATE NIGHT/TRADITIONAL FRENCH   Their famous onion soup and namesake specialty (grilled pigs' feet with béarnaise sauce) still lure visitors, and where else in Paris can you get such a good meal at 3am? Other specialties include a platter named after the medieval patron saint of sausage makers, *la temptation de St-Antoine,* which includes grilled pig's tail, pig's snout, and half a pig's foot, all served with béarnaise and *pommes frites;* and *andouillettes* (chitterling sausages) with béarnaise. Two flavorful but less unusual dishes: a *jarret* (shin) of pork, caramelized in honey and served on a bed of sauerkraut, and grilled pork ribs with sage sauce. On the street outside, you can buy some of the freshest oysters in town.

6 rue Coquillière, 1er. ℂ **01-40-13-77-00.** www.pieddecochon.com. Reservations recommended for lunch and dinner hours. Main courses 17€–48€. AE, DC, MC, V. Daily 24 hr. Métro: Les Halles or Louvre.

Cabaret ASIAN/MODERN FRENCH   You'll either admire this restaurant for its sense of cutting-edge glamour or become irritated with its inflated sense of grandeur, its artfully vague lack of organization, and, in some cases, its genuinely silly sense of chichi. Depending on when you arrive, your meal will be served either on the street level or in the cellar, where a well-publicized team of hot designers (including Jacques Garcia and Ora-Ito) have installed a postmodern decor that's coy, minimalist, and thought-provoking. A bar crafted from mirrors, exotic hardwoods, and replicas of beds are spread across the lounge-disco area. Recommended dishes include carpaccio of scallops with truffle oil, fried slices of foie gras with toast, and roast lamb flavored with thyme and citrus and served with flap mushrooms and eggplant.

2 place du Palais-Royal, 1er. (📞 **01-58-62-56-25.** www.cabaret.fr. Reservations recommended. Main courses 14€–35€. AE, MC, V. Restaurant Tues–Sat 8–11:30pm. Club Tues–Sat 11:30pm–5 or 6am. Métro: Palais-Royal.

Joe Allen ★ ☺ AMERICAN   The first American restaurant in Les Halles is aging well. Joe Allen long ago invaded the place with his hamburger. Though the New York restaurateur admits "it's a silly idea," it works, and this place serves Paris's best burger. While listening to the jukebox, you can order black-bean soup, chili, sirloin steak, ribs, or apple pie. Joe Allen is getting more sophisticated, catering to modern tastes with dishes such as grilled salmon with coconut rice and sun-dried tomatoes. His saloon is the only place in Paris serving New York cheesecake and real pecan pie. A very popular brunch is served Saturday and Sunday from noon to 4pm, costing 20€. Without a dinner reservation, expect a 30-minute wait at the New York Bar.

30 rue Pierre-Lescot, 1er. (📞 **01-42-36-70-13.** www.joeallenrestaurant.com. Reservations recommended for dinner. Main courses 13€–21€; fixed-price menu 14€–26€. AE, MC, V. Daily noon–1am; Sat–Sun brunch noon–4pm. Métro: Etienne-Marcel.

L'Absinthe MODERN FRENCH   Charming and airy, its pair (upstairs/downstairs) of dining rooms are gracefully paneled, and an enormous antique clock dominates a panorama over the chattering and animated dining room. Best of all for foodies who follow this sort of thing, this upscale bistro is associated with one of the mightiest names of megacelebrity French gastronomy: It's owned and its dining room is supervised by Caroline, daughter of Michel Rostang. In summer, tables spill outside onto an all-pedestrian, see-and-be-seen stretch of street with dauntingly upscale boutiques. Come here for well-prepared, but not particularly innovative, bistro-style food. The best examples are tender veal in a red-wine sauce, scallops sautéed with bacon and sherry, poached codfish with a garlicky aioli sauce, and a served-pink version of standing rack of veal. Service is quirky, a wee bit judgmental, and at its worst a bit cranky.

24 place du Marché St-Honoré, 1er. (📞 **01-49-26-90-04.** www.restaurantabsinthe.com. Reservations recommended. Main courses 22€; fixed-price menu 31€–39€. AE, DC, MC, V. Mon–Fri noon–2pm; Mon–Sat 7:15–10:30pm. Métro: Tuileries.

La Poule au Pot LATE NIGHT/TRADITIONAL FRENCH   Established in 1935, this bistro welcomes late-night carousers and showbiz personalities looking for a meal after a performance. (Past aficionados have included the Rolling Stones, Prince, and Dustin Hoffman.) The decor is authentically Art Deco; the ambience, nurturing. Time-tested and savory menu items include salmon with champagne sauce, onion soup, a tripe casserole Norman style, Burgundy-style snails, country pâté on a bed of onion marmalade, and a succulent version of the restaurant's namesake—chicken in a pot, with slices of pâté and fresh vegetables.

9 rue Vauvilliers, 1er. ☏ **01-42-36-32-96.** www.lapouleaupot.fr. Reservations recommended. Main courses 21€–36€; fixed-price menu 35€. MC, V. Tues–Sun 7pm–5am. Métro: Louvre or Les Halles.

L'Assaggio ★ ITALIAN/MEDITERRANEAN   Just before press time for this edition, the respected Hotel Castille terminated its contract with overpriced culinary superstar Alain Ducasse, giving the nod to the highly competent Italy-born wunderkind Vittoria Beltramelli instead. Today, within an indigo and pistachio-colored dining room overlooking the fountain of the hotel's interior courtyard, you'll find a succulent array of Italian dishes prepared in ways you might expect in Italy itself—always with respect for the waistlines of the politicos and supermodels who frequent this posh address. Expect an especially sophisticated array of risottos and pastas which change with the season, salads and vegetables that evoke sunnier climes, and an excellent tiramisu.

In the Hôtel Castille, 37 rue Cambon, 1er. ☏ **01-44-58-45-67.** www.castille.com. Reservations recommended. Main courses 18€–36€, pastas and risottos 20€–24€. Fixed-price lunches 38€–45€. AE, DC, MC, V. Mon–Fri noon–2pm and 7–10pm. Métro: Concorde or Madeleine.

Le Fumoir ★ INTERNATIONAL   This upscale brasserie is in an antique building a few steps from the Louvre. It's one of the most fashionable places in Paris for a bite or drink. You can order salads, pastries, and drinks at off-hours, and platters of more substantial food at mealtimes. Examples are Argentine beefsteak, rack of veal simmered in its own juices with tarragon, calves' liver with onions, and herring in mustard-flavored cream sauce.

6 rue de l'Amiral-Coligny, 1er. ☏ **01-42-92-00-24.** www.lefumoir.com. Reservations recommended. Main courses 18€–23€. AE, MC, V. Salads, pastries, and snacks daily 11am–2am; full menu Mon–Fri 7:30–11:30pm, Sat–Sun 7:30pm–midnight. Métro: Louvre-Rivoli.

Pinxo ★ 🍴 SOUTHWESTERN FRENCH   This is the cost-conscious brasserie that's associated with megachef Alain Dutournier's terribly stylish, and much more expensive, Carré des Feuillants, which is on a nearby street. Within Pinxo, a good-looking waitstaff encourages clients to share their starters and platters with their tablemates. This becomes relatively easy because anytime something appears on a plate, it's replicated, sometimes with variations, three times. The setting manages to elevate kitchen drudgery to a high, and high-tech, art form. Expect a wooden floor, white walls, and views that extend directly into an all-black open kitchen-cum-theater. Most foods here are grilled or at least prepared with heart-healthy cooking oils. Examples include a mixture of Aquitaine beef on the same plate as a steak, a tartare, and a blood sausage, all of them accompanied by a slice of foie gras. Other dishes to sample include rare sesame-glazed tuna and sautéed squid with garlic chips.

In the Plaza-Paris-Vendôme Hôtel, 9 rue d'Alger, 1er. ☏ **01-40-20-72-00.** www.pinxo.fr. Reservations recommended. Main courses 13€–28€; fixed-price lunch 21€. AE, MC, V. Daily 12:15–2:30pm and 7:15–11:30pm. Métro: Tuileries.

Yam' 'Tcha ★★★ TRADITIONAL FRENCH/CHINESE   This sweet little restaurant lies on an ancient side street in Les Halles, feeding only 20 diners a night. In spite of its lack of pretension, it is one of the hottest dining tickets in Paris, so try to reserve a table as far in advance as possible. French food critics have made chef Adeline Grattard the queen of Les Halles and a darling of the media, including *Le Figaro,* whose reporters first discovered her amazing talents. Her pre-fixe menus are regularly changing and adjusted to the season. You might begin with such delights as an appetizer of broad beans with sautéed pork dressed with ginger, garlic, and sesame-seed oil. Try also the fat Mozambique shrimp or the sublime duckling with sautéed eggplant (aubergine). Finish, perhaps, with a delightful dessert of homemade ginger ice cream with avocado slices and passion fruit.

4 rue Sauval, 1er. ✆ **01-40-26-08-07.** Reservations required. Fixed-price lunch 30€–65€; fixed-price dinner 65€. AE, MC, V. Métro: Louvre-Rivoli.

INEXPENSIVE

Angélina ★★ TEA/TRADITIONAL FRENCH   In the high-rent area near the InterContinental, this *salon de thé* (tea salon) combines fashion-industry glitter and bourgeois respectability. The carpets are plush, the ceilings high, and the accessories have the right amount of patina. This place has no equal when it comes to viewing the lionesses of haute couture over tea and sandwiches. The waitresses bear silver trays with pastries, drinks, and tea or coffee to marble-topped tables. Lunch usually offers a salad and a *plat du jour* (dish of the day) such as *salade gourmande* (gourmet salad) with foie gras and smoked breast of duck on a bed of fresh salad greens. An enduring specialty here is hot chocolate. Another specialty, designed to go well with tea, is the Mont Blanc, a combination of chestnut cream and meringue.

226 rue de Rivoli, 1er. ✆ **01-42-60-82-00.** Reservations not accepted for tea. Pot of tea for one 7€; sandwiches and salads 10€–15€; main courses 16€–30€. AE, MC, V. Mon–Fri 8am–6:45pm; Sun 9am–6:45pm. Métro: Tuileries or Concorde.

Juveniles SCOTTISH/INTERNATIONAL   A short stroll from the Louvre and the Opéra, Juveniles is the domain of Tim Johnston, a Scot, who has opened this tiny wine bar, featuring the best Australian wine *carte* in Paris. You can even order that famous (infamous?) Scottish dish, haggis here—it's a delicacy for some. The menu also includes sausages and mashed potatoes, Puy lentils (the best in the world), and charcuterie plates. He even serves Indian chicken tikka masala. The cheeses are pungent, the staff bilingual and friendly.

47 rue de Richelieu, 1er. ✆ **01-42-97-46-49.** Reservations recommended. Set-lunch menu 17€; fixed-price dinner 28€; main dishes 17€; tapas from 7€. MC, V. Tues–Sat noon–3pm and 7–11pm. Métro: Pyramide or Palais Royal.

Le Béarn SOUTHWESTERN FRENCH   This is the most famous of the workingman's "zinc cafes" of the 1st arrondissement. It was created in 1945 at the end of the war and installed in what had been a butcher's shop. The kitchen and the flowery Art Nouveau tiles still here from the day it opened will surely appeal to those who like to dine in the scruffy, gritty zincs of Paris. Patrons squeeze together on burgundy leather banquettes at Formica tables. The menu is based on regional products, and the food is prepared country style. Familiar fare to Parisians for decades includes veal kidneys in Madeira sauce and fresh mushrooms; perch with a white butter sauce, and strip steak with béarnaise sauce. For an appetizer, you can order the old-fashioned hard-boiled eggs with mayonnaise or smoked herring marinated in oil.

8 rue Halles, 1er. ✆ **01-42-36-93-35.** Reservations recommended. Main courses 8€–16€; fixed-price menu 17€. AE, DC, MC, V. Mon–Sat 8am–11pm. Métro: Châtelet.

2nd Arrondissement (La Bourse)

MODERATE

Aux Lyonnais ★ LYONNAIS/TRADITIONAL FRENCH After a meal here, you'll know why Lyon is called the gastronomic capital of France. There is no better Lyonnais bistro in Paris than this time-mellowed place vaguely associated with Alain Ducasse. The day's menu is based on the freshest produce in the market that morning. It's offered against an 1890s bistro backdrop of potted palms, etched glass, and globe lamps. Inventiveness and solid technique characterize such dishes as parsleyed calves' liver, pike dumplings (the best in Paris), skate meunière, and peppery *coq au vin* (chicken stewed in red wine) with *crème fraîche* (fresh cream) macaroni. Foie gras is a starter, or you can opt for a charcuterie (deli meat) platter. The best for last: a heaven-sent Grand Marnier soufflé.

32 rue St-Marc, 2e. ✆ **01-42-96-65-04.** www.auxlyonnais.com. Reservations required. Main courses 22€–25€; 3-course fixed-price menu 26€–34€. AE, DC, MC, V. Tues–Fri noon–1:30pm and Tues–Sat 7:30–10pm. Métro: Grands-Boulevards.

Chez Georges TRADITIONAL FRENCH Three generations of the same family run this bistro, which opened in 1964 near La Bourse (the stock exchange). At lunch it's packed with stock-exchange members. It serves *la cuisine bourgeoise* (comfort food). Waiters bring around bowls of appetizers, such as celery rémoulade, to get you started. You can follow with grilled turbot in a béarnaise sauce, duck breast with cèpe mushrooms, cassoulet, or *pot-au-feu* (beef simmered with vegetables). The sole filet with a sauce made from Pouilly wine and crème fraîche (fresh cream) is a delight.

1 rue du Mail, 2e. ✆ **01-42-60-07-11.** Reservations required. Main courses 23€–34€. AE, MC, V. Mon–Fri noon–2pm and 7:30–10pm. Closed Aug and last week of Dec. Métro: Bourse.

Le Vaudeville LATE NIGHT/TRADITIONAL FRENCH Adjacent to La Bourse (stock exchange), this bistro retains its marble walls and Art Deco carvings from 1918. In summer, tables dot a terrace among banks of geraniums. The place is boisterous and informal, often welcoming groups of six or eight diners at a time. The roster of platters includes a salad of crayfish and asparagus points, grilled Dover sole, smoked salmon, sauerkraut, and grilled meats, even stewed calf's head. Three dishes reign as enduring favorites: fresh grilled codfish with mashed potatoes and truffle juice, fresh *escalope* of warm foie gras with grapes or raspberries, and fresh pasta with morels. The prix-fixe menu is a good deal.

29 rue Vivienne, 2e. ✆ **01-40-20-04-62.** www.vaudevilleparis.com. Reservations recommended in the evenings. Main courses 16€–30€; fixed-price menu 40€–50€. AE, DC, MC, V. Daily noon–3pm and 7pm–1am. Métro: Bourse.

3rd Arrondissement (Le Marais)

EXPENSIVE

L'Ami Louis ★ TRADITIONAL FRENCH L'Ami Louis is in one of central Paris's least fashionable neighborhoods, far removed from the part of the Marais that has become chic, and its facade has seen better days. It was one of Paris's most famous brasseries in the 1930s, thanks to its excellent food served in copious portions and its old-fashioned decor. Its traditions, including the hostile waiters, are fervently maintained today, and Bill Clinton loves it. Amid a "brown gravy" decor (the walls retain a smoky patina), dishes such as game in season, grilled veal kidneys, milk-fed lamb, confit of duckling, and slices of foie gras are served on marble-topped tables. The whole roasted chicken is served with a mountain of french fries. Though some say the ingredients aren't as good as in the restaurant's heyday, the sauces are as thick as they were between the wars.

32 rue du Vertbois, 3e. ✆ **01-48-87-77-48.** Reservations required far in advance. Main courses 35€–65€. AE, DC, MC, V. Wed–Sun noon–1:30pm and 8–11:30pm. Closed July 19–Aug 25. Métro: Temple.

MODERATE

Le Pamphlet ★ ✦ SOUTHWESTERN FRENCH/TRADITIONAL FRENCH
This is the kind of rustic, country-comfortable inn where Parisians book a table at least 48 hours in advance and then schedule the event in their appointment books as a midweek break from urban life. Part of the charm here involves discussing the political theories of strong-willed and gruffly charming owner and chef Alain Carrère. The menu changes at least once a week. Your meal might begin with *rillettes* (a rough-textured terrine) of rabbit with crayfish, a thick cream of crabmeat soup garnished with baby peas, or a thin potato tart with marinated wild salmon and fine herbs. Recommended main courses include a rack of Pyrenean lamb served with *croustillant* (a crisp pastry) enriched with Rocamadour goat cheese, or a mixed grill of meats.

38 rue Debelleyme, 3e. ✆ **01-42-72-39-24.** Reservations required, usually 48 hr. in advance for dinner. Fixed-price menu 30€–45€. MC, V. Tues–Fri noon–2:30pm; Mon–Sat 7:30–11pm. Closed first 2 weeks of Jan and 2 weeks in mid-Aug. Métro: Filles du Calvaire.

INEXPENSIVE

Au Bascou ★ 🏠 BASQUE   The succulent cuisine of France's "deep southwest" is the specialty here, where art objects, paintings, and tones of ocher celebrate the beauty of the region, and hanging clusters of pimentos add spice to the air. For a ray of sunshine, try *pipérade basquaise* (a spicy omelet loaded with peppers and onions), pimentos stuffed with purée of codfish, and *axoa* of veal (shoulder of calf) served with pimento-and-pepper-based green sauce. Also noteworthy is the sautéed shrimp with fennel salad.

38 rue Réaumur, 3e. ✆ **01-42-72-69-25.** Reservations recommended. Main courses 17€; fixed-price lunch menu 19€. AE, DC, MC, V. Mon–Sat noon–2pm and 7:30–10:30pm. Closed Aug and week of Christmas. Métro: Arts-et-Métiers.

Chez Janou PROVENÇAL   On one of the 17th-century streets behind place des Vosges, a pair of cramped but cozy dining rooms filled with memorabilia from Provence make up this loud and somewhat raucous bistro. The service is brusque and sometimes hectic. But the food will remind you of a visit to your French grandmother's kitchen—dishes such as crayfish, grilled sea bass with pesto, spinach salad with goat cheese, fondue of ratatouille, gratin of mussels, and simple but savory *magret* (breast) of duck with rosemary.

2 rue Roger-Verlomme, 3e. ✆ **01-42-72-28-41.** www.chezjanou.com. Reservations recommended. Main courses 14€–18€; fixed-price lunch 15€. AE, MC, V. Daily noon–3pm and 7:30pm–midnight. Métro: Chemin Vert.

Chez Jenny ✦ ALSATIAN   One of the city's most famous Alsatian restaurants was established in 1930 by members of the Jenny family. Little has changed since its inauguration except that the clientele is a lot more contemporary-looking than in the old days. Up to 220 diners can fit into this nostalgia-laden setting, where Alsatian *Gemütlichkeit* prevails. An ongoing specialty is the *choucroute* (sauerkraut) *de chez Jenny,* piled high with sausages, tender pork knuckles, and slices of ham. Also available are salmon with sorrel, grilled meats, grilled fish, and chicken supreme flavored with Riesling. Any of these tastes wonderful accompanied by one of the Alsatian wines that fill the wine list.

39 bd. du Temple, 3e. ✆ **01-44-54-39-00.** www.chez-jenny.com. Reservations recommended. Main courses 20€–25€; fixed-price menu 24€. AE, DC, MC, V. Sun–Thurs noon–midnight; Fri–Sat noon–1am. Métro: République.

L'Ambassade d'Auvergne ★ AUVERGNAT/TRADITIONAL FRENCH
You enter this rustic tavern through a bar with heavy oak beams, hanging hams, and ceramic plates. It showcases the culinary bounty of France's most isolated region, the Auvergne, whose pork products are widely celebrated. Try chicory salad with apples and pieces of country ham; pork braised with cabbage, turnips, and white beans; or grilled tripe sausages with mashed potatoes and Cantal cheese with garlic. Nonpork specialties are pan-fried duck liver with gingerbread, perch steamed in verbena tea, and roasted rack of lamb with wild mushrooms.

22 rue de Grenier St-Lazare, 3e. ✆ **01-42-72-31-22.** www.ambassade-auvergne.com. Reservations recommended. Main courses 14€–23€; fixed-price menu 28€. AE, MC, V. Daily noon–2pm and 7:30–10:30pm. Métro: Rambuteau.

4th Arrondissement (Ile De La Cité/ Ile St-Louis & Beaubourg)

VERY EXPENSIVE

L'Ambroisie ★ ✋ FRENCH   One of Paris's most talented chefs, Bernard Pacaud, drew attention with his vivid flavors and gastronomic skill, but culinary standards here are declining. At this 17th-century town house, the decor resembles an Italian palazzo. Pacaud's tables are nearly always filled with diners drawn here by all that praise in Michelin. The dishes change seasonally and may include escargot cannelloni in a creamy star anise–flavored broth, roasted foie gras glazed with onion caramels, lobster gazpacho, or *poulard de Bresse demi-deuil homage à la Mère Brazier* (chicken roasted with black truffles and truffled vegetables). There is a rather snobby attitude here: It's a bit shocking when one calls for a reservation to be asked to state one's nationality.

9 place des Vosges, 4e. ✆ **01-42-78-51-45.** www.ambroisie-placedesvosges.com. Reservations required far in advance. Main courses 100€–140€. AE, MC, V. Tues–Sat noon–1:30pm and 8–9:30pm. Métro: St-Paul or Chemin Vert.

EXPENSIVE

Benoit ★ TRADITIONAL FRENCH   There's something weighty about this historical monument; every mayor of Paris has dined here since the restaurant was founded in 1912. Today Benoit is owned by the Alain Ducasse Group. This fabled chef claims that he wants "to use more products from the soil." The setting is theatrical, and the service can be attentive or arrogant, depending on a delicate chemistry that only longtime fans of this place understand. Prices are higher than you'd expect for bistro fare, but it all seems part of the self-satisfied norm here, and clients keep coming back for more. The satisfying cuisine is full of flavor, based on time-tested classics. Traditional crowd-pleasers include turbot roasted

Taking an Ice-Cream Break at Berthillon

A landmark on Ile St-Louis after more than 3 dozen years in business, the *salon de thé* Berthillon ★★★, 29 rue St-Louis-en-l'Ile, 4e (📞 01-43-54-31-61; www.berthillon.fr; Métro: Pont Marie), offers the world's best selection of ice cream. Try gingerbread, bitter-chocolate mousse, rhubarb, melon, kumquat, black currant, or any fresh fruit in season—there are more than 70 flavors and nothing artificial (but only 35 are available at any given moment). Parisians flock here in such numbers that gendarmes have been called out to direct the traffic of ice-cream aficionados. It's open Wednesday to Sunday 10am to 8pm. Closed late July and August.

in the Basque style, filet of sole Nantua, or a traditional head of veal with a *ravigote* sauce. One of the best dishes is a filet of beef in a bordelaise sauce served with macaroni and cheese. The chefs also make a satisfying cassoulet with white beans.

20 rue St-Martin, 4e. 📞 **01-42-72-25-76.** Reservations required. Main courses 24€–43€; fixed-price lunch 38€. AE, DC, MC, V. Daily noon–2pm and 7:30–10pm. Métro: Hôtel-de-Ville.

MODERATE

Bofinger ✋ ALSATIAN/MODERN & TRADITIONAL FRENCH   Opened in the 1860s, Bofinger is the oldest Alsatian brasserie in town, but it's grown tired and stale over the years. Nonetheless, it's packed every night with visitors because of its world fame. If the food isn't what it used to be, the atmosphere for some will be worth trekking over here. It's a Belle Epoque dining palace, resplendent with brass and stained glass. Affiliated with La Coupole, Julien, and Brasserie Flo, the restaurant has updated its menu, retaining the most popular traditional dishes, such as sauerkraut and sole meunière (sole in lemon butter sauce). Other items include roasted leg of lamb with fondant of artichoke hearts and parsley purée, grilled turbot with a fennel sauce, and bouillabaisse Bofinger. Fresh oysters and lobster are almost always available in season. You can dine on an outdoor terrace, weather permitting. In light of the restaurant's rich history, a staff member conducts brief complimentary tours.

5–7 rue de la Bastille, 4e. 📞 **01-42-72-87-82.** www.bofingerparis.com. Reservations recommended. Main courses 15€–35€; fixed-price menu 25€–32€. AE, DC, MC, V. Mon–Fri noon–3pm and 6:30pm–1am; Sat–Sun noon–1am. Métro: Bastille.

Georges ★ INTERNATIONAL   The Centre Pompidou is again in the spotlight; all of artsy Paris is talking about this place. Georges is in a large space on the top floor of Paris's most comprehensive arts complex, with views through bay windows over most of the city. The decor is minimalist and postmodern, with lots of brushed aluminum and stainless steel. Tables are made from sandblasted glass, lit from below, and accessorized with hypermodern cutlery. Menu items are mostly Continental, with hints of Asia. Some combinations surprise—macaroni with lobster, for example. Others seem exotic, including roasted ostrich steak. Aside from these dishes, one of the best items on the menu is king crab with coconut milk and curry. To get here, head for the exterior elevator to the left of the Centre's main entrance. Tell the guard you have a reservation; otherwise, you might not be allowed up.

A PARISIAN pique-nique

One of the best ways to save money while still enjoying Parisian cuisine is to picnic. Go to a *fromagerie* for cheese; to a *boulangerie* for a baguette; to a charcuterie for pâté, sausage, or salad; and to a patisserie for luscious pastries. Add a bottle of Côtes du Rhone—it goes well with picnics—and you'll have the makings of a delightful, typically French meal you can take to the nearest park or along the banks of the Seine. Pretend you're in Manet's *Déjeuner sur l'herbe,* and enjoy! (Don't forget the corkscrew!)

The best spot for a picnic is at any number of cozy nooks along the **Seine.**

Another great place for picnics (also boating, walks, and jogging) is the **Bois de Boulogne** (Métro: Porte Maillot), covering some 809 hectares (2,000 acres) at the western edge of Paris. At night it becomes a twilight zone of sex and drugs, but it's lovely during the day. Even though they're in a state of restoration, the splendid gardens of **Versailles** are another fine picnic spot. You can also enjoy your meal on the grass on a day trip to the cathedral city of **Chartres.** Go to bucolic **Parc André Gagon,** a 5-minute walk northwest of the fabled cathedral.

Centre Pompidou, 6th floor, 14 rue Beaubourg, 4e. ☎ **01-44-78-47-99.** www.centrepompidou. fr. Reservations required for dinner, recommended for lunch. Main courses 37€–47€. AE, DC, MC, V. Wed–Mon noon–2am. Métro: Rambuteau.

9th Arrondissement (Opera Garnier/Pigalle)

As with its counterparts from Hong Kong to Reykjavík, the **Hard Rock Cafe,** 14 bd. Montmartre, 9e (☎ **01-53-24-60-00;** Métro: Grands-Boulevards or Richelieu-Drouot), offers musical memorabilia as well as musical selections from 35 years of rock. The crowd appreciates the juicy steaks, hamburgers, veggie burgers, salads, pastas, and heaping platters of informal French-inspired food. It's open Sunday to Thursday 8:30am to 1am and Friday to Saturday 8:30am to 2am.

MODERATE

Au Petit Riche ★ LOIRE VALLEY (ANJOU)/TRADITIONAL FRENCH   No, that's not Flaubert or Balzac walking through the door, but should they miraculously return, the decor of old Paris, with the original gas lamps and time-mellowed paneling, will make them feel at home. This place opened in 1865 as the restaurant associated with the very large and then-solvent Café Riche next door. After Café Riche burned down, the restaurant continued to attract lawyers, set designers, and machinists from the nearby Opéra Garnier, eventually becoming a well-known restaurant. Charles Aznavour is an occasional patron, along with politicians and anyone interested in the nostalgia of *La Vieille France.* Expect an impressive roster of Loire Valley wines and food that combines Loire Valley classics with traditional French fare. The house is famous for its Gillardeau oysters. Other examples include roasted rack of veal prepared *à l'ancienne,* a long-standing house special of tartare of beef, roasted whitefish in meat drippings, and seasonal game dishes such as civet of rabbit.

25 rue Le Peletier, 9e. ☎ **01-47-70-68-68.** www.aupetitriche.com. Reservations recommended. Main courses 16€–32€; fixed-price menu 33€–34€. AE, DC, MC, V. Daily noon–2:15pm and 7pm–12:15am. Métro: Le Peletier or Richelieu-Drouot.

Casa Olympe ★ ★ 🍴 PROVENÇAL/CORSICAN   Serious Paris foodies and peripatetic gourmets such as Francis Ford Coppola make their way to the 9th to feast on the wares of an original cook. Olympe Versini earned a Michelin star at the age of 29 and dazzled some of the most discerning palates of *tout* Paris in Montparnasse before opening this unassuming 32-seat dining room. Critics cite the earthiness of her cooking as evoked by her duck ravioli bathed in a jus reduction or her heavenly foie gras terrine brazenly studded with split vanilla beans. From head to hoof, she serves most parts of the pig—and does so with gutsiness. Her langoustine ravioli is modish but not excessively so, and her beef tenderloin with peppercorn sauce is one of the best versions of this time-honored dish.

48 rue St-Georges, 9e. ✆ **01-42-85-26-01.** Reservations required. Fixed-price menu 28€–35€. MC, V. Mon–Fri noon–2pm and 8–11pm. MC, V. Closed 3 weeks in Aug, 1 week in May, and 10 days in Dec. Métro: St-Georges.

Chez Jean ★ TRADITIONAL FRENCH   The crowd is young, the food is sophisticated, and the vintage 1950s aura makes you think that American expatriate novelist James Baldwin will arrive any minute. Surrounded by well-oiled pine panels and polished copper, you can choose from some of grandmother's favorites as well as more modern dishes. Owner Jean-Frederic Guidoni worked for more than 20 years at one of the world's most expensive restaurants, Taillevent, but within his own milieu, he demonstrates his own innovative touch at prices that are much more reasonable. For starters, consider a chicken consommé with endives and chorizo; a savory version of a cheesy alpine staple, *raclette,* made with mustard sauce and *Curé Nantais* cheese; and slow-braised pork cooked for 7 hours and served on a bed of carrots, apricots, and confit of lemon.

8 rue St-Lazare, 9e. ✆ **01-48-78-62-73.** www.restaurantjean.fr. Reservations recommended far in advance. Main courses 27€–38€; fixed-price lunch 46€; fixed-price dinner 70€–95€. AE, DC, MC, V. Mon–Fri noon–2:30pm and 7:30–10:30pm. Métro: Notre-Dame de Lorette, Opéra, or Cadet.

Wally Le Saharien ALGERIAN   Head to this dining room—lined with desert photos and tribal artifacts crafted from ceramics, wood, and weavings—for an insight into the spicy, slow-cooked cuisine that fueled the colonial expansion of France into North Africa. The prix-fixe dinner menu begins with a trio of starters: spicy soup, stuffed and grilled sardines, and a savory *pastilla* of pigeon in puff pastry. Next comes any of several kinds of couscous or a *méchouia* (slow-cooked tart) of lamb dusted with an optional coating of sugar. *Merguez,* the cumin-laden spicy sausage of the North African world, factors importantly into any meal, as do homemade pastries.

36 rue Rodier, 9e. ✆ **01-42-85-51-90.** Reservations recommended. Main courses (lunch only) 35€–57€; fixed-price dinner 44€. MC, V. Tues–Sat noon–2pm and 7–10:30pm. Closed Aug. Métro: Anvers.

INEXPENSIVE

Chartier TRADITIONAL FRENCH   Opened in 1896, this unpretentious *fin-de-siècle* restaurant is now an official historic monument featuring a whimsical mural with trees, a flowering staircase, and an early depiction of an airplane (it was painted in 1929 by an artist who traded his work for food). The menu follows brasserie-style traditions, including items you might not dare to eat—tartare of beef, chitterling sausages, tongue of beef with spicy sauce—as well as some old-time tempters. The waiter will steer you through such dishes as *choucroute* (sauerkraut) or Bolognese spaghetti, *pavé* (a thick slice of rump steak), and at least five kinds of fish.

7 rue du Faubourg Montmartre, 9e. ✆ **01-47-70-86-29.** www.restaurant-chartier.com. Main courses 9€–12€. AE, DC, MC, V. Daily 11:30am–10pm. Métro: Grands-Boulevards.

10th Arrondissement (Gare De L'est)

MODERATE

Brasserie Flo ★ ALSATIAN   This remote restaurant is hard to find, but after you arrive (after walking through passageway after passageway), you'll see that *fin-de-siècle* Paris lives on. The restaurant opened in 1860 and has changed its decor very little. The specialty is *la formidable choucroute* (a mound of sauerkraut with boiled ham, bacon, and sausage) for two. Onion soup and sole meunière (sole in lemon butter sauce) are always good, as are warm foie gras and guinea hen with lentils. Look for the *plats du jour,* ranging from roast pigeon to tuna steak with hot peppers.

7 cour des Petites-Ecuries, 10e. ✆ **01-47-70-13-59.** www.flobrasseries.com. Reservations recommended. Main courses 18€–36€; fixed-price dinner 23€–28€; fixed-price lunch 19€. AE, DC, MC, V. Daily noon–3pm and 7pm–1am. Métro: Château d'Eau or Strasbourg-St-Denis.

Chez Michel BRETON   Adapting to the tastes and income of its loyal crowd, this restaurant near the Gare du Nord serves generous portions of well-prepared Breton dishes. In a pair of dining rooms accented with exposed wood, you'll enjoy the fruits of the fields and seacoast, densely flavored and traditional; they include veal chops fried in butter and served with gratin of potatoes enriched with calf's foot gelatin, and codfish filets served on a bed of tomatoes and onions with a tapenade of black olives. Other regional choices include a Celtic stew (*kig ha farz,* in Breton dialect) made from stewed veal and pork, and served with grilled lard, herbs, and baby vegetables; and *les craquelins de Saint Mâlo* (small Breton-style tarts) stuffed with aromatic goat cheese.

10 rue de Belzunce, 10e. ✆ **01-44-53-06-20.** Reservations required. Fixed-price menu 32€. MC, V. Tues–Fri 11:45am–3pm and Mon–Fri 6:45pm–midnight. Métro: Gare du Nord.

La Grille 🍴 SEAFOOD/TRADITIONAL FRENCH   Few other moderate restaurants are as hotly pursued by Parisians as this nine-table holdover from another age. For at least a century after the French Revolution, fishermen from Dieppe used this place as a springboard for carousing and cabaret-watching after delivering their fish to Les Halles market. Since the late 1960s, the charming, outspoken M. and Mme Cullérre, who in 2005 received an award from the French tourist office for their contribution to tourism in Paris, have run this restaurant. They have become distinctive, albeit slightly eccentric, neighborhood fixtures. The holy grail at La Grille is an entire turbot prepared tableside with an emulsified white-butter sauce. Other recommended dishes are seafood terrine, *boeuf bourguignon* (braised beef in red-wine sauce), and a brochette of scallops in white butter. (The restaurant name derives from the 200-year-old wrought-iron grills in front, classified as national treasures.)

80 rue du Faubourg-Poissonnière, 10e. ✆ **01-47-70-89-73.** Reservations required. Main courses 17€–66€. AE, MC, V. Mon–Sat noon–2:15pm and 7:30–9:30pm. Métro: Poissonnière.

INEXPENSIVE

Café Panique ★ 🏛 MODERN FRENCH   Welcome to the New France and one of Paris's best-kept secrets. Although this cafe opened its doors in the '90s, it was only really discovered post-millennium when word seeped out about its easy-going atmosphere and affordable prices. Come here for the mellow ambience and the scrumptious food. The Café has improved its kitchen since its debut, and today's chefs offer such delights as coast veal kidney or filet of cod with fried shrimp. A marvelous monkfish flavored with fresh basil is also featured, as is a lamb flavored with mint.

12 rue des Messagerie, 10e. 📞 **01-47-70-06-84.** www.cafepanique.com. Reservations recommended. Main courses 22€; fixed-price lunch 20€; fixed-price dinner 35€. MC, V. Mon–Fri noon–2pm and 7:30–10pm. Closed Aug. Métro: Poissonnière.

11th Arrondissement (Opéra Bastille)

EXPENSIVE

Blue Elephant ★ THAI   At this branch of a chain of Thai restaurants, the decor evokes the jungles of Southeast Asia, interspersed with sculptures and paintings. The menu items are succulent, infused with lemon grass, curries, and the aromas that make Thai cuisine distinctive. Examples are chicken satay; large grilled shrimp; pastry with chicken, crab and ginger or grilled fish with passion fruit. If you have trouble deciding which delicacy is for you, consider a *plateau royal*, a main course that contains five different specialties of the Thai repertoire (shrimp, chicken, fish, and vegetable dishes), all of them artfully arranged.

43 rue de la Roquette, 11e. 📞 **01-47-00-42-00.** www.blueelephant.com. Reservations recommended. Main courses 25€–30€; fixed-price menu 48€–52€. AE, DC, MC, V. Mon–Fri noon–2:30pm; Sun 2 brunches noon–2pm and 2:30–4:30pm; Mon–Wed 7–11pm; Thurs–Sun 7pm–midnight. Métro: Bastille.

MODERATE

Au Petit Monsieur ★ 🏛 TRADITIONAL FRENCH   A meal at this restaurant, tucked away in the 11th arrondissement, is like dining in the French countryside. Under wooden beams held up by old stone walls, the three dining rooms are decorated with country crockery. Patrons dine at bare wooden tables, using kitchen towels as napkins. Both modernists and upholders of French culinary tradition find a happy home here. Everything is served by a capable staff sensitive to your needs and orders. The fixed-price lunch and dinner menus are changed every day. Appetizers often begin with a tureen of soup from which you help yourself. Appetizers feature such dishes as a risotto with artichokes and tomatoes, followed by a *tournedos* of duckling in the Provençal style, or else delicate veal in a white sauce.

50 rue Amelot, 11e. 📞 **01-43-55-54-04.** Reservations required. Fixed-price lunch 12€–22€; fixed-price dinner 35€. AE, MC, V. Mon–Fri noon–2pm and Mon–Sat 7–10pm. Métro: Chemin Vert. Closed in Aug and last week of Sept.

Chez Ramulaud ★ TRADITIONAL FRENCH   This establishment may seem like the average Parisian restaurant from the outside, but on any given day, you will encounter the friendlier side of Paris in this almost completely gentrified neighborhood. A trio of musicians *chante* French golden oldies, and a few empty wine bottles later, the foodies are singing along. The wine prices are reasonable, and you tip for the musicians. Tried-and-true specialties lure a list of habitués. Rump steak is perfectly prepared with a nutty sauce, or else you can order *andouillette*, *sole meunière* with French green beans, or veal sweetbreads.

269 rue du Faubourg-Saint-Antoine, 11e. ✆ **01-43-72-23-29.** www.chez-ramulaud.fr. Reservations recommended. Main courses 19€; fixed-price lunch 14€–16€; fixed-price dinner 29€. MC, V. Mon–Fri noon–3pm; Mon–Sat 8–11pm. Métro: Faidherbe-Chaligny.

Mansouria MOROCCAN One of Paris's most charming Moroccan restaurants occupies a much-restored building midway between place de la Bastille and place de la Nation. The minimalist decor combines futuristic architecture with bare sand-colored walls, accented only with sets of antique doors and portals from the sub-Sahara. Look for seven kinds of couscous, including versions with chicken; beef brochettes; or lamb, onions, and almonds. *Tagines* are succulent dishes of chicken or fish prepared with aromatic herbs and slow-cooked in clay pots that are carried to your table.

11 rue Faidherbe, 11e. ✆ **01-43-71-00-16.** Reservations recommended. Main courses 15€–24€; fixed-price lunch 29€–45€; fixed-price dinner 30€–46€. AE, MC, V. Wed–Sat noon–2pm; Mon–Sat 7–11pm. Métro: Faidherbe-Chaligny.

INEXPENSIVE

Le Chateaubriand ★ 🏠 MODERN FRENCH The owner, Inaki Aizpitarte, calls this time-tested old eatery a "neo bistro," and so it is. The dark 1930s decor looks relatively intact, but this native of the Basque Country, where he learned his culinary skills, has completely changed the cuisine. Today instead of the classic coq au vin or steak with frites, you are treated to rare tuna slices in pink beet foam flavored with pomegranate seeds or steamed cod with Moroccan spices.

At dinner the only choice is a prix-fixe and it's a winner, perhaps featuring such dishes as eel flavored with orange juice and olive oil, warm cockles and mussels, teriyaki salmon, and mint lamb tagine. Some of the dishes are very daring indeed, including pork belly flavored with licorice.

129 av. Parmentier, 11e. ✆ **01-43-57-45-95.** Reservations required. Main courses at lunch 12€–35€; fixed-price lunch 16€; 5-course fixed-price dinner 30€–39€. AE, DC, MC, V. Tues–Fri noon–2pm and Tues–Sat 8–10:30pm. Métro: Goncourt.

Le Manguier SENEGALESE Many of the patrons who dine here don't know much about Senegalese cuisine, but thanks to a charming welcome and good food, they tend to come back. The decor evokes a West African fishing village. You can order zesty fare such as roast chicken marinated with lime and served with onions; lamb with a nutty sauce; and the national dish, *tieboudiene* (a blend of fish, rice, and fresh vegetables). The medley is perked up with a selection of fiery sauces you apply yourself.

67 av. Parmentier, 11e. ✆ **01-48-07-03-27.** Reservations recommended. Main courses 12€–14€; fixed-price lunch 12€. AE, DC, MC, V. Tues–Sat noon–3pm and 7pm–2am. Métro: Parmentier.

Le Pure Café TRADITIONAL FRENCH The decor around this horseshoe-shaped zinc bar is dated, but the dishes are modern and often served in innovative combinations. These grimy yellowed bistro walls are the real thing, not the faux impression so often created by designers today. Local drunks along with fashionable families crowd in here to sample such specialties as lamb gigot with confit carrots or perhaps grilled squid flavored with sesame seeds and served with rhubarb compote. Other delightful dishes include crunchy shrimp in fresh herbs or sea bass cooked with fennel and baby vegetables.

14 rue Jean-Macé, 11e. ℂ **01-43-71-47-22.** Reservations recommended. Main courses 15€–18€. MC, V. Daily noon–3pm and 7:30–10:30pm. Métro: Charonne or Faidherbe-Chaligny.

Mélac TRADITIONAL FRENCH   Emile Zola in his *The Belly of Paris* may have coined the term zinc bar, which by 1880 came into common usage, and this is one of the most time-honored zinc cafe-bars in Paris. One of our all-time favorites, it dates from 1938, and not much has changed here since. You still have to walk through the kitchen to get to the main dining room. Many of the hearty dishes of Jacque Mélac's Aveyron (a department of the Auvergne) are served, including the likes of confit of pig's liver, veal tripe bundles, fresh and cured sausages, and a *poêlon aveyronnais* (a cast-iron casserole of chicken liver and fried eggs in a sauce made with red wine and shallots). Of course, the tasty wines of the Aveyron are served here.

42 rue Léon-Frot, 11e. ℂ **01-43-70-59-27.** www.melac.fr. Reservations recommended. Main courses 14€–20€; fixed-price lunch (Tues–Fri) 15€. DC, MC, V. Tues–Sat noon–4pm and 8–11pm. Closed Aug. Métro: Charonne.

12th Arrondissement (Bois de Vincennes/ Gare de Lyon)

EXPENSIVE

Au Trou Gascon ★★★ GASCONY   One of Paris's most acclaimed chefs, Alain Dutournier, lures fashionable palates to an unchic area. He launched his career in southwest France's Gascony region. His parents mortgaged their inn to allow Dutournier to open an early 1900s-style bistro in a little-known part of the 12th arrondissement. Word spread of a savant in the kitchen who practiced authentic *cuisine moderne*. His wife, Nicole, is the welcoming hostess, and the wine steward has distinguished himself for his exciting cave containing several little-known wines along with a fabulous collection of Armagnacs. You can start with duck foie gras cooked in a terrine or Gascony-cured ham. The best main courses include a casserole of scallops with endive; tender lamb from the Pyrenees; or the chef's favorite dish, le Cassoulet, made with duckling, pork, lamb, and sausage. Other starters feature foie gras with raisins or else grilled shrimp.

40 rue Taine, 12e. ℂ **01-43-44-34-26.** www.autrougascon.fr. Reservations recommended. Main courses 28€–42€; fixed-price lunch 38€; fixed-price dinner 49€. AE, DC, MC, V. Mon–Fri noon–2pm and 8–10pm. Closed Aug, and 6 days in Nov. Métro: Daumesnil.

INEXPENSIVE

L'Ebauchoir ★ 🎁 TRADITIONAL FRENCH   Tucked into a neighborhood rarely visited by foreigners and featuring a 1950s decor that is so out it's in, this bistro attracts carpenters, plumbers, and electricians, as well as an occasional journalist and screenwriter. With buffed aluminum trim and plaster-and-stucco walls tinted dark orange-yellow and bordeaux, the place might remind you of a factory canteen. You can order surprisingly generous and well-prepared smoked herring and potato salad for starters, even tuna tartare. One of the most unusual main courses is a grilled tuna steak with white chocolate. Too much for you? There's always the more traditional roast chicken (flavored with thyme) or rack of lamb with turmeric, along with red snapper filet with olive oil and fresh garlic.

43 rue de Citeaux, 12e. ✆ **01-43-42-49-31.** Reservations recommended for dinner. Main courses 14€–25€; fixed-price lunch 14€; fixed-price dinner 23€. AE, MC, V. Tues–Sat noon–2:30pm; Mon–Sat 8–11pm. Métro: Faidherbe-Chaligny.

18th Arrondissement (Montmartre)
MODERATE
La Famille ★ MODERN FRENCH   The ambience is like New York's East Village, and this place attracts fashionistas and photographers who climb the hill to Montmartre to sample the tasty food. The bartender makes *mojitos* like Hemingway drank them, while Edith Piaf records spin in the background. Each dish arrives like a sensation, including the oyster terrine made with seaweed, cappuccino, and cilantro mousse. Other offerings include a terrine of duck confit or a special mackerel dish. For dessert, finish off, perhaps, with a lemon tart with lemon verbena jus. Always count on the chefs offering some surprise combinations every night.

41 rue des Trois Freres, 18e. ✆ **01-42-52-11-12.** Reservations required. Fixed-price menu 29€–50€. MC, V. Tues–Sat 8–11:30pm. Closed 3 weeks in Aug. Métro: Abesses.

INEXPENSIVE
Le Grain de Folie ORGANIC/VEGETARIAN   Simple and wholesome, this cuisine is inspired by France, Greece, California, Turkey, and India. The menu includes an array of theme salads, cereals, tarts, terrines, and casseroles. Dessert selections might include an old-fashioned tart or a fruit salad. The decor includes potted plants and exposed stone. You can choose one of an array of wines or a frothy glass of vegetable juice to accompany your meal. This place may be a bit difficult to find, but it's worth the search. Marie-Cécite is the charming owner.

24 rue de La Vieuville, 18e. ✆ **01-42-58-15-57.** Reservations recommended. Main courses 11€–14€; fixed-price menu 8€–15€. No credit cards. Tues–Sun 12:30–2pm and 7–11pm. Métro: Abbesses.

8th Arrondissement (Champs-Elysees/Madeleine)
VERY EXPENSIVE
Lasserre ★★★ MODERN & TRADITIONAL FRENCH   It's so old, it's new again. This elegant restaurant was a bistro before World War II and has since become a legend. The main salon stretches two stories high, with a mezzanine on each side. Tall, silk-draped, arched windows frame the tables set with fine porcelain, gold-edged crystal glasses, and silver candelabras. The ceiling is painted with white clouds and a cerulean sky, but in good weather, the staff slides back the roof to reveal the real sky. The faces of Audrey Hepburn, Maria Callas, and Marlene Dietrich have given way to young British royals and statuesque models from Brazil. A spectacular chef, Jean-Louis Nomicos, is a master of taste and texture, and he's brought renewed life to this swank citadel. The appetizers are among Paris's finest, including macaroni with black truffles and foie gras or marinated scallops with caviar. The main course specialty is poached sole filets *Club de la Casserole,* in puff pastry with asparagus tips and asparagus-flavored cream sauce; also wonderful are the veal kidneys flambé and pigeon André Malraux. The wine cellar, with some 160,000 bottles, is one of Paris's most remarkable.

17 av. Franklin D. Roosevelt, 8e. ☎ **01-43-59-02-13.** Fax 01-45-63-72-23. www.restaurant-lasserre.com. Reservations required far in advance. Main courses 56€–95€; fixed-price lunch 75€; fixed-price dinner 185€. AE, MC, V. Thurs–Fri noon–2pm; Mon–Sat 7:30–10pm. Closed Aug. Métro: Franklin-D-Roosevelt.

Le Cinq ★★★ TRADITIONAL FRENCH   Since it was established in 1928 in honor of the king of England, there has always been a world-class dining venue associated with the Hotel George V. The configuration today dates from its acquisition by Toronto's Four Seasons group, which poured time, money, talent, and taste into a high-ceilinged room whose majestic decor evokes the Grand Trianon at Versailles. Within a gray and very pale pink dining room that shimmers with gold inlays, your dining needs will be supervised by a sophisticated staff that intuitively understands the needs and priorities of the hotel's widely divergent international clientele. Within 3 years of this restaurant's rebirth in 1999, it had been awarded three coveted stars by the Guide Michelin. The menu changes frequently, but enduring favorites include farm-raised veal sweetbreads; and a classic that has been on the menu since the days of Mistinguett and Piaf—Bresse chicken "in the style of the George V," stuffed with crayfish and herbs.
In the Four Seasons Hotel George V, 31 av. George V, 8e. ☎ **01-49-52-71-54.** Fax 01-49-52-71-81. www.fourseasons.com. Reservations recommended 4 weeks in advance for dinner, 1 week in advance for lunch. Main courses 78€–135€; fixed-price lunch 78€–160€; fixed-price dinner 160€–230€. AE, DC, MC, V. Daily 12:30–2:30pm and 7–10:30pm. Métro: George V.

Pierre Gagnaire ★★★ MODERN FRENCH   If you're able to get a reservation, it's worth the effort. The menus are seasonal to take advantage of France's rich bounty; owner Pierre Gagnaire demands perfection, and the chef has a dazzling way with flavors and textures. Stellar examples are roast duck, and turbot cooked in a bag and served with fennel and Provençal lemons. Chicken with truffles comes in two stages—first the breast in wine-based aspic and then the thighs, chopped into roughly textured pieces.
6 rue Balzac, 8e. ☎ **01-58-36-12-50.** Fax 01-58-36-12-51. www.pierre-gagnaire.com. Reservations required. Main courses 65€–165€; fixed-price lunch 105€; fixed-price dinner 255€. AE, DC, MC, V. Mon–Fri noon–1:30pm; Sun–Fri 7:30–10pm. Métro: George V.

Restaurant Plaza Athénée (Alain Ducasse) ★★★ MODERN & TRADITIONAL FRENCH   Few other chefs have been catapulted to international fame as quickly as Alain Ducasse. There's a lot of marketing and glitter involved, but what you'll find in this world-renowned hotel is a lobby-level hideaway that top-notch decorator Patrick Jouin originally decorated around the turn of the millennium and then artfully redecorated, much to the fascination of haute Paris. The six-star chef, Alain Ducasse, who supervises the kitchens here, divides his time among Paris, Monaco, Las Vegas, New York, and Tokyo. In this, his Parisian stronghold, he places a special emphasis on "rare and precious ingredients," whipping up flavorful and very expensive combinations of caviar, lobster, crayfish, truffles (both black and white), and shellfish. Cuisine is vaguely Mediterranean and decidedly contemporary, yet based on traditional models. Some of the best examples include smoked, tea-glazed pigeon or line-caught sea bass with mushrooms. For appetizers, try the creamy pasta with truffles and giblets. Desserts are perhaps the finest in all of Paris's luxe restaurants. The wine list is superb, with some selections deriving from the best vintages of France, Germany, Switzerland, Spain, California, and Italy.

Where to Dine on the Right Bank (8 & 16–17e)

17e

16e

7e

Palais des Congrès de Paris

place de la Porte Maillot

Ternes

place des Ternes

Arc de Triomphe

place Charles de Gaulle

Champs Élysées

American Cathedral in Paris

Musée Guimet

Palais Galliera

Musée d'Art Moderne

Palais de Tokyo

CHAILLOT

Palais de Chaillot

Jardins du Trocadéro

place de Varsovie

place de Costa Rica

Cimetière de Passy

Musée du Quai Branly

Tour Eiffel

Champ de Mars-Tour Eiffel

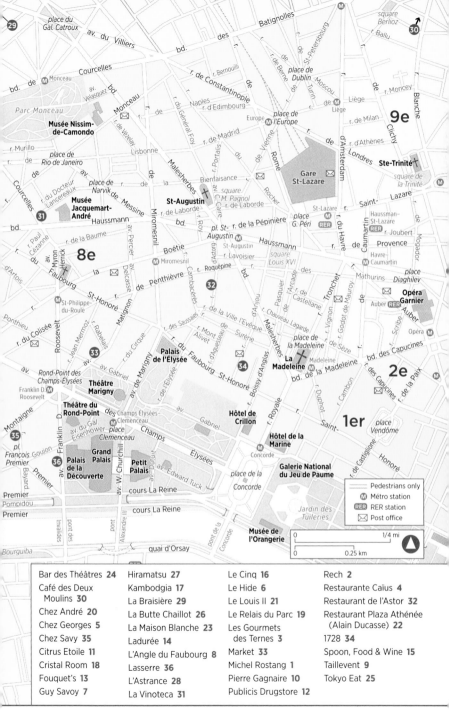

Bar des Théâtres **24**	Hiramatsu **27**	Le Cinq **16**	Rech **2**
Café des Deux Moulins **30**	Kambodgia **17**	Le Hide **6**	Restaurante Caïus **4**
Chez André **20**	La Braisière **29**	Le Louis II **21**	Restaurant de l'Astor **32**
Chez Georges **5**	La Butte Chaillot **26**	Le Relais du Parc **19**	Restaurant Plaza Athénée (Alain Ducasse) **22**
Chez Savy **35**	La Maison Blanche **23**	Les Gourmets des Ternes **3**	1728 **34**
Citrus Etoile **11**	Ladurée **14**	Market **33**	Spoon, Food & Wine **15**
Cristal Room **18**	L'Angle du Faubourg **8**	Michel Rostang **1**	Taillevent **9**
Fouquet's **13**	Lasserre **36**	Pierre Gagnaire **10**	Tokyo Eat **25**
Guy Savoy **7**	L'Astrance **28**	Publicis Drugstore **12**	
	La Vinoteca **31**		

In the Hôtel Plaza Athénée, 25 av. Montaigne, 8e. ☎ **01-53-67-65-00.** Fax 01-53-67-65-12. www.
alain-ducasse.com. Reservations required 4–6 weeks in advance. Main courses 70€–175€; fixed-
price menu 260€–360€. AE, DC, MC, V. Thurs–Fri 12:45–2:15pm; Mon–Fri 7:45–10:15pm. Closed
mid-July to Aug 25 and 10 days in late Dec. Métro: Alma-Marceau.

Taillevent ★★★ MODERN & TRADITIONAL FRENCH   This is the Parisian *ne plus ultra* of gastronomy. Taillevent opened in 1950 and has climbed
steadily in excellence; today it ranks as Paris's outstanding all-around restaurant,
challenged only by Lucas-Carton and Pierre Gagnaire. It's in a grand 19th-cen-
tury town house off the Champs-Elysées, with paneled rooms and crystal chandeliers. The place is small, which permits the owner to give personal attention to
every facet of the operation and maintain a discreet atmosphere. Each dish is
supreme in flavor, including John Dory with olives or lamb saddle seasoned with
wild herbs. A cassoulet of crayfish, if featured, is also divine. Chefs dare to serve
that old standard, *baba au rhum,* but it's perhaps the best you'll ever taste. The
wine list is among the best in Paris.

15 rue Lamennais, 8e. ☎ **01-44-95-15-01.** Fax 01-42-25-95-18. www.taillevent.com. Reservations required 4–6 weeks in advance. Main courses 34€–90€; fixed-price lunch 80€; *menu
dégustation* (tasting menu) 190€. AE, DC, MC, V. Mon–Fri 12:15–2:30pm and 7:15–10pm. Closed
Aug. Métro: George V.

EXPENSIVE

La Maison Blanche ★★ PROVENÇAL/TRADITIONAL FRENCH   Jacques
and his twin brother, Lauren Pourcel, were two of the most famous chefs in the
southerly province of Languedoc before heading north to Paris. The setting
would be the envy of any restaurant in the world: Positioned on the uppermost
(seventh) floor of the Art Deco–style Theatre des Champs-Elysées, it has contemporary, all-white-and-purple decor, sweeping views across the Seine, and two
dining rooms. Clientele tends to be rich, non-French, and a bit pretentious, but
in light of the brilliant food and the sublime setting, who cares? The menu
changes with the inspiration of the chefs and the seasons, but stellar examples
include such starters as crispy filet of red mullet with coriander-flavored baby
vegetables or a small tart of duck foie gras with roasted rhubarb and peach. An
especially good fish specialty is filet of John Dory in candied lemon vinaigrette
with stuffed olives, or else a rack of Aveyron lamb with cracked wheat and mushroom compote.

15 av. Montaigne, 8e. ☎ **01-47-23-55-99.** Reservations required. Main courses 38€–73€; fixed-
price lunch 55€. AE, DC, MC, V. Mon–Fri noon–2pm; daily 8–11pm. Métro: Alma-Marceau.

L'Angle du Faubourg ★★ TRADITIONAL FRENCH   Throughout the
1980s and early 1990s, a reservation at the ultra-upscale Taillevent was sought
after by diplomats, billionaires, and *demi-mondains* from around Europe. In
2001, the Taillevent's owner, M. Vrinat, opened this cost-conscious bistro that
capitalizes on Taillevent's reputation, but at much lower prices. Lunches here
tend to be efficient, relatively quick, and businesslike; dinners are more leisurely,
even romantic. The restaurant has an ultramodern dining room, additional seating in the cellar, and a menu that simplifies Taillevent's lofty culinary ideas.
The best examples include braised lamb with the juice of black olives;
risotto with ingredients that change weekly (during our visit, it was studded with
braised radicchio); and a grilled, low-fat version of *daurade* (bream), served with

Master chef Alain Ducasse continues to expand his empire with the opening of **BE**, 73 bd. de Courcelles, 8e (✆ **01-46-22-20-20**; Métro: Courcelles). Short for *Boulangerie Epicerie,* BE is part bakery and part upmarket deli. As a baker, Eric Kayser is famous in Paris, and he sells some 400 products from all over the globe, including 15 varieties of French bread baked fresh at least eight times a day. You can stop off here for the makings of a picnic, costing about 20€ to 30€ per person, depending on your selection. There are only 22 seats. If a table is free, grab it. You can eat an array of freshly made salads for 6€ to 9€, delicious homemade soups at 5€, and some of the best and most delectable sandwiches in Paris, costing from 4 € to 8€. Of course, if you want some walnut oil from the Dordogne or some lavender honey from Moustiers-Ste-Marie, they are standing on the shelves as well. Open Monday to Saturday 7am to 8pm.

artichokes and a reduction of mushrooms, appreciated by the many diet-conscious *photo-modèles* who stop in.

195 rue du Faubourg St-Honoré, 8e. ✆ **01-40-74-20-20.** www.taillevent.com. Reservations required. Main courses 25€–47€; fixed-price menu 38€–75€. AE, DC, MC, V. Mon–Fri noon–2:30pm and 7:30–10:30pm. Closed Aug. Métro: Terme or Etoile.

La Vinoteca ★ ITALIAN   Market-fresh cuisine, backed up by an impressive Italian wine *carte*, is served here in an intimate, modern atmosphere. You will taste dishes both simple and complicated. Chef Sene Tapha trained at the swanky Hotel Meurice. His well-chosen menu is full of flavor, and his imaginative pastas are succulent. Try such starters as a "cappuccino" of fresh asparagus or a risotto with porcini mushrooms of the day. One of his best pastas is *tagliolini* with fresh truffles in summer. Fish and meat courses, forever changing on the menu, are also first rate.

32 rue de Courcelles, 8e. ✆ **01-53-96-07-68.** Reservations recommended. Main courses 28€–32€. MC, V. Mon–Sat noon–3pm and 7:30–10:30pm. Métro: St. Philippe-du-Roule.

Le Louis II ★ INTERNATIONAL   A power lunch venue, this restaurant is in the revamped La Trémoille. On exquisitely beautiful dishes, some of the most delectable food in Paris is served, including such treats as shellfish soup with marinated shrimp or scallops a la plancha (grilled). The contemporary and traditional French cuisine also features chateaubriand served with beef tartare or foie gras with caramelized onions. Designed by the famous Brit, Sir Terrence Conrad, the restaurant is ultramodern in appointments. The fashionably cool bar area is decorated with ivory leather sofas and subtle lighting, which changes from blue to red throughout the day.

In the Hotel La Trémoille, 14 rue de la Trémoille, 8e. ✆ **01-56-52-14-14.** www.hotel-tremoille.com. Reservations required. Main courses 17€–28€; fixed-price lunch 23€–33€; fixed-price dinner 50€. Mon–Fri noon–3pm and Mon–Sat 7–11pm. Métro: Alma-Marceau.

Restaurant de l'Astor ★ MODERN FRENCH   The vaguely Art Deco decor by superstar Frederick Mechiche includes tones of black and champagne. The restaurant attracts some of the leading politicians of France, many of whom walk the short distance from the dining room to the Elysée Palace and government ministries. The cuisine, as conceived and concocted by Nicolas Clavier, is utterly sublime. Menus change with the season but are likely to feature such specialties as scallops carpaccio marinated with green lemon or roast prawns, perhaps an oyster risotto. In the autumn look for game dishes. Everything here is artfully presented, with a sort of reverential hush.

In the Hôtel Saint-Honoré, 11 rue d'Astorg, 8e. ✆ **01-53-05-05-05.** www.astorsainthonore.com. Reservations recommended. Main courses 25€–32€; fixed-price lunch 42€; fixed-price dinner 52€. AE, DC, MC, V. Mon–Fri 12:30–2pm and 7:30–10pm. Métro: Madeleine.

1728 ★ 🍴 JAPANESE/MODERN FRENCH   An 18th-century town house, just off Faubourg-St-Honoré where the Marquis de Lafayette lived, has been turned into this chic rendezvous. The decor is sumptuous, just like it was in the 1700s, with paintings on the wall—each for sale—and low marble dining tables and chairs. Call the place what you like—upmarket tea salon or cafe. Start with the tuna tartare or even a well-stuffed club sandwich at lunch. The tiger shrimp are savory and scented with malt whisky. For a main course, one of the most delightful offerings is steamed sea bass, flavored with ginger and served with snow peas and zucchini. Other fine selections include filet of sole with a saffron-laced sauce and filet of beef in a sauce made of Chinese truffles. The pastries are supplied from the famous Pierre Hermé bakeries.

8 rue d'Anjou, 8e. ✆ **01-40-17-04-77.** www.restaurant-1728.com. Reservations recommended for main meals. Main courses 15€–48€; fixed-price lunch 45€. AE, MC, V. Mon–Fri noon–midnight; Sat 2:30pm (tearoom only); dinner 8pm–midnight. Closed 3 weeks in Aug. Métro: Concorde.

Spoon, Food & Wine ★ INTERNATIONAL   This hypermodern venture by star chef Alain Ducasse is both hailed as a "restaurant for the millennium" and condemned as surreal and a bit absurd. Despite that, there can be a 2-week wait for a dinner reservation. This upscale but affordable restaurant may be the least pretentious and most hip of Ducasse's ventures. The somewhat claustrophobic dining room blends Parisian and Californian references, and the menu (which changes every 2 months) roams the world. Examples include deliberately under-cooked grilled squid (part of it evokes sushi) with curry sauce; grilled lamb cutlets; and hake with potatos, capers, lemon and watercress. Vegetarians appreciate stir-fried dishes in which you can mix and match up to 15 ingredients.

In the Hôtel Marignan-Elysée, 12 rue Marignan, 8e. ✆ **01-40-76-34-44.** www.spoon.tm.fr. Reservations recommended 1–2 weeks in advance. Main courses 29€–47€; fixed-price lunch 36€. AE, DC, MC, V. Mon–Fri 12:15–2:30pm and 7:30–10:30pm. Closed Aug and last week of Dec. Métro: Franklin-D-Roosevelt.

MODERATE

Chez André TRADITIONAL FRENCH   Chez André is one of the neighborhood's favorite bistros with an ambience that evokes France in the 1950s and a clientele that includes everyday folk, as well as some of the most prosperous residents of this extremely upscale neighborhood. Outside, a discreet red awning stretches over an array of shellfish on ice; inside, an Art Nouveau decor includes etched glass and masses of flowers. This has been a landmark on rue Marbeuf since 1937. It remains as it was when it was founded (thanks to an agreement made with the original owners). The old-style cuisine on the menu includes frogs' legs, grilled veal kidneys, roast rack of lamb, fresh shellfish, and on Fridays, bouillabaisse. Several reasonably priced wines are offered as well.

12 rue Marbeuf (at rue Clément-Marot), 8e. ℂ **01-47-20-59-57.** Reservations recommended. Main courses 15€–34€; fixed-price menu 34€. AE, DC, MC, V. Daily noon–1am. Métro: Franklin-D-Roosevelt.

Citrus Etoile ★ FRENCH   It's a good example of a hip, well-connected, and stylish restaurant-of-the-minute, where part of the fun involves seeing and being seen by the politically connected and trend-conscious crowd. The decor is minimalist, black, white, and orange, a bemused blend of the best of California (former home of the owners and inspiration for some of the cuisine) and France. If you opt for a meal here, you'll be in good hands: Chef Gilles Epié used to be a caterer and private chef in Hollywood before returning to Paris with his fashion-model wife Elizabeth (an American, who supervises the dining room) to open this en vogue dining venue near the Arch of Triumph. Menu items are health-conscious, artfully simple, "uncluttered," and flavorful. Try such delights as rabbit leg, grilled tuna with foie gras, plumb oysters with fresh asparagus, or lobster cooked in tarragon-flavored bouillon.

6 rue Arsène Houssaye, 8e. ℂ **01-42-89-15-51.** www.citrusetoile.fr. Reservations recommended. Main courses 42€–69€; fixed-price menu 49€–85€. AE, MC, V. Mon–Fri noon–3pm and 7:30–10:30pm. Métro: Etoile.

Ladurée ★ TRADITIONAL FRENCH   Acclaimed since 1862 as one of Paris's grand cafes, Ladurée adds a touch of class to the neighborhood. This offshoot of the original near La Madeleine caters to an international set. The stylish, somewhat chaotic venue changes from tearoom to full-fledged restaurant at least twice each day. The Belle Epoque setting is ideal for sampling Ladurée's macaroons—not the coconut version familiar to Americans, but two almond meringue cookies, flavored with vanilla, coffee, strawberry, pistachio, or another flavor, held together with butter cream. The talented chefs constantly adjust to take advantage of the freshest ingredients. After starting with the hot duck foie gras with crystallized dates, you might follow with the red mullet filet with tabouleh, salmon with mozzarella or perhaps saddle lamb and melon. One downside: Service isn't always efficient.

75 av. des Champs-Elysées, 8e. ℂ **01-40-75-08-75.** www.laduree.fr. Reservations required for restaurant. Main courses 15€–44€; fixed-price breakfast 18€–27€; fixed-price lunch or dinner 25€–29€; pastries from 6€. AE, DC, MC, V. Daily 7:30am–12:30am. Métro: George V.

Les Gourmets des Ternes ✦ TRADITIONAL FRENCH   This restaurant caters to hordes who appreciate its affordable prices and lack of pretension. Despite the brusque service, diners have included the mayor of Atlanta (who wrote the bistro a thank-you letter), Sean Penn, and Oliver Stone, as well as hundreds of folks from this neighborhood. Thriving in this spot since 1892, the place retains an early-1900s paneled decor, with some additions from the 1950s, including bordeaux-colored banquettes, mirrors, wooden panels, touches of brass, and paper tablecloths. The finely grilled signature dishes include rib steak with marrow sauce and fries; sole meunière; sole, turbot, and monkfish; and desserts such as crème caramel and *baba au rhum* (rum cake with raisins).

87 bd. de Courcelles, 8e. ℂ **01-42-27-43-04.** www.lesgourmetsdesternes.com. Main courses 18€–36€. AE, DC, MC, V. Mon–Fri noon–2:30pm and 7–10pm. Métro: Ternes.

Market ★ FUSION   The creative force here is Alsatian Jean-Georges Vongerichten, whose restaurants in New York, Hong Kong, London, and Las Vegas are classified by local critics as both megahip and top tier. The Paris gemstone in the Vongerichten empire holds 130 diners in a richly paneled postmodern decor, designed by decorating mogul Christian Liaigre, dotted with carved masks from Polynesia and Borneo and with art objects on loan from the Paris branch of Christie's auction house. Menu items include a pizza with black truffles and Fontina cheese; foie gras with a purée of quince, corn pancakes, and wild cranberries; or crabmeat salad with mango. Main courses might feature *daurade* (bream or porgy) baked in a salt crust; a faux-filet with exotic mushrooms; or a "black plate" for two diners, loaded high with shellfish and their garnishes. There's a wine list that most oenophiles consider extremely interesting.

15 av. Matignon, 8e. ℂ **01-56-43-40-90.** Reservations required. Main courses 29€–46€; fixed-price lunch 34€; pizzas 19€–29€. AE, MC, V. Mon–Fri noon–3pm and daily 7:30–11:30pm; Sat–Sun brunch noon–4:30pm. Métro: Champs-Elysées-Clemenceau.

Publicis Drugstore MODERN FRENCH   In 1958 the founder of this company, Marcel Bleustein-Blanchet, following a visit to the United States, created a new concept for Paris that became a legend. Years later, a fire in one drugstore and a bombing in a Left Bank branch ended its glory. But le Drugstore has made a spectacular comeback. Truman Capote once defined a city as a place where you can purchase a canary at 3 o'clock in the morning. In Paris, the Drugstore is a place where you can purchase a 200€ teddy bear or order a deluxe hamburger with foie gras in the wee hours. The Drugstore stands on the site of the old Astoria Hotel, the home of General Eisenhower when he was supreme commander of the Allied Forces in Europe. Today it houses a brasserie, a bookshop, a wine shop, two cinemas, a newsstand, and a high-end grocery store. The famed chef, Alain Ducasse, planned the menu. Every food item from grilled scallops to ham with truffles Ducasse-style is served here.

133 av. des Champs-Elysées, 8e. ℂ **01-44-43-77-64.** www.publicisdrugstore.com. Main courses 16€–34€. AE, DC, MC, V. Mon–Fri 8am–2am. Sat–Sun 10am–2am. Métro: Charles-de-Gaulle-Etoile or Georges V.

INEXPENSIVE

Bar des Théâtres TRADITIONAL FRENCH   Its local patrons in the 8th arrondissement have long called this bar/restaurant "The Temple of the God Steak Tartare." For those daring souls who still eat this blood-rare red meat specialty, this long-established restaurant is said to make the best dish. Even though it's situated in the most lethally priced district of Paris, over the years it has kept its prices reasonable. Across the street is the Théâtre des Champs-Elysées, and many of its performers, especially actors and musicians, make the bar their "local" while appearing here. The chef also specializes in a delectable *magret de canard* (breast of duckling), and you can even order caviar and foie gras, but those items would put this into a very expensive category. Better settle for the sauerkraut.

6 av. Montaigne, 8e. ℂ **01-47-23-34-63.** Reservations recommended. Main courses 13€–22€. AE, DC, MC, V. Daily noon–1am. Closed Aug. Métro: Alma Marceau.

Chez Savy ★ 🍴 AUVERGNAT   Set within one of Paris's most stratospherically expensive neighborhoods, this old-time brasserie has prices that, compared to nearby competitors, seem modest. Founded in 1923 and with an old-fashioned bistro decor (mirrors, brass hardware, polished paneling, banquettes) that hasn't changed much since the Jazz Age, it has a pair of long and narrow dining rooms, the first of which is known as *le wagon* (the dining car). Come here for the kind of hearty, flavorful food that your great-grandmother (had she been from the Auvergne) would have prepared for a holiday meal around 1910. Sauces here are likely enriched with bone marrow; pork chitterlings are laboriously processed into earthy versions of *andouillettes*; and accompaniments to a main course might include a *petit farçou*, a thick crepe enriched with such green leafy vegetables as chard, spinach, and leeks. Lamb here is superb, especially the slow-cooked haunches, cooked with rosemary until the meat is literally falling off the bone.

23 rue Bayard, 8e. ✆ **01-47-23-46-98.** Reservations required for lunch. Main courses 22€–28€; fixed-price lunch 28€; fixed-price dinner 35€. AE, DC, MC, V. Mon–Fri noon–2:30pm and 7:30–10:30pm. Closed Aug. Métro: Franklin-D-Roosevelt.

16th Arrondissement (Trocadero/ Bois de Boulogne)

VERY EXPENSIVE

Hiramatsu ★ 🍴 TRADITIONAL FRENCH   Other than the fact that chef Hiroyuki Hiramatsu and most of his staff are Japanese, the only Asian touch at this restaurant is a hot, wet towel that arrives before the meal, in the Japanese style. Everything else is unabashedly French: the contemporary dining room, seating just 40, that's outfitted in mostly monochromatic tones of black and white; the rows of windows, each of which is set with shimmering panes of red-and-blue cut glass; and a polite staff wearing gray-and-white uniforms. Menu items change frequently, but are always artfully presented. Try pigeon breast with foie gras (flavored with strong coffee and cocoa), lobster with spinach wine sauce and chops of veal with vegetables.

52 rue de Longchamps, 16e. ✆ **01-56-81-08-80.** www.hiramatsu.co.jp. Reservations required. Main courses 47€–72€; fixed-price menu 95€–130€. AE, DC, MC, V. Mon–Fri 12:30–1:30pm and 7:30–9:30pm. Métro: Trocadéro.

EXPENSIVE

Cristal Room ★★ MODERN FRENCH   The Taittinger family of champagne fame has opened this Baccarat crystal–laden room in a former town house of the art patroness, Marie-Laure de Noailles. She was known as the benefactor of such artists as Man Ray and Salvador Dalí. For the new restaurant setting, Philippe Starck was called in to create the minimalist decor, with a bow to the surrealists. The chef is the brilliant Guy Martin, a total original, creating his own take on such classics as lobster ravioli or even a chocolate soufflé, each dish having a distinctive flavor. Start, perhaps, with a delectable chestnut *veloute* and follow with such delights as roast scallops, roast pigeon, or roast lobster flavored with pepper.

11 place des Etats-Unis, 16e. ✆ **01-40-22-11-10.** Reservations required. Main courses 30€–45€; fixed-price lunch 29€–55€; fixed-price dinner 99€–149€. AE, MC, V. Mon–Sat 12:15–2:15pm and 7:15–10:30pm. Closed last week in Dec. Métro: Boissière.

L'Astrance ★★★ MODERN FRENCH   It's small, it's charming, and its creative flair derives from the partnership of two former employees (some say "disciples") of megachef Alain Passard, scion of L'Arpège, an ultraglam restaurant in the 7th arrondissement. The perfectly mannered Christophe Rohat, supervising the dining room, is the more visible of the two, but Pascal Barbot, the chef

FAMILY-FRIENDLY restaurants

Meals at Paris's grand restaurants are rarely suitable for young children. Nevertheless, many parents drag their kids along, often to the annoyance of other diners. You may have to make some compromises, such as dining earlier than most Parisians. **Hotel dining rooms** can be another good choice for family dining. They usually have children's menus or at least one or two *plats du jour* cooked for children, such as spaghetti with meat sauce.

If you take your child to a **moderate** or an **inexpensive restaurant,** ask if they will serve a child's plate. If not, order a *plat du jour* or *plat garni* (a garnished main-course platter), which will be suitable for most children, particularly if a dessert is to follow. Most **cafes** welcome children during the day and early evening. At a cafe, children seem to like the

sandwiches (try a *croque monsieur,* or toasted ham and cheese), the omelets, and the *pommes frites* (french fries).

Crémerie-Restaurant Polidor (p. 199) One of the most popular restaurants on the Left Bank, this reasonably priced dining room is so family friendly, it calls its food *cuisine familiale.* This might be the best place to introduce your child to bistro food.

Hard Rock Cafe (p. 170)   At the Paris branch of this chain, good old American burgers and more are served against a background of rock memorabilia and music.

Joe Allen (p. 163)   This American restaurant in Les Halles delivers everything from chili to chocolate-mousse pie to the best burgers in Paris.

creating the food that emerges from the kitchens, has become a true culinary force. Expect a crisply contemporary dining room. The menu, from which flavors practically jump off the plates, might include an unusual form of "ravioli," wherein thin slices of avocado encase a filling of seasoned crabmeat, all of it accompanied by salted almonds and a splash of almond oil. Other delights to the palate include turbot flavored with lemon and ginger, or sautéed pigeon with potatoes au gratin.

4 rue Beethoven, 16e. ☎ **01-40-50-84-40.** Reservations required 3 or 4 weeks in advance. Main courses 24€–38€; fixed-price lunch 70€–120€; fixed-price dinner 120€–290€. AE, DC, MC, V. Tues–Fri 12:15–1:30pm and 8:15–9pm. Closed Aug. Métro: Passy.

Le Relais du Parc ★★ MODERN FRENCH   The two most celebrated chefs of France, Alain Ducasse and Joël Robuchon, buried the hatchet and launched this joint venture. The Paris press hailed them as the dynamic duo. But Batman and Robin they aren't. The marriage did not last. Ducasse is still in charge, though not the actual chef, of course, but Robuchon bolted for reasons unknown.

In fair weather, you dine alfresco among white magnolia trees in the inner courtyard, or else in the intimate and elegant dining room set in neutral hues. Each dish is a delight, including pigeon with cabbage and foie gras, or langoustines from Southern Brittany enhanced by Iranian caviar. The wild hare from the Loire Valley is stuffed with foie gras and roasted. Enjoy Ducasse's signature baked macaroni with butter, ham, and truffles, or his Pompadour potato casserole with crispy bacon.

In the Hotel Sofitel Le Parc, 55–57 av. Raymond-Poincaré, 16e. ☎ **01-44-05-66-10.** Reservations required. Main courses 36€–49€; fixed-price lunch 49€–59€; fixed-price dinner 85€. AE, DC, MC, V. Tues–Sat noon–2pm and 7:30–10pm. Closed Aug. Métro: Trocadéro or Victor Hugo.

MODERATE

La Butte Chaillot ★ 🍴 TRADITIONAL FRENCH   This baby bistro showcases culinary high priest Guy Savoy and draws a crowd from the affluent neighborhood's corporate offices. Diners congregate in posh but congested areas. Menu items change weekly (sometimes daily) and betray a strange sense of mass production not unlike that found in a luxury cruise ship's dining room. You might begin with a terrine of rabbit studded with nuts and served with red onion compote, or perhaps crayfish tartare flavored with lemon. For main dishes, filet of sea bass is served with green lentils from the Pyrenees, or else you might go for the duckling confit with mushrooms.

110 bis av. Kléber, 16e. ☎ **01-47-27-88-88.** www.guysavoy.com. Reservations recommended. Main courses 16€–28€; fixed-price menu 36€. AE, DC, MC, V. Sun–Fri noon–2pm; daily 7–11pm. Métro: Trocadéro.

Tokyo Eat MODERN FRENCH   Ignore the name. There is no Japanese food served here. What is called the "glam-funk fashion-and-design crowd" fills up the tables at the daringly avant-garde museum, Palais de Tokyo. Like miniature space ships, large pink spheres overhead flash in time to the booming music. The spacious Art Deco terrace is the most sought-after place to dine in fair weather.

Each day the chefs prepare a series of tasty *plats du jour*. The most expensive item on the menu is filet of beef with morels and a yellowish Jura wine. In their innovative recipes, the chefs are as modern as the museum itself—take the minestrone of sardines, for example. Mains might include gilt-head bream tartare with fruit chutney and ginger-and-vanilla oil or else satay-crusted loin of lamb with baby eggplant.

13 av. du Président Wilson, 16e. ☎ **01-47-20-00-29.** Reservations recommended. Main courses 12€–29€. AE, DC, MC, V. Tues–Sun noon–3pm and 8–11:30pm. Métro: Iéna.

INEXPENSIVE

Kambodgia ASIAN/CAMBODIAN   The waiters, all dressed in black cotton tunics, will welcome you to this excellent eatery that serves some of the best and most flavorful Asian dishes in Paris. The basement atmosphere has been called "Zen-like," but the service is welcoming, and it's a good choice for a romantic dinner not far from the Champs-Elysées. Two of our favorite dishes: a superb seafood *pot-au-feu* (stew) and chicken roasted with honey and lemon. One Cambodian dish that's a delight is the ginger fish wrapped in a banana leaf.

15 rue de Bassano, 16e. ☎ **01-47-20-03-50.** www.kambodgia.com. Reservations required. Main courses 15€–22€; fixed-price lunch 20€–25€. AE, MC, V. Mon–Fri noon–2:30pm; Mon–Sat 7:30–10:30pm. Closed Aug. Métro: George V.

17th Arrondissement (Parc Monceau/ Place Clichy)

VERY EXPENSIVE

Guy Savoy ★★★ TRADITIONAL FRENCH   One of the hottest chefs in Europe, Guy Savoy serves the kind of food he likes to eat, prepared with consummate skill. We think he has a slight edge over his rival Michel Rostang (see below), though Ducasse, at least in media coverage, surpasses them both. The superb meals comprise as many as nine courses, but portions are small; you won't necessarily be satiated at the end. The menu changes seasonally and may include oven-roasted sole steaks with smoked seaweed, roasted rib of veal, purée potatoes with truffles, or steam-baked Bresse chicken breast with lemon grass and Swiss chard. If you come in the right season, you may have a chance to order game, such as mallard and venison. Savoy is fascinated with mushrooms and has been known to serve a dozen types, especially in autumn.

18 rue Troyon, 17e. ✆ **01-43-80-40-61.** Fax 01-46-22-43-09. www.guysavoy.com. Reservations for dinner required 1 month in advance; 2–3 days in advance for lunch. Main courses 75€–230€; *menu dégustation* (tasting menu) 285€–450€. AE, DC, MC, V. Tues–Fri noon-2pm; Tues–Sat 7-10:30pm. Métro: Charles-de-Gaulle-Etoile or Ternes.

Michel Rostang ★★★ MODERN & TRADITIONAL FRENCH   Michel Rostang is one of Paris's most creative chefs, the fifth generation of a distinguished French "cooking family." His restaurant contains four dining rooms paneled in mahogany, cherrywood, or pearwood; some have frosted Lalique crystal panels. Changing every season, the menu offers modern improvements on *cuisine bourgeoise.* Truffles are the dish of choice in midwinter, and in spring you'll find racks of suckling lamb from the salt marshes of France's western coast; in game season, look for pheasant and venison. Year-round staples are quail eggs with sea urchins, fricassee of sole, quenelles of whitefish with a lobster sauce, roast scallops with chestnut gnocchi, or hot foie gras with roast mandarines.

20 rue Rennequin, 17e. ✆ **01-47-63-40-77.** Fax 01-47-63-82-75. www.michelrostang.com. Reservations required 1 week in advance. Main courses 48€–98€; fixed-price lunch 74€–285€; fixed-price dinner 169€–285€. AE, DC, MC, V. Tues–Fri noon-2:30pm; Mon–Sat 7:30-10:30pm. Closed 3 weeks in Aug. Métro: Ternes.

EXPENSIVE

Rech ★ TRADITIONAL FRENCH/SEAFOOD   Fabled chef Alain Ducasse has brought new life to this brasserie founded in 1925 and specializing in shellfish. The original Alsatian brasserie features have been retained, including the Art Deco furnishings—even the oyster shucker on the sidewalk. The previous owner, August Rech, believed in keeping the menu limited but choice, a tradition that has been respected. Ducasse was inspired to create some of the recipes here while vacationing in Brittany. The *pièce de résistance* is a platter of *fruits de mer,* but you can also order half a dozen different kinds of succulent fresh oysters. Poached skate wing appears with garlic and caper butter, and you can also order a grilled entrecôte with béarnaise sauce. For dessert, patrons order the largest éclair served in Paris.

62 av. des Ternes, 17e. ✆ **01-45-72-29-47.** Reservations required. Main courses 24€–45€; fixed-price lunch 34€. AE, DC, MC, V. Mon–Sat noon-3pm and 7-10pm. Closed July 25–Aug 15. Métro: Ternes.

MODERATE

Chez Georges TRADITIONAL FRENCH   Not to be confused with a bistro of the same name in the 2nd arrondissement, this is a worthy choice. It has flourished since 1926 despite an obscure location. The setting has changed little—cheerfully harassed waiters barge through a dining room sheathed with old-fashioned paneling and etched glass, and savory odors emerge from the busy kitchen. Two enduring specialties are head of veal with ravigote sauce and standing rib roast with herbs (especially thyme) in its own juices and au gratin of potatoes. Preceding these might be duckling foie gras; a gilthead sea bream tartare; or a selection of sausages and pork products eaten with bread, butter, and sour pickles.

273 bd. Pereire, 17e. ℰ **01-45-74-31-00.** www.restaurant-chezgeorges.fr. Reservations recommended. Main courses 21€–38€. MC, V. Daily noon–3pm and 7–11:30pm. Métro: Porte Maillot.

La Braisière ★★ 🏠 SOUTHWESTERN FRENCH   In this very residential arrondissement, Jacques Faussat is all the rage, winning his first Michelin star in 2004. Born in the Pyrenees, he brings the savory cuisine of the southwest to this 40-seat restaurant, whose entrance is dominated by an enormous vase of flowers in a Médici-inspired Renaissance vase. The decor is cozy, warm, and intimate, with the restaurant evoking upscale chic in one of the French provinces. From the first bite, we fell in love with Faussat's savory, ambitious cuisine, and with its contrast in texture and flavor. Nothing is finer for a starter than his signature appetizer of foie gras terrine with apricot. You can then go on to one of the beautifully prepared and seasoned fish dishes, such as "lacquered" red tuna served with onions, braised endive, and Szechuan peppers. The lamb from the Pyrenees is among the best we've ever had. The dessert specialty, familiar to residents of Gascony, is *tortière,* made with a light phyllo pastry over stewed prunes flavored with Armagnac and cinnamon, and garnished with the world's best fig ice cream.

54 rue Cardinet, 17e. ℰ **01-47-63-40-37.** Reservations required. Main courses 22€–31€. Fixed-price lunch 38€. AE, DC, MC, V. Mon–Sat noon–2:30pm and Mon–Fri 7:30–10:30pm. Closed Aug. Métro: Malesherbes.

Le Hide ★ 🏠 TRADITIONAL FRENCH   This is a real discovery, a bistro with superlative food near the Arc de Triomphe. Some expats living in Paris claim that Le Hide is their favorite bistro in the whole capital. The restaurant takes its name from its Japanese chef, Hide Kobayashi. He describes his food as French bistro, but that is too plebian a name for the dishes he concocts. The cuisine is certainly French, but many of his recipes also reflect his Japanese origins. The chef perfected his craft in the kitchens of some of the world's greatest chefs, including Joël Robuchon. The menu changes daily, and all the main courses, listed under *plats du jour,* cost the same. Main courses include a fricassee of rabbit flavored with mustard, sweetbreads in cream with truffles, and a succulent entrecôte.

10 rue du General Lanrezac, 17e. ℰ **01-45-74-15-81.** www.lehide.fr. Reservations required. Main courses 16€; fixed-price menu 22€–29€. MC, V. Mon–Fri noon–2pm and Mon–Sat 7:30–10:30pm. Métro: Charles-de-Gaulle–Etoile.

Restaurant Caïus ★ 🍴 TRADITIONAL FRENCH   This chic place, popular for business lunches and dinners, also draws residents and shoppers. It's ringed with wood paneling, banquettes, and teakwood chairs. The new owner, Jean-Marc Notelet, has brought renewed vigor to the kitchen. His cuisine, however, remains traditionally French and is based on spices and a judicious use of pepper. The dining room is a showcase for the chef's enticing cuisine, which is based on authentically flavor-filled local foodstuffs. To whet your appetite, try such dishes as grilled flap mushrooms or duckling foie gras. Among other masterful offerings are dorado braised with Belgian endives and root vegetables, and a confit of beef with fava beans and aged vinegar along with celery whipped into almond milk.

6 rue d'Armaillé, 17e. ☎ **01-42-27-19-20.** Reservations recommended. Main courses 19€–31€; fixed-price lunch 23€; fixed-price dinner 39€. AE, DC, MC, V. Mon–Sat noon–2:30pm; Mon–Sat 7:30–11pm. Métro: Argentine.

ON THE LEFT BANK

We begin with the most centrally located arrondissements on the Left Bank and then work our way through the more outlying neighborhoods and to the area near the Eiffel Tower.

5th Arrondissement (Quartier Latin)

VERY EXPENSIVE

La Tour d'Argent 🖐 TRADITIONAL FRENCH   This penthouse restaurant, a national institution, enjoys a panoramic view over the Seine and Notre-Dame. Although its reputation as the best in Paris has long been eclipsed, dining here remains an unsurpassed event, not because of the diminishing culinary reputation of this place, but because of the view of those flying buttresses of Notre-Dame. A restaurant of some sort has stood on this site since 1582: Mme de Sévigné refers to a cafe here in her letters, and Dumas used it in one of his novels. The fame of La Tour d'Argent spread during its ownership by Frédéric Delair, who in the 1890s started the practice of issuing certificates to diners who ordered *caneton* (pressed duckling). The birds are numbered: The first was served to Edward VII in 1890, and now the number has surpassed 1.2 million! For decades, the restaurant was owned by Claude Terrail, who became the most famous restauranteur in Europe. He died in 2006, and today management is handled by his son, André. A good part of the menu is devoted to duck, but the kitchen, of course, knows how to prepare other dishes. There are plenty of other places nearby where you can order food even better than that served here—and at only half the price.

15–17 quai de la Tournelle, 5e. ☎ **01-43-54-23-31.** Fax 01-44-07-12-04. www.latourdargent.com. Reservations required far in advance. Main courses 60€–75€; fixed-price lunch 65€. AE, DC, MC, V. Tues–Sat noon–1pm; Tues–Sat 7:30–9pm. Métro: St-Michel or Pont Marie.

MODERATE

Al Dar LEBANESE   This well-respected restaurant works hard to popularize the savory cuisine of Lebanon. Within a modern decor whose colors might remind you of the arid scrublands of the Middle East, you'll dine on such dishes as tabbouleh, a refreshing combination of finely chopped parsley, mint, milk, tomatoes, onions, lemon juice, olive oil, and salt; baba ghanouj (pulverized and seasoned eggplant); and hummus (pulverized chickpeas with herbs). These can be followed with savory roasted chicken or tender minced lamb with mint, cumin, and Mediterranean herbs.

8 rue Frédéric-Sauton, 5e. ☎ **01-43-25-17-15.** Reservations recommended. Main courses 13€–17€; fixed-price lunch 17€–30€; fixed-price dinner 40€–53€. AE, DC, MC, V. Daily noon–3pm and 7pm–midnight. Métro: Maubert-Mutualité.

Brasserie Balzar ★ TRADITIONAL FRENCH   Opened in 1898, Brasserie Balzar is battered but cheerful, with some of Paris's most colorful waiters. The menu makes almost no concessions to modern cuisine; it includes onion soup, pepper steak, sole meunière, sauerkraut with ham and sausage, pigs' feet, and fried calves' liver served without garnish. Be warned that if you want just coffee or a drink, you probably won't get a table at mealtimes. But the staff, accustomed to many patrons' odd hours, will be happy to serve you dinner in the midafternoon. Guests have included Sartre and Camus (who often got into arguments), James Thurber, and countless professors from the nearby Sorbonne.

49 rue des Ecoles, 5e. ✆ **01-43-54-13-67.** www.brasseriebalzar.com. Reservations strongly recommended. Main courses 18€–35€. AE, DC, MC, V. Daily noon–11:45pm. Métro: Odéon or Cluny–La Sorbonne.

Itineraire ★ TRADITIONAL FRENCH   There's always a danger when a successful restaurant moves and expands. Often its original charm and patrons are lost. Not so with acclaimed chef Sylvain Sendra and his wife, Sarah, who closed their 26-seat Le Temps au Temps in the 11th arrondissement and opened another restaurant in the Latin Quarter. Their new place is twice as large, and the cuisine is just as good as it always was. Specialties include everything from Jerusalem artichoke soup to pheasant breast accompanied by dates, pistachios, fruit compote, and the odd nugget of buckshot. One specialty is morchella mushrooms served with bacon crisps and a soft-boiled egg. They have a distinctive strong taste and come in a creamy sauce. Salmon is cooked on one side only and served with cannelloni stuffed with risotto. You might also order a delightful sea bass stuffed with white asparagus and served with a creamy Parmesan vanilla sauce.

5 rue de Pontoise, 5e. ✆ **01-46-33-60-11.** Reservations required. Fixed-price menu 36€. AE, MC, V. Tues–Sat noon–2pm and 7:30–10:30pm (11:30pm Fri–Sat). Métro: Maubert-Mutualité.

Le Petit Pontoise ★ ☝ TRADITIONAL FRENCH   Lying on a little-visited side street, off quai de la Tournelle, this restaurant is frequented by both professors and students from the Sorbonne. It's tiny, but the portions are big and generous. The clientele—often made up of regulars—is pampered with comfort food. Fine ingredients and a technique honed to perfection have made this a citadel of fine dining. You could take your grandmother here, even your great-grandmother, and she would likely be pleased with the roast quail with almonds or the fresh chicken cooked in wine and mushrooms. Tender, well-flavored duckling comes with foie gras, and you can also take delight in the stew of pigs' cheeks and fresh vegetables, served in an iron casserole.

9 rue de Pontoise, 5e. ✆ **01-43-29-25-20.** Main courses 18€–27€. AE, MC, V. Daily noon–2:30pm and 7:30–10:30pm. Métro: Maubert-Mutualité.

Le Pré Verre ★ 🍴 ASIAN/TRADITIONAL FRENCH   Around the corner from the Sorbonne in the heart of the Latin Quarter comes a refreshing restaurant where you can get seriously good food at an affordable price. Even if this is not an earth-shattering gastronomic experience, it is solid and reliable, with good cooking and market-fresh ingredients. The Delacourcelle brothers are firmly based in the French tradition, but they have added innovative modern twists by giving extra spicing to the food, many of the flavorings inspired by Asia. In a welcoming, relaxed, and convivial atmosphere, tables are placed so close together that you're literally dining and rubbing elbows with the same people. For something bourgeois, dig into the well-flavored terrines for starters. One of these—and the most delectable—is made with layers of foie gras and mashed potatoes. Your meal might begin with oysters marinated with ginger and poppy seeds or

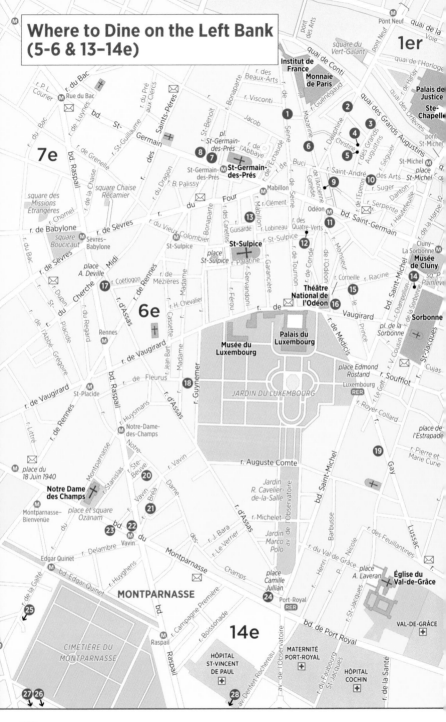

Where to Dine on the Left Bank (5-6 & 13–14e)

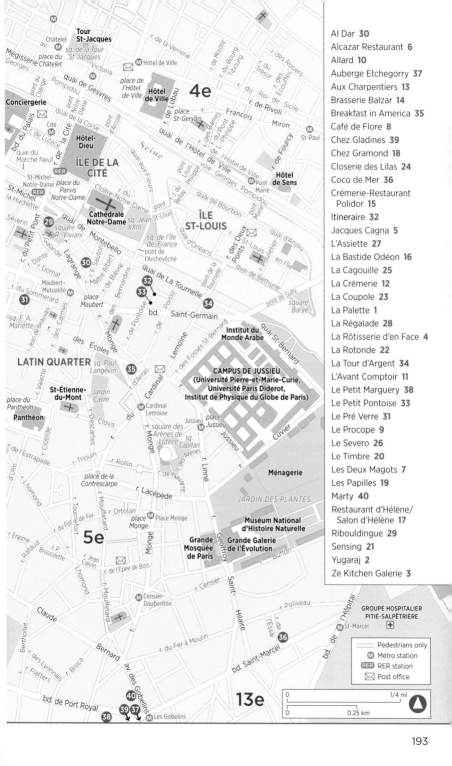

Al Dar **30**
Alcazar Restaurant **6**
Allard **10**
Auberge Etchegorry **37**
Aux Charpentiers **13**
Brasserie Balzar **14**
Breakfast in America **35**
Café de Flore **8**
Chez Gladines **39**
Chez Gramond **18**
Closerie des Lilas **24**
Coco de Mer **36**
Crémerie-Restaurant
  Polidor **15**
Itineraire **32**
Jacques Cagna **5**
L'Assiette **27**
La Bastide Odéon **16**
La Cagouille **25**
La Crémerie **12**
La Coupole **23**
La Palette **1**
La Régalade **28**
La Rôtisserie d'en Face **4**
La Rotonde **22**
La Tour d'Argent **34**
L'Avant Comptoir **11**
Le Petit Marguery **38**
Le Petit Pontoise **33**
Le Pré Verre **31**
Le Procope **9**
Le Severo **26**
Le Timbre **20**
Les Deux Magots **7**
Les Papilles **19**
Marty **40**
Restaurant d'Hélène/
  Salon d'Hélène **17**
Ribouldingue **29**
Sensing **21**
Yugaraj **2**
Ze Kitchen Galerie **3**

scallops with cinnamon. Main courses might include suckling pig with aromatic spices and crisp-cooked cabbage, or roasted codfish.

8 rue Thenard, 5e. ✆ **01-43-54-59-47.** www.lepreverre.com. Reservations required. Main courses 18€; fixed-price lunch 14€–29€; fixed-price dinner 29€. MC, V. Tues–Sat noon–2pm and 7:30–10:30pm. Closed Aug. Métro: Maubert-Mutualité.

Les Papilles ★ MODERN FRENCH One of the most exciting additions to Paris's culinary scene is this deli, bistro, and wine shop all at one address. It features an appetizer (called *entrée* in French), a *plat du jour,* and dessert for an affordable price. Wine is available by the glass, but patrons are encouraged to order by the bottle since these bottles have some of the cheapest retail prices in France. Near Jardin de Luxembourg, Les Papilles offers superb food, including a four-course *dégustation menu* at night that blends the cookery of the Garonne with the chef's imagination of the day.

30 rue Gay-Lussac. ✆ **01-43-25-20-79.** Reservations not needed. Market menu 31€; fixed-price dinner 80€. AE, MC, V. Mon–Sat noon–3pm and 7–11pm. Métro: Luxembourg.

Marty ★ MODERN FRENCH Charming, with a stone-trimmed decor that's authentic to the era (1913) when it was established, this restaurant has been "discovered" by new generations of restaurant-goers. Named after its founders, Etienne and Marthe Marty, its fame now extends beyond the 5th arrondissement. Service is attentive, and lots of Jazz Age murals grace the walls. Food is savory, satisfying, and unfussy. Views from the hideaway tables on the mezzanine sweep over the entire human comedy, which is loud, large, and animated, unfolding above and below you. Begin a meal with duckling terrine or Andalusian gazpacho. Continue with *suprême* of guinea fowl with vegetable moussaka, a rump steak in black pepper sauce, or perhaps fried scallops sautéed in the Provençal style.

20 av. des Gobelins, 5e. ✆ **01-43-31-39-51.** www.marty-restaurant.com. Main courses 21€–35€; fixed-price menu 35€. AE, DC, MC, V. Daily noon–midnight. Métro: Gobelins.

Ribouldingue TRADITIONAL FRENCH Offal lovers flock to this bistro near St-Julien-le-Pauvre church to enjoy such old-fashioned fare as the tip of a pig's snout or thinly breaded and sautéed slices of a cow's udder. If those are unappealing, how about lamb's brain meunière or tripe cooked in white wine, even veal kidneys in garlic sauce? For the offal timid, there are many other dishes, including veal rib with fried potatoes; Pollock with eggplant caviar and crispy lardons (bacon cubes), or even a blanquette of monkfish. We adore their mascarpone crumble, but you might want the ice cream made of ewe's milk. This Latin Quarter bistro is the creation of Nadège Varigny, the daughter of a butcher in the

---

Can You Dine Badly in Paris?

The answer is an emphatic yes. Our mailbox fills with complaints from readers who've encountered haughty service and paid outrageous prices for swill. Often, these complaints are about restaurants catering to tourists. Avoid them by following our suggestions or looking in nontouristy areas for new discoveries. If you ask Parisians for recommendations, specify that you're looking for restaurants where *they* would dine, not where they think you, as a tourist, would dine.

French Alps. This woman is definitely not afraid of the sight of blood. She'll seat you in two cozy rooms, and will do so with a great sense of humor.

10 rue Saint-Julien-le-Pauvre, 5e. ℂ **01-46-33-98-80.** Reservations required. Main courses 17€–26€; fixed-price lunch 27€; fixed-price dinner 29€. MC, V. Tues–Fri noon–2:30pm and Tues–Sat 7:30–10:30pm. Closed 3 weeks in Aug. Métro: Cluny La Sorbonne or St-Michel.

INEXPENSIVE

Breakfast in America AMERICAN   Connecticut-born Hollywood screen-writer Craig Carlson opened this replica of a down-home U.S.-based diner in 2003, building it with funds from members of the California film community who donated memorabilia from their films. Its self-proclaimed mission involves dispensing proper, rib-sticking American breakfasts and diner food to a genera-tion of Parisians who assume, prior to their visits here, that coffee comes only as espresso, and that quantities, per meal, are rigidly limited. The venue replicates a 1950s-era railway car, replete with scarlet-and-black Naugahyde banquettes, faux windows with mirrored insets, and an unabashedly Americanized staff. Breakfast (heaping portions of the egg-and-waffle-and-bacon combinations, as well as omelets) is served throughout the day and evening. Also available are half a dozen variations of burgers, as well as tacos, club sandwiches, and BLTs.

17 rue des Ecoles, 5e. ℂ **01-43-54-50-28.** Reservations not accepted. Breakfast platters 7€–11€; lunch and dinner platters and "blue-plate specials" 8€–12€; fixed-price Sun brunch 16€. MC, V. Daily 8:30am–10:30pm. Métro: Cardinal Lemoine or Jussieu.

Coco de Mer ★ 🎁 SEYCHELLE ISLANDS   The theme of this restaurant tugs at the emotions of Parisians who have spent their holidays on the beaches of the Seychelles, in the Indian Ocean. It contains several dining rooms, one of which is outfitted like a beach, with a sand-covered floor, replicas of palm trees, and a scattering of conch shells. Menu items feature such exotic dishes as tartare of tuna flavored with ginger, olive oil, salt, and pepper; and smoked swordfish, served as carpaccio or in thin slices with mango mousse and spicy sauce. Main courses focus on fish, including a species of red snapper (*boirzoes*) imported from the Seychelles.

34 bd. St-Marcel, 5e. ℂ **01-47-07-06-64.** Reservations recommended. Main courses 14€–17€; fixed-price menu 23€–30€. AE, DC, MC, V. Tues–Sat noon–3pm; Mon–Sat 7:30pm–midnight. Métro: Les Gobelins or St-Marcel.

6th Arrondissement (St-Germain/Luxemburg)
VERY EXPENSIVE

Jacques Cagna ★★★ MODERN & TRADITIONAL FRENCH   St-Ger-main knows no finer dining than at Jacques Cagna, a sophisticated restaurant in a 17th-century town house with massive timbers, burnished paneling, and 17th-century Dutch paintings. Jacques Cagna is one of the best classically trained chefs in Paris, though he has become a half-apostle to *cuisine moderne.* This is evident in his delectable standing roast of veal with a lime-and-ginger sauce, his turbot with Granny Smith apples, his Vendée pigeon with green Chartreuse, or his pan-seared duckling with foie gras.

14 rue des Grands-Augustins, 6e. ℂ **01-43-26-49-39.** Fax 01-43-54-54-48. www.jacquescagna. com. Reservations required in advance. Main courses 27€–67€; fixed-price lunch 45€–95€; fixed-price dinner 95€. AE, DC, MC, V. Tues–Fri noon–2pm; Mon–Sat 7:30-10:15pm. Closed 3 weeks in Aug. Métro: St-Michel or Odéon.

Restaurant d'Hélène/Salon d'Hélène ★★★ SOUTHWESTERN FRENCH   Hélène Darroze is the most famous female chef in Paris, a Basque-born wunderkind whose southwestern French cuisine is a superb modern take on a classic. Be very clear about what you want before entering: The upstairs dining room (Le Restaurant d'Hélène, with elaborately set round tables) is more formal, horrendously expensive, and more sedate than the bistro (Le Salon d'Hélène). In both areas, expect bright, pop-influenced decor and relatively slow service. Upstairs, menus are artfully composed and presented as part of fixed-price meals that contain, among other things, Basque lamb saddle stuffed with chorizo and toasted with fresh bay leaves; wild river salmon grilled just on one side; or pan-fried, milk-fed lamb sweetbreads with tandoori spices. On street level, food focuses on an array of *plats du jour* (skate *Grenobloise* with lemon and capers) and tapas, two or three of which can be combined to create a meal. Tapas might include raw marinated tuna with Basque-derived red pepper sauce or cannelloni gratinéed with Basque sheep's milk cheese and smoked Basque ham.

4 rue d'Assas, 6e. ✆ **01-42-22-00-11.** www.helenedarroze.com. Reservations required. Restaurant fixed-price lunch 52€–145€; fixed-price dinner 125€–145€. Salon fixed-price lunch 28€–35€; fixed-price dinner 105€. AE, MC, V. Tues–Sat 12:30–2:30pm and 7:30–10pm. Métro: Sèvres-Babylone.

EXPENSIVE

Closerie des Lilas ★ TRADITIONAL FRENCH   Opened in 1847, the Closerie was a social and culinary magnet for the avant-garde. The famous people who have sat in the "Pleasure Garden of the Lilacs" include Gertrude Stein and Alice B. Toklas, Ingres, Henry James, Chateaubriand, Picasso, Hemingway, Apollinaire, Lenin and Trotsky (at the chessboard), and Whistler. Today, the crowd consists of tourists or members of the Paris publishing world. The place resounds with the sometimes-loud sounds of a jazz pianist every night after 7pm, making the interior seem more claustrophobic than it is. If you're asked to wait for a table, you can make the wait more enjoyable by ordering the world's best champagne julep at the bar. The cuisine has been improved, offering such dishes as roast turbot with Provençal vegetables or lightly pan-fried king prawns with a saffron-flavored linguine pasta, or perhaps braised sweetbreads of veal with a morels sauce. You'll be more comfortable here if you realize in advance that there are two distinctly different seating areas inside this place: the crowded and relatively inexpensive brasserie (also known as *le bateau*, the boat), and the more expensive and nominally more sedate *restaurant*, where service is a bit more formal and attentive.

171 bd. du Montparnasse, 6e. ✆ **01-40-51-34-50.** www.closeriedeslilas.fr. Reservations recommended 2–3 days in advance (for restaurant only). Restaurant main courses 22€–49€; brasserie main courses 22€–27€. AE, DC, MC, V. Restaurant daily noon–2:30pm and 7–11:30pm. Brasserie daily noon–1am. Métro: Port Royal or Vavin.

Sensing ★★ MODERN FRENCH   This eatery is devoted to the five senses. One of the most famous chefs in Paris, Guy Martin, who continues to enjoy his three stars granted by Michelin at Grand Véfour, is also the inspiration for this chicly modern Left Bank restaurant. Wisely, he's hired a talented on-site chef, Rémy Van Péthegem, to rattle those pots and pans, and he's full of innovative surprises.

The decor relies on video projections on the walls and blond sycamore tables. Videos celebrate women's beauty, showing lips, curvature of the shoulder, hairdos, and eyes, as well as fields of blooming flowers. When plates are served, they are like statements from a museum of modern art—geometric arrangements of rectangles and cylinders along with Miró-like squiggles of sauce. Dishes are sublime, ranging from herb-crusted veal with tubes of macaroni stuffed with fresh mushrooms to fresh squab coated with a muscovado sugar caramel crust.

19 rue Bréa, 6e. ☎ **01-43-27-08-80.** www.restaurantsensing.com. Reservations required. Main courses 29€–36€; fixed-price lunch 35€–55€; 7-course fixed-price dinner 75€–95€. AE, MC, V. Tues–Sat noon–2:30pm and Mon–Sat 7:30–10:30pm. Closed Aug. Métro: Vavin.

MODERATE

Alcazar Restaurant ★ MODERN FRENCH   Paris's highest-profile *brasserie de luxe* is this high-tech place funded by British restaurateur Sir Terence Conran. It features a red-and-white futuristic decor in a street-level dining room and a busy upstairs bar (La Mezzanine de l'Alcazar). The menu includes rack of veal sautéed with wild mushrooms, roasted rack of lamb with thyme, and shellfish and oysters from the waters of Brittany. The wines are as stylish and diverse as you'd expect.

62 rue Mazarine, 6e. ☎ **01-53-10-19-99.** Reservations recommended. Main courses 17€–33€; fixed-price lunch 20€–32€; fixed-price dinner 43€; Sun brunch 32€. AE, DC, MC, V. Daily noon–2:30pm and 7pm–1am. Métro: Odéon.

Allard ★ TRADITIONAL FRENCH   This old-time bistro, opened in 1931, is still going strong. It was once the city's leading bistro, although today the competition is too great for it to reclaim that reputation. Over the years, the front room's zinc bar has been a haven for many celebrities, including Mme Pompidou; actor Alain Delon; and, since then, a gaggle of French celebrities. Allard serves all the old specialties, with quality ingredients deftly handled by the kitchen. Try snails, foie gras, Challans duck with olives, or frogs' legs or turbot in a *beurre blanc* sauce. We head here on Monday for the *cassoulet Toulousian* (casserole of white beans and goose and other meats) and on Saturday for coq au vin.

41 rue St-André-des-Arts, 6e. ☎ **01-43-26-48-23.** Reservations required. Main courses 19€–39€; fixed-price lunch 25€; fixed-price dinner 34€. AE, DC, MC, V. Daily noon–2:30pm and 7–11:30pm. Métro: St-Michel or Odéon.

Chez Gramond ★ 🎁 TRADITIONAL FRENCH   Aficionados of the way France used to be seek out this place, and if you're looking for the kind of cuisine that used to satisfy the *grands intellectuels* of the Latin Quarter in the 1960s, you might find it appealing. It seats only 20 people, each of whom is treated to the savoir-faire of Auvergne-born Jean-Claude Gramond and his wife, Jeannine. Listed in purple ink that's duplicated on an old-time mimeograph machine, the menu items may include at various times a marinade of mushrooms with coriander; a *navarin* (rich stew) of lamb with scotch beans; roasted grouse with figs; leeks, and shallots; partridge (this is increasingly rare and expensive) served with an *émincé* (shredded mixture) of cabbage; sautéed pheasant with a Calvados-flavored cream sauce; two different preparations of rabbit, one of which is a traditional *civet* (a wild hare); or duckling with orange sauce.

5 rue de Fleurus, 6e. ☎ **01-42-22-28-89.** Reservations recommended. Main courses 21€–35€. MC, V. Mon–Sat noon–3pm and 7–10:30pm. Closed in Aug. Métro: Notre-Dame des Champs.

La Rôtisserie d'en Face ★ 🍴 TRADITIONAL FRENCH   This is Paris's most popular baby bistro, operated by Jacques Cagna, whose expensive namesake restaurant is across the street. The informal place features a postmodern decor with high-tech lighting, yellow walls, and red banquettes. The simply prepared food is very good and employs high-quality ingredients. Tantalizing starters include red tuna and sea bream tartare flavored with ginger and soy or else rabbit pâté with pine kernels. Main dish favorites include the signature spit-roasted, free-range chicken served with the traditional buttery mashed potatoes. Other mains include cold grilled salmon with coriander-marinated fresh vegetables. Few desserts top "the red berry bowl," with Cassis sauce and whipped cream.

2 rue Christine, 6e. ☎ **01-43-26-40-98.** Reservations recommended. Main courses 22€–27€; fixed-price lunch 25€–31€. AE, DC, MC, V. Mon–Fri noon–2:30pm; Mon–Sat 7–11pm. Métro: Odéon or St-Michel.

Le Timbre ★ 🏠 TRADITIONAL FRENCH   A Brit running a restaurant in Paris? That's practically unheard of, at least to former President Jacques Chirac, who once denounced British cooking as the worst in the world. Surprisingly, a Brit, Chris Wright, has opened the tiniest restaurant on the tiniest street in Paris near Montparnasse. The Manchester-born chef shops for only the finest of French regional products, including truffles and foie gras, and he gets by with no microwave or freezer. In this postage stamp restaurant Wright prepares faultless dishes, including trout stuffed with fresh fava beans and country ham, andouillette sausages with lentils from Puy, or a filet of white fish with olives. In spite of all these *à la française* dishes, he likes to put English cheddar on his cheeseboard. If not the cheese, you might end your meal with the ruby-red strawberry soup.

3 rue Sainte Beuve, 6e. ☎ **01-45-49-10-40.** www.restaurantletimbre.com. Reservations required. Main courses 15€–21€; fixed-price lunch 24€–28€. MC, V. Tues–Sat noon–2pm and 7:30–10:30pm. Closed 3 weeks in Aug. Métro: Notre-Dame-des-Champs or Vavin.

Yugaraj INDIAN   On two floors of an old Latin Quarter building, Yugaraj serves flavorful food based on the recipes of northern and (to a lesser degree) southern India. In recently renovated rooms done in vivid shades of ocher, with a formally dressed staff and lots of intricately carved Kashmiri panels and statues, you can sample the spicy, aromatic tandoori dishes that are all the rage in France. Seafood specialties are usually made with warm-water fish imported from the Seychelles, including *thiof, capitaine,* and *bourgeois,* prepared as they would be in Calcutta, with tomatoes, onions, cumin, coriander, ginger, and garlic.

14 rue Dauphine, 6e. ☎ **01-43-26-44-91.** www.yugaraj.com. Reservations recommended. Main courses 20€–32€; fixed-price lunch 19€–31€; fixed-price dinner 31€–66€. AE, DC, MC, V. Tues–Wed and Fri–Sun noon–2pm; Tues–Sun 7–10:15pm. Métro: Pont-Neuf or Odéon.

Ze Kitchen Galerie ★ 🏠 INTERNATIONAL/MODERN FRENCH   The owner and head chef of this restaurant, William Ledeuil, trained in haute Parisian gastronomy under culinary czar Guy Savoy. The setting is a colorful loft space in an antique building, with an open-to-view showcase kitchen. Most of the paintings on display are for sale (the place doubles as an art gallery). Menu items, as with the paintings, change about every 5 weeks; appetizers are subdivided into pastas, soups, and fish; and main courses are divided into meats and fish that are usually *à la plancha* (grilled). For starters, ever had beet gazpacho with candied ginger, cucumber, and fresh shrimp? The grilled chicken and veal sweetbreads with a carrot-and-mustard jus (flavored with ginger) are heavenly, as are platters of oysters, mussels, and sea urchins. Sometimes grilled shoulder of wild boar with tamarind sauce is featured. A meal might also be followed with the restaurant's "cappuccino of the month," a frothy dessert concoction with ingredients that change with the seasons.

4 rue des Grands-Augustins, 6e. ☎ **01-44-32-00-32.** www.zekitchengalerie.fr. Reservations recommended. Main courses 30€–35€; fixed-price lunch with wine 24€–39€; fixed-price dinner 76€. AE, DC, MC, V. Mon–Fri noon–2:30pm; Mon–Sat 7–11pm. Métro: St-Michel or Pont-Neuf.

INEXPENSIVE

Aux Charpentiers TRADITIONAL FRENCH   This old bistro, which opened more than 150 years ago, attracts those seeking the Left Bank of yesteryear. It was once the rendezvous spot of the master carpenters, whose guild was next door. Nowadays, it's where young men take dates. Though the food isn't imaginative, it's well prepared in the best tradition of *cuisine bourgeoise*—hearty but not effete. Appetizers include pâté of duck, rabbit terrine, and homemade foie gras. Recommended as a main course is roast duck with olives. The *plats du jour* recall French home cooking: salt pork with lentils, *pot-au-feu,* and stuffed cabbage. The wine list has a selection of bordeaux, including Château Gaussens.

10 rue Mabillon, 6e. ☎ **01-43-26-30-05.** www.auxcharpentiers.fr. Reservations required. Main courses 18€–36€; fixed-price lunch 20€; fixed-price dinner 28€. AE, DC, MC, V. Daily noon–3pm and 7–11:30pm. Métro: St-Germain-des-Prés or Mabillon.

Crémerie-Restaurant Polidor ★ ☺ TRADITIONAL FRENCH   Crémerie Polidor is the most traditional bistro in the Odéon area, serving *cuisine familiale.* Its name dates from the early 1900s, when it specialized in frosted cream desserts, but the restaurant can trace its history to 1845. The Crémerie was André Gide's favorite, and Joyce, Hemingway, Valéry, Artaud, and Kerouac also dined here. Peer beyond the lace curtains and brass hat racks to see drawers where in olden days, regular customers used to lock up their cloth napkins. Try the day's soup followed by kidneys in Madeira sauce, *boeuf bourguignon, confit de canard,* or *blanquette de veau.* For dessert, order a chocolate, raspberry, or lemon tart.

39 rue Monsieur-le-Prince, 6e. ☎ **01-43-26-95-34.** www.polidor.com. Main courses 11€–48€; fixed-price menu 22€–32€. No credit cards. Daily noon–2:30pm; Mon–Sat 7pm–12:30am; Sun 7–11pm. Métro: Odéon.

La Bastide Odéon ★ 🎒 PROVENÇAL   The sunny climes of Provence come through in the pale yellow walls, oak tables, and bouquets of wheat and dried roses. Chef Gilles Ajuelos prepares a market-based cuisine. His simplest first courses are the most satisfying, such as scallop risotto with Parmesan, and eggplant-stuffed roasted rabbit with olive toast and balsamic vinegar. Main courses include a warm napoleon of grilled eggplant served "in the style of the Riviera," and roasted chicken with a confit of Provençal garlic and fried potatoes.

7 rue Corneille, 6e. ☎ **01-43-26-03-65.** www.bastide-odeon.com. Reservations recommended. Fixed-price menu 32€–45€. AE, MC, V. Tues–Sat 2:15–2pm and 7:30–10:30pm. Métro: Odéon. RER: Luxembourg.

La Crèmerie ★ 🎒 TRADITIONAL FRENCH   A New Yorker, Serge Mathieu was an architect when he first entered La Crèmerie. But after one dinner here, he decided to buy the joint and transform this tiny 19th century "creamery" in the Latin Quarter into his own place. He had done so admirably. Today under a ceiling of handpainted silk under glass, he attracts the neighborhood locals to his precincts. They know they can get great bargains from his wine cellar, which showcases artisanal bottlings from all over the country. His charcuterie and cheeses are also exceptional. You can dine on foie gras, oysters, delicately smoked tuna, and a spectacular chocolate fondant. Take note that La Crémerie doesn't serve any hot food except for grilled vegetables. The cost, of course, depends on what you order.

9 rue des Quatre Vents, 6e. ℰ **01-43-54-99-30.** www.lacremerie.fr. Reservations not needed. Meals from 20€. MC, V. Tues–Sat 10:30am–10pm, Sun 11am–2:30pm, Mon 2–8pm. Métro: Odéon.

L'Avant Comptoir ★ TRADITIONAL FRENCH/SPANISH   This hole-in-the-wall is just steps from the Odéon. Here you will encounter bistro maestro Yves Camdeborde, who operates a crêperie by day and a cocktail and hors d'oeuvres bar by night. Next door to his seminal restaurant Le Comptoir. His latest business lies in a short, narrow, standing-room space with an open kitchen. His small plates are Basque and Béarnais-inspired "nibbles." There's a great selection of French wines by the glass. Try such hearty fare as a shellfish bouillon with octopus; deep-fried pigs' foot croquettes; oxtail canapés with horseradish cream, or chicken hearts grilled with garlic and parsley. No more than a dozen people can crowd into this place at a time. It's really narrow.

3 Carrefour de l'Odéon, 6e. ℰ **08-26-10-10-87.** No reservations accepted. Main courses 12€–22€. MC, V. Daily 9am–1am. Métro: Odéon.

13th Arrondissement (Gare d'Austerlitz)
MODERATE

Auberge Etchegorry BASQUE   Its windows overlook a verdant patch of lawn that's so green, you might for a moment imagine you've entered a rustic countryside inn. The building was once a cabaret frequented by Victor Hugo. Dark paneling, deep colors, hanging hams and pigtails of garlic, and lacy curtains emulate the Basque country, the corner of southwestern France adjacent to Spain. The cramped tables are a drawback, but not much of one in this rich atmosphere. The menu includes such specialties as cassoulet, squid in its own ink, *magret* (breast) of duckling, beef filet with wild mushrooms, a peppery omelet known as *pipérades*, paella with seafood, and terrines or pan-fried slices of foie gras.

41 rue Croulebarbe, 13e. ℰ **01-44-08-83-51.** www.etchegorry.com. Reservations recommended. All courses 16€–20€; fixed-price lunch 18€; fixed-price dinner 27€. AE, MC, V. Tues–Sat noon–2:30pm and 7:30–10:30pm. Métro: Gobelins or Corvisart.

Le Petit Marguery POITEVINE/TRADITIONAL FRENCH   This place feels like a turn-of-the-20th-century bistro, with antique floor tiles, banquettes, vested waiters, and a color scheme of dark rose. Menu items are based in old-fashioned traditions, especially those from the Poitou region of west-central France, with emphasis on game dishes in autumn and fresh produce in summer. The finest examples include duck and rosemary terrine with foie gras; slices of wild duck breast dusted with white pepper and strewn over mounds of shredded cabbage; a *petit salé* (family-style stew) of duckling that's served with braised cabbage and garlic-flavored cream sauce; and a variety of homemade terrines (including an excellent version from blood sausage). There are also two very fine dishes, classics from *la cuisine bourgeoise* (comfort food) of the late 19th century: roasted pigeon with red cabbage and chestnuts or rooster (*coq*), which is deboned,

> ## Chinatown Paris Style
>
> More and more visitors are discovering that Paris, as with New York, has a Chinatown. Take the Métro to Porte d'Ivry or Place d'Italie in the 13th arrondissement. **Quartier Chinois,** a 5-minute walk from Place d'Italie, centers on avenue d'Ivry. Here you will find 250,000 Asians (the population grows all the time) living in a center of food stores, Asian restaurants and markets, and rows of teas and spices straight from China. The center of the sector is **Tang Frères,** the largest Asian-food market in Europe. Spend a morning exploring here and stick around for lunch. We'd recommend **Le Mer de Chine** at 159 des Rentiers, 13e ((𝒞 **01-45-84-22-49;** Métro: Place d'Italie), serving the best Cantonese cuisine in Paris.

marinated, roasted, and served in a sauce that combines red wine, some of the animal's blood, and foie gras.

9 bd. du Port-Royal, 13e. 𝒞 **01-43-31-58-59.** www.petitmarguery.com. Reservations recommended. 2- or 3-course lunch 23€–26€; 3-course dinner 30€–35€. AE, DC, MC, V. Daily noon–2:45pm and Mon–Sat 7:15–10:15pm. Closed Aug. Métro: Gobelins.

INEXPENSIVE

Chez Gladines ⌁ BASQUE   For one of the great "tuck-ins" of Paris, all at affordable prices, even students from the Latin Quarter cross the Seine to dine on the large portions at this dive. The setting is laid back (actually a bit grimy), but the food is hearty and authentic. Who can forget the enormous mixed salads served in giant metal bowls? Its convivial atmosphere has been called "somewhere between old-school Paris and hip." This is not the place to go to impress a date—go here to eat to your stomach's delight on such recommendable main dishes as *pipérade* (Basque-style scrambled eggs with vegetables), cassoulet, potatoes with ham and Cantal cheese, and our favorite, ham in a creamy sauce with layers of gratin style potatoes that have been fried in duck fat. Okay, so it's a bit leaden, but devotees love it.

30 rue des Cinq Diamants, 13e. 𝒞 **01-45-80-70-10.** Reservations not accepted. Main courses 8€–15€; fixed-price lunch 9€. No credit cards. Daily noon–3pm and 7pm–midnight; Sun noon–4pm. Closed 3 weeks in July. Métro: Corvisart or Place d'Italie.

14th Arrondissement (Montparnasse)

MODERATE

La Cagouille ★ ◈ TRADITIONAL FRENCH/SEAFOOD   Don't expect to find meat at this temple of seafood—owner Gérard Allamandou refuses to feature it. Everything about La Cagouille is a testimonial to a modern version of the culinary arts of La Charente, the flat sandy district on the Atlantic south of Bordeaux. In a trio of oak-sheathed dining rooms, you'll sample seafood prepared as naturally as possible, with no fancy sauces or elaborate techniques. Try such dishes as fried filet of sole, grilled John Dory, or warm cockles. Red mullet might be sautéed in oil or baked in rock salt. The name derives from the regional symbol of La Charente, the sea snail, whose preparation elevates its namesake to a fine culinary art. Look for a vast assemblage of wines and cognacs.

10–12 place Constantin-Brancusi, 14e. ☎ **01-43-22-09-01.** www.la-cagouille.fr. Reservations recommended. Main courses 16€–60€; fixed-price menu 23€–38€. MC, V. Daily noon–2:30pm and 7:30–10:30pm. Métro: Gaité.

La Régalade FRENCH TRADITIONAL   The setting is a bistro with banquettes the color of aged bordeaux wine, congenial service, and unexpectedly good food. The prix-fixe menu presents a choice of at least 10 starters, 10 main courses, and about a dozen fresh desserts or selections from a cheese tray. The menu changes weekly (sometimes daily) according to the availability of the ingredients, but likely offerings might include foie gras flan in a creamy chanterelle mushroom broth, pigeon breast roasted on the bone, roast Pyrenean lamb served with thyme and a confit of roasted garlic, or filet of wild boar with a red-wine sauce.

14 av. Jean-Moulin, 14e. ☎ **01-45-45-68-58.** Reservations required 3 days in advance. Fixed-price menu 30€–50€. MC, V. Tues–Fri noon–2:30pm; Mon–Fri 7–11:30pm. Closed Aug. Métro: Alésia.

L'Assiette MODERN FRENCH   Everything here appeals to a nostalgic crowd seeking down-to-earth prices and flavorful food. The place was a charcuterie (pork butcher's shop) in the 1930s and maintains some of its old accessories. Mitterrand used to drop in for oysters, crayfish, sea urchins, and clams. The food is inspired by Paris's long tradition of bistro cuisine, with a few twists. The new chef and owner was once a student of Alain Ducasse, the master chef. You might begin with an appetizer of smoked ham or else sardines marinated in citrus. The chef also makes a good tasting *pot-au-feu* or stew, and works wonders with pepper steak. Escargots arrive in a pot sprinkled with homemade croutons. The duck pâté is another good choice, followed by such desserts as crème caramel or *riz au lait* (rice with milk).

181 rue du Château, 14e. ☎ **01-43-22-64-86.** www.restaurant-lassiette.com. Reservations recommended. Main courses 21€–37€; fixed-price lunch 23€. AE, MC, V. Wed–Sun noon–2:30pm and 7:30–10:30pm. Closed Aug. Métro: Gaité.

Le Severo ★ TRADITIONAL FRENCH   This place is a carnivore's delight—in fact, its owner was a butcher from Nivernaises before turning restaurateur. Come here to experience the way Parisians ate back in the 1890s. No one seems to do fried pigs' feet as crunchy crisp as the cooks here do. They're served with hand cut and expertly prepared *frites*. On the blackboard menu, you are likely to encounter some of the choicest cuts of meats in Paris. Farmhouse blood pudding (*boudin noir*), steak tartare, and grilled rib-eye steaks are just some of the bloody offerings at this joint. Most beef arrives to table blood rare and beautifully marbled. Parisians order their steak *saignant* (underdone). If you want it medium rare, ask for it *à point*.

8 rue des Plantes, 14e. ☎ **01-40-44-73-09.** Reservations required. Main courses 20€–27€. Mon–Sat noon–2pm and Tues–Fri 7:30–10pm. Closed Aug. Métro: Mouton-Duvernet or Alésia.

7th Arrondissement (Eiffel Tower/ Musee d'Orsay)

If you're in the 7th arrondissement for breakfast or lunch, perhaps visiting the Musée d'Orsay, a good refueling stop is the bakery, bar, and cafe, **Eric Kayser ★★**, 18 rue du Bac, 7e (☎ **01-42-61-27-63;** Métro: Bac or Musée d'Orsay).

Where to Dine on the Left Bank (7 & 15e)

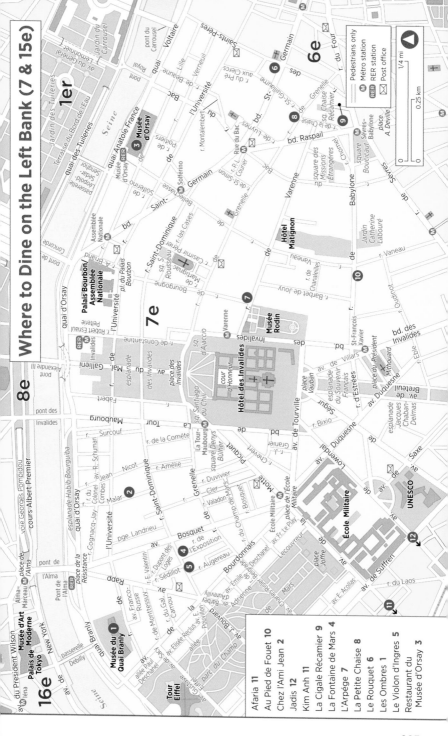

Afaria **11**
Au Pied de Fouet **10**
Chez l'Ami Jean **2**
Jadis **12**
Kim Anh **11**
La Cigale Récamier **9**
La Fontaine de Mars **4**
L'Arpège **7**
La Petite Chaise **8**
Le Rouquet **6**
Les Ombres **1**
Le Violon d'Ingres **5**
Restaurant du
Musée d'Orsay **3**

Pedestrians only
Ⓜ Metro station
RER RER station
☒ Post office

Kayser's forte is bread making—he is known for the long fermentation of his dough. He's always coming up with new ideas for his breads, including one made with apricots and pistachios or else chorizo. This Alsatian baker offers many luxe breads and pastries, and breakfast is a delight here. At lunch you have a choice of 20 different combinations of *tartines* (open-faced sandwiches), and teatime features gourmet snacks such as a sweet tartine with meringue and chestnuts. Open Tuesday to Sunday 7am to 8pm.

VERY EXPENSIVE

L'Arpège ★★★ MODERN FRENCH   L'Arpège is best known for Alain Passard's specialties—no restaurant in the 7th serves better food. Surrounded by etched glass, burnished steel, monochromatic oil paintings, and pearwood paneling, you can enjoy such specialties as couscous of vegetables and shellfish, lobster braised in the yellow wine of the Jura, braised monkfish in an Orléans mustard sauce, pigeon roasted with almonds and honey-flavored mead, and carpaccio of crayfish with caviar-flavored cream sauce. Although Passard is loath to include red meat on his menus, Kobe beef and venison sometimes appear. He focuses on fish, shellfish, poultry, and his passion—vegetables. These he elevates to levels unequaled by any other chef in Paris.

84 rue de Varenne, 7e. ✆ **01-47-05-09-06.** Fax 01-44-18-98-39. www.alain-passard.com. Reservations required 2 weeks in advance. Main courses 48€–180€; fixed-price lunch 135€; fixed-price dinner 420€. AE, DC, MC, V. Mon–Fri 12:30–2:30pm and 8–10:30pm. Métro: Varenne.

EXPENSIVE

La Fontaine de Mars ★ TRADITIONAL FRENCH   When President Obama and his First Lady dined at the classic French bistrot, **La Fontaine de Mars,** visiting Americans began booking tables here. One of the "ancient" bistrots of Paris, it's been a venerable institution since it first opened in 1908, but it's never had this kind of business before. The menu is about the same as it was when your French grandfather (if you had one) dined here before World War I. Believe it or not, the chef still cooks that Burgundian appetizer of two eggs baked in red wine with shallots and served with a bacon sauce. Homemade duck foie gras is on the menu, with such main dishes as free range chicken breast with fresh morels or the classic sole menuière. Obama went for the black chocolate mousse.

129 rue Saint Dominique, 7e. ✆ **01-47-05-46-44.** www.fontainedemars.com. Reservations required. Main courses 32€–45€. AE, MC, V. Daily noon–3pm and 7:30–11pm. Métro: Ecole Militaire.

Les Ombres ★ INTERNATIONAL/MODERN FRENCH   Les Ombres in French means "the Shadows." Architect Jean Nouvel named this museum rooftop restaurant for the shadows cast by the Eiffel Tower looming nearby. A late dinner is practically a spectacle, as the tower twinkles for the first 10 minutes of every hour. Fortunately, the chefs don't just rely on the view. The head chef, Arno Busquet, trained under the great Joël Robuchon, and for his ingenious cuisine he sails the seas, from Oceania to Asia and the Americas. You dine under a canopy of "metallic lace" inspired by the tower itself. Feast on such dishes as foie gras with spiced mango chutney or guinea fowl stuffed with creole sausage and served with an apple cabbage purée. Other delights include a shellfish risotto flavored with lemon, duck seasoned with rosemary, or seared tuna belly with onion rings flavored with sesame. The cuisine is invariably based on fresh produce.

Musée du Quai Branly, 27 quai Branly, 7e. ℂ **01-47-53-68-00.** www.lesombres-restaurant.com. Reservations required. Main courses 32€–45€; fixed-price menu 38€–145€. MC, V. Daily noon–2:30pm and 7–10:30pm. Métro: Pont de l'Alma.

Le Violon d'Ingres ★★★ MODERN FRENCH   This restaurant is Paris's *pièce de résistance.* Chef-owner Christian Constant is "the new Robuchon." Those fortunate enough to dine in Violon's warm atmosphere rave about the artistic dishes. They range from wood pigeon cooked on the grill and served with a fricassee of mushrooms to such hearty fare as veal's head with the tongue and brain poached in a sauce of capers and hard-boiled eggs. If you're not man (or woman) enough for that, you can opt for sea bass under a crust of almonds. The service is charming and discreet; the wine selection, well chosen. The Constant family has tied up the dining rituals along this street, with less expensive, less formal restaurants flanking Le Violon d'Ingres.

135 rue St-Dominique, 7e. ℂ **01-45-55-15-05.** Fax 01-45-55-48-42. www.leviolondingres.com. Reservations required. All main courses 27€; fixed-price menu 49€. AE, DC, MC, V. Tues–Sat noon–2:30pm and 7–10:30pm. Métro: Invalides or Ecole-Militaire.

MODERATE

La Cigale Récamier ★ 🍴 TRADITIONAL FRENCH   The Obamas dined at La Fontaine de Mars (see p. 204), but the following day, Mrs. Obama dined with her daughters at La Cigale Récamier, a Left Bank bistro that had been recommended to her by some members of the American Embassy. A former First Lady, Laura Bush, had also dined here. Once news spread of Mrs. Obama's visit, this humble Left Bank bistro was put on the culinary map. Chef Ferard Idoux is a new chef, having taken over from a man who ran the place for 3 decades. He served the Obama women his famous Camembert soufflé and beef filet grilled in fresh basil.

4 rue Récamier, 7e. ℂ **01-45-48-86-58.** Reservations required. Main courses 21€–35€. AE, MC, V. Mon–Sat noon–3pm and 7–11pm. Métro: Sèvres-Babylone.

La Petite Chaise TRADITIONAL FRENCH   This is Paris's oldest restaurant, opened as an inn in 1680 by the baron de la Chaise at the edge of a hunting preserve. (According to lore, the baron used the upstairs bedrooms for afternoon dalliances, btw. fox and pheasant hunts.) Very Parisian, the "Little Chair" invites you into a world of cramped but attractive tables, old wood paneling, and ornate wall sconces. A vigorous chef has brought renewed taste and flavor to this longtime favorite, and the four-course set menu offers a large choice of dishes in each category. Examples are *magret* (breast) of duck with sweet-and-sour sauce, *pot-au-feu* with seasonal ingredients, and grilled sea bass on a bed of fennel with a light butter sauce.

36 rue de Grenelle, 7e. ℂ **01-42-22-13-35.** www.alapetitechaise.fr. Reservations recommended. Main courses all 20€. Fixed-price menu 31€. MC, V. Daily noon–2pm and 7–11pm. Métro: Sèvres-Babylone or Rue du Bac.

Restaurant du Musée d'Orsay ★ MODERN FRENCH   If you can overlook the hysterical and rude staff—a big if—you can treat yourself to a sumptuous Belle Epoque dining room overlooking the Seine. Perhaps Marcel Proust and his gay comrades once sat under the magnificent frescoed ceiling. In such a glamorous setting, you can enjoy a traditional cuisine, though it has been given a decidedly modern interpretation. Escoffier it isn't. The best bargain is the two-course

IN PURSUIT OF THE PERFECT
parisian pastry

Could it be true, as rumor has it, that more eggs, sugar, cream, and butter per capita are consumed in Paris than in any other city? From a modern-day Proust sampling a *madeleine* to a child munching a *pain au chocolat* (chocolate-filled croissant), everyone in Paris seems to be looking for two things: the perfect lover and the perfect pastry, not necessarily in that order. As a Parisian food critic once said, "A day without a pastry is a day in hell!"

Who'd think of beginning a morning in Paris without a **croissant** or two—freshly baked, flaky, light, and made with real butter, preferably from Norman cows. The Greeks may have invented pastry making, but the French perfected it. Some French pastries have made a greater impact than others. The croissant and the **brioche,** a yeasty sweet breakfast bread, are baked around the world today, as is the fabled **éclair au chocolat** (chocolate éclair), a pastry filled with whipped cream or pastry cream and topped with chocolate. Another pastry you should sample on its home turf is the **Napolitain**—layers of cake flour and almonds alternating with fruit purée. (Don't confuse this term with *Neapolitan,* meaning sweets and cakes made with layers of two or more colors, each layer flavored differently.) Very much in vogue is the **mille-feuille** ("thousand leaves"), made by arranging thin layers of flaky pastry on top of one another, along with layers of cream or fruit purée or jam; the American version is the napoleon.

Here are some of our favorite patisseries:

Stohrer. 51 rue Montorgueil, 2e (℡ **01-42-33-38-20;** www.stohrer.fr; Métro: Sentier or Les Halles), has been going strong ever since it was opened by Louis XV's pastry chef in 1730. A pastry always associated with this place is *puits d'amour* (well of love), which consists of caramelized puff pastry filled with vanilla ice cream. Available at any time is one of the most luscious desserts in Paris, **baba au rhum,** made with rum-soaked sponge cake, or its even richer cousin, **un Ali Baba,** which also incorporates cream-based rum-and-raisin filling. Stohrer boasts an interior decor classified as a national historic treasure, with frescoes of damsels in 18th-century costume bearing flowers and (what else?) pastries.

Ladurée Royale. 16 rue Royale, 8e (℡ **01-42-60-21-79;** www.laduree.fr; Métro: Concorde or Madeleine), is Paris's dowager tearoom, opened in 1862, and just a few steps from La Madeleine. Its

prix-fixe lunch. The menu is ever changing, but basically it consists of a more simplified version of a traditional French cuisine. Expect such savory dishes as grilled sea bream filet or perhaps the duck and peaches supreme served with *gratin dauphinois.*

1 rue de Bellechasse, 7e. ℡ **01-45-49-42-33.** Reservations recommended. 2-course lunch 17€; Sun brunch 23€; Thurs evening gourmet menu 42€; children's menu 8€. AE, MC, V. Tues–Sun 11:45am–5:45pm. Tea 2:45–5:45pm. Thurs 11:45am–9:30pm. Métro: Solférino. RER: Musée d'Orsay.

pastry chefs are known for the *macaroon,* a pastry for which this place is celebrated. Karl Lagerfeld comes here and raves about them, as did the late U.S. ambassador Pamela Harriman. This isn't the sticky coconut-version macaroon known to many, but two almond meringue cookies, flavored with chocolate, vanilla, pistachio, coffee, or other flavors, stuck together with butter cream. You may also want to try *Le Faubourg,* a lusciously dense chocolate cake with layers of caramel and apricots.

Dalloyau. 101 rue du Faubourg St-Honoré, 8e (☎ **01-42-99-90-00;** www. dalloyau.fr; Métro: St-Philippe du Roule). In business since Napoleon was in power, Dalloyau has a name instantly recognizable throughout Paris; it supplies pastries to the Elysée Palace (the French White House) and many Rothschild mansions nearby. Its specialties are *Le Dalloyau,* praline cake filled with almond meringue that's marvelously light-textured; and *un Opéra,* composed of an almond-flavored biscuit layered with butter cream, chocolate, coffee, and cashews. Unlike Stohrer, Dalloyau has a tearoom (open daily 8:30am–7:30pm) one floor above street level, where ladies who lunch can drop in for a slice of pastry that Dalloyau warns is "too fragile to transport, or to mail, over long distances."

Fauchon. 26–30 place de la Madeleine, 8e (☎ **01-70-39-38-00;** www. fauchon.com; Métro: Madeleine). As readers of French literature know, the taste of the *madeleine* (a scalloped tea cake) triggered the memory of the narrator in Marcel Proust's *Remembrance of Things Past.* Known since the 18th century, the madeleine also inspired chef Christophe Adam at Fauchon to tinker with the classic cookie recipe. Today he prepares madeleines in such flavors as orange, coffee-sesame, and pistachio.

Pierre Hermé. 72 rue Bonaparte, 6e (☎ **01-43-54-47-77;** www.pierreherme. com; Métro: St-Sulpice). We always head here for truffles with chocolate and pistachios or truffles praline. The macaroons, probably of Venetian origin, are worth crossing town to sample, especially if the cream filling is flavored with fresh raspberries or litchis.

Sadaharu Aoki. 56 bd. Port Royale, 13e (☎ **01-45-35-34-19;** www.sadaharu. com; Métro: Les Gobelins). Parisians started eating éclairs, that cream-filled chocolate-covered shell of choux pastry, in the 1800s. Surprisingly it is a Japanese chef who makes the best éclairs in today's Paris. He even does a mâcha green tea version, with green tea powder imported from Kyoto.

INEXPENSIVE

Au Pied de Fouet TRADITIONAL FRENCH   This is one of the neighborhood's oldest and most reasonably priced restaurants. In the 1700s, it was a stopover for carriages en route to Paris, offering wine, food, and stables. Don't expect a leisurely or attentive meal: Food and drink will disappear quickly from your table, under the gaze of others awaiting their turn. The dishes are solid and unpretentious and include *blanquette de veau* (veal stew), chicken in vinegar sauce (a house specialty), *petit salé* (a savory family style stew made from pork and vegetables and served with lentils), and filet of sea wolf or filet of codfish. If you demand a polite staff, go elsewhere. The waiters are among the rudest in Paris. Some visitors claim that's part of the charm of this place. You decide.

45 rue de Babylone, 7e. ☎ **01-47-05-12-27.** Main courses 8€–13€. MC, V. Mon–Sat noon–2:30pm and 7–11pm. Closed Aug. Métro: Vaneau.

Chez l'Ami Jean BASQUE/SOUTHWESTERN FRENCH   This restaurant was opened by a Basque nationalist in 1931, and fans claim its Basque cuisine and setting are the most authentic on the Left Bank. Decorative details include wood panels; memorabilia from *pelote* (a Basque game similar to jai alai), rugby, and soccer. Dishes include herb-laden Béarn-influenced vegetable soups; confit of duck with small sautéed potatoes; and fine slices of veal with fresh herbs, onions, red peppers, and a light tomato sauce. In springtime, look for a specialty rarely found elsewhere: *saumon de l'Adour* (Adour salmon) with béarnaise sauce.

27 rue Malar, 7e. ☎ **01-47-05-86-89.** www.amijean.eu. Reservations recommended. Main courses 20€–40€; 3-course Basque dinner 35€. MC, V. Tues–Sat noon–2pm and 7pm–midnight. Closed Aug. Métro: Invalides.

15th Arrondissement (Eiffel Tower)

MODERATE

Jadis ★★ 🍴 TRADITIONAL FRENCH   In the autumn of 2009, *Le Figaro* hailed Jadis as "the best bistrot of the autumn." *Le Fooding* went even farther, calling it "the best bistrot in Paris." We won't go that far except to say that Jadis still has the same high standards that brought it so much early acclaim. In the up-and-coming 15th arrondissement, Chef Guillaume Delage in his culinary showroom dazzles some of the finest palates of Paris. He is known for giving his own interpretation to what some food critics call "soulful Neoclassical flavors." A typical example of that is his *épaule d'agneau* (a shoulder of lamb for two). It comes in a copper casserole a top a quasi-cassoulet of flat mogette beans. His set menu is based on the classic "snout-to-tail" type of cooking. Yes, he's not afraid to use an animal's brains and feet.

208 rue de la Croix Nivert, 15e. ☎ **01-45-57-73-20.** Reservations required. Fixed-price lunch or dinner 32€. AE, MC, V. Mon–Fri 12:15–2:30pm and 7:15–10:30pm. Métro: Convention.

Kim Anh VIETNAMESE   This is one of the best addresses in Paris for the savory, spicy cuisine of its former colony. It's a bit lost down in the 15th, but many Parisian foodies journey here anyway. The cuisine includes the sharp, spicy, sour, and succulent flavors of Vietnam, as prepared in pork, chicken, fish, and beef dishes, many of them excellent. Waiters are very patient in explaining various dishes to newcomers. We are especially fond of the caramelized langoustines and most definitely the stuffed crabs and steamed stuffed snails.

51 av. Emile Zola, 15e. ☎ **01-45-79-40-96.** www.kimanh-restaurant.com. Reservations recommended. Main courses 20€–37€; fixed-price menu 34€. AE, MC, V. Tues–Sat noon–2pm, Tues–Sun 7–11pm. Closed last 2 weeks of Aug. Métro: Charles-Michels.

INEXPENSIVE

Afaria ★ BASQUE   Many visitors skip the 15th arrondissement, but Afaria is a good reason to go there. Julien Duboue, born in Southwest France, is the chef, and he once worked in Le Carré des Feuillants, one of Paris's most famous restaurants. Together with his wife, Celine, they run the brightest "light" on this dull street. Up front is a communal table, and in back are bistro-style wooden tables decked in traditional red and white tablecloths. Traditional recipes are revisited with an imaginative twist, including such specialties as jarret of pork braised; spicy pumpkin soup with scallops and artichokes; terrine of venison with fig chutney, and rosy charred duck breast on the bone served over "smoking" grapevines.

15 rue Desnouettes, 15e. (✆) **01-48-56-15-36.** Reservations required. Main courses 17€–19€; fixed-price lunch 22€–26€. MC, V. Tues–Sat noon–2:30pm and 7–11pm. Métro: Convention.

THE TOP CAFES

As surely everyone knows, the cafe is a Parisian institution. Parisians use cafes as combination club/tavern/snack bars, almost as extensions of their living rooms. They're spots where you can sit alone and read your newspaper, do your homework or write your memoirs; meet a friend or lover; nibble on a hard-boiled egg; or drink yourself into oblivion. At cafes, you meet your dates, and then go on to a show or stay and talk. Above all, cafes are for people-watching.

Coffee, of course, is the chief drink. It comes black, in a small cup, unless you specifically order it *au lait* (with milk). *Thé* (tea, pronounced *tay*) is also fairly popular but generally not high quality. If you prefer beer, we advise you to pay a bit more for the imported German, Dutch, or Danish brands, which are much better than the local brew. If you insist on a French beer, at least order it *à pression* (draft), which is superior. There's also a vast variety of fruit drinks, as well as Coca-Cola, which can be rather expensive. French chocolate drinks—either hot or iced—are absolutely superb and on par with the finest Dutch brands. They're made from ground chocolate, not a chemical compound.

Now, just a few words on cafe etiquette: You don't pay when you get your order—only when you intend to leave. Payment indicates you've had all you want. *Service compris* means the tip is included in your bill, so it isn't necessary to tip extra; still, most people leave an extra euro or so. You'll hear the locals call for the "*garçon,*" but as a foreigner, it would be more polite to say "*monsieur.*" All waitresses, on the other hand, are addressed as "*mademoiselle,*" regardless of age or marital status. In the smaller cafes, you may have to share your table. In that case, even if you haven't exchanged a word with your table companion, when you leave it's customary to bid him or her *au revoir*.

For the locations of these cafes, see the corresponding arrondissement maps earlier in this chapter.

EXPENSIVE

Café de Flore ★★   It's the most famous cafe in the world, still fighting to maintain a Left Bank aura despite hordes of visitors from around the world. Sartre—the granddaddy of existentialism, a key figure in the Resistance, and a renowned cafe-sitter—often came here during World War II. Wearing a leather jacket and beret, he sat and wrote his trilogy *Les Chemins de la Liberté* (*The Roads to Freedom*). Camus, Picasso, and Apollinaire also frequented the Flore. The cafe is still going strong, though the famous patrons have moved on and tourists have taken up all the tables. According to the spokeswoman, "We will never change the decor." The menu offers omelets, salads, club sandwiches, and more.

172 bd. St-Germain, 6e. (✆) **01-45-48-55-26.** www.cafe-de-flore.com. Café espresso 5€; glass of beer 9€; snacks from 16€; full meal 25€–45€. AE, DC, MC, V. Daily 7:30am–1:30am. Métro: St-Germain-des-Prés.

Fouquet's ★   For people-watching, this is definitely on the see-and-be-seen circuit. Fouquet's has been collecting anecdotes and a patina since it was founded in 1901. A celebrity favorite, it has attracted Chaplin, Chevalier, Dietrich, Churchill, Roosevelt, and Jackie Onassis. The premier cafe on the Champs-Elysées sits behind a barricade of potted flowers at the edge of the sidewalk. Today, it's owned by the well-managed hotel and dining conglomerate Lucien Barrière. You can choose a table in the sunshine or retreat to the glassed-in elegance of the leather banquettes and rattan furniture of the grillroom. This is a full-fledged restaurant, with a beautiful formal dining room on the second floor.

99 av. des Champs-Elysées, 8e. ℭ **01-40-69-60-50.** Glass of wine from 9€; sandwiches 19€–21€; main courses 26€–55€; fixed-price lunch or dinner 78€. AE, DC, MC, V. Daily 8am–2am. Restaurant daily noon–3pm and 7pm–midnight. Bar and brasserie 8am–1am. Métro: George V.

MODERATE

Café Beaubourg   Next to the all-pedestrian plaza of the Centre Pompidou, this is a trendy cafe with soaring concrete columns and a minimalist decor. Many of the regulars work in the neighborhood's eclectic shops and galleries. You can order salads, omelets, grilled steak, chicken *cordon bleu,* pastries, and daily platters. In warm weather, tables are set up on the sprawling outdoor terrace, providing an appropriate niche for watching the young and the restless go by.

100 rue St-Martin, 4e. ℭ **01-48-87-63-96.** Glass of wine 5€–9€; beer 6€; American breakfast 15€–24€; sandwiches and platters 12€–29€. AE, DC, MC, V. Mon–Fri 8am–1am; Sat–Sun 8am–2am. Métro: Rambuteau or Hôtel-de-Ville.

Café de la Musique   This cafe's location, in one of the grandest of Mitterrand's *grands travaux,* guarantees a crowd passionately devoted to music; the recorded sounds that play in the background are likely to be more diverse and more eclectic than those in any other cafe in Paris. The red-and-green velour setting might remind you of a modern opera house. Although it originated in the late 1990s as a cafe serving light platters, sandwiches, and drinks, its cuisine became dramatically more sophisticated in 2002, the year it was taken over by culinary legend and nightlife impresario Alain Poudou. The menu was inspired by the cuisine served in one of Paris's trendiest hotels, the Costes, and is likely to include lobster-studded risotto, roasted rack of lamb with thyme, fresh salads of the type you'd find in Italy, brochettes of shrimp with spinach, and baked salmon in a white-wine cream sauce. As the evening progresses, this place takes on more of the ambience of a hip nightclub as DJs spin various kinds of music.

 Did You Know?

You'll pay substantially less in a cafe if you stand at the counter rather than sit at a table, partly because there's no service charge, and partly because clients tend to linger at tables.

In the Cité de la Musique, place Fontaine aux Lions, 213 av. Jean-Jaurès, 19e. ℭ **01-48-03-15-91.** www.cafe-de-la-musique.com. Main courses 12€–24€. AE, DC, MC, V. Daily 8am–2am. Restaurant daily 8am–1am. Métro: Porte de Pantin.

La Belle Hortense   This is the most literary cafe in a neighborhood (the Marais) that's loaded with literary antecedents and references. It contains an erudite and accessible staff; an inventory of French literary classics as well as modern tomes about art, psychoanalysis, history, and culture; and two high-ceilinged, 19th-century rooms with little changed since the days of Baudelaire and Balzac.

Near the entrance is a zinc-covered bar that sells glasses of wine. If you're fluent in French, you might be interested in attending a reading, a book signing, or a lecture. Some kind of public gathering, conducted only in rapid, colloquial French, is scheduled every Tuesday, Wednesday, and Thursday, usually at 8pm. One particularly intriguing and ongoing series involves three trained actors, each reading sequential passages from a book.

31 rue Vieille du Temple, 4e. ℂ **01-48-04-71-60.** Glass of wine 4€–10€; coffee 1.50€; plats du jour 12€–24€. MC, V. Daily 5pm–2am. Métro: Hôtel-de-Ville or St-Paul.

La Coupole ★   Born in 1927 and once a leading center of artistic life, La Coupole is now the epitome of the grand Paris brasserie in Montparnasse. Former patrons include Josephine Baker, Henry Miller, Dalí, Calder, Hemingway, Fitzgerald, and Picasso. At one of its sidewalk tables, you can sit and watch the passing scene and order a coffee or a cognac VSOP. The food is quite good, despite the fact that the dining room resembles an enormous rail-station waiting room. Try main dishes such as sole meunière, a very good rump steak, fresh oysters, shellfish, grilled lobster with flambéed whisky sauce, or curried lamb. The waiters are as rude and inattentive as ever, and the patrons would have it no other way.

102 bd. du Montparnasse, 14e. ℂ **01-43-20-14-20.** www.flobrasseries.com. Breakfast buffet 14€–19€; main courses 20€–40€. AE, DC, MC, V. Daily 8am–1am (breakfast buffet Mon–Fri 8:30–10:30am). Métro: Vavin.

La Palette ★★   The staff here defiantly maintains old-fashioned Parisian traditions that haven't changed much since the days of Picasso and Braque—the same drinks (Ricard and Pernod, among others) are still popular. A bustle of comings and goings makes La Palette an insider's version of a battered, artistically evocative Latin Quarter cafe. The interior, inhabited by amiably crotchety waiters, consists of tiled murals, installed around 1935, advertising the virtues of a brand of liqueur that's no longer manufactured. If you happen to drop in during mealtime, you'll have a limited selection of salads and *croque monsieur* (toasted ham and cheese), plus one *plat du jour* per day, always priced at 15€, which may include roast beef, lamb stew, fish, or gigot of lamb. The food is well prepared, and the dish of the day is usually announced as a kind of surprise to the joint's devoted fans.

43 rue de Seine, 6e. ℂ **01-43-26-68-15.** Sandwiches, omelets, and plats du jour 6€–15€. MC, V. Cafe and bar daily 8am–2am. Restaurant daily noon–3pm. Métro: Mabillon or St-Germain-des-Prés.

La Rotonde   Once patronized by Hemingway, the original Rotonde faded into history but is immortalized in the pages of *The Sun Also Rises,* in which Papa wrote, "No matter what cafe in Montparnasse you ask a taxi driver to bring you to from the right bank of the river, they always take you to the Rotonde." Lavishly upgraded, its reincarnation has a paneled Art Deco elegance and shares the site with a cinema. The menu includes such hearty fare as pepper steak with *pommes frites* (french fries), shellfish in season, a superb and genuinely succulent version of sole meunière, and sea-bass filets with herb-flavored lemon sauce.

105 bd. du Montparnasse, 6e. ℂ **01-43-26-48-26.** www.rotondemontparnasse.com. Glass of wine 4€–11€; main courses 10€–38€; fixed-price lunch 18€–35€; fixed-price dinner 35€. AE, MC, V. Cafe daily 7:15am–2am; food service daily noon–1am. Métro: Vavin.

Le Procope ★★   To fans of French history, this is the holy grail of Parisian cafes. Opened in 1686, it occupies a three-story town house categorized as a historic monument. Inside, nine salons and dining rooms, each of whose 300-year-old walls have been carefully preserved and painted a deep red, are available for languorous afternoon coffee breaks or well-presented meals. Menu items include platters of shellfish, onion soup au gratin, coq au vin (chicken stewed in wine), duck breast in honey sauce, and grilled versions of various meats and fish. Every day between 3 and 6pm, the place makes itself available to sightseers who come to look but not necessarily eat and drink at the site that welcomed such movers and shakers as Diderot, Voltaire, George Sand, Victor Hugo, and Oscar Wilde. Of special charm is the ground-floor room outfitted like an antique library.

13 rue de l'Ancienne-Comédie, 6e. ☎ **01-40-46-79-00.** www.procope.com. Reservations recommended. Coffee 3€; glass of beer 5€–7€; main courses 20€–29€. AE, DC, MC, V. Daily 10:30am–1am. Métro: Odéon.

Les Deux Magots ★★   This legendary hangout for the sophisticated residents of St-Germain-des-Prés becomes a tourist favorite in summer. Visitors monopolize the few sidewalk tables as the waiters rush about, seemingly oblivious to anyone's needs. Regulars from around the neighborhood reclaim it in the off season. Les Deux Magots was once a gathering place of the intellectual elite, such as Sartre, de Beauvoir, and Giraudoux. Inside are the two large statues of *magots* (Confucian wise men) that give the cafe its name. The crystal chandeliers are too brightly lit, but the regulars are used to the glare. After all, some of them even read their daily papers here. You can order salads, pastries, ice cream, or one of the daily specials; the fresh fish is usually good.

6 place St-Germain-des-Prés, 6e. ☎ **01-45-48-55-25.** www.lesdeuxmagots.fr. Café au lait 6€; whisky soda 12€–16€; main courses 22€–36€. AE, DC, V. Daily 7:30am–1am. Métro: St-Germain-des-Prés.

INEXPENSIVE

Café des Deux Moulins   *Amélie* was a quirky low-budget film that was nominated for five Oscars and was seen by more than 25 million people around the world following its release in 2001. The film was set in Montmartre, and the cafe featured in the film has developed into a mandatory stopping-off place for the constantly arriving "cult of *Amélie*." In the film, Amélie worked as a waitress at the Café des Deux Moulins. The musty atmosphere, with its 1950s decor, mustard-colored ceiling, and lace curtains, has been preserved—even the wall lamps and unisex toilet. The menu remains much the same as it always was—beef filets, calf's liver, green frisée salad with bacon bits and warm goat cheese, and pigs' brains with lentils. The kitchen serves hamburgers, but with an egg on top. Of course, the classic dish is a demi-Camembert with a glass of Côtes du Rhône.

15 rue Lepic, 18e. ☎ **01-42-54-90-50.** Main courses 11€–17€. MC, V. Daily 7am–2am. Métro: Blanche.

Le Rouquet ★ 🎁   Despite its conventional food, Le Rouquet enjoys an enviable cachet and sense of chic, partly because it competes on a less flamboyant scale with the nearby Café de Flore and Les Deux Magots and partly because the decor hasn't changed since a 1954 remodeling. Less than 60 yards from St-Germain church, you can sit for as long as you want, watching a crowd of stylish Italians and Americans performing rituals of shopping and people-watching, which have barely altered since Le Rouquet's founding in 1922.

188 bd. St-Germain, 7e. ☎ **01-45-48-06-93.** Café au lait 3€ at counter, 5€ at table; *plats du jour* at lunch 16€. MC, V. Mon–Sat 7am–9pm. Métro: St-Germain-des-Prés.

7

EXPLORING PARIS

P

aris is a city where taking in the street life—shopping, strolling, and hanging out—should claim as much of your time as sightseeing in churches or museums. Having a picnic in the Bois de Boulogne, taking a sunrise stroll along the Seine, spending an afternoon at a flea market—Paris bewitches you with these kinds of experiences. For all of the Louvre's beauty, you'll probably remember the Latin Quarter's crooked alleyways better than the 370th oil painting of your visit.

ATTRACTIONS BY ARRONDISSEMENT

For the locations of these sights, see the **"Top Paris Attractions"** map on p. 218 and the individual **arrondissement maps** that follow.

The Right Bank

1ST ARRONDISSEMENT
Forum des Halles (p. 285)
Jardin des Tuileries ★★ (p. 270)
Jardin du Carrousel (p. 270)
Les Halles ★ (p. 285)
Musée de l'Orangerie ★ (p. 244)
Musée des Arts Décoratifs ★ (p. 245)
Musée du Louvre ★★★ (p. 234)
Palais Royal ★★ (p. 267)
St-Eustache ★★ (p. 261)
St-Germain l'Auxerrois ★★ (p. 262)

3RD ARRONDISSEMENT
Hôtel de Clisson (p. 254)
Hôtel de Rohan (p. 255)
Hôtel le Peletier de St-Fargeau (p. 244)
Musée Carnavalet-Histoire de Paris ★★ (p. 244)
Musée Cognacq-Jay ★ (p. 250)
Musée d'Art et Histoire du Judaisme ★★ (p. 254)
Musée de l'Histoire de France ★ (p. 254)

4TH ARRONDISSEMENT
Atelier Brancusi ★ (p. 241)
Cathédrale de Notre-Dame ★★★ (p. 225)

Centre Pompidou ★★★ (p. 241)
Conciergerie ★★ (p. 264)
Hôtel de Lauzun (p. 284)
Hôtel de Ville ★ (p. 265)
Hôtel Dieu (p. 283)
Hôtel Lambert (p. 284)
Maison de Victor Hugo ★ (p. 269)
Place des Vosges (p. 310)
Pont Neuf (p. 283)
Rue des Rosiers (p. 314)
Sainte-Chapelle ★★★ (p. 237)
Square du Vert Galant (p. 284)
St-Louis-en-l'Ile (p. 285)

8TH ARRONDISSEMENT
American Cathedral of the Holy Trinity (p. 258)
Arc de Triomphe ★★★ (p. 216)
Champs-Elysées (p. 92)
Jeu de Paume (p. 242)
La Madeleine ★★ (p. 260)
Musée Jacquemart-André ★★ (p. 246)
Musée Nissim de Camondo ★ (p. 252)
Parc Monceau ★ (p. 274)
Place de la Concorde (p. 92)

PREVIOUS PAGE: **The Chapelle des Anges (Chapel of the Angels) at St-Sulpice, with its frescoes by Eugène Delacroix.**

Attractions by Arrondissement

EXPLORING PARIS

9TH ARRONDISSEMENT
Fragonard Musée du Parfum (p. 256)
Musée Grévin ★ (p. 291)
Paris-Story (p. 255)

11TH ARRONDISSEMENT
Musée Edith Piaf (p. 251)
Villa Calte (p. 251)

16TH ARRONDISSEMENT
Bois de Boulogne ★★ (p. 272)
Cimetière de Passy (p. 276)
Hippodrome d'Auteuil (p. 273)
Hippodrome de Longchamp ★★★
     (p. 273)
Jardin d'Acclimatation ★ (p. 273)
La Cité de l'Architecture et du Patri-
     moine ★ (p. 242)
La Grande Arche de La Défense ★
     (p. 266)
Maison de Balzac (p. 269)
Musée d'Art Moderne de la Ville de
     Paris (p. 251)
Musée des Enfants (p. 251)
Musée du Vin (p. 257)
Musée Marmottan Monet ★★
     (p. 247)
Musée National des Arts Asiatiques-
     Guimet ★★ (p. 252)
Palais de Tokyo ★ (p. 253)

18TH ARRONDISSEMENT
Basilique du Sacré-Coeur ★★
     (p. 217)
Cimetière de Montmartre ★ (p. 274)
Cimetière St-Vincent (p. 278)
Musée de l'Erotisme (p. 256)

19TH ARRONDISSEMENT
Cité des Sciences et de l'Industrie
     ★★ (p. 290)
La Géode (p. 290)
Musée de la Musique (p. 251)
Parc de La Villette (p. 290)

20TH ARRONDISSEMENT
Cimetière du Père-Lachaise ★★★
     (p. 276)

The Left Bank

5TH ARRONDISSEMENT
Arènes de Lutèce (p. 263)
La Grande Mosquée de Paris ★
     (p. 259)
Musée de l'Institut du Monde Arabe
     (p. 257)

Musée National d'Histoire Naturelle ★
     (p. 291)
Musée National du Moyen Age/
     Thermes de Cluny ★★ (p. 248)
Panthéon ★★ (p. 267)
Roman Baths (p. 248)
Rue de la Huchette (p. 268)
St-Etienne-du-Mont ★★ (p. 260)
Val-de-Grâce ★★ (p. 263)

6TH ARRONDISSEMENT
Hôtel du Vieux-Paris (p. 268)
Institut de France ★ (p. 265)
Jardin du Luxembourg ★★ (p. 271)
Musée National Eugène Delacroix
     (p. 249)
Musée Zadkine (p. 253)
Palais du Luxembourg (p. 271)
Rue Monsieur-le-Prince (p. 268)
Rue Visconti (p. 287)
St-Germain-des-Prés ★★ (p. 261)
St-Sulpice ★★ (p. 262)
20 rue Jacob (p. 287)
27 rue de Fleurus (p. 287)

7TH ARRONDISSEMENT
Champ de Mars (p. 289)
Eglise du Dôme/Napoleon's Tomb
     (p. 232)
Hôtel des Invalides ★★★ (p. 230)
Le Musée du quai Branly ★★★
     (p. 243)
Les Egouts ★ (p. 278)
Musée de l'Armée (p. 230)
Musée des Plans-Reliefs (p. 231)
Musée d'Orsay ★★★ (p. 232)
Musée Rodin ★★ (p. 249)
Palais Bourbon/Assemblée
     Nationale ★ (p. 266)
Tour Eiffel ★★★ (p. 239)

13TH ARRONDISSEMENT
Bibliothèque Nationale de France
     (p. 263)
Manufacture Nationale des
     Gobelins ★ (p. 253)

14TH ARRONDISSEMENT
Cimetière du Montparnasse ★
     (p. 276)
Les Catacombes ★ (p. 278)
Tour Montparnasse (p. 288)

15TH ARRONDISSEMENT
Musée Bourdelle ★ (p. 250)

Arc de Triomphe.

THE TOP ATTRACTIONS:
Arc de Triomphe to the Tour Eiffel

Arc de Triomphe ★★★   At the western end of the Champs-Elysées, the Arc de Triomphe suggests an ancient Roman arch, only it's larger. Actually, it's the biggest triumphal arch in the world, about 49m (161 ft.) high and 44m (144 ft.) wide. To reach it, *don't try to cross the square,* Paris's busiest traffic hub. With a dozen streets radiating from the "Star," the roundabout has been called by one writer "vehicular roulette with more balls than numbers," death is certain! Take the underground passage, and live a little longer.

Commissioned by Napoleon in 1806 to commemorate the victories of his Grand Armée, the arch wasn't ready for the entrance of his empress, Marie-Louise, in 1810 (he divorced Joséphine because she couldn't provide him an heir). It wasn't completed until 1836, under the reign of Louis-Philippe. Four years later, Napoleon's remains, brought from St. Helena, passed under the arch on their journey to his tomb at the Hôtel des Invalides. Since then, it has become the focal point for state funerals. It's also the site of the tomb of the Unknown Soldier, in whose honor an eternal flame burns.

The greatest state funeral was Victor Hugo's in 1885; his coffin was placed under the arch, and much of Paris came to pay tribute. Another notable funeral was in 1929 for Ferdinand Foch, commander of the Allied forces in World War I. The arch has been the centerpiece of some of France's proudest moments and some of its most humiliating defeats, notably in 1871 and 1940. The memory of German troops marching under the arch is still painful to the French. Who can forget the 1940 newsreel of the Frenchman standing on the Champs-Elysées weeping as the Nazi storm troopers goose-stepped through Paris? The arch's happiest moment occurred in 1944, when the liberation-of-Paris parade passed beneath it. That same year, Eisenhower paid a visit to the tomb of the Unknown Soldier, a new tradition among leaders of state and important figures. After

Charles de Gaulle's death, the French government (despite protests from anti-Gaullists) voted to change the name of this site from place de l'Etoile to place Charles de Gaulle. Nowadays it's often known as place Charles de Gaulle–Etoile.

Of the sculptures on the monument, the best known is Rude's *Marseillaise*, or *The Departure of the Volunteers*. J. P. Cortot's *Triumph of Napoléon in 1810* and Etex's *Resistance of 1814* and *Peace of 1815* also adorn the facade. The monument is engraved with the names of hundreds of generals (those underlined died in battle) who commanded French troops in Napoleonic victories.

You can take an elevator or climb the stairway to the top, where there's an exhibition hall with lithographs and photos depicting the arch throughout its history, as well as an observation deck with a fantastic view.

Place Charles de Gaulle–Etoile, 8e. ☎ **01-55-37-73-77.** www.monum.fr. Admission 9€ adults, 5.50€ for those 18–24. Apr–Sept daily 10am–11pm; Oct–Mar daily 10am–10:30pm. Métro: Charles-de-Gaulle–Etoile. Bus: 22, 30, 31, 52, 73, or 92.

Basilique du Sacré-Coeur ★★   Sacré-Coeur is one of Paris's most characteristic landmarks and has been the subject of much controversy. One Parisian called it "a lunatic's confectionery dream." An offended Zola declared it "the basilica of the ridiculous." Sacré-Coeur has had warm supporters as well, including poet Max Jacob and artist Maurice Utrillo. Utrillo never tired of drawing and painting it, and he and Jacob came here regularly to pray. Atop the *butte* (hill) in Montmartre, its multiple gleaming white domes and campanile (bell tower) loom over Paris like a 12th-century Byzantine church. But it's not that old. After France's 1870 defeat by the Prussians, the basilica was planned as a votive offering to cure France's misfortunes. Rich and poor alike contributed money to build it. Construction began in 1876, and though the church wasn't consecrated until 1919, perpetual prayers of adoration have been made here day and night since 1885. The interior is brilliantly decorated with mosaics: Look for the striking Christ on the ceiling and the mural of his Passion at the back of the altar. The stained-glass windows were shattered during the struggle for Paris in 1944 but have been well replaced. The crypt contains what some of the devout believe is Christ's sacred heart—hence, the name of the church.

 Best City View

From the observation deck of the Arc de Triomphe, you can see up the Champs-Elysées and such landmarks as the Louvre, the Eiffel Tower, Sacré-Coeur, and La Défense. Although we don't want to get into any arguments about this, we think the view of Paris from this perspective is the grandest in the entire city.

Insider's tip: Although the view from the Arc de Triomphe is the greatest panorama of Paris, we also want to endorse the view from the gallery around the inner dome of Sacré-Coeur. On a clear day, your eyes take in a sweep of Paris extending for 48km (30 miles) into the Ile de France. You can also walk around the inner dome, an attraction even better than the interior of Sacré-Coeur itself.

Place St-Pierre, 18e. ☎ **01-53-41-89-00.** www.sacre-coeur-montmartre.com. Free admission to basilica, joint ticket to dome and crypt 5€. Basilica daily 6am–11pm; dome and crypt daily 9am–6pm. Métro: Abbesses; take elevator to surface and follow signs to funicular.

Top Paris Attractions

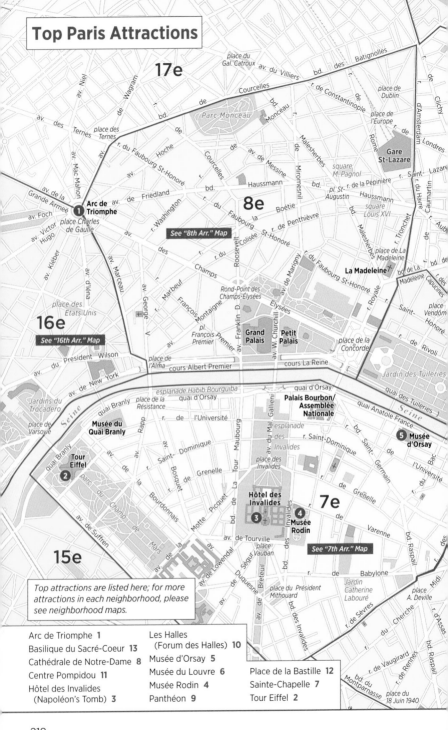

17e

place du Gal. Catroux — av. du Villiers — bd. — des — Batignolles

Courcelles — place de Dublin — d'Amsterdam — Clichy

de — Monceau — place de l'Europe — r. — Rome — Londres

Parc Monceau — Malesherbes — **Gare St-Lazare**

av. des Ternes — place des Ternes — r. du Faubourg St-Honore — Hoche — av. de Messine — square M. Pagnol — Saint-Lazare — r. du Havre

av. de la Grande Armée — Haussmann — pl. St-Augustin — r. de la Pépinière — Haussmann — Caumartin

Arc de Triomphe 1 — av. de Friedland — r. du Faubourg — Boétie — square Louis XVI — r. Tronchet

place Charles de Gaulle — r. Washington — **8e** — la — r. de Penthièvre — place de La Madeleine — bd. de la

av. Victor Hugo — av. Kléber — *See "8th Arr." Map* — des — Roosevelt — Colisée — St-Honoré — **La Madeleine** 7 — Madeleine — Capucines

av. d'Iéna — av. Marceau — Champs — Matbeuf — François — r. du Faubourg St-Honoré — r. Royale — Saint- — place Vendôme

16e — place des États Unis — av. George V — pl. François Premier — Rond-Point des Champs-Elysées — Elysées — r. — de — Rivoli — Honoré

See "16th Arr." Map — place de l'Alma — cours Albert Premier — **Grand Palais** — **Petit Palais** — W. Churchill — place de la Concorde — Jardin des Tuileries

av. du Président Wilson — av. de New York — cours La Reine — Seine — quai des Tuileries

Jardins du Trocadéro — quai Branly — esplanade Habib Bourguiba — quai d'Orsay — **Palais Bourbon/ Assemblée Nationale** — quai Anatole France — Seine

place de Varsovie — place de la Résistance — r. de l'Université — Galliéni — esplanade des Invalides — r. Saint-Dominique — **Musée d'Orsay** 5

Musée du Quai Branly — Rapp — av. Saint-Dominique — Tour — place des Invalides — Saint-Germain — de — l'Université

Tour Eiffel 2 — Parc du Champ de Mars — de Grenelle — Bosquet — La Motte-Picquet — **Hôtel des Invalides** 3 — **Musée Rodin** 4 — Grenelle — de — Varenne — bd. Raspail

15e — av. de Suffren — Bourdonnais — av. de Tourville — place Vauban — **7e** — *See "7th Arr." Map* — de — Babylone

av. de Lowendal — Ségur — Duquesne — Breteuil — place du Président Mithouard — des Invalides — Jardin Catherine Labouré — place A. Deville — r. de Sèvres — r. de Cherche — r. d'Assas

Top attractions are listed here; for more attractions in each neighborhood, please see neighborhood maps.

bd. du Montparnasse — place du 18 Juin 1940 — r. de Vaugirard — r. de Rennes — bd. Raspail — Midi

Arc de Triomphe **1**

Basilique du Sacré-Coeur **13**

Cathédrale de Notre-Dame **8**

Centre Pompidou **11**

Hôtel des Invalides (Napoléon's Tomb) **3**

Les Halles (Forum des Halles) **10**

Musée d'Orsay **5**

Musée du Louvre **6**

Musée Rodin **4**

Panthéon **9**

Place de la Bastille **12**

Sainte-Chapelle **7**

Tour Eiffel **2**

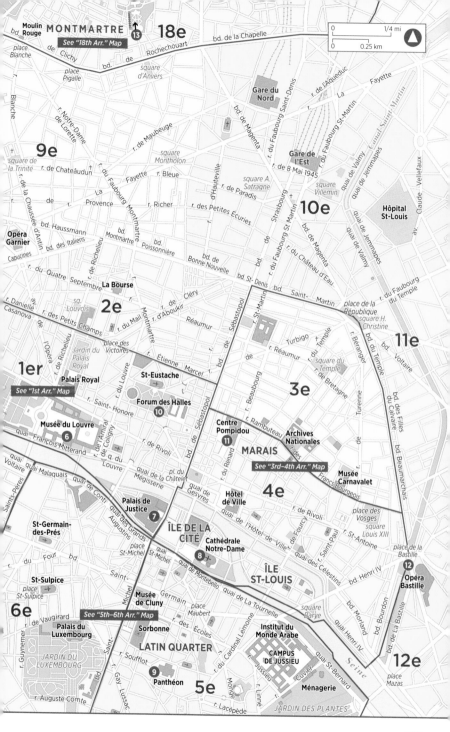

Attractions in the 1st Arrondissement

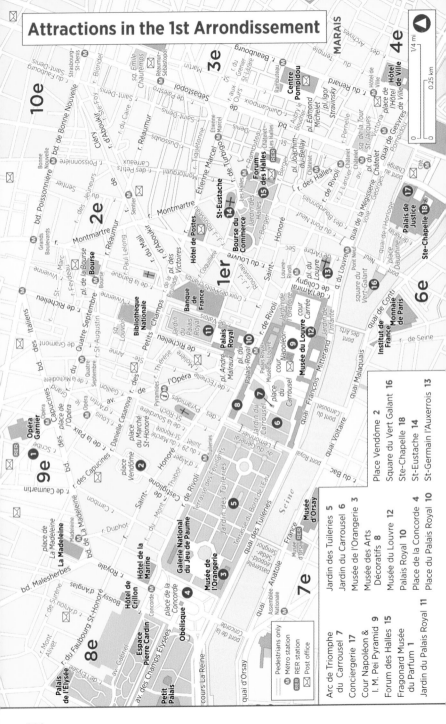

Arc de Triomphe
du Carrousel **7**
Conciergerie **17**
Cour Napoléon &
I. M. Pei Pyramid **9**
Forum des Halles **15**
Fragonard Musée
du Parfum **1**
Jardin du Palais Royal **11**

Jardin des Tuileries **5**
Jardin du Carrousel **6**
Musée de l'Orangerie **3**
Musée des Arts
Décoratifs **8**
Musée du Louvre **12**
Palais Royal **10**
Place de la Concorde **4**
Place du Palais Royal **10**

Place Vendôme **2**
Square du Vert Galant **16**
Ste-Chapelle **18**
St-Eustache **14**
St-Germain l'Auxerrois **13**

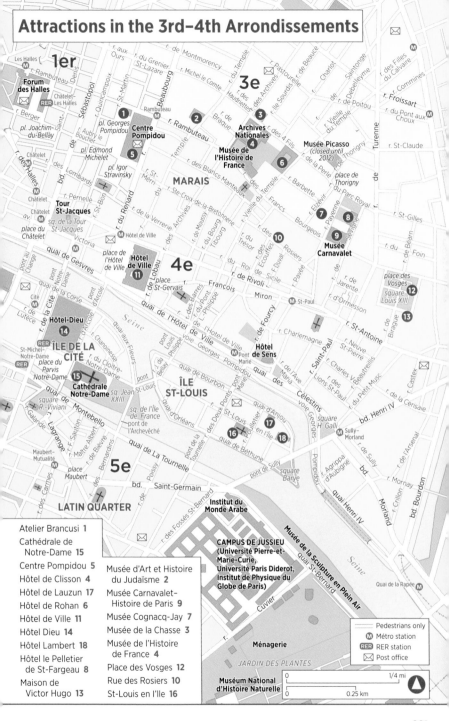

Attractions in the 3rd–4th Arrondissements

1er

Les Halles

Forum
des Halles

Châtelet-
Les Halles

3e

Archives
Nationales

Musée Picasso
*(closed until
2012)*

MARAIS

Musée de
l'Histoire de
France

Musée
Carnavalet

Tour
St-Jacques

place du
Châtelet

Hôtel de Ville

Hôtel
de Ville

place de
l'Hôtel
de Ville

4e

place
St-Gervais

place des
Vosges

square
Louis XIII

Hôtel-Dieu

**ÎLE DE LA
CITÉ**

place du
Parvis
Notre-Dame

Cathédrale
Notre-Dame

**ÎLE
ST-LOUIS**

Hôtel
de Sens

Hôtel
Marie

5e

place
Maubert

LATIN QUARTER

Institut du
Monde Arabe

**CAMPUS DE JUSSIEU
(Université Pierre-et-
Marie-Curie,
Université Paris Diderot,
Institut de Physique du
Globe de Paris)**

Ménagerie

JARDIN DES PLANTES

Muséum National
d'Histoire Naturelle

Quai de la Rapée

Atelier Brancusi 1

Cathédrale de
  Notre-Dame 15

Centre Pompidou 5

Hôtel de Clisson 4

Hôtel de Lauzun 17

Hôtel de Rohan 6

Hôtel de Ville 11

Hôtel Dieu 14

Hôtel Lambert 18

Hôtel le Pelletier
  de St-Fargeau 8

Maison de
  Victor Hugo 13

Musée d'Art et Histoire
  du Judaïsme 2

Musée Carnavalet–
  Histoire de Paris 9

Musée Cognacq-Jay 7

Musée de la Chasse 3

Musée de l'Histoire
  de France 4

Place des Vosges 12

Rue des Rosiers 10

St-Louis en l'Ile 16

Pedestrians only
Ⓜ Métro station
RER RER station
✉ Post office

0   1/4 mi
0   0.25 km

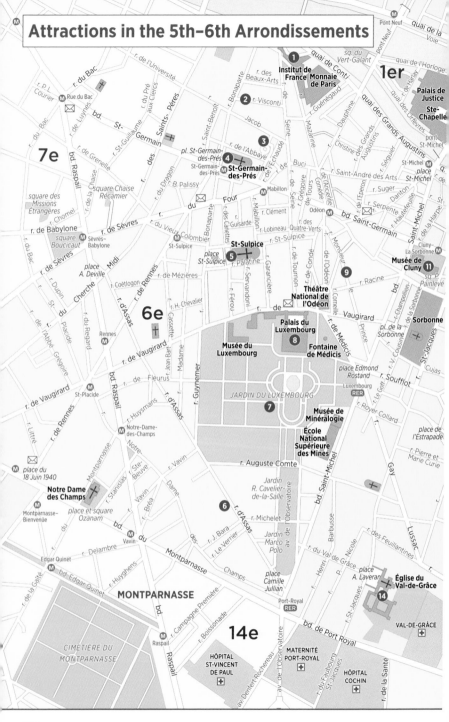

Attractions in the 5th–6th Arrondissements

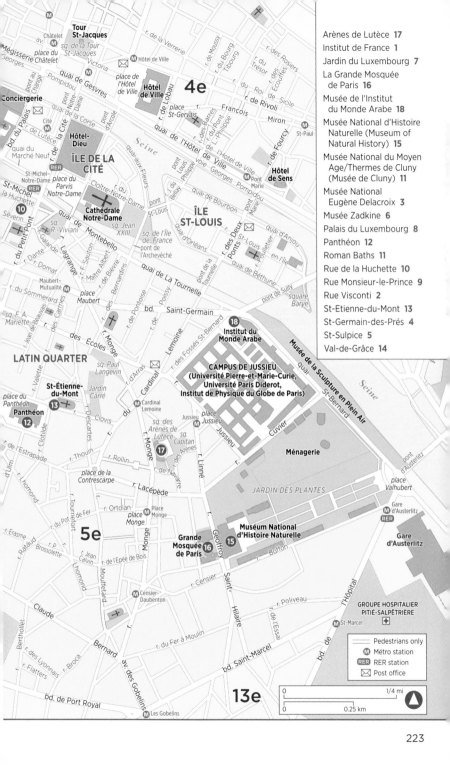

Arènes de Lutèce 17
Institut de France 1
Jardin du Luxembourg 7
La Grande Mosquée
  de Paris 16
Musée de l'Institut
  du Monde Arabe 18
Musée National d'Histoire
  Naturelle (Museum of
  Natural History) 15
Musée National du Moyen
  Age/Thermes de Cluny
  (Musée de Cluny) 11
Musée National
  Eugène Delacroix 3
Musée Zadkine 6
Palais du Luxembourg 8
Panthéon 12
Roman Baths 11
Rue de la Huchette 10
Rue Monsieur-le-Prince 9
Rue Visconti 2
St-Etienne-du-Mont 13
St-Germain-des-Prés 4
St-Sulpice 5
Val-de-Grâce 14

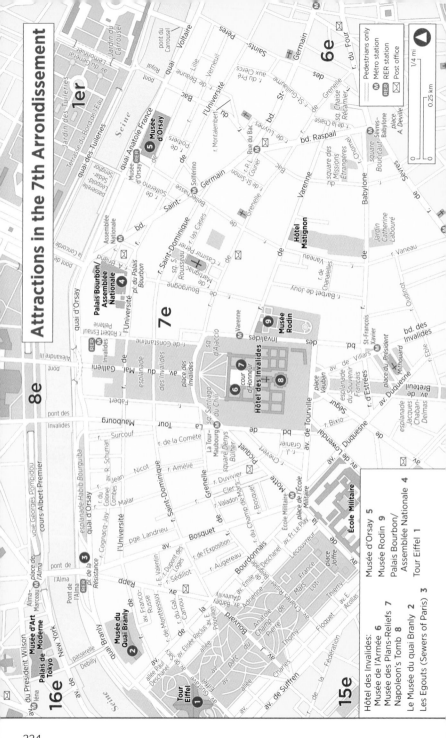

Attractions in the 7th Arrondissement

Pedestrians only
Ⓜ Metro station
RER RER station
☒ Post office

1/4 mi
0.25 km

Hôtel des Invalides:
Musée de l'Armée **6**
Musée des Plans-Reliefs **7**
Napoleon's Tomb **8**
Le Musée du quai Branly **2**
Les Egouts (Sewers of Paris) **3**

Musée d'Orsay **5**
Musée Rodin **9**
Palais Bourbon/
Assemblée Nationale **4**
Tour Eiffel **1**

Attractions in the 8th Arrondissement

American Cathedral of the Holy Trinity **6**

Arc de Triomphe **4**

Avenue des Champs-Elysées **5**

La Madeleine **8**

Musée Jacquemart-André **3**

Musée Nissim de Camondo **1**

Parc Monceau **2**

Place de la Concorde **7**

Pedestrians only

Ⓜ Métro station

RER RER station

✉ Post office

0 ——— 1/4 mi

0 ——— 0.25 km

Cathédrale de Notre-Dame ★★★   Notre-Dame is the heart of Paris and even of the country itself: Distances from the city to all parts of France are calculated from a spot at the far end of place du Parvis, in front of the cathedral, where a circular bronze plaque marks **Kilomètre Zéro.**

The cathedral's setting on the banks of the Seine has always been memorable. Founded in the 12th century by Maurice de Sully, bishop of Paris, Notre-Dame has grown over the years, changing as Paris has changed; often falling victim to whims of taste. Its flying buttresses (the external side supports, giving the massive interior a sense of weightlessness) were rebuilt in 1330. Though many disagree, we feel Notre-Dame is more interesting outside than in, and you'll want to walk all around it to fully appreciate this "vast symphony of stone."

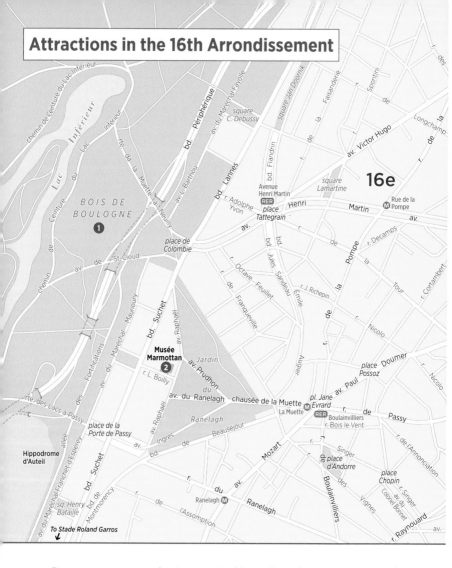

Attractions in the 16th Arrondissement

BOIS DE BOULOGNE ❶

Musée Marmottan ❷

16e

Hippodrome d'Auteil

To Stade Roland Garros ↓

Better yet, cross over the Pont au Double to the Left Bank and view it from the quai.

The histories of Paris and Notre-Dame are inseparable. Many prayed here before going off to fight in the Crusades. The revolutionaries who destroyed the Galerie des Rois and converted the building into a secular temple didn't spare "Our Lady of Paris." Later, Napoleon crowned himself emperor here, yanking the crown out of Pius VII's hands and placing it on his own head before crowning his Joséphine empress (see David's *Coronation of Napoléon* in the Louvre). But carelessness, vandalism, embellishments, and wars of religion had already demolished much of the previously existing structure.

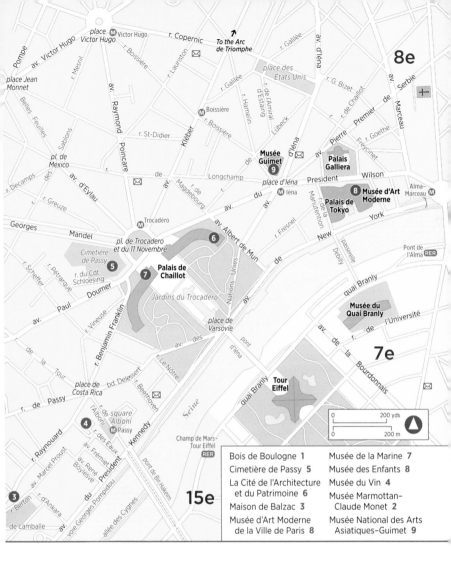

place Victor Hugo
M Victor Hugo
r. Copernic
To the Arc de Triomphe
r. Galilée
av. d'Iéna
8e

av. Victor Hugo
r. Mesnil
r. Boissière
r. Lauriston
place des États Unis
r. G. Bizet
av. de Serbie

Pompe

place Jean Monnet
r. Boissière
r. de l'Amiral d'Estaing
r. de Chaillot
av. Marceau

Belles Feuilles
av. Raymond Poincaré
av. d'Eylau
r. Boissière
r. Hamelin
r. Premier
r. de Chaillot

Sablons

r. St-Didier
Kléber
de
av. de Magdebourg
de
Lübeck
d'Iéna
Pierre
r. Goethe
Freycinet

pl. de Mexico
r. Decamps
r. Greuze
Longchamp
Musée Guimet 9
place d'Iéna
President Wilson
Palais Galliera
Alma-Marceau

Georges Mandel
Trocadéro
M Iéna
8 Musée d'Art Moderne
Palais de Tokyo
York

pl. de Trocadéro et du 11 Novembre
av. Albert de Mun
r. Fresnel
New
Pont de l'Alma RER

Cimetière de Passy 5
7 Palais de Chaillot
6
passerelle Debilly

r. Scheffer
r. Pétrarque
r. du Cdt. Schloesing
Jardins du Trocadéro
Nations Unies
quai Branly
Musée du Quai Branly
r. de l'Université

Paul Doumer
av.
place de Varsovie
7e

r. Vineuse
r. Benjamin Franklin
av. des
pont d'Iéna

r. de la Tour
bd. Delessert
r. Beethoven
r. Le Nôtre
av. de la Bourdonnais

place de Costa Rica
square Alboni
M Passy
Kennedy
Tour Eiffel

4 r. des Eaux
President
quai Branly

r. Raynouard
av. Marcel Proust
av. Frémiet
av. René Boylesve
Champ de Mars–Tour Eiffel RER
0 ____ 200 yds
0 ____ 200 m

3
r. Berton
r. d'Ankara
du
voie Georges Pompidou
pont de Bir-Hakeim
15e

de Lamballe
av.
allée des Cygnes

Bois de Boulogne **1**	Musée de la Marine **7**
Cimetière de Passy **5**	Musée des Enfants **8**
La Cité de l'Architecture et du Patrimoine **6**	Musée du Vin **4**
Maison de Balzac **3**	Musée Marmottan– Claude Monet **2**
Musée d'Art Moderne de la Ville de Paris **8**	Musée National des Arts Asiatiques–Guimet **9**

The cathedral was once scheduled for demolition, but because of the popularity of Victor Hugo's *Hunchback of Notre-Dame* and the revival of interest in the Gothic period, a movement mushroomed to restore the cathedral to its original glory. The task was completed under Viollet-le-Duc, an architectural genius. The houses of old Paris used to crowd in on Notre-Dame, but during his redesign of the city, Baron Haussmann ordered them torn down to show the cathedral to its best advantage from the parvis. This is the best vantage for seeing the three sculpted 13th-century portals (the Virgin, the Last Judgment, and St. Anne).

On the left, the **Portal of the Virgin** depicts the signs of the zodiac and the coronation of the Virgin, an association found in dozens of medieval churches. The restored central **Portal of the Last Judgment** depicts three levels: the first

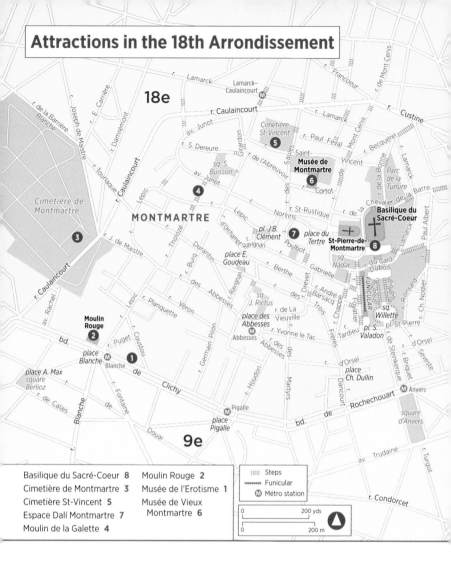

Attractions in the 18th Arrondissement

Basilique du Sacré-Coeur	8	Moulin Rouge	2
Cimetière de Montmartre	3	Musée de l'Erotisme	1
Cimetière St-Vincent	5	Musée de Vieux	
Espace Dalí Montmartre	7	Montmartre	6
Moulin de la Galette	4		

ⅢⅢ	Steps
⤳	Funicular
Ⓜ	Métro station

shows Vices and Virtues; the second, Christ and his Apostles; and above that, Christ in triumph after the Resurrection. The portal is a close illustration of the Gospel according to Matthew. Over it is the remarkable **west rose window** ★★, 9.5m (31 ft.) wide, forming a showcase for a statue of the Virgin and Child. On the far right is the **Portal of St. Anne,** depicting scenes such as the Virgin enthroned with Child; it's Notre-Dame's best-preserved and most perfect piece of sculpture. Equally interesting (though often missed) is the **Portal of the Cloisters** (around on the left), with its dour-faced 13th-century Virgin, a survivor among the figures that originally adorned the facade. (Alas, the Child she's holding has been decapitated.) Finally, on the Seine side of Notre-Dame, the **Portal of St. Stephen** traces that saint's martyrdom.

Basilique du Sacré-Coeur.

The interior of Sacré-Coeur's dome.

If possible, see Notre-Dame at sunset. Inside of the three giant medallions warming the austere cathedral, the **north rose window ★★** in the transept, from the mid–13th century, is best. The main body of the church is typically Gothic, with slender, graceful columns. In the **choir,** a stone-carved screen from the early–14th century depicts such biblical scenes as the Last Supper. Near the altar stands the 14th-century *Virgin and Child* ★, highly venerated among Paris's faithful. In the **treasury** are displayed vestments and gold objects, including crowns. Exhibited is a cross presented to Haile Selassie, former emperor of Ethiopia, and a reliquary given by Napoleon. Notre-Dame is especially proud of its relics of the True Cross and the Crown of Thorns.

To visit the **gargoyles ★★** immortalized by Hugo, you have to scale steps leading to the twin **towers,** rising to a height of 68m (223 ft.). When there, you can inspect devils (some giving you the raspberry), hobgoblins, and birds of prey. Look carefully, and you may see hunchback Quasimodo with Esmeralda.

Kilomètre Zéro.

Approached through a garden behind Notre-Dame is the **Mémorial des Martyrs Français de la Déportation de 1945 (Deportation Memorial),** out on the tip of Ile de la Cité. Here, birds chirp and the Seine flows gently by, but the memories are far from pleasant. The memorial commemorates the French citizens who were deported to concentration camps during World War II. Carved into stone are these blood-red words (in French): "Forgive, but don't forget."

The memorial is open Monday to Friday 8:30am to 9:45pm, and Saturday to Sunday 9am to 9:45pm. Admission is free.

6 place du Parvis Notre-Dame, 4e. *(℃)* **01-53-10-07-02.** www.notredame deparis.fr. Admission free to cathedral. Towers 8€ adults, 5€ seniors and ages 13–25, free for children 12 and younger. Treasury 3€ adults, 2.20€ seniors, 1.60€ ages 13–25, free for children 12 and younger. Cathedral year-round daily 8am–6:45pm (Sat–Sun 7:15pm). Towers and crypt daily 10am–6pm (until 11pm Sat–Sun June–Aug). Museum Wed and Sat–Sun 2–5pm. Treasury Mon–Fri 9:30am–6pm; Sat 9:30am–6:30pm; Sun 1:30–6:30pm. Métro: Cité or St-Michel. RER: St-Michel.

Hôtel des Invalides/Napoleon's Tomb ★★★ In 1670, the Sun King decided to build this "hotel" to house soldiers with disabilities. It wasn't an entirely benevolent gesture, considering that the men had been injured,

Notre-Dame de Paris

Statue of Louis XIV — Ambulatory — Statue of Louis XIII
Pietà
High Altar
→ To Treasu
Choir
Virgin & Child (13th cent.) — Statue of St. Denis — Virgin & Child (14th cent.)
Portal of the Cloisters — North Transept — Crossing — South Transept — Portal o St. Step
North Rose Window — South Rose Window
North Aisle — Nave — South Aisle
Entrance to the Towers — West Rose Window
Portal of the Virgin — Portal of the Last Judgment — Portal of St. Anne

crippled, or blinded while fighting his battles. When the building was finally completed (Louis XIV had long been dead), a gilded dome by Jules Hardouin-Mansart crowned it, and its corridors stretched for miles. The best way to approach the Invalides is by crossing over the Right Bank via the early-1900s Pont Alexander-III and entering the cobblestone forecourt, where a display of massive cannons makes a formidable welcome.

Before rushing on to Napoleon's Tomb, you may want to visit the world's greatest military museum, the **Musée de l'Armée.** In 1794, a French inspector started collecting weapons, uniforms, and equipment, and with the accumulation of war material over time, the museum has become a documentary of man's self-destruction. Viking swords, Burgundian battle axes, 14th-century blunderbusses, Balkan *khandjars,* American Browning machine guns, war pitchforks, salamander-engraved Renaissance serpentines, a 1528 Griffon, musketoons, grenadiers…if it can kill, it's enshrined here. As a sardonic touch, there's even the wooden leg of General Daumesnil, the governor of Vincennes who lost his leg in the battle of Wagram. Oblivious to the irony of committing a crime against a place that documents man's evil nature, the Nazis looted the museum in 1940.

Among the outstanding acquisitions are suits of armor worn by the kings and dignitaries of France, including Louis XIV. The best are in the new Arsenal. The most famous one, the "armor suit of the lion," was made for François I. Henri II ordered his suit engraved with the monogram of his mistress, Diane de Poitiers, and (perhaps reluctantly) that of his wife, Catherine de Médici. Particularly fine are the showcases of swords and the World War I mementos, including

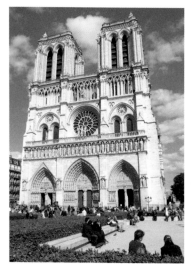

Cathédrale de Notre-Dame.

Notre-Dame's rose window.

those of American and Canadian soldiers—seek out the Armistice Bugle, which sounded the cease-fire on November 7, 1918, before the general cease-fire on November 11. The west wing's Salle Orientale has arms of the Eastern world, including Asia and the Mideast Muslim countries, from the 16th century to the 19th century. Turkish armor (look for Bajazet's helmet) and weaponry, and Chinese and Japanese armor and swords are on display.

Then there's that little Corsican who became France's greatest soldier. Here you can see the death mask Antommarchi made of him, as well as an oil by Delaroche painted at the time of Napoleon's first banishment (Apr 1814) and depicting him as he probably looked, paunch and all. The First Empire exhibit displays

Napoleon's Tomb.

Napoleon's field bed with his tent; in the room devoted to the Restoration, the 100 Days, and Waterloo, you can see his bedroom as it was at the time of his death on St. Helena. The Turenne Salon contains other souvenirs, such as the hat Napoleon wore at Eylau; the sword from his Austerlitz victory; and his "Flag of Farewell," which he kissed before departing for Elba.

You can gain access to the **Musée des Plans-Reliefs** through the west wing. This collection shows French towns and monuments done in scale models (the model of Strasbourg fills an

Engraving of Napoleon's return from St. Helena.

entire room), as well as models of military fortifications since the days of the great Vauban.

A walk across the Cour d'Honneur (Court of Honor) delivers you to the **Eglise du Dôme,** designed by Hardouin-Mansart for Louis XIV. The architect began work on the church in 1677, though he died before its completion. The dome is the second-tallest monument in Paris (the Tour Eiffel is the tallest, of course). The hearse used at the emperor's funeral on May 9, 1821, is in the Napoleon Chapel.

To accommodate **Napoleon's Tomb ★★★,** the architect Visconti had to redesign the church's high altar in 1842. First buried on St. Helena, Napoleon's remains were exhumed and brought to Paris in 1840 on the orders of Louis-Philippe, who demanded that the English return the emperor to French soil. The remains were locked inside six coffins in this tomb made of red Finnish porphyry, with a green granite base. Surrounding it are a dozen Amazon-like figures representing Napoleon's victories. Almost lampooning the smallness of the man, everything is done on a gargantuan scale. In his coronation robes, the statue of Napoleon stands 2.5m (8¼ ft.) high. The grave of the "King of Rome," his son by second wife Marie-Louise, lies at his feet. Surrounding Napoleon's Tomb are those of his brother, Joseph Bonaparte; the great Vauban, who built many of France's fortifications; World War I Allied commander Foch; and the *vicomte* de Turenne, the republic's first grenadier (actually, only his heart is entombed here).

Place des Invalides, 7e. ⓒ **01-44-42-37-72.** www.invalides.org. Admission to Musée de l'Armée, Napoleon's Tomb, and Musée des Plans-Reliefs 8.50€ adults, 6.50€ students, free for children 17 and younger. Oct 1–Mar 31 Mon–Sat 10am–5pm, Sun 10am–5:30pm; Apr 1–Sept 30 Mon, Wed–Sat 10am–6pm, Sun 10am–6:30pm, Tues 10am–9pm; June–Aug daily 10am–7pm. Closed Jan 1, May 1, Nov 1, and Dec 25. Métro: Latour-Maubourg, Varenne, Invalides, or St-Francois-Xavier.

Musée d'Orsay ★★★ Architects created one of the world's great museums from an old rail station, the neoclassical Gare d'Orsay, across the Seine from the Louvre and the Tuileries. Don't skip the Louvre, of course, but come here even if you have to miss all the other art museums in town. The Orsay boasts an astounding collection devoted to the watershed years 1848 to 1914, with a treasure-trove by the big names plus all the lesser-known groups (the symbolists, pointillists, nabis, realists, and late romantics). The 80 galleries also include Belle Epoque furniture, photographs, objets d'art, and architectural models. A cinema shows classic films.

A monument to the Industrial Revolution, the Orsay is covered by an arching glass roof allowing in floods of light. It displays works ranging from the creations of academic and historic painters such as Ingres to romanticists such as Delacroix, to neorealists including Courbet and Daumier. The Impressionists and post-Impressionists, including Manet, Monet, Cézanne, Van Gogh, and Renoir, share space with the fauves, Matisse, the cubists, and the expressionists in a setting once used by Orson Welles to film a nightmarish scene in *The Trial*, based on Kafka's unfinished novel. You'll find Millet's sunny wheat fields, Barbizon landscapes, Corot's mists, and Tahitian Gauguins all in the same hall.

But it's the Impressionists who draw the crowds. When the nose-in-the-air Louvre chose not to display their works, a great rivalry was born. Led by Manet, Renoir, and Monet, the Impressionists shunned ecclesiastical and mythological set pieces for a light-bathed Seine, faint figures strolling in the Tuileries, pale-faced women in hazy bars, and even vulgar rail stations such as the Gare St-Lazare. And the Impressionists were the first to paint that most characteristic feature of Parisian life: the sidewalk cafe, especially in the artists' quarter of Montmartre.

The most famous painting from this era is Manet's 1863 **Déjeuner sur l'herbe (Picnic on the Grass),** whose forest setting with a nude woman and two fully clothed men sent shock waves through respectable society when it was first exhibited. Two years later, Manet's **Olympia** created another scandal by

Ball at the Moulin de la Gallette by Renoir at Musée d'Orsay.

depicting a woman lounging on her bed and wearing nothing but a flower in her hair and high-heeled shoes; she's attended by an African maid in the background. Zola called Manet "a man among eunuchs."

One of Renoir's most joyous paintings is here: the **Moulin de la Galette** (1876). Degas is represented by his paintings of racehorses and dancers; his 1876 cafe scene, **Absinthe,** remains one of his most reproduced works. Paris-born Monet was fascinated by the effect of changing light on Rouen Cathédrale and brought its stone bubbles to life in a series of five paintings; our favorite is **Rouen Cathédrale: Full Sunlight.** Another celebrated work is by an American, Whistler's **Arrangement in Grey and Black: Portrait of the Painter's Mother,** better known as **Whistler's Mother.** It's said that this

Cour Carrée at the Louvre.

painting heralded modern art, though many critics denounced it at the time because of its funereal overtones. Whistler was content to claim he'd made "Mummy just as nice as possible."

1 rue de Bellechasse or 62 rue de Lille, 7e. ℂ **01-40-49-48-14.** www.musee-orsay.fr. Admission 8€ adults, 5.50€ ages 18–24, free ages 17 and younger. Tues–Wed and Fri–Sun 9:30am–6pm; Thurs 9:30am–9:45pm. Closed Jan 1 and Dec 25. Métro: Solférino. RER: Musée d'Orsay.

Musée du Louvre ★★★ The Louvre is the world's largest palace and museum. As a palace, it leaves us cold except for the **Cour Carrée.** As a museum, it's one of the greatest art collections ever. To enter, pass through I. M. Pei's controversial 21m (69-ft.) **glass pyramid** ★—a startling though effective contrast of the ultramodern against the palace's classical lines. Commissioned by the late president François Mitterrand and completed in 1989, it allows sunlight to shine on an underground reception area with a complex of shops and restaurants. Ticket machines relieve the long lines of yesteryear.

People on one of those "Paris-in-a-day" tours try to break track records to get a glimpse of the Louvre's two most famous ladies: the beguiling **Mona Lisa** and the armless **Venus de Milo** ★★★. The herd then dashes on a 5-minute stampede in pursuit of **Winged Victory** ★★★, the headless statue discovered at Samothrace and dating from about 200 B.C. In defiance of the assembly-line theory of art, we head instead for David's **Coronation of Napoleon,** showing Napoleon poised with the crown aloft as Joséphine kneels before him, just across from his **Portrait of Madame Récamier** ★, depicting Napoleon's opponent at age 23; she reclines on her sofa agelessly in the style of classical antiquity.

Then a big question looms: Which of the rest of the 30,000 works on display would you like to see?

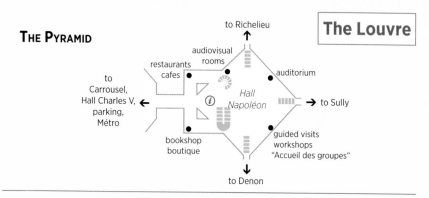

The Louvre

The Pyramid

to Richelieu

audiovisual rooms

restaurants cafes

to Carrousel, Hall Charles V, parking, Métro

auditorium

Hall Napoléon

(i)

to Sully

bookshop boutique

guided visits workshops "Accueil des groupes"

to Denon

The Wings

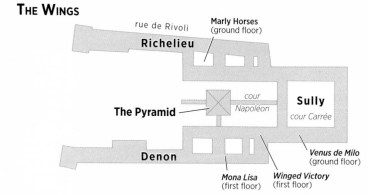

rue de Rivoli

Marly Horses (ground floor)

Richelieu

The Pyramid

cour Napoléon

Sully

cour Carrée

Denon

Venus de Milo (ground floor)

Mona Lisa (first floor)

Winged Victory (first floor)

Between the Seine and rue de Rivoli, the Palais du Louvre suffers from an embarrassment of riches, stretching for almost a kilometer (half a mile). In the days of Charles V, it was a fortress, but François I, a patron of Leonardo da Vinci, had it torn down and rebuilt as a royal residence. Less than a month after Marie Antoinette's head and body parted company, the Revolutionary Committee decided the king's collection of paintings and sculpture should be opened to the public. At the lowest point in its history, in the 18th century, the Louvre was home for anybody who wanted to set up housekeeping. Laundry hung in the windows, corners were pigpens, and families built fires to cook their meals in winter. Napoleon ended all that, chasing out the squatters and restoring the palace. In fact, he chose the Louvre as the site of his wedding to Marie-Louise.

So where did all these paintings come from? The kings of France, notably François I and Louis XIV, acquired many of them, and others were willed to or purchased by the state. Many contributed by Napoleon were taken from reluctant donors: The church was one especially heavy and unwilling giver. Much of Napoleon's plunder had to be returned, though France hasn't yet seen its way clear to giving back all the booty.

The collections are divided into seven departments: Egyptian Antiquities; Oriental Antiquities; Greek, Etruscan, and Roman Antiquities; Sculpture; Painting; Decorative Arts; and Graphic Arts. A number of galleries devoted to Italian paintings, Roman glass and bronzes, Oriental antiquities, and Egyptian antiquities

Da Vinci's *Virgin and Child with St. Anne.*

Venus de Milo.

were opened in 1997 and 1998. If you don't have to do Paris in a day, you might want to visit several times, concentrating on different collections or schools of painting. Those with little time should take a guided tour.

Acquired by François I to hang above his bathtub, Leonardo's **La Gioconda (Mona Lisa)** ★★★ has been the source of legend for centuries. Note the guard and bulletproof glass: The world's most famous painting was stolen in 1911 and found in Florence in 1913. At first, both the poet Guillaume Apollinaire and Picasso were suspected, but it was discovered in the possession of a former Louvre employee, who'd apparently carried it out under his overcoat. Two centuries after its arrival at the Louvre, the *Mona Lisa* in 2003 was assigned a new gallery of her own. Less well known (but to us even more enchanting) are Leonardo's **Virgin and Child with St. Anne** ★ and the **Virgin of the Rocks.**

After paying your respects to the "smiling one," allow time to see some French works stretching from the Richelieu wing through the entire **Sully wing** and even overflowing into the **Denon wing.** It's all here: Watteau's *Gilles* with the mysterious boy in a clown suit staring at you; Fragonard's and Boucher's rococo renderings of the aristocracy; and the greatest masterpieces of David, including his stellar 1785 **The Oath of the Horatii** and the vast and vivid **Coronation of Napoleon.** Only Florence's Uffizi rivals the Denon wing for its Italian Renaissance collection—everything from Raphael's **Portrait of Balthazar Castiglione** to Titian's **Man with a Glove.** Veronese's gigantic **Wedding Feast at Cana** ★, a romp of Venetian high society in the 1500s, occupies an entire wall (that's Paolo himself playing the cello).

 Leaping over the Louvre Line

If you don't want to wait in line at the entrance to the Louvre pyramid or use the automatic ticket machines, you can order tickets over the phone (☎ **08-92-68-46-94**) or online (http://louvre.fnacspectacles.com) with a credit card. You can also order advance tickets and take a virtual tour at www.louvre.fr. Tickets can be mailed to you in the U.S., or you can pick them up at any Paris branch of the FNAC electronics chain.

The Secret of Her Smile

Nat King Cole sang of the secret of her smile. For centuries, the most famous painting in the world, Leonardo da Vinci's *Mona Lisa,* has dazzled viewers with her enigmatic smile. Since 1804 the artist's masterpiece has been hanging in the Louvre. Now researchers feel they have solved the riddle of Mona Lisa's smug look. Using three-dimensional technology to study the masterpiece, they conducted the most extensive examination ever made of the painting. For the first time, they discovered a very fine gauze veil worn over the dress. Such a veil was worn by women who were either pregnant or had just given birth. Incidentally, the lady depicted in the painting is not named Mona. Mona is the equivalent of Madame, so she is "Madame Lisa." The model was actually Lisa Gherardini, the wife of an obscure Florentine merchant.

Of the Greek and Roman antiquities, the most notable collections, aside from the *Venus de Milo* and *Winged Victory,* are fragments of a **Parthenon frieze** (in the Denon wing). In Renaissance sculpture, you'll see Michelangelo's **Esclaves (Slaves),** originally intended for the tomb of Julius II but sold into other bondage. The Denon wing houses masterpieces such as Ingres's **The Turkish Bath,** the **Botticelli frescoes** from the Villa Lemmi, Raphael's **La Belle Jardinière,** and Titian's **Open Air Concert.** The Sully wing is also filled with old masters, such as Boucher's **Diana Resting After Her Bath** and Fragonard's **Bathers.**

The **Richelieu wing ★★★** reopened in 1993 after lying empty for years. Now, with an additional 69,000 sq. m (743,000 sq. ft.) of exhibition space, it houses northern European and French paintings, along with decorative arts, sculpture, Oriental antiquities (including a rich collection of both Islamic and Far Eastern Art), and the Napoleon III salons. One of its galleries displays 21 works that Rubens painted in a space of only 2 years for Marie de Médici's Palais de Luxembourg. The masterpieces here include Dürer's **Self-Portrait,** van Dyck's **Portrait of Charles I of England,** and Holbein the Younger's **Portrait of Erasmus of Rotterdam.**

When you tire of strolling the galleries, you may like a pick-me-up at the Richelieu Wing's **Café Richelieu** (ⓒ **01-47-03-99-68**) or at **Café Marly,** 93 rue de Rivoli, 1er (ⓒ **01-49-26-06-60**). Boasting Napoleon III opulence, the Marly is a perfect oasis. Try a café crème, a club sandwich, a pastry, or something from the bistro menu.

34–36 quai du Louvre, 1er. Main entrance in the glass pyramid, Cour Napoléon. ⓒ **01-40-20-53-17,** 01-40-20-50-50 for operator, or 08-92-68-46-94 for advance credit card sales. www.louvre. fr. Admission 9€, children 17 and younger free, free to all 1st Sun of every month. Sat–Mon and Thurs 9am–6pm; Wed and Fri 9am–10pm. 1½-hr. English-language tours (Mon and Wed–Sun) 6€, free for children 12 and younger with museum ticket. Métro: Palais-Royal-Musée du Louvre.

Sainte-Chapelle ★★★ Countless writers have called this tiny chapel a jewel box, yet that hardly suffices, nor can it be called "a light show." Go when the sun is shining, and you'll need no one else's words to describe the remarkable

7

EXPLORING PARIS

The Top Attractions

Veronese's *Marriage Feast at Cana*.

effects of natural light on Sainte-Chapelle. You approach the church through the Cour de la Sainte-Chapelle of the Palais de Justice. If it weren't for the chapel's 74m (243-ft.) spire, the law courts here would almost swallow it up.

Begun in 1246, the bi-level chapel was built to house relics of the True Cross, including the Crown of Thorns acquired by St. Louis (the Crusader King, Louis IX) from the emperor of Constantinople. (In those days, cathedrals throughout Europe were busy acquiring relics for their treasuries, regardless of their authenticity. It was a seller's, perhaps a sucker's, market.) Louis IX is said to have paid heavily for his relics, raising the money through unscrupulous means. He died of the plague on a crusade and was canonized in 1297.

You enter through the *chapelle basse* (**lower chapel**), used by the palace servants; it's supported by flying buttresses and ornamented with fleur-de-lis designs. The king and his courtiers used the *chapelle haute* (**upper chapel**), one of the greatest achievements of Gothic art; you reach it by ascending a narrow spiral staircase. On a bright day, the 15 stained-glass windows seem to glow with Chartres blue and with reds that have inspired the saying "wine the color of Sainte-Chapelle's windows." The walls consist almost entirely of the glass, 612 sq. m (6,588 sq. ft.) of it, which had to be removed for safekeeping during the Revolution and again during both world wars. In the windows' Old and New Testament designs are embodied the hopes

Detail of stained glass panel from Sainte-Chapelle.

and dreams (and the pretensions) of the kings who ordered their construction. The 1,134 scenes depict the Christian story from the Garden of Eden through the Apocalypse; you read them from bottom to top and from left to right. The great rose window depicts the Apocalypse.

Sainte-Chapelle stages **concerts** from March to November, daily at 7 and 8:30pm; tickets cost 19€ to 25€. Call ℂ **01-44-07-12-38** from 11am to 6pm daily for details.

Palais de Justice, 4 bd. du Palais, 4e. ℂ **01-53-40-60-80.** www.monum.fr. 8€ adults, 5€ ages 18–25, free 17 and younger. Mar–Oct daily 9:30am–6pm; Nov–Feb daily 9am–5pm. Métro: Cité, St-Michel, or Châtelet–Les Halles. RER: St-Michel.

Tour Eiffel ★★★   This is without doubt one of the most recognizable structures in the world. Weighing 7,000 tons, but exerting about the same pressure on the ground as an average-size person sitting in a chair, the wrought-iron tower wasn't meant to be permanent. Gustave-Alexandre Eiffel, the French engineer whose fame rested mainly on his iron bridges, built it for the 1889 Universal Exhibition. (Eiffel also designed the framework for the Statue of Liberty.) Praised by some and denounced by others (some called it a "giraffe," the "world's greatest lamppost," or the "iron monster"), the tower created as much controversy in the 1880s as I. M. Pei's glass pyramid at the Louvre did in the 1980s. What saved it from demolition was the advent of radio—as the tallest structure in Europe, it made a perfect spot to place a radio antenna (now a TV antenna).

The tower, including its TV antenna, is 317m (1,040 ft.) high. On a clear day you can see it from 65km (40 miles) away. An open-framework construction, the tower unlocked the almost unlimited possibilities of steel construction, paving the way for skyscrapers. Skeptics said it couldn't be built, and Eiffel actually wanted to make it soar higher. For years it remained the tallest man-made structure on earth, until skyscrapers such as the Empire State Building surpassed it.

We could fill an entire page with tower statistics. (Its plans spanned 5,400 sq. m/58,000 sq. ft. of paper, and it contains 2.5 million rivets.) But forget the

 TIME OUT AT the tower

To see the Eiffel Tower best, don't sprint—approach it gradually. We suggest taking the Métro to the Trocadéro stop and walking from the Palais de Chaillot to the Seine to get the full effect of the tower and its surroundings; then cross the Pont d'Iéna and head for the base, where you'll find elevators in two of the pillars—expect long lines. (When the tower is open, you can see the 1889 lift machinery in the east and west pillars.) You visit the tower in three stages: The first landing provides a view over the rooftops, as well as a cinema museum showing films, restaurants, and a bar. The second landing offers a panoramic look at the city. The third landing gives the most spectacular view; Eiffel's office has been re-created on this level, with wax figures depicting the engineer receiving Thomas Edison.

Tour Eiffel Bargain

The least expensive way to see the Tour Eiffel (www.tour-eiffel.fr) is to walk up the first two floors at a cost of 4.50€ adults, or 3.10€ ages 25 and younger. That way, you also avoid the long lines waiting for the elevator—although the views are less spectacular from this platform. If you dine at the tower's own **Altitude 95** (🕿 **01-45-55-20-04**), an Eiffel restaurant on the first floor, management allows patrons to cut to the head of the line.

numbers. Just stand beneath the tower, and look straight up. It's like a rocket of steel lacework shooting into the sky.

In 2004 it became possible to ice-skate inside the Eiffel Tower, doing figure eights while taking in views of the rooftops of Paris. Skating takes place on an observation deck 57m (188 ft.) above ground. The rectangular rink, open December to February, is a bit larger than an average tennis court, holding 80 skaters at once—half the capacity of New York City's Rockefeller Center rink. Rink admission and skate rental are free, after you pay the initial entry fee below.

To get to **Le Jules Verne** (🕿 **01-45-55-61-44**), the second-platform restaurant, take the private south foundation elevator. You can enjoy an aperitif in the piano bar and then take a seat at one of the dining room's tables, all of which provide an inspiring view. The menu changes seasonally, offering fish and meat dishes that range from filet of turbot with seaweed and buttered sea urchins to veal chops with truffled vegetables. Reservations are recommended.

Champ de Mars, 7e. 🕿 **01-44-11-23-23.** www.tour-eiffel.fr. Admission to 1st landing 4.80€, 2nd landing 8€, 3rd landing 13€. Stairs to 2nd floor 4.50€. Sept–May daily 9:30am–11:45pm; June–Aug daily 9am–12:45am. Sept–June stairs open only to 6:30pm. Métro: Trocadéro, Ecole Militaire, or Bir Hakeim. RER: Champ de Mars–Tour Eiffel.

Tour Eiffel.

Tour Eiffel under construction.

THE MAJOR MUSEUMS

Turn to "The Top Attractions," earlier, for a comprehensive look at the **Musée du Louvre** and the **Musée d'Orsay.**

Centre Pompidou ★★★   Reopened in January 2000 in what was called in the 1970s "the most avant-garde building in the world," the restored Centre Pompidou is packing in the art-loving crowds again. The dream of former president Georges Pompidou, this center for 20th- and 21st-century art, designed by Richard Rogers and Renzo Piano, opened in 1977 and quickly became the focus of controversy. Its bold exoskeletal architecture and the brightly painted pipes and ducts crisscrossing its transparent facade (green for water, red for heat, blue for air, and yellow for electricity) were jarring in the old Beaubourg neighborhood. Perhaps the detractors were right all along—within 20 years, the building began to deteriorate so badly that a major restoration was necessary. The renovation added 450 sq. m (4,844 sq. ft.) of exhibit space and a rooftop restaurant, a cafe, and a boutique; in addition, a series of auditoriums were created for film screenings and dance, theater, and musical performances. Access for visitors with disabilities has also been improved.

The Centre Pompidou encompasses five attractions:

Musée National d'Art Moderne (National Museum of Modern Art) ★★★ has a large collection of 20th- and 21st-century art. With some 40,000 works, this is the big attraction, though only about 850 works can be displayed at one time. If you want to view some real charmers, seek out Calder's 1926 *Josephine Baker,* one of his earlier versions of the mobile, an art form he invented. You'll also find two examples of Duchamps's series of Dada-style sculptures he invented in 1936: *Boîte en Valise* (1941) and *Boîte en Valise* (1968). And every time we visit, we have to see Dalí's *Hallucination partielle: Six images de Lénine sur un piano* (1931), with Lenin dancing on a piano.

In the **Bibliothèque Information Publique (Public Information Library),** people have free access to a million French and foreign books, periodicals, films, records, slides, and microfilms in nearly every area of knowledge. The **Centre de Création Industriel (Center for Industrial Design)** emphasizes the contributions made in the fields of architecture, visual communications, publishing, and community planning; and the **Institut de Recherche et de Coordination Acoustique-Musique (Institute for Research and Coordination of Acoustics/Music)** brings together musicians and composers interested in furthering the cause of contemporary and traditional music. Finally, you can visit a re-creation of the Jazz Age studio of Romanian sculptor Brancusi, the **Atelier Brancusi ★**, a mini-museum slightly separated from the rest of

---

 The Museum Discount Card

If you're a culture buff, consider buying a **Paris Museum Pass,** which admits you to some 70 museums in Paris and its environs. You do the math—if you plan to visit three or four museums, the card is usually worth the investment. A pass good for 2 days costs 32€; for 4 consecutive days, 48€; and for 6 consecutive days, 64€. Cards are available at all major museums. For more information, contact **Association Inter-Musees,** 4 rue Brantôme, 3e (𝒞 **01-44-61-96-60;** www.parismuseumpass.fr; Métro: Rambuteau).

the action. Open Wednesday to Monday 2 to 6pm.

The museum's **forecourt** is a free "entertainment center" featuring mimes, fire-eaters, circus performers, and sometimes musicians. Don't miss the nearby **Stravinsky fountain,** containing mobile sculptures by Tinguely and Saint Phalle.

Place Georges-Pompidou, 4e. ✆ **01-44-78-12-33.** www.centrepompidou.fr. Admission 12€ adults, 9€ students, free for children 17 and younger. Wed–Mon 11am–10pm. Métro: Rambuteau, Hôtel de Ville, or Châtelet–Les Halles.

Jeu de Paume After knowing many roles, this museum has become a center for photography and video, exploring "the world of images, their uses, and the issues they raise." Its exhibitions not only display photography but also mechanical or electronic images. It is one of the finest museums of its type in the world, and it presents ever-changing exhibitions, many of them daringly avant-garde.

FROM TOP: **Centre Pompidou; Stravinsky fountain.**

For years the National Gallery in the Jeu de Paume, in the northeast corner of the Tuileries gardens, was one of the treasures of Paris, displaying some of the finest works of the Impressionists. In 1986 that collection was hauled off to the Musée d'Orsay, much to the regret of many. Following a $14-million face-lift, this Second Empire building has been transformed into state-of-the-art galleries.

Originally, in this part of the gardens, Napoleon III built a ball court on which *jeu de paume,* an antecedent of tennis, was played—hence the museum's name. The most infamous period in the National Gallery's history came during the Nazi occupation, when it served as an "evaluation center" for works of modern art. Paintings from all over France were shipped to the Jeu de Paume; art condemned by the Nazis as "degenerate" was burned.

1 Place de la Concorde, 8e. ✆ **01-47-03-12-50.** www.jeudepaume.org. Admission 7€ adults, 5€ students and children. Tues noon–9pm; Wed–Fri noon–7pm; Sat–Sun 10am–7pm. Métro: Concorde.

La Cité de l'Architecture et du Patrimoine ★ ☺ After a decade-long makeover, the City of Architecture and Heritage was opened by President Nicolas Sarkozy in 2007. With its trio of galleries and vast space, the museum is the largest architectural museum in the world. It lies in the east wing of the Palais de Chaillot on a hill overlooking a curve of the Seine, with panoramic views of Paris in all directions. The Eiffel Tower looms just across the river.

Exhibits are devoted to 12 centuries of French architecture, the most stunning of which is the reproduction of the stained-glass window ★★ in the Gothic cathedral at Chartres. Other exhibits include a walk-in replica of Le Corbusier's mid-20th-century Cité Radieuse in Marseille.

In all there are 350 plaster cast reproductions of some of the greatest achievements in French architecture, going back to the Middle Ages. One gallery reproduces France's remarkable paintings and frescoes from the 12th to 16th centuries. A third gallery is devoted to modern architecture right up to a turn-of-the-millennium cultural center in New Caledonia in the South Pacific. Children can build their own architectural masterpieces with Legos and other materials.

1 place du Trocadéro, 16e. ☎ **01-58-51-52-00.** www.citechaillot.fr. Admission 8€ adults, 5€ students, free ages 18 and younger. Wed and Fri–Mon 11am–7pm; Thurs 11am–9pm. Métro: Trocadéro.

Le Musée du quai Branly ★★★   The architect, Jean Nouvel, said he wanted to create something "unique, poetic, and disturbing." And so he did with the opening of this $265-million museum, which took a decade to launch. There was even scandal: The terra-cotta figures from Nigeria turned out to be smuggled. At long last, under one roof nearly 300,000 tribal artifacts from Africa, Asia, Oceania, and the Americas have been assembled. Galleries stand on sculpted pillars that evoke totem poles. Set in a lush, rambling garden on the Left Bank in the shadow of the Eiffel Tower, this is the greatest museum to open in Paris since Pompidou.

Housed in four spectacular buildings with a garden walled off from the quai Branly are the art, sculpture, and cultural materials of a vast range of non-Western civilizations, separated into different sections that represent the traditional cultures of Africa, East and Southeast Asia, Oceania, Australia, the Americas, and New Zealand. The pieces here come from the now-defunct Musée des Arts Africains et Oceaniens, from the Louvre, and from the Musée de l'Homme. Temporary exhibits are shown off in boxes all along the 183m-long (600-ft.) exhibition hall.

Incredible masterpieces are on display made by some very advanced traditional civilizations; some of the most impressive exhibits present tribal masks of different cultures, some of which are so lifelike and emotional in their creation that you can feel the fear and elation involved in their use, which is well documented by descriptions in English. Allow 2 hours for a full visit; also take a stroll

FROM LEFT: **Multimedia exhibit at Jeu de Paume; historic shot of place de la Bastille.**

in the carefully manicured garden, or have a café au lait in the small cafeteria across from the main building. There are numerous entrances to the museum grounds from the area near the Eiffel Tower; the main entrance is on quai Branly.

27–37 quai Branly and 206–208 rue de Université, 7e. ℂ **01-56-61-70-00.** www.quaibranly.fr. Admission 8.50€ adults, 6€ senior and students 18–26, free for children 17 and younger. Tues–Wed and Sun 11am–7pm; Thurs–Sat 11am–9pm. Métro: Alma-Marceau. RER: Pont d'Alma.

Musée Carnavalet-Histoire de Paris ★★ ☺ If you enjoy history, but history tomes bore you, spend some time here for insight into Paris's past, which comes alive in such details as the chessmen Louis XVI used to distract himself while waiting to go to the guillotine. The

Exhibit at Musée du quai Branly.

comprehensive and lifelike exhibits are great for kids. The building, a Renaissance palace, was built in 1544 and later acquired by Mme de Carnavalet. The great François Mansart transformed it between 1655 and 1661.

The palace is best known for one of history's most famous letter writers, Mme de Sévigné, who moved here in 1677. Fanatically devoted to her daughter (she moved in with her because she couldn't bear to be apart), she poured out nearly every detail of her life in her letters, virtually ignoring her son. A native of the Marais district, she died at her daughter's château in 1696. In 1866, the city of Paris acquired the mansion and turned it into a museum. Several salons cover the Revolution, with a bust of Marat, a portrait of Danton, and a model of the Bastille (one painting shows its demolition). Another salon tells the story of the captivity of the royal family at the Conciergerie, including the bed in which Mme Elisabeth (the sister of Louis XVI) slept and the Dauphin's exercise book.

Exhibits continue at the **Hôtel le Peletier de St-Fargeau,** across the courtyard. On display is furniture from the Louis XIV period to the early 20th century, including a replica of Marcel Proust's cork-lined bedroom with his actual furniture, including his brass bed. This section also exhibits artifacts from the museum's archaeological collection, including some Neolithic pirogues, shallow oak boats used for fishing and transport from about 4400 to 2200 B.C.

23 rue de Sévigné, 3e. ℂ **01-44-59-58-58.** www.carnavalet.paris.fr. Free admission. Special exhibits from 5€ adults, 4.20€ students and children. Tues–Sun 10am–6pm. Métro: St-Paul or Chemin Vert.

Musée de l'Orangerie ★ In the Tuileries stands this gem among galleries. It has an outstanding collection of art and one celebrated painting on display: Claude Monet's exquisite *Nymphéas* (1915–27), in which water lilies float amorphously on the canvas. The water lilies are displayed as the artist intended them to be—lit by sunlight in large oval galleries that evoke the shape of the garden ponds at his former Giverny estate.

Musée Carnavalet-Histoire de Paris.

Creating his effects with hundreds and hundreds of minute strokes of his brush (one irate 19th-c. critic called them "tongue lickings"), Monet achieved unity and harmony, as he did in his Rouen Cathedral series and his haystacks. Artists with lesser talent might have stirred up "soup." But Monet, of course, was a genius. See his lilies and evoke for yourself the mood and melancholy as he experienced them so many years ago. Monet continued to paint his water landscapes right up until his death in 1926, although he was greatly hampered by failing eyesight.

The renovated building also houses the art collections of two men, John Walter and Paul Guillaume, who are not connected to each other, except that they were both married at different times to the same woman. Their collection includes more than 24 Renoirs, including *Young Girl at a Piano*. Cézanne is represented by 14 works, notably *The Red Rock,* and Matisse by 11 paintings. The highlight of Rousseau's nine works displayed here is *The Wedding*, and the dozen paintings by Picasso reach the pinnacle of their brilliance in *The Female Bathers.* Other outstanding paintings are by Utrillo (10 works in all), Soutine (22), and Derain (28).

Jardin des Tuileries, 1er. ℰ **01-44-77-80-07.** www.musee-orangerie.fr. Admission 7.50€ adults, 5.50€ students 25 and younger. Free 1st Sun of every month. Wed–Mon 9am–6pm. Métro: Concorde.

Musée des Arts Décoratifs   In the northwest wing of the Louvre's Pavillon de Marsan, this museum holds a treasury of furnishings, fabrics, wallpaper, objets d'art, and items displaying living styles from the Middle Ages to the present. Notable are the 1920s Art Deco boudoir, bath, and bedroom done for couturier Jeanne Lanvin by the designer Rateau, plus a collection of the works donated by Jean Dubuffet. Decorative art from the Middle Ages to the Renaissance is on the second floor; collections from the 17th, 18th, and 19th centuries occupy the

An exhibit at the Musée des Arts Décoratifs.

third and fourth floors. The fifth floor has specialized centers, such as wallpaper and drawings, and exhibits detailing fashion, textiles, toys, crafts, and glass trends.

Palais du Louvre, 107 rue de Rivoli, 1er. ☎ **01-44-55-57-50.** www.lesartsdecoratifs.fr. Admission 8€ adults, 6.50€ ages 18–25, free for children 17 and younger. Tues, Wed, Fri 11am–6pm; Thurs 11am–6pm; Sat–Sun 10am–6pm. Métro: Palais-Royal or Tuileries.

Musée Jacquemart-André.

Musée Jacquemart-André ★★   This is the finest museum of its type in Paris, the treasure-trove of a couple devoted to 18th-century French paintings and furnishings, 17th-century Dutch and Flemish paintings, and Italian Renaissance works. Edouard André, the last scion of a family that made a fortune in banking and industry in the 19th century, spent most of his life as an army officer stationed abroad; he eventually returned to marry a well-known portraitist of government figures and the aristocracy, Nélie Jacquemart, and they went on to compile a collection of rare decorative art and paintings in this 1850s town house.

In 1912, Mme Jacquemart willed the house and its contents to the Institut de France, which paid for an extensive renovation and enlargement. The salons drip with gilt and are the ultimate in *fin-de-siècle* style. Works by Bellini, Carpaccio, Uccelo, Van Dyck, Rembrandt (*The Pilgrim of Emmaus*), Tiepolo,

Rubens, Watteau, Boucher, Fragonard, and Mantegna are complemented by Houdon busts, Savonnerie carpets, Gobelin tapestries, Della Robbia terra cottas, and an awesome collection of antiques. The 18th-century Tiepolo frescoes of spectators on balconies viewing Henri III's 1574 arrival in Venice are outstanding.

Take a break with a cup of tea in Mme Jacquemart's high-ceilinged dining room, adorned with 18th-century tapestries. Salads, tarts, *tourtes* (pastries filled with meat or fruit), and Viennese pastries are served during museum hours.

158 bd. Haussmann, 8e. ✆ **01-45-62-11-59.** www.musee-jacquemart-andre.com. Admission 10€ adults, 7.50€ children 7–17, free for children 6 and younger. Daily 10am–6pm. Métro: Miromesnil or St-Philippe-du-Roule.

Musée Marmottan Monet ★★   In the past, an art historian or two would sometimes venture here to the edge of the Bois de Boulogne to see what Paul Marmottan had donated to the Académie des Beaux-Arts. Hardly anyone else did until 1966, when Claude Monet's son Michel died in a car crash, leaving a then $10-million bequest of his father's art to the little museum. The Académie suddenly found itself with 130-plus paintings, watercolors, pastels, and drawings. Monet lovers could now trace the evolution of the great man's work in a single museum. The collection includes more than 30 paintings of Monet's house at Giverny and many of water lilies, his everlasting fancy, plus ***Willow*** (1918), ***House of Parliament*** (1905), and a **Renoir portrait** of a 32-year-old Monet. The museum had always owned Monet's ***Impression: Sunrise*** (1872), from which the Impressionist movement got its name. Paul Marmottan's original collection includes fig-leafed nudes, First Empire antiques, assorted objets d'art, Renaissance tapestries, bucolic paintings, and crystal chandeliers. You can also see countless miniatures donated by Daniel Waldenstein. The works of other

Impression: Sunrise at Musée Marmottan Monet.

Impressionists are also included, among them Degas, Manet, Pissarro, Renoir, Auguste Rodin, and Alfred Sisley.

2 rue Louis-Boilly, 16e. ℭ **01-44-96-50-33.** www.marmottan.com. Admission 9€ adults, 5€ ages 8-24, free for children 7 and younger. Wed-Sun 11am–6pm, Tues 11am–9pm. Métro: La Muette. RER: Bouilainvilliers, line C.

Musée National du Moyen Age/Thermes de Cluny (Musée de Cluny) ★★

Along with the Hôtel de Sens in the Marais, the Hôtel de Cluny is all that remains of domestic medieval architecture in Paris. Enter through the cobblestoned **Cour d'Honneur (Court of Honor),** where you can admire the flamboyant Gothic building with its vines, turreted walls, gargoyles, and dormers with seashell motifs. First, the Cluny was the mansion of a rich 15th-century abbot, built on top of/next to the ruins of a Roman bath. By 1515, it was the residence of Mary Tudor, widow of Louis XII and daughter of Henry VII and Elizabeth of York. Seized during the Revolution, the Cluny was rented in 1833 to Alexandre du Sommerard, who adorned it with medieval artworks. After his death in 1842, the government bought the building and the collection.

This collection of medieval arts and crafts is superb. Most people come to see *The Lady and the Unicorn* tapestries ★★★, the most acclaimed tapestries of their kind. All the romance of the age of chivalry—a beautiful princess and her handmaiden, beasts of prey, and house pets—lives on in these remarkable yet mysterious tapestries discovered only a century ago in Limousin's Château de Boussac. Five seem to deal with the senses (one, for example, depicts a unicorn looking into a mirror held by a dour-faced maiden). The sixth shows a woman under an elaborate tent with jewels, her pet dog resting on an embroidered cushion beside her, with the lovable unicorn and his friendly companion, a lion, holding back the flaps. The background forms a rich carpet of spring flowers, fruit-laden trees, birds, rabbits, donkeys, dogs, goats, lambs, and monkeys.

The other exhibits range widely: Flemish retables; a 14th-century Sienese John the Baptist and other sculptures; statues from Sainte-Chapelle (1243–48); 12th- and 13th-century crosses, chalices, manuscripts, carvings, vestments, leatherwork, jewelry, and coins; a 13th-century Adam; and recently discovered heads and fragments of statues from Notre-Dame de Paris. In the fan-vaulted medieval chapel hang tapestries depicting scenes from the life of St. Stephen.

Downstairs are the ruins of the **Roman baths,** from around A.D. 200. The best-preserved section is seen in room X, the frigidarium (where one bathed in cold water). Once it measured 21×11m (69×36 ft.), rising to a height of 15m (49 ft.), with stone walls nearly 1.5m (5 ft.) thick. The ribbed

Religious art at Musée de Cluny.

vaulting here rests on consoles evoking ships' prows. Credit for this unusual motif goes to the builders of the baths, Paris's boatmen. During Tiberius's reign, a column to Jupiter was found beneath Notre-Dame's chancel and is now on view in the court; called the "Column of the Boatmen," it's believed to be the oldest sculpture created in Paris.

6 place Paul Painlevé, 5e. ✆ **01-53-73-78-00.** www.musee-moyenage.fr. Admission 8€ adults, free 25 and under. Daily 10am–6pm. Métro: Miromesnil or St-Philippe-du-Roule.

Musée National Eugène Delacroix　This museum is for Delacroix groupies, among whom we include ourselves. If you want to see where he lived, worked, and died, this is worth at least an hour. Delacroix (1798–1863) is something of an enigma to art historians. Even his parentage is a mystery. Many believe Talleyrand was his father. One biographer saw him "as an isolated and atypical individualist—one who respected traditional values, yet emerged as the embodiment of Romantic revolt." Baudelaire called him "a volcanic crater artistically concealed beneath bouquets of flowers." The museum is on one of the Left Bank's most charming squares, with a romantic garden. A large arch on a courtyard leads to Delacroix's studio—no poor artist's studio, but the creation of a solidly established man. Sketches, lithographs, watercolors, and oils are hung throughout. If you want to see more of Delacroix's work, head to the Chapelle des Anges in St-Sulpice (p. 263).

6 place de Furstenberg, 6e. ✆ **01-44-41-86-50.** www.musee-delacroix.fr. Admission 5€ adults, free for children 17 and younger. Wed–Mon 9:30am–5pm. Métro: St-Germain-des-Prés or Mabillon.

Musée Rodin ★★　Today Rodin is acclaimed as the father of modern sculpture, but in a different era, his work was labeled obscene. The world's artistic taste changed, and in due course, in 1911, the French government purchased Rodin's studio in this gray-stone, 18th-century mansion in the Faubourg St-Germain. The government restored the rose gardens to their 18th-century splendor, making them a perfect setting for Rodin's most memorable works.

In the courtyard are three world-famous creations. Rodin's first major public commission, **The Burghers of Calais,** commemorated the heroism of six citizens of Calais who in 1347 offered themselves as a ransom to Edward III in return for ending his siege of their port. Perhaps the single best-known work, **The Thinker,** in Rodin's own words, "thinks with every muscle of his arms, back, and legs, with his clenched fist and gripping toes." Not completed when Rodin died, **The Gate of Hell,** as he put it, is "where I lived for a whole year in Dante's *Inferno.*"

 Looking for a Quick Escape?

The little alley behind the Musée Rodin winds its way down to a pond with fountains, flower beds, and even sand pits for children. It's one of the most idyllic hidden spots in Paris.

Inside, the sculptures, plaster casts, reproductions, originals, and sketches reveal the freshness and vitality of a remarkable artist. You can almost see his works emerging from marble into life. Everybody is attracted to **Le Baiser (The Kiss),** of which one critic wrote, "The passion is timeless." Upstairs are two versions of the celebrated and

condemned ***Nude of Balzac,*** his bulky torso rising from a tree trunk (Albert E. Elsen commented on the "glorious bulging" stomach). Included are many versions of his ***Monument to Balzac*** (a large one stands in the garden), Rodin's last major work. Other significant sculptures are the soaring ***Prodigal Son; The Crouching Woman*** (the "embodiment of despair"); and ***The Age of Bronze,*** an 1876 study of a nude man modeled after a Belgian soldier. (Rodin was falsely accused of making a cast from a living model.) Generally overlooked is a room devoted to Rodin's mistress, Camille Claudel, a towering artist in her own right. She was his pupil, model, and lover, and created such works as ***Maturity, Clotho,*** and the recently donated ***The Waltz*** and ***The Gossips.***

In the Hôtel Biron, 79 rue de Varenne, 7e. ✆ **01-44-18-61-10.** www.musee-rodin.fr. Admission 6€ adults, 5€ ages 18–25, free for children 17 and younger. Apr–Sept Tues–Sun 9:30am–5:45pm; Oct–Mar Tues–Sun 10am–5:45pm. Métro: Varenne, Invalides, or St-Francois-Xavier.

The Thinker at Musée de Rodin.

SPECIALTY MUSEUMS

Be sure to turn to "The Top Attractions" and "The Major Museums," both earlier in this chapter, for the cream of the crop. "Especially for Kids," later in this chapter, includes museums that parents and kids alike will love. The museums below represent the curious, fascinating, and sometimes arcane balance of Paris's offerings.

Art & Music Museums

Musée Bourdelle ★ 🏛 Here you can see works by Rodin's star pupil, Antoine Bourdelle (1861–1929), who became a celebrated artist in his own right. Along with changing exhibitions, the museum permanently displays the artist's drawings, paintings, and sculptures, and lets you wander through his studio, garden, and house. The original plaster casts of some of his greatest works are on display, but what's most notable here are the 21 studies of Beethoven. Though some of the exhibits are poorly captioned, you'll still feel the impact of Bourdelle's genius.

18 rue Antoine-Bourdelle, 15e. ✆ **01-49-54-73-73.** www.bourdelle.paris.fr. Admission 7€ adults, 3.50€ ages 14–26, free for children 13 and younger. Tues–Sun 10am–6pm. Métro: Montparnasse-Bienvenüe.

Musée Cognacq-Jay ★ The founders of La Samaritaine department store, Ernest Cognacq and his wife, Louise Jay, were fabled for their exquisite taste. To see what they accumulated from around the world, head for this museum in the

16th-century Hôtel Denon, with its Louis XV and Louis XVI paneled rooms. Some of the 18th century's most valuable decorative works are exhibited, ranging from ceramics and porcelain to delicate cabinets and paintings by Canaletto, Fragonard, Greuze, Chardin, Boucher, Watteau, and Tiepolo.

In the Hôtel Donon, 8 rue Elzévir, 3e. ℭ **01-40-27-07-21.** www.paris.fr/musees. Free admission to permanent collection; variable charges for temporary shows. Tues–Sun 10am–6pm. Métro: St-Paul.

Musée d'Art Moderne de la Ville de Paris & Musée des Enfants This museum bordering the Seine has a permanent collection of paintings and sculpture owned by the city, but come here only if visits to the d'Orsay and Louvre haven't satiated you. It presents ever-changing exhibits on individual artists from all over the world or on trends in international art. You'll find works by Chagall, Matisse, Léger, Rothko, Braque, Dufy, Picasso, Utrillo, and Modigliani. Seek out Pierre Tal Coat's *Portrait of Gertrude Stein,* and keep Picasso's version of this difficult subject in mind. The Musée des Enfants has exhibits and shows for children.

11 av. du Président-Wilson, 16e. ℭ **01-53-67-40-00.** www.mam.paris.fr. Free admission to general collections, temporary exhibition admission 5€–7€. Tues–Sun 10am–6pm. Métro: Iéna or Alma-Marceau.

Musée de la Musique In the stone-and-glass Cité de la Musique, this museum serves as a tribute and testament to music. You can view 4,500 instruments from the 16th century to the present, as well as paintings, engravings, and sculptures that relate to musical history. It's all here: cornets disguised as snakes, mandolins, lutes, zithers, music boxes, even an early electric guitar. Models of the world's great concert halls and interactive display areas give you a chance to hear and better understand musical art and technology.

In the Cité de la Musique, 221 av. Jean-Jaurès, 19e. ℭ **01-44-84-44-84.** www.cite-musique.fr. Admission 8€ adults, 6€ students 18–25, 6€ children 17 and younger. Tues–Sat noon–6pm; Sun 10am–7pm. Métro: Porte de Pantin.

Musée Edith Piaf 📶 This privately run museum is filled with Piaf memorabilia such as photos, costumes, and personal possessions. The daughter of an acrobat, Giovanna Gassion grew up in this neighborhood and assumed the name of Piaf ("little sparrow"); her songs, such as "La Vie en Rose" and "Non, Je Ne Regrette Rien," eventually were heard around the world. You must phone in advance for the security code you need to buzz your way in. Nearby is the **Villa Calte,** a beautiful example of the architecture many locals are trying to save (ask for directions at the Piaf museum). Fronted by an intricate wrought-iron fence, the house has a pleasant garden where parts of Truffaut's *Jules et Jim* was filmed.

5 rue Crespin-du-Gast, 11e. ℭ **01-43-55-52-72.** Free admission but donations appreciated. Mon–Wed 1–6pm, but only by reservation. Métro: Ménilmontant.

Some of the many instruments on display at Musée de la Musique.

Musée National des Arts Asiatiques-Guimet ★★   This is one of the most beautiful Asian museums in the world, and it houses one of the world's finest collections of Asian art. Some 3,000 pieces of the museum's 45,000 works are on display. The Guimet, opened in Lyon but transferred to Paris in 1889, received the Musée Indochinois du Trocadéro's collections in 1931 and the Louvre's Asian collections after World War II. The most interesting exhibits are Buddhas, serpentine monster heads, funereal figurines, and antiquities from the temple of Angkor Wat. Some galleries are devoted to Tibetan art, including fascinating scenes of the Grand Lamas entwined with serpents and demons.

6 place d'Iéna, 16e. ℂ **01-56-52-53-00.** www.guimet.fr. Admission 7.50€. Free for ages 17 and younger. Wed-Mon 10am-6pm. Métro: Iéna.

Musée Nissim de Camondo ★   Visit this museum for keen insight into the decorative arts of the 18th century. The pre–World War I town house was donated to the Musée des Arts Décoratifs by Comte Moïse de Camondo in memory of his son, Nissim, a French aviator killed in combat during World War I. The museum is like the home of an aristocrat—rich with needlepoint chairs, tapestries (many from Beauvais or Aubusson), antiques, paintings, bas-reliefs, silver, Chinese vases, crystal chandeliers, Sèvres porcelain, Savonnerie carpets, and even an Houdon bust. The Blue Salon, overlooking Parc Monceau, is most impressive. The kitchen of the original mansion has been reopened in its original form, capable of serving hundreds of dinner guests at one time, with few alterations from its original Belle Epoque origins. Fittings and many of the cooking vessels are in brass or copper, and the walls are tiled.

63 rue de Monceau, 8e. ℂ **01-53-89-06-40.** www.lesartsdecoratifs.fr. Admission 7€ adults, 5€ ages 18-25, free for children 17 and younger. Wed-Sun 10am-5:30pm. Closed Jan 1, May 1, Bastille Day (July 14), and Dec 25. Métro: Villiers.

Musée Nissim de Camondo.

Musée National des Arts Asiatiques-Guimet.

Musée Zadkine   This museum near the Jardin du Luxembourg was once the home of sculptor Ossip Zadkine (1890–1967), and his collection has been turned over to the city for public viewing. Included are some 300 pieces of sculpture, displayed in the museum and the garden. Some drawings and tapestries are also exhibited. At these headquarters, where he worked from 1928 until his death, you can see how he moved from "left wing" cubist extremism to a renewed appreciation of the classic era. You can visit his garden for free even if you don't want to go into the museum—in fact, it's one of the finest places to relax in Paris on a sunny day, sitting on a bench taking in the two-faced *Woman with the Bird.*

100 bis rue d'Assas, 6e. (🖉) **01-55-42-77-20.** www.zadkine.paris.fr. Free admission to permanent collections. Tues–Sun 10am–6pm. Métro: Notre-Dame des Champs or Vavin.

Palais de Tokyo ★   This art center is the most daringly avant-garde in Europe. Not since the opening of the Pompidou Center has there been such excitement among Paris's art community. The artworks are so contemporary here that they're defined as "up to the minute." Miracle of miracles, the museum stays open until midnight. A rotating series of exhibitions is staged, many quite controversial. Sometimes the *palais* exhibits works by artists so daring that they might find no other showcase. The museum has been called an "art incubator."

Always check when you're in Paris to see what's showing, perhaps a video or sculpture show, fashion events, or various artistic or "performance art" events. The curators stay in close touch with art communities of the world, including what's happening in the art scenes of Beijing and Shanghai.

13 av. du Président-Wilson, 16e. (🖉) **01-47-23-54-01.** www.palaisdetokyo.com. Admission 6€ adults, 4.50€ students, free for ages 18 and younger. Tues–Sun noon–midnight. Métro: Iéna.

Craft & Industry Museums

Manufacture Nationale des Gobelins ★   Did you know a single tapestry can take 4 years to complete, employing as many as three to five full-time weavers? The founder of this dynasty, Jehan Gobelin, came from a family of dyers and clothmakers; in the 15th century, he discovered a scarlet dye that made him famous. By 1601, Henri IV imported 200 weavers from Flanders to make tapestries full time. Until this endeavor, the Gobelin family hadn't made any tapestries. Colbert, Louis XIV's minister, bought the works, and under royal patronage the craftsmen set about executing designs by Le Brun. After the Revolution, the industry was reactivated by Napoleon. Today, Les Gobelins is a viable business entity, weaving tapestries for museums and historical restorations around the world. Throughout most of the week, the factories are closed to casual visitors, who are never allowed to wander at will. But if you'd like insight into this medieval craft, you can participate, 3 days a week, in one of

Exhibition at the Palais de Tokyo.

two guided tours, each lasting 90 minutes and each conducted in French. The tour guide will showcase the history of the enterprise and expose you to views of weavers and needlepoint artisans as they painstakingly ply their craft, patiently inserting stitch after laborious stitch, often while standing or seated behind huge screens of thread. If you don't speak French, pamphlets in English are distributed, each outlining the context of the lecture.

42 av. des Gobelins, 13e. (✆ **01-40-13-46-46.** www. monum.fr. Tours in French (with English pamphlets) 6€ adults, 4€ ages 8–25, free for children 17 and younger. Tues–Thurs 2 and 2:45pm, reservation only. Métro: Gobelins.

A weaver demonstrates his craft at Manufacture Nationale des Gobelins.

Musée d'Art et Histoire du Judaisme ★★   Security is tight, but it's worth the effort. In the Hôtel de St-Aignan, dating from the 1600s, this museum of Jewish history has been handsomely and impressively installed. The development of Jewish culture is traced not only in Paris, but also in France itself, as well as in Europe. Many of the exhibitions are devoted to religious subjects, including menorahs, Torah ornaments, and ark curtains, in both the Ashkenazi and Sephardic traditions. For us, the most interesting documents relate to the notorious Dreyfus case. Also on parade is a collection of illuminated manuscripts, Renaissance Torah arks, and paintings from the 18th and 19th centuries, along with Jewish gravestones from the Middle Ages. The best display is of the artwork by leading Jewish painters and artists ranging from Soutine to Zadkine, from Chagall to Modigliani.

Hôtel de St-Aignan, 71 rue du Temple, 3e. (✆ **01-53-01-86-53.** www.mahj.org. Admission 6.80€ adults, 4.50€ ages 18–26, free for children 17 and younger. Mon–Fri 11am–6pm; Sun 10am–6pm. Métro: Rambuteau.

History Museums

Musée de l'Histoire de France (Musée des Archives Nationales) ★   The official home of the archives that reflect the convoluted history of France, this small but noteworthy palace was first built in 1371 as the **Hôtel de Clisson** and later acquired by the ducs de Guise, who figured prominently in France's bloody wars of religion. In 1705, most of it was demolished by the prince and princesse de Soubise, through their architect, the much-underrated Delamair, and rebuilt with a baroque facade. The princesse de Soubise was once the mistress of Louis XIV, and apparently, the Sun King was very generous, giving her the funds to remodel and redesign the palace into one of the most beautiful buildings in the Marais. *Tip:* Before entering through the building's main entrance, the gracefully colonnaded Cour d'Honneur (Court of Honor), walk around the corner to 58 rue des Archives, where you'll see the few remaining vestiges—a turreted medieval gateway—of the original Hôtel de Clisson.

In the early 1800s, the site was designated by Napoleon as the repository for his archives, and it has served that function ever since. The archives contain documents that predate Charlemagne. But depending on the policies of the curator, only some of them are on display at any given moment, and usually as part of an ongoing series of temporary exhibitions that sometimes spill out into the **Hôtel de Rohan,** just around the corner on the rue Vieille du Temple.

Within these exhibitions, you're likely to see the facsimiles of the penmanship of Marie Antoinette in a farewell letter she composed just before her execution; Louis XVI's last will and testament; and documents from Danton, Robespierre, Napoleon I, and Joan of Arc. The archives have the only known sketch of the Maid of Orléans that was completed during her lifetime. Even the jailers' keys from the long-since-demolished Bastille are here. Despite the undeniable appeal of the documents it shelters, one of the most intriguing aspects of this museum involves the layout and decor of rooms that have changed very little since the 18th century. One of the finest is the **Salon de la Princesse** (aka the Salon Ovale), an oval room with sweeping expanses of gilt and crystal and a series of artfully executed ceiling frescoes by Van Loo, Boucher, and Natoire.

In the Hôtel de Soubise, 60 rue des Francs-Bourgeois, 3e. ✆ **01-40-27-60-96.** Admission 3€ adults, 2.30€ ages 18–25, free for children 17 and younger. Mon and Wed–Fri 10am–12:30pm and 2–5:30pm; Sat–Sun 2–5:30pm. Métro: Hôtel-de-Ville or Rambuteau.

Paris-Story ☺   This very touristy, 45-minute multimedia show retraces the city's history in a state-of-the-art theater. The 2,000 years since Paris's birth unroll to the music of such musicians as Wagner and Piaf. Maps, portraits, and scenes from dramatic times are projected on the large screen as a running commentary (heard through headphones in one of 13 languages) gives details about art, architecture, and events. Many visitors come here for a preview of what they want to see; others stop for an in-depth look at what they've already visited.

Musée d'Art et Histoire du Judaisme.

The medieval turrets of the Musée des Archives Nationales.

11 bis rue Scribe, 9e. © **01-42-66-62-06.** www.paris-story.com. Admission 10€ adults, 6€ students or children ages 6–17, free for children 5 and younger. Family ticket 26€. Daily 10am–6pm. Shows begin every hour on the hour. Métro: Opéra. RER: Auber.

The Offbeat

Fragonard Musée du Parfum 🛍 This perfume museum is in a 19th-century theater on one of Paris's busiest thoroughfares. As you enter the lobby through a courtyard, the scented air will remind you of why you're there—to appreciate perfume enough to buy a bottle in the ground-floor shop. But first, a short visit upstairs introduces you to the rudiments of perfume history. The copper containers with spouts and tubes were used in the distillation of perfume oils, and the exquisite collection of perfume bottles from the 17th to the 20th century is impressive.

9 rue Scribe, 9e. © **01-4742-04-56.** www.fragonard.com. Free admission. Mon–Sat 9am–6pm, Sun 9am–5pm. Métro: Opéra.

Musée de l'Erotisme A tribute to the primal appeal of human sexuality, this art gallery/museum is in a 19th-century town house that had been a raunchy cabaret. It presents a tasteful but risqué collection of art and artifacts, with six floors boasting an array of exhibits such as erotic sculptures and drawings. The oldest object is a palm-size Roman *tintinabulum* (bell), a phallus-shaped animal with the likeness of a nude woman riding astride it. Modern objects include resin, wood, and plaster sculptures by French artist Alain Rose and works by American, Dutch, German, and French artists. Also on-site is a collection of erotic and satirical cartoons by well-known Dutch artist Willem. Also look for everyday items with erotic themes from South America (terra-cotta pipes shaped like phalluses) and the United States (a 1920s belt buckle that resembles a praying nun when it's fastened and a nude woman when it's open). The gift shop sells

Fragonard Musée du Parfum.

Risqué sculpture at Musée de l'Erotisme.

The striking exterior walls of the Musée de l'Institute du Monde Arabe.

Asian amulets, African bronzes, and terra-cotta figurines from South America. There's also a gallery where serious works of art are sold.

72 bd. de Clichy, 18e. ✆ **01-42-58-28-73.** www.musee-erotisme.com. Admission 9€ adults, children 17 and younger not permitted. Daily 10am–2am. Métro: Blanche.

Musée de l'Institut du Monde Arabe   Many factors have contributed to France's preoccupation with the Arab world, but three of the most important include trade links that developed during the Crusades, a large Arab population living today in France, and the memories of France's lost colonies in North Africa. For insights into the way France has handled its relations with the Arab world, consider making a trek to this bastion of Arab intellect and aesthetics. Designed in 1987 by architect Jean Nouvel and funded by 22 different, mostly Arab countries, it includes expositions on calligraphy, decorative arts, architecture, and photography produced by the Arab/Islamic world, as well as insights into its religion, philosophy, and politics. There's a bookshop on-site, a replica of a Medina selling high-quality gift and art objects, and archival resources that are usually open only to bona-fide scholars. Views from the windows of the on-site Moroccan restaurant encompass Notre-Dame, l'Ile de la Cité, and Sacré-Coeur. Guided tours start at 3pm Tuesday to Friday or at 4:30pm on Saturday and Sunday.

1 rue des Fossés St-Bernard, 5e. ✆ **01-40-51-38-38.** www.imarabe.org. Admission to permanent exhibitions 4€, free for children 11 and younger; temporary exhibits 8.50€ adults, 6.50€ students 12–25, free for children 11 and younger. Tues–Sun 10am–6pm. Métro: Jussieu, Cardinal Lemoine, Sully-Morland.

Musée du Vin   This museum is in an ancient stone-and-clay quarry used by 15th-century monks as a wine cellar. It provides an introduction to the art of winemaking, displaying various tools, beakers, cauldrons, and bottles in a series of exhibits. The quarry is right below Balzac's house (p. 269), and the ceiling contains a trap door he used to escape from his creditors.

5 rue des Eaux, 16e. ✆ **01-45-25-63-26.** www.museeduvinparis.com. Admission 12€ adults, 9.90€ seniors and students, free for children 13 and under. Tues–Sun 10am–6pm. Métro: Passy.

7 THE MAJOR CHURCHES

Turn to "The Top Attractions," earlier in this chapter, for a full look at the **Cathédrale de Notre-Dame, Basilique du Sacré-Coeur,** and **Sainte-Chapelle.**

American Cathedral of the Holy Trinity   This cathedral is one of Europe's finest examples of Gothic Revival architecture and a center for the presentation of music and art. It was consecrated in 1886, and George Edmund Street, best known for the London Law Courts, created it. Aside from the architecture, you'll find remarkable pre-Raphaelite stained-glass windows illustrating the *Te Deum,* an early-15th-century triptych by an anonymous painter (probably a monk) known as the Roussillon Master; a needlepoint collection including kneelers depicting the 50 state flowers; and the 50 state flags in the nave. A **Memorial Cloister** commemorates Americans who died in Europe in World War I and all the victims of World War II. Documentation in several languages explains the highlights. The cathedral is also a center of worship, with a schedule of Sunday and weekday services in English. Les Arts George V, a cultural organization, presents reasonably priced choral concerts, lectures, and art shows.

23 av. George V, 8e. ✆ **01-53-23-84-00.** www.americancathedral.org. Free admission. Mon–Fri 9am–5pm. Métro: Alma-Marceau or George V.

Interior of Basilique St-Denis.

Basilique St-Denis ★★   In the 12th century, Abbot Suger placed an inscription on the bronze doors here: "Marvel not at the gold and expense, but at the craftsmanship of the work." France's first Gothic building that can be precisely dated, St-Denis was constructed between 1137 and 1281 and was the "spiritual defender of the State" during the reign of Louis VI ("the Fat"). The facade has a rose window and a crenellated parapet on the top similar to the fortifications of a castle. The stained-glass windows—in stunning mauve, purple, blue, and rose—were restored in the 19th century.

The first bishop of Paris, St. Denis became the patron saint of the monarchy, and royal burials began here in the 6th century and continued until the Revolution. The sculpture designed for the **tombs**— some two stories high—spans French artistic development from the Middle Ages to the Renaissance. (There are guided tours in French of the Carolingian-era crypt.) François I was entombed at St-Denis, and his

Playing checkers and drinking mint tea at the Restaurant de la Mosquée de Paris.

funeral statue is nude, though he demurely covers himself with his hand. Other kings and queens here include Louis XII and Anne de Bretagne, as well as Henri II and Catherine de Médici. Revolutionaries stormed through the basilica during the Terror, smashing many marble faces and dumping royal remains in a lime-filled ditch in the garden. (These remains were reburied under the main altar during the 19th c.) Free organ concerts are given on Sundays at 11:15am.

1 rue de la Légion d'honneur, St-Denis. ☎ **01-48-09-83-54.** Admission 7€ adults, 4.50€ seniors and students 18–25, free for children 17 and younger. Apr–Sept Mon–Sat 10am–6:15pm, Sun noon–6:15pm; Oct–Mar Mon–Sat 10am–5pm, Sun noon–5:15pm. Closed Jan 1, May 1, Dec 25. Métro: St-Denis.

La Grande Mosquée de Paris ★   This beautiful pink marble mosque was built in 1922 to honor the North African countries that had given aid to France during World War I. Today, North Africans living in Paris gather on Friday, the Muslim holy day, and during Ramadan to pray to Allah. Short tours are given of the building, its central courtyard, and its Moorish garden; guides present a brief history of the Islamic faith. However, you may want to just wander around on your own and then join the students from nearby universities for couscous and sweet mint tea at the Muslim **Restaurant de la Mosquée de Paris** (☎ **01-43-31-18-14**), adjoining the grounds, open daily from noon to 3pm and 7 to 10:30pm.

2 bis place du Puits-de-l'Ermite, 5e. ☎ **01-45-35-97-33.** www.mosquee-de-paris.net. Admission 3€, free for children 7 and younger. Sat–Thurs 9am–noon and 2–6pm. Métro: Place Monge.

 The Royal Heart of the Boy Who Would Be King

In a bizarre twist, following a Mass in 2004, the heart of the 10-year-old heir to the French throne, Louis XVII, was laid to rest at **Saint-Denis Basilica, 2 rue de Strasbourg, St-Denis** (☎ **01-48-09-83-54**), near the graves of his parents, Marie Antoinette and Louis XVI. The heart was pickled, stolen, returned, and, 2 centuries later, DNA tested. More than 2 centuries of rumor and legend surrounding the child's death were put to rest. Genetic testing has persuaded even the most cynical historians that the person who might have been the future Louis XVII never escaped prison. The boy died of tuberculosis in 1795, his body ravaged by tumors. The child's corpse was dumped into a common grave, but not before a doctor secretly carved out his heart and smuggled it out of prison in a handkerchief. The heart of the dead boy was compared with DNA of hair trimmed from Marie Antoinette during her childhood in Austria. It was a perfect match.

La Madeleine ★★   La Madeleine is one of Paris's minor landmarks, dominating rue Royale, which culminates in place de la Concorde. Though construction began in 1806, it wasn't consecrated until 1842. Resembling a Roman temple, the building was intended as a monument to the glory of the Grande Armée (Napoleon's idea, of course). Later, several alternative uses were considered: the National Assembly, the Bourse, and the National Library. Climb the 28 steps to the facade, and look back: You'll be able to see rue Royale, place de la Concorde and its obelisk, and (across the Seine) the dome of the Hôtel des Invalides. Don't miss Rude's *Le Baptême du Christ,* to the left as you enter.

Place de la Madeleine, 8e. ℭ **01-42-65-52-17.** www.eglise-lamadeleine.com. Free admission. Mon–Sat 9:30am–7pm; Sun services at 9:30, 11am, 7pm. Métro: Madeleine.

St-Etienne-du-Mont ★★   Once there was an abbey here, founded by Clovis and later dedicated to St. Geneviève, the patroness of Paris. Such was the fame of this popular saint that the abbey proved too small to accommodate the pilgrimage crowds. Now part of the Lycée Henri IV, the Tour de Clovis (Tower of Clovis) is all that remains of the ancient abbey—you can see the tower from rue Clovis. Today, the task of keeping St. Geneviève's cult alive has fallen on this church, practically adjoining the Panthéon. The interior is Gothic, an unusual style for a 16th-century church. Building began in 1492 and was plagued by delays until the church was finally finished in 1626.

Besides the patroness of Paris, such men as Pascal and Racine were entombed here. Because of the destruction of church records during the French Revolution, church officials aren't sure of the exact locations in which they're buried. St. Geneviève's tomb was destroyed during the Revolution, but the stone on which her coffin rested was discovered later, and her relics were gathered for

Rude's *Le Baptême du Christ.*

The 16th-century rood screen at St-Etienne-du-Mont.

The black-marble tomb of Jean-Baptiste Colbert.

a place of honor at St-Etienne. The church possesses a remarkable early-16th-century **rood screen:** Crossing the nave, it's unique in Paris—called spurious by some and a masterpiece by others. Another treasure is a wood **pulpit,** held up by Samson, clutching a bone in one hand, with a slain lion at his feet. The fourth chapel on the right when you enter contains impressive 16th-century stained glass.

1 place St-Geneviève, 5e. ☎ **01-43-54-11-79.** Free admission. With the exception of some of France's school holidays, when hours may vary slightly, the church is open year-round as follows: Mon noon–7:30pm; Tues–Fri 8:45am–7:30pm; Sat 8:45am–7:45pm; Sun 8:45am–12:15pm and 2:30–7:45pm. Métro: Cardinal Lemoine or Luxembourg.

St-Eustache ★★   This Gothic and Renaissance church completed in 1637 is rivaled only by Notre-Dame. Mme de Pompadour and Richelieu were baptized here, and Molière's funeral was held here in 1673. The church has been known for organ recitals ever since Liszt played in 1866. Inside rests the **black-marble tomb** of Jean-Baptiste Colbert, the minister of state under Louis XIV; atop the tomb is his marble effigy flanked by statues of *Abundance* by Coysevox and *Fidelity* by Tuby. The church's most famous painting is Rembrandt's ***The Pilgrimage to Emmaus.*** There's a side entrance on rue Rambuteau.

2 impasse St-Eustache, 1er. ☎ **01-42-36-31-05.** www.st-eustache.org. Free admission. Daily 9am–7pm; Sun 9am–7pm; Sun organ recitals 5:30pm. Métro: Les Halles.

> ### ○ Gregorians Unplugged
>
> St-Germain-des-Prés stages wonderful concerts on the Left Bank; it boasts fantastic acoustics and a marvelous medieval atmosphere. The church was built to accommodate an age without microphones, and the sound effects will thrill you. For more information, call ☎ 01-55-42-81-33 (www.eglise-sgp.org). Arrive about 45 minutes before the performance if you'd like a front-row seat. Tickets are 15€ to 50€.

St-Germain-des-Prés ★★   It's one of Paris's oldest churches, from the 6th century, when a Benedictine abbey was founded here by Childebert, son of Clovis. Alas, the marble columns in the triforium are all that remain from that period. The Normans nearly destroyed the abbey at least four times. The present building has a Romanesque nave and a Gothic choir with fine capitals. At one time, the abbey was a pantheon for Merovingian kings. Restoration of the site of their tombs, **Chapelle de St-Symphorien,** began in 1981, and unknown Romanesque paintings were discovered on the triumphal arch. Among the others interred here

are Descartes (his heart, at least) and Jean-Casimir, the king of Poland who abdicated his throne. The Romanesque tower, topped by a 19th-century spire, is the most enduring landmark in St-Germain-des-Prés. Its church bells, however, are hardly noticed by the patrons of Les Deux Magots across the way.

When you leave the church, turn right on rue de l'Abbaye and have a look at the 17th-century pink **Palais Abbatial.**

3 place St-Germain-des-Prés, 6e. ℭ **01-55-42-81-33.** www.eglise-sgp. org. Free admission. Mon–Sat 8am–7:45pm; Sun 9am–8pm. Métro: St-Germain-des-Prés.

St-Germain l'Auxerrois ★★ Once it was the church for the Palais du Louvre, drawing an assortment of royalty, courtesans, men of art and law, and local artisans. Sharing place du Louvre with Perrault's colonnade, the church contains only the foundation stones of its original 11th-century belfry. The chapel that had stood here was greatly

FROM TOP: **A Delacroix fresco in St-Sulpice's Chapelle des Anges; the angel-filled dome of Val-de-Grâce.**

enlarged in the 14th century by the addition of side aisles and became a beautiful church, with 77 sq. m (829 sq. ft.) of stained glass, including some rose windows from the Renaissance. The intricately carved **church-wardens' pews** are outstanding, based on 17th-century Le Brun designs. Behind them is a **15th-century triptych** and **Flemish retable,** so poorly lit you can hardly appreciate it. The organ was ordered by Louis XVI for Sainte-Chapelle. Many famous men were entombed here, including the sculptor Coysevox and the architect Le Vau. Around the chancel is an intricate **18th-century grille.**

The saddest moment in the church's history was on August 24, 1572, the evening of the St. Bartholomew Massacre. The tower bells rang, signaling the supporters of Catherine de Médici, Marguerite de Guise, Charles IX, and the future Henri III to launch a slaughter of thousands of Huguenots, who'd been invited to celebrate the marriage of Henri de Navarre to Marguerite de Valois.

2 place du Louvre, 1er. ℭ **01-42-60-13-96.** Free admission. Daily 8am-7pm. Métro: Louvre-Rivoli.

St-Sulpice ★★ Pause first outside St-Sulpice. The 1844 fountain by Visconti displays the sculpted likenesses of four bishops of the Louis XIV era: Fenelon, Massillon, Bossuet, and Flechier. Work on the church, at one time Paris's largest,

7

EXPLORING PARIS | The Major Churches

began in 1646. Though laborers built the body by 1745, work on the bell towers continued until 1780, when one was finished and the other left incomplete. One of the priceless treasures inside is Servandoni's rococo **Chapelle de la Madone (Chapel of the Madonna),** with a Pigalle statue of the Virgin. The church has one of the world's largest organs, comprising 6,700 pipes; it has been played by musicians such as Marcel Dupré and Charles-Marie Widor.

The real reason to come here is to see the Delacroix frescoes in the **Chapelle des Anges (Chapel of the Angels),** the first on your right as you enter. Look for his muscular Jacob wrestling (or dancing?) with an effete angel. On the ceiling, St. Michael is having some troubles with the Devil, and yet another mural depicts Heliodorus being driven from the temple. Painted in Delacroix's final years, the frescoes were a high point in his baffling career. If these impress you, pay the painter tribute by visiting the Musée Delacroix (see "The Major Museums," earlier this chapter).

Rue St-Sulpice, 6e. ✆ **01-42-34-59-98.** Free admission. Daily 8:30am–8pm. Métro: St-Sulpice.

Val-de-Grâce ★★ According to an old proverb, to understand the French you must like Camembert cheese, the Pont Neuf, and the dome of Val-de-Grâce. Its origins go back to 1050, when a Benedictine monastery was built here. In 1619, Louis XIII appointed as abbess Marguerite Veni d'Arbouze, who asked Louis's wife, Anne of Austria, for a new monastery. After 23 years of a childless marriage, Anne gave birth to a boy who went on to be known as the Sun King. To express his gratitude, Louis XIII approved the rebuilding of the church, and at the age of 7, on April 1, 1645, the future Louis XIV laid Val-de-Grâce's first stone. Mansart was the main architect, and to him we owe the facade in the Jesuit style. Le Duc, however, designed the dome, and Mignard added the frescoes. Le Mercier and Le Muet also had a hand in the church's fashioning. The church was turned into a military hospital in 1793 and an army school in 1850.

1 place Alphonse-Laveran, 5e. ✆ **01-40-51-47-28.** Admission 5€ adults, 2.50€ children and students, free for children 5 and younger. Daily 1:30–5:30pm. Métro: Port Royal.

ARCHITECTURAL & HISTORIC HIGHLIGHTS

Arènes de Lutèce Discovered and partially destroyed in 1869, this amphitheater is Paris's most important Roman ruin after the baths in the Musée de Cluny (p. 248). Today, the site is home to a small arena, not as grand as the original, and gardens. You may feel as if you've discovered a private spot in the heart of the city, but don't be fooled. Your solitude is sure to be interrupted, if not by groups of students playing soccer, then by parents pushing strollers down the paths. This is an ideal spot for a picnic; bring a bottle of wine and baguettes to enjoy in this vestige of the ancient city of Lutétia.

At rues Monge and Navarre, 5e. ✆ **01-40-71-76-60.** www.paris.fr. Free admission. Mon–Fri 8am–9pm; Sat–Sun 9am–9pm. Métro: Jussieu.

Bibliothèque Nationale de France, Site Tolbiac/François Mitterrand The French National Library opened in 1996 with a futuristic design by Dominique Perrault (a quartet of 24-story towers evoking the look of open books); this is the last of the *grands projets* of the late François Mitterrand. It boasts the same grandiose scale as the Cité de la Musique and houses the nation's literary and historic archives; it's regarded as a repository of the French soul, replacing outmoded facilities on rue des Archives. The library incorporates space for 1,600 readers at a time, many of whom enjoy views over two levels of a garden-style courtyard that seems far removed from Paris's urban congestion.

This is one of Europe's most user-friendly academic facilities, emphasizing computerized documentation and microfiche—a role model that will set academic and literary priorities well into the future. The public has access to as many as 180,000 books, plus thousands of periodicals, with an additional 10 million historic (including medieval) documents available to qualified experts. Though the appeal of this place extends mainly to serious scholars, a handful of special exhibits might interest you, as well as concerts and lectures. Concert tickets rarely exceed 15€ for adults and 10€ for students, seniors, and children; a schedule is available at the library.

Quai François-Mauriac, 13e. ℰ **01-53-79-59-59.** www.bnf.fr. Admission 7€. Children 15 and under not admitted. Mon 2–8pm; Tues–Sat 10am–7pm; Sun 1–7pm. Closed Sept 8–21. Métro: Bibliothèque François-Mitterrand.

Conciergerie ★★   London has its Bloody Tower, and Paris has its Conciergerie. Even though the Conciergerie had a long regal history before the Revolution, it was forever stained by the Reign of Terror and lives as an infamous symbol of the time when carts pulled up constantly to haul off fresh supplies of victims of Dr. Guillotin's wonderful little invention.

Much of the Conciergerie was built in the 14th century as an extension of the Capetian royal Palais de la Cité. You approach through its landmark twin towers, the **Tour d'Argent** (where the crown jewels were stored at one time) and **Tour de César,** but the **Salle des Gardes (Guard Room)** is the actual entrance. Even more interesting is the dark and foreboding Gothic **Salle des Gens d'Armes (Room of People at Arms),** utterly changed from the days when the king used it as a banquet hall. However, architecture plays a secondary role to the list of prisoners who spent their last days here. Few in its history endured tortures as severe as those imposed on Ravaillac, who assassinated Henri IV in 1610. In the Tour de César, he received pincers in the flesh and had hot lead and boiling oil poured on him like bath water before being executed. During the Revolution, the Conciergerie became a symbol of terror to the nobility and enemies of the State. A short walk away, the Revolutionary Tribunal dispensed a skewed, hurried justice—if it's any consolation, the jurists didn't believe in

The foreboding Conciergerie.

Skating in front of the Hôtel de Ville.

torturing their victims, only in decapitating them.

After being seized by a crowd of peasants who stormed Versailles, Louis XVI and Marie Antoinette were brought here to await their trials. In failing health and shocked beyond grief, *l'Autrichienne* ("the Austrian," as she was called with malice) had only a small screen (sometimes not even that) to protect her modesty from the gaze of guards stationed in her cell. By accounts of the day, she was shy and stupid, though the evidence is that on her death, she displayed the nobility of a true queen. (What's more, the famous "Let them eat cake," which she supposedly uttered when told the peasants had no bread, is probably apocryphal—besides, at the time, cake flour was less expensive than bread flour, so even if she said this, it wasn't meant coldheartedly.) It was shortly before noon on the morning of October 16, 1793, when the executioners arrived, grabbing her and cutting her hair, as was the custom for victims marked for the guillotine.

Later, the Conciergerie housed other prisoners, including Mme Elisabeth; Mme du Barry, mistress of Louis XV; Mme Roland ("O Liberty! Liberty! What crimes are committed in thy name!"); and Charlotte Corday, who killed Marat while he was taking a sulfur bath. In time, the Revolution consumed its own leaders, such as Danton and Robespierre. Finally, one of Paris's most hated men, public prosecutor Fouquier-Tinville, faced the guillotine to which he'd sent so many others. Among the few interned here who lived to tell the tale was American Thomas Paine, who reminisced about his chats in English with Danton.

1 quai de l'Horloge, 4e. ☎ **01-53-40-60-80.** www.monum.fr. Admission 7€ adults, 4.50€ ages 18–25, free for children 17 and younger. Mar–Oct daily 9:30–6pm; Nov–Feb daily 9am–5pm. Métro: Cité, Châtelet, or St-Michel. RER: St-Michel.

Hôtel de Ville ★   On a large square with fountains and early-1900s lampposts, the 19th-century Hôtel de Ville isn't a hotel, but Paris's grandiose City Hall. The medieval structure it replaced had witnessed countless municipally ordered executions. Henri IV's assassin, Ravaillac, was quartered alive on the square in 1610, his body tied to four horses that bolted in opposite directions. On May 24, 1871, the Communards doused the City Hall with petrol, creating a blaze that lasted for 8 days. The Third Republic ordered the structure rebuilt, with many changes, even creating a Hall of Mirrors evocative of that at Versailles. For security reasons, the major splendor of this building is closed to the public.

29 rue de Rivoli, 4e. No phone for information. Free admission. Métro: Hôtel-de-Ville.

Institut de France ★   Designed by Louis Le Vau, this dramatic baroque building with an enormous cupola is the seat of all five academies that dominate

France's intellectual life—Française, Sciences, Inscriptions et Belles Lettres, Beaux Arts, and Sciences Morales et Politiques. The members of the Académie Française (limited to 40), guardians of the French language referred to as "the immortals," gather here. Many are unfamiliar figures (though Jacques Cousteau and Marshall Pétain were members), and the academy is remarkable for the great writers and philosophers who have *not* been invited to join—Balzac, Baudelaire, Diderot, Flaubert, Descartes, Proust, Molière, Pascal, Rousseau, and Zola, to name only a few. The cenotaph was designed by Coysevox for Mazarin.

23 quai de Conti, 6e. ☎ **01-44-41-44-47.** www.institut-de-france.fr. Free admission (guests can walk into courtyard only). Daily 9am–6pm. Métro: Louvre-Rivoli.

La Grande Arche de La Défense ★ Designed as the architectural centerpiece of the sprawling satellite suburb of La Défense, outside the 16th arrondissement, this massive steel-and-masonry arch rises 35 stories. It was built with the blessing of the late François Mitterrand and extends the magnificently engineered straight line linking the Louvre, Arc de Triomphe du Carrousel, Champs-Elysées, Arc de Triomphe, avenue de la Grande Armée, and place du Porte Maillot. The arch is ringed with a circular avenue patterned after the one around the Arc de Triomphe. The monument is tall enough to shelter Notre-Dame beneath its heavily trussed canopy. An elevator carries you up to an observation platform, where you get a view of the carefully planned geometry of the surrounding streets.

You'll notice nets rigged along the Grande Arche. When pieces of Mitterrand's *grand projet* started falling to the ground, they were erected to catch the falling fragments. If only such protection existed for all politicians' follies!

1 place du parvis de La Défense, Puteaux, 16e. ☎ **01-49-07-27-27.** www.grandearche.com. Admission 10€ adults, 8.50€ ages 6–25, free 5 and younger. Daily 10am–7pm (until 8pm Apr–Sept). Métro: Grande Arche de la Défense.

Palais Bourbon/Assemblée Nationale ★ The French parliament's lower house, the Chamber of Deputies, meets at this 1722 mansion built by the duchesse de Bourbon, a daughter of Louis XIV. You can make reservations for one of two types of visits as early as 6 months in advance. Hour-long tours on art, architecture, and basic French government processes are given Monday, Friday, and Saturday. They're in French (in English with advance booking). You may also

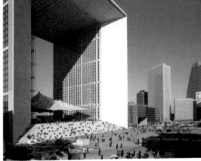

FROM LEFT: **Fountains at Palais Royal; La Grande Arche de La Défense.**

The Panthéon.

observe sessions of the National Assembly, held Tuesday afternoon and all day Wednesday and Thursday beginning at 9:30am. Remember, this is a working government building, and all visitors are subject to rigorous security checks.

33 quai d'Orsay, 7e. ℗ **01-40-63-64-08.** www.assemblee-nationale.fr. Free admission. Hours vary, so call ahead. Métro: Assemblée Nationale.

Palais Royal ★★   The Palais Royal was originally known as the Palais Cardinal, for it was the residence of Cardinal Richelieu, Louis XIII's prime minister. Richelieu had it built, and after his death it was inherited by the king, who died soon after. Louis XIV spent part of his childhood here with his mother, Anne of Austria, but later resided at the Louvre and Versailles. The palace was later owned by the duc de Chartres et Orléans (see the entry for Parc Monceau under "Parks & Gardens"), who encouraged the opening of cafes, gambling dens, and other public entertainment. Though government offices occupy the Palais Royal and are not open to the public, do visit the **Jardin du Palais Royal,** an enclosure bordered by arcades. Don't miss the main courtyard, with the controversial 1986 Buren sculpture—280 prison-striped columns, oddly placed.

Rue St-Honoré, 1er. No phone. Free admission. Gardens daily 7:30am–dusk. Métro: Palais Royal-Musée du Louvre.

Panthéon ★★   Some of the most famous men in French history (Victor Hugo, for one) are buried here on the crest of the mount of St. Geneviève. In 1744, Louis XV vowed that if he recovered from a mysterious illness, he'd build a church to replace the Abbaye de St. Geneviève. He recovered but took his time fulfilling his promise. It wasn't until 1764 that Mme de Pompadour's brother hired Soufflot to design a church in the form of a Greek cross with a dome reminiscent of St. Paul's in London. When Soufflot died, his pupil Rondelet carried out the work, completing the structure 9 years after his master's death.

After the Revolution, the church was converted to a "Temple of Fame" and became a pantheon for the great men of France. Mirabeau was buried here, though his remains were later removed. Likewise, Marat was only a temporary tenant. Voltaire's body was exhumed and placed here—and allowed to remain. In the 19th century, the building changed roles so many times—a church, a pantheon, a church again—that it was hard to keep its function straight. After Hugo was buried here, it became a pantheon once again. Other notable men entombed within are Rousseau, Soufflot, Zola, and Braille. Only one woman has so far been deemed worthy of placement here: Marie Curie, who joined her husband, Pierre. Most recently, the ashes of André Malraux were transferred to the Panthéon because, according to President Jacques Chirac, he "lived [his] dreams and made them live in us." As Charles de Gaulle's culture minister, Malraux decreed the arts should be part of the lives of all French people, not just Paris's elite.

Before entering the crypt, note the striking frescoes: On the right wall are scenes from Geneviève's life, and on the left is the saint with a white-draped head looking out over medieval Paris, the city whose patron she became, as well as Geneviève relieving victims of famine with supplies.

Place du Panthéon, 5e. ✆ **01-44-32-18-00.** www.monum.fr. Admission 8€ adults, 5€ ages 18–25, free for children 17 and younger. Apr–Sept daily 10am–6:30pm; Oct–Mar daily 10am–6pm (last entrance 45 min. before closing). Métro: Cardinal Lemoine or Maubert-Mutualité.

LITERARY LANDMARKS

If there's a literary bone in your body, you'll feel a vicarious thrill on discovering the haunts of the writers and artists who've lived, worked, and played in Paris.

Take the Métro to place St-Michel to begin your tour. As you wander away from the Seine, you'll encounter **rue de la Huchette,** one of the Left Bank's most famous streets. Its inhabitants were immortalized in Eliot Paul's *The Last Time I Saw Paris.* Continuing on, you'll enter the territory of the Beat Generation, home to the **Café Gentil-homme** (no longer there) described by Jack Kerouac in *Satori in Paris.* Allen Ginsberg's favorite, the **Hôtel du Vieux-Paris** (9 rue Gît-le-Coeur, 6e; www.vieuxparis.com), still attracts those in search of the Beats.

Stroll down **rue Monsieur-le-Prince,** the "Yankee alleyway," where Richard Wright, James McNeill Whistler, Henry Wadsworth Longfellow, and Oliver Wendell Holmes lived at one time or another. During a visit in 1959, Martin Luther

Rue de la Huchette.

King, Jr., came to call on Richard Wright, the Mississippi-born African-American novelist famous for *Native Son.* King climbed to the third-floor apartment at **no. 14** to find that Wright's opinions on the civil-rights movement conflicted with his own. Whistler rented a studio at **no. 22,** and in 1826, Longfellow lived at **no. 49.** Oliver Wendell Holmes, Sr., lived at **no. 55.** After strolling along this street, you can dine at the haunts of Kerouac and Hemingway. (See our recommendation of

Harry's New York Bar.

Maison de Victor Hugo.

Crémerie-Restaurant Polidor, 41 rue Monsieur-le-Prince, 6e, on p. 199.) Or cross back over to the Right Bank for a drink at the famed **Hôtel de Crillon,** 10 place de la Concorde, 8e (p. 124), where heroine Brett Ashley broke her promise to rendezvous with Jake Barnes in Hemingway's *The Sun Also Rises.* Zelda and F. Scott Fitzgerald lifted their glasses here as well.

For details on **Harry's New York Bar,** 5 rue Daunou, 2e, see "Literary Haunts" in chapter 10. For a description of **Les Deux Magots, Le Procope,** and **La Rotonde,** see "The Top Cafes" in chapter 6. For coverage of the bookstore **Shakespeare and Company,** see "Shopping A to Z," in chapter 9.

Here are two great museums for hard-core literary fans:

Maison de Balzac   In the residential district of Passy, near the Bois de Boulogne, sits this modest house with a courtyard and garden. Honoré de Balzac fled to this house in 1840, after his possessions and furnishings were seized, and lived there for 7 years (to see him, you had to know a password). If a creditor knocked on the rue Raynouard door, Balzac was able to escape through the rue Berton exit. The museum's most notable memento is Balzac's "screech-owl" (his nickname for his tea kettle), which he kept hot throughout the night as he wrote *La Comédie Humaine.* Also enshrined are Balzac's writing desk and chair, and a library of special interest to scholars. The little house is filled with caricatures of Balzac. A biographer once wrote: "With his bulky baboon silhouette, his blue suit with gold buttons, his famous cane like a golden crowbar, and his abundant, disheveled hair, Balzac was a sight for caricature."

47 rue Raynouard, 16e. ℭ **01-55-74-41-80.** www.balzac.paris.fr. Admission free for permanent collection. Special exhibition admission 4.50€ adults, 3.80€ seniors, 2€ ages 14–26, free for children 13 and younger. Tues–Sun 10am–6pm. Métro: Passy or La Muette.

Maison de Victor Hugo ★   Today, theatergoers who've seen *Les Misérables,* even those who haven't read anything by Paris's 19th-century novelist, come to place des Vosges to see where Hugo lived and wrote. Some thought him a genius, but Cocteau called him a madman, and an American composer discovered that in his old age, he was carving furniture with his teeth! From 1832 to 1848, the novelist/poet lived on the second floor of the Hôtel Rohan Guéménée. The museum owns some of Hugo's furniture, as well as pieces that once belonged to Juliette Drouet, the mistress with whom he lived in exile on Guernsey, one of the Channel Islands.

Worth the visit are Hugo's drawings, more than 450, illustrating scenes from his own works. Mementos of the great writer abound, including samples of his handwriting, his inkwell, and first editions of his works. A painting of Hugo's 1885 funeral procession at the Arc de Triomphe is on display, as are many portraits and souvenirs of his family. Of the furnishings, a chinoiserie salon stands out. The collection even contains Daumier caricatures and a bust of Hugo by David d'Angers, which, compared with Rodin's, looks saccharine.

6 place des Vosges, 4e. ☎ **01-42-72-10-16.** www.musee-hugo.paris.fr. Free admission. Tues-Sun 10am–6pm. Métro: St-Paul, Bastille, or Chemin-Vert.

PARKS & GARDENS
Jardin des Tuileries

The spectacular statue-studded **Jardin des Tuileries ★★**, bordering place de la Concorde, 1er (☎ **01-40-20-90-43;** Métro: Tuileries or Concorde), is as much a part of Paris as the Seine. Le Nôtre, Louis XIV's gardener and planner of the Versailles grounds, designed the gardens. Some of the gardens' most distinctive statues are the 18 enormous bronzes by Maillol, installed within the Jardin du Carrousel, a subdivision of the Jardin des Tuileries, between 1964 and 1965, under the direction of Culture Minister André Malraux.

About 400 years before that, Catherine de Médici ordered a palace built here, the **Palais des Tuileries;** other occupants have included Louis XVI (after he left Versailles) and Napoleon. Twice attacked by Parisians, it was burned to

An early-19th-century painting of the Tuileries Palace.

La Fontaine de Médici in the Jardin du Luxembourg.

Rowing in the Bois de Boulogne.

the ground in 1871 and never rebuilt. The gardens, however, remain. In orderly French manner, the trees are arranged according to designs, and even the paths are arrow-straight. Bubbling fountains break the sense of order and formality. It's open daily: April to May 7am to 9pm, June to August 7am to 11pm, September 7am to 9pm, October to March 7:30am to 7:30pm, and admission is free.

Jardin du Luxembourg

Hemingway once told a friend that the **Jardin du Luxembourg ★★**, in the 6th arrondissement (Métro: Odéon; RER: Luxembourg), "kept us from starvation." He related that in his poverty-stricken days in Paris, he wheeled a baby carriage (the vehicle was considered luxurious) through the garden because it was known "for the classiness of its pigeons." When the gendarme went across the street for a glass of wine, the writer would eye his victim, preferably a plump one; lure him with corn; "snatch him, wring his neck"; and hide him under the blanket. "We got a little tired of pigeons that year," he confessed, "but they filled many a void."

The Luxembourg has always been associated with artists, though children, students, and tourists predominate nowadays. Watteau came this way, as did Verlaine. Balzac didn't like the gardens at all. In 1905, Gertrude Stein would cross them to catch the Batignolles/Clichy/Odéon omnibus, pulled by three gray mares, to meet Picasso in his studio at Montmartre, where he painted her portrait.

Marie de Médici, the wife of Henri IV, ordered the **Palais du Luxembourg** built on this site in 1612, shortly after she was widowed. A Florentine by birth, the regent wanted to create another Pitti Palace, where she could live with her "witch" friend, Leonora Galigal. Architect Salomon de Brossee wasn't entirely successful, though the overall effect is Italianate. Alas, the queen didn't get to enjoy the palace, as her son, Louis XIII, forced her into exile when he discovered she was plotting to overthrow him. She died in poverty in Cologne. For her palace, she'd commissioned 21 paintings from Rubens, which glorified her life, but they're now in the Louvre. It is extremely difficult to visit the palace, because it is the chamber of French senators. A few visits are organized throughout the year but there is no schedule. But you can call ℂ **01-44-54-19-49** and take a chance. Even so, when tours are offered only 30 tickets are available. The cost is 8€ per person.

You don't really come to the Luxembourg to visit the palace; the gardens are the attraction. For the most part, they're in the classic French tradition: well groomed and formally laid out, the trees planted in patterns. Urns and statuary on pedestals—one honoring Paris's patroness, St. Geneviève, with pigtails reaching to her thighs—encircle a central water basin. Kids can sail a toy boat, ride a pony, or attend an occasional Grand Guignol puppet show. And you can play *boules* (lawn bowling) with a group of elderly men who wear black berets and have Gauloises dangling from their mouths.

Bois de Boulogne

One of the most spectacular parks in Europe is the **Bois de Boulogne ★★**, Porte Dauphine, 16e (ℂ **01-40-67-90-82;** Métro: Les Sablons, Porte Maillot, or Porte Dauphine), often called the "main lung" of Paris. Horse-drawn carriages traverse it, but you can also drive through. You can discover its hidden pathways, however, only by walking. You could spend days in the Bois de Boulogne and still not see everything.

Porte Dauphine is the main entrance, though you can take the Métro to Porte Maillot as well. West of Paris, the park was once a forest kept for royal hunts. It was in vogue in the late 19th century: Along avenue Foch, carriages with elegantly attired and coiffured Parisian damsels would rumble along with their foppish escorts. Nowadays, it's more likely to attract run-of-the-mill picnickers. (Be careful at night, when hookers and muggers proliferate.)

When Napoleon III gave the grounds to the city in 1852, they were developed by Baron Haussmann. Separating Lac Inférieur from Lac Supérieur is the **Carrefour des Cascades ★** (you can stroll under its waterfall). The Lower Lake contains two islands connected by a footbridge. From the east bank, you can take a boat to these idyllically situated grounds, perhaps stopping off at the cafe/restaurant on one of them.

FROM LEFT: **Races at the Hippodrome de Longchamp;** the teacup ride in the Jardin d'Acclimatation.

The lovely Parc de Bagatelle.

Restaurants in the *bois* are numerous, elegant, and expensive. The **Pré Catelan** ★ contains a deluxe restaurant of the same name (© **01-44-14-41-00**; www.precatelanparis.com), occupying a gem of a Napoleon III–style château, and also a Shakespearean theater in a garden planted with trees mentioned in the bard's plays. Nearby is **La Grande Cascade** (© **01-45-27-33-51**; www. grandcascade.com), once a hunting lodge for Napoleon III.

Jardin d'Acclimatation (© **01-40-67-90-82**; www.jardindacclimatation. fr), at the northern edge of the park, is for children, with a zoo, an amusement park, and a narrow-gauge railway (see "Especially for Kids," later in this chapter, for more details). Two racetracks, the **Hippodrome de Longchamp** ★★★ and the **Hippodrome d'Auteuil,** are in the park. The Grand Prix is run in June at Longchamp (the site of a medieval abbey). Fashionable Parisians always turn out for this, the women in their finest haute couture. To the north of Longchamp is the **Grand Cascade,** an artificial waterfall.

In the western section of the *bois,* the 24-hectare (59-acre) **Parc de Bagatelle** ★ (© **01-43-28-47-63**) owes its existence to a bet between the comte d'Artois (later Charles X) and Marie Antoinette, his sister-in-law. The comte wagered he could erect a small palace in less than 3 months, so he hired nearly 1,000 craftsmen (cabinetmakers, painters, Scottish landscape architect Thomas Blaikie, and others) and irritated the locals by requisitioning all shipments of stone and plaster arriving through Paris's west gates. He won his bet. If you're here in late April, it's worth visiting the Bagatelle just for the tulips. In late May, one of the finest rose collections in Europe is in full bloom. For some reason, as the head gardener confides to us, "This is the major rendezvous point in Paris for illicit couples."

Some of Parc Monceau's famed flowers.

Dramatic Chinese-style building near Parc Monceau.

The park is open in summer daily 9:30am to 6:30pm (winter closing can be at 5pm). Admission is 2.90€ for adults, 1.50€ for students and children, free under 3.

Park Monceau

Much of **Parc Monceau** ★, 8e (✆ **01-42-27-39-56;** www.parcmonceau.org; Métro: Monceau or Villiers), is ringed with 18th- and 19th-century mansions, some evoking Proust's *Remembrance of Things Past.* Carmontelle designed it in 1778 as a private hideaway for the duc d'Orléans (who came to be known as Philippe-Egalité), at the time the richest man in France. The duke was noted for his debauchery and pursuit of pleasure, so no ordinary park would do. It was opened to the public in the days of Napoleon III's Second Empire.

Monceau was laid out with an Egyptian-style obelisk, a medieval dungeon, a thatched farmhouse, a Chinese pagoda, a Roman temple, an enchanted grotto, various chinoiseries, and a waterfall. These fairy-tale touches have largely disappeared except for a pyramid and an oval naumachia fringed by a colonnade. Now the park is filled with solid statuary and monuments, including one honoring Chopin. In spring, the red tulips and magnolias are worth the airfare to Paris.

CEMETERIES

Sightseers often view Paris's cemeteries as being somewhat like parks—suitable places for strolling. The graves of celebrities are also major lures. Père-Lachaise, for example, is a major attraction; the other cemeteries are of lesser interest.

Cimetière de Montmartre ★   This cemetery, established in 1795, lies west of Montmartre and north of boulevard de Clichy. Russian dancer **Vaslav Nijinsky,** novelist **Alexandre Dumas** *fils,* Impressionist **Edgar Degas,** and composers **Hector Berlioz** and **Jacques Offenbach** are interred here, along with **Stendhal** and lesser literary lights such as **Edmond** and **Jules de Goncourt** and **Heinrich Heine.** A more recent tombstone honors **François Truffaut,**

Cimetière du Père-Lachaise

Abélard & Héloïse **37**

Guillaume Apollinaire **5**

Pierre-Auguste
  Beaumarchais **30**

Hans Bellmer **24**

Sarah Bernhardt **9**

Georges Bizet **17**

Maria Callas **3**

Frédéric Chopin **36**

Colette **23**

Auguste Comte **34**

Jean Baptiste
  Camille Corot **11**

Honoré Daumier **10**

Jacques-Louis David **19**

Honoré de Balzac **16**

Eugène Delacroix **15**

Gustave Doré **14**

Isadora Duncan **6**

Paul Eluard **26**

Max Ernst **2**

Théodore Géricault **20**

Jean-Auguste-
  Dominique Ingres **13**

Jean La Fontaine **33**

René Lalique **12**

Lefebvre Masséna **29**

Amedeo Modigliani **28**

Molière **32**

Jim Morrison **35**

Alfred de Musset **21**

Edith Piaf **27**

Camille Pissarro **38**

Marcel Proust **4**

Gioacchio Antonio
  Rossini **22**

Rothschild family plot **39**

Henri de Saint-Simon **31**

Georges Seurat **18**

Simone Signoret &
  Yves Montand **8**

Gertrude Stein &
  Alice B. Toklas **25**

Oscar Wilde **1**

Richard Wright **7**

film director of the *nouvelle vague* (new wave). We like to pay our respects at the tomb of **Alphonsine Plessis,** heroine of *La Dame aux Camélias,* and **Mme Récamier,** who taught the world how to lounge. **Emile Zola** was buried here, but his corpse was exhumed and promoted to the Panthéon in 1908. In 1871, the cemetery was used for mass burials of victims of the Siege and the Commune.

20 av. Rachel (west of the Butte Montmartre and north of bd. de Clichy), 18e. ℂ **01-53-42-36-30.** Mon–Fri 8am–6pm; Sat 8:30am–6pm; Sun 9am–6pm. Métro: La Fourche.

Cimetière de Passy   This cemetery runs along Paris's old northern walls, south and southwest of Trocadéro. It's a small graveyard sheltered by chestnut trees, but it contains many gravesites of the famous—a concierge at the gate can guide you. Painters **Edouard Manet** and **Romaine Brooks** and composer **Claude Debussy** are tenants. Many great literary figures since 1850 were interred here, including **Tristan Bernard, Jean Giraudoux,** and **François de Croisset.** Also present are composer **Gabriel Fauré;** aviator **Henry Farman;** actor **Fernandel;** and high priestess of the city's most famous literary salon, **Natalie Barney,** along with **Renée Vivien,** one of her many lovers.

2 rue du Comandant-Schloesing, 16e. ℂ **01-53-70-40-80.** Free admission. Mar–Nov Mon–Fri 8am–6pm, Sat 8:30am–6pm, Sun 9am–6pm; Nov–Feb Mon–Fri 8am–5:30pm, Sat 8:30am–5:30pm, Sun 9am–5:30pm. Métro: Trocadéro.

Cimetière du Montparnasse ★   In the shadow of the Tour Montparnasse, this debris-littered cemetery is a burial ground of yesterday's celebrities. A map to the left of the main gateway will direct you to the gravesite of its most famous couple, **Simone de Beauvoir** and **Jean-Paul Sartre.** Others resting here include **Samuel Beckett; Guy de Maupassant; Pierre Larousse** (famous for his dictionary); **Capt. Alfred Dreyfus;** auto tycoon **André Citroën;** sculptors **Ossip Zadkine** and **Constantin Brancusi;** actress **Jean Seberg;** composer **Camille Saint-Saëns;** photographer **Man Ray;** and poet **Charles Baudelaire,** who wrote about "plunging into the abyss, Heaven or Hell." In 2005, the cemetery interred the remains of American intellectual and activist **Susan Sontag,** who wanted to be buried in the same cemetery as some of her favorite writers.

3 bd. Edgar-Quinet, 14e. ℂ **01-44-10-86-50.** Mon–Fri 8am–6pm; Sat 8:30am–6pm; Sun 9am–6pm (closes at 5:30pm Nov–Mar). Métro: Edgar-Quinet.

Cimetière du Père-Lachaise ★★★   When it comes to name-dropping, this cemetery knows no peer; it has been called the "grandest address in Paris." A free map of Père-Lachaise is available at the newsstand across from the main entrance (additional map on p. 275).

Everybody from **Sarah Bernhardt** to **Oscar Wilde** to **Richard Wright** is resting here, along with **Honoré de Balzac, Jacques-Louis David, Eugène Delacroix, Maria Callas, Max Ernst,** and **Georges Bizet.** Colette was taken here in 1954; her black granite slab always sports flowers, and legend has it that cats replenish the roses. In time, the "little sparrow," **Edith Piaf,** followed. The lover of George Sand, poet **Alfred de Musset,** was buried under a weeping willow. Napoleon's marshals, **Ney** and **Masséna,** lie here, as do **Frédéric Chopin** and **Molière.** Marcel Proust's black tombstone rarely lacks a tiny bunch of violets (he wanted to be buried beside his friend/lover, composer **Maurice Ravel,** but their families wouldn't allow it).

Chopin's gravesite.

Surprisingly lively avenues traverse Père-Lachaise.

Some tombs are sentimental favorites: Love-torn graffiti radiates 1km (half a mile) from the grave of Doors singer **Jim Morrison.** The great dancer **Isadora Duncan** came to rest in the Columbarium, where bodies have been cremated and "filed" away. If you search hard enough, you can find the tombs of that star-crossed pair **Abélard** and **Héloïse,** the ill-fated lovers of the 12th century—at Père-Lachaise, they've found peace at last. Other famous lovers also rest here: A stone is marked **"Alice B. Toklas"** on one side and **"Gertrude Stein"** on the other; and eventually, France's First Couple of film were reunited when **Yves Montand** joined his wife, **Simone Signoret.** (Montand's gravesite attracted much attention in 1998: His corpse was exhumed in the middle of the night for DNA testing in a paternity lawsuit. He wasn't the father.)

Covering more than 44 hectares (109 acres), Père-Lachaise was acquired by the city in 1804. Nineteenth-century sculpture abounds, as each family tried to outdo the others in ostentation. Monuments also honor Frenchmen who died in the Resistance or in Nazi concentration camps. Some French Socialists still pay tribute at the **Mur des Fédérés,** the anonymous gravesite of the Communards who were executed in the cemetery on May 28, 1871. When these last-ditch fighters of the Commune, the world's first anarchist republic, made their final desperate stand against the troops of the French government, they were overwhelmed, lined up against the wall, and shot in groups. A handful survived and lived hidden in the cemetery for years, venturing into Paris at night to forage for food.

16 rue de Repos, 20e. *C* **01-55-25-82-10.** www.pere-lachaise.com. Mon–Fri 8am–6pm; Sat–Sun 8:30am–6pm (closes at 5pm Nov–early Mar). Métro: Père-Lachaise or Philippe Auguste.

Cimetière St-Vincent   Because of the artists and writers who have their resting places in the modest burial ground of St-Vincent, with a view of Sacré-Coeur on the hill, it's sometimes called "the most intellectual cemetery in Paris"—but that epithet seems more apt for other graveyards. Artists **Maurice Utrillo** and **Théopile-Alexandre Steinien** were buried here, as were musician **Arthur Honegger** and writer **Marcel Aymé.** More recently, burials have included the remains of French actor **Gabriello,** film director **Marcel Carné,** and painter **Eugène Boudin.**

6 rue Lucien-Gaulard, 18e. 🕿 **01-46-06-29-78.** Mar 6–Nov 5 Mon–Fri 8am–6pm, Sat 8:30am–6pm, Sun 9am–6pm; Nov 6–Mar 5 Mon–Fri 8am–5:15pm, Sat 8:30am–5:15pm, Sun 9am–5:15pm. Métro: Lamarck-Caulaincourt.

PARIS UNDERGROUND

Les Catacombes ★   Every year, an estimated 50,000 visitors explore some 910m (2,986 ft.) of tunnel in these dank catacombs to look at six million ghoulishly arranged, skull-and-crossbones skeletons. First opened to the public in 1810, this "empire of the dead" is now illuminated with electric lights over its entire length. In the Middle Ages, the catacombs were quarries, but by the end of the 18th century, overcrowded cemeteries were becoming a menace to public health. City officials decided to use the catacombs as a burial ground, and the bones of several million persons were transferred here. In 1830, the prefect of Paris closed the catacombs, considering them obscene and indecent. During World War II, the catacombs were the headquarters of the French Resistance.

1 place du Colonel Henri Rol-Tanguy, 14e. 🕿 **01-43-22-47-63.** www.catacombes-de-paris.fr. Admission 8€ adults, 6€ seniors, 4€ ages 14–25, free for children 13 and younger. Tues–Sun 10am–5pm. Métro: Denfert-Rochereau.

Les Egouts ★   Some sociologists assert that the sophistication of a society can be judged by the way it disposes of waste. If so, Paris receives good marks for its mostly invisible sewer network. Victor Hugo is credited with making them famous in *Les Misérables:* Jean Valjean takes flight through them, "all dripping with slime, his soul filled with a strange light." Hugo also wrote, "Paris has beneath it another Paris, a Paris of sewers, which has its own streets, squares, lanes, arteries, and circulation."

In the early Middle Ages, drinking water was taken directly from the Seine, and wastewater poured onto fields or thrown onto the unpaved streets transformed the urban landscape into a sea of rather smelly mud. Around 1200, the streets were paved with cobblestones, and open sewers ran down the center of each. These open sewers helped spread the Black Death, which devastated the city. In 1370, a vaulted sewer was built on rue Montmartre, draining effluents into a Seine tributary. During Louis XIV's reign, improvements were made, but the state of waste disposal in Paris remained deplorable.

Les Catacombes.

During Napoleon's reign, 31km (19 miles) of sewer were constructed beneath Paris. By 1850, as the Industrial Revolution made the manufacture of iron pipe and steam-digging equipment more practical, Baron Haussmann developed a system that used separate channels for drinking water and sewage. By 1878, it was 580km (360 miles) long. Beginning in 1894, the network was enlarged, and laws required that discharge of all waste and storm-water runoff be funneled into the sewers. Between 1914 and 1977, an additional 966km (600 miles) were added. Today, the network of sewers is 2,093km (1,300 miles) long.

The city's sewers are constructed around four principal tunnels, one 5.5m (18 ft.) wide and 4.5m (15 ft.) high. It's like an underground city, with the street names clearly labeled. Sewer tours begin at Pont de l'Alma on the Left Bank, where a stairway leads into the city's bowels. Visiting times might change during bad weather, as a storm can make the sewers dangerous. The tour consists of a film, a small museum visit, and then a short trip through the maze. **Warning:** The smell is pretty bad, especially in summer.

Pont de l'Alma, 7e. 🕾 **01-53-68-27-81.** Admission 4.20€ adults; 3.40€ seniors, students, and children 5–16; free for children 4 and younger. May–Sept Sat–Wed 11am–5pm; Oct–Apr Sat–Wed 11am–4pm. Métro: Alma-Marceau. RER: Pont de l'Alma.

SPORTS & RECREATION

Cycling

Bicycling through the streets and parks of Paris, perhaps with a baguette tucked under your arm, might have become your fantasy after seeing your first Maurice Chevalier film. In recent years, the city has added many miles of right-hand lanes designated for cyclists, as well as hundreds of bike racks. (When these aren't available, many Parisians simply chain their bikes to fences or lampposts.) Cycling is especially popular in the larger parks and gardens.

Following a model set by Copenhagen, Paris in 2007 became a cycling town. Thousands of bikes became available at hundreds of self-service docking stations, with the introduction of Vélib bikes. Bikes are available at more than 1,000 stations scattered throughout central Paris.

The Vélib system is simple: You swipe your credit card in a kiosk by the bike stand. The first half-hour is free; after that, you pay 1€ for another 30 minutes, 2€ for the next 30 minutes, and 4€ for each remaining half-hour you use the bike. You can leave the cycle at any Vélib station in Paris.

When you swipe the card, the system takes a 150€ deposit to ensure the bike's safe return. The Métro stops running around 1am, but Vélib kiosks are open all night.

Bikes are one size fits all, with adjustable seats; children 13 and younger are not permitted to use the cycles. Maps showing the locations of Vélib stations throughout Paris are available at the city hall in each of the 20 arrondissements. For more information, call 🕾 **01-30-79-79-30,** or see www.velib.paris.fr.

Some of the best-orchestrated bike tours in Paris are conducted in English and offered by **Fat Tire Bike Tours** (🕾 **01-56-58-10-54;** www.fattirebiketours paris.com); they depart from a spot that's immediately adjacent to the south leg (*pilier sud*) of the Eiffel Tower. (Look for a large yellow sign advertising the tours.) Between mid-February and mid-December, bike tours depart daily at 11am, and between May and September, an additional tour is offered at 3:30pm. Between April and October, a night tour is also offered, departing at 7pm from the same spot. The cost of any tour includes use of a bike and a protective helmet. **Hint:** If you're interested in participating in one of these bike tours, we recommend that you schedule your ascent to the upper levels of the Eiffel Tower for either immediately before or after your bike tour and that you arrive in clothing appropriate for a two-wheeled, self-propelled jaunt through the monumental avenues of central Paris. The cost is 24€ per person for the day tour and 28€ for the night tour. The night tour is more festive than the day tour and includes a complimentary ride aboard the *bateaux mouches,* the big-windowed panoramic boats that chug along the Seine beneath some of the most famous bridges in Europe.

Fitness Centers

Body Gym   Evoking a long and narrow corridor within one of the nearby Métro stations, this gym occupies the street level of an older building near the Gare de Lyon. The machines are modern and up to date, however, with equal emphasis on cardio and weight training. Patronized mostly by office workers and residents of this sometimes gritty neighborhood, it offers views of Paris many visitors don't often see.

157 rue du Faubourg St-Antoine, 11e. ✆ **01-43-42-42-33.** www.bodygymparis.com. 1-time entrance 17€. Mon–Fri 8am–9:30pm; Sat 9am–7pm; Sun 10am–2pm. Métro: Ledru Rollin.

Club Med Gyms   This chain of state-of-the-art fitness centers is the largest in France, with 22 of them scattered throughout Paris and its suburbs. The two noted here are the largest on the Left and Right Banks of the Seine and incorporate within their busy premises every conceivable kind of fitness, body-building, and cardio training machine, as well as squash courts. For additional addresses of gyms within this respected chain, check out www.clubmedgym.fr.

149 rue de Rennes, 6e. ✆ **01-45-44-24-35.** 1-time visit 26€. Mon–Fri 8am–10pm; Sat 8am–8pm; Sun 9am–2pm. Métro: Montparnasse or St-Sulpice.

16 rue des Colonnes du Trône, 12e. ✆ **01-43-45-93-12.** 1-time visit 26€. Mon–Fri 7:30am–10pm; Sat 8am–8pm; Sun 9am–5pm. Métro: Nation.

Horse Racing

Paris boasts an army of avid horse-racing fans who get to the city's eight racetracks whenever possible. Information on current races is available in newspapers and magazines such as ***Tierce, Paris-Turf, France-Soir,*** and *L'Equipe,* all sold at kiosks throughout the city.

The epicenter of Paris horse racing is the **Hippodrome de Longchamp** ★★★, in the Bois de Boulogne, 16e (✆ **01-44-30-75-00;** RER or Métro: Porte Maillot and then a free shuttle bus on race days only). Established in 1855, during the autocratic and pleasure-loving reign of Napoleon III, it's the most prestigious track, boasts the greatest number of promising thoroughbreds, and awards the largest purse in France. The most important events at Longchamp are the **Grand Prix de Paris** in late June and the **Prix de l'Arc de Triomphe** in early October.

Another racing venue is the **Hippodrome d'Auteuil,** also in the Bois de Boulogne (✆ **01-40-71-47-47;** Métro: Porte Auteuil; then walk). Known for its steeplechases and obstacle courses, it sometimes attracts more than 50,000 Parisians at a time. Spectators appreciate the park's promenades as much as they do the equestrian events. Races are conducted from early March to late November.

The steeplechase at Hippodrome d'Auteuil.

Ice-Skating

In the deep of winter (usually around Christmas to Feb), Paris officials set up two huge outdoor rinks, each of which is free, though you'll pay 4€ for skate rental. The best is in front of the **Hotel de Ville** in the 4th (Métro: Hôtel-de-Ville). It's open Monday to Thursday noon to 10pm, Friday noon to midnight, and Sunday 9am to 10pm. Smaller and not as attractive is the one on the esplanade facing the ugly old **Gare Montparnasse** in the 14th (Métro: Montparnasse). It's open Monday to Friday noon to 8pm and Saturday and Sunday 9am to 8pm.

Jogging

The French call jogging *le footing,* and it is not as popular here as in such cities as Los Angeles and New York. The most popular place for jogging is along the **quays of the Seine.** Of course, you might have to suck in a few exhaust fumes along the way.

Our favorite route is the **Promenade Plantée ★** starting east of the Bastille and continuing all the way to the Bois de Vincennes on the converted and now green rooftop of the old train trestle route. The entrance is just behind the opera house at Bastille along avenue Daumesnil where a staircase climbs to this long, narrow "green lung" of Paris.

Other spots are around the lakes in the **Bois de Boulogne** and the **Bois de Vincennes.** You might also try Hemingway's favorite **Jardin du Luxembourg,** where he strolled, not jogged.

Public Swimming Pools

Paris offers some three dozen public swimming pools called *piscines.* They are found throughout the city, and a complete list of them is available if you surf www.sport.paris.fr to find one near your hotel. Admission to all these municipal pools is 3€; you can also purchase a *carnet* granting 10 visits for 24€.

FROM LEFT: Enjoying the outdoors on the Promenade Plantée; Ile de la Cité.

Our favorite Right Bank pool is **Suzanne Berlioux** ★★, 10 place de la Rotonde, Forum des Halles in the 1st (✆ **01-42-36-98-44;** Métro: Les Halles). This vast pool is in the underground forum with a wall of windows for natural light. On the Left Bank, **St-Germain** ★ is a standout, at 12 rue Lobineau in the 6th (✆ **01-56-81-25-40;** Métro: Mabillon or Odéon). This 25m (82-ft.) pool is in a modern underground space near Marché St-Germain.

NEIGHBORHOOD HIGHLIGHTS

Some of Paris's neighborhoods are attractions unto themselves. The 1st arrondissement probably has a higher concentration of attractions per block than anywhere else. Though all Paris's neighborhoods are worth wandering, some are more interesting than others. This is especially true of Montmartre, the Latin Quarter, and the Marais, so we've featured them as walking tours in chapter 8.

Islands in the Stream: Ile de la Cité & Ile St-Louis

For a map of Ile de la Cité and Ile St-Louis, please refer to the map of the same name in the color insert at the beginning of this book.

ILE DE LA CITÉ: WHERE PARIS WAS BORN ★★★   Medieval Paris, that blend of grotesquerie and Gothic beauty, bloomed on this island in the Seine (Métro: Cité). Ile de la Cité, which the Seine protects like a surrounding moat, has been known as "the cradle" of Paris ever since. As Sauval once observed, "The Island of the City is shaped like a great ship, sunk in the mud, lengthwise in the stream, in about the middle of the Seine."

Few have written more movingly about its heyday than Victor Hugo, who invited the reader "to observe the fantastic display of lights against the darkness of that gloomy labyrinth of buildings; cast upon it a ray of moonlight, showing the city in glimmering vagueness, with its towers lifting their great heads from that foggy sea." Medieval Paris was a city not only of legends and lovers, but also of blood-curdling tortures and brutalities. No story illustrates this better than the affair of Abélard and his charge Héloïse, whose jealous uncle hired ruffians to castrate her lover. (The attack predictably quelled their ardor; he became a monk, and she, an abbess.) You can see their graves at Père-Lachaise (see "Cemeteries," above).

Because you'll want to see all the attractions on Ile de la Cité, begin at the cathedral of Notre-Dame. Proceed next to the Sainte-Chapelle, moving west. After a visit there, you can head northeast to the Conciergerie. To cap off your visit, and for the best scenic view, walk to the northwestern end of the island for a view of the bridge, Pont Neuf, seen from square du Vert Galant.

The island's stars, as mentioned, are **Notre-Dame, Sainte-Chapelle,** and the **Conciergerie**—all described earlier. Across from Notre-Dame is the **Hôtel Dieu,** built from 1866 to 1878 in neo-Florentine style. This is central Paris's main hospital, replacing the 12th-century hospital that ran the island's entire width. Go in the main entrance, and take a break in the spacious neoclassical courtyard whose small garden and fountain make a quiet oasis.

Don't miss the ironically named **Pont Neuf (New Bridge)** at the tip of the island opposite from Notre-Dame. The span isn't new—it's Paris's oldest bridge, begun in 1578 and finished in 1604. In its day, it had two unique features: It was paved, and it wasn't flanked with houses and shops. Actually, with 12 arches, it's not one bridge but two (they don't quite line up)—one from the Right Bank to the island and the other from the Left Bank to the island. At the **Musée Carnavalet** (p. 244), a painting called *The Spectacle of Buffoons* shows what the bridge was like between 1665 and 1669. Duels were fought on it, the nobility's great coaches crossed it, peddlers sold their wares, and entertainers such as Tabarin went there to seek a few coins from the gawkers. As public facilities were lacking, the bridge also served as a *de facto* outhouse.

Square du Vert Galant.

Just past Pont Neuf is the "prow" of the island, the **square du Vert Galant.** Pause to look at the equestrian statue of beloved Henri IV, who was assassinated by Ravaillac (see the entry for the Conciergerie). A true king of his people, Henri was also (to judge from accounts) regal in the boudoir—hence the nickname "Vert Galant" (Old Spark). Gabrielle d'Estrées and Henriette d'Entragues were his best-known mistresses, but they had to share him with countless others, some of whom would casually catch his eye as he was riding along the streets. In fond memory of the king, the little triangular park continues to attract lovers. It appears to be a sunken garden because it remains at its natural level; the rest of the Cité has been built up during the centuries.

ILE ST-LOUIS ★★   Cross the Pont St-Louis, the footbridge behind Notre-Dame, to Ile St-Louis, and you'll find a world of tree-shaded quays, town houses with courtyards, restaurants, and antiques shops. (You can also take the Métro to Sully-Morland or Pont Marie and cross the bridge.) The fraternal twin of Ile de la Cité, Ile St-Louis is primarily residential; nearly all the houses were built from 1618 to 1660, lending the island a remarkable architectural unity. Plaques on the facades identify the former residences of the famous. **Marie Curie** lived at 36 quai de Béthune, near Pont de la Tournelle, and sculptor **Camille Claudel** (Rodin's mistress) lived and worked in the Hôtel de Jassaud, 19 quai de Bourbon.

The most exciting mansion—though perhaps with the saddest history—is the 1656-to-1657 **Hôtel de Lauzun,** 17 quai d'Anjou, built for Charles Gruyn des Bordes. He married Geneviève de Mouy and had her initials engraved on much of the interior decor; their happiness was short-lived, because he was convicted of embezzlement and sent to prison in 1662. The next occupant was the duc de Lauzun, who resided there for only 3 years. He had been a favorite of Louis XIV until he asked for the hand of the king's cousin, the duchesse de Montpensier. Louis refused and had Lauzun tossed into the Bastille. Eventually, the duchesse pestered Louis into releasing him, and they married secretly and moved here in 1682, but domestic bliss eluded them—they fought often and separated in 1684. Lauzun sold the house to the grandnephew of Cardinal Richelieu and his wife, who had such a grand time throwing parties they went bankrupt. Baron Pichon bought it in 1842 and rented it out to a hashish club. Tenants Baudelaire and Gaultier regularly held hashish soirees in which Baudelaire did research for his *Les Paradis Artificiels* and Gaultier for his *Le Club des Hachichins.* Now the mansion belongs to the city and is used to house official guests. The interior is sometimes open for temporary exhibits, so call the tourist office.

Hôtel Lambert, 2 quai d'Anjou, was built in 1645 for Nicholas Lambert de Thorigny. The portal on rue St-Louis-en-l'Ile gives some idea of the splendor within, but the house's most startling element is the oval gallery extending into the garden. Designed to feature a library or art collection, it's best viewed from the beginning of quai d'Anjou. Voltaire and his mistress, Emilie de Breteuil, lived here; their quarrels were legendary. The mansion also housed the Polish royal family for more than a century before becoming the residence of actress Michèle Morgan. It now belongs to the Rothschild family and isn't open to the public.

Nos. 9, 11, 13, and 15 quai d'Anjou also belonged to the Lamberts. At **no. 9** is the house where painter/sculptor/lithographer Honoré Daumier lived from 1846 to 1863, producing hundreds of caricatures satirizing the bourgeoisie and attacking government corruption. He was imprisoned because of his 1832 cartoon of Louis-Philippe swallowing bags of gold extracted from the people.

Near the Hôtel de Lauzun is the church of **St-Louis-en-l'Ile,** no. 19 bis rue St-Louis-en-l'Ile. Despite a dour exterior, the ornate interior is one of the finest examples of Jesuit baroque. Built between 1664 and 1726, this church is still the site of many weddings—with all the white stone and gilt, you'll feel as if you're inside a wedding cake. Look for the 1926 plaque reading "In grateful memory of St. Louis in whose honor the city of St. Louis, Missouri, USA, is named."

Right Bank Highlights

LES HALLES ★   For 8 centuries, **Les Halles** (Métro: Les Halles; RER: Châtelet–Les Halles) was the city's major wholesale fruit, meat, and vegetable market. In the 19th century, Zola called it "the belly of Paris." The smock-clad vendors, beef carcasses, and baskets of vegetables all belong to the past, for the original market, with zinc-roofed Second Empire "iron umbrellas," has been torn down. Today the action has moved to a steel-and-glass edifice at Rungis, a suburb near Orly. In 1979 the **Forum des Halles,** 1–7 rue Pierre-Lescot, 1er, opened. This large complex, much of it underground, contains shops, restaurants, and movie theaters. Many of the shops are unattractive, but others contain a wide display of merchandise that has made the mall popular with residents and visitors.

For many visitors, a night on the town still ends in the wee hours with a bowl of onion soup at Les Halles, usually at **Au Pied de Cochon (The**

The bustling street life of Les Halles.

A late-night stop at Au Pied de Cochon is nearly de rigueur.   Les Deux Magots.

Pig's Foot), 6 rue Coquillière, 1er ((𝄪 **01-40-13-77-00;** p. 162), or at **Au Chien Qui Fume (The Smoking Dog),** 33 rue du Pont-Neuf, 1er ((𝄪 **01-42-36-07-42**). One of the classic scenes of old Paris was elegantly dressed Parisians (many fresh from Maxim's) standing at a bar drinking cognac with blood-smeared butchers. Some writers have suggested that 19th-century poet Gérard de Nerval introduced the custom of frequenting Les Halles at such an unearthly hour.

A newspaper correspondent described today's scene: "Les Halles is trying to stay alive as one of the few places where one can eat at any hour of the night."

Left Bank Highlights

ST-GERMAIN-DES-PRES ★★   This neighborhood in the 6th arrondissement (Métro: St-Germain-des-Prés) was the postwar home of existentialism, associated with Sartre, De Beauvoir, Camus, and an intellectual bohemian crowd that gathered at **Café de Flore** or **Les Deux Magots** (see chapter 6). Among them, black-clad poet and singer Juliette Greco was known as *la muse de St-Germain-des-Prés,* and to Sartre, she was the woman who had "millions of poems in her throat." Her long hair, black slacks, black sweater, and black sandals launched a fashion trend adopted by young women everywhere. In the 1950s, new names appeared, such as Françoise Sagan, Gore Vidal, and James Baldwin, but by the 1960s, tourists were firmly entrenched.

St-Germain-des-Prés still retains an intellectually stimulating bohemian street life, full of many interesting bookshops, art galleries, *caveau* (basement) clubs, bistros, and coffeehouses. But the stars of the area are two churches, **St-Germain-des-Prés,** 3 place St-Germain-des-Prés, and **St-Sulpice,** rue St-Sulpice (for both, see "The Major Churches," earlier in this chapter), and the **Musée National Eugène Delacroix,** 6 place de

Furstenberg (p. 249). Nearby, **rue Visconti** was designed for pushcarts and is worth visiting today. At **nos. 20–24** is the residence where dramatist Jean-Baptiste Racine died in 1699. And at **no. 17** is the house where Balzac established his printing press in 1825. (The venture ended in bankruptcy, forcing the author back to his writing desk.) Such celebrated actresses as Champmeslé and Clairon also lived here.

MONTPARNASSE ★★   For the "Lost Generation," life centered around the cafes of Montparnasse, at the border of the 6th and 14th arrondissements (Métro: Montparnasse-Bienvenüe). Hangouts such as the **Dôme, Coupole, Rotonde,** and **Sélect** became legendary, as artists—especially American expats—turned their backs on touristy Montmartre. Picasso, Modigliani, and Man Ray came this way, and Hemingway was also a popular figure. So was Fitzgerald when he was poor (when he wasn't, you'd find him at the Ritz). Faulkner, MacLeish, Duncan, Miró, Joyce, Ford Maddox Ford, and even Trotsky spent time here.

The most notable exception was Gertrude Stein, who never frequented the cafes. To see her, you had to wait for an invitation to her salon at **27 rue de Fleurus.** She bestowed this favor on Sherwood Anderson, Elliot Paul, Ezra Pound, and, for a time, Hemingway. When Pound launched himself into a beloved chair and broke it, he incurred Stein's wrath, and Hemingway decided there wasn't "much future in men being friends with great women."

American expatriate writer Natalie Barney, who moved to Paris as a student in 1909 and stayed for more than 60 years, held her grand salons at **20 rue Jacob** (actually in St-Germain-des-Prés). Every Friday, her salon attracted the literati of her day, such as Gertrude Stein, Djuna Barnes, Colette, Sherwood Anderson, T. S. Eliot, Janet Flanner, James Joyce, Sylvia Beach, Marcel Proust, and William Carlos Williams. The group met on and off for half a century, interrupted only by two world wars. Near place de Furstenberg, Barney's former residence is landmarked but not open to the public. In the garden you can see a small Doric temple bearing the inscription *A l'Amitié,* "to friendship."

Aside from the literary legends, one of the most notable characters was **Kiki de Montparnasse** (actually named Alice Prin). She was raised by her grandmother in Burgundy until her mother called her to Paris to work. She became an artist's model and adopted her new name; soon she became a prostitute and would bare her breasts for anyone who'd pay three francs. She sang at **Le Jockey,** 127 bd. du Montparnasse, which no longer exists. In her black hose and garters, she captivated dozens of

Gertrude Stein and Alice B. Toklas held court at 27 rue de Fleurus.

men, among them Frederick Kohner, who went so far as to title his memoirs *Kiki of Montparnasse*. Kiki later wrote her own memoirs, with an introduction by Hemingway. Papa called her "a Queen," noting that it was "very different from being a lady."

Completed in 1973 and rising 206m (676 ft.) above the skyline, the **Tour Montparnasse** (**©** **01-45-38-52-56;** www.tourmontparnasse56. com; Métro: Montparnasse-Bienvenüe) was denounced by some as "bringing Manhattan to Paris." The city soon passed an ordinance outlawing any further structures of this size in the heart of Paris. Today, the modern tower houses an underground shopping mall, as well as much of the infrastructure for the Gare de Montparnasse rail station. You can ride an elevator up to the 56th floor (where you'll find a bar and restaurant) and then climb three flights to the roof terrace. The view encompasses virtually every important Paris monument, including Sacré-Coeur, Notre-Dame, and La Défense. Admission is 11€ for adults, 7.50€ for students, and 4.50€ for kids 7 to 15. Free for children 6 and younger. It's open April to September daily 9:30am to 11:30pm, October to March daily 9:30am to 10:30pm (Métro: Montparnasse-Bienvenüe).

The life of Montparnasse still centers on its cafes and exotic nightclubs, many only a shadow of what they used to be. Its heart is at the crossroads of **boulevard Raspail** and **boulevard du Montparnasse,** one of the settings of *The Sun Also Rises*. Hemingway wrote that "boulevard Raspail always made dull riding." Rodin's controversial statue of Balzac swathed in a large cape stands guard over the prostitutes who cluster around the pedestal. Balzac seems to be the only one in Montparnasse who doesn't feel the weight of time.

Memorial to a Princess

Place de l'Alma (Métro: Alma-Marceau) has been turned into a tribute to the late Diana, princess of Wales, killed in an auto accident August 31, 1997, in a nearby underpass. The bronze flame in the center is a replica of the one in the Statue of Liberty and was a gift from the *International Herald Tribune* to honor Franco-American friendship. Many bouquets and messages (and even graffiti) are still placed around the flame.

Paris has also opened the **Center for Nature Discovery, Garden in Memory of Diana, Princess of Wales,** at 21 rue des Blancs-Manteaux in the Marais. The small park, which you can visit on weekends during daylight hours, is devoted to teaching children about nature and gardening and contains flowers, vegetables, and decorative plants.

Cafe culture was a central part of life for the Lost Generation.

ESPECIALLY FOR KIDS

If you're staying on the Right Bank, take the children for a stroll through the **Jardin des Tuileries** (p. 270), where there are donkey rides, ice-cream stands, and a marionette show; at the circular pond, you can rent a toy boat. On the Left Bank, similar treats exist in the **Jardin du Luxembourg** (p. 271). After a visit to the Eiffel Tower, you can take the kids for a donkey ride in the **Champ de Mars.**

A Paris tradition, **puppet shows** are worth seeing for their colorful productions; they're a genuine French child's experience. At the Jardin du Luxembourg, puppets re-enact plots set in Gothic castles and Oriental palaces; many critics say the best puppet shows are held in the Champ de Mars.

On Sunday afternoon, French families head to the **Butte Montmartre** to bask in the fiesta atmosphere. You can join in: Take the Métro to Anvers, and walk to the *funiculaire* (the cable car that carries you up to Sacré-Coeur). When up top, follow the crowds to place du Tertre, where a Sergeant Pepper–style band will usually be blasting off-key and you can have the kids' pictures sketched by local artists. You can take in the views of Paris from the various vantage points and treat your children to ice cream. For a walking tour of Montmartre, see chapter 8.

Your kids may want to check out the Gallic versions of Mickey Mouse and his pals, so see chapter 11, "Side Trips from Paris," for **Disneyland Paris.**

Temple de Sibylle at Parc des Buttes Chaumont, 19e.

Museums

Cité des Sciences et de l'Industrie ★★ ☺   A city of science and industry has risen here from unlikely ashes. When a slaughterhouse was built on the site in the 1960s, it was touted as the most modern of its kind. It was abandoned in 1974, and the location on the city's northern edge presented the government with a problem. What could be built in such an unlikely place? In 1986, the converted premises opened as the world's most expensive ($642-million) science complex, designed to "modernize mentalities" in the service of modernizing society.

The place is so vast, with so many exhibits, that a single visit gives only an idea of the scope of the Cité. Busts of Plato, Hippocrates, and a double-faced Janus gaze silently at a tube-filled riot of high-tech girders, glass, and lights. The sheer dimensions pose a challenge to the curators of its constantly changing exhibits. Some exhibits are couched in Gallic humor—imagine using the comic-strip adventures of a jungle explorer to explain seismographic activity. **Explora,** a permanent exhibit, occupies the three upper levels of the building and examines four themes: the universe, life, matter, and communication. The Cité also has a **multimedia library,** a **planetarium,** and an **"inventorium"** for kids. The silver-skinned geodesic dome called **La Géode**—a 34m-high (112-ft.) sphere with a 370-seat theater—projects the closest thing to a 3-D cinema in Europe and has several surprising additions, including a real submarine.

The Cité is in the **Parc de La Villette,** an ultramodern science park surrounding some of Paris's newest housing developments. This is Paris's largest park—twice the size of the Tuileries. The playgrounds, fountains, and sculptures are all innovative. Here you'll find a belvedere, a video workshop for children, and information about exhibits and events, along with a cafe and restaurant.

In the Parc de La Villette, 30 av. Corentine-Cariou, La Villette, 19e. ✆ **01-40-05-70-00.** www. cite-sciences.fr. Varied ticket options 8€–20€ adults, 6€–16€ ages 7–24, free 6 and younger. Tues–Sat 10am–6pm; Sun 10am–7pm. Métro: Porte de La Villette.

FROM LEFT: **A puppet show; the festive atmosphere at Butte Montmartre.**

FROM TOP: Place du Tertre; wax figures at Musée Grévin.

Musée Grévin ★ ☺ The Grévin is Paris's number-one waxworks. Comparisons with Madame Tussaud's are almost irresistible, but it isn't all blood and gore and doesn't shock as much as Tussaud's. It presents French history in a series of tableaux. Depicted are the 1429 consecration of Charles VII in the Cathédrale de Reims (armored Joan of Arc, carrying her standard, stands behind the king); Marguerite de Valois, first wife of Henri IV, meeting on a secret stairway with La Molle, who was soon to be decapitated; Catherine de Médici with Florentine alchemist David Ruggieri; Louis XV and Mozart at the home of the marquise de Pompadour; and Napoleon on a rock at St. Helena, reviewing his victories and defeats. Visitors will also find displays of contemporary sports and political figures, as well as 50 of the world's best-loved film stars.

Two shows are staged frequently throughout the day. The first, called the **"Palais des Mirages,"** starts off as a sort of Temple of Brahma and, through magically distorting mirrors, changes first into an enchanted forest and then into a fête at the Alhambra in Granada. A magician is the star of the second show, **"Le Cabinet Fantastique"**; he entertains children of all ages.

10 bd. Montmartre, 9e. ✆ **01-47-70-85-05.** www.grevin.com. Admission 20€ adults, 17€ students, 12€ children 6–14, 10€ children 5 and younger. Mon–Fri 10am–6:30pm; Sat–Sun 10am–7pm. Ticket office closes at 5:30pm. Métro: Grands Boulevards.

Musée National d'Histoire Naturelle (Museum of Natural History) ★ ☺ This museum in the Jardin des Plantes, founded in 1635 as a research center by Guy de la Brosse, physician to Louis XIII, has a range of science and nature exhibits. At the entrance of the **Grande Gallery of Evolution,** two 26m (85-ft.) skeletons of whales greet you. One display containing the skeletons of dinosaurs and mastodons is dedicated to endangered and vanished species. Galleries specialize in paleontology, anatomy, mineralogy, and botany. Within the museum's grounds are **tropical hothouses** containing thousands of species of unusual plant life and a **menagerie** with small animals in simulated natural habitats.

36 rue Geoffrey, 5e. ✆ **01-40-79-54-79.** www.mnhn.fr. Admission 9€ adults; 7€ students, seniors 60 and older, and children 4–13. Wed–Mon 10am–6pm. Métro: Jussieu or Gare d'Austerlitz.

Swing ride at the Jardin d'Acclimatation.

An Amusement Park

Jardin d'Acclimatation ★ ☺   Paris's definitive children's park is the 20-hectare (49-acre) Jardin d'Acclimatation in the northern part of the Bois de Boulogne. This is the kind of place that amuses tykes and adults but not teenagers. The visit starts with a ride on a green-and-yellow or green-and-red narrow-gauge train from Porte Maillot to the Jardin entrance, through a stretch of wooded park. The train operates at 10-minute intervals daily from 10:30am until the park closes; one-way fare costs 1.25€. En route you'll find a **house of mirrors,** an **archery range,** a **miniature-golf course, zoo animals,** a **puppet theater** (performances Wed, Sat–Sun, and holidays), a **playground,** a **hurdle-racing course, junior-scale rides, shooting galleries,** and **waffle stalls.** You can trot the kids off on a **pony** (Sat–Sun only) or join them in a **boat** on a mill-stirred lagoon. **La Prévention Routière** is a miniature roadway operated by the Paris police: Youngsters drive through in small cars equipped to start and stop, and are required to obey two genuine gendarmes to obey street signs and light changes. Inside the gate is an easy-to-follow map.

In the Bois de Boulogne, 16e. ☎ **01-40-67-90-82.** www.jardindacclimatation.fr. Admission 2.90€, free for children 3 and younger. Apr–Sept daily 10am-7pm; Oct–Mar daily 10am-6pm. Métro: Sablons.

ORGANIZED TOURS
By Bus

Before plunging into sightseeing on your own, you may like to take the most popular get-acquainted tour in Paris: **Cityrama,** 2 rue des Pyramides, 1er (☎ **01-44-55-61-00;** Métro: Musée du Louvre-Rivoli). On a double-decker bus with enough windows for Versailles, you take a 2-hour ride through the city. You don't

Relaxing under a palm tree on a chaise lounge sounds more Caribbean than Parisian, but a nearly 4.8km (3-mile) stretch of sandy shore has opened along the Seine. With the Eiffel Tower looming in the background, visitors and locals can splash in fountains, swing in hammocks, play volleyball, or enjoy a picnic. Just don't go into the polluted water of the murky Seine. The Paris beach opened in the late summer of 2003, after tons of sand were poured into concrete bases along the river.

go inside any attractions, but you get a look at the outside of Notre-Dame and the Eiffel Tower, among other sites, and it helps you get a feel for the city. There's commentary in eight languages on earphones. Tours depart daily at 10, 11:30am, and 2:30pm. A 1½-hour orientation tour is 20€ adults, 10€ children. A morning tour with interior visits to the Louvre costs 42€. Half-day tours to Versailles (64€) and Chartres (63€) are a good value and relieve some of the hassle associated with visiting those monuments. A joint ticket that includes Versailles and Chartres costs 110€. A tour of the nighttime illuminations leaves daily at 10pm in summer, 7pm in winter, and costs 30€; it tends to be tame and touristy.

The **RATP** (☎ **08-92-68-77-14;** www.ratp.fr), which runs regular public transportation, also operates the **Balabus,** a fleet of orange-and-white big-windowed motorcoaches. The only drawback is their limited operating times: Sunday and national holidays from 12:30 to 8:30pm, from April to the end of September. Itineraries run in both directions between Gare de Lyon and the Grand Arche de La Défense. Three Métro tickets will carry you along the entire route. You'll recognize the bus, and the route it follows, by the *Bb* symbol on its side and on signs posted along its route.

Cruises on the Seine

A boat tour on the Seine provides vistas of the riverbanks and some of the best views of Notre-Dame. Many boats have sun decks, bars, and restaurants. **Bateaux-Mouche** (☎ **01-42-25-96-10;** www.bateaux-mouches.fr; Métro: Alma-Marceau) cruises depart from the Right Bank of the Seine, adjacent to Pont de l'Alma, and last about 75 minutes. Tours leave daily at 20- to 30-minute

Parisian monuments make a great backdrop for romance.

Cycling along picturesque Canal St-Martin.

intervals from 10:15am to 11pm between April and September. Between October and March, there are at least five departures daily between 11am and 9pm, with a schedule that changes according to demand and the weather. Fares are 10€ for adults and 5€ for children 4 to 12. Dinner cruises depart daily at 8:30pm, last 2 hours, and cost 95€ to 135€. On dinner cruises, jackets and ties are required for men. Lunch cruises are on Saturday and Sunday at 1pm, costing 50€ for adults or 25€ for ages 11 and younger.

Friday Night "Rando" Fever

The Paris Roller Rando takes over the city on Friday nights, "rando" being short for *randonnée,* meaning tour or excursion. The starting time is around 10pm at the place d'Italie (also the name of the Métro stop). Roller folk from Paris and throughout Ile de France amass here to begin their 3-hour weekly journey through the city on rollerblades. Every Friday three motorcycle policemen lead the way with dome lights flashing, signaling moving cars to get out of the way. First-aid wagons follow the "rollers." On an average night in Paris, some 20,000 rollers show up.

Many visitors like to stay up late that night to watch these mad, mad Parisians in all their crazed rollermania.

A typical scene in many of Paris's parks.

Shopping on one of Paris's elegant boulevards.

Some people enjoy excursions on the Seine and its canals. The 2½-hour **Seine et le Canal St-Martin** tour, offered by **Paris Canal** (☎ **01-42-40-96-97**; www.pariscanal.com), requires reservations. The tour begins at 9:30am on the quays in front of the Musée d'Orsay (Métro: Solférino) and at 2:30pm in front of the Cité des Sciences et de l'Industrie at Parc de la Villette (Métro: Porte de la Villette). Excursions negotiate the waterways of Paris, including the Seine, an underground tunnel below place de la Bastille, and the Canal St-Martin. Tours are offered twice daily from mid-March to mid-November; the rest of the year, on Sunday only. As you glide along the waterways, recorded commentary in French and English relates how building supplies and food staples were hauled, with relative efficiency, into central Paris during the capital's building boom in the Napoleonic age of the 19th century. The cost is 17€ for adults, 14€ for seniors 60 and older and students ages 12 to 25, 10€ ages 4 to 11, and free for children 3 and younger.

The Tour Eiffel during Bastille Day celebrations.

Other Tours

Context:Paris (☎ **215/609-4471** in the U.S., or 01-72-81-36-35; www.contextparis.com) is an organization of graduate students and art-history professors who lead thematic walking tours of the city. Tours range from 1-hour orientation "chats" to 4-hour in-depth visits of the Louvre. Being academics, the guides try to create a college seminar feeling without being too obscure and scholarly. Context:Paris also rents cellphones, arranges transportation, and organizes culinary excursions. Prices vary widely depending on what itinerary you select, but many tours cost 35€ to 90€ per person.

STROLLING AROUND PARIS

The best way to discover Paris is on foot. Our favorite walks are along the Seine and down the Champs-Elysées from the Arc de Triomphe to the Louvre. In this chapter we highlight the attractions of Montmartre, the Latin Quarter, and the Marais.

For more walking tours in the City of Light, see *Frommer's 24 Great Walks in Paris.*

WALKING TOUR 1: **MONTMARTRE**

START:	**Place Pigalle (Métro: Pigalle).**
FINISH:	**Place Pigalle.**
TIME:	**5 hours, more if you break for lunch. It's a 4km (2½-mile) trek.**
BEST TIME:	**Any day it isn't raining. Set out by 10am at the latest.**
WORST TIME:	**After dark.**

Soft-white three-story houses and slender barren trees stick up from the ground like giant toothpicks—that's how Utrillo, befogged by absinthe, saw Montmartre. Toulouse-Lautrec painted it as a district of cabarets, circus freaks, and prostitutes. Today, Montmartre remains truer to Toulouse-Lautrec's conception than it does to Utrillo's.

PREVIOUS PAGE: **Cobblestone street in Montmartre.** ABOVE: **Place Pigalle.**

Before the late 1800s, Montmartre was a sleepy farm community with windmills dotting the landscape. The name has always been the subject of disagreement, some arguing it originated from the "mount of Mars," a Roman temple at the top of the hill, others asserting it's from "mount of martyrs," a reference to the martyrdom of St. Denis, who was beheaded here with fellow saints Rusticus and Eleutherius.

Turn right after leaving the Métro station and go down boulevard de Clichy; turn left at the Cirque Medrano, and begin the climb up rue des Martyrs. On reaching rue des Abbesses, turn left and walk along this street, crossing place des Abbesses. Go uphill along rue Ravignan, which leads to tree-studded place Emile-Goudeau, in the middle of rue Ravignan. At no. 13, across from the Timhôtel, is the:

1 Bateau-Lavoir (Boat Washhouse)

Though gutted by fire in 1970, this building, known as the cradle of cubism, has been reconstructed by the city. While Picasso lived here (1904–12), he painted one of the world's most famous portraits, *The Third Rose* (of Gertrude Stein), as well as *Les Demoiselles d'Avignon.* Other residents were van Dongen, Jacob, and Gris; Modigliani, Rousseau, and Braque had studios nearby.

Rue Ravignan ends at place Jean-Baptiste-Clément. Go to the end of the street and cross onto rue Norvins (on your right). Here rues Norvins, St-Rustique, and des Saules collide a few steps from rue Poulbot, a scene captured in a famous Utrillo painting. Turn right and go down rue Poulbot. At no. 11 you come to:

2 Espace Dalí Montmartre

The phantasmagoric world of Espace Dalí Montmartre (✆ **01-42-64-40-10;** www.daliparis.com) features 300 original Dalí works, including his famous 1956 lithograph of Don Quixote. Note that there are indeed 300

Le Bateau-Lavoir.

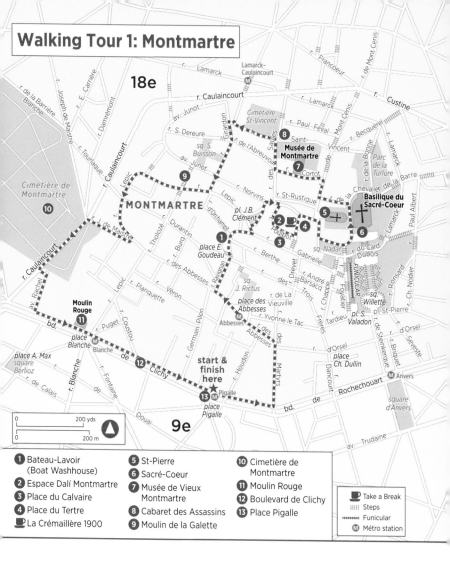

Walking Tour 1: Montmartre

18e

MONTMARTRE

9e

① Bateau-Lavoir (Boat Washhouse)	⑤ St-Pierre	⑩ Cimetière de Montmartre	
② Espace Dalí Montmartre	⑥ Sacré-Coeur	⑪ Moulin Rouge	
③ Place du Calvaire	⑦ Musée de Vieux Montmartre	⑫ Boulevard de Clichy	
④ Place du Tertre	⑧ Cabaret des Assassins	⑬ Place Pigalle	
☕ La Crémaillère 1900	⑨ Moulin de la Galette		

☕ Take a Break
‖‖‖ Steps
⋯⋯⋯ Funicular
Ⓜ Métro station

works by Dalí on permanent exposition and in that capacity, this is very much a museum/gallery where nothing is for sale. There's also a boutique on-site selling copies of Dalí lithographs, and gift items which include scarves with Dalí designs and housewares inspired by Dalí.

Rue Poulbot crosses tiny:

3   Place du Calvaire

Here you have a panoramic view of Paris. On this square once lived artist/painter/lithographer Maurice Neumont (a plaque marks the house).

A street musician entertains a crowd in Montmartre.

From place du Calvaire, head east along rue Gabrielle, taking the first left north along the tiny rue du Calvaire, which leads to:

4 Place du Tertre

This old town square is tourist central. All around the square are terrace restaurants with dance floors and colored lights, while Sacré-Coeur gleams through the trees. The cafes overflow with people, as do the indoor and outdoor art galleries. Some of the "artists" still wear berets (you'll be asked countless times if you want your portrait sketched). The square is so loaded with local color that it can seem gaudy and inauthentic.

☕ Take a Break

Many restaurants in Montmartre, especially those around place du Tertre, are unabashed tourist traps. An exception is **La Crémaillère 1900,** 15 place du Tertre, 18e (✆ **01-46-06-58-59;** www.cremaillere1900.com). As its name suggests, this is a Belle Epoque dining room, retaining much of its original look, including many paintings. You can sit on the terrace opening onto the square or retreat to the courtyard garden. A full menu is served throughout the day, including a standard array of French classics. Go any time daily from 9am to 12:30am.

Espace Dalí Montmartre.

Right off the square fronting rue du Mont-Cenis is:

5 St-Pierre

Originally a Benedictine abbey, this church has played many roles: a Temple of Reason during the Revolution, a food depot, a clothing store, and even a munitions factory. These days, one of Paris's oldest churches is back to being a church.

Facing St-Pierre, turn right and follow rue Azaïs to:

6 Sacré-Coeur

The basilica's Byzantine domes and bell tower loom above Paris and present a wide vista (see "The Top Attractions: From the Arc de Triomphe to the Tour Eiffel" in chapter 7). Behind the church, clinging to the hillside, are steep, crooked little streets that have survived the march of progress.

Facing the basilica, take the street on the left (rue du Cardinal-Guibert); then go left onto rue du Chevalier-de-la-Barre and right onto rue du Mont-Cenis. Continue on this street to rue Cortot; then turn left. At no. 12 is the:

Having coffee at La Crémaillère 1900.

7 Musée Montmartre

Musée Montmartre (✆ **01-69-25-89-37**) presents a collection of mementos of the neighborhood. Luminaries such as Dufy, Van Gogh, Renoir, and Suzanne Valadon and her son, Utrillo, occupied this 17th-century house, and it was here that Renoir put the final touches on his *Moulin de la Galette* (see below).

From the museum, turn right, heading up rue des Saules past a winery, a reminder of the days when Montmartre was a farming village on the outskirts of Paris. A grape-harvesting festival is held here every October. The intersection of rue des Saules and rue St-Vincent is one of the most visited and photographed corners of the butte. Here, on one corner, sits what was the famous old:

8 Cabaret des Assassins

This was long ago renamed **Au Lapin Agile** (see "Chansonniers" in chapter 10). Picasso and Utrillo frequented this little cottage, which numerous artists have patronized and painted. On any given afternoon, French folk tunes, love ballads, army songs, sea chanteys, and music-hall ditties stream out of the cafe and onto the street.

Turn left on rue St-Vincent, passing the Cimetière St-Vincent on your right (see "Cemeteries" in chapter 7). Take a left onto rue Girardon and climb the stairs. In a minute or two, you'll spot on your right two of the moulins (windmills) that used to dot the butte. One of these, at no. 75, is the:

Show at the Moulin Rouge.

9 Moulin de la Galette

This windmill (entrance at 1 av. Junot) was built in 1622 and was immortalized in oil by Renoir (the painting is in the Musée d'Orsay). When it was turned into a dance hall in the 1860s, it was named for the *galettes* (cakes made with flour ground inside the mills) that were sold here. Later, Toulouse-Lautrec, Van Gogh, and Utrillo visited the dance hall. A few steps away, at the angle of rue Lepic and rue Girardon, is the Moulin Radet, now part of a restaurant.

Turn right onto rue Lepic and walk past no. 54. In 1886, Van Gogh lived here with his brother, Guillaumin. Take a right turn onto rue Joseph-de-Maistre and then left again on rue Caulaincourt until you reach the:

10 Cimetière de Montmartre

This final resting place is second in fame only to Père-Lachaise and is the haunt of Nijinsky, Dumas *fils*, Stendhal, Degas, and Truffaut, among others (see "Cemeteries" in chapter 7).

From the cemetery, take av. Rachel; turn left onto blvd. de Clichy; and go to place Blanche, where stands a windmill even better known than the one in Renoir's painting, the:

11 Moulin Rouge

One of the world's most-talked-about nightclubs, the Moulin Rouge was immortalized by Toulouse-Lautrec. The windmill is still here, and so is the cancan, but the rest has become an expensive, slick variety show with an emphasis on undraped women (see "Nightclubs & Cabarets" in chapter 10).

From place Blanche, you can begin a descent on:

12 Boulevard de Clichy

En route, you'll have to fight off the pornographers and hustlers trying to lure you into sex joints. With some rare exceptions, notably the citadels of the chansonniers (songwriters), boulevard de Clichy is one gigantic tourist trap. But everyone who comes to Paris invariably winds up here.

The boulevard strips and peels its way down to where you started:

13 Place Pigalle

The center of nudity in Paris was named after a French sculptor, Pigalle, whose closest brush with nudity was a depiction of Voltaire in the buff. Toulouse-Lautrec had his studio right off the square at 5 av. Frochot. Of course, place Pigalle was the notorious "Pig Alley" of World War II. When Edith Piaf was lonely and hungry, she sang in the alleyways, hoping to earn a few francs for the night.

WALKING TOUR 2: **THE LATIN QUARTER**

START:	**Place St-Michel (Métro: St-Michel).**
FINISH:	**The Panthéon.**
TIME:	**3 hours, not counting stops. The distance is about 2.5km (1½ miles).**
BEST TIME:	**Any weekday from 9am to 4pm.**
WORST TIME:	**Sunday morning, when everybody else is asleep.**

Place St-Michel.

This is the precinct of the Université de Paris (known for its most famous branch, the Sorbonne), where students meet and fall in love over café crème and croissants. Rabelais named it the Quartier Latin after the students and professors who spoke Latin in the classroom and on the streets. The sector teems with restaurants, cafes, bookstalls, *caveaux* (basement nightclubs), *étudiants* (students), *clochards* (bums), and *gamins* (kids).

A good starting point for your tour is:

1 Place St-Michel

Balzac used to draw water from the fountain (Davioud's 1860 sculpture of St-Michel slaying the dragon) when he was a youth. This was the scene of frequent skirmishes between the Germans and the Resistance in the summer of 1944, and the names of those who died here are engraved on plaques around the square.

☕ Take a Break

Open 24 hours, **Café le Départ St-Michel,** 1 place St-Michel (✆ **01-43-54-24-55**), lies on the banks of the Seine. The decor is warmly modern, with etched mirrors reflecting the faces of a diversified crowd. If you want to fortify yourself for your walk, opt for one of the warm or cold snacks, including sandwiches.

To the south, you find:

2 Boulevard St-Michel

Also called by locals Boul' Mich, this is the main street of the Latin Quarter as it heads south. It's a major tourist artery and won't give you great insight into local life. For that, you can branch off to any streets that feed into the boulevard and find cafes, bars, gyro counters, ice cream stands, crepe stands, and bistros such as those seen in movies set in Paris in the 1950s. The Paris Commune began here in 1871, as did the student uprisings of 1968.

From place St-Michel, with your back to the Seine, turn left down:

3 Rue de la Huchette

This typical street was the setting of Elliot Paul's *The Last Time I Saw Paris* (1942). Paul first wandered here "on a soft summer evening, and entirely by chance," in 1923 and then moved into no. 28, the Hôtel Mont-Blanc. Though much has changed, some of the buildings are so old that they have to be propped up by timbers. Paul captured the spirit of the street more

One of rue de la Huchette's many Greek restaurants.

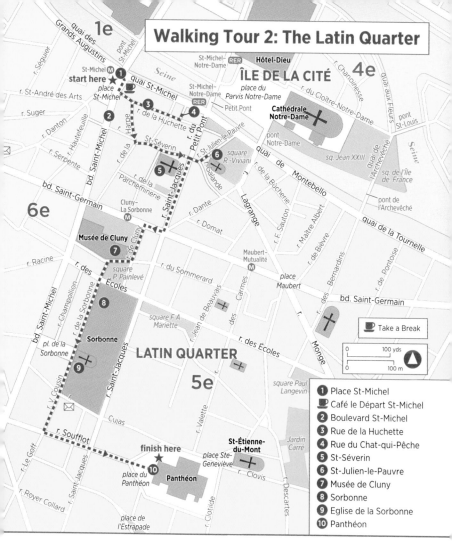

ÎLE DE LA CITÉ

4e

1e

Cathédrale Notre-Dame

6e

Musée de Cluny

LATIN QUARTER

5e

Sorbonne

Panthéon

Take a Break

❶	Place St-Michel
🍵	Café le Départ St-Michel
❷	Boulevard St-Michel
❸	Rue de la Huchette
❹	Rue du Chat-qui-Pêche
❺	St-Séverin
❻	St-Julien-le-Pauvre
❼	Musée de Cluny
❽	Sorbonne
❾	Eglise de la Sorbonne
❿	Panthéon

evocatively than anyone, writing of "the delivery wagons, makeshift vehicles propelled by pedaling boys, pushcarts of itinerant vendors, knife-grinders, umbrella menders, a herd of milk goats, and the neighborhood pedestrians." (The local bordello has closed, however.) Today, you see lots of Greek restaurants.

Branching off this street to your left is:

4 Rue du Chat-qui-Pêche

This is said to be the shortest, narrowest street in the world, with not one door and only a handful of windows. It's usually filled with garbage or lovers or both. Before the quai was built, the Seine sometimes flooded the cellars of the houses, and legend has it that an enterprising cat took advantage of its good fortune and went fishing in the confines of the cellars—hence the street's name, which means "Street of the Cat Who Fishes."

Now retrace your steps toward place St-Michel and turn left at the intersection with rue de la Harpe, which leads to rue St-Séverin. At the intersection, take a left to see:

5 St-Séverin

A flamboyant Gothic church named for a 6th-century recluse, St-Séverin was built from 1210 to 1230 and was reconstructed in 1458, over the years adopting many of the features of Notre-

Rue du Chat-qui-Pêche.

Dame, across the river. The tower was completed in 1487 and the chapels from 1498 to 1520; Hardouin-Mansart designed the Chapelle de la Communion in 1673 when he was 27, and it contains some beautiful Roualt etchings from the 1920s. Before entering, walk around the church to examine the gargoyles, birds of prey, and reptilian monsters projecting from its roof. To the right, facing the church, is the 15th-century "garden of ossuaries." The stained glass inside St-Séverin, behind the altar, is a stunning adornment using great swaths of color to depict the seven sacraments.

After visiting the church, go back to rue St-Séverin and follow it to rue Galande; then continue on until you reach:

6 St-Julien-le-Pauvre

This church is on the south side of square René-Viviani. First, stand at the gateway and look at the beginning of rue Galande, especially the old houses with the steeples of St-Séverin rising across the way; it's one of the most frequently painted scenes on the Left Bank. Enter the courtyard, and you'll be in medieval Paris. The garden to the left has the best view of Notre-Dame. Everyone from Rabelais to Thomas Aquinas has passed through the doors of this church. Before the 6th century, a chapel stood on this spot. The present church goes back to the Longpont monks, who began work on it in 1170 (making it the oldest church in Paris). In 1655, it was given to the Hôtel Dieu and in time became a small warehouse for salt. In 1889, it was presented to the followers of the Melchite Greek rite, a branch of the Byzantine church.

Students at the Sorbonne.

Return to rue Galande and turn left at the intersection with rue St-Séverin. Continue until you reach rue St-Jacques, turn left, and turn right when you reach boulevard St-Germain. Follow this boulevard to rue de Cluny, turn left, and head toward the entrance to the:

7 Musée de Cluny

Even if you're rushed, see *The Lady and the Unicorn* tapestries and the remains of the Roman baths. (See "The Major Museums" in chapter 7.)

After your visit to the Cluny, exit onto boulevard St-Michel, but instead of heading back to place St-Michel, turn left and walk to place de la Sorbonne and the:

8 Sorbonne

One of the most famous academic institutions in the world, the Sorbonne was founded in the 13th century by Robert de Sorbon, St. Louis's confessor, for poor students who wished to pursue theological studies. By the next century it had become the most prestigious university in the West, attracting such professors as Thomas Aquinas and Roger Bacon and such students as Dante, Calvin, and Longfellow. The courtyard and galleries are open to the public when the university is in session. In the Cour d'Honneur are statues of Hugo and Pasteur. At first glance from place de la Sorbonne, the Sorbonne seems architecturally undistinguished. In truth, it was rather indiscriminately reconstructed in the early 1900s. A better fate lay in store for the:

9 Eglise de la Sorbonne

Built in 1635 by Le Mercier, this church contains the marble tomb of Cardinal Richelieu, a work by Girardon based on a design by Le Brun. At his feet is the remarkable statue *Learning in Tears*.

From the church, go south on rue Victor-Cousin and turn left at rue Soufflot. At the street's end is place du Panthéon and the:

10 Panthéon

Sitting atop Mont St-Geneviève, this nonreligious temple is the final resting place of such distinguished figures as Hugo, Zola, Rousseau, Voltaire, and Curie. (See "Architectural & Historic Highlights" in chapter 7.)

START:	Place de la Bastille (Métro: Bastille).
FINISH:	Place de la Bastille.
TIME:	4½ hours, with only brief stops en route. The distance is about 4.5km (2¾ miles).
BEST TIME:	Monday to Saturday, when more buildings and shops are open. If interiors are open, often you can walk into courtyards.
WORST TIME:	Toward dusk, when shops and museums are closed and it's too dark to admire the architectural details.

When Paris began to overflow the confines of Ile de la Cité in the 13th century, the citizenry started to settle in Le Marais, a marsh that was once flooded by the Seine. By the 17th century, the Marais had become the center of aristocratic Paris, and some of its great *hôtels particuliers* (mansions), many now restored or still being spruced up, were built by the finest craftsmen in France. In the 18th and 19th centuries, fashion deserted the Marais for the expanding Faubourg St-Germain and Faubourg St-Honoré. Industry took over and once-elegant *hôtels* deteriorated into tenements. There was talk of demolishing the neighborhood, but in 1962 the community banded together and saved the historic district.

Today, the 17th-century mansions are fashionable once again. The *International Herald Tribune* called this area the latest refuge for the Paris artisan fleeing the tourist-trampled St-Germain-des-Prés. (However, that doesn't mean the area doesn't get its share of tourist traffic—quite the contrary.) The "marsh" sprawls across the 3rd and 4th arrondissements, bounded by the Grands Boulevards, rue du Temple, place des Vosges, and the Seine. It has become Paris's center of gay/lesbian life, particularly on rues St-Croix-de-la-Bretonnerie, des Archives, and Vieille-du-Temple, and is a great area for window-shopping at trendy boutiques, up-and-coming galleries, and eclectic stores.

Begin your tour at the site that spawned one of the most celebrated and abhorred revolutions in human history:

1 Place de la Bastille

On July 14, 1789, a mob attacked the Bastille prison here, igniting the French Revolution. Now, nothing of this symbol of despotism remains. Built in 1369, it loomed over Paris with eight huge towers. Within them, many prisoners, some sentenced by Louis XIV for "witchcraft," were kept, the best known being the "Man in the Iron Mask." Yet when the revolutionary mob stormed the fortress, only seven prisoners were discovered. (The Marquis de Sade had been shipped to the madhouse 10 days earlier.) The authorities had discussed razing it, so the attack meant little. But what it symbolized and what it unleashed can never be undone, and each July 14 the country celebrates Bastille Day with great festivity. Since the late 1980s, what had been scorned as a grimy-looking traffic circle has become an artistic focal point, thanks to the construction of the Opéra Bastille on its eastern edge.

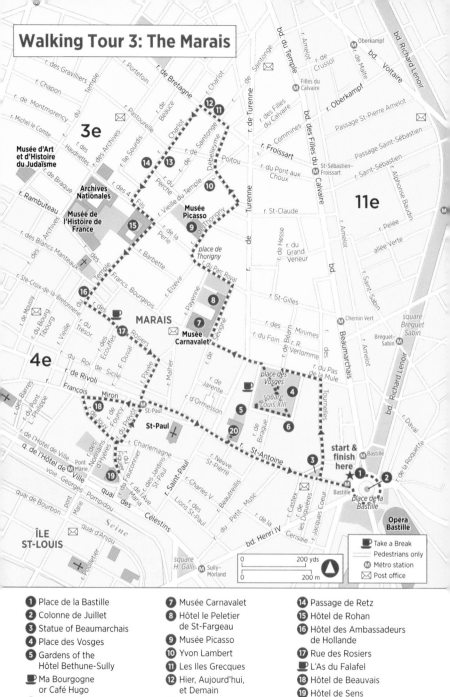

Walking Tour 3: The Marais

1. Place de la Bastille
2. Colonne de Juillet
3. Statue of Beaumarchais
4. Place des Vosges
5. Gardens of the Hôtel Bethune-Sully
   Ma Bourgogne or Café Hugo
6. Maison de Victor Hugo
7. Musée Carnavalet
8. Hôtel le Peletier de St-Fargeau
9. Musée Picasso
10. Yvon Lambert
11. Les Iles Grecques
12. Hier, Aujourd'hui, et Demain
13. Dominique Picquier
14. Passage de Retz
15. Hôtel de Rohan
16. Hôtel des Ambassadeurs de Hollande
17. Rue des Rosiers
    L'As du Falafel
18. Hôtel de Beauvais
19. Hôtel de Sens
20. Hôtel de Bethune-Sully

It was probably easier to storm the Bastille in 1789 than it is now to cross over to the center of the square for a close-up view of the:

2 Colonne de Juillet

The July Column doesn't commemorate the Revolution, but honors the victims of the July Revolution of 1830, which put Louis-Philippe on the throne after the heady but wrenching victories and defeats of Napoleon Bonaparte. The winged God of Liberty, whose forehead bears an emerging star, crowns the tower.

Colonne de Juillet in place de la Bastille.

From place de la Bastille, walk west along rue St-Antoine for about a block. Turn right and walk north along rue des Tournelles, noting the:

3 Statue of Beaumarchais

Erected in 1895, it honors the 18th-century author of *The Barber of Seville* and *The Marriage of Figaro,* set to music by Rossini and Mozart, respectively.

Continue north for a long block along rue des Tournelles; then turn left at medieval-looking rue Pas-de-la-Mule (Footsteps of the Mule), which will open suddenly onto the northeastern corner of enchanting:

4 Place des Vosges

This is Paris's oldest square and was once its most fashionable, boasting 36 brick-and-stone pavilions rising from covered arcades that allowed people to shop no matter what the weather. The buildings were constructed according to a strict plan: The height of the facades is equal to their width, and the height of the triangular roofs is half the height of the facades. In 1559, Henri II was killed while jousting on a spot near the Hôtel des Tournelles; his widow, Catherine de Médici, had the place torn down. The current square was begun in 1605 on Henri IV's orders and called place Royal; the king intended the square to be the scene of businesses and social festivities and even planned to live there, but Ravaillac had other plans and assassinated Henri 2 years before its completion in 1612. By the 17th century, the square was the home of many aristocrats. During the Revolution, it was renamed place de l'Invisibilité, and its statue of Louis XIII was stolen (and probably melted down). A replacement now stands in its place.

In 1800, the square was renamed place des Vosges because the Vosges *département* (an administrative unit) was the first in France to pay its taxes to Napoleon. The addition of chestnut trees sparked a controversy; critics say they spoil the perspective. Even though its fortunes waned when the Marais went out of fashion, place des Vosges is back big-time. Over the years, the famous often took up residence: Descartes, Pascal, Cardinal Richelieu, courtesan Marion Delorme, Gautier, Daudet, and Mme de Sévigné all lived here. But its best-known occupant was Victor Hugo (his home, now a museum, is the only house open to the public).

We'll visit the Hotel de Bethune-Sully later on (see no. 20 in this tour). However, we'll let you in on a secret:

5 Gardens of the Hôtel Bethune-Sully

The back garden of this mansion contains an entrance into the place des Vosges. It's entered by the corner door at the right of the south face of the square near no. 5 place des Vosges. You might want to visit it for a bit of R&R before continuing on with the tour. There are benches and a formal garden here. It's one of our favorite places in all of Paris to rest, contemplate, and dream.

☕ Take a Break

Two cafes hold court from opposite sides of place des Vosges, both serving café au lait, wine, eaux de vie (brandies), sandwiches, pastries, and tea: **Ma Bourgogne** at no. 19 (𝄞 **01-42-78-44-64**), on the western edge, and **Café Hugo,** at no. 22 (𝄞 **01-42-72-64-04**).

Near the square's southeastern corner at 6 place des Vosges, commemorating the life and times of a writer whose works were read with passion in the 19th century, is the:

6 Maison de Victor Hugo

Hugo's former home is now a museum (𝄞 **01-42-72-10-16;** www.musee-hugo.paris.fr) and literary shrine (see "Literary Landmarks" in chapter 7). Hugo lived here from 1832 to 1848, when he went into voluntary exile on the Channel Islands after the rise of the despotic Napoleon III.

Exit place des Vosges from its northwestern corner (opposite the Maison de Victor Hugo) and walk west along rue des Francs-Bourgeois until you reach the intersection with rue de Sévigné; then make a right. At no. 23 is the:

7 Musée Carnavalet

This 16th-century mansion is now a museum (𝄞 **01-44-59-58-58;** www.carnavalet.paris.fr) devoted to the history of Paris and the French Revolution (see "The Major Museums" in chapter 7).

Continue to a point near the northern terminus of rue de Sévigné, noting no. 29 (now part of the Carnavalet). This is the:

8 Hôtel le Peletier de St-Fargeau

The structure bears the name of its former occupant, who was considered responsible for the death sentence of Louis XVI. It's used for offices and can't be visited.

At the end of the street, make a left onto lovely rue du Parc-Royal, lined with 17th-century mansions. It leads to place de Thorigny, where at no. 5 you'll find the:

The museum occupies the **Hôtel Salé,** built by a salt-tax collector. The museum is currently closed for renovations; check on its status at the time of your visit.

Walk northeast along rue Thorigny and turn left onto rue Debelleyme. After a block, near the corner of rue Vieille-du-Temple, at 108 rue Vieille-du-Temple, is a particularly worthwhile art gallery (among dozens in this neighborhood):

10 Yvon Lambert

This gallery (© **01-42-71-09-33**) specializes in contemporary and sometimes radically avant-garde art by international artists including many American artists, thanks to a branch they maintain in the Chelsea neighborhood of New York City. The art is displayed in a cavernous main showroom, spilling over into an annex room. An excellent primer for the local arts scene, it provides an agreeable contrast to the 17th-century trappings all around you.

Continue north for 2 short blocks along rue Debelleyme until you reach rue de Bretagne. Anyone who appreciates a really good deli will want to stop at 14 rue de Bretagne:

11 Les Iles Grecques

This deli (© **01-42-71-00-56**) is the most popular of the area's ethnic takeout restaurants, a perfect place to buy picnic supplies before heading to square du Temple (up rue de Bretagne) or place des Vosges. You'll find moussaka, stuffed eggplant, stuffed grape leaves, olives, *tarama* (a savory paste made from fish roe), and both meatballs and vegetarian balls. It's open Monday from 4 to 8pm and Tuesday to Sunday from 10am to 2pm and 4 to 8pm.

Delis and traiteurs provide the makings of a gourmet picnic.

Fabrics at one of Paris's boutiques.

After you fill up on great food, note that at the same address is:

12 Hier, Aujourd'hui, et Demain

At this shop (☎ **01-42-77-69-02**) you can appreciate France's love affair with 1930s Art Deco. Michel, the owner, provides an array of bibelots and art objects, with one of the widest selections of colored glass in town. Works by late-19th-century glassmakers such as Daum, Gallé, and Legras are shown. Some items require special packing and great care in transport; others can be carted home as souvenirs.

Now walk southeast along rue Charlot to no. 10 at the corner of rue Pastourelle, where you'll be tempted by the fabrics of:

13 Dominique Picquier

Looking to redo your settee? This stylish shop (☎ **01-42-72-23-32;** www. dominiquepicquier.com) sells a wide roster of fabric (50% cotton, 50% linen) that stands up to rugged use. Most patterns are based on some botanical inspiration, such as ginkgo leaves, vanilla pods and vines, and magnolia branches.

Nearby, at 9 rue Charlot, adjacent to the corner of rue Charlot and rue du Perche, is the Marais's large experimental art gallery, the:

14 Passage de Retz

Opened in 1994, this avant-garde gallery (☎ **01-48-04-37-99**) has about 630 sq. m (6,781 sq. ft.) of space to show off its exhibits. Its shows have included such selections as Japanese textiles, American abstract expressionist paintings, modern Venetian glass, and contemporary Haitian paintings.

Walk 1 block farther along rue Charlot, turn left for a block onto rue des 4 Fils; then go right on rue Vieille-du-Temple to no. 87, where you'll come across Delamair's:

15 Hôtel de Rohan

The fourth Cardinal Rohan, the larcenous cardinal of the "diamond necklace scandal" that led to a flood of destructive publicity for Marie Antoinette, once lived here. The first occupant of the hotel was reputed to be the son of Louis XVI. The interior is usually closed to the public except during an occasional exhibit. If it's open, check out the amusing **Salon des Singes (Monkey Room).** Sometimes you can visit the courtyard, which boasts one of the finest sculptures of 18th-century France, *The Watering of the Horses of the Sun,* with a nude Apollo and four horses against a background of

A traiteur on rue des Rosiers.

exploding sunbursts. (If you want to see another Delamair work, detour to 60 rue des Francs-Bourgeois to see the extraordinary Hôtel de Soubise, now housing the **Musée de l'Histoire de France** [p. 254].)

Along the same street, at no. 47, is the:

16 Hôtel des Ambassadeurs de Hollande

Here, Beaumarchais wrote *The Marriage of Figaro.* It's one of the most splendid mansions in the Marais and, despite its name, was never occupied by the Dutch embassy.

Continue walking south along rue Vieille-du-Temple until you reach:

17 Rue des Rosiers

Rue des Rosiers (Street of the Rosebushes) is one of the most colorful and typical streets remaining from Paris's old Jewish quarter, and you'll find an intriguing blend of living memorials to Ashkenazi and Sephardic traditions. The Star of David shines from some of the shop windows; Hebrew letters appear, sometimes in neon; couscous is sold from shops run by Moroccan, Tunisian, or Algerian Jews; restaurants serve kosher food; and signs appeal for Jewish liberation. You'll come across many delicacies you might have read about but never seen, such as sausage stuffed in a gooseneck, roots of black horseradish, and pickled lemons.

Take a Break

The street offers a cornucopia of ethnic restaurants that remain steadfast to their national origins. The most frequented is **L'As du Falafel,** 34 rue des Rosiers (☎ **01-48-87-63-60**). This is both a kosher falafel kiosk and a small restaurant. Some clients have claimed that it serves the "best falafel on the planet." Because we haven't tasted all versions, we're not sure. It's open Monday to Thursday and Sunday noon to midnight; Friday noon to 5pm.

Hôtel de Sens.

Take a left onto rue des Rosiers and head down to rue Pavée, which gets its name because it was the first street in Paris, sometime during the 1300s, to have cobblestones placed over its open sewer. At this "paved street," turn right and walk south until you reach the St-Paul Métro stop. Make a right along rue François-Miron and check out no. 68, the 17th-century:

18 Hôtel de Beauvais

Though the facade was damaged in the Revolution, it remains one of Paris's most charming *hôtels*. A plaque announces that Mozart lived here in 1763 and played at the court of Versailles. (He was 7 at the time.) Louis XIV presented the mansion to Catherine Bellier, wife of Pierre de Beauvais and lady-in-waiting to Anne of Austria; she reportedly had the honor of introducing Louis, then 16, to the facts of life. To visit the interior, apply to the **Association du Paris Historique** on the ground floor.

Continue your walk along rue François-Miron until you come to a crossroads, where you take a sharp left along rue de Jouy, cross rue Fourcy, and turn onto rue du Figuier, where at no. 1 you'll see the:

19 Hôtel de Sens

The structure was built between the 1470s and 1519 for the archbishops of Sens. Along with the Cluny on the Left Bank, it's the only domestic architecture remaining from the 15th century. Long after the archbishops had departed in 1605, the wife of Henri IV, Queen Margot, lived here. Her new lover, "younger and more virile," slew her old lover as she looked on in amusement. Today, the hotel houses the Bibliothèque Forney (© **01-42-78-14-60**). Leaded windows and turrets characterize the facade; you can go into the courtyard to see more ornate stone decoration—the gate is open Tuesday to Friday 1 to 7pm.

Retrace your steps to rue de Fourcy, turn right, and walk up the street until you reach the St-Paul Métro stop again. Turn right onto rue St-Antoine and continue to no. 62:

20 Hôtel de Bethune-Sully

Work began on this mansion in 1625, on the order of Jean Androuet de Cerceau. In 1634, it was acquired by the duc de Sully, once Henri IV's minister of finance. After a straight-laced life as the "accountant of France," Sully broke loose in his declining years, adorning himself with diamonds and garish rings and a young bride who had a thing for very young men. The hotel was acquired by the government just after World War II and is now the seat of the National Office of Historical Monuments and Sites, with an information center and a bookshop inside. The relief-studded facade is especially appealing. You can visit the interior with a guide on Saturday or Sunday at 3pm and can visit the courtyard and the garden any day; chamber-music concerts are frequently staged here.

9

SHOPPING IN PARIS

Y ou don't have to buy anything to appreciate shopping in Paris—just soak up the art form the French have made of rampant consumerism. Peer in the *vitrines* (display windows), absorb cutting-edge ideas, witness new trends, and take home with you a whole new education in style.

THE SHOPPING SCENE

Best Buys

FOODSTUFFS Nothing makes a better souvenir than a product of France brought home to savor later. Supermarkets are located in tourist neighborhoods; stock up on coffee, designer chocolates, mustards (try Maille or Meaux brands), and perhaps American products in French packages for the kids. However, to be sure you don't try to bring home a prohibited foodstuff, consider "Entry Requirements," in chapter 3, "Planning Your Trip to Paris."

FUN FASHION Sure, you can buy couture or *prêt-à-porter* (ready-to-wear), but French teens and trendsetters have their own stores where the latest looks are affordable. Even the dime stores in Paris sell designer copies. In the stalls in front of the department stores on boulevard Haussmann, you'll find some of the latest accessories, guaranteed for a week's worth of small talk after you get home.

PERFUMES, MAKEUP & BEAUTY TREATMENTS A discount of 20% to 30% makes these items a great buy; qualify for a VAT refund (see below), and you'll save 40% to 45% off the Paris retail price, allowing you to bring home goods at about half the U.S. price. Duty-free shops abound in Paris and are always less expensive than the ones at the airports.

For bargain cosmetics, try out French dime-store and drugstore brands such as **Bourjois** (made in the Chanel factories), **Lierac,** and **Galenic. Vichy,** famous for its water, has a skincare and makeup line. A retail trend in Paris is the *parapharmacie,* a type of discount drugstore loaded with inexpensive brands, health cures, beauty regimes, and diet plans. These usually offer a 20% discount.

Getting a VAT Refund

The French **value-added tax** (**VAT—TVA** in French) is 16.38%, but you can get most of that back if you spend 176€ or more in any store that participates in the VAT refund program. Most stores participate.

When you meet your required minimum purchase amount, you qualify for a tax refund. The amount of the refund varies with the way the refund is handled and the fee some stores charge you for processing it. So the refund at a department store may be 13%, whereas at a small shop it may be 15% or even 18%.

PREVIOUS PAGE: **Window shopping at Pierre Hardy.**

You'll receive **VAT refund papers** in the shop; some stores, such as Hermès, have their own, while others provide a government form. Fill in the forms before you arrive at the airport and expect to stand in line at the Customs desk for as long as half an hour. You must show the goods at the airport, so have them on you or visit the Customs office before you check your luggage. After the papers are mailed, a credit will appear, often months later, on your credit card bill. All refunds are processed at the point of departure from the **European Union (E.U.)**, so if you're going to another E.U. country, don't apply for the refund in France.

Be sure to mark the paperwork to request that your refund be applied to your credit card so you aren't stuck with a check in euros, which may be hard to cash. This also ensures the best rate of exchange. In some airports, you're offered the opportunity to get your refund back in cash, which is tempting. But if you accept cash in any currency other than euros, you'll lose money on the conversion rate.

To avoid refund hassles, ask for a Global Refund form (Shopping Checque) at a store where you make a purchase. When leaving an E.U. country, have it stamped by Customs, after which you take it to a Global Refund counter at one of more than 700 airports and border crossings in France. Your money is refunded on the spot. For information, contact **Global Refund,** 18 rue de Calais, 75009 Paris (**℗ 01-41-61-51-51;** www.globalrefund.com).

 Shopping Etiquette

When you walk into a French store, it's traditional to greet the owner or sales clerk with a direct address, not a fey smile or even a weak *"Bonjour."* Only a clear and pleasant *"Bonjour, madame/monsieur"* will do.

And if you plan to enter the rarefied atmospheres of the top designer boutiques (to check out the pricey merchandise, if not to buy anything), be sure to dress the part. You don't need to wear couture, but do leave the sneakers and sweat suit back at your hotel. The sales staff will be much more accommodating if you look as if you belong there.

Duty-Free Boutiques

The advantage of duty-free shops is that you don't have to pay the VAT, so you avoid the red tape of getting a refund. Both Charles de Gaulle and Orly airports have shopping galore (de Gaulle has a virtual mall with crystal, cutlery, chocolates, luggage, wine, pipes and lighters, lingerie, silk scarves, perfume, knitwear, jewelry, cameras, cheeses, and even antiques). You'll also find duty-free shops on the avenues branching out from the Opéra Garnier, in the 1st arrondissement. Sometimes bargains can be found, but most often not.

Business Hours

Usual shop hours are Monday to Saturday from 10am to 7pm, but hours vary, and Monday mornings don't run at full throttle. Small shops sometimes close for a 2-hour lunch break and some do not open at all until after lunch on Monday. Thursday is the best day for late-night shopping, with stores open to 9 or 10pm.

Sunday shopping is limited to tourist areas and flea markets, though there's growing demand for full-scale Sunday hours. The department stores are now open on the five Sundays before Christmas. The **Carrousel du Louvre**

(📞 **01-43-16-47-10**), a mall adjacent to the Louvre, is open daily 10am to 8pm. The tourist shops lining rue de Rivoli across from the Louvre are open on Sunday, as are the antiques villages, flea markets, and specialty events. Several food markets enliven the streets on Sunday. For our favorites, see the box "Food Markets" (p. 333). The **Virgin Megastore** on the Champs-Elysées, a big teen hangout, pays a fine to stay open on Sunday.

Great Shopping Neighborhoods

Here are the best of the shopping arrondissements:

1ST & 8TH ARRONDISSEMENTS   These two arrondissements adjoin each other and form the heart of Paris's best Right Bank shopping strip—they're one big hunting ground. This area includes the **rue du Faubourg St-Honoré,** where the big designer houses are, and the **Champs-Elysées,** with hot mass-market and teen scenes. At one end of the 1st is the **Palais Royal,** one of the best shopping secrets in Paris, where an arcade of boutiques flanks each side of the garden of the former palace.

Also here is **avenue Montaigne,** Paris's most glamorous shopping street, boasting 2 blocks of ultrafancy shops, where you float from big name to big name and in a few hours can see everything from Dior to Caron. Avenue Montaigne is also the address of **Joseph,** a British design firm, and **Porthault,** maker of the poshest sheets in the world.

2ND ARRONDISSEMENT   Right behind the Palais Royal is the **Garment District (Sentier),** as well as a few sophisticated shopping secrets, such as **place des Victoires.**

In the 19th century, this area became known for its *passages,* glass-enclosed shopping streets—in fact, the world's first shopping malls. They were also the city's first buildings to be illuminated by gaslight. Many have been torn down, but a dozen or so have survived. Of them all, we prefer **Passage de Grand Cerf,** between 145 rue St-Denis and 10 rue Dussoubs (Métro: Bourse), lying a few blocks from the Beaubourg. It's a place of wonder, filled with everything from retro-chic boutiques to (increasingly) Asian-themed shops. What's exciting is to come upon a discovery, perhaps a postage-stamp-size shop with a special jeweler who creates unique products such as jewel-toned safety pins.

3RD & 4TH ARRONDISSEMENTS   The border between these two arrondissements gets fuzzy, especially around **place des Vosges,** center stage of the Marais. The districts provide several dramatically different shopping experiences.

On the surface, the shopping includes the "real people stretch" (where all the nonmillionaires shop) of **rue de Rivoli** and **rue St-Antoine,** featuring everything from Gap and a branch of Marks & Spencer to local discount stores and mass merchants. Many shoppers will also be looking for **La Samaritaine,** 19 rue de la Monnaie, once the most famous department store in France. It occupied four noteworthy buildings erected between 1870 and 1927. These buildings have been sold and are undergoing renovation to be completed in 2012. The owner has not made his intentions clear about the future of this Parisian landmark, but it is currently closed. Hidden in the Marais is a medieval warren of twisting streets chockablock with cutting-edge designers and up-to-the-minute fashions and trends. Start by

Shops in the Viaduc des Arts.

walking around place des Vosges for galleries, designer shops, and special finds; then dive in and lose yourself in the area leading to the Musée Picasso.

Finally, the 4th is the home of the **Bastille,** an up-and-coming area for artists and galleries, where you'll find the newest entry on the retail scene, the **Viaduc des Arts** (which actually stretches into the 12th). It's a collection of about 30 stores occupying a series of narrow vaulted niches under what used to be railroad tracks. They run parallel to avenue Daumesnil, centered on boulevard Diderot.

6TH & 7TH ARRONDISSEMENTS   Though the 6th is one of the most famous shopping districts in Paris—it's the soul of the Left Bank—a lot of the good stuff is hidden in the zone that turns into the residential district of the 7th. **Rue du Bac,** stretching from the 6th to the 7th in a few blocks, stands for all that wealth and glamour can buy.

9TH ARRONDISSEMENT   To add to the fun of shopping the Right Bank, the 9th sneaks in behind the 1st, so if you choose not to walk toward the Champs-Elysées and the 8th, you can head to the city's big department stores, all built in a row along **boulevard Haussmann** in the 9th. Department stores include not only the two big French icons, **Au Printemps** and **Galeries Lafayette,** but also a large branch of Britain's **Marks & Spencer.**

SHOPPING A TO Z

Antiques

Le Louvre des Antiquaires ★★   Across from the Louvre, this store offers three levels of fancy knickknacks and 250 vendors. It's just the place if you're looking for 30 matching Baccarat-crystal champagne flutes from the 1930s, a Sèvres tea service from 1773, or a signed Jean Fouquet gold-and-diamond pin. Too stuffy? No problem. There's always the 1940 Rolex with the aubergine crocodile strap. Prices can be high, but a few reasonable items are hidden here. What's more, the Sunday scene is fabulous, and there's a cafe with a variety of lunch menus. Pick up a free map and brochure of the premises from the information desk. Open Tuesday to Sunday 9am to 7pm. Closed Sunday July to August. 2 place du Palais Royal, 1er. ☎ **01-42-97-27-27.** www.louvre-antiquaires.com. Métro: Palais-Royal.

Village St-Paul   This isn't an antiques center, but a cluster of dealers in their own hole-in-the-wall hideout. It really hops on Sunday. Bring your camera, because inside the courtyards and alleys is a dream vision of hidden Paris: dealers in a courtyard selling furniture and other decorative items in French-country and formal styles. The rest of the street, stretching from the river to the Marais, is also lined with dealers. Open Thursday to Monday 11am to 7pm. 23-27 rue St-Paul, 4e. No phone. www.village-saint-paul.com. Métro: St-Paul.

Art

Artcurial ★★   Set within minimalist showrooms in one of the most spectacular 19th-century mansions in Paris, this is one of the best outlets in Europe for contemporary art. Since it was established in 1975, it has represented megastars such as Man Ray and the "enfant terrible" of France's postwar intelligentsia, Jean Cocteau. Today, the names of showcased artists read like a *Who's Who* of contemporary art: Arman, Sonia Delaunay, and Niki de Saint Phalle for painting and sculpture; Claude Lalanne for jewelry design; and Matta for contemporary carpets. Technically, it's an auction house, similar in some ways to Sotheby's and Christie's, albeit with a specialization in modern and contemporary art, vintage photographs by "important" photographers, antique books and posters, and sculpture. The staff is well versed in the merits of each individual artist on display. The more expensive works are usually displayed in anticipation of a scheduled auction, but there's also a boutique selling reproductions and gift items, and an overwhelming sense of an association with the inner workings of the international art investment community. Despite an address that might be among the most expensive in the world (the intersection of av. Montaigne and Champs-Elysées), the place is more welcoming than, and not as forbidding as, its location implies. Open Monday to Friday 10am to 7pm; Saturday 11am to 7pm. 7 rond-point des Champs-Elysées, 8e. ✆ **01-42-99-20-20.** www.artcurial.com. Métro: Franklin-D-Roosevelt.

Galerie Adrien Maeght ★★★   This art house is among the most famous names, selling contemporary art on a fancy Left Bank street that's far more fashionable than the bohemian Left Bank that Picasso knew. Open Monday 10am to 6pm; Tuesday to Saturday 9:30am to 7pm. 42 rue du Bac, 7e. ✆ **01-45-48-45-15.** www.maeght.com. Métro: Rue du Bac.

Galerie 27   This tiny closet sells etchings and lithographs by famous artists of the early 20th century, including Picasso, Miró, Braque, and Léger. Contemporary artists are also represented. Open Tuesday to Saturday 11am to 1pm and 2:30 to 7pm. 27 rue de Seine, 6e. ✆ **01-43-54-78-54.** Métro: St-Germain-des-Prés, Odéon, or Mabillon.

J. C. Martinez ★   In its way, this is one of the most charming and old-fashioned art galleries in Paris. Established in the mid-1970s within a single room that's loaded with at least 400 separate boxes, it specializes in antique prints and engravings, most of them crafted between the late 1700s and around 1910, and some even earlier. You can rummage randomly through the inventories here, depending on how rare they are. But if your parameters are more specialized, the staff will guide you toward whatever subject interests you the most. If you're interested in engravings of birds, botany, fashion, sailing ships, floral arrangements, architectural renderings, or horse races, there's at least one box devoted to that particular subject. And if you're interested in the way the borders of

An Open-Air Canvas Gallery

The **Paris Art Market** (☎ **01-53-57-42-60**) is "the place to go" on a Sunday. At the foot of Montparnasse Tower, this market is like an open-air gallery and has done much to restore the reputation of Montparnasse (14e) as a *quartier* for artists. Some 100 artists participate, including painters, sculptors, and photographers, even jewelers and hat makers. Head for the mall along the boulevard Edgar Quinet for the best work. Go anytime on Sunday between 9am and 7pm (Métro: Montparnasse).

France and its internal regions have been organized and reorganized since the days of the *ancien régime,* there's a wondrous collection of maps crafted at different times of the nation's complicated history. Open Monday 10:30am to 12:30pm and 2 to 7pm; Tuesday to Saturday 10:30am to 7pm. 21 rue St-Sulpice, 6e. ☎ **01-43-26-34-53.** www.jean-claude-martinez.fr.   Métro: Odéon or Mabillon.

La Maison Rouge ★   The so-called Red House, created by Antoine de Galbert, has an ever-changing decor, as well as a constantly rotating display of the latest work of the "hot" artists of Paris. A large, well-laid-out, avant-garde space awaits you. Open Wednesday to Sunday 11am to 7pm (9pm on Thurs). Because this place is a virtual museum of art, an admission is charged: 7€ adults, 5€ ages 3 to 18 and senior citizens. 10 bd. de la Bastille, 12e. ☎ **01-40-01-08-81.** www.lamaisonrouge.org. Métro: Quai de la Rapée.

Viaduc des Arts   This complex of boutiques and crafts workshops occupies the vaulted spaces beneath one of the 19th-century railway access routes into the Gare de Lyon. Around 1990, crafts artists, including furniture makers, potters, glassblowers, and weavers, began renting the niches beneath the viaduct, selling their wares to homeowners and members of Paris's decorating trades. Several trendsetting home-furnishing outfits have rented additional spaces. Stretching for more than 2 blocks between the Opéra Bastille and the Gare de Lyon, it allows one to see what Parisians consider chic in terms of home decorating. Open Monday to Saturday 11am to 7pm. 119 av. Daumesnil, 12e. ☎ **01-44-75-80-66.** www.viaduc-des-arts.com. Métro: Bastille, Ledru-Rollin, Reuilly-Diderot, or Gare-de-Lyon.

Books

If you like rare and unusual books, patronize one of the *bouquinistes,* the owners of those army-green stalls that line the Seine. This is where tourists in the 1920s and 1930s went to buy "dirty" French postcards. You might get lucky and come across some treasured book, such as an original edition of Henry Miller's *Tropic of Cancer,* which was banned for decades in the United States.

Brentano's   A block from the Opéra Garnier, Brentano's is a large English-language bookstore selling guides, maps, novels, and nonfiction as well as greeting cards, postcards, holiday items, and gifts. Open Monday to Saturday 10am to 7:30pm; Sunday 1 to 7pm. 37 av. de l'Opéra, 2e. ☎ **01-42-61-52-50.** www.brentanos.fr. Métro: Opéra or Pyramides.

Galignani   Sprawling over a large street level and supplemented by a mezzanine, this venerable wood-paneled bookstore has thrived since 1810. Enormous numbers of books are available in French and English, with a special emphasis on French classics, modern fiction, sociology, and fine arts. Looking for English-language translations of works by Balzac, Flaubert, Zola, or Colette? Most of them are here; if not, they can be ordered. Open Monday to Saturday 10am to 7pm. 224 rue de Rivoli, 1er. ✆ **01-42-60-76-07.** www.galignani.com. Métro: Tuileries.

Les Mots à la Bouche   This is Paris's largest, best-stocked gay bookstore. You can find French- and English-language books as well as gay-info magazines such as *Illico, Blue, e.m@le, Carol's Girlfriends,* and *Lesbia.* You'll also find lots of free pamphlets advertising gay/lesbian venues and events. Open Monday to Saturday 11am to 11pm; Sunday 1 to 9pm. 6 rue Ste-Croix-la-Bretonnerie, 4e. ✆ **01-42-78-88-30.** www.motsbouche.com. Métro: Hôtel-de-Ville.

Librairie le Bail-Weissert   Paris is filled with rare book shops, but this one has the best collection of atlases, rare maps, and engravings from the 15th century to the 19th century. The shop sells original topographical maps of European and world cities, along with various regions of Europe. There's also a superb collection of architectural engravings. Open Monday to Friday 10am to 12:30pm and 2 to 7pm; Saturday 2 to 6pm. 13 rue Frederic Sauton, 5e. ✆ **01-43-29-72-59.** www.librairie-lebail.fr. Métro: Cluny–La Sorbonne.

Shakespeare and Company ★   The most famous bookstore on the Left Bank is Shakespeare and Company, on rue de l'Odéon, home to Sylvia Beach, "mother confessor to the Lost Generation." Hemingway, Fitzgerald, and Stein were frequent patrons, as was Anaïs Nin, the diarist noted for her description of struggling American artists in 1930s Paris. Nin helped her companion, Henry Miller, publish *Tropic of Cancer,* a book so notorious in its day that returning Americans who tried to slip copies through Customs often had them confiscated as pornography. (When times were hard, Nin herself wrote pornography for a dollar a page.) Long ago, the shop moved to rue de la Bûcherie, a musty old place where expatriates still swap books and literary gossip and foreign students work in exchange for modest lodgings. Check out the lending library upstairs. Open daily 10am to 11pm. 37 rue de la Bûcherie, 5e. ✆ **01-43-25-40-93.** www.shakespeareco.org. Métro: St-Michel.

Taschen   This store is a Germany-based publishing house that's known for coffee-table books. Erudite, high-profile, and glossy, most of them focus on architecture, art, photography, or eroticism. If you're in the market for a sweeping overview of the organization's past projects, this is the store for you. It is one of only two retail outlets in the world solely devoted to Taschen products (the other is in Cologne). Open Tuesday to Saturday 11am to 7pm. 2 rue de Buci, 6e. ✆ **01-40-51-79-22.** www.taschen.com. Métro: Odéon.

Tea & Tattered Pages   At this largely English-language paperback bookshop, you can take a break from browsing to have tea. Though it's out of the way, an extra dose of charm makes it worth the trip. Open Monday to Saturday 11am to 7pm; Sunday noon to 6pm. 24 rue Mayet, 6e. ✆ **01-40-65-94-35.** www.teaandtatteredpages.com. Métro: Duroc.

Shopping along glamorous avenue Montaigne.

Village Voice Bookshop This favorite of expatriate Yankees is on a side street in the heart of the best Left Bank shopping district, near some of the gathering places described in Gertrude Stein's *The Autobiography of Alice B. Toklas.* Opened in 1981, the shop is a hangout for literati. Its name has nothing to do with the New York weekly. Open Monday 2 to 8pm; Tuesday to Saturday 10am to 8pm; Sunday 2 to 7pm. 6 rue Princesse, 6e. ℂ **01-46-33-36-47.** www.villagevoice bookshop.com. Métro: Mabillon.

W. H. Smith France This store provides books, magazines, and newspapers published in English (most titles are from Britain). You can get the *Times* of London, of course, and the Sunday *New York Times* is available every Monday. There's a fine selection of maps and travel guides, plus a special children's section that includes comics. Open Monday to Saturday 9am to 7:30pm; Sunday 1 to 7:30pm. 248 rue de Rivoli, 1er. ℂ **01-44-77-88-99.** Métro: Concorde.

Ceramics, China & Porcelain

La Maison Ivre This charming shop is perfect for country-style ceramics that add authenticity to French-country decor. It carries an excellent selection of handmade pottery from all over France, with an emphasis on Provençal and southern French ceramics, including ovenware, bowls, platters, plates, pitchers, mugs, and vases. Open Monday to Saturday 10:30am to 7pm. 38 rue Jacob, 6e. ℂ **01-42-60-01-85.** www.maison-ivre.com. Métro: St-Germain-des-Prés.

Limoges-Unic/Madronet Housed in two shops on the same street, this store is crammed with crystal of Daum, Baccarat, Lalique, Haviland, and Bernardaud. You'll also find other table items: glass and crystal, silver, whatever your heart desires. They'll ship your purchases, and English is widely spoken. Open Monday to Saturday 11am to 6pm. 34 and 58 rue de Paradis, 10e. ℂ **01-47-70-34-59.** Métro: Gare de l'Est.

Manufacture Nationale de Sèvres ★★★ Once endorsed and promoted by the mistresses of Louis XV, Sèvres today manufactures only 4,000 to 5,000 pieces of porcelain every year. Of these, many are reserved as replacements for government and historical entities. Located a short walk beyond the western edge of Paris's 16th arrondissement, in the suburb of Sèvres, it maintains a sales outlet for the porcelain manufactured inside. Open Monday to Friday 10am to 5pm. 2 place de la Manufacture, 92310 Sèvres. ℂ **01-46-29-22-10.** Métro: Pont-de-Sèvres. More centrally located is the organization's sales outlet near the Louvre, at place André Malraux, 1er (ℂ **01-47-03-40-20**). Métro: Palais-Royal. Tues–Fri 11am–7pm, Mon–Sat 2–7pm.

Children: Fashion & Toys

Au Nain Bleu ★ This is the largest, oldest, and most centrally located toy store in Paris. More important, it's probably the fanciest toy store in the world. But don't panic—in addition to the expensive stuff, you'll find rows of cheaper items on the first floor. Open Monday 2 to 7pm; Tuesday to Saturday 10am to 7pm. 5 bd. Malesherbes, 8e. ℂ **01-42-65-20-00.** www.aunainbleu.com. Métro: Concorde or Madeleine.

Bonpoint This outlet is part of a chain that helps parents transform their darlings into models of well-tailored conspicuous consumption. Though you'll find some garments for real life, the primary allure of the place lies in its tailored, traditional—and expensive—garments by the "Coco Chanel of the children's garment industry," Marie-France Cohen. The shop sells clothes for boys and girls from newborn to age 16. Open Monday to Saturday 10am to 6pm. 15 rue Royale, 8e. ⓒ **01-47-42-52-63.** Métro: Concorde.

Crystal

Baccarat ★★★   Opened in 1764, Baccarat is one of Europe's leading purveyors of full-lead crystal. You won't be able to comparison-shop Baccarat crystal at its four branches—a central organization sets rigid prices. The most prestigious outlet is on place de la Madeleine, but the outlet at 11 place des Etats-Unis, 16e, is larger and contains the **Musée Baccarat.** A third branch at rue de la Paix sells only women's jewelry, in which real gemstones (usually colored stones such as rubies and sapphires) are sometimes interspersed with cut crystal for that flashy "is it real or is it fake?" look. A fourth branch is in the Hotel Concorde La Fayette at the Palais des Congrès–Côté Ternes, at place du Général Koenig. Branches are open Tuesday to Friday 10am to 7pm; Monday and Saturday 10am to 7:30pm. 11 place de la Madeleine, 8e. ⓒ **01-42-65-36-26.** www.baccarat.fr. Métro: Madeleine. Also: 11 place des Etats-Unis, 16e. ⓒ **01-40-22-11-22.** Métro: Boissière.

Lalique ★★   Lalique is known for its smoky frosted-glass sculpture, Art Deco crystal, and unique perfume bottles. The shop sells a wide range of merchandise, including leather belts with Lalique buckles and silk scarves, designed to compete directly with those sold by Hermès. Open Monday to Saturday 10am to 7pm. 11 rue Royale, 8e. ⓒ **01-53-05-12-81.** www.cristallalique.fr. Métro: Concorde.

Department Stores

Au Bon Marché   Don't be fooled by the name ("low-budget" or "cheap") of this two-part Left Bank department store—for about 20 years, it has worked hard to position itself in the luxury market, selling fashion for men, women, and children; furniture; upscale gifts; and housewares. Some visitors compare it with Bloomingdale's. This is the oldest department store in Paris, dating from 1852. Of course, it can't compete with the *grands magasins* (department stores) such as Galeries Lafayette (see below), except in one category: Au Bon Marché has a superior rug department, which it has fine-tuned as its specialty since 1871. It also has one of the largest food halls in Paris. Open Monday to Wednesday and Saturday 10am to 8pm; Thursday and Friday 10am to 9pm. 22-24 rue de Sèvres, 7e. ⓒ **01-44-39-80-00.** www.lebonmarche.fr. Métro: Sèvres-Babylone.

Au Printemps ★★   Take a look at the facade of this store for a reminder of the Gilded Age. Inside, the merchandise is divided into housewares (**Printemps Maison),** women's fashion (**Printemps de la Mode),** and men's clothes (**Le Printemps de l'Homme).** This is better for women's and children's fashions than is Galeries Lafayette. As for the top names in perfume, it's in a dead heat with Galeries Lafayette. Although visitors feel more pampered in Galeries Lafayette, Au Printemps's customer service is dazzling, putting all major department stores in Paris to shame. Check out the magnificent stained-glass dome, through which turquoise light cascades into the sixth-floor **Café Flo,** where you can have a coffee or a full meal. Interpreters at the Welcome Service in Printemps de la Mode will help you find what you're looking for, claim your VAT refund, and so on. Au Printemps also has a tourist discount card, offering a flat 10% discount. Open Monday to Wednesday and Friday to Saturday 9:35am to 7pm; Thursday

9:35am to 9pm. 64 bd. Haussmann, 9e. ☏ **01-42-82-50-00.** www.printemps.com. Métro: Havre-Caumartin. RER: Auber or Haussmann–St-Lazare.

Colette   Named after the great French writer, Colette is a swank citadel for a la mode fashion. It buzzes with excitement, displaying fashions by some of the city's most promising young talent, including Marni and Lucien Pellat-Finet. This is for the sophisticated shopper who'd never be caught dead shopping at Galeries Lafayette and the like. Not to be overlooked are home furnishings by such designers as Tom Dixon and even zany Japanese accessories. Even if you don't plan to buy anything, patronize the tea salon, with its fresh quiches, salads, and cakes, plus three-dozen brands of bottled water. Open Monday to Saturday 11am to 7pm. 213 rue St-Honoré, 1er. ☏ **01-55-35-33-90.** www.colette.fr. Métro: Tuileries or Pyramides.

Galeries Lafayette ★★★   Opened in 1896, with a lobby capped by an early-1900s stained-glass cupola classified as a historic monument, Galeries Lafayette is Europe's largest department store. If you have time for only one department store, make it this one. This store could provision a small city with everything from perfume to fashion. It is even more user-friendly than Au Printemps, and in fashion it places more emphasis on upcoming designers. It also concentrates on an upscale roster of everything you need to furnish and maintain a home; thousands of racks of clothing for men, women, and children; and a staggering array of cosmetics, makeup products, and perfumes. Menswear is concentrated in a section called **Galfa;** also in the complex is **Lafayette Gourmet,** one of the fanciest grocery stores in Paris, selling culinary exotica at prices usually lower than those at Fauchon (see "Food: Chocolate, Honey, Pâtés & More," later in this chapter); **Lafayette Sports; Galeries Lafayette Mariage** (for wedding accessories); and two other general-merchandise stores, both known simply as **"GL."** The floor above street level has a concentration of high-end, semi-independent boutiques, including Cartier, Vuitton, and Prada Sport. A fashion show is held at least once daily, usually in the **Salon Opéra.** At the street-level **Welcome Desk,** a multilingual staff will tell you where to find various items in the store, where to get a taxi back to your hotel, and so on. Open Monday to Wednesday and Friday to Saturday 9:30am to 8pm; Thursday 9:30am to 9pm. 40 bd. Haussmann, 9e. ☏ **01-42-82-34-56.** Métro: Chaussée d'Antin. RER: Auber.

Talmaris ★ 🛍   This is called the world's smallest department store. Actually, it's a boutique showcase for Alain-Paul Ruzé, who spends 6 months a year traveling the world picking up treasures, which he brings back to Paris and sells at this outlet. He's likely to turn up with just about anything, perhaps an American flag from the 1700s, discovered in a Greenwich Village flea market in Manhattan. Both costly and less expensive items are sold. Open Monday to Saturday 10am to 7pm. 59–61 av. Mozart, 16e. ☏ **01-42-88-20-20.** Métro: Ranelagh.

Fabrics

Souleiado ★   This is the only Paris branch of one of Provence's most successful purveyors of the bright fabrics and thick pottery of France's southern tier. Fabrics are measured out by scissors-wielding saleswomen and then sold by the meter for seamstresses to whip into curtains, tablecloths, or whatever. In a separate shop just around the corner, at 78 rue de Seine (same phone), there are displays of table settings, housewares, and gift items, each reflecting the bright

A Touch of Africa in the Marais

A stroll down rue Elzévir in the Marais is like a trip to Senegal. Valeria Schlumberger, a Frenchwoman who lives for part of the year on Ile de Gorée, off the coast of Dakar, has opened up several storefronts on this street in the Marais, all under the umbrella organization of **La Compagnie du Sénégal et de l'Afrique de l'Ouest** (www.csao.fr). You can find beautiful hand-woven and hand-dyed bolts of cloth that make fabulous curtains, cushion covers, or quilts. Many decorative items are made of recycled material, such as metallic bits and pieces from tin cans, or even aerosol sprays. Multicolored carpets are sold, along with basketwork and paintings. The leading outlets, all in the 3rd arrondissement, include **La boutique de la CSAQ**, 9 rue Elzévir (✆ **01-42-71-33-17**); and **La Garerie 3A**, 9 rue Elzévir (✆ **01-42-77-66-42**). La Jokko, 5 rue Elzévir (✆ **01-42-74-35-96**), is a languid bar, ideal for drinking between rounds of shopping. At the association's restaurant, **Le Petit Dakar**, 6 rue Elzévir (✆ **01-44-59-34-74**), you can order such native specialties as grouper with cassava and rice, topped off by litchi ice cream.

sunshine and colors (usually ocher, cerulean blue, and a strong medium green) of the Midi. Open Monday to Saturday 10:30am to 7pm. 3 rue Lobineau, 6e. ✆ **01-43-54-62-25.** www.souleiado.com. Métro: Odéon or Mabillon.

Fashion
CUTTING-EDGE CHIC

Azzedine Alaïa Alaïa, who became the darling of French fashion in the 1970s, is the man who put body consciousness back into Paris chic. If you can't afford the current collection, try the **stock shop** around the corner at 18 rue de la Verrerie, 4e (✆ **01-42-72-54-97**; Métro: Hôtel-de-Ville), where last year's leftovers are sold at serious discounts. Both outlets sell leather trench coats, knit dresses, pleated skirts, cigarette pants, belts, purses, and fashion accessories. Open Monday to Saturday 10am to 7pm. 18 rue Verrerie, 4e. ✆ **01-42-72-19-19.** Métro: Hôtel-de-Ville.

BCBG/Max Azria You'll quickly get the sense that someone spent hours meticulously selecting the women's clothing and accessories featured on three floors of this stylish boutique where everything is "BCBG" (*bon chic, bon genre*— a designation for things chic, restrained, and tasteful). Things here are indeed "BCBG," but in brighter colors than you might expect, judging from the samba-inspired and highly theatrical front windows. Come here for women's sportswear, evening wear (at least some of it in silk mousseline), costume jewelry, and accessories. The staff seems thoughtful and sensitive to its clientele. The place stocks European sizes 34 to 44, which translate roughly to U.S.-derived sizes 0 to 12. It's open Monday to Saturday 10am to 7:30pm. 412–414 rue St-Honoré, 8e. ✆ **01-40-20-16-50.** www.bcbg.com. Métro: Concorde or Madeleine.

Courrèges The house of Courrèges, founded in 1961, now maintains only one retail outlet in all of France: a sprawling, futuristic-looking showcase where the combined fashion statements of more than 40 years of fashion design are assembled into one blockbuster venue. The designs, once associated with moonwalks and the expanding space-age programs, are back and hot again. Even those white vinyl go-go boots and disco purses in silver metallic cloth are back in style, with special emphasis on neon tones of red and white, plastic, and a sense of whimsy and fun. André Courrèges, the founder, is in semiretirement: Coqueline, his wife, boldly forges ahead with ideas and venues for the 21st century. Open Monday to Saturday 10am to 7pm. 40 rue François Premier, 8e. (*) **01-53-67-30-00.** Métro: Alma-Marceau.

Jean-Paul Gaultier   Supporters of this high-camp, high-fashion mogul describe him as an avant-garde classicist without allegiance to any of the aesthetic restrictions of the bourgeoisie. Detractors call him a glorified punk rocker with a gimmicky allegiance to futurist models as interpreted by *Star Trek*. Whatever your opinion, it's always refreshing and insightful, especially for fashion buffs, to check out France's most iconoclastic designer. Gaultier's purses are available in luxurious textures of leather, silk, or satin and are directly inspired by street fashion as it evolved in the urban environments of Los Angeles and New York. There's a franchise branch of his store at 6 rue Vivienne, 2e (*) **01-42-86-05-05;** Métro: Bourse), but the company's main branch, and the site of its biggest inventories, is at avenue George V. Open Monday and Saturday 10:30am to 7pm; Tuesday to Friday 10am to 7pm. 44 av. George V, 8e. (*) **01-44-43-00-44.** Métro: George V.

DESIGNER BOUTIQUES & FASHION FLAGSHIPS

There are two primary fields of dreams in Paris when it comes to showcasing the international big names: rue du Faubourg St-Honoré and avenue Montaigne. Though the Left Bank is gaining in status, with such recent additions as Dior, Armani, and Vuitton, the heart of the international designer parade is on the Right Bank.

   Rue du Faubourg St-Honoré is so famous and fancy, it's simply known as "the Faubourg." It was the traditional miracle mile until recent years, when the really exclusive shops shunned it for the wider and even more deluxe avenue Montaigne at the other end of the arrondissement. (It's a long but pleasant walk from one fashion strip to the other.) **Avenue Montaigne** is filled with almost unspeakably fancy shops, but a few of them have affordable cafes (try Joseph at no. 14), and all have sales help who are usually cordial to well-dressed customers.

   The mix is quite international—from British (**Joseph**) to German (**Jil Sander**) to Italian (**Krizia**). **Chanel, Lacroix, Porthault, Ricci, Dior,** and **Ungaro** are a few of the big French names. Also check out some of the lesser-known creative powers, and don't miss a visit to **Caron.** Most of the designer shops sell men's and women's clothing. The Faubourg hosts other traditional favorites: **Hermès, Lanvin, Jaeger, Rykiel,** and the upstart **Façonnable,** which sells preppy men's clothing in the United States through a business deal with Nordstrom. Lanvin has its own men's shop **(Lanvin Homme),** with a cafe perfect for a light (and affordable) lunch.

Alain Figaret   Alain Figaret is one of France's foremost designers of men's shirts and women's blouses. Though this store has a broad range of fabrics, 100% cotton is its specialty. Also, check out the silk neckties in distinctively designed prints and the silk scarves for women. In recent years, inventories have been expanded to include pajamas, polo shirts, undergarments, and vests for both men and women. If you're comparison-shopping, Figaret and Charvet (see below) are half a block apart. Open Monday to Saturday 10am to 7:30pm. 21 rue de la Paix, 2e. ✆ **01-42-65-04-99.** www.alain-figaret.fr. Métro: Opéra.

Chanel ★   If you can't have the sun, the moon, and the stars, at least buy something with Coco Chanel's initials on it—either a serious fashion statement (drop-dead chic) or something fun and playful (tongue-in-chic). Karl Lagerfeld's designs come in all flavors and have added a subtle twist to Chanel's classicism. This store is adjacent to the Chanel couture house and behind the Ritz, where Mlle Chanel once lived. Check out the beautiful staircase of the *maison* before you shop the two-floor boutique—it's well worth a peek. Open Monday to Saturday 10am to 7pm. 29 rue Cambon, 1er. ✆ **01-42-86-28-00.** www.chanel.fr. Métro: Concorde or Tuileries.

Charvet   The duke of Windsor made Charvet famous, but Frenchmen of distinction have been buying their shirts here for years. The store sells ties, pocket squares, underwear, and pajamas as well, plus women's shirts, all custom-tailored or straight off the peg. Open Monday to Saturday 10:30am to 7pm. 28 place Vendôme, 1er. ✆ **01-42-60-30-75.** Métro: Opéra.

Christian Dior   This fashion house is set up like a small department store, selling men's, women's, and children's clothing, as well as affordable gift items, makeup, and perfume on the street level. For several years, cutting-edge Brit designer John Galliano has been in charge of the collections. Unlike some of the other big-name fashion houses, Dior is very approachable. Open Monday to Saturday 10am to 7pm. 30 av. Montaigne, 8e. ✆ **01-40-73-73-73.** www.dior.fr. Métro: Franklin-D-Roosevelt.

Givenchy ★   Hubert de Givenchy made fashion news around the world with his establishment, in 1962, of the company that continues its lonely role as a *couturier* (custom-made clothier) for elegant women. Today, from chic premises set one floor above street level, the art form of custom-made women's clothing continues, a tradition that has died out except for just a handful of other practitioners. Be forewarned that if you're interested in custom-made clothing, advance appointments are necessary, and prices are stratospheric. But on the street level of the same premises, you'll find the flagship of the Givenchy empire, specializing in women's ready-to-wear. Just across the street, you'll find the official outlet for Givenchy's women's accessories, including purses and bags, scarves, shoes, and whatever it takes to keep a stylish woman-of-a-certain-age looking fabulous. A short walk away is **Givenchy Hommes,** where upscale, ready-to-wear clothing is inventoried for men. Both outlets maintain the same hours: Monday to Saturday 10am to 7pm. 3 av. George V, 8e. ✆ **01-44-31-50-00.** www.givenchy.fr. Métro: George V. Givenchy Hommes: 56 rue François Premier, 8e. ✆ **01-40-76-07-27.** Métro: Alma-Marceau.

Hermès ★★   France's single most important status item is a scarf or tie from Hermès. Patterns on these illustrious scarves, retailing for about 240€, have recently included the galaxies, Africa, the sea, the sun, and horse racing and breeding. But the choices don't stop there—this large flagship store has beach towels and accessories, dinner plates, clothing for men and women, a large collection of Hermès fragrances, and even a saddle shop; a package of postcards is the least expensive item sold. Ask to see the private museum upstairs. Outside, note the horseman on the roof with his scarf-flag flying. Open Monday to Saturday 10:30am to 6:30pm. 24 rue du Faubourg St-Honoré, 8e. ✆ **01-40-17-46-00.** www. hermes.com. Métro: Concorde.

Louis Vuitton ★   Its luggage is among the most famous and prestigious in the world, a standard accessory aboard the first-class cabins of aircraft flying transatlantic and transpacific. Not content to cover the world's luggage with his initials, Vuitton has branched into leather goods, writing instruments, travel products, and publishing. Look for the traditional collection of leather, including Vuitton's monogrammed brown-on-brown bags in printed canvas, on the street level. The mezzanine showcases upscale pens, writing supplies, and stationery. The top floor carries the company's newest line: women's shoes and bags. Open Monday to Saturday 10am to 7pm. 6 place St-Germain-des-Prés, 6e. ✆ **01-45-49-62-32.** Métro: St-Germain-des-Prés.

Yves Saint Laurent   Long gone are the 1970s, when anything the late Yves Saint Laurent did was touted by the international press as a sign of his genius and the fashionable French dressed up in his luxurious versions of Cossack costumes, replete with boleros, riding boots, and copies of antique jewelry from the Russian steppes. With the shutdown in 2003 of his couture department and the worldwide availability of off-the-rack Saint Laurent franchises selling mass-market clothing around the world, there are now only four outlets in Paris that sell his clothing. Hours of all branches are Monday 11am to 7pm; Tuesday to Saturday 10:30am to 7pm. 6 place St-Sulpice, 6e. ✆ **01-43-29-43-00** and 01-43-26-84-40. www.ysl.com. Métro: St-Sulpice. Other locations at 32 (men) and 38 (women) rue du Faubourg St-Honoré, 8e. ✆ **01-53-05-80-80** and 01-42-65-74-59. Métro: Madeleine or Concorde.

DISCOUNT & RESALE

Anna Lowe ★   Adjacent to the Bristol Hotel, one of the most expensive addresses in Paris, is one of the city's premier boutiques for women who want to purchase heavily discounted clothing (new, with labels intact) from some of the world's best-known fashion designers. Expect discounts of up to 50% on last year's collections from such artists as Valentino, Thierry Mugler, John Galliano, Chanel, Versace, and many more. Your find might be what a model wore down the runway at last year's fashion show, excess inventories from factories that—for whatever reason—never got paid, or overstock from boutiques looking to make room for new inventories. Prices are reasonable, and the labels, in many cases, still retain their old magic and sense of chic. Open Monday to Saturday 10am to 7pm. 104 rue du Faubourg St-Honoré, 8e. ✆ **01-42-66-11-32.** www.annalowe.com. Métro: Miromesnil.

> ### Cutting Edge in the Marais
>
> With the world currencies as bad as they are, even some wealthy shoppers are skipping the Dior or Chanel boutiques and heading instead for the Haute-Marais section of Paris, which is cutting edge in fashion and design. To get you started on a shopping spree here, try such trendy shops as **Gaspard Yurkievich**, 243 rue St-Martin, 3e (✆ **01-42-77-42-46**; Métro: Temple). This shop is known for its flashy fashion statements, including silvery rock-'n'-roll boots.

Annexe des Créateurs ★★   Few stores in Paris receive as much publicity as this high-end, ultraglamorous discount outlet, where the collections of top-drawer designers are discounted by 30% to 70%. Charming owner and founder Edwige Meister inventories the only slightly worn but out-of-date women's wear of Stella McCartney, Versace, Moschino, Gaultier, Vivienne Westwood, and others. The staff insists that garments are in "perfect or near-perfect condition" and usually derive from terribly wealthy, obsessively stylish women who refuse to wear any garment more than once. It "isn't inconceivable," according to Mlle Meister, for a client to sell (on consignment) a garment in one of these two boutiques and then immediately pass through the interconnecting door to buy a secondhand but mint-condition garment in the boutique's counterpart a few steps away. Open Tuesday to Saturday 11am to 7pm. 19 rue Godot de Mauroy, 9e. ☎ **01-42-65-46-40.** www.annexedescreateurs.com. Métro: Madeleine.

Défilé des Marques   French TV stars often shop here, picking up Saint Laurent, Dior, Lacroix, Prada, Chanel, Versace, Hermès, and others at a fraction of the price. Yes, it sells discounted Hermès scarves as well. Low prices here derive from the owners' skill at picking up used clothing from last year's collections in good condition and, in some cases, retro-chic clothing from collections of many years ago, sometimes from estate sales. Open Tuesday to Saturday 11am to 8pm. 171 rue de Grenelles, 7e. ☎ **01-45-55-63-47.** Métro: Latour-Maubourg.

Limoges-Unic & Madronet   In two shops a 3-minute walk from each other, you'll find Limoges china and anything else you might need for the table—glass, crystal, and silver. It pays to drop into both stores, whose inventories vary according to the season and the whims of the buyers. Open Monday to Saturday 10am to 7pm. 34 and 58 rue de Paradis, 10e. ☎ **01-47-70-34-59.** Métro: Gare-de-l'est.

Réciproque   Forget about serious bargains, but celebrate what could be your only opportunity to own designer clothing of this caliber. Within a series of six storefronts side by side along the same avenue, you'll find used clothing from every major name in fashion, along with shoes, accessories, menswear, and wedding gifts. Everything has been worn, but some items were worn only on fashion runways or during photo shoots. Open Tuesday to Saturday 11am to 7pm. 89-101 rue de la Pompe, 16e. ☎ **01-47-04-30-28.** Métro: Pompe.

VINTAGE COUTURE

Didier Ludot   Fashion historians salivate when they're confronted with an inventory of vintage haute couture. In this frenetically stylish shop, albeit at prices that rival what you'd expect to pay for a serious antique, you'll find a selection of gowns and dresses created between 1900 and 1980 for designing women who looked *faaabulous* at Maxim's, at chic cocktail parties on the avenue Foch, in Deauville, or wherever. Open Monday to Saturday 11am to 7pm. 24 Galerie de Montpensier, in the arcades surrounding the courtyard of the Palais Royal, 1er. ☎ **01-42-96-06-56.** Métro: Palais-Royal.

Food: Chocolate, Honey, Pates & More

Christian Constant ★★   Opened in 1970, Christian Constant sells some of Paris's most delectable chocolates by the kilo. Each is a blend of ingredients from Ecuador, Colombia, or Venezuela, usually mingled with scents of spices and flowers such as orange blossoms, jasmine, the Asian blossom ylang-ylang, and vetiver and *verveine* (herbs usually used to brew tea). Open daily 9am to 8pm. 37 rue d'Assas, 6e. ☎ **01-53-63-15-15.** Métro: St-Placide.

Fauchon ★★★   At place de la Madeleine stands one of the city's most popular sights—not the church, but Fauchon, a hyper-upscale mega-delicatessen that thrives within a city famous for its finicky eaters. It's divided into three divisions that include an *épicerie* (for jams, crackers, pastas, and exotic canned goods), a

food MARKETS

Outdoor markets are plentiful in Paris. Some of the better known are the **Marché Buci** (see "Markets," later in this chapter); the **rue Mouffetard market,** open Tuesday to Sunday from 9:30am to 1pm and Tuesday to Saturday from 4 to 7pm (6e; Métro: Monge or Censier-Daubenton); and the **rue Montorgueil market,** behind the St-Eustache church, open Monday to Saturday from 9am to 7pm (1er; Métro: Les Halles). The trendiest market is **Marché Biologique,** along boulevard Raspail, a tree-lined stretch lying between rue de Rennes and rue du Cherche-Midi, 6e. It's open Sunday from 8:30am to 6:30pm (Métro: Montparnasse).

pâtissier (for breads, pastries, and chocolates), and a *traiteur* (for cheeses, terrines, pâtés, caviar, and fruits). Prices are steep, but the inventories—at least to serious foodies—are fascinating. At some of the counters, you'll indicate to attendants what you want from behind glass display cases and get an electronic ticket, which you'll carry to a *caisse* (cash register). Surrender your tickets, pay the tally, and then return to the counter to pick up your groceries. In other cases, you simply load up a shopping basket with whatever you want and pay for your purchases at a cash register, just as you would at any grocery store.

On the same premises, Fauchon has a restaurant, **Brasserie Fauchon,** and a tea salon, which showcases the pastry-making talents of its chefs. Among the many offerings is a *Paris-Brest*, a ring in the shape of a bicycle wheel that's loaded with pastry cream, almond praline, butter cream, and hazelnut paste capped with almonds. Open Monday to Saturday 9:30am to 7pm. 26 place de la Madeleine, 8e. ✆ **01-70-39-38-00.** www.fauchon.com. Métro: Madeleine.

Hédiard   This 1850 temple of *haute gastronomie* has been renovated, perhaps to woo visitors away from Fauchon. The decor is a series of salons filled with almost Disneyesque displays meant to give the store the look of an early-1900s spice emporium. Hédiard is rich in coffees, teas, jams, and spices. The decor changes with whatever holiday (Halloween, Easter, Bastille Day) or special promotion (the coffees of Brazil, the teas of Ceylon) is in effect at the time. Upstairs, you can eat at the Restaurant de l'Epicerie. Open Monday to Friday 8am to 10pm, Saturday noon to 10:30pm. 21 place de la Madeleine, 8e. ✆ **01-43-12-88-99.** www.hediard.fr. Métro: Madeleine.

Jadis et Gourmande   This chain of chocolatiers has a less lofty reputation than Christian Constant and more reasonable prices. It's best known for its alphabetical chocolate blocks, which allow you to spell out any message (well . . . almost), in any language. *"Merci"* comes prepackaged. Specialties that are even more delectable are *pralines fondants*, a mixture of praline, nuts, and chocolate that begins to melt the moment it hits your taste buds. Open Monday 1 to 7pm; Tuesday to Saturday 10am to 7pm. 27 rue Boissy d'Anglais, 8e. ✆ **01-42-65-23-23.** www.jadisetgourmande.fr. Métro: Madeleine. An even larger premises, with greater quantities of the same inventories, is at 88 bd. du Port-Royal, 5e. ✆ **01-43-26-17-75.** RER: Port-Royal. Métro: Gobelins.

Jean-Paul Hévin   One of the great chocolatiers of Paris, its owner has mastered the fusion of *chocolat* with *fromage* (cheese, of course). Sweet luscious

Marché Biologique.

chocolates with tart cheeses such as Camembert or Roquefort are infused to satisfy both the cheese fan and the chocolate lover's sweet tooth. Savory chocolates are also served without cheese. New offerings—unique in Paris—have caused this place to become one of the most acclaimed in Europe for chocolate devotees. Open Monday to Saturday 10am to 7:30pm. 231 rue St-Honoré, 1er. ☏ **01-55-35-35-96.** www.jphevin.com. Métro: Tuileries or Concorde.

Le Maison du Miel Running "The House of Honey" has been a family tradition since before World War I. The entire store is devoted to products made from honey: honey oil, honey soap, and various honeys to eat, including one made from heather. This store owes a tremendous debt to the busy bee. Monday to Saturday 9:30am to 7pm. 24 rue Vignon, 9e. ☏ **01-47-42-26-70.** www.lamaisondumiel.com. Métro: Madeleine, Havre-Caumartin, or Opéra.

Maison de la Truffe ★ 🎁 Cramped and convivial, the layout of this shop was modeled after a Parisian's fantasy of an affable, cluttered, old-fashioned butcher shop in Lyon. It's *the* source for foie gras, caviar, black and white truffles, and other high-end foodstuffs. Artfully assembled gift baskets are a house specialty. One corner is devoted to a restaurant where many (but not all) of the dishes contain the costly items (especially truffles) sold in the shop. Examples include noodles or risottos with truffles and caviar with all the fixings. The restaurant is open Monday to Saturday noon to 6pm and 7 to 11pm. The store is open Monday to Saturday 10am to 9pm. 19 place de la Madeleine, 8e. ☏ **01-42-65-53-22.** www.maison-de-la-truffe.com. Métro: Madeleine or Auber.

Pietrement-Lambret ★ Serious foodies are flocking to this tiny gourmet shop at Les Halles. It sells products from the Lot Valley, especially goose and duck offerings such as foie gras or confit. You can also purchase cassoulet here. Since many of these products are in tin cans, you can bring them through Customs. Open Monday to Friday 9am to 7pm; Saturday 9am to 1pm. 58 rue Jean-Jacques Rousseau, 1er. ☏ **01-42-33-30-50.** Métro: Les Halles.

Poilâne ★★ One of Paris's best-loved bakeries, Poilâne hasn't changed much since it opened in 1932. Come here to taste and admire the beautiful loaves of bread decorated with simple designs of leaves and flowers that'll make you yearn for an all-but-vanished Paris. Specialties include apple tarts, butter cookies, and a chewy sourdough loaf cooked in a wood-burning oven. Breads can be specially wrapped to stay fresh during your journey home. Cherche-Midi location open Monday to Saturday 7:15am to 8:15pm; Grenelle location Tuesday to Sunday 7:15am to 8:15pm. 8 rue du Cherche-Midi, 6e. ☏ **01-45-48-42-59.** www.poilane.fr. Métro: St-Sulpice. Also: 49 bd. de Grenelle, 15e. ☏ **01-45-79-11-49.** Métro: Dupleix.

Home Accessories

La Quincaillerie ★ This is one of those shopping oddities that seem to exist only in Paris. The owners specialize in doorknobs for front doors, windows, and cupboards. There are knobs for almost any piece of furniture, and dozens of accessories, often by top designers such as Philippe Starck. The wares in their stores at no. 3 and no. 4 are modern and designed by some of Europe's top names, including the Italian legend Gio Ponti or Portuguese architect Alvaro Siza. Open Monday to Friday 10am to 1pm and 2 to 7pm; Saturday 10am to 1pm and 2 to 6pm. 3-4 bd. St-Germain-des-Prés, 5e. ✆ **01-46-33-66-71.** www.laquincaillerie. com. Métro: St-Germain-des-Prés.

Jewelry

Bijoux Blues ★ 🎁   This Marais boutique offers unique jewelry handmade in Paris with a variety of different materials, including Austrian and bohemian crystals, natural and semiprecious stones, pearls, coral, and mother-of-pearl. Custom requests are welcomed for individually designed pieces. The store offers jewelry at what the staff calls "atelier prices." Open Tuesday to Saturday noon to 7pm, Sunday 2 to 6pm. 30 rue St-Paul, 4e. ✆ **01-48-04-00-64.** www.bijouxblues.com. Métro: St. Paul.

Bijoux Burma   If you can't afford any of the spectacular and expensive bijoux at the city's world-famous jewelers, come here to console yourself with some of the best fakes anywhere. This quality costume jewelry is the secret weapon of many a Parisian woman. Open Monday to Saturday 10:30am to 6:45pm. 50 rue François-Premier, 8e. ✆ **01-47-23-79-93.** www.bijouxburma.com. Métro: Franklin-D-Roosevelt.

Cartier ★★   One of the most famous jewelers in the world, Cartier has prohibitive prices to match its glamorous image. Go to gawk, and if your pockets are deep enough, pick up an expensive trinket. Open Monday to Saturday 10:30am to 7pm. 23 place Vendôme, 1er. ✆ **01-44-55-32-20.** www.cartier.com. Métro: Opéra or Tuileries.

Van Cleef & Arpels ★★   Years ago, Van Cleef's designers came up with an intricate technique that remains a vital part of its allure—the invisible setting, wherein a band of sparkling gemstones, each cut to interlock with its neighbor, creates an uninterrupted flash of brilliance. Come browse with the rich and famous. Open Monday to Friday 10:30am to 7pm; Saturday 11am to 7pm. 22 place Vendôme, 1er. ✆ **01-53-45-35-50.** www.vancleef-arpels.com. Métro: Opéra or Tuileries.

Kitchenware

Dehillerin   Established in 1820, Dehillerin is Paris's most famous cookware shop, in the "kitchen corridor" alongside A. Simon and several other kitchenware stores. The shop has more of a professional feel to it than beginner-friendly A. Simon, but don't be intimidated. Equipped with the right tools from Dehillerin, you, too, can learn to cook like a master chef. Open Monday 9am to 12:30pm and 2 to 6pm; Tuesday to Saturday 9am to 6pm. 18-20 rue Coquillière, 1er. ✆ **01-42-36-53-13.** www.e-dehillerin.fr. Métro: Les Halles.

Leather goods

Morabito   This glamorous leather purveyor was originally established by an Italian entrepreneur on the place Vendôme in 1905. In the 1990s, it was partially acquired by an organization in Tokyo. Today, from a site on the glamorous rue François-Premier, it sells chicer-than-thou handbags. Morabito also has suitcases—some of the best in Paris—for men and women. Open Monday to

Saturday 10am to 7pm. 259 rue St-Honoré, 1er. ℂ **01-53-23-90-40.** www.morabitoparis. com. Métro: George V.

Lingerie

Cadolle   Herminie Cadolle invented the brassiere in 1889. Today, her family manages the store she founded, and they still make specialty brassieres for the Crazy Horse Saloon. This is the place to go if you want made-to-order items or are hard to fit. Open Monday to Saturday 9:30am to 1pm and 2 to 6:30pm. 4 rue Cambon, 1er. ℂ **01-42-60-94-22.** www.cadolle.com. Métro: Concorde.

Nikita   This is the discount sales outlet for all the big names in women's lingerie, including Bolero, Lise Charmel, Lejaby, Simone Pérèle, and Aubade. Most of the lingerie sold here is 20% to 30% less than its counterparts in Right Bank boutiques. Open Monday to Saturday 9:30am to 7:30pm; Sunday 9:30am to 1:30pm. 25 rue Lévis, 17e. ℂ **01-47-66-72-41.** Métro: Villiers.

Sabbia Rosa   Everything here is filmy, silky, and sexy. Look for undergarments (slips, brassieres, and panties) and the kind of negligees that might have been favored by Brigitte Bardot in *And God Created Woman*. Even Madonna has been spotted shopping for panties here. Open Monday to Saturday 10am to 7pm. 73 rue des Sts-Pères, 6e. ℂ **01-45-48-88-37.** Métro: Sèvres-Babylone or St-Germain.

Malls

Carrousel du Louvre   If you want to combine an accessible location, a fun food court, boutiques, and plenty of museum gift shops with a touch of culture, don't miss the Carrousel. Always mobbed, this is one of the few venues allowed to open on Sunday. There's a Virgin Megastore, a branch of The Body Shop, and several other emporiums for conspicuous consumption. Check out Diane Claire for the fanciest souvenirs you've ever seen. Open Tuesday to Sunday 10am to 8pm. 99 rue de Rivoli, 1er. ℂ **01-43-16-47-10.** www.carrouseldulouvre.com. Métro: Palais-Royal or Musée du Louvre.

Les Trois Quartiers   Named after the junction of the three neighborhoods (Madeleine, Opéra, and Concorde) where it sits, this is a mall of at least 13 upscale boutiques specializing in clothing, perfume, cosmetics for men and women, and household accessories. The largest is Madelios, a menswear store that stocks more than 50 brand names, including Ralph Lauren, Hugo Boss, and Burberry. Open Monday to Saturday 10am to 5pm. 23 bd. de la Madeleine, 1er. ℂ **01-42-97-80-00.** Métro: Madeleine.

 A Discount Shopping Village Outside Paris

Just 35 minutes from the center of Paris, **La Vallée Village, 3 Cours de la Garonne, 77700 Serris** (ℂ **01-60-42-35-00;** www.lavalleevillage.com), is home to some 75 boutiques in this chic Outlet Shopping Village. Sometimes brand names such as Lacoste or Waterford are sold at 70% less than retail prices in the center of Paris—just ask such patrons as Sir Mick Jagger, Victoria Beckham (Posh Spice), or even the Duchess of York. From the center of Paris you can take RER to the Val d'Europe station; by car, follow the A4 motorway out of Paris to exit 12.1 (signposted from there).

Porte de Clignancourt market.

Montparnasse Shopping Centre

This shopping center is sort of a quick-fix mini mall in a business center and hotel (Le Méridien) complex, with a small branch of Galeries Lafayette and some inexpensive boutiques. Visiting it is really worthwhile only if you also take a trip across the street to Inno, with its deluxe supermarket in the basement. Open Monday to Saturday 10am to 7pm. Btw. rue de l'Arrivée and 22 rue du Départ, 14e. No phone. Métro: Montparnasse-Bienvenüe.

Markets

Marché aux Fleurs Artists and photographers love to capture the Flower Market on canvas or film. The stalls are ablaze with color, and each is a showcase of flowers, most of which escaped the perfume factories of Grasse on the French Riviera. The Flower Market is along the Seine, behind the Tribunal de Commerce. On Sunday, it becomes the **Marché aux Oiseaux (Bird Market).** Open daily 8:30am to 4pm. Place Louis-Lépine, Ile de la Cité, 4e. No phone. Métro: Cité.

Marché aux Puces de la Porte de Vanves This weekend event sprawls along two streets and is the best flea market in Paris—dealers swear by it. There's little in terms of formal antiques and furniture. It's better for old linens, used Hermès scarves, toys, ephemera, costume jewelry, perfume bottles, and bad art. Asking prices tend to be high, as dealers prefer to sell to nontourists. On Sunday, there's a food market one street over. Open Tuesday to Sunday 7am to 5pm. Av. Georges-Lafenestre, 14e. No phone. Métro: Porte de Vanves.

Marché aux Puces St-Ouen de Clignancourt ★ Paris's most famous flea market is a grouping of more than a dozen flea markets—a complex of 2,500 to 3,000 open stalls and shops on the northern fringe of the city, selling everything from antiques to junk, from new to vintage clothing. The market begins with stalls of cheap clothing along avenue de la Porte de Clignancourt. As you proceed, various streets will tempt you. Hold on until you get to rue des Rosiers; then turn left. Vendors start bringing out their offerings around 9am Saturday to Monday and take them in around 6pm. Hours are a tad flexible, depending on weather and crowds. Monday is traditionally the best day for bargain seekers—attendance is smaller and merchants demonstrate a greater desire to sell.

First-timers always want to know two things: "Will I get any real bargains?" and "Will I get fleeced?" It's all relative. Obviously, dealers (who often have a prearrangement to have items held for them) have already skimmed the best buys. And it's true that the same merchandise displayed here will sell for less in the provinces. But for the visitor who has only a few days to spend in Paris—and only half a day for shopping—the flea market is worth the experience.

Dress casually and show your knowledge if you're a collector. Most dealers are serious and get into the spirit of things only if you speak French or make it clear you know what you're doing. The longer you stay, the more you chat and show your respect for the goods, the more you'll have for negotiating. Most of the markets have restroom facilities; some have central offices to arrange shipping.

Cafes, pizza joints, and even a few restaurants are scattered around. Almost without exception, they are bad. The exception is **Le Soleil,** 109 av. Michelet, St-Ouen (© **01-40-10-08-08;** www.restaurantlesoleil.com), which was converted from a cafe into a family run restaurant by Louis-Jacques Vannucci. Catering to flea-market shoppers, the restaurant looks as if it were flea market–decorated as well. The French food is excellent, especially the sautéed chicken in a light cream sauce, the green-bean salad tossed with tomato cubes, and the fresh Norman cod and the tiny mussels cooked in a rich broth. Le Soleil is open daily for lunch and Thursday to Saturday for dinner. *Note:* Beware of pickpockets and teenage troublemakers while shopping the market. Open Saturday to Monday 9am to 7pm. Av. de la Porte de Clignancourt, 18e. No phone. www.marchesauxpuces.fr. Métro: Porte de Clignancourt (turn left, cross bd. Ney, and then walk north on av. de la Porte Montmartre). Métro: Porte de Clignancourt.

Marché Ave du Président Wilson Even if you don't buy anything, browsing this market is a city attraction. Parisians flock to this open-air market to purchase some of the most exotic kinds of vegetables sold in the city; everything from purple cauliflower to sunflower yellow zucchini. One stallmaster even sells a type of heirloom pea, "Kelvedon Marvel," that was a particular favorite of Louis XIV, who preferred eating them to bedding one of his mistresses. A major attraction here is a stall operated by **Joel Thiebault** (© **01-44-24-05-77;** www.joel thiebault.fr). Serious foodies will love his vegetables. Open Wednesday and Saturday from 7am to 2:30pm. On av. du Président Wilson btw. Place d'Iena and Rue Debrousse, 16e. No phone. Métro: Iena or Alma-Marceau.

Marché Buci This traditional French food market is set up at the intersection of two streets and is only a block long, but what a block it is! Seasonal fruits and vegetables cover tabletops, and chickens spin on the rotisserie. One stall is entirely devoted to big bouquets of fresh flowers. Monday mornings are light; Sunday is best. Open daily 9am to 7pm. Rue de Buci, 6e. No phone. Métro: St-Germain-des-Prés or Mabillon.

Music

FNAC This is a large chain of music and book stores known for their wide selection and discounted prices. Eight branches are in Paris, with the largest being at 136 rue de Rennes, Montparnasse. Other locations include rue St-Lazare, avenue des Champs-Elysées, Forum des Halles, avenue des Ternes, and avenue d'Italie. All are open Monday to Saturday 10am to 7:30pm except Champs-Elysées, which is open daily noon to midnight. 136 rue de Rennes, 6e. © **08-25-02-00-20.** www.fnac.com. Métro: St-Placide.

Virgin Megastore Paris has three branches of Europe's biggest, most widely publicized CD and record store. The Champs-Elysées branch is the city's largest music store; a bookstore and cafe are downstairs. The store's opening in a landmark building helped to rejuvenate the avenue. You'll find a Virgin Megastore at each airport. Open Monday to Saturday 10am to midnight; Sunday noon to midnight (other locations: Carrousel du Louvre, Sun–Tues 10am–8pm; Wed–Saturday 10am–10pm; Gare Montparnasse, Mon–Thurs 7am–8pm; Fri 7am–9pm;

THE scent OF A PARISIAN

If there's one reason international shoppers come to Paris, it's cosmetics—after all, the City of Light is the world capital of fragrances and beauty supplies. These are a few of our favorite perfume and makeup shops:

Although you can buy **Parfums Caron** scents in any duty-free or discount *parfumerie*, it's worth visiting the source of some of the world's most famous perfumes. The tiny shop is at 34 av. Montaigne, 8e (*(C)* **01-47-23-40-82;** www. parfumscaron.com; Métro: Franklin-D-Roosevelt), boasting old-fashioned glass beakers filled with fragrances and a hint of yesteryear. Fleur de Rocaille, a Caron scent, was the featured perfume in the movie *Scent of a Woman*. Store hours are Monday to Saturday from 10am to 6:30pm.

Although there are other branches, and you can test Goutal bathroom amenities at many upscale hotels, the sidewalk mosaic tile and the unique scents make the **Annick Goutal,** at 14 rue Castiglione, 1er (*(C)* **01-42-60-52-82;** www. annickgoutal.com; Métro: Concorde), worth stopping by. Try Eau d'Hadrien for

a unisex splash of citrus and summer. Store hours are Monday to Saturday from 10am to 7pm.

Shiseido, the world's fourth-largest maker of cosmetics and skincare goods, has become more prominent thanks to the efforts of the **Salons du Palais Royal Shiseido,** 142 Galerie de Valois, Palais Royal, 1er (*(C)* **01-49-27-09-09;** www. salons-shiseido.com; Métro: Palais-Royal). In addition to an awesome array of skincare products and cosmetics, it stocks more than 20 exclusive unisex fragrances created by the company's creative director, Serge Lutens, including one of its latest, Les Sarrasins, a jasmine-based scent which was introduced in September 2007. Don't be afraid to wander in and ask for some scent strips. Open Monday to Saturday from 10am to 7pm.

Sat 7am–8pm). 52-60 av. des Champs-Elysées, 8e. *(C)* **01-49-53-50-00.** Métro: Franklin-D-Roosevelt.

Perfume & Makeup (Discount)

Catherine 👜 This family owned shop sells an impressive stock of all the big-name perfumes and cosmetics at discounts of 20% to 25%. In addition, its paperwork is usually extremely well organized, allowing refunds of the value-added tax (VAT) to be cleared quickly through Customs. Many of the staff speak English. Open Tuesday to Saturday 9am to 7pm; Monday 10:30am to 7pm. 7 rue Castiglione, 1er. *(C)* **01-42-61-02-89.** Métro: Concorde.

The Different Company ★ 👜 Many fashionistas are deserting the fabled houses of scent and heading for this corner of counterculture chic on a hot new shopping street that's midway between place de la Bastille and the Hôtel de Ville. The perfume shop is run by the father-daughter team of Jean-Claude and Céline Ellana. Scents which include Osmanthus, Sel de Vétiver, and Rose Poivrée, have been called "fragrances for the 21st century." Tuesday to Saturday noon to between 7:30 and 8pm. 10 rue Ferdinand Duval, 4e. *(C)* **01-47-83-65-88.** www.the differentcompany.com. Métro: Saint-Paul.

Editions de Parfums Fréderic Malle ★ 🎁   If the big brand-name perfumes that are sold at every duty-free airport in Europe bore you, consider a visit to this boutique where brands are more personalized. This is the only outlet of an organization founded in 2000 by master perfumer Fréderic Malle, whose nose is as sensitive as that of any wine expert. Each of the scents sold here comes in a standardized bottle in either a 50ml size or a 100ml size. Scents are designed for either men or women; come in varying intensities of floral, spice, or Oriental motifs; and carry names that include Iris Poudre, Noir Epices, En Passant, and one of the bestsellers, Musc Ravageur. There's a lot of elegant chichi about this place (the paneled decor was designed by superdecorators Andrée Putnam and Olivier Lempereur), but the scents inside are often lovely. One of the things we like best about the place is the display of framed photographic portraits of each of the men and women who created the original scents sold within the boutique. Open Monday 1pm to 7pm; Tuesday to Saturday 11am to 7pm. 37 rue de Grenelle, 7e. ✆ **01-42-22-76-40.** www.editionsdeparfums.com. Métro: Rue du Bac.

Maki   You get some of the best deals in cosmetics and makeup here. In fact, it's the place where French actors and many models come for quality makeup products at discounted prices. The shop lies in the middle of a theater area. The staff often advises you about makeup. Open Tuesday to Saturday 11am to 1pm and 2:30 to 6:30pm. 9 rue Mansart, 9e. ✆ **01-42-81-33-76.** Métro: Blanche.

Souvenirs & Gifts

Au Nom de la Rose   Tasteful and frilly, this flower shop and gift boutique sells many of the floral arrangements that decorate local hotels and restaurants, as well as gift objects that are scented, emblazoned, or permeated with "the spirit or scent of the rose." Expect an overwhelming mass of flowers, many of them temporarily resting in glassed-in coolers, as well as rose-hip jams and marmalades, scented soaps and candles, rosewater-based perfumes, and decorative items for the home and kitchen. A "refinement" (their words) that you might consider either hopelessly decadent or whimsical and charming, depending on your point of view, is a perfume that's specifically designed to enhance the allure of your bedsheets. Open Monday to Saturday 9am to 9pm; Sunday 9am to 2pm. 46 rue du Bac, 7e. ✆ **01-42-22-22-12.** www.aunomdelarose.fr. Métro: Rue du Bac.

La Tuile à Loup   This emporium has been selling authentic examples of all-French handcrafts since around 1975, making a name through its concentration of hand-produced woven baskets, cutlery, and woodcarvings. Especially appealing are the hand-painted crockery and charming stoneware from such traditional manufacturers as Quimper and Malicorne and from small-scale producers in the Savoie Alps and Alsace. Open Monday 1 to 7pm; Tuesday to Saturday 10:30am to 7pm. 35 rue Daubenton, 5e. ✆ **01-47-07-28-90.** www.latuilealoup.com. Métro: Censier-Daubenton.

Stationery

Cassegrain ★   Nothing says elegance more than thick French stationery and notecards. Cassegrain, originally an engraver in 1919, offers beautifully engraved stationery, most often in traditional patterns, and business cards engraved to order. Several other items for the desk, many suitable for gifts, are for sale as well; there are even affordable pencils and pens, leather wallets, and small desktop

A shop such as **La Plaque Emaillées et Gravée Jacquin** stands in sharp contrast to the mass merchandise in most department stores. Established in 1908, when the Art Nouveau craze swept Paris, the outfit has done a respectable business promoting turn-of-the-20th-century Parisian charm ever since. Its specialty is the custom manufacture of cast-iron plaques, enameled and baked, commemorating virtually any event, person (including yourself), or piece of real estate that appeals to you. Phillippe Jacquin, the owner, offers a variety of shapes, sizes, and colors for the finished product. It will take 3 to 4 weeks for your plaque to be manufactured, after which it can be shipped. Shipping can be expensive and, in our opinion (because of the cast-iron nature of what's in the package), complicated. Much smaller plaques, some ready-made, are also available. Open Monday to Friday 9am to 1pm and 2 to 6pm. It's located at 18 bd. des Filles-du-Calvaire, 11e (𝒞 01-47-00-50-95; www.la-plaque-emaillee.com; Métro: St-Sébastien).

accessories. Open Monday to Saturday 10am to 7pm. 422 rue St-Honoré, 8e. 𝒞 **01-42-60-20-08.** www.cassegrain.fr. Métro: Concorde.

Tableware

Conran Shop This shop might remind you of an outpost of the British Empire, valiantly imposing Brit aesthetics and standards on the French-speaking world. Inside, you'll find articles for the kitchen and dining room; glass and crystal vases; fountain pens and stationery; reading material and postcards; and even a selection of chocolates, teas, and coffees to help warm up a foggy English day. Open Monday to Friday 10am to 7pm; Saturday 10am to 7:30pm. 117 rue du Bac, 7e. 𝒞 **01-42-84-10-01.** www.conranshop.fr. Métro: Sèvres-Babylone.

Geneviève Lethu This Provençal designer has shops all over France, with 19 others in and around Paris, all selling her clever and colorful Pottery Barn–meets–French Mediterranean tableware. The newer designs stress influences from India, South America, and Africa as well. Energy, style, and verve are rampant, and the prices are moderate. Open Monday to Saturday 10:15am to 7pm. 95 rue de Rennes, 6e. 𝒞 **01-45-44-40-35.** www.genevievelethu.com. Métro: St-Sulpice.

Wines

Lavinia ★ This is the largest wine-and-spirits store in Europe, opened in 2002 to great acclaim in Paris. Spread over three floors near place de la Madeleine, it stocks more than 3,000 brands of French wine and spirits, along with more than 2,000 brands from other parts of the world. A simple lunch-only restaurant is on-site, as well as a tasting bar. Wine sales here are big business and reflective of France's marketing ideas that regard wine as its favorite beverage. This is the only place in Paris where you can buy a good bottle of South Dakota wine. But who would want to? Open Monday to Saturday 10am to 8pm. 3-5 bd. de la Madeleine, 1er. 𝒞 **01-42-97-20-20.** www.lavinia.fr. Métro: Madeleine.

Les Caves Taillevent This is a temple to the art of making fine French wine. Associated with one of Paris's grandest restaurants, Taillevent, it occupies the street level and cellar of an antique building. Stored here are more than 25,000 bottles of wine, with easy access in nearby warehouses to almost a million more. Open Monday 2 to 7:30pm; Tuesday to Saturday 9am to 7:30pm. 199 rue du Faubourg St-Honoré, 8e. ✆ **01-45-61-14-09.** www.taillevent.com. Métro: Charles-de-Gaulle–Etoile.

Nicolas 🎁 This is the flagship store of this chain of wine boutiques, and as such, its vintages are likely to be more esoteric and rare than what you'd find in any of the other 400 or so members of its chain. Scattered over three floors of a large space near La Madeleine are fairly priced bottles of mainstream wines such as Alsatian Gewürztraminers and Collioures from Languedoc-Roussillon. Nicolas also stocks some exceptionally rare vintages, such as a Romanée-Conti from Burgundy. Open Monday to Saturday 9:30am to 8pm. 31 place de la Madeleine, 8e. ✆ **01-42-68-00-16.** www.nicolas.com. Métro: Madeleine.

PARIS AFTER DARK

10

W hen darkness falls, the City of Light lives up to its name—the monuments and bridges are illuminated, and the glow of old-fashioned and modern street lamps, the blaze of sidewalk-cafe windows, and the glare of neon signs flood the avenues and boulevards. Parisians start the serious part of their evenings as most western tourists stretch, yawn, and announce it's time for bed. After the workday is over, most people go to a cafe to meet with friends over a drink and perhaps a meal (see "The Top Cafes," in chapter 6); then, they may head home or proceed to a restaurant or the theater; and much later, they may show up at a bar or a dance club.

In this chapter, we describe Paris's after-dark diversions—from attending a Molière play at the Comédie-Française to catching a cancan show at the Moulin Rouge to sipping a Sidecar at Harry's New York Bar to partying at Le Queen with all the boys.

THE PERFORMING ARTS

LISTINGS Announcements of shows, concerts, and operas are plastered on kiosks all over town. You'll find listings in the weekly ***Pariscope,*** an entertainment guide with a section in English, or the English-language bimonthly ***Boulevard.*** Performances start later in Paris than in London or New York—from 8 to 9pm—and Parisians tend to dine after the theater. You may not want to do the same, because many of the less-expensive restaurants close as early as 9pm.

TICKETS Paris has many ticket agencies, most near the Right Bank hotels. *Avoid them if possible.* You can buy the cheapest tickets at the box office of the theater or at discount agencies that sell tickets at discounts of up to 50%. One is the **Kiosque Théâtre,** 15 place de la Madeleine, 8e (no phone; www.kiosquetheatre.com; Métro: Madeleine), offering leftover tickets for about half-price on the day of performance. Tickets for evening performances are sold Tuesday to Saturday from 12:30 to 8pm, for matinees, Sunday 12:30 to 4pm. Other branches are in the basement of the Châtelet–Les Halles Métro station and in front of Gare Montparnasse.

Students with ID can often get last-minute tickets by applying at the box office an hour before curtain time.

The easiest (and most expensive) way to get tickets, especially if you're staying in a first-class or deluxe hotel, is to ask your concierge to arrange for

PREVIOUS PAGE: **Parisian musician.**

them. A service fee is added, but it's a lot easier if you don't want to waste precious hours in Paris trying to secure often hard-to-get tickets.

Tickets for festivals, concerts, and the theater are easy to obtain through one of these locations of the **FNAC** record store chain: 136 rue de Rennes, 6e (☎ **08-25-02-08-02;** Métro: St. Placide); or 1–7 rue Pierre-Lescot, in the Forum des Halles, 1er (☎ **08-25-02-00-20;** Métro: Châtelet–Les Halles).

For information and tickets to just about any show in Paris (also Dijon, Lyon, and Nice), **Keith Prowse** has a New York office if you'd like to make arrangements before you go. It's at 234 W. 44th St., Ste. 1000, New York, NY 10036 (☎ **800/669-8687;** www.keithprowse.com). The Paris office is at 7 rue de Clichy, 9e (☎ **01-42-81-88-98;** Métro: Place de Clichy). They will mail tickets to your home, fax confirmation, or leave tickets at the box office in Paris. There's a markup of 20% (excluding opera and ballet) over box-office price, plus a U.S. handling charge of $8. Hotel and theater packages are also available.

Theater

Comédie-Française ★★ Those with even a modest understanding of French can delight in a sparkling production of Molière at this national theater, established to keep the classics alive and to promote important contemporary authors. Nowhere else will you see the works of Molière and Racine so beautifully staged. The box office is open daily from 11am to 6pm, but the hall is dark from mid-July to early September. In 1993 a Left Bank annex was launched, the **Comédie Française-Théâtre du Vieux-Colombier,** 21 rue du Vieux-Colombier, 4e (☎ **01-44-39-87-00**). Though its repertoire varies, it's known for presenting serious French dramas. Discounts are available if you reserve in advance. 2 rue de Richelieu, 1er. ☎ **08-25-10-16-80.** www.comedie-francaise.fr. Tickets 28€ adults, 11€ 26 and younger. Métro: Palais-Royal or Musée du Louvre.

Opera, Dance & Classical Concerts

Cité de la Musique ★★★ This testimony to the power of music has been the most widely applauded, the least criticized, and the most innovative of the late François Mitterrand's *grands projets.* At the city's northeastern edge in what used to be a run-down neighborhood, this $120-million stone-and-glass structure incorporates a network of concert halls, a library and research center for the study of all kinds of music, and a museum (see "Specialty Museums," in chapter 7). The complex hosts a rich variety of concerts, ranging from Renaissance music through 19th- and 20th-century works, including jazz and traditional music from nations around the world. 221 av. Jean-Jaurès, 19e. ☎ **01-44-84-45-00,** or 01-44-84-44-84 for tickets. www.cite-musique.fr. Tickets 20€–39€ for 4:30 and 8pm concerts. Métro: Porte de Pantin.

Opéra Bastille ★★★ This controversial building—it has been called a "beached whale"—was designed by Canadian architect Carlos Ott, with curtains by Japanese designer Issey Miyake. Since the house's grand opening in July 1989, the Opéra National de Paris has presented works such as Mozart's *Marriage of Figaro* and Tchaikovsky's *Queen of Spades.* The main hall is the largest of any French opera house, with 2,700 seats, but music critics have lambasted the acoustics. The building contains two other concert halls, including an intimate

A soirée at Opéra Garnier.

250-seat room that usually hosts chamber music. Both traditional opera performances and symphony concerts are presented here, as well as both classical and modern dance. Several concerts are given for free in honor of certain French holidays. Write ahead for tickets. 2 place de la Bastille, 4e. ☎ 08-92-89-90-90 or 01-40-01-17-89. www.operadeparis.fr. Tickets 10€–175€ opera, 12€–80€ dance. Métro: Bastille.

Opéra Comique This is a charming venue for light opera, on a smaller scale than Paris's major opera houses. Built in the late 1890s in an ornate style that might remind you of the Opéra Garnier, it's the site of small productions of operas such as *Carmen, Don Giovanni, Tosca,* and *Palleas & Melisande.* There are no performances from mid-July to late August. The box office, however, is open year-round Monday to Saturday 11am to 7pm; Sunday 11am to 5pm. 5 rue Favart, 2e. ☎ 01-42-44-45-40. www.opera-comique.com. Tickets 5€–115€. Métro: Richelieu-Drouot.

Opéra Garnier ★★★ Once the haunt of the Phantom, this is the premier venue for dance and once again for opera. Charles Garnier designed this 1875 rococo wonder during the heyday of the French Empire; the facade is adorned with marble and sculpture, including *The Dance* by Carpeaux. Following a year-long renovation, during which the Chagall ceiling was cleaned and air-conditioning was added, the facade gleams as it did for Napoleon III. You can see the original gilded busts and statues, the rainbow-hued marble pillars, and the mosaics. The Opéra Garnier combines ballet and opera, and provides one of the most elegant evenings you can spend in the City of Light. Because of the competition from the Opéra Bastille, the Garnier has made great efforts to present more up-to-date dance works such as choreography by Twyla Tharp, Agnes de Mille, and

The Music of Angels

Some of the most moving music in Paris echoes through its churches, with sounds that can take you back to the Middle Ages. At **Eglise de St-Eustache,** 2 impasse St-Eustache, 1er (☎ **01-42-36-31-05;** www.saint-eustache.org; Métro: Rambuteau), High Mass with the organ playing and the choir singing is at 11am on Sunday. In summer, concerts are played on the organ, marking the church's role in holding the premiere of Berlioz's *Te Deum* and Liszt's *Messiah.* Tickets to these special concerts sell for 12€ to 40€. The church is open daily 9:30am to 7pm.

The **American Church in Paris,** 65 quai d'Orsay, 7e (☎ 01-40-62-05-00; www.acparis.org; Métro: Invalides or Alma-Marceau), sponsors concerts from September to June on Sundays at 5pm. You can also attend free concerts at **Eglise St-Merry,** 76 rue Verrerie, 4e (☎ 01-42-71-93-93; Métro: Hôtel-de-Ville). These performances are staged with variable musicians based on their availability, from September to July on Saturdays at 8:30pm, and again on Sundays at 4pm.

White Nights (Nuit Blanche) in Paris

Beginning in Paris in 2002, *Nuit Blanche,* a frenetic all-night multivenue cultural bash, was launched. Since then, the concept has swept such European capitals as Madrid and Rome. Dates for this event vary from year to year. In 2010, it occurs on October 2. Check its website for late-changing information: www. nuitblanche.paris.fr or call ✆ **01-42-76-65-26.**

What to expect: The offerings seem endless, everything from street entertainers such as circus acts to jazz jam sessions. Of course, there are modern art shows, theatrical presentations, and music of every genre, even old-fashioned French ballads. "Nuit Blanche is the greatest party ever thrown in the streets of Paris," said Pierre Monosiet. "We dance the night away until dawn's early light."

White Night events are free and take place, often spontaneously, throughout Paris—not just in the historic core. As many as two million people might take to the streets in the next White Night extravaganza. Many museums and art galleries will remain open around the clock.

There might even be all-night dancing in one of the giant terminals of a Paris rail station. The axis of events will follow the course of the no. 14 Métro (subway) line from the Batignolles sector in northwest Paris, cutting through the heart of the city to the fringes of Les Olympiades in the southwest.

George Balanchine. The box office is open Monday to Saturday from 10:30am to 6:30pm. Place de l'Opéra, 9e. ✆ **08-92-89-90-90** or 01-40-01-18-50. www.operadeparis. fr. Tickets 8€–160€ opera, 12€–80€ dance. Métro: Opéra.

Salle Pleyel ★★★   New York has its Carnegie Hall but for years Paris lacked a permanent home for its orchestra. That is, until 2006 when the restored Salle Pleyel opened once again. Built in 1927 by the piano-making firm of the same name, Pleyel was the world's first concert hall designed exclusively for a symphony orchestra. Ravel, Debussy, and Stravinsky performed their masterpieces here, only to see the hall devastated by fire less than 9 months after its opening. The original sound quality was never recovered because of an economic downturn. In 1998, real estate developer Hubert Martigny purchased the concert hall and pumped $38 million into it, restoring the Art Deco spirit of the original and also refining the acoustics it once knew. Nearly 500 seats were removed to make those that remained more comfortable. The Orchestre Philarmonique de Radio France and the Orchestre de Paris now have a home worthy of their reputations, and the London Symphony Orchestra makes Pleyel its venue in Paris. The box office is open Monday to Friday 10am to 6pm. 252 rue du Faubourg-St-Honoré, 8e. ✆ **01-42-56-13-13.** www.sallepleyel.fr. Tickets 10€–160€. Métro: Miromesnil.

Théâtre des Champs-Elysées   This Art Deco theater, attracting the haute couture crowd, hosts both national and international orchestras (such as the Vienna Philharmonic) as well as opera and ballet. The box office is open Monday to Saturday from 1 to 7pm. There are no performances in August. 15 av. Montaigne, 8e. ☎ **01-49-52-50-50** for box office. www.theatrechampselysees.fr. Tickets 8€–160€. Métro: Alma-Marceau.

Théâtre National de Chaillot   Part of the architectural complex facing the Eiffel Tower, this is one of the city's largest concert halls, hosting cultural events that are announced on billboards in front. Sometimes (rarely) dance is staged here, or you might see a brilliantly performed play by Marguerite Duras. The box office is open Monday to Saturday from 11am to 7pm, Sunday 1 to 5pm. 1 place du Trocadéro, 16e. ☎ **01-53-65-30-00.** www.theatre-chaillot.fr. Tickets 17€–35€ adults, 15€–21€ seniors 60 and older, 9€–18€ 24 and younger. Métro: Trocadéro.

THE CLUB & MUSIC SCENE

Paris is still a late-night mecca, and both the quantity and variety of nightlife exceed that of other cities. Nowhere else will you find such a huge, mixed array of nightclubs, bars, dance clubs, cabarets, jazz dives, music halls, and honky-tonks.

A Music Hall

Olympia   Charles Aznavour and other big names appear in this cavernous hall. The late Yves Montand performed once, and the show was sold out 4 months in advance. Today, you're more likely to catch Gloria Estefan. A typical lineup might include an English rock group, Italian acrobats, a French singer, a dance troupe, juggling American comedians (doing much of their work in English), and the featured star. A witty master of ceremonies and an onstage band provide smooth transitions. Performances usually begin at 8:30pm Tuesday to Saturday, with Sunday matinees at 5pm. 28 bd. des Capucines, 9e. ☎ **01-55-27-10-00** or 08-92-68-33-68. www.olympiahall.com. Tickets 25€–99€. Métro: Opéra or Madeleine.

Chansonniers

Chansonniers (literally, songwriters) provide a bombastic musical satire of the day's events. This combination of parody and burlesque is a time-honored Gallic amusement and a Parisian institution. Songs are often created on the spot, inspired by the "disaster of the day."

Au Lapin Agile ★   Picasso and Utrillo patronized this little cottage near the top of Montmartre, then known as the Cabaret des Assassins, and it has been painted by many artists, including Utrillo. You'll sit at carved wooden tables in a dimly lit room with walls covered by bohemian memorabilia and listen to French folk tunes, love ballads, army songs, sea chanteys, and music-hall ditties. You're encouraged to sing along, even if it's only the *"oui, oui, oui—non, non, non,"* the refrain of "Les Chevaliers de la Table Ronde." Open Tuesday to Sunday 9pm to 2am. 22 rue des Saules, 18e. ☎ **01-46-06-85-87.** www.au-lapin-agile.com. Cover (includes 1 drink) 24€, 17€ students. Métro: Lamarck Caulaincourt.

Théâtre des Deux Anes   Since 1920, this theater has staged satires of the foibles, excesses, and stupidities of French governments. Favorite targets are President Nicolas Sarkozy and other mandarins of the *hexagone française*. Cultural icons, French and foreign, receive a grilling that's very funny and sometimes caustic. The place considers itself more of a theater than a cabaret and doesn't serve drinks or refreshments. The 2½-hour show is conducted in rapid-fire French slang, so if your syntax isn't up to par, you won't appreciate its charms.

Performances are given Tuesday through Saturday at 8:30pm, with matinees on Sunday at 3pm; closed July to September. 100 bd. de Clichy, 18e. ℭ **01-46-06-10-26.** www.2anes.com. Tickets 33€–41€. Métro: Place Clichy.

Nightclubs & Cabarets

Decidedly expensive, these places give you your money's worth by providing lavishly spectacular floor shows. They generally attract an older crowd and are definitely not youth-oriented.

Chez Michou   The setting is blue, the master of ceremonies wears blue, and the spotlights bathe performers in yet another shade of blue. Cross-dressing belles bear names such as Hortensia and DuDuche; they lip-sync in costumes from haute couture to haute concierge, paying tribute to such Americans as Whitney Houston and Tina Turner and to French stars such as Mireille Mathieu, Sylvie Vartan, and Brigitte Bardot. If you don't want dinner, you'll have to stand at the bar, paying a compulsory 35€ for the first drink. Dinner is served nightly at 8:30pm (reservations required); shows begin nightly at 11pm. 80 rue des Martyrs, 18e. ℭ **01-46-06-16-04.** www.michou.com. Cover (including dinner, aperitif, wine, coffee, and show) 135€. Métro: Pigalle.

Crazy Horse Saloon   Since 1951, this sophisticated strip joint has thrived, thanks to good choreography and a sly, coquettish celebration of the female form. The theme binding each of the 5-minute numbers (featuring gorgeous dancers in erotic costumes) is La Femme in her various states: temperamental, sad, dancing/bouncy, or joyful. Dance numbers that endure season after season include "Le Laser" and "The Erotic Lesson." Dinner is served at Chez Francis, a restaurant under separate management a few steps away. Shows last less than 2 hours. You'll find a small number of women among the audience of mainly businessmen. Shows Sunday to Friday 8:15 and 10:45pm; Saturday at 7, 9:30, and 11:45pm. 12 av. George V, 8e. ℭ **01-47-23-32-32.** www.lecrazyhorseparis.com. Reservations recommended. Cover (includes 2 drinks) 65€ for seat at the bar, 100€–150€ for table (dinner spectacle). Métro: George V or Alma Marceau.

Folies-Bergère   The Folies-Bergère has been an institution since 1869. Josephine Baker, the African-American singer who danced in a banana skirt and threw bananas into the audience, became "the toast of Paris" here. According to legend, the first GI to reach Paris at the 1944 Liberation asked for directions to the club. Don't expect the naughty and slyly permissive, skin-and-glitter revue that used to be the trademark of this place. In 1993, that all ended with a radical restoration of the theater and a reopening under new management. Today, it's a conventional 1,600-seat theater devoted to a frequently changing roster of big-stage performances in French, many of which are adaptations of Broadway blockbusters. Recent examples have included restagings of *Fame* and *Saturday Night Fever,* and a revue of male strippers inspired by America's Chippendales. There's even been a relatively highbrow re-enactment of one of the classics of the French-language repertory, *L'Arlésienne,* by 19th-century playwright Alphonse Daudet. True, there's always an acknowledgment of the nostalgia value of the old-time, much naughtier Folies-Bergère, and endless nods to the stars of yesterday (especially Josephine Baker and her topless act with bananas), but if you're looking for artful nudity presented with unabashed Parisian permissiveness, head for the Crazy Horse Saloon or the Lido. An on-site restaurant serves dinners in one of the theater's salons, but most spectators opt just for the show, and not the meal. Shows are usually given Tuesday to Saturday at 9pm and Sunday at 3pm. 32 rue Richer, 9e. ☎ **01-44-79-98-60** or 08-92-68-16-50. www.foliesbergere.com. Tickets 25€–84€. Métro: Grands-Boulevards or Cadet.

L'Ane Rouge   This red-and-black minitheater has been a showcase for French satire and humor since it opened shortly after World War II. You'll enjoy a well-flavored dinner of French specialties, followed by a 2-hour medley of French-language standup comedy, ribald stories, and politicized jokes. If your knowledge of French is zero, you won't enjoy this place; ditto if you hate being singled out by a comedian in front of a crowd. Dinner served nightly at 8pm; shows nightly 10pm to midnight. 3 rue Laugier, 17e. ☎ **01-47-64-45-77.** www.diners-spectacles.com. Reservations recommended. Tickets 35€–45€; fixed-price dinner (includes access to show) 55€–100€, which includes 1 drink. Métro: Ternes.

Le Paradis Latin   Built in 1889 by Alexandre-Gustave Eiffel, with the same metallic skeleton as the famous tower, Le Paradis Latin represents the architect's only venture into theater design. The place is credited with introducing vaudeville and musical theater to Paris. In 1903 the building was a warehouse, but in the 1970s it was transformed into a successful cabaret whose singers, dancers, and special effects extol the fun, frivolity, and permissiveness of the City of Light. The show includes tasteful nudity (they contrast their more dignified nudity—breasts only—with the more blatant and unabashed nudity at Crazy Horse), a ventriloquist, and a trapeze artist. The master of ceremonies speaks in French and English. Dinner Wednesday to Monday 8pm; reviews at 9:30pm. 28 rue Cardinal-Lemoine, 5e. ☎ **01-43-25-28-28.** www.paradis-latin.com. Cover 85€ including a glass of champagne, dinner and show 123€–179€. Métro: Jussieu or Cardinal Lemoine.

Lido de Paris   The Lido competes with the best Las Vegas has to offer. Its 10€-million production, *C'est Magique*, reflects a dramatic reworking of the classic Parisian cabaret show, with eye-popping special effects, water technology using more than 60,000 gallons per minute, and even aerial and aquatic ballet. The show, the most expensive ever produced in Europe, uses 70 performers, $4 million in costumes, and a $2-million lighting design with lasers. There's even an ice rink and swimming pool that appears and disappears. The 45 topless Bluebell Girls, those legendary showgirls, are still here. 16 av. des Champs-Elysées, 8e. ☎ **800/227-4884** in the U.S., or 01-40-76-56-10. www.lido.fr. Dinner dance (7pm) and show (11:30pm) 140€–210€, show only (9:30 and 11:30pm) 90€. Price includes half-bottle of champagne per person. Métro: George V.

Moulin Rouge   This is a camp classic. The establishment that Toulouse-Lautrec immortalized is still here, but the artist would probably have a hard time recognizing it. Colette created a scandal here by offering an on-stage kiss to Mme de Morny, but shows today have a harder time shocking audiences. Try to get a table—the view is much better on the main floor than from the bar. What's the theme? It's strip routines and the saucy sexiness of *la Belle Epoque*, and of permissive Paris between the wars. Handsome men and girls, girls, girls, virtually all topless, keep the place going. Dance finales usually include two dozen of the belles doing a topless cancan. Revues begin nightly at 9 and 11pm. 82 bd. Clichy, place Blanche, 18e. ☎ **01-53-09-82-82.** www.moulinrouge.fr. Cover including champagne 92€–102€, 7pm dinner and show 150€–180€. Métro: Blanche.

Nouveau Casino   Some Paris-watchers consider this the epitome of the hyperhip countercultural scene that blossoms along the rue Oberkampf every night. In a former movie theater adjacent to the Café Charbon, it's a large, drafty

PARIS AFTER DARK   The Club & Music Scene

space centered on a dance floor and an enormous bar crafted to resemble an iceberg. Live concerts take place nightly between 8pm and 1am; on Friday and Saturday, the party continues from 1am till dawn, with a DJ who spins some of the most avant-garde dance music in Paris. Celebrity spotters have picked out Prince Albert of Monaco and such French-language film stars as Vincent Cassel and Mathieu Kassovitz. 109 rue Oberkampf, 9e. ☎ **01-43-57-57-40.** www.nouveau casino.net. Admission to concerts 16€–27€, to disco 7€–20€. Métro: St-Maur, Parmentier, or Ménilmontant.

Jazz, Salsa, Rock & More

The great jazz revival that long ago swept America is still going strong here, with Dixieland, Chicago, bop, and free-jazz rhythms being pounded out in dozens of jazz cellars, mostly called *caveaux*. Most clubs are between rue Bonaparte and rue St-Jacques on the Left Bank. The crowds that attend clubs to hear rock, salsa, and the like are definitely young, often in their late teens, 20s, or early 30s. The exception to that is in the clubs offering jazz nights, where jazz-lovers span all ages.

Baiser Salé   In a cellar lined with jazz-related paintings, a large bar, and videos that show jazz greats of the past (Charlie Parker, Miles Davis), this is an appealing club. Everything is mellow and laid-back, with an emphasis on the music. Genres include Afro-Caribbean, Afro-Latino, salsa, merengue, rhythm and blues, and sometimes fusion. Open daily 5:30pm to 6am. 58 rue des Lombards, 1er. ☎ **01-42-33-37-71.** www.lebaisersale.com. Cover Mon 7€, Tues-Sun 10€–20€ after 10pm. Free Mon. Métro: Châtelet.

Caveau de la Huchette ★   This celebrated jazz *caveau*, reached by a winding staircase, draws a young crowd, mostly students, who dance to the music of well-known jazz combos. In pre-jazz days, Robespierre and Marat frequented the place. It's open Sunday to Wednesday 9:30pm to 2:30am; Thursday to Saturday and holidays 9:30pm to 4am. 5 rue de la Huchette, 5e. ☎ **01-43-26-65-05.** www.caveau delahuchette.fr. Cover 12€ Sun-Thurs, 14€ Fri-Sat; students 24 and younger 10€. Métro/RER: St-Michel.

Caveau des Oubliettes ★   It's hard to say which is more intriguing—the entertainment and drinking or the setting. An oubliette is a dungeon with a trap door at the top as its only opening, and the name is accurate. Located in the Latin Quarter, just across the river from Notre-Dame, this night spot is housed in a genuine 12th-century prison, complete with dungeons, spine-tingling passages, and scattered skulls, where prisoners were tortured and sometimes pushed through portholes to drown in the Seine. The *caveau* is beneath the subterranean vaults that many centuries ago linked it with the fortress prison of Petit Châtelet. Today patrons laugh, drink, talk, and flirt in the narrow *caveau* or else retreat to the jazz lounge. There's a free jam session every night, perhaps Latin jazz or rock. At some point on Friday and Saturday nights concerts are staged (a cover is assessed at this time). Open daily 5pm to 2am. 52 rue Galande, 5e. ☎ **01-46-34-23-09.** www.caveaudesoubliettes.fr. Cover 15€ Fri-Sat. Métro: St-Michel.

La Chapelle des Lombards 🎁   The club's proximity to the Opéra Bastille seems incongruous, considering the African/Caribbean jazz and Brazilian samba that's the norm. It's a magnet for South American and African expatriates, and the rhythms and fire of the music propel everyone onto the dance floor. Open Tuesday to Sunday 11:30pm to 6am; June to August daily 11:30pm to 6am. 19 rue de Lappe, 11e. ☎ **01-43-57-24-24.** www.la-chapelle-des-lombards.com. Cover 15€–19€

including first drink. Women free Thurs before midnight. Métro: Bastille.

Le Duc des Lombards Comfortable and appealing, this low-key jazz club replaced an older club 10 years ago. Performances begin nightly at 9pm and continue (with breaks) for 5 hours, touching on everything from free jazz to more traditional forms such as hard bop. Concerts begin at 9:30pm. 42 rue des Lombards, 1er. ℓ **01-42-33-22-88.** www.ducdeslombards. com. Cover 20€–30€. Métro: Châtelet.

Olivier Durand and Elliott Murphy perform at New Morning.

Le Gibus Attracting a pulsating under-30 crowd, this is one of the best-known rock clubs in Paris, patronized by both gays and straights. It opens every night as late as a dance club, entertaining its diverse medley of counterculture Parisians and visitors. Depending on the week's schedule, visitors will be confronted with a rotating series of themes, ranging from "Club Trance" to "Party Up." There might be a live rock band or even a drag show presented as part of the evening's rhythms. Times designated as specifically gay vary, but at press time, the gay venue was usually on Sunday from midnight to 6am. Open Friday to Sunday midnight to 6am, depending on business. Other nights of the week this place tended to be the venue for private parties or for loosely scheduled rock or pop concerts. 18 rue du Faubourg du Temple, 11e. ℓ **01-47-00-78-88.** www.gibus.fr. Cover 20€. Métro: République.

Le Petit Journal Sometimes French jazz aficionados refer to this jazz club and restaurant by its English name—"The Small Newspaper of Saint-Michel." The club lies in the center of the Latin Quarter, opposite the Jardin du Luxembourg. Created in 1971, it is the "high temple" in Paris for the jazz of New Orleans. Some of the country's top artists appear here, including Claude Bolling. The music is downstairs in an underground cellar. Open Monday to Saturday 9:15pm to 2am. 71 bd. St-Michel, 5e. ℓ **01-43-26-28-59.** www.petitjournalsaintmichel. com. Cover 17€–20€ including a drink; dinner and show 48€–53€. Closed Aug. RER: Luxembourg. Métro: Cluny–La Sorbonne.

Le Petit Journal Montparnasse This is one of the best jazz supper clubs in Paris. It's also a showcase for R&B, rock, and Latino music as well. Music lovers come here for a dinner and floor show, although you can also visit just for drinks and the music (a lot cheaper). Dinner guests are given preferred seating; other patrons usually sit at the bar. Some big names are often booked here. Open 8pm to 2am Monday to Saturday. 13 rue du Commandant Mouchotte, 14e. ℓ **01-43-21-56-70.** www.petitjournal-montparnasse.com. 3-course dinner and show 60€–85€, cover (without dinner) 25€ including first drink. Métro: Gare Montparnasse.

Le Sunset/Le Sunside ★ This is a dual temple of jazz, one of the hottest addresses on the after-dark scene in Paris, lying between the Forum des Halles and the Centre George Pompidou. The Sunset Jazz Club, created in 1983, is dedicated to electric jazz and international music, whereas Sunside, launched in 2001, is devoted to acoustic jazz for the most part. Some of the most innovative names in European jazz appear here regularly, along with jazz legends, many from abroad. Both clubs form a single complex with two concerts every night. Open Monday to Saturday 9:30pm to 1am. 60 rue des Lombards, 1er. ℓ **01-40-26-46-60.** www.sunset-sunside.com. Tickets 20€–22€. Métro: Châtelet.

10

PARIS AFTER DARK | The Club & Music Scene

New Morning   Jazz maniacs come to drink, talk, and dance at this enduring club. It's sometimes a scene, attracting such guests as Spike Lee and Prince. The place is especially popular with jazz groups from central and southern Africa. It opens nightly at 8pm, with concerts beginning at 9pm. 7 rue des Petites-Ecuries, 10e. ✆ **01-45-23-51-41.** www.newmorning.com. Cover 18€-26€. Métro: Château-d'Eau.

Dance Clubs

The following nightspots are among hundreds of places where people in their 20s or early 30s go to dance—distinct from others where the main attraction is the music. The area around the church of **St-Germain-des-Prés** is full of dance clubs, but they come and go so quickly that you could arrive to find a hardware store in the place of last year's white-hot club—but as with all things in nature, the new springs up to replace the old. Check *Time Out: Paris* or *Pariscope* to get a sense of current trends. Most of these clubs don't really get going until well after 10pm.

Batofar ★   Self-consciously proud of its status as a club that virtually every-body views as hip, Batofar sits on a converted barge that floats on the Seine, sometimes attracting hundreds of gyrating dancers, most of whom are in their 20s and 30s. House, garage, techno, and live jazz by groups that hail from (among other places) Morocco, Senegal, and Germany sometimes add to the mix. Come here for an insight into late-night Paris at its most raffish and countercultural, and don't even try to categorize the patrons. Beer will cost around 8.50€ a bottle. Open Tuesday to Saturday from 6pm to 3 or 4am, depending on business. Closed November to March. Facing 11 quai François Mauriac, 13e. ✆ **01-53-14-76-59.** www.batofar.org. Cover 10€-14€. Métro: Quai de la Gare.

Cab ★★   If you've ever wanted to dance in a basement under the Louvre, it doesn't get much classier than this joint patronized by French models, Arab busi-nessmen, women with a past, and children of the rich. Dim lighting illuminates black leather furniture, and there are two bars with shiny black or glass surfaces. There is also a trio of different seating areas. Music is house and electro, with various hip-hop songs and other American hits mixed in. We even heard Michael Jackson one night (remember him?). Open Wednesday to Saturday 11:30pm to 6am. 2 Place du Palais Royal, 1er. ✆ **01-58-62-56-25.** www.cabaret.fr. Cover 20€, including 1 drink. Métro: Palais Royal-Musée du Louvre.

Chacha Club★★   For the chic and sophisticated of all ages, this hot spot draws a crowd that the French press labeled "international slutterati." In addition to a cavernous bar and dance hall, there are several small salons, even a passcode-restricted bedroom. The über-trendy place is also a restaurant serving a range of finger foods such as tapas and antipasti. DJs keep the sound track on high through-out the night. Some of the most beautiful models in Paris arrange themselves on the leather armchairs. It's better to go early if you want to get in; the doorman is one tough bully. Open Monday to Saturday 8pm to 6am for the club, 8pm to mid-night for the restaurant. 47 rue Berger. ✆ **01-40-13-12-12.** www.chachaclub.fr. Food plat-ters 15€-25€. Metro: Louvre-Rivoli.

Club Zed 🎁   Hip, breezy, and very French, this popular nightspot in a former bakery with a vaulted masonry ceiling may surprise you with its mix of musical offerings, including samba, rock, 1960s pop, and jazz. Specific theme parties, such as the one at Halloween where virtually everyone comes in costume, are a delight. Open Thursday 9:30pm to 2:30am, Friday and Saturday 11pm to

5:30am. 2 rue des Anglais, 5e. ☎ **01-43-54-93-78.** Cover 10€ Thurs, 18€ Fri–Sat, including 1st drink. Métro: Maubert-Mutualité.

Favela Chic The hot sounds of Brazil permeate this nighttime party at this bar and restaurant that makes the best *mojitos* in town (surely even Ernest Hemingway would approve). Weekends are packed with an under-35 crowd. At times you'll think you've been transplanted to Rio de Janeiro. Bossa jazz and samba rap are also heard on some nights. A *favela*, incidentally, is a ghetto in Brazil. Open Tuesday to Thursday 8pm to 2am. 18 rue du Faubourg du Temple, 11e. ☎ **01-40-21-38-14.** www.favelachic.com. Cover 10€ Fri–Sat 8pm to 4am. Métro: République.

Dancing the night away at a trendy club.

La Balajo Established in 1936, this dance club is where Edith Piaf won the hearts of Parisian music lovers. Today, it's easy to compare La Balajo with New York City's Roseland—an old-fashioned venue steeped in Big Band nostalgia, which sometimes manages to shake the dust out for special parties and events. Afternoon sessions focus on tangos, *pasodobles,* and waltzes, and are more staid than their late-night counterparts. Evenings attract a younger crowd (age 20–35-ish), who groove to a mixture, depending on the DJ, of house, garage, techno, and old-fashioned disco. Open Tuesday to Thursday 7pm to 2am, Friday and Saturday 11pm to 6am, and Sunday 3 to 7pm. 9 rue de Lappe, 11e. ☎ **01-47-00-07-87.** www.balajo.fr. Cover (includes 1 drink) 8€ for afternoon sessions, 16€–20€ for night sessions. Métro: Bastille.

La Java This *bal-musette* dance hall was once one of the most important in Paris; Piaf and Maurice Chevalier made their names here. Today, you can still waltz on what one critic called "retro fetish night," or even tango on Sunday afternoon. Brazilian and Latin themes predominate on some nights. Overall, it's one of the best places in Paris for the old-fashioned pleasures of couples arm-in-arm on a dance floor. 105 rue du Faubourg du Temple, 11e. ☎ **01-42-02-20-52.** www.la-java.fr. Cover 17€. Métro: Belleville or Goncourt.

La Loco Next to the Moulin Rouge, this club is popular with American students and is especially busy on Sunday. People dance to rock and techno, though occasionally metal concerts are staged. La Loco is one of the largest clubs in Paris. In the *sous-sol* (the basement, the coolest of the three levels), you can even see the remnants of an old railway line (hence the name). The Bar Americain looks more Roman with fake statuary and columns crowned by lions. Daily 11pm to 6am. 90 bd. De Clichy, 18e. ☎ **01-53-41-88-88.** www.laloco.com. Cover 12€–26€. Métro: Blanche.

Le Baron ★ If there's such a thing as a speakeasy in the 21st century, this bastion of cool is it. Once it was the most expensive brothel in Paris, and much of its original decor remains, including the 1920s-era tile of frolicking nude ladies, the sexy red walls, and the tasseled lamps. Today, however, the Gucci crowd in thick shades turns up, an equal mix of both sexes, including some customers who

AFTER-DARK diversions:
DIVES, DRAG & MORE

On a Paris night, the cheapest entertainment, especially if you're young, is "the show" at the tip of Ile de la Cité, behind Notre-Dame. A sort of Gallic version of the Sundowner Festival in Key West, Florida, it attracts just about everyone who ever wanted to try his or her hand at performance. The spontaneous entertainment usually includes magicians, fire-eaters, jugglers, mimes, and music makers from all over, performing against the backdrop of the illuminated cathedral. This is one of the greatest places in Paris to meet young people in a sometimes-euphoric setting.

Also popular is a stroll along the Seine after 10pm. Take a graveled pathway down to the river from the Left Bank side of Pont de Sully, close to the Institut du Monde Arabe, and walk to the right, away from Notre-Dame. This walk, which ends near place Valhubert, is the best place to see spontaneous Paris in action at night. Joggers and saxophone players come here, and many Parisians arrive for impromptu dance parties.

To quench your thirst, wander onto Ile St-Louis and head for the **Café-Brasserie St-Regis,** 6 rue Jean-du-Bellay, 4e, across from Pont St-Louis (℗ **01-43-54-59-41;** Métro: Pont Marie). If you want to linger, you can order a *plat du jour* or a coffee at the bar. But try doing as the Parisians do: Get a 3€ beer to go *(une bière à emporter)* in a cup and take it with you on a stroll around the island. The cafe is open daily until midnight.

If you're caught waiting for the Métro to start running again at 5am, try the **Sous-Bock Tavern,** 49 rue St-Honoré, 1er (℗ **01-40-26-46-61;** Métro: Les Halles or Louvre-Rivoli), open Monday to Saturday from 11am to 5am, Sunday 5pm to 5am. Young drinkers gather here to sample from 250 varieties of beer or 20 varieties

of whiskey. The dish to order is a platter of mussels—curried, with white wine, or with cream sauce; they go well with the brasserie-style fries.

If drag shows aren't your cup of tea, how about *Last Tango in Paris?* At **Le Tango,** 11 rue au Maire, 3e (℗ **01-42-72-17-78;** Métro: Arts et Métiers), memories of Evita and Argentina live on. On-site is a ballroom called *La Boîte à Frissons.* The evening starts at 10:30pm, with couples dancing until 12:30am, featuring the waltz, the tango, *pasodoble,* the polka, rock 'n' roll, and cha-cha. After that, the dance floor turns into a disco. The cover is 8€. It's open Friday and Saturday from midnight to 5am.

If you're looking for a sophisticated, laid-back venue, consider the **Sanz-Sans,** 49 rue du Faubourg St-Antoine, 4e (℗ **01-44-75-78-78;** www.sanzsans.com; Métro: Bastille or Ledru Rollin), a multi-ethnic playground where the children of prominent Parisians mingle, testifying to the unifying power of jazz. In this red-velvet duplex, the most important conversations seem to occur over margaritas on the stairway or the backroom couches. The later it gets, the sexier the scene becomes. No cover is charged.

haven't decided which sex to be. The dance floor is one of the most packed in Paris with some of the world's most beautiful people. Drinks are costly but so is being trendy. It's open daily 11pm to 6am, although hours can vary. 6 av. Marceau, 8e. ℗ **01-47-20-04-01.** www.clublebaron.com. Cover ranges from free to 15€ depending on the venue and the night of the week. Métro: Champs-Elysées.

Le Saint   Occupying three medieval cellars in the university area, this place attracts a crowd of people in their 20s and 30s who dance (to music from the U.S. and Europe), drink, and soak up the Left Bank student-dive scene. Vacationers will enjoy this fun spot, and its "young love beside the Seine" vibe can be a hoot. Thursday 7pm to 1am, Friday to Sunday 11pm to 6am. 7 rue St-Séverin, 5e. ✆ **01-40-20-43-23.** www.lesaintdisco.com. Cover (includes 1 drink) 10€–15€. Métro: St-Michel or Cluny–La Sorbonne.

Les Bains Douches   The name, "the Baths," comes from this hot spot's former function as a Turkish bath that attracted gay clients, none more notable than Marcel Proust. It may be hard to get in if the doorman doesn't think you're trendy and *très chic*. Yes, that was Jennifer Lopez we saw whirling around the floor. Dancing begins at midnight, and a supper club–like restaurant is upstairs. Meals cost 32€ to 120€. On certain nights this is the hottest party atmosphere in Paris, and Mondays are increasingly gay, although sexual preference is hardly an issue at this club. "We all walk the waterfront," one DJ enigmatically told us. Open Wednesday to Sunday 9pm to 2am. 7 rue du Bourg-l'Abbé, 3e. ✆ **01-53-01-40-60.** www.lesbainsdouches.net. Cover 10€–20€. Métro: Etienne Marcel.

Les Coulisses   Montmartre has more tourist traps than anywhere in Paris, but this fairly new club has some legitimacy; it's a good spot for drinking and dancing. It consists of a basement-level dance club, a first-floor bar, and a restaurant on the second floor. The decor changes all the time, but management usually sticks to baroque and medieval themes. The restaurant is open Monday to Saturday 9pm to midnight. The club is open from 11pm to 5am. 1 rue St. Rustique, 18e. ✆ **01-42-62-89-99.** Cover 20€–30€ Fri–Sat; no cover for restaurant patrons. Métro: Abbesses or Funiculaire de Montmartre.

Rex Club   This echoing blue-and-orange space emulates the techno-grunge clubs of London, complete with an international mood-altered crowd enjoying the kind of music that only those ages 18 to 28 could love. A host of DJs, including techno-circuit celeb Laurent Garnier, is on hand. Open Thursday to Saturday midnight to 6am. 5 bd. Poissonnière, 2e. ✆ **01-42-36-10-96.** www.rexclub.com. Cover 15€. Métro: Bonne Nouvelle.

BARS, PUBS & CLUBS
Wine Bars

Many Parisians now prefer wine bars to traditional cafes or bistros. The food is often better, and the ambience more inviting. For cafes, see "The Top Cafes," in chapter 6.

Au Sauvignon   This tiny spot has tables overflowing onto a covered terrace and a decor that features old ceramic tiles and frescoes done by Left Bank artists. Wines range from the cheapest Beaujolais to the most expensive Puligny-Montrachet. A glass of wine costs 4.50€ to 6€. To go with your wine, choose an Auvergne specialty, such as goat cheese or a terrine. Fresh Poilâne bread is ideal with ham, pâté, or goat cheese. Open Monday to Saturday 8am to 10pm, Sunday 10am to 9pm. Closed in August. 80 rue des Sts-Pères, 7e. ✆ **01-45-48-49-02.** Métro: Sèvres-Babylone or St-Sulpice.

Cavesteve   This is a *cave à manger*—that is, a wine shop where you are served food. Near the place du Trocadéro, this outlet is a branch of the original in the Bastille. It is a wine shop first, a place to eat second. The wine selection boasts about 300 labels, choices ranging from France to Chile, from New Zealand to California. Food is served upstairs and down (often at a communal table). Everything from Spanish ham to a foie gras terrine is featured, along with five hot daily specials. For dessert, try one of the chef's delectable lemon-glazed pound cakes. Open Tuesday to Saturday 10am to 8pm. 15 rue Longchamps, 16e. ℰ **01-47-04-01-45.** www.caveeteve.com. Métro: Iena or Trocadéro.

5e Cru ★ 🎁 This is a real local Parisian dive patronized mostly by foodies and wine connoisseurs who come to sample owner Jean de Toalier's *carte*. He serves more wines than just "fifth-growth" bottles as the name suggests. The ochre-hued wine bar and restaurant has only three pine tables as well as a few barrels converted to dining stations. De Rotaliers boasts that he's got "every *terroir* of France covered" in his kitchen. *Terroir* is the French name for regional products from deep in the countryside, ranging from charcuterie to local cheeses and tartines. The food is hearty, simple, natural and the product of local growers. More than 150 different French wines are sold. You can get a simple menu for 13€; a glass of wine for 3 to 8€, with bottles priced as low as 8€, rarely more than 60€. Open Monday to Friday 10:30am to midnight, Saturday 2:30pm to 1am. 7 rue du Cardinal Lemoine, 5e. ℰ **01-40-46-86-34.** www.5ecru.com. Métro: Jussieu.

La Tartine Mirrors, brass details, and frosted-globe chandeliers make La Tartine look like a movie set of old Paris. At least 60 wines are offered at reasonable prices, including seven kinds of Beaujolais and a large selection of bordeaux by the glass. Glasses of wine cost 3.50€ to 6.50€, and the charcuterie platter costs 9€ to 16€. We recommend the light Sancerre wine and goat cheese from the Loire Valley. Open daily 8am to 1am. 24 rue de Rivoli, 4e. ℰ **01-42-72-76-85.** Métro: St-Paul.

Le Porte Pot One of the best wine bars in the Latin Quarter often fills with students from the Sorbonne. In the cellar are some 60 different wines from all the regions of France, many from relatively new winemakers. The staff is helpful guiding you through the wine *carte*. You can also dine here, enjoying such dishes as sausage and duck confit, salt-pork flavored lentils, or a salad with chicken livers, perhaps hot meat pie. Lunch menus cost 9.90€ to 11€, a fixed-price dinner 10€ to 14€. Open Tuesday to Saturday 6pm to midnight. 14 rue Boutebrie, 5e. ℰ **01-43-25-24-24.** Métro: Cluny–La Sorbonne.

Le Sancerre Engagingly old-fashioned, with an agreeable staff and food prepared fresh every day, this wine bar specializes in vintages from the Loire Valley and Sancerre. The latter, produced in red, rosé, and white, is known for its not-too-dry fruity aroma and legions of fans who believe it should be more celebrated. Other wine choices include chinon and saumur wine (both from the Loire Valley), as well as pinot de Bourgogne (from Burgundy), gamay (from the Ardèche Valley in France's southwest), and chenas (from the Beaujolais). Food items usually include *andouillettes* (chitterling sausages), omelets with flap mushrooms, fresh oysters, and quiches. Glasses of wine cost 3.10€ to 5.20€; simple platters of food cost 8.50€ to 15€ each. Open Monday to Friday 8am to 4pm and 6:30 to 11pm, Saturday 8:30am to 4pm. 22 av. Rapp, 7e. ℰ **01-45-51-75-91.** Métro: Alma-Marceau.

Les Bacchantes This place prides itself on offering more wines by the glass—at least 90—than any other wine bar in Paris; prices range from 3€ to 6€. It also does a hefty restaurant trade in well-prepared *cuisine bourgeoise*, with main courses costing 14€ to 25€. Its cozy, rustic setting—with paneling, and chalkboards announcing vintages and platters—attracts theatergoers before and after performances at the Théâtre Olympia, as well as anyone interested in carefully chosen vintages from esoteric or small-scale winemakers. Wines are mainly from France, but you'll also find examples from neighboring countries. Open Monday to Saturday noon to 3pm and 7pm to 2am. 21 rue Caumartin, 9e. ℰ **01-42-65-25-35.** Métro: Havre-Caumartin.

Versant Vins ★ 🎁   For the flavor of a real authentic Parisian wine bar, head here to this spruced-up wine booth at the Marché des Enfants Rouges, the oldest food market in Paris. Here the sommelier Jeanne Galinié will suggest a bottle to go with some of the ethnic fare from the neighboring stalls. Perhaps she'll suggest a bottle of Mano a Mano Grenache blend to go with those *merguez* meatballs from the Moroccan stand next door. The shop specializes in organic and natural wines, with bottles costing from 6€ to 40€. Open Tuesday noon to 8pm, Wednesday to Saturday 10am to 8pm, Sunday 10am to 4pm. 39 rue de Bretagne, 3er. ℰ **01-42-72-34-85.** www.versantvins.com. Métro: Filles du Calvaire or Temple.

Willi's Wine Bar ★★   Journalists and stockbrokers head for this popular wine bar in the financial district. It offers about 300 kinds of wine, including a dozen specials you can taste by the glass for 4€ to 18€. Lunch is the busiest time; on quiet evenings, you can better enjoy the warm ambience. Daily specials are likely to include fricassee of guinea fowl with mushrooms or bacon salad with chestnuts, plus a spectacular dessert such as chocolate terrine. A fixed-price menu costs 19€ to 25€ at lunch, 34€ at dinner. The restaurant is open Monday to Saturday noon to 2:30pm and 7 to 11pm; the bar, Monday to Saturday noon to midnight. 13 rue des Petits-Champs, 1er. ℰ **01-42-61-05-09.** www.williswinebar.com. Métro: Bourse, Pyramides, or Palais-Royal.

Bars, Pubs & Clubs

These "imported" places trying to imitate American cocktail bars or British pubs mostly strike an alien chord. But that doesn't prevent fashionable Parisians from barhopping (not to be confused with cafe-sitting). Many bars in Paris are youth-oriented. But if you're an older traveler who prefers to take your expensive drink in one of the grand-luxe bars of the world, Paris has those as well. The bars at the **Plaza Athénée** or **Ritz,** for example, are among the grandest in the world and provide a uniquely Parisian experience for those who want to don their finest apparel and take along a gold-plated credit card. In general, bars and pubs are open daily from 11am to 1:30am.

Académie de la Bière 🍺   The decor is paneled and rustic, an appropriate foil for an "academy" whose curriculum includes more than 153 kinds of beer from microbreweries. More than half of the dozen beers on tap are from small-scale breweries in Belgium that deserve to be better known than that country's best-seller, Stella Artois. Snack-style food is available, including platters of mussels, assorted cheeses, and sausages with mustard. Open Sunday to Thursday 10am to 2am and Friday and Saturday noon to 3am. 88 bis bd. du Port-Royal, 5e. ℰ **01-43-54-66-65.** RER: Port Royal. Métro: Raspail.

Andy Whaloo   A play on Andy Warhol's name, this bar would be at home in Marrakesh, the most chic city today in North Africa. Enjoy tapas Mediterranean or smoke a hookah. The background music might be *raï* from old Algiers. Patterned Moroccan rugs are thrown over banquettes, which fill up nightly with some of the most fashionable young people of Paris. The stools are made from

Some of the many beers on tap at Académie de la Bière.

Willi's Wine Bar.

paint barrels. The ambience is definitely of the souk. Open Tuesday to Saturday 6pm to 2am. 69 rue des Gravilliers, 3e. ✆ **01-42-71-20-38.** Métro: Arts et Métiers.

Bar Hemingway/Bar Vendôme   In 1944, during the liberation of Paris, Ernest Hemingway made history by ordering a drink at the Ritz Bar while gunfire from retreating Nazi soldiers was still audible in the streets. Today the Ritz commemorates the event with bookish memorabilia, rows of newspapers, and stiff drinks. Look for the bar's entrance, and homages to other writers such as Proust, near the hotel's rue Cambon entrance. If you develop a thirst in the daytime, when the Bar Hemingway isn't open, head for the Bar Vendôme, near the hotel's place Vendôme entrance. The setting is just as cozy and woodsy, albeit a bit more grand. Open daily 6:30pm to 2am. In the Hôtel Ritz, 15 place Vendôme, 1er. ✆ **01-43-16-30-30.** Métro: Opéra or Concorde.

Barrio Latino   This multilevel emporium of good times, Gallic flair, and Latin charm occupies a space designed by Gustav Eiffel in the 19th century. Tapas bars and dance floors are on the street level (*rez-de-chaussée*) and third floor (*3eme étage*); a Latin restaurant is on the second floor (*2eme étage*). Staff members roll carts loaded with tapas around the floors, selling them like hot dogs at an American baseball game. The restaurant specializes in food that French palates find refreshing: Argentine steaks, Brazilian *feijoada* (a bean-based dish that's similar to cassoulet), and Mexican chili, all of which taste wonderful with beer, *caipirinhas*, cuba libres, or rum punches. The clientele is mixed, mostly straight, partly gay, and 100% blasé about matters such as an individual's sexuality. Open Sunday through Thursday noon to 2am, Friday noon to 2:30am, Saturday noon to 3am. 46 rue du Faubourg St-Antoine, 12e. ✆ **01-55-78-84-75.** Cover 20€ for nondiners after 9pm. Métro: Bastille.

Buddha Bar   The food is mediocre, but that doesn't seem to matter to the fashionistas on the see-and-be-seen circuit. A giant Buddha presides over the vast dining room, where a combination of Japanese sashimi, Vietnamese spring rolls, Chinese lacquered duck, and various Asian fusion dishes are served. Many patrons come here to drink at the lacquered bar, found upstairs from the street-level dining room. From the upper perch you can observe the action of the swanky international patrons below. The music is spacey, the atmosphere electric, and some of the prettiest women and handsomest hunks in Paris are in

10

PARIS AFTER DARK

Bars, Pubs & Clubs

attendance nightly. The location is near the Champs-Elysées and place de la Concorde. Open Monday to Friday 5pm to 2am, Saturday and Sunday 4pm to 2am. 8 rue Boissy d'Anglais, 8e. © **01-53-05-90-00.** www.buddha-bar.com. Métro: Concorde.

Café de l'Industrie This is a bizarre, only-in-Paris type of complex—a restaurant, cafe, and shop of provocative lingerie. The original cafe branched out with a second restaurant across the street known as Cafés de l'Industrie as well as a shop called L'Industrie Lingerie. Good Parisian food and drink are served in the main branch with an interior decorated with photos of movie stars. Open daily 9:30am to 2am. 16 rue Saint-Sabin, 11e. © **01-47-00-13-53.** www.cafedelindustrie.com. Métro: Bréguet-Savin or Bastille.

La Belle Hortense There are dozens of other bars and cafes near this one, but none maintains a bookstore in back, and few seem so self-consciously aware of their roles as ersatz literary salons. Come for a glass of wine and participation in a discussion within what's defined as "a literary bar." It's named after a pulpy 19th-century romance (*La Belle Hortense*) set within the neighborhood. Glasses of wine cost 3€ to 7€. Open daily 5pm to 2am. 31 rue Vieille-du-Temple, 4e. © **01-48-04-71-60.** Métro: Hôtel-de-Ville.

Le Bar de L'Hôtel A Left Bank hotel is home to the city's most romantic bar. Oscar Wilde checked out long ago, but the odd celebrity still shows up: We were once 15 minutes into a conversation before realizing we were speaking to Jeanne Moreau. Drinks are expertly mixed, the place sleek and chic, and conversations are held at a discreet murmur. It would be hard to find a better place for a romantic rendezvous. Usually open from noon to 1am. In L'Hôtel, 13 rue des Beaux-Arts, 6e. © **01-44-41-99-00.** Métro: St-Germain-des-Prés.

Le China There's been a club on this site for years. Back in the 1930s, it was an opium den and jazz club. Today, in its latest incarnation, it is all dark colors, candles, soft lights, and intimacy. Upstairs, patrons can play backgammon; there is also a fireplace and library plus a winter garden with big rattan chairs further setting a homey mood. The on-site restaurant evokes 1930s Shanghai with red-painted walls. A long zinc bar is found on the ground floor and a bar in the basement hosts jazz concerts. It's an ideal place to have a drink. Cocktails cost from 10€. Open daily 6pm to 2am. 50 rue de Charenton, 12e. © **01-43-46-08-09.** www.lechina.eu. Metro: Ledru Rollin.

Le Forum Patrons, who include frequent business travelers, compare this place with a private club in London. The comparison is due partly to the polished oak paneling and ornate stucco, and partly to the selection of single-malt whiskeys. You can also try 180 cocktails, including many that haven't been popular since the Jazz Age. Champagne by the glass is common, as is that social lubricant, the martini. Open Monday to Thursday noon to 1am, Friday noon to 2am, Saturday 5:30pm to 2am. 4 bd. Malesherbes, 8e. © **01-42-65-37-86.** www.bar-le-forum.com. Métro: Madeleine.

Le Fumoir At Le Fumoir, the well-traveled crowd that lives or works in the district provides a kind of classy raucousness. The decor is a lot like that of an English library, with about 6,000 books providing a backdrop to the schmoozing. A Swedish chef prepares an international menu featuring meal-size salads, roasted codfish with zucchini, and roasted beef in red-wine sauce. Main courses cost 19€ to 24€. Open daily 11am to 2am. 6 rue de l'Amiral-de-Coligny, 1er. © **01-42-92-00-24.** www.lefumoir.com. Métro: Louvre-Rivoli.

Le Lèche-Vin   If you're sacrilegious and like to pub crawl in the Bastille sector, head here. Expect a blasphemous, kitschy mix of religious icons, such as Christ or his mother, in the bar, and XXX-rated porno in the toilets. Patrons are an international crowd, both gay and straight, and a lot of French students. Open Tuesday to Saturday 6:30pm to 2am, closed Sunday and Monday. 13 rue Daval, 11e. ☏ **01-43-55-06-70.** Métro: Bastille.

Le Piano Vache   A student hangout since the uprising of 1969, this enduring Latin Quarter favorite attracts a counterculture clientele; even Johnny Depp has been known to show up. You can lose yourself here around the old *déglingué* piano. It's where the Paris of yesterday meets the Paris of today as piano music graces the night. Music begins on most nights after 8pm. DJs play everything from punk to rock; the '80s often live again. Open Monday to Friday noon to 2am and Saturday and Sunday 6pm to 2am. 8 rue Laplace, 5e. ☏ **01-46-33-75-03.** www.lepianovache.com. Métro: Maubert Mutualité.

Louis² ★   In the swanky Hotel de Trémoille, this bar since 1883 has always been a chic rendezvous for a drink. In its latest restoration, it still evokes the 1930s with thick carpets and embroidered fabrics. With its private alcoves, the bar is intimate with both a library and a fireplace, with seating around a live piano player. Near the Champs-Elysées, the bar attracts chic Parisians. Cocktails range in price from 18€ to 20€. Open daily 7am to midnight. 16 rue de la Trémoille, 8e. ☏ **01-56-52-14-14.** Métro: George V or Franklin D. Roosevelt.

Mojito Habana   Amid a decor that evokes colonial Havana under Batista, with lots of green upholsteries, wood panels, and deep sofas, you'll find a three-tiered place with a restaurant (it charges around 50€ for a full meal) and a piano bar (music begins at 11pm every night the place is open, and at 10pm on Tuesday). Jazz concerts are featured on Tuesday nights. Cocktails, including cuba libres, cost 13€ each. Entrance is always free. And the music that's in the background is international rock and pop, not solely salsa and merengue. It's open Monday to Friday from noon to 5am and Saturday 6pm to 5am. And it attracts a lot of nattily dressed business travelers. 19 rue de Presbourg, 16e. ☏ **01-45-00-84-84.** Métro: Etoile.

The Moose   This sports bar is the major Canadian outpost in Paris. The drink of choice, of course, is Moosehead. Canadian rugby and hockey games are all the rage on TV here. Depending on the weather and the mood of the organizers, theme nights here include country-western bashes or "beach parties" at which the less inhibited clients strip down to their Calvin Kleins. If you get the munchies, burgers and delicious salads are offered. Incidentally, a pitcher of Moosehead costs 16€ to 20€. Open Monday to Thursday 4pm to 2am, Friday to Sunday 11am to 2pm. 16 rue des Quatre Vents, 6e. ☏ **01-46-33-77-00.** www.canadianbarsparis.com. Métro: Odéon.

The Quiet Man   Named after a famous John Wayne movie set in Ireland, this is the best Irish pub in Paris. Naturally, it's the watering hole for all Irish expats who gravitate to their Guinness, Irish music, and, of course, darts. Open daily 5pm to 2am. 5 rue des Haudriettes, 3e. ☏ **01-48-04-02-77.** www.thequietman.eu. Métro: Rambuteau.

Le Scopiton ★   This is a chic bar operated by the owners of another well-established night spot, Le Baron. The atmosphere is sexy and at times a bit intoxicating (or is that the champagne talking?). This subterranean club is installed in a former Chinese restaurant, and attracts *Parisiens aristo-branchés* (plugged in jet-setters). DJs rule over the intimate dance space. If you get by the doormen, you descend a staircase lit by red lights as in an old bordello. Drinks range from 8€ to 18€, and the music is a bit rock electro. Open Tuesday to Sunday 7pm to 2am, until 6am Friday and Saturday. 5 av. de l'Opéra, 5e. ☎ **01-42-60-64-65.** Métro: Palais-Royal or Pyramides-Ligne.

GAY & LESBIAN BARS & CLUBS

Gay life is centered on **Les Halles** and **Le Marais,** with the greatest concentration of gay and lesbian clubs, restaurants, bars, and shops between the Hôtel-de-Ville and Rambuteau Métro stops. Gay dance clubs come and go so fast that even the magazines devoted to them, such as **Illico**—distributed free in the gay bars and bookstores—have a hard time keeping up. For lesbians, there is **Lesbian Magazine.** Also look for Gai Pied's **Guide Gai** and **Pariscope**'s regularly featured English-language section, "A Week of Gay Outings." Also important for both men and women is **Têtu** magazine, sold at most newsstands.

    Café Cox, 15 rue des Archives, 4e (☎ **01-42-72-08-00;** see below), gets so busy in the early evening that the crowd stands on the sidewalk. This is where you'll find the most mixed gay crowd in Paris—from hunky American tourists to sexy Parisian men. Another hot place in Les Halles is **Le Tropic Café,** 66 rue des Lombards, 1er (☎ **01-40-13-92-62;** Métro: Châtelet–Les Halles), where the trendy, good-looking crowd parties until dawn. A restaurant with a bar popular with women is **Okawa,** 40 rue Vieille-du-Temple, 4e (☎ **01-48-04-30-69;** Métro: Hôtel-de-Ville), where trendy lesbians (and some gay men) enjoy happy hour.

Banana Café   This popular bar is a stop for gays visiting or doing business in Paris. Occupying two floors of a 19th-century building, it has walls the color of an overripe banana, dim lighting, and a policy of raising the drink prices after 10pm, when things become really interesting. There's a street-level bar and a cellar dance floor that features a live pianist and recorded music—sometimes with dancing. On many nights, go-go dancers perform from spotlit platforms in the cellar. Open daily from 5:30pm to 4 or 5am. 13 rue de la Ferronnerie, 1er. ☎ **01-42-33-35-31.** www.bananacafeparis.com. Métro: Châtelet–Les Halles.

La Champmeslé   With dim lighting, background music, and comfortable banquettes, La Champmeslé offers a cozy meeting place for women and a few (about 5%) "well-behaved" men. Paris's leading women's bar is in a 300-year-old building with exposed stone, ceiling beams, and 1950s-style furnishings. Thursday night, one of the premier lesbian events in Paris, a cabaret begins at 10pm. Open daily 4pm until dawn. 4 rue Chabanais, 2e. ☎ **01-42-96-85-20.** www.lachampmesle.com. Métro: Pyramides or Bourse.

Le Central   Established in 1980 in a 300-year-old town house, Le Central is a staple of gay men's life in the Marais. Outfitted with decor of battered paneling and windows that wrap around on two sides, it attracts local residents who make the place their hangout, along with goodly numbers of attractive male tourists and the Parisians who appreciate them. Don't be surprised if the friendships you forge here are with other Yanks, Aussies, or Brits. A small gay hotel is upstairs. Open Monday to Friday from 4pm to 2am, Saturday to Sunday from 2pm to 2am. 33 rue Vieille-du-Temple, 4e. ☎ **01-48-87-99-33.** www.hotelcentralmarais.com. Métro: Hôtel-de-Ville.

Le Depot This gay pleasure palace stages everything from Queer Mother Nights to Putanas at Work. Patrons wander the rooms downstairs searching for their companions of the night. After 11pm, lesbians patronize the upstairs dance floor. The age range here is from 18 to 50. The post-Sunday-brunch gay tea dance, starting at 5pm, is one of the happening events of Paris. Open daily from 2pm to 8am. 10 rue aux Ours, 3e. *(C)* **01-44-54-96-96.** Cover 8.50€–13€. Métro: Etienne-Marcel.

Le Queen Should you miss gay life a la New York, seek out the flashing purple sign near the corner of avenue George V. This

Dancing at Le Queen.

place is often mobbed, primarily by gay men and, to a lesser degree, chic women who work in fashion and film. Look for drag shows, muscle shows, striptease by danseurs atop the bars, and everything from '70s-style disco nights to foam parties (only in summer), when cascades of suds descend onto the dance floor. Go very, very late: The place opens at midnight and stays open until 6 or 7am. 102 av. des Champs-Elysées, 8e. *(C)* **01-53-89-08-90.** www.queen.fr. Cover 15€–20€ Fri–Sat. Métro: Franklin-D-Roosevelt or George V.

Le Raidd ★ The bartenders are handsome hunks and so are most of the patrons. A special feature is a Plexiglas shower box where nude shower boys flaunt their assets throughout the night. It's shoulder-to-shoulder action all night, with pickup possibilities galore. Dress cool to get by the ax murderer at the door. Open daily 5pm to 5am. 23 rue du Temple, 4e. *(C)* **01-92-77-09-88.** www.raiddbar.com. Métro: Hôtel-de-Ville or Rambuteau.

Le 3w Kafe The 3w means "Woman with Woman." This is the best-known lesbian bar in the Marais, where an unattached woman can usually find a drinking buddy. On weekends there's dancing downstairs with a DJ in control of the sounds. Straight men are welcome but only if accompanied by a female. Gay men are admitted without any problem. At this dive, theme evenings are often presented. Open Wednesday to Sunday 5pm to 2am, Friday and Saturday 5pm to 4am. 8 rue des Ecouffes, 4e. *(C)* **01-48-87-39-26.** Métro: St. Paul.

Open Café/Café Cox Although this side-by-side pair of gay men's bars are each independent, their clienteles are so interconnected, and there's such traffic between them, that we—as with many other residents of this neighborhood—usually jumble them together. Both define themselves as bars rather than dance clubs, but on particularly busy nights, one or another couple might actually begin to dance. Simple cafe-style food is served from noon to around 5pm. Patrons can include just about every type of man that roams the streets of gay Europe today. Open daily from 11am to 2am, Friday and Saturday to 3am. 17 rue des Archives, 4e. *(C)* **01-42-72-26-18.** Métro: Hôtel-de-Ville.

LITERARY HAUNTS

Harry's New York Bar ★ At *sank roo doe noo,* as the ads tell you to instruct your cabdriver, is the most famous bar in Europe—possibly in the world. Opened on Thanksgiving Day 1911 by an expatriate named MacElhone, it's where members of the World War I ambulance corps drank themselves silly. In addition to being Hemingway's favorite, Harry's is where the White Lady and Sidecar cocktails were invented; it's also the reputed birthplace of the bloody mary and the headquarters of a loosely organized fraternity of drinkers known as the International Bar Flies.

The historic core is the street-level bar, where CEOs and office workers loosen their ties on more or less equal footing. Daytime crowds are from the neighborhood's insurance, banking, and travel industries; evening crowds include pre- and post-theater groupies and night owls who aren't bothered by the gritty setting and unflattering lighting. A softer, somewhat less macho ambience reigns in the cellar, where a pianist provides music Tuesday to Saturday from 10pm to 2am. Open daily noon until between 2 and 4am. 5 rue Daunou, 2e. ℂ **01-42-61-71-14.** www.harrys-bar.fr. Métro: Opéra.

Rosebud   The popularity of this place, known for a bemused and indulgent attitude toward anyone looking for a drink and some talk, hasn't diminished since the 1950s. The name refers to the beloved sled of Orson Welles's *Citizen Kane.* Around the corner from Montparnasse's famous cafes and thick in associations with Sartre and de Beauvoir, Ionesco, and Duras, Rosebud draws a 35- to 65-year-old crowd, though the staff has noticed the appearance of literary-minded students. Drop in at night for a glass of wine, a shot of whiskey, or a hamburger or chili con carne. Open daily 7pm to 2am. 11 bis rue Delambre, 14e. ℂ **01-43-35-38-54.** Métro: Vavin.

SIDE TRIPS
FROM PARIS

Paris is the center of a curious landlocked island known as the **Ile de France.** Shaped roughly as a saucer, it's encircled by a thin ribbon of rivers: the **Epte, Aisne, Marne,** and **Yonne.** Fringing these rivers are forests with famous names—**Rambouillet, St-Germain, Compiègne,** and **Fontainebleau.** These forests are said to be responsible for Paris's clear, gentle air and the unusual length of its spring and fall. This may be debatable, but there's no argument that they provide the capital with a fine series of day trips, all within easy reach.

The forests surrounding Paris were once the domain of royalty and the aristocracy, and they're still sprinkled with the magnificent châteaux of their former masters. Together with ancient villages, glorious cathedrals, and cozy country inns, they make the Ile de France irresistible. In this chapter, we offer only a handful of the possibilities for day jaunts. For a more extensive list, see *Frommer's France 2011.*

VERSAILLES ★

21km (13 miles) SW of Paris, 71km (44 miles) NE of Chartres

For centuries, the name of the Parisian suburb of Versailles resounded through the consciousness of every aristocratic family in Europe. The palace here outdazzled every other kingly residence in Europe—it was a horrendously expensive scandal and a symbol to later generations of a regime obsessed with prestige above all else.

Back in the *grand siècle* (the 17th c.), all you needed was a sword, a hat, and a bribe for the guard at the gate. Provided you didn't look as if you had smallpox, you'd be admitted to the **Château de Versailles,** where you could stroll through salon after glittering salon—watching the Sun King rise—and dress and dine and do even more intimate things while you gossiped, danced, plotted, flirted, and trysted.

You get to see only half of the palace's treasures; the rest are closed to the public. Some 3.2 million visitors arrive annually; on average, they spend 2 hours.

Essentials

GETTING THERE To get to Versailles, catch the **RER** line C1 to Versailles–Rive Gauche at the Gare d'Austerlitz, St-Michel, Musée d'Orsay, Invalides, Ponte de l'Alma, Champ de Mars, or Javel stop, and take it to the Versailles–Rive Gauche station. The trip takes 35 to 40 minutes. Do not get off at Versailles Chantier, which will leave you on the other end of town, a long

PREVIOUS PAGE: Fountain statuary at Versailles.

walk from the château. The round-trip fare is 5.60€; Eurailpass holders travel free on the RER but need to show the pass at the ticket kiosk to receive an RER ticket. **SNCF trains** (Société Nationale des Chemins de Fer) make frequent runs from Gare St-Lazare and Gare Montparnasse in Paris to Versailles: Trains departing from Gare St-Lazare arrive at the Versailles Rive Droite railway station; trains departing from Gare Montparnasse arrive at Versailles Chantiers station, a long walk as mentioned.

You can purchase the **Château Passeport,** which from April to October costs 20€ Monday to Friday, rising to 25€ Saturday and Sunday. From November to March its daily cost is 16€. The pass is sold at the tourist office in Versailles and with it you can avoid the long lines at the château itself.

The tourist office doesn't sell tickets to each of the sights so you should purchase the pass if you want to see the whole Versailles complex. If you hold the **Paris Museum Pass** (p. 241), admission is free to the château. You can also avoid the long ticket lines with the Paris Museum Pass.

An even better deal to consider is a combined RER train fare and château entrance ticket. These are sold at any SNCF (train) or Transilien (RER) station 7 days a week. Called *forfait,* the packet costs 22€, including the round-trip train fare from Paris and a 1-day Passeport. This is a great deal considering the cost of the Passeport itself (see above). The combined deal also allows you to avoid the long lines at the palace entrance.

Château de Versailles.

The Versailles–Rive Gauche station is within a 10-minute walk of the château, and we recommend the walk as a means of orienting yourself to the town, its geography, its scale, and its architecture. If you can't or don't want to walk, you can take bus B, or (in midsummer) a shuttle bus marked CHATEAU from either station to the château for either a cash payment of around 2€ (drop the coins directly into the coin box near the driver) or the insertion of a valid ticket for the Paris Métro. Because of the vagaries of the bus schedules, we highly recommend the walk. Directions to the château are clearly signposted from each railway station.

If you're **driving,** exit the *périphérique* (the ring road around Paris) on N10 (av. du Général-Leclerc), which will take you to Versailles; park on place d'Armes in front of the château.

VISITOR INFORMATION The **Office de Tourisme** is at 2 bis av. de Paris (✆ **01-39-24-88-88;** fax 01-39-24-88-89; www.versailles-tourisme.com). Closed Sunday and Monday.

EVENING SPECTACLES Recognizing the value of the palace as a national symbol, the French government offers a program of fireworks and illuminated fountains, "Les Fêtes de Nuit de Versailles," on about 7 to 10 widely publicized dates between late August and early September, usually beginning at 9:30pm. Observers, who sit in bleachers near the palace's boulevard de la Reine entrance, close to the Fountain *(Bassin)* of Neptune, are treated to a display of fireworks, prerecorded classical music, and up to 200 players (none of whom utters a line) in period costume, portraying the glories of France as symbolized by Louis XIV and the courtiers of the *ancien régime.* Shows are big on pomp and visuals, and last about 90 minutes. Tickets range from 45€ to 85€. Gates open around 90 minutes prior to showtime. For information, call ✆ **01-30-83-78-89.**

DAYTIME SPECTACLES Saturdays and Sundays from April to early October, between 11:30am and noon and 3:30 and 5pm, the French government broadcasts classical music throughout the park and opens the valves on as many fountains as are currently in operation as part of a program known as *Les Grandes Eaux Musicales de Versailles.* The spectacles showcase the landscaping vision of the palace's designers and encourage participants to walk, promenade, or meander the vast park, enjoying the juxtaposition of supremely grand architecture with lavish waterworks. Afternoon events include water coming out of more jets than during the somewhat less lavish morning events. Admission to any part of the park during these spectacles can vary widely from 6€ to 10€. For information, call ✆ **01-30-83-78-88.**

Versailles

allée des Matelots
Grand Canal
allée St-Antoine

allée d'Appolon
allée d'Appolon

Bassin d'Apollon

allée d'Appolon
allée d'Appolon

allée de Bacchus

Bassin du Miroir

allée du   allée du Printemps

et de Saturne

allée de l'Eté
allée de l'Eté

Bassin de Latone

allée de Céres

et de Flore

allée du Petit Pont

av. du Trianon

allée du Mail

Château
SOUTH WING   NORTH WING
Chapel
Royal Opera
Crusaders Gallery

Bassin de Neptune

Ballroom Grove **6**	Fountain of Enceladus **17**	Green Carpet **13**	Parterre of Latona **4**
Baths of Apollo **24**	Fountain of Neptune **30**	Grove of the Domes **16**	Pyramid Fountain **26**
Chestnut Grove **11**	Fountain of Spring **19**	King's Garden **9**	Queen's Grove **7**
Colonnade **12**	Fountain of Summer **23**	North Parterre **25**	South Parterre **1**
Diana's Bathing Nymphs **27**	Fountain of the	North Quincunx **20**	South Quincunx **5**
Dragon Fountain **29**	Blissful Ode **22**	Obelisk Fountain **18**	Star Grove **21**
Fountain of Apollo **14**	Fountain of Winter **10**	Orangery and Lake of	Water Avenue **28**
Fountain of Autumn **8**	Grand Canal **15**	the Swiss Guards **2**	Water Parterre **3**

You can purchase tickets to all spectacles at Versailles up until about a half-hour prior to the day or night of any performance from the ticket office in the *Accueil-Billeterie* on Place d'Armes, immediately across from the main facade of the palace, or from any French branch of the FNAC department store (FNAC's central phone number is ✆ **01-55-21-57-93**).

Hall of Mirrors.

Touring Versailles

Château de Versailles ★★★ Begun in 1661, its construction involved 32,000 to 45,000 workmen, some of whom had to drain marshes and move forests. Louis XIV set out to build a palace that would be the envy of Europe and created a symbol of opulence copied, yet never duplicated, the world over. Within 50 years, the Château de Versailles was transformed from Louis XIII's hunting lodge into an extravagant palace.

Wishing (with good reason) to keep an eye on the nobles of France, Louis XIV summoned them to live at his court. Here he amused them with constant entertainment and lavish banquets. To some he awarded such tasks as holding the hem of his robe. While the aristocrats played at often-silly intrigues and games, the peasants on the estates sowed the seeds of the Revolution.

When Louis XIV died in 1715, his great-grandson Louis XV succeeded him and continued the outrageous pomp, though he is said to have predicted the outcome: *"Après moi, le déluge"* ("After me, the deluge"). His wife, Marie Leszczynska, was shocked by the blatant immorality at Versailles.

The next monarch, Louis XVI, found his grandfather's behavior scandalous—in fact, on gaining the throne, he ordered that the "stairway of indiscretion" (secret stairs leading to the king's bedchamber) be removed. The well-intentioned but weak king and his queen, Marie Antoinette, were well liked at first, but the queen's frivolity and spending led to her downfall. Louis and Marie Antoinette were at Versailles on October 6, 1789, when they were notified that mobs were marching on the palace. As predicted, *le déluge* had arrived.

Napoleon stayed at Versailles but never seemed fond of it. Louis-Philippe (who reigned 1830–48) prevented the destruction of the palace by converting it into a museum dedicated to the glory of France. To do that, he had to surrender some of his own riches. Decades later, John D. Rockefeller contributed toward the restoration of Versailles, and work continues today.

The magnificent **Grands Appartements** ★★★ are in the Louis XIV style; each bears the name of the allegorical painting on the ceiling. The best-known and largest is the **Hercules Salon** ★★, with a ceiling painted by François Lemoine depicting the Apotheosis of Hercules. In the **Mercury Salon** (with a ceiling by Jean-Baptiste Champaigne), the body of Louis XIV was put on display in 1715; his 72-year reign was one of the longest in history.

The most famous room at Versailles is the 71m-long (233-ft.) **Hall of Mirrors** ★★★. Begun by Mansart in 1678 in the Louis XIV style, it was decorated by Le Brun with 17 arched windows faced by beveled mirrors in simulated arcades. The German Empire was proclaimed here in 1871. On June 28, 1919, the treaty ending World War I was signed in this corridor.

The royal apartments were for show, but Louis XV and Louis XVI retired to the **Petits Appartements ★★** to escape the demands of court etiquette. Louis XV died in his bedchamber in 1774, a victim of smallpox. In a second-floor apartment, which you can visit only with a guide, he stashed away first Mme de Pompadour and then Mme du Barry. Attempts have been made to return the Queen's Apartments to their appearance in the days of Marie Antoinette, when she played her harpsichord in front of special guests.

Louis XVI had a sumptuous **Library,** designed by Jacques-Ange Gabriel. Its panels are delicately carved, and the room has been restored and refurnished. The **Clock Room** contains Passement's astronomical clock, encased in gilded bronze. Twenty years in the making, it was completed in 1753. The clock is supposed to keep time until the year 9999. At age 7, Mozart played for the court in this room.

Gabriel designed the **Opéra ★★** for Louis XV in 1748, though it wasn't completed until 1770. In its heyday, it took 3,000 candles to light the place. Hardouin-Mansart built the harmoniously gold-and-white **Royal Chapel** in 1699, dying before its completion. Louis XVI married Marie Antoinette here in 1770, while he was the Dauphin.

Spread across 100 hectares (247 acres), the **Gardens of Versailles ★★★** were laid out by landscape artist André Le Nôtre. At the peak of their glory, 1,400

fountains spewed forth. *The Buffet* is an exceptional fountain, designed by Mansart. One fountain depicts Apollo in his chariot pulled by four horses, surrounded by Tritons rising from the water. Le Nôtre created a Garden of Eden using ornamental lakes and canals, geometrically designed flower beds, and avenues bordered with statuary. On the mile-long **Grand Canal,** Louis XV used to take gondola rides with his favorite of the moment.

CLOCKWISE FROM TOP: One of the Grands Appartements; a performance of *Pygmalion* at the Opéra; the elegant grounds of the château.

A RETURN TO faded glory

The French government is going to pour $455 million into a grand restoration of Versailles and its splendid gardens. The project, it is estimated, will take until 2024, but the attraction—one of the most visited in Europe—will remain open during the work in progress. The grand design of the architects is to make the palace, dating from the 17th century, look much as it did when it was home to Louis XIV, XV, and the ill-fated XVI. Some features will be removed, such as a wide staircase ordered built by King Louis-Philippe in the château's last major rebuilding in the 1830s. Other features will be added, including a replica of the *grille royale* that was torn out after the 1789 Revolution. Facilities for those with disabilities will also improve.

Developments within the sprawling infrastructure created by the monarchs of France include *Les Grandes Écuries* (the Stables), avenue Rockefeller, immediately opposite the château's main front facade, where the horses and carriages of the kings were housed. Visitors can watch a team of up to a dozen students, with their mounts, strut their stuff during hour-long riding demonstrations within the covered, 17th-century amphitheater of the historic stables. Horse lovers will appreciate the equestrian maneuvers that this riding school shows off during these presentations, but they shouldn't go with any expectations that the horsemanship will re-create exclusively 17th- and 18th-century styles. With a painted backdrop that reflects a circus theme, and with costumes that are colorful and artful but not exclusive to Versailles during its heyday, the focus is on showmanship and equestrian razzmatazz rather than exact replication of period costumes or riding styles. Each demonstration lasts about an hour. Demonstrations are conducted Tuesday to Thursday, and Saturday and Sunday, at 11:15am. There's an additional presentation every Saturday and Sunday at 2pm. Depending on what's happening, the price of tickets can vary, perhaps 20€ to 25€. There are no discounts for students or seniors, but children 9 and younger, accompanied by an adult, enter free. For additional information, contact the château directly at ✆ **01-30-83-78-00.**

Incidentally, participation in this event provides the only official way a visitor to Versailles can easily gain entrance to the stables, which contain a warren of narrow stalls for horses, as well as a large space with a plastered ceiling that's used as the amphitheater for displays of horsemanship.

On Christmas 1999, one of the worst storms in France's history destroyed some 10,000 historic trees on the grounds. Blowing at 161kmph (100 mph), gusts uprooted 80% of the trees planted during the 18th and 19th centuries. They included pines from Corsica planted during Napoleon's reign, tulip trees from Virginia, and a pair of junipers planted in honor of Marie Antoinette. Still, much remains to enchant you, and the restored gardens get better every month.

Place d'Armes. ✆ **01-30-83-78-00.** www.chateauversailles.fr. Palace 15€ adults; 13€ adults after 3pm; free for 18 and under. Both Trianons and Le Hameau (see listing below) 10€ adults; free for 26 and under. Everything free for children 17 and younger. Palace Apr–Oct Tues–Sun 9am–6:30pm; Nov–Mar Tues–Sun 9am–5:30pm. Trianons and Le Hameau Tues–Sun noon–6pm. Grounds daily dawn–dusk.

Grand Trianon.

Musée Lambinet ★   Often overlooked by visitors to Versailles, the Musée Lambinet is filled with treasures seized from the French court during the Revolution. Here are all the antiques, the carved wood paneling, and even religious art and other objets d'art so beloved by Marie Antoinette and the mistresses of Louis XV such as Mme de Pompadour and Mme du Barry. The sumptuous mansion from 1751 is also filled with paintings (no great masterpieces, however), along with weaponry, and rare porcelain (look for the Du Barry rose). Also on view are rare displays illustrating the lives of Jean-Paul Marat, the radical journalist, and his murderer, Charlotte Corday, as depicted in stage plays and films.

54 bd. de la Reine. ℂ **01-39-50-30-32.** www.musee-lambinet.fr. Admission 5.50€ adults; 2.50€ ages 6–18. Tues, Thurs, Sat–Sun 2–6pm; Wed 1–6pm; Fri 2–5pm.

The Trianons & The Hamlet A long walk across the park will take you to the **Grand Trianon (Grand Pavilion)** ★★, in pink-and-white marble. Le Vau built a Porcelain Trianon here in 1670, covered with blue-and-white china tiles, but it was fragile and soon fell into ruin. So, in 1687, Louis XIV commissioned Hardouin-Mansart to build the Grand Trianon. Traditionally, it has been a place where France has lodged

> ## Impressions
>
> *When Louis XIV finished the Grand Trianon (Grand Pavilion), he told [Mme de] Maintenon he had created a paradise for her, and asked if she could think of anything now to wish for . . . She said she could think of but one thing—it was summer, and it was balmy France—yet she would like well to sleigh ride in the leafy avenues of Versailles! The next morning found miles and miles of grassy avenues spread thick with snowy salt and sugar, and a procession of those quaint sleighs waiting to receive the chief concubine of the gaiest and most unprincipled court that France has ever seen!*
>
> —Mark Twain,
> *The Innocents Abroad* (1869)

important guests, though de Gaulle wanted to turn it into a weekend retreat. Nixon once slept here in the room where Mme de Pompadour died. Mme de Maintenon also slept here, as did Napoleon. The original furnishings are gone, of course, with mostly Empire pieces there today.

Marie Antoinette's Hamlet.

Gabriel, the designer of place de la Concorde in Paris, built the **Petit Trianon** ★★ in 1768 for Louis XV. Louis used it for his trysts with Mme du Barry. When he died, Louis XVI presented it to his wife, and Marie Antoinette adopted it as her favorite residence, a place to escape the rigid life and oppressive scrutiny at the main palace. Many of the current furnishings, including a few in her rather modest bedchamber, belonged to the ill-fated queen.

Rousseau's theories about recapturing the natural beauty and noble simplicity of life were much in favor in the late 18th century, and they prompted Marie Antoinette to have Mique build her the 12-house **Le Hameau (Hamlet)** on the banks of the Grand Trianon Lake in 1783. She wanted a chance to experience the simplicity of peasant life—or at least peasant life as seen through the eyes of a frivolous queen. Dressed as a shepherdess, she would come here to watch sheep being tended and cows being milked, men fishing, washerwomen beating their laundry in the lake, and donkey carts bringing corn to be ground at the mill. The interiors of the hamlets cannot be visited, but the surrounding informal landscaping—in obvious contrast to the formality of the other gardens at Versailles—and bizarre origins make views of their exteriors one of the most popular attractions here.

Follow the signs from the place d'Armes (to the immediate right after entering the Palace of Versailles). See previous entries for admission times and hours to visit.

Where to Dine

Gordon Ramsay au Trianon ★★★ FRENCH/INTERNATIONAL The *enfant terrible* of chefs, Gordon Ramsay, has invaded Versailles and is king of the roost at this Art Deco modernized restaurant inside the swanky Trianon Palace Hotel. He is a master at traditional French cooking done in a modern style, and changes his menu frequently to take advantage of the best and the freshest in any season. No one does filet of turbot like Ramsay. But the same could be said of his roast sea bass with asparagus cooked in foie gras. He stuffs delectable ravioli with langoustines, and if you toss a pork belly his way, he'll create a culinary masterpiece for you. The service, the setting—everything here is a delight. The food is of the highest order—and so are the prices. In summer, you can dine under the canopy on the front terrace.

In the Hotel Trianon Palace, 1 bd. de la Reine. ℂ **01-30-84-55-55.** www.gordonramsay.com. Reservations required. Main courses 55€–72€; fixed-price menu 150€. AE, DC, MC, V. Fri–Sat 12:30–2:30pm and Tues–Sat 7–10:30pm. Closed Jan and 1 week in Mar.

Le Potager du Roy ★ MODERN FRENCH   Philippe Letourneur spent years perfecting a distinctive cuisine and now adds novelty to the dining scene in Versailles. Letourneur rotates his skillfully prepared menu with the seasons. Examples are foie gras with vegetable-flavored vinaigrette, *pot-au-feu* of vegetables with foie gras, cream of lentil soup with scallops, roasted duck with *navarin* of vegetables, and roasted codfish with roasted peppers in the style of Provence. Looking for something unusual and earthier? Try fondant of pork jowls with fresh vegetables.

1 rue du Maréchal-Joffre. ✆ **01-39-50-35-34.** www.potager-du-roi.fr. Reservations required. Main courses 28€; fixed-price menu 34€–42€. AE, MC, V. Tues–Sat 12:30–2pm and 7:30–9:30pm.

Le Resto du Roy FRENCH   This informal bistro lies in an 18th-century building overlooking the western facade of the palace at Versailles. Orange and apricot tones prevailing in the main dining room evoke an autumnal theme. The chef prepares an appetizing array of dishes, including specialties such as duck foie gras with caramelized apples or salmon smoked with birch branches. For a main course, we recommend such dishes as fresh sole or sautéed scallops in a parsley sauce. A seasonal specialty is wild doe with chestnuts. For dessert, there are such grand choices as a souffle flambé with mandarin oranges or omelet Norwegian (called baked Alaska in the U.S.).

1 av. de St-Cloud. ✆ **01-39-50-42-26.** www.restaurant-versailles.com. Reservations required. Main courses 15€–16€; fixed-price menu 19€–36€. AE, MC, V. Daily 11:45am–2:30pm and 7–10:30pm.

THE FOREST & CHATEAU OF RAMBOUILLET ★

55km (34 miles) SW of Paris, 42km (26 miles) NE of Chartres

Château de Rambouillet.

Once known as La Forêt d'Yveline, the **Forest of Rambouillet** ★ is one of the loveliest forests in France. More than 19,000 hectares (46,950 acres) of greenery stretch from the valley of the Eure to the high valley of Chevreuse, the latter rich in medieval and royal abbeys. Lakes, copses of deer, and even wild boar are some of the attractions of this "green lung." Most people, however, come here to see the château, which you can visit when it's not in use as a "Camp David" for French presidents.

GETTING THERE   Trains depart from Paris's Gare Montparnasse every 20 minutes throughout the day for a 35-minute ride. Information and train schedules can be obtained by contacting **La Gare de Rambouillet,** place Prud'homme (✆ **08-91-36-20-20**). By **car,** take N10 southwest from Paris, passing Versailles along the way.

Château de Rambouillet.

VISITOR INFORMATION   The **tourist office** is at the Hôtel de Ville, place de la Libération (✆ **01-34-83-21-21;** www.ot-rambouillet.fr).

Seeing the Chateau

Château de Rambouillet ★   Dating from 1375, the château is surrounded by a park in one of the most famous forests in France. Superb woodwork is used throughout, and the walls are adorned with tapestries, many from the era of Louis XV. Before it became a royal residence, the marquise de Rambouillet kept a house here; it's said she taught Paris's cultured ladies and gentlemen how to talk, introducing them to poets and painters. François I, the Chevalier king, died of a fever here in 1547 at age 52. When the château was later occupied by the comte de Toulouse, Rambouillet was often visited by Louis XV, who was amused (in more ways than one) by the comte's high-spirited wife. Louis XVI, eventually acquired the château, but Marie Antoinette found it boring and called it "the toad." In his surprisingly modest boudoir are four panels representing the continents.

In 1814, Napoleon's second wife, Marie-Louise (daughter of Francis II, emperor of Austria), met at Rambouillet with her father, who convinced her to abandon Napoleon and France after her husband's defeats at Moscow and Leipzig. Afterward, she fled to her original home, the royal court in Vienna, with Napoleon's 3-year-old son, François-Charles-Joseph Bonaparte (also known as l'Aiglon—the Young Eagle—and, at least in title, the King of Rome). Before his death in Vienna at age 21, his claim on the Napoleonic legacy was rejected by France's enemies, despite the fact that his father had had a special annex to the château at Rambouillet built especially for his use. Before his final exile to the remote island of St. Helena, Napoleon insisted on spending a final night at Rambouillet, where he secluded himself with his meditations and memories.

In 1830, the elderly Charles X, Louis XVI's brother, abdicated the throne at Rambouillet as a mob marched on the château and his troops began to desert him. From Rambouillet, he embarked for a safe but controversial haven in England. Afterward, Rambouillet fell into private hands. At one time it was a fashionable

Through an Enchanted Forest

Rambouillet and its forests can provide a verdant interlude. If you've exhausted by the idea of a ramble through the gardens that surround the château (or if they're closed because of a visit from the president of France), consider a visit to the **Rochers d'Angennes,** rocky hillocks that remain as leftovers from the Ice Age. To reach them, park your car on the D107, where you'll see a sign pointing to the **Rochers et Etang d'Angennes,** about 4km (2½ miles) north of the hamlet of Epernon. Walk along a clearly marked trail through a pine forest before you eventually reach a rocky plateau overlooking the hills and a pond (*l'Etang d'Angennes*) nestled into the surrounding countryside. Round-trip, from the site of your parked car to the plateau and back, your promenade should take between 30 and 45 minutes.

restaurant attracting Parisians by offering gondola rides. Napoleon III returned it to the Crown. In 1897, it was designated a residence for the presidents of the republic. In 1944, Charles de Gaulle lived here briefly before giving the order for what was left of the French army to join the Americans in liberating Paris.

It takes about 2 hours to see the château at Rambouillet.

Parc du Château. ✆ **01-34-83-00-25.** Admission 5€ adults, 3.50€ students 18–25, free for children 18 and younger. Apr–Sept Wed–Mon 10am–noon and 2–6pm; Oct–Mar Wed–Mon 10am–noon and 2–5pm.

Where to Dine

La Poste TRADITIONAL FRENCH   On a corner in the town's historic center, this restaurant dates from the mid–19th century, when it provided meals and shelter for the region's mail carriers. The two dining rooms have rustic beams and old-fashioned accents that complement the flavorful old-fashioned food. Good-tasting menu items include a fricassee of chicken and crayfish; and noisettes of lamb "prepared in the style of a roebuck," with a *grand Veneur* sauce (that's made with red wine, autumn berries, a touch of vinegar, and crème fraîche). Also popular are civets of both *une biche* (female venison) and rabbit.

101 rue du Général-de-Gaulle. ✆ **01-34-83-03-01.** Reservations recommended Sat–Sun. Main courses 18€–20€; fixed-price menu 23€–40€. AE, MC, V. Tues–Thurs and Sat noon–2pm; Fri–Sat and Tues–Wed 7–9:30pm. Closed 1 week of Jan.

THE CATHEDRAL AT CHARTRES ★★★

97km (60 miles) SW of Paris, 76km (47 miles) NW of Orléans

Many observers feel the architectural aspirations of the Middle Ages reached their highest expression in the glorious Cathédrale de Chartres. Come to see its soaring architecture; highly wrought sculpture; and above all, its stained glass, which gave the world a new color: Chartres blue. It takes a full day to see Chartres.

GETTING THERE   From Paris's Gare Montparnasse, **trains** run directly to Chartres, taking less than an hour. Tickets cost 27€ round-trip. Call 🕾 **08-92-35-35-35.** If **driving,** take A10/A11 southwest from the *périphérique* and follow signs to Le Mans and Chartres. (The Chartres exit is clearly marked.)

VISITOR INFORMATION   The **Office de Tourisme** is on place de la Cathédrale (🕾 **02-37-18-26-26;** fax 02-37-21-51-91; www.chartres-tourisme.com).

Seeing the Cathedral

Cathédrale Notre-Dame de Chartres ★★★   Reportedly, Rodin once sat for hours on the sidewalk, admiring this cathedral's Romanesque sculpture. His opinion: Chartres is the French Acropolis. When it began to rain, a kind soul offered him an umbrella, which he declined, so transfixed was he by this place.

The cathedral's origins are uncertain; some have suggested it grew up over an ancient Druid site that later became a Roman temple. As early as the 4th century, there was a Christian basilica here. An 1194 fire destroyed most of what had by then become a Romanesque cathedral but spared the western facade and crypt. The cathedral you see today dates principally from the 13th century, when it was rebuilt with the efforts and contributions of kings, princes, churchmen, and pilgrims from all over Europe. One of the world's greatest high Gothic cathedrals, it was the first to use flying buttresses to support the soaring dimensions within.

French sculpture in the 12th century broke into full bloom when the **Royal Portal ★★★** was added. A landmark in Romanesque art, the sculptured bodies are elongated, often stylized, in their long, flowing robes. But the faces are

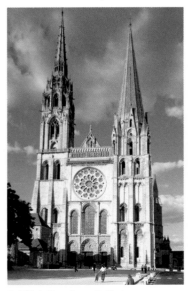

Cathédrale Notre-Dame de Chartres.

Magnificent stained glass at Chartres.

amazingly (for the time) lifelike, occasionally winking or smiling. In the central tympanum, Christ is shown at the Second Coming, with his descent depicted on the right and his ascent on the left. Before entering, walk around to both the **North Portal** and the **South Portal,** each from the 13th century. They depict such biblical scenes as the expulsion of Adam and Eve from the Garden of Eden.

Inside is a celebrated **choir screen;** work on it began in the 16th century and lasted until 1714. The niches, 40 in all, contain statues illustrating scenes from the life of the Madonna and Christ—everything from the *Massacre of the Innocents* to the *Coronation of the Virgin.*

However, few rushed visitors ever notice the screen because they're too transfixed by the light from the **stained glass ★★★**.

Covering an expanse of more than 2,500 sq. m. (26,910 sq. ft.), the glass is unlike anything else in the world. The stained glass, most of which dates from the 12th and 13th centuries, was spared in both world wars by being painstakingly removed, piece by piece, and stored away. See the windows in the morning, at noon, in the afternoon, at sunset—as often as you can. Like the petals of a kaleidoscope, they constantly change. It's difficult to single out one panel or window above the others, but an exceptional one is the 12th-century *Vierge de la Belle Verrière* (**Our Lady of the Beautiful Window**) on the south side. Of course, there are three fiery rose windows, but you couldn't miss those if you tried.

The **nave,** the widest in France, still contains its ancient floor labyrinth, which formed a mobile channel of contemplation for monks. The wooden *Notre-Dame du Piller* (**Virgin of the Pillar**), to the left of the choir, dates from the 14th century. The crypt was built over 2 centuries, beginning in the 9th. Enshrined within is *Our Lady of the Crypt,* a 1976 Madonna that replaced one destroyed during the Revolution.

Try to take a tour conducted by Malcolm Miller (*©* **02-37-28-15-58;** fax 02-37-28-33-03; millerchartres@aol.com), an Englishman who has spent 3 decades studying the cathedral and giving tours in English. His rare blend of scholarship, enthusiasm, and humor will help you understand and appreciate the cathedral. He usually conducts 75-minute tours at noon and 2:45pm Monday to Saturday for 10€ for adults or 5€ students. Tours are canceled during pilgrimages, religious celebrations, and large funerals.

If you're fit enough, don't miss the opportunity, especially in summer, to climb to the top of the tower.

After your visit, stroll through the **Episcopal Gardens** and enjoy yet another view of this remarkable cathedral.

16 Cloître Notre-Dame. © **02-37-21-22-07.** www.monum.fr. Admission 7€ adults; 4.50€ adults 18–25; free for children 17 and under. Daily 8:30am–7:30pm.

Exploring the Old Town

If time remains, you may want to explore the medieval cobbled streets of the **Vieux Quartier (Old Town)** ★. At the foot of the cathedral are lanes containing gabled houses and humped bridges spanning the Eure River. From the Pont de Bouju, you can see the lofty spires in the background. Try to find **rue Chantault,** which boasts houses with colorful facades, one of which is 8 centuries old.

Musée des Beaux-Arts de Chartres ★ Located next to the cathedral, a stop here will be a highlight of your visit. A former Episcopal palace, the building at times competes with its exhibitions—one part dates from the 15th century and encompasses a courtyard. This museum of fine arts boasts a collection covering the 16th to the 20th centuries, including the work of masters such as Zurbarán, Watteau, and Brósamer. Of particular interest is David Ténier's *Le Concert*.

29 Cloître Notre-Dame. © **02-37-90-45-80.** May 3–Oct 30 Wed–Mon 10am–noon and 2–6pm (closed Sun mornings); the rest of the year, until 5pm. Admission 3€ adults, 1.50€ 18 and under.

Where to Stay

Grand Monarque Best Western The most appealing and desirable hotel in Chartres occupies an imposing civic monument whose 600-year-old foundations and infrastructures were gentrified some time in the 19th century with white stucco, neoclassical detailing, and touches of the baroque. Functioning as an inn since its original construction in the 15th century, and expanded and improved many times since then, it's a grand hotel that remains under the direction of the hardworking members of the Jallerat family. It

attracts guests who enjoy its old-world charm—such as Art Nouveau stained glass and Louis XV chairs in the dining room. The guest rooms are decorated with reproductions of antiques; most have sitting areas. The hotel provides solid and reliable comfort but not great style.

22 place des Epars, 28005 Chartres. © **800/528-1234** in the U.S., or 02-37-18-15-15. Fax 02-37-36-34-18. www.bw-grand-monarque.com. 60 units. 104€–180€ double; 210€–240€ suite. AE, DC, MC, V. Parking 8€. **Amenities:** 2 restaurants; bar; room service. *In room:* A/C (in some), TV, hair dryer, minibar, Wi-Fi (free).

Where to Dine

La Vieille Maison ★★ MODERN FRENCH Even if the food here weren't superb, the 14th-century building would still be visited for its historic value. The dining room, outfitted in the Louis XIII style, is centered on a narrow ceiling vault, less than 2m (6½ ft.) across, crafted of chiseled white stone blocks during the 9th century. Bruno

Chartres's Vieux Quartier.

Music of the Spheres

If you're visiting Chartres on a Sunday afternoon, the cathedral has a free 1-hour organ concert at 4:45pm, when the filtered light of the Ile de France sunset makes the western windows come thrillingly alive.

Letartre, the only *maître cuisinier de France* in Chartres, supervises the cuisine. The menu changes four or five times a year, reflecting the seasonality of the Ile de France and its produce. Some good examples include foie gras of duckling, roasted crayfish with Indian spices, foie gras served on sliced rye bread, brochettes of lobster and scallops with spaghetti, *suprême* of turbot with baby vegetables and saffron, and noisettes of venison fried with Jamaican and Szechuan pepper and wild mushrooms. Dessert fans should go with the thin apple-and-fig tart served with walnut-flavored ice cream.

5 rue au Lait. ☎ **02-37-34-10-67.** www.lavieillemaison.fr. Reservations recommended. Main courses 32€–38€; fixed-price menu 20€–45€. MC, V. Tues–Sun noon–2:15pm; Tues–Sat 7–10pm. Closed 1 week in Aug.

Le Geôrges ★★ FRENCH   The best food and the most upscale dining ambience in Chartres is now found at the town's best hotel, an also-recommended establishment with roots that go back to the 15th century, when the site served food and drink (not as elegant as what you'll find today) to weary travelers and postal workers. Menu items change with the seasons but usually include savory portions of *pâté de Chartres,* made with a combination of minced meats that includes wild duck baked in a giant puff pastry; a steamed combination of crayfish with scallops in wine sauce; and a superb version of roasted veal "Grand Monarque," served with a casserole of mushrooms and cheese. Also interesting is lobster "prepared in the style of perch," with a reduction of apple-flavored Calvados and Newburg (specifically, lobster) sauce. Desserts are sumptuous, and the cheese trolley will warm the heart of any Francophile.

In the Grand Monarque Best Western, 22 place des Epars. ☎ **02-37-18-15-15.** www.bw-grand-monarque.com. Reservations recommended. Main courses 18€–36€; fixed-price menu 48€–85€. AE, DC, MC, V. Tues–Sun noon–2:45pm; Tues–Sat 7–10pm.

GIVERNY ★

80km (50 miles) NW of Paris

On the border between Normandy and the Ile de France, Giverny—now the home of the Claude Monet Foundation—is where the great painter lived for 43 years. The restored house and its gardens are open to the public. Budget 2 hours to spend at Giverny.

GETTING THERE   It takes a morning to get to Giverny and to see its sights. Take the Paris-Rouen **train** from Paris's Gare St-Lazare to the Vernon station, where a taxi can take you the 5km (3 miles) to Giverny. Vernon itself lies 40km (25 miles) southeast of Rouen. Perhaps the easiest way to get there is on a 5-hour **bus tour** from Paris, for 70€ per person, that focuses on Monet's house and garden. For ages 3 to 11, the fare is 36€. Tours depart at 1:45pm Monday to Saturday between April and October. You can arrange tours in the summer through **Cityrama,** 149 rue St-Honoré, 1er (☎ **01-44-55-61-00;** www.pariscityrama.com; Métro: Palais-Royal–Musée du Louvre), or year-round through **American Express,** 11 rue Scribe, 9e (© **01-47-14-50-00;** Métro: Opéra).

If you're **driving,** take the Autoroute de l'Ouest (Port de St-Cloud) toward Rouen. Leave the autoroute at Bonnières, and then cross the Seine on the Bonnières Bridge. From here, a direct road with signs leads to Giverny. Expect it to take about an hour; try to avoid weekends. Another approach is to leave the highway at the Bonnières exit and go toward Vernon. Once there, cross the bridge over the Seine and follow signs to Giverny or Gasny (Giverny is before Gasny). This is easier than going through Bonnières, where there aren't many signs.

VISITOR INFORMATION The **Office de Tourisme des Portes de l'Eure** is shared by Giverny and the nearby hamlet of Vernon (36 Carnot 27200 Vernon; © **02-32-51-39-60;** http://www.cape-tourisme.fr/web/index.php). Open October to April Tuesday to Saturday 9am to 12:30pm and 2 to 5:30pm, May to September 9am to 6pm.

Show Me the Monet

Claude Monet Foundation ★★★ Born in 1840, the French Impressionist was a brilliant innovator, who excelled at presenting the effects of light at different times of the day. Some critics claim that he "invented light." His paintings of the Rouen cathedral and of water lilies, which one critic called "vertical interpretations of horizontal lines," are just a few of his masterpieces.

Monet first came to Giverny in 1883. Many of his friends used to visit him here at Le Pressoir, including Clemenceau, Cézanne, Rodin, Renoir, Degas, and Sisley. When Monet died in 1926, his son, Michel, inherited the house, but left it

Monet's house.

Monet's garden pond.

abandoned until it decayed. The gardens became almost a jungle, inhabited by river rats. In 1966, Michel died and left it to the Académie des Beaux Arts. It wasn't until 1977 that Gerald van der Kemp, who restored Versailles, decided to work on Giverny. A large part of it was restored with gifts from U.S. benefactors, especially the late Lila Acheson Wallace, former head of *Reader's Digest*.

You can stroll the garden and view the thousands of flowers, including the *nymphéas*. The Japanese bridge, hung with wisteria, leads to a setting of weeping willows and rhododendrons. Monet's studio barge was installed on the pond.

84 rue Claude-Monet Parc Gasny. ⓒ **02-32-51-28-21.** www.fondation-monet.com. Admission 6€ adults, 4.50€ students, 3.50€ children 7–12, free for children 6 and younger. Apr–Oct daily 9:30am–6pm. Closed Nov–Mar.

Where to Stay

La Musardiere   Giverny has become so popular with visitors that many local homes are opening as B&Bs to accommodate the overnight flow. We find this small inn to be the best of the lot. Just a short walk from Monet's museum and gardens, it is a former manor house opening onto a scenic park filled with ancient trees. The building with its mansard roof dates from 1880 and was around in Monet's time. Many of the antique features and architectural adornments are still in place. Bedrooms are medium in size, attractively and comfortably furnished, each with a small bathroom with tub or shower. The hotel also operates its own restaurant and crêperie.

123 rue Claude-Monet, 27620 Giverny. ⓒ **02-32-21-03-18.** www.lamusardiere.fr. Fax 02-32-21-60-00. 10 units. 81€–89€ double; 130€ suite. AE, DC, MC, V. Free parking. Closed: Jan. **Amenities:** Restaurant; bar. *In room:* TV, hair dryer, Wi-Fi (free).

Where to Dine

Baudy FRENCH   We hesitate to recommend this place because of the never-ending buses arriving from Paris, but it's a local legend and deserves a look. During the town's 19th-century heyday, the American painters used the pink villa as their lodging. In Monet's time, this place was an *epicerie-buvette* (casual hangout) run by the painter's friends Angelina and Gaston Baudy. Metcalf was the first artist to arrive on Mme Baudy's doorstep, and in time a string of other painters followed. Artists such as Cézanne could be found wandering around the rose garden here. The place no longer has its "legendary two tables," at which Mme Baudy fed the artists, but it now plays host to virtually all visitors to Giverny, feeding them simply prepared, traditional French cuisine, including big, freshly made salads and a changing array of hot food.

81 rue Claude-Monet. ☎ **02-32-21-10-03.** Reservations recommended. Main courses 14€–21€; fixed-price menu 24€. MC, V. daily 10am–9:30pm; Sun 10am–3pm. Closed Nov–Mar.

Restaurant Les Fleurs ★ FRENCH   Capably managed by Bernard Lefebvre, this pleasant, popular restaurant does a large percentage of its business with art lovers. The Claude Monet Foundation is just across the river in Giverny. On the main street of Vernon, 4.8km (3 miles) southwest of the museum, the restaurant focuses on flavorful, familiar *cuisine bourgeoise* that many diners remember fondly from their childhoods. Chef Bernard served an apprenticeship with culinary megastar Alain Ducasse. Menu items include fresh fish such as sea bass served with saffron sauce and a flavorful risotto of the day, and sweetbreads braised with Parmesan. Other dishes include an array of homemade terrines and pâtés; fresh scallops with spice cocoa sauce; a platter devoted to different preparations of duckling; and a variety of meats grilled, simply and flavorfully, *à la plancha.*

71 rue Sadi-Carnot, Vernon. From the Claude Monet Foundation in Giverny, drive 5km (3 miles) southwest, crossing the Seine, and follow signs to Vernon. ☎ **02-32-51-16-80.** Reservations recommended. Main courses 18€–30€; fixed-price menu 18€–47€. AE, MC, V. Wed–Sun noon–2pm; Tues–Sat 7:30–10pm.

DISNEYLAND PARIS

32km (20 miles) E of Paris

After provoking some of the most enthusiastic and controversial reactions in recent French history, the multimillion-dollar Disneyland Paris opened in 1992. It's one of the world's most lavish theme parks, conceived on a scale rivaling that of Versailles. European journalists initially accused it of everything from cultural imperialism to the death knell of French culture.

But after goodly amounts of public relations and financial juggling, Disneyland Paris has become France's number-one tourist attraction, with 50 million visitors annually. It surpasses the Eiffel Tower and the Louvre in the number of visitors and accounts for 4% of the French tourism industry's foreign currency sales. About 40% of the visitors are French, half from Paris. Disneyland Paris looks, tastes, and feels like the ones in California and Florida—except the expensive cheeseburgers come *"avec pommes frites."*

Situated on a 2,000-hectare (4,942-acre) site (about one-fifth the size of Paris) in the suburb of Marne-la-Vallée,

Sleeping Beauty Castle.

Fast Pass Those Long Lines

Disneyland Paris has instituted a program that's done well at the other parks. With the Fast Pass system, visitors to the various rides reserve a 1-hour time block. Within that block, the waiting is usually no more than 8 minutes.

the park incorporates the most successful elements of its Disney predecessors combined with European flair. In terms of the other Disney parks (excluding Tokyo), Disneyland Paris definitely lies in the middle, with top honors going to Florida. The California Disneyland emerges as a distant third. The Florida park is larger than the Paris property, with more attractions and rides. But Disneyland Paris does a decent job of re-creating the Magic Kingdom. In 2002, the Paris park added **Walt Disney Studios,** focusing on the role of movies in popular culture.

Take 1 day for the highlights, 2 days for more depth.

GETTING THERE   The RER commuter express **rail** network (Line A) stops within walking distance of the park. Board the RER in Paris at Charles-de-Gaulle–Etoile, Châtelet–Les Halles, or Nation. Get off at Line A's last stop, Marne-la-Vallée/Chessy, 45 minutes from central Paris. The round-trip fare is 12€ or 6.30€ one-way. Trains run daily, every 10 to 20 minutes from 5:30am to midnight.

   Shuttle buses connect Orly and Charles de Gaulle airports with each hotel in the resort. Buses depart the airports every 30 to 45 minutes. One-way transport to the park from either airport is 14€ for adults, 12€ for children 3 to 11.

   If you're **driving,** take A4 east from Paris and get off at exit 14, DISNEYLAND PARIS. Parking begins at 8€ per day, but is free if you stay at one of the park hotels. A series of moving sidewalks speeds up pedestrian transit from parking areas to the park entrance.

VISITOR INFORMATION   All the hotels we recommend offer general information on the theme park. For details and reservations at any of its hotels, contact the **Disneyland Paris Guest Relations Office,** located in City Hall on Main Street, U.S.A. (© **01-60-30-60-53** in English, or 08-25-30-60-30 in French; www.disneylandparis.com). For information on Disneyland Paris and specific details on the many other attractions and monuments in the Ile de France and the rest of the country, contact the **Maison du Tourisme,** Disney Village (B.P. 77705), Marne-la-Vallée (© **01-60-43-33-33**).

ADMISSION   Admission varies depending on the season. In peak season, a 1-day park ticket costs 52€ for adults, 44€ for children 3 to 12, free for children 2 and younger; a 2-day park-hopper ticket is 110€ for adults, 96€ for kids; and a 3-day park-hopper ticket is 159€ for adults, 117€ for kids. Peak season is from mid-June to mid-September as well as Christmas and Easter weeks. Entrance to Disney Village is free, though there's usually a cover charge at the dance clubs.

HOURS   Hours vary throughout the year, but most frequently they are 10am to 7pm. Be warned that autumn and winter hours vary the most; it depends on the weather and national holidays. It's a good idea to phone ahead if you're contemplating a visit at this time.

Spending the Day at Disney

Disneyland Paris ★★★   The resort was designed as a total vacation destination: In one enormous unit, the park includes five "lands" of entertainment, a dozen hotels, a campground, an entertainment center (**Disney Village,** with six restaurants of its own), a 27-hole golf course, and dozens of restaurants, shows, and shops. The Disney Village entertainment center is illuminated inside by a spectacular gridwork of lights suspended 18m (59 ft.) above the ground. The complex contains dance clubs, shops, restaurants (one of which offers a dinner spectacle based on the original *Buffalo Bill's Wild West Show*), bars for adults trying to escape their children, a French Government Tourist Office, a post office, and a marina.

Visitors stroll among flower beds, trees, reflecting ponds, fountains, and a large artificial lake flanked with hotels. An army of smiling employees and Disney characters—many of whom are multilingual, including Buffalo Bill, Mickey and Minnie Mouse, and of course, the French-born Caribbean pirate Jean Laffite—are on hand to greet the thousands of *enfants.*

Main Street, U.S.A., abounds with horse-drawn carriages and barbershop quartets. Steam-powered railway cars embark from the Main Street Station for a trip through a Grand Canyon diorama to **Frontierland,** with its paddlewheel steamers reminiscent of Mark Twain's Mississippi River. Other attractions include a petting zoo—the Critter Corral—at the Cottonwood Creek Ranch, and

---

FOR THOSE WITH ANOTHER DAY:
walt disney studios

Walt Disney Studios takes guests on a behind-the-scenes interactive discovery of film, animation, and television.

The main entrance to the studios, called the **Front Lot,** consists of "Sunset Boulevard," an elaborate sound stage complete with hundreds of film props. The **Animation Courtyard** allows visitors to learn the trade secrets of Disney animators, and the **Production Courtyard** lets guests take a look behind the scenes of film and TV production. At **Catastrophe Canyon,** guests are plunged into the heart of a film shoot. Finally, the **Back Lot** is home to special effects and stunt workshops. A live stunt show features cars, motorbikes, and jet skis.

This ode to Hollywood and the films it produced since the end of its "golden age" has a rollercoaster, the Rock 'n'

Roller Coaster, featuring the music of Aerosmith, that combines rock memorabilia with high-speed scary twists and turns (completely in the dark); and a reconstruction of one of the explosion scenes in the Hollywood action film *Armageddon.*

Admission is 59€ for adults, 43€ for children. Hours are daily from 10am to 7pm.

Adventureland.

the Lucky Nugget Saloon, inspired by the Gold Rush era. The steps and costumes of the saloon's cancan show originated in the cabarets of turn-of-the-20th-century Paris.

The park's steam trains chug past **Adventureland**—with its swashbuckling pirates, Swiss Family Robinson treehouse, and re-enacted Arabian Nights legends—to **Fantasyland.** Here you'll find the **Sleeping Beauty Castle (*Le Château de la Belle au Bois Dormant*),** whose pinnacles and turrets are an idealized (and spectacular) interpretation of French châteaux. In its shadow are Europeanized versions of *Blanche Neige et Les Sept Nains* (*Snow White and the Seven Dwarfs*), Peter Pan, Dumbo, Alice (from Wonderland), the Mad Hatter's Teacups, and Sir Lancelot's Magic Carousel.

Visions of the future are in **Discoveryland,** where tributes to invention and imagination draw from the works of Leonardo da Vinci, Jules Verne, H. G. Wells, the modern masters of science fiction, and the *Star Wars* series.

You'll see characters from *Aladdin, The Lion King, Pocahontas, Toy Story,* and *Chicken Little.* As Disney continues to churn out animated blockbusters, look for the newest stars to appear in the theme park.

Where to Stay

You can easily make Disneyland a day trip from Paris—the transportation links are excellent—or spend the night.

The resort's six theme hotels share a reservation service. In North America, call ✆ **407/W-DISNEY** (934-7639). In France, contact the **Central Reservations Office,** Euro Disney Resort, S.C.A., B.P. 105, F-77777 Marne-la-Vallée Cedex 4 (✆ **08-25-30-60-30;** www.disneylandparis.com).

VERY EXPENSIVE

Disneyland Hotel ★★ Mouseketeers who have rich daddies and mommies frequent Disney's poshest resort. At the park entrance, this flagship four-story hotel is Victorian, with red-tile turrets and jutting balconies. The spacious guest rooms are plushly furnished but evoke the image of Disney, with cartoon depictions and candy-stripe decor. The beds are king-size, double, or twin; in some rooms armchairs convert to beds. Accommodations in the rear overlook Sleeping Beauty Castle and Big Thunder Mountain. Some less desirable units open onto a parking lot. The luxurious bathrooms have marble vanities, showers and tubs, and twin basins. On the Castle Club floor, you get free newspapers, all-day beverages, and access to a well-equipped private lounge.

Disneyland Paris, B.P. 111, F-77777 Marne-la-Vallée Cedex 4. ☎ **01-60-45-65-89.** Fax 01-60-45-65-33. www.disneylandparis.com. 495 units. 526€–853€ double; from 770€ suite. Rates include breakfast. AE, DC, MC, V. **Amenities:** 2 restaurants; bar; babysitting; health club & spa; pool (indoor); room service. *In room:* A/C, TV, TV/DVD player, hair dryer, minibar, Wi-Fi (10€ for 3 hr.).

EXPENSIVE

Newport Bay Club ★★   You expect to see the reincarnation of Joe Kennedy walking along the veranda with its slated roofs, awnings, and pergolas. It's very Hyannisport here. It's also the biggest hotel in France. With a central cupola, balconies, and a blue-and-cream color scheme, it recalls a harborfront New England hotel (ca. 1900). The layout features nautically decorated rooms in various shapes and sizes. The most spacious are the corner units.

Disneyland Paris, B.P. 105, F-77777 Marne-la-Vallée Cedex 4. ☎ **01-60-45-55-00.** Fax 01-60-45-55-33. www.disneylandparis.com. 1,093 units. 240€–454€ double; 500€–840€ suite. Rates include breakfast. AE, DC, MC, V. **Amenities:** 2 restaurants; bar; state-of-the-art health club; 2 pools (indoor and outdoor); room service. *In room:* A/C, TV/DVD player, minibar, Wi-Fi (15€ per day).

MODERATE

Hotel Cheyenne/Hotel Santa Fe ☺   Next door to each other near a re-creation of Texas's Rio Grande, these Old West–style lodgings are the resort's least expensive hotels. The Cheyenne consists of 14 two-story buildings along Desperado Street; the desert-themed Santa Fe encompasses four "nature trails" winding among 42 adobe-style pueblos. The Cheyenne is a favorite among families, offering a double bed and bunk beds. Children have an array of activities, including a play area in a log cabin with a lookout tower and a section where you can explore the "ruins" of an ancient Anasazi village. The only disadvantage is the absence of a pool.

More recently constructed, but charging the same prices, is the nearby **Kyriad Hotel,** a government-rated two-star hotel designed for families, that evokes the aesthetics and layout of a French country inn. Whenever the Cheyenne and the Santa Fe are full, Disney usually directs the overflow to the Kyriad.

Disneyland Paris, B.P. 115, F-77777 Marne-la-Vallée Cedex 4. ☎ **01-60-45-63-12** (Cheyenne) or 01-60-45-79-22 (Santa Fe). Fax 01-60-45-62-33 (Cheyenne) or 01-60-45-78-33 (Santa Fe). www.disneylandparis.com. 2,000 units. Hotel Cheyenne 131€–279€ double; Hotel Santa Fe 112€–249€ double. Rates include breakfast. AE, DC, MC, V. **Amenities:** Restaurant; bar; babysitting. *In room:* A/C, TV, Wi-Fi (15€ per 100 min.).

Where to Dine

Disneyland Paris offers a gamut of cuisine in more than 45 restaurants and snack bars. You can live on burgers and fries, or you can experiment at the following upscale restaurants.

California Grill ★★ ☺ CALIFORNIAN/FRENCH   The resort's showcase restaurant serves cuisine that's equal to the fare at a one-Michelin-star restaurant. Focusing on the lighter specialties for which the Golden State is famous, with many concessions to French palates, the elegant restaurant accommodates both adults and children gracefully. Even French food critics are impressed with the oysters prepared with leeks and salmon. We also embrace the appetizer of foie gras with roasted red peppers, and rate as simply fabulous the roasted pigeon with braised Chinese cabbage and black-rice vinegar. Another winning selection is fresh salmon roasted over beechwood and served with a sprinkling of walnut oil, sage sauce, asparagus, and fricassee of forest mushrooms. Many items are specifically for children. If you want a quiet, mostly adult venue, go here as late as your hunger pangs will allow.

In the Disneyland Hotel. ☎ **01-60-45-65-76.** Reservations required. Fixed-price menu 57€–71€; children's menu 17€–20€. AE, DC, MC, V. Daily 6:30–10:30pm.

Inventions 🏄 INTERNATIONAL   This may be the only buffet restaurant in Europe where animated characters from the Disney films (including Mickey and Minnie) go table-hopping. With views over a park, the restaurant contains four enormous buffet tables devoted to starters, shellfish, main courses, and desserts. Selections are wide, portions can be copious, and no one leaves hungry. Don't expect *grande cuisine*—that's the domain of the more upscale California Grill (see the previous listing), in the same hotel. What you'll get is a sense of American bounty and culinary generosity, with ample doses of cartoon fantasy.

In the Disneyland Hotel. ☎ **01-60-45-65-83.** Buffet 49€ adults, 25€ children 7–11, 19€ children 3–6. AE, DC, MC, V. Daily 12:30–3pm and 6–10:30pm.

Disneyland After Dark

The premier theatrical venue is **Le Legende de Buffalo Bill** in Disney Village (☎ **01-60-45-71-00**). The twice-per-night stampede of entertainment recalls the show that once traveled the West with Buffalo Bill and Annie Oakley. You'll dine at tables arranged amphitheater-style around a rink where sharpshooters, runaway stagecoaches, and dozens of horses and Indians ride fast and perform alarmingly realistic acrobatics. A Texas-style barbecue, served in an assembly line by waiters in 10-gallon hats, is part of the experience. Despite its corny elements, it's not without its charm. Wild Bill is dignified and the Indians are suitably brave. Shows start at 6:30 and 9:30pm; the cost (dinner included) is 59€ for adults, 45€ for children 3 to 11.

FONTAINEBLEAU ★

60km (37 miles) S of Paris, 74km (46 miles) NE of Orléans

Within the forest that bears its name (Forêt de Fontainebleau), this suburb of Paris has offered refuge to French monarchs throughout the country's history. Renaissance kings valued it because of its nearness to rich hunting grounds and its distance from the slums and smells of the city. Napoleon referred to the Palais de Fontainebleau, which he embellished with his distinctive monogram and decorative style, as "the house of the centuries." Many pivotal and decisive events have occurred inside, perhaps none more memorable than when Napoleon stood on the horseshoe-shaped exterior stairway and bade farewell to his shattered army before departing for Elba.

After the glories of Versailles, a visit to Fontainebleau can be a bit of a letdown, especially if you visit on the day after you saw Versailles. But Fontainebleau, although a grand château, actually looks like a place where a king could live, whereas Versailles is more of a production. If you stay for lunch, a trip to Fontainebleau should last a half-day.

Château de Fontainebleau.

GETTING THERE **Trains** to Fontainebleau depart from the Gare de Lyon in Paris. The trip takes 45 minutes each way and costs 7.50€ one-way. Fontainebleau's railway station lies 3km (1¾ miles) north of the château, in the suburb of Avon. A local bus (marked simply CHATEAU and part of line A) makes the trip to the château at 15-minute intervals Monday through Saturday and at 30-minute intervals on Sunday; the fare is 1.40€ each way. If you're **driving,** take A6 south from Paris, exit onto N191, and follow the signs.

VISITOR INFORMATION The **Office de Tourisme** is at 4 rue Royale, Fontainebleau (✆ **01-60-74-99-99;** www.fontainebleau-tourisme.com), opposite the main entrance to the château.

Seeing the Place

Musée National du Château de Fontainebleau ★★★ Napoleon's affection for this palace was understandable. He followed the pattern of a succession of French kings in the pre-Versailles days who used Fontainebleau as a resort and hunted in its forests. François I tried to turn the hunting lodge into a royal palace in the Italian Renaissance style, bringing artists, including Benvenuto Cellini, there to work for him. Under this patronage, the School of Fontainebleau gained prestige, led by painters Rosso Fiorentino and Primaticcio. The artists adorned the 63m-long (207-ft.) **Gallery of François I ★★★**, where stucco-framed panels depict such scenes as *The Rape of Europa* and the monarch holding a pomegranate, a symbol of unity. The salamander, the symbol of the Chevalier king, is everywhere.

Sometimes called the Gallery of Henri II, the **Ballroom ★★★** displays the interlaced initials "H&D," referring to Henri and his mistress, Diane de Poitiers. Competing with this illicit tandem are the initials "H&C," symbolizing Henri and his ho-hum wife, Catherine de Médici. At one end of the room is a monumental fireplace supported by two bronze satyrs, made in 1966 (the originals were melted

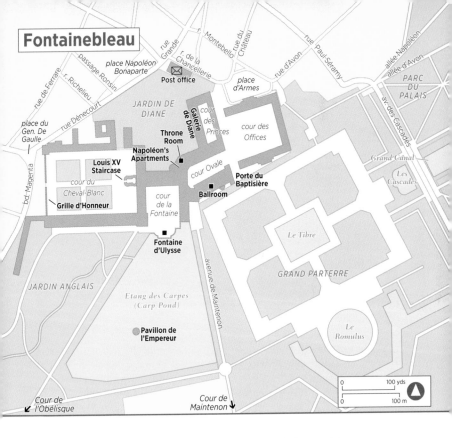

Fontainebleau

place Napoléon Bonaparte
place d'Armes
JARDIN DE DIANE
Galerie de Diane
cour des Princes
cour des Offices
Throne Room
Napoléon's Apartments
Louis XV Staircase
cour Ovale
Porte du Baptisière
cour du Cheval-Blanc
cour de la Fontaine
Ballroom
Grille d'Honneur
Fontaine d'Ulysse
Grand Canal
Les Cascades
Le Tibre
GRAND PARTERRE
JARDIN ANGLAIS
Etang des Carpes (Carp Pond)
avenue de Maintenon
Le Romulus
Pavillon de l'Empereur
PARC DU PALAIS
Cour de l'Obélisque
Cour de Maintenon

down during the Revolution). At the other side is the balcony of the musicians, with sculptured garlands. The ceiling displays octagonal coffering adorned with rosettes. Above the wainscoting is a series of frescoes, painted between 1550 and 1558, that depict subjects such as *The Feast of Bacchus*. An architectural curiosity is the richly adorned **Louis XV Staircase ★★**. The room above it was originally decorated by Primaticcio for the bedroom of the duchesse d'Etampes, but when an architect was designing the stairway, he simply ripped out her floor. Of the Italian frescoes that were preserved, one depicts the queen of the Amazons climbing into Alexander the Great's bed.

When Louis XIV ascended to the throne, he neglected Fontainebleau because of his preoccupation with Versailles. However, he wasn't opposed to using the palace for houseguests, specifically such unwanted ones as Queen Christina, who had abdicated the throne of Sweden in a fit of religious fervor. Under the assumption that she still had "divine right," she ordered the brutal murder of her companion Monaldeschi, who had ceased

Detail of the Ballroom.

Gallery of François I.

to please her. Though Louis XV and then Marie Antoinette took an interest in Fontainebleau, the château found its renewed glory under Napoleon. You can wander around much of the palace on your own, visiting sites evoking the Corsican's 19th-century imperial heyday. They include the **throne room** where he abdicated rule of France, his **offices,** his monumental **bedroom,** and his **bathroom.** Some of the smaller Napoleonic rooms contain his personal mementos and artifacts.

After your trek through the palace, visit the **gardens** and especially the **carp pond;** the gardens, however, are only a prelude to the Forest of Fontainebleau.

Place du Général-de-Gaulle. ☎ **01-60-71-50-60.** www.musee-chateau-fontainebleau.fr. Combination ticket including private *appartements* 8€ adults, 6€ students 18–25; ticket to *petits appartements* and Napoleonic rooms 4.50€ adults, 3€ students 18–25, free 17 and under. Apr–Sept Wed–Mon 9:30am–6pm; Oct–Mar Wed–Mon 9:30am–5pm.

Hiking Along Trails Left by French Kings

The Forest of Fontainebleau is riddled with *sentiers* (hiking trails) made by French kings and their entourages who went hunting in the forest. A *Guide des Sentiers* is available at the tourist information center (see above). Bike paths also cut through the forest. You can rent bikes at the Fontainebleau-Avon rail depot. At the station, go to the kiosk, **A La Petite Reine** (☎ **01-60-74-57-57**). The cost of a bike is 13€ per half-day, 16€ for a full day. The kiosk is open Monday to Friday from 9:30am to 6pm, Saturday and Sunday from 10am to 7pm.

Where to Stay

Grand Hôtel de l'Aigle-Noir (The Black Eagle) ★   This mansion, once the home of Cardinal de Retz, sits opposite the château. The formal courtyard entrance has a high iron/board grille and pillars crowned by black eagles. It became a hotel in 1720 and is the finest lodging in Fontainebleau. The rooms are decorated with Louis XVI, Empire-, or Regency-era antiques or reproductions, with plush beds and elegant bathroom amenities. Enjoy a drink in the Napoleon III–style piano bar before dinner.

27 place Napoleon-Bonaparte, 77300 Fontainebleau. ✆ **01-60-74-60-00.** Fax 01-60-74-60-01. www.hotelaiglenoir.fr. 15 units. 170€–240€ double; 280€–380€ suite. AE, DC, MC, V. Parking 10€. Closed 2 last weeks of Dec. **Amenities:** Restaurant; bar; exercise room; pool (indoor); room service. *In room:* A/C, hair dryer, minibar, Wi-Fi (free).

Where to Dine

Le Caveau des Ducs TRADITIONAL FRENCH   This reasonably priced restaurant occupies a former storage cellar. It sits underground, beneath a series of 17th-century stone vaults built by the same masons who laid the cobblestones of rue de Ferrare. Although the food is simple, the setting—with lots of wood and flickering candles—is dramatic. Menu items include staples such as snails in garlic butter, roast leg of lamb with garlic-and-rosemary sauce, and virtually everything that can be concocted from the body of a duck (terrines, magret, and confits). Filet of rump steak with brie sauce is tasty, as are platters of sole, crayfish tails, and salmon on a bed of pasta. Especially flavorful are strips of veal in morel-studded cream sauce on a bed of pasta.

24 rue de Ferrare. ✆ **01-64-22-05-05.** www.caveaudesducs.com. Reservations recommended. Main courses 15€–23€; fixed-price menu 22€–41€. AE, MC, V. Daily noon–2pm and 7–10pm.

Cycling through the Forest of Fontainebleau.

Château de Fontainebleau.

Le François-1er (Chez Bernard) ★ TRADITIONAL FRENCH   The premier dining choice in Fontainebleau has Louis XIII decor, winemaking memorabilia, and walls that the owners think are about 200 years old. If weather permits, sit on the terrace overlooking the château and the cour des Adieux. In game season, the menu features hare, duck liver, and partridge. Other choices include a cassoulet of snails with flap mushrooms and garlic-flavored cream sauce, magret of duckling with cassis sauce, *rognon de veau* (veal kidneys) with mustard sauce, and a salad of baby scallops with crayfish. Chef Bernard Crogiez's cuisine is meticulous, with an undeniable flair.

3 rue Royale. ✆ **01-64-22-24-68.** Reservations required. Main courses 23€–45€; fixed-price lunch Mon–Fri only 15€; fixed-price dinner daily 25€. AE, MC, V. Tues–Sun noon–2pm; Mon–Sat 7:30–10pm. Closed 2 weeks in Aug and 1 week in Dec.

FAST FACTS: PARIS

ATM Networks See "Money & Costs," p. 68.

Babysitters The best deal comes from **Babychou** Services, 31 rue Moulin de la Pointe, 13e (📞 **01-43-13-33-23;** fax 01-43-13-33-20). You pay 17€ for the booking, plus 9€ per hour for one kid, 10€ per hour for two kids, and 11€ for three.

Business Hours Opening hours in Paris are erratic. Most museums close 1 day a week (often Tues) and national holidays; hours tend to be from 9:30am to 5pm. Some museums, particularly the smaller ones, close for lunch from noon to 2pm. Most museums are open Saturday, but many close Sunday morning and reopen in the afternoon (see chapter 7 for specific times). Generally, **offices** are open Monday to Friday from 9am to 5pm, but don't count on it—always call first. **Large stores** are open from 9 or 9:30am (often 10am) to 6 or 7pm without a break for lunch. Some **shops,** particularly those operated by non-native French owners, open at 8am and close at 8 or 9pm. In some **small stores,** the lunch break can last 3 hours, beginning at 1pm.

Cellphones (Mobile Phones) See "Staying Connected," p. 79.

Drinking Laws Supermarkets, grocery stores, and cafes sell alcoholic beverages. The legal drinking age is 18, but persons under that age can be served alcohol in a bar or restaurant if accompanied by a parent or legal guardian. Wine and liquor are sold every day of the week, year-round. Hours of cafes vary. Some open at 6am, serving drinks to 3am; others are open 24 hours. Bars and nightclubs may stay open as late as they wish. The Breathalyzer test is used in France, and a motorist is considered "legally intoxicated" with .5 grams of alcohol per liter of blood (the more liberal U.S. law varies among states, with many states in the range of .6 to .8g per liter). If convicted, a motorist faces a stiff fine and a possible prison term of 2 months to 2 years.

Driving Rules See "Getting There & Getting Around," p. 62.

Drugstores After regular hours, have your concierge contact the Commissariat de Police for the nearest 24-hour pharmacy. French law requires one pharmacy in each neighborhood to stay open 24 hours. You'll find the address posted on the doors or windows of all other drugstores. One of the most central all-nighters is **Pharmacie Les Champs,** 84 av. des Champs-Elysées, 8e (📞 **01-45-62-02-41;** Métro: George V).

Electricity   In general, expect 200 volts AC (60 cycles), though you'll encounter 110 and 115 volts in some older establishments. Adapters are needed to fit sockets. Many hotels have two-pin (in some cases, three-pin) sockets for electric razors.

Embassies & Consulates   If you have a passport, immigration, legal, or other problem, contact your consulate. Call before you go—they often keep odd hours and observe both French and home-country holidays. The Embassy of the **United States,** 2 av. Gabriel, 8e (☎ **01-43-12-22-22;** http://france.usembassy.gov; Métro: Concorde), is open Monday to Friday 8:30am to 5pm. The Embassy of **Canada** is at 35 av. Montaigne, 8e (☎ **01-44-43-29-00;** www.international.gc.ca/canada-europa/france/menu-en.asp; Métro: Franklin-D-Roosevelt or Alma-Marceau), open Monday to Friday 9am to noon and 2 to 5pm. The Embassy of the **United Kingdom** is at 35 rue du Faubourg St-Honoré, 8e (☎ **01-44-51-31-00;** http://ukinfrance.fco.gov.uk; Métro: Concorde or Madeleine), open Monday to Friday 9:30am to 1pm and 2:30 to 5pm. The Embassy of **Ireland** is at 4 rue Rude, 75116 Paris (☎ **01-44-17-67-00;** www.embassyofireland.fr; Métro: Etoile), open Monday to Friday 9:30am to 1pm and 2:30 to 5:30pm. The Embassy of **Australia** is at 4 rue Jean-Rey, 15e (☎ **01-40-59-33-00;** www.france.embassy.gov.au; Métro: Bir Hakeim), open Monday to Friday 9:15am to noon and 2:30 to 4:30pm. The embassy of **New Zealand** is at 7 ter rue Léonard-de-Vinci, 16e (☎ **01-45-01-43-43;** www.nzembassy.com; Métro: Victor Hugo), open Monday to Friday 9am to 1pm and 2:30 to 6pm. The embassy of **South Africa,** at 59 quai d'Orsay, 7e (☎ **01-53-59-23-23;** www.afriquesud.net; Métro: Invalides), is open Monday to Friday 9am to noon.

Emergencies   For the police, call ☎ **17;** to report a fire, call ☎ **18.** For an ambulance, call ☎ **15** or 01-45-67-50-50.

Etiquette & Customs   The French are known for a certain classic stylishness and conservatism in dress. Parisians like pleasantries: Say *Bonjour Madame/Monsieur* when entering an establishment and *Au revoir* when you depart. Always say *Pardon* when you accidentally bump into someone. Bread is served with each meal, and it's polite to wipe your plate with it. Waiters will not bring the check until asked. French etiquette requires you to keep your hands above the table and not below, in your lap. For more information, refer to *The Global Etiquette Guide to Europe: Everything You Need to Know for Business and Travel Success* by Dean Foster (Wiley Publishing).

Holidays   Major holidays are January 1 (New Year's Day), Easter, Ascension Day (40 days after Easter), Pentecost (seventh Sun after Easter), May 1 (May Day), May 8 (VE Day), July 14 (Bastille Day), August 15 (Assumption of the Virgin Mary), November 1 (All Saints Day), November 11 (Armistice Day), and December 25 (Christmas). For more information on holidays, see "Paris Calendar of Events," p. 56.

Hospitals   Open Monday to Saturday from 8am to 7pm, **Central Médical Europe,** 44 rue d'Amsterdam, 9e (☎ **01-42-81-93-33;** www.centre-medical-europe.com; Métro: Liège or Europe), maintains contacts with medical and dental practitioners in all fields. Appointments are recommended. Another choice is the **American Hospital of Paris,** 63 bd. Victor-Hugo, Neuilly, 17e (☎ **01-46-41-25-25;** www.american-hospital.org; Métro: Pont de Levallois or Pont de Neuilly; Bus: 82), which operates 24-hour medical and dental services. An additional clinic is the **Centre Medico-Social,** 2 rue du Figuier, 4e (☎ **01-49-96-62-70;** Métro: St-Paul). Call before visiting.

Hot Lines   S.O.S. Help hotline for English-speaking callers in crisis at ☎ **01-46-21-46-46.** The 24-hr. pharmacy hot line is ☎ **01-45-62-02-41.** S.O.S. Dentaire (dentist) is ☎ **01-43-37-51-00.**

Internet Access See "Staying Connected," p. 80.

Language English is widely understood. It is more understood by young people than their elders. English is common in all the tourist areas—museums, hotels, restaurants, cafes, and nightclubs. For handy French words and phrases, as well as food and menu terms, refer to chapter 13, "Useful Terms & Phrases." A good phrasebook is *Frommer's French PhraseFinder & Dictionary.*

Legal Aid In an emergency, especially if you get into trouble with the law, your country's embassy or consulate will provide legal advice. For serious emergencies, the staff might even advance you some money. See "Embassies & Consulates" above.

Lost & Found To speed the process of replacing your personal documents if they're lost or stolen, make a photocopy of the first few pages of your passport and write down your credit card numbers (and the serial numbers of your traveler's checks, if you're using them). Leave this information with someone at home—to be faxed to you in an emergency—and swap it with your traveling companion. Be sure to tell all your credit card companies the minute you discover your wallet has been lost or stolen, and file a report at the nearest police precinct. Your credit card company or insurer may require a police report number or record of the loss.

Use the following numbers in France to report your lost or stolen credit card: **American Express** (call collect) ☏ **336/393-1111; MasterCard** ☏ **08-00-90-13-87,** www.mastercard.com; **Visa** ☏ **08-00-90-11-79,** www.visaeurope.com. Your credit card company may be able to wire you a cash advance immediately or deliver an emergency card in a day or two.

If you need emergency cash over the weekend when all banks and American Express offices are closed, you can have money wired to you via **Western Union** (☏ **800/325-6000;** www.westernunion.com). **Travelers Express/MoneyGram** is the largest company in the U.S. for money orders (☏ **800/MONEY-GRAM** [666-3947]; www.moneygram.com).

Identity theft and fraud are potential complications of losing your wallet, especially if you lose your driver's license with your cash and credit cards. Notify the major credit-reporting bureaus immediately; placing a fraud alert on your records may protect you against liability for criminal activity. The three major U.S. credit-reporting agencies are **Equifax** (☏ **800/766-0008;** www.equifax.com), **Experian** (☏ **888/397-3742;** www.experian.com), and **TransUnion** (☏ **800/680-7289;** www.transunion.com).

Mail Most post offices in Paris are open Monday to Friday from 8am to 5pm and every Saturday from 8am to noon. One of the biggest and most central of them is the main post office for the 1st arrondissement, at 52 rue du Louvre (☏ **01-40-28-21-51;** Métro: Musée du Louvre). It maintains the hours noted above for services including the sale of postal money orders, mail collection and distribution, and the expedition of faxes. For the purposes of selling stamps and accepting packages, it's open on a limited basis 24 hours a day. Stamps are also sold at the reception desks of many hotels and at cafes designated with red TABAC signs.

Newspapers & Magazines See "Staying Connected," p. 80.

Passports Allow plenty of time before your trip to apply for a passport; processing normally takes 3 weeks but can take longer during busy periods (especially spring). Keep in mind that if you need a passport in a hurry, you'll pay a higher processing fee.

For Residents of the United States: Whether you're applying in person or by mail, you can download passport applications from the U.S. State Department website at http://travel.state.gov. To find your regional passport office, either check the U.S. State

Department website or call the toll-free number of the **National Passport Information Center** (☎ **877/487-2778;** http://travel.state.gov) for automated information.

For Residents of Canada: Passport applications are available at travel agencies throughout Canada or from the central **Passport Office,** Department of Foreign Affairs and International Trade, Ottawa, ON K1A 0G3 (☎ **800/567-6868;** www.ppt.gc.ca).

For Residents of Ireland: You can apply for a 10-year passport at the **Passport Office,** Setanta Centre, Molesworth St., Dublin 2 (☎ **01/671-1633;** www.irlgov.ie/iveagh). Those 17 and under or 66 and up must apply for a 12€ 3-year passport. You can also apply at 1A South Mall, Cork (☎ **021/494-4700**) or at most main post offices.

For Residents of Australia: You can pick up an application from your local post office or any branch of Passports Australia, but you must schedule an interview at the passport office to present your application materials. Call the **Australian Passport Information Service** at ☎ **131-232** or visit the government website at www.passports.gov.au.

For Residents of New Zealand: You can pick up a passport application at any New Zealand Passports Office or download it from their website. Contact the **Passports Office** at ☎ **0800/225-050** in New Zealand or 04/474-8100, or log on to www.passports.govt.nz.

For Residents of the United Kingdom: To pick up an application for a standard 10-year passport (5-year passport for children age 15 and under), visit your nearest passport office, major post office, or travel agency, or contact the **United Kingdom Passport Service** at ☎ **0870/521-0410,** or log on to www.UKPA.gov.uk.

Police In an emergency, call ☎ **17.** For non-emergency situations, the principal préfecture is at 9 bd. du Palais, 4e (☎ **01-53-73-53-73;** Métro: Cité).

Smoking Smoking is no longer acceptable in restaurants and cafes, museums, or other public areas.

Taxes As a member of the European Union, France routinely imposes a value-added tax (VAT in English; TVA in French) on many goods and services. The standard VAT is 19.6% on merchandise, including clothing, appliances, liquor, leather goods, shoes, furs, jewelry, perfumes, cameras, and even caviar. Refunds are made for the tax on certain goods and merchandise, but not on services. The minimum purchase is 184€ at one time for nationals or residents of countries outside the E.U. Hotel taxes in Paris range from around .70€ to around 1.50€ (Ritz rate) per person per day.

Telephones See "Staying Connected," p. 80.

Time France is usually 6 hours ahead of Eastern Standard Time and 9 hours ahead of Pacific Standard Time in the United States. French daylight saving time lasts from around April to September, when clocks are set 1 hour ahead of the standard time.

Tipping By law, all bills show *service compris,* which means the tip is included; additional gratuities are customarily given as follows: For **hotel staff,** tip the porter 1.00€ to 1.50€ per item of baggage and 1.50€ per day for the chambermaid. You're not obligated to tip the concierge, doorman, or anyone else unless you use his or her services. In **cafes** and **restaurants,** waiter service is usually included, though you can leave some small change, if you like. In **theaters** and **restaurants,** give cloakroom attendants at least .75€ per item. Give **restroom attendants** in nightclubs and such places about .30€. Tip the **hairdresser** about 15%, and don't forget to tip the person who gives you a shampoo or a manicure 1.50€. For **guides** of group visits to museums and monuments, .75€ to 1.50€ is a reasonable tip.

Toilets If you're in dire need, duck into a cafe or brasserie to use the toilet. It's customary to make some small purchase if you do so. In the street, the domed self-cleaning lavatories are a decent option if you have small change; Métro stations and underground garages may have public lavatories, but the degree of cleanliness varies.

Water Drinking water is generally safe, though some who were unused to it have gotten diarrhea. If you ask for water in a restaurant, it will be bottled water (for which you'll pay) unless you specifically request *une carafe d'eau* (tap water).

AIRLINE WEBSITES

MAJOR AIRLINES

Air France
www.airfrance.com

Air India
www.airindia.com

Air Tahiti Nui
www.airtahitinui-usa.com

Alitalia
www.alitalia.com

American Airlines
www.aa.com

British Airways
www.british-airways.com

China Airlines
www.china-airlines.com

Continental Airlines
www.continental.com

Delta Air Lines
www.delta.com

EgyptAir
www.egyptair.com

El Al Airlines
www.elal.co.il

Emirates Airlines
www.emirates.com

Finnair
www.finnair.com

Iberia Airlines
www.iberia.com

Icelandair
www.icelandair.com

Japan Airlines
www.jal.co.jp

Korean Air
www.koreanair.com

Lan Airlines
www.lan.com

Lufthansa
www.lufthansa.com

Qantas Airways
www.qantas.com

South African Airways
www.flysaa.com

Swiss Air
www.swiss.com

Thai Airways International
www.thaiair.com

Turkish Airlines
www.thy.com

United Airlines
www.united.com

US Airways
www.usairways.com

BUDGET AIRLINES

Aegean Airlines
www.aegeanair.com

Aer Lingus
www.aerlingus.com

Air Berlin
www.airberlin.com

BMI Baby
www.bmibaby.com

easyJet
www.easyjet.com

Ryanair
www.ryanair.com

13

USEFUL TERMS & PHRASES

FRENCH-LANGUAGE TERMS

Although Parisians often seem to carry upon their backs a burden of misery that they famously dole out to immigrants and foreigners, it's often amazing how a word or two of halting French will change their dispositions. At the very least, try to learn a few numbers, basic greetings, and—above all—the life-raft, *"Parlez-vous anglais?"* As it turns out, many Parisians do speak passable English and will use it liberally if you demonstrate the basic courtesy of greeting them in their language. Go out, try our glossary on, and don't be bashful. *Bonne chance!*

BASICS

English	French	Pronunciation
Yes/No	Oui/Non	**Wee/Nohn**
Okay	D'accord	**Dah-*core***
Please	S'il vous plaît	**seel voo *play***
Thank you	Merci	**Mair-*see***
You're welcome	De rien	**duh ree-*ehn***
Hello (during daylight hours)	Bonjour	**Bohn-*jhoor***
Good evening	Bonsoir	**bohn-*swahr***
Good-bye	Au revoir	**O ruh-*vwahr***
What's your name?	Comment vous appellez-vous?	**Ko-*mahn* voo *za*-pell-ay-*voo*?**
My name is . . .	Je m'appelle . . .	**Jhuh ma-*pell* . . .**
Happy to meet you	Enchanté(e)	**Ohn-shahn-tay**
Miss	Mademoiselle	**Mad-mwa-*zel***
Mr.	Monsieur	**muh-*syuh***
Mrs.	Madame	**Ma-*dam***
How are you?	Comment allez-vous?	**Kuh-*mahn* tahl-ay-*voo*?**
Fine, thank you, and you?	Très bien, merci, et vous?	**Tray bee-*ehn*, mare-*ci*, ay *voo*?**
Very well, thank you	Très bien, merci	**tray bee-ehn, mair-*see***
So-so	Comme ci, comme ça	**Kum-*see*, kum-*sah***
I'm sorry/excuse me	Pardon	**pahr-*dohn***
I'm so very sorry	Désolé(e)	**Day-zoh-*lay***
That's all right	Il n'y a pas de quoi	**Eel nee ah pah duh kwah**

GETTING AROUND/STREET SMARTS

English	French	Pronunciation
Do you speak English?	Parlez-vous anglais?	**Par-lay-*voo* ahn-*glay*?**
I don't speak French	Je ne parle pas français	**Jhuh ne parl pah frahn-*say***
I don't understand	Je ne comprends pas	**Jhuh ne kohm-*prahn* pas**
Could you speak more loudly/more slowly?	Pouvez-vous parler un peu plus fort/plus lentement?	**Poo-vay-*voo* par-*lay* un puh ploo for/ploo lan-te-*ment*?**
Could you repeat that?	Répétez, s'il vous plaît?	**Ray-pay-*tay*, seel voo *play***
What is it?	Qu'est-ce que c'est?	**Kess kuh *say*?**
What time is it?	Qu'elle heure est-il?	**Kel uhr eh-*teel*?**
What?	Quoi?	**Kwah?**

English	French	Pronunciation
How? or What did you say?	Comment?	**Ko-*mahn*?**
When?	Quand?	**Kahn?**
Where is . . . ?	Où est . . . ?	**Ooh eh . . . ?**
Who?	Qui?	**Kee?**
Why?	Pourquoi?	**Poor-*kwah*?**
Here/there	ici/là	**ee-*see*/lah**
Left/right	à gauche/à droite	**a goash/a drwaht**
Straight ahead	tout droit	**too drwah**
I'm American/Canadian/ British	Je suis américain(e)/ canadien(e)/anglais(e)	**Jhe sweez a-may-ree-*kehn*/can-ah-dee-*en*/ ahn-glay (*glaise*)**
I'm sick	Je suis malade	**Jhuh swee mal-*ahd***
Fill the tank (of a car), please	Le plein, s'il vous plaît	**Luh plan, seel voo play**
I'm going to . . .	Je vais à . . .	**Jhe vay ah . . .**
I want to get off at . . .	Je voudrais descendre à . . .	**Jhe voo-*dray* day-*son*-drah ah**
airport	l'aéroport	**lair-o-*por***
bank	la banque	**lah bahnk**
bridge	pont	**pohn**
bus station	la gare routière	**lah gar roo-tee-*air***
bus stop	l'arrêt de bus	**lah-*ray* duh boohss**
by means of a bicycle	en vélo/par bicyclette	**uh *vay*-low/par bee-see-*clet***
by means of a car	en voiture	**ahn vwa-*toor***
cashier	la caisse	**lah *kess***
cathedral	cathédral	**ka-tay-*dral***
church	église	**ay-*gleez***
dead end	une impasse	**ewn am-*pass***
driver's license	permis de conduire	**per-*mee* duh con-*dweer***
elevator	l'ascenseur	**lah-sahn-*seuhr***
entrance (to a building or a city)	une porte	**ewn port**
exit (from a building or a freeway)	une sortie	**ewn sor-*tee***
fortified castle or palace	château	**sha-*tow***
garden	jardin	**jhar-*dehn***
gasoline	du pétrol/de l'essence	**duh pay-*trol*/de lay-*sahns***
ground floor	rez-de-chausée	**ray-de-show-*say***

English	French	Pronunciation
highway to . . .	la route pour	**la root por**
hospital	l'hôpital	**low-pee-*tahl***
insurance	les assurances	**lez ah-sur-*ahns***
luggage storage	consigne	**kohn-*seen*-yuh**
museum	le musée	**luh mew-*zay***
no entry	sens interdit	**sehns ahn-ter-*dee***
no smoking	défense de fumer	**day-*fahns* de fu-may**
on foot	à pied	**ah pee-*ay***
one-day pass	ticket journalier	**tee-kay jhoor-nall-ee-*ay***
one-way ticket	aller simple	**ah-*lay sam*-pluh**
police	la police	**lah po-*lees***
rented car	voiture de location	**vwa-*toor* de low-ka-see-*on***
round-trip ticket	aller-retour	**ah-*lay*-re-*toor***
second floor	premier étage	**prem-ee-*ehr* ay-*taj***
slow down	ralentir	**rah-lahn-*teer***
store	magasin	**luh ma-ga-*zehn***
street	rue	**roo**
suburb	banlieu/environs	**bahn-*liew*/en-veer-*ohns***
subway	le Métro	**le *May*-tro**
telephone	le téléphone	**luh tay-lay-*phone***
ticket	un billet	**uh *bee*-yay**
ticket office	vente de billets	**vahnt duh bee-*yay***
toilets	les toilettes/les WC	**lay twa-*lets*/les Vay-*Say***
tower	tour	**toor**

NECESSITIES

English	French	Pronunciation
I'd like . . .	Je voudrais . . .	**Jhe voo-*dray* . . .**
a room	une chambre	**ewn *shahm*-bruh**
the key	la clé (la clef)	**la *clay***
I'd like to buy . . .	Je voudrais acheter . . .	**Jhe voo-dray ahsh-*tay* . . .**
aspirin	des aspirines/des aspros	**dayz ahs-peer-*eens*/deyz ahs-*prohs***
cigarettes	des cigarettes	**day see-ga-*ret***
condoms	des préservatifs	**day pray-ser-va-*teefs***
dictionary	un dictionnaire	**uh deek-see-oh-*nare***

English	French	Pronunciation
dress	une robe	ewn robe
envelopes	des envelopes	days ahn-veh-*lope*
gift (for someone)	un cadeau	uh kah-*doe*
handbag	un sac	uh sahk
hat	un chapeau	uh shah-*poh*
magazine	une revue	ewn reh-*vu*
map of the city	un plan de ville	unh plahn de *veel*
matches	des allumettes	dayz a-loo-*met*
necktie	une cravate	uh cra-*vaht*
newspaper	un journal	uh zhoor-*nahl*
phone card	une carte téléphonique	uh cart tay-lay-fone-*eek*
postcard	une carte postale	ewn carte pos-*tahl*
road map	une carte routière	ewn cart roo-tee-*air*
shirt	une chemise	ewn che-*meez*
shoes	des chaussures	day show-*suhr*
skirt	une jupe	ewn jhoop
soap	du savon	dew sah-*vohn*
socks	des chaussettes	day show-*set*
stamp	un timbre	uh *tam*-bruh
trousers	un pantalon	uh pan-tah-*lohn*
writing paper	du papier à lettres	dew pap-pee-*ay a let*-ruh
How much does it cost?	C'est combien?/Ça coûte combien?	Say comb-bee-*ehn?*/Sah coot comb-bee-*ehn?*
That's expensive	C'est cher/chère	Say share
That's inexpensive	C'est raisonnable/C'est bon marché	Say ray-son-*ahb*-bluh/Say bohn mar-*shay*
Do you take credit cards?	Est-ce que vous acceptez les cartes de credit?	Es-*kuh* voo zak-sep-*tay* lay kart duh creh-*dee?*

IN YOUR HOTEL

English	French	Pronunciation
Are taxes included?	Est-ce que les taxes sont comprises?	*Ess*-keh lay taks son com-*preez?*
balcony	un balcon	uh bahl-*cohn*
bathtub	une baignoire	ewn bayn-*nwar*
bedroom	une chambre	ewn *shawm*-bruh

English	French	Pronunciation
for two occupants	pour deux personnes	**poor duh pair-*sunn***
hot and cold water	l'eau chaude et froide	**low showed ay fwad**
Is breakfast included?	Petit dé jeuner inclus?	**Peh-*tee* day-jheun-*ay* ehn-*klu*?**
room	une chambre	**ewn *shawm*-bruh**
shower	une douche	**ewn dooch**
sink	un lavabo	**uh la-va-*bow***
suite	une suite	**ewn sweet**
We're staying for . . . days with	On reste pour . . . jours avec	**Ohn rest poor . . . jhoor ah-*vek***
with air-conditioning	avec climatisation	**ah-*vek* clee-mah-tee-zah-see-*on***
without	sans	**sahn**
youth hostel	une auberge de jeunesse	**oon oh-*bayrhj* duh jhe-*ness***

IN THE RESTAURANT

English	French	Pronunciation
I would like . . .	Je voudrais	**Jhe voo-*dray***
to eat	manger	**mahn-*jhay***
to order	commander	**ko-mahn-*day***
Please give me . . .	Donnez-moi, s'il vous plaît . . .	**Doe-nay-*mwah,* seel voo play . . .**
a bottle of . . .	une bouteille de . . .	**ewn boo-*tay* duh . . .**
a cup of . . .	une tasse de . . .	**ewn tass duh . . .**
a glass of . . .	un verre de . . .	**uh vair duh . . .**
an ashtray	un cendrier	**uh sahn-dree-*ay***
a plate of . . .	une assiette de . . .	**ewn ass-ee-*et* duh . . .**
bread	du pain	**dew pan**
breakfast	le petit déjeuner	**luh puh-*tee* day-zhuh-*nay***
butter	du beurre	**dew burr**
check/bill	l'addition/la note	**la-dee-see-*ohn*/la noat**
Cheers!	à votre santé	***ah* vo-truh sahn-*tay***
Can I buy you . . .	Puis-je vous payer . . .	***Pwee*-jhe voo pay-*ay***
. . . a drink?	. . . un verre?	**uh *vairh*?**
. . . a cocktail?	. . . un apéritif	**uh ah-pay-ree-*teef***
coffee	du café	**dew ka-*fay***
coffee (black)	un café noir	**uh ka-*fay* nwahr**

English	French	Pronunciation
coffee (decaf)	un café décaféiné	uh ka-*fay* day-kah-fay-*nay*
coffee (espresso)	un café express	uh ka-fay ek-*sprehss*
coffee (with cream)	un café crème	uh ka-*fay* krem
coffee (with milk)	un café au lait	uh ka-*fay* o *lay*
dinner	le dîner	luh dee-*nay*
fixed-price menu	un menu	uh may-new
fork	une fourchette	ewn four-*shet*
Is the tip/service included?	Est-ce que le service est compris?	*Ess*-ke luh ser-*vees* eh com-*pree*?
knife	un couteau	uh koo-*toe*
napkin	une serviette	ewn sair-vee-*et*
pepper	du poivre	dew *pwah*-vruh
platter of the day	un plat du jour	uh plah dew jhoor
salt	du sel	dew sell
soup	une soupe/un potage	ewn soop/uh poh-*tahj*
spoon	une cuillère	ewn kwee-*air*
sugar	du sucre	dew *sook*-ruh
tea	un thé	uh tay
tea (with lemon)	un thé au citron	uh tay o see-*tron*
tea (herbal)	une tisane	ewn tee-*zahn*
Waiter!/Waitress!	Monsieur!/Mademoiselle!	Mun-*syuh*/Mad-mwa-*zel*
wine list	une carte des vins	ewn cart day *van*
appetizer	une entrée	ewn en-*tray*
main course	un plat principal	uh plah pran-see-*pahl*
tip included	service compris	sehr-*vees* cohm-*preez*
wide-range sample of the chef's best efforts	menu dégustation	may-new day-gus-ta-see-*on*
drinks not included	boissons non comprises	bwa-*sons* no com-*preez*
cheese tray	plâteau de fromage	plah-*tow* duh fro-*mahj*

SHOPPING

English	French	Pronunciation
antiques store	un magasin d'antiquités	uh maga-*zan* don-tee kee-*tay*
bakery	une boulangerie	ewn boo-lon-zhur-*ree*
bank	une banque	ewn bonk
bookstore	une librairie	ewn lee-brehr-*ree*

English	French	Pronunciation
butcher	une boucherie	**ewn boo-shehr-*ree***
cheese shop	une fromagerie	**ewn fro-mazh-*ree***
dairy shop	une crémerie	**ewn krem-*ree***
delicatessen	une charcuterie	**ewn shar-koot-*ree***
department store	un grand magasin	**uh grah maga-*zan***
drugstore	une pharmacie	**ewn far-mah-*see***
fishmonger shop	une poissonerie	**ewn pwas-son-*ree***
gift shop	un magasin de cadeaux	**uh maga-*zan* duh ka-*doh***
greengrocer	un marchand de légumes	**uh mar-*shon* duh lay-*goom***
hairdresser	un coiffeur	**uh kwa-*fuhr***
market	un marché	**uh mar-*shay***
pastry shop	une pâtisserie	**ewn pa-tee-*sree***
supermarket	un supermarché	**uh soo-pehr-mar-*shay***
tobacconist	un tabac	**uh ta-*bah***
travel agency	une agence de voyages	**ewn azh-*ahns* duh vwa-*yazh***

COLORS, SHAPES, SIZES & ATTRIBUTES

English	French	Pronunciation
black	noir	**nwahr**
blue	bleu	**bleuh**
brown	marron/brun	**mar-*rohn*/bruhn**
green	vert	**vaihr**
orange	orange	**o-*rahnj***
pink	rose	**rose**
purple	violet	**vee-o-*lay***
red	rouge	**rooj**
white	blanc	**blahnk**
yellow	jaune	**jhone**
bad	mauvais(e)	**moh-*veh***
big	grand(e)	**gron/gronde**
closed	fermé(e)	**fer-*meh***
down	en bas	**on *bah***
early	de bonne heure	**duh bon *urr***
enough	assez	**as-*say***
far	loin	**lwan**
free, unoccupied	libre	***lee*-bruh**

English	French	Pronunciation
free, without charge	gratuit(e)	**grah-*twee*/grah-*tweet***
good	bon/bonne	**bon/bun**
hot	chaud(e)	**show/shoad**
near	près	**preh**
open (as in "museum")	ouvert(e)	**oo-*ver*/oo-*vert***
small	petit(e)	**puh-*tee*/puh-*teet***
up	en haut	**on *oh***
well	bien	**byehn**

NUMBERS & ORDINALS

English	French	Pronunciation
zero	zéro	**zare-*oh***
one	un	**uh**
two	deux	**duh**
three	trois	**twah**
four	quatre	***kaht*-ruh**
five	cinq	**sank**
six	six	**seess**
seven	sept	**set**
eight	huit	**wheat**
nine	neuf	**nuf**
ten	dix	**deess**
eleven	onze	**ohnz**
twelve	douze	**dooz**
thirteen	treize	**trehz**
fourteen	quatorze	**kah-*torz***
fifteen	quinze	**kanz**
sixteen	seize	**sez**
seventeen	dix-sept	**deez-*set***
eighteen	dix-huit	**deez-*wheat***
nineteen	dix-neuf	**deez-*nuf***
twenty	vingt	**vehn**
twenty-one	vingt-et-un	**vehnt-ay-*uh***
twenty-two	vingt-deux	**vehnt-*duh***
thirty	trente	**trahnt**
forty	quarante	**ka-*rahnt***

English	French	Pronunciation
fifty	cinquante	**sang-*kahnt***
sixty	soixante	**swa-*sahnt***
sixty-one	soixante-et-un	**swa-sahnt-et-*uh***
seventy	soixante-dix	**swa-sahnt-*deess***
seventy-one	soixante-et-onze	**swa-sahnt-et-*ohnze***
eighty	quatre-vingts	**kaht-ruh-*vehn***
eighty-one	quatre-vingt-un	**kaht-ruh-vehn-*uh***
ninety	quatre-vingt-dix	**kaht-ruh-venh-*deess***
ninety-one	quatre-vingt-onze	**kaht-ruh-venh-*ohnze***
one hundred	cent	**sahn**
one thousand	mille	**meel**
one hundred thousand	cent mille	**sahn meel**
first	premier	***preh*-mee-ay**
second	deuxième	***duhz*-zee-em**
third	troisième	***twa*-zee-em**
fourth	quatrième	**kaht-ree-em**
fifth	cinquième	***sank*-ee-em**
sixth	sixième	***sees*-ee-em**
seventh	septième	***set*-ee-em**
eighth	huitième	***wheat*-ee-em**
ninth	neuvième	***neuv*-ee-em**
tenth	dixième	***dees*-ee-em**

THE CALENDAR

English	French	Pronunciation
January	janvier	***jhan*-vee-ay**
February	février	***feh*-vree-ay**
March	mars	**marce**
April	avril	**a-*vreel***
May	mai	**meh**
June	juin	**jhwehn**
July	juillet	***jhwee*-ay**
August	août	**oot**
September	septembre	**sep-*tahm*-bruh**
October	octobre	**ok-*toh*-bruh**
November	novembre	**no-*vahm*-bruh**

English	French	Pronunciation
December	decembre	**day-*sahm*-bruh**
Sunday	dimanche	**dee-*mahnsh***
Monday	lundi	***luhn*-dee**
Tuesday	mardi	***mahr*-dee**
Wednesday	mercredi	***mair*-kruh-dee**
Thursday	jeudi	***jheu*-dee**
Friday	vendredi	***vawn*-druh-dee**
Saturday	samedi	***sahm*-dee**
yesterday	hier	**ee-*air***
today	aujourd'hui	**o-jhord-*dwee***
this morning/this afternoon	ce matin/cet après-midi	**suh ma-*tan*/set ah-preh-mee-*dee***
tonight	ce soir	**suh *swahr***
tomorrow	demain	**de-*man***

BASIC MENU TERMS

Note: To order any of these items from a waiter, simply preface the French-language name with the phrase *"Je voudrais"* (jhe voo-*dray*), which means, "I would like . . ." Also see the previous "In the Restaurant" entries. *Bon appétit!*

MEATS

English	French	Pronunciation
beef stew	du pot au feu	**dew poht o *fhe***
marinated beef braised with red wine and served with vegetables	du boeuf à la mode	**dew bewf ah lah *mhowd***
brains	de la cervelle	**duh lah ser-*vel***
chicken	du poulet	***dew poo*-lay**
rolls of pounded and baked chicken, veal, or fish, often pike, usually served warm	des quenelles	**day ke-*nelle***
chicken, stewed with mushrooms and wine	du coq au vin	**dew cock o *vhin***
ham	du jambon	**dew jham-bohn**
haunch or leg of an animal, especially that of a lamb or sheep	du gigot	**dew *jhi*-goh**
kidneys	des rognons	**day *row*-nyon**
lamb	de l'agneau	**duh lahn-*nyo***

English	French	Pronunciation
lamb chop	une cotelette de l'agneau	**ewn koh-te-*let* duh lahn-*nyo***
rabbit	du lapin	**dew lah-*pan***
sirloin	de l'aloyau	**duh lahl-why-*yo***
steak	du bifteck	**dew beef-*tek***
filet steak, embedded with fresh green or black pepper-corns, flambéed and served with a cognac sauce	un steak au poivre	**uh stake o *pwah*-vruh**
double tenderloin, a long muscle from which filet steaks are cut	du chateaubriand	**dew *sha*-tow-bree-ahn**
stewed meat with white sauce, enriched with cream and eggs	de la blanquette	**duh lah blon-*ket***
sweetbreads	des ris de veau	**day *ree* duh voh**
veal	du veau	**dew *voh***

FISH

English	French	Pronunciation
herring	du hareng	**dew ahr-*rahn***
lobster	du homard	**dew oh-*mahr***
mussels	des moules	**day *moohl***
mussels in herb-flavored white wine with shallots	des moules marinières	**day moohl mar-ee-nee-*air***
oysters	des huîtres	**dayz hoo-*ee*-truhs**
pike	du brochet	**dew broh-*chay***
shrimp	des crevettes	**day kreh-*vette***
smoked salmon	du saumon fumé	**dew sow-*mohn* fu-*may***
trout	de la truite	**duh lah tru-eet**
tuna	du thon	**dew tohn**
wolffish, a Mediterranean sea bass	du loup de mer	**dew loo duh *mehr***

SIDES/APPETIZERS

English	French	Pronunciation
bread	du pain	**dew pan**
butter	du beurre	**dew bhuhr**
gooseliver	du foie gras	**dew fwah grah**
liver	du foie	**dew fwah**

English	French	Pronunciation
potted and minced pork and pork by-products, prepared as a roughly hopped pâté	des rillettes	**day ree-*yet***
rice	du riz	**dew ree**
snails	des escargots	**dayz ess-car-*goh***

BEVERAGES

English	French	Pronunciation
beer	de la bière	**duh lah bee-*aire***
milk	du lait	**dew lay**
orange juice	du jus d'orange	**dew joo d'or-*ahn*-jhe**
water	de l'eau	**duh lo**
red wine	du vin rouge	**dew vhin *rooj***
white wine	du vin blanc	**dew vhin *blahn***
coffee	un café	**uh ka-*fay***
coffee (black)	un café noir	**uh ka-fay *nwahr***
coffee (decaf)	un café décaféiné (slang: un déca)	**un ka-*fay* day-kah-fay-*nay* (uh *day*-kah)**
coffee (espresso)	un café espresso (un express)	**uh ka-*fay* e-*sprehss*-o (un ek-*sprehss*)**
coffee (with cream)	un café crème	**uh ka-fay *krem***
coffee (with milk)	un café au lait	**uh ka-fay o *lay***
tea	du thé	**dew *tay***
herbal tea	une tisane	**ewn tee-*zahn***

SPICES/CONDIMENTS

English	French	Pronunciation
mustard	de la moutarde	**duh lah moo-*tard*-uh**
pepper	du poivre	**dew *pwah*-vruh**
salt	du sel	**dew *sel***
sour heavy cream	de la crème fraîche	**duh lah krem *fresh***
sugar	du sucre	**dew *sooh*-kruh**

Index

A

Above and Beyond Tours, 74
Académie de la Bière, 358
Accommodations, 103–150. *See also* Accommodations Index
1st Arrondissement (Louvre/ Les Halles), 110–113
2nd Arrondissement (La Bourse), 113–114
3rd Arrondissement (Le Marais), 114–115
4th Arrondissement (Ile de la Cité/Ile St-Louis & Beaubourg), 116–119
5th Arrondissement (Quartier Latin), 133–138
6th Arrondissement (St-Germain/ Luxembourg), 138–143
7th Arrondissement (Eiffel Tower/Musée d'Orsay), 145–149
8th Arrondissement (Champs-Elysées/Madeleine), 124–125, 128–130
9th Arrondissement (Opera Garnier/Pigalle), 119–121
10th Arrondissement (Gare de l'Est), 121
11th Arrondissement (Opera Bastille), 121–122
12th Arrondissement (Bois de Vincennes/Gare de Lyon), 122
13th Arrondissement (Gare d'Austerlitz), 143–144
14th Arrondissement (Montparnasse), 144
15th Arrondissement (Eiffel Tower), 144–145
16th Arrondissement (Trocadéro/Bois de Boulogne), 130–131
17th Arrondissement (Parc Monceau/Place Clichy), 131–132
18th Arrondissement (Montmartre), 123–124
alternatives to hotels, 106–107
bathrooms, 112
best, 5–9, 105–106
Chartres, 380
condos, villas, houses and apartments, 103–105
Disneyland Paris, 387–388
family-friendly, 117
Fontainebleau, 393
Giverny, 383
hotel chains, 104

Left Bank, 104–105, 132–149
near the airports, 149–150
on the Right Bank, 104–105, 107–132
Addresses, finding, 65
Advantage Tennis Tours, 78
Aéroport d'Orly, 62–63
accommodations near, 149–150
Aéroport Roissy-Charles de Gaulle, 62
accommodations near, 150
African immigrants, 74
Air France
buses
Orly, 63
Roissy, 62
senior discounts, 75–76
Airports, accommodations near, 149–150
Air travel, 62–63
Alain Figaret, 329–330
A La Petite Reine (Fontainebleau), 392
Alcôve & Agapes, 106
Alliance Française, 78
American Cathedral of the Holy Trinity, 258
American Church in Paris, 346
American Express traveler's checks, 71
Amusement park, 292
Andy Whaloo, 358–359
Anna Lowe, 331
Annexe des Créateurs, 331–332
Annick Goutal, 339
Antiques, 321–322
Appartement de Ville, 107
Arc de Triomphe, 216–217
Architecture, 38–42
Arènes de Lutèce, 263
Armistice Day, 59
Arrondissements (neighborhoods), 65
attractions by, 214–215
best, for getting lost, 17–19
brief descriptions of, 83–88
highlights, 282–288
shopping, 320–321
Art, 35–38
Artcurial, 322
Art galleries, 322–323
Art museums, 250–253
Assemblée Nationale, 266–267
Association des Paralysés de France, 75
Atelier Brancusi, 241–242
ATMs (automated teller machines), 68

Attractions. *See* Sights and attractions
Au Bon Marché, 326
Au Chien Qui Fume, 286
Auditorium du Louvre, 56
Au Lapin Agile, 301, 348–351
Au Nain Bleu, 325
Au Nom de la Rose, 340
Au Pied de Cochon, 285–286
Au Printemps, 326–327
Au Sauvignon, 356
Autumn Festival, 59
Avenue des Champs-Elysées, 65
Avenue Montaigne, 329
Azzedine Alaïa, 328

B

Babysitters, 395
Baccarat, 326
Baiser Salé, 351
Balabus, 66–67, 293
Balzac, Honoré de, 287, 303
Maison de, 269
Banana Café, 362
Barclay International Group, 103–104
Bar Hemingway/Bar Vendôme, 359
Barney, Natalie, 287
Barrio Latino, 359
Bars, 356–364
gay and lesbian, 362–363
wine, 356–358
Basilique du Sacré-Coeur, 217
Basilique St-Denis, 258–259
Bastille Day, 58
Bateau-Lavoir (Boat Washhouse), 298
Bateaux-Mouche, 293–294
Batobus, 67–68
Batofar, 353
BCBG/Max Azria, 328
Beach along the Seine, 293
Beaujolais Nouveau, Release of the, 59
Beaumarchais, Statue of, 310
BE (Boulangerie Epicerie), 181
Bed & breakfasts (B&Bs), 106
Bibliothèque Information Publique, 241
Bibliothèque Nationale de France, Site Tolbiac/ François Mitterrand, 263–264
Biennale des Antiquaires, 59
Bijoux Blues, 335
Bijoux Burma, 335
Biking, 68, 279–280

GENERAL INDEX

Boat travel and cruises, 67–68, 293–295
Body Gym, 280
Bois de Boulogne, 272–273
Bonpoint, 325
Books, recommended, 42–44
Bookstores, 323–325
Boulevard de Clichy, 303
Boulevard St-Michel, 304
Bourdelle, Antoine, Musée, 250
Brasserie Fauchon, 333
Brentano's, 323
Britanny Ferries, 64
Buddha Bar, 359–360
Business hours, 319–320, 395
Bus tours, 292–293
Bus travel, 63, 66–67
Butte Montmartre, 289

C

Cab, 353
Cabaret des Assassins, 301
Cadolle, 336
Café Cox, 362
Café de l'Industrie, 360
Cafes, 209–212
Calder, 241
Calendar of events, 56–59
Carrefour des Cascades, 272
Carrousel du Louvre, 319–320, 336
Carte Mobilis, 67
Carte Orange, 67
Cartier, 335
Car travel, 64
Cassegrain, 340
Cathédrale de Notre-Dame, 225–230
Cathédrale Notre-Dame de Chartres, 377–380
Catherine, 339–340
Caveau de la Huchette, 351
Caveau des Oubliettes, 351
Cavesteve, 356–357
Cellphones, 79–80
Cemeteries, 274–278
Center for Nature Discovery, Garden in Memory of Diana, Princess of Wales, 288
Centers for Disease Control and Prevention, 72
Centre de Création Industriel (Center for Industrial Design), 241
Centre Pompidou, 241–242
Ceramics, china and porcelain, 325
Cézanne, Paul, 38
Chacha Club, 353
Chanel, 330
Chansonniers, 348–349

Chapelle de la Madone, 263
Chapelle de St-Symphorien, 261
Chapelle des Anges, 263
Chapelle St-Piat (Chartres), 379
Chapelle St-Sacrement (Chartres), 379–380
Chapel of the Angels, 263
Chapel of the Madonna, 263
Charles de Gaulle Airport (Roissy), 62
   accommodations near, 150
Chartres, 377–381
Charvet, 330
Château de Rambouillet, 375–377
Château de Versailles, 370–372
Chez Michou, 349
Children, families with, 75
   accommodations, 117
   Disneyland Paris, 384–389
   Musée des Enfants, 251
   restaurants, 186
   shopping for fashion and toys, 325–326
   sights and attractions, 289–292
Chip and PIN credit cards, 71
Chocolates, 332–334
Christian Constant, 332
Christian Dior, 330
Churches, major, 258–263
Cimetière de Montmartre, 274, 302
Cimetière de Passy, 276
Cimetière du Montparnasse, 276
Cimetière du Père-Lachaise, 275–277
Cimetière St-Vincent, 278
5e Cru, 357
Citadines, 107
Cité de la Musique, 56, 345
Cité de l'Architecture et du Patrimoine, 242–243
Cité des Sciences et de l'Industrie, 290
Cityrama, 292–293
Classical music, 345–348
Claudel, Camille, 284
Claude Monet Foundation (Giverny), 382–383
Clock Room (Versailles), 371
Club and music scene, 348–356
Club Med Gyms, 280
Club Zed, 353–354
Coach House Rentals, 106
Colette, 327
Colonne de Juillet, 310
Comédie-Française, 345
Comédie Française-Théâtre du Vieux-Colombier, 345

Concerts, 345–348
   at churches
      American Church in Paris, 346
      St-Denis, 259
      Sainte-Chapelle, 239
      St-Eustache, 346
      St-Germain-des-Prés, 261
      St-Merry, 346
Conciergerie, 264–265
Conran Shop, 341
Context:Paris, 295
Cooking schools, 77
Cour d'Honneur (Court of Honor), 248
Courrèges, 328–329
Craft and industry museums, 253–254
Crazy Horse Saloon, 349
Credit cards, 70–71
Crime and safety, 72–74
Crystal, 326
Cuisine and food, 49–51, 153–154. See also Restaurants
   stores and markets, 181, 318, 332–334
Curie, Marie, 284
Currency and currency exchange, 68–70
Customs regulations, 60–61
Cycling, 68, 279–280

D

Dailey-Thorp Travel, 78
Dalí, Salvador, Espace Dalí Montmartre, 298–299
Debit cards, 70–71
Défilé des Marques, 332
Degas, Edgar, 37–38
Dehillerin, 335
Delacroix, Eugène, Musée National, 249
Department stores, 326–327
Deportation Memorial (Mémorial des Martyrs Français de la Déportation de 1945), 229–230
Diana, Princess of Wales, 288
Didier Ludot, 332
Dining, 49–50, 152–212. See also Restaurants Index
   1st Arrondissement (Louvre/Les Halles), 158–165
   2nd Arrondissement (La Bourse), 166
   3rd Arrondissement (Le Marais), 166–168
   4th Arrondissement (Ile De La Cité/Ile St-Louis & Beaubourg), 168–170
   5th Arrondissement (Quartier Latin), 190–195

6th Arrondissement (St-Germain/Luxemburg), 195
7th Arrondissement (Eiffel Tower/Musée d'Orsay), 202–208
8th Arrondissement (Champs-Elysées/Madeleine), 176–185
9th Arrondissement (Opera Garnier/Pigalle), 170–172
10th Arrondissement (Gare de l'Est), 172–173
11th Arrondissement (Opéra Bastille), 173–175
12th Arrondissement (Bois de Vincennes/Gare de Lyon), 175–176
13th Arrondissement (Gare d'Austerlitz), 200–201
14th Arrondissement (Montparnasse), 201–202
15th Arrondissement (Eiffel Tower), 208–209
16th Arrondissement (Trocadero/Bois de Boulogne), 185–187
17th Arrondissement (Parc Monceau/Place Clichy), 187–190
18th Arrondissement (Montmartre), 176
best, 9–11, 152–153
cafes, 209–212
Chartres, 380–381
Chinatown, 201
by cuisine, 156–158
Disneyland Paris, 388–389
family-friendly, 186
Fontainebleau, 393–394
Giverny, 383–384
Left Bank, 190–212
Rambouillet, 377
range of, 154, 156
Right Bank, 158–190
Versailles, 374–375
Disabilities, travelers with, 74–75
Discrimination, 74
Disneyland Paris, 384–389
Dominique Picquier, 313
Drag shows, 355
Drawbridge to Europe, 104
Drinking laws, 395
Drugstores, 395
Duty-free boutiques, 319

E

Editions de Parfums Fréderic Malle, 340
Eglise de la Sorbonne, 307
Eglise de St-Eustache, 261, 346
Eglise du Dôme, 232
Eglise St-Merry, 346
EHIC (European Health Insurance Card), 72
Eiffel Tower, 239–240

Electricity, 396
Embassies and consulates, 396
Episcopal Gardens (Chartres), 380
Escorted tours, 79
Espace Dalí Montmartre, 298–299
Etiquette and customs, 396
Eurolines France station, 63
European Health Insurance Card (EHIC), 72
Eurostar Express, 64
Eurotunnel, 64
Explora, 290

F

Fabrics, 327–328
Families with children, 75
accommodations, 117
Disneyland Paris, 384–389
Musée des Enfants, 251
restaurants, 186
shopping for fashion and toys, 325–326
sights and attractions, 289–292
Fashion (clothing), 318, 328–332
for kids, 325–326
Fat Tire Bike Tours, 279
Fauchon, 207, 332
Favela Chic, 354
Ferries, from England, 64
Festival Musique en l'Ile, 58
Fête d'Automne, 59
Fête de la Musique, 57–58
Fête de St-Denis, 57
Fête de St-Sylvestre, 59
Films, 44–47
Fitness centers, 280
Flea markets, 337–338
FNAC, 338, 345
Foire du Trône, 56
Folies-Bergère, 349–350
Fontainebleau, 389–394
Food and cuisine, 49–51, 153–154
stores and markets, 181, 318, 332–334
Forest of Rambouillet, 375–377
Forum des Halles, 285
Fragonard Musée du Parfum, 256
France Lodge, 107
Franceway, 78
Free or almost free activities, 12–15
French Open Tennis Championship, 57
FUSAC, 107

G

Galerie Adrien Maeght, 322
Galeries Lafayette, 327
Galerie 27, 322

Galignani, 323–324
Gallery of François I (Fontainebleau), 390
Gardens of Versailles, 371
Gare d'Austerlitz, 63
Gare de l'Est, 63
Gare de Lyon, 63
Gare du Nord, 63
Gare Montparnasse, 63, 281
Gare St-Lazare, 63
Gargoyles, Notre-Dame, 229
Gaspard Yurkievich, 331
Gauguin, Paul, 38
Gay Pride Parade, 58
Gay and lesbian travelers, 74
bars and clubs, 362–363
Geneviève Lethu, 341
Gifts and souvenirs, 340
Ginsberg, Allen, 268
Givenchy, 330
Givenchy Hommes, 330
Giverny, 381–384
Global Refund, 319
Globus + Cosmos Tours, 79
Good Morning Paris, 106
Grand Canal (Versailles), 371–372
Grand Cascade, 273
Grand Prix de Paris, 280
Grands Appartements (Versailles), 370
Grand Steeplechase de Paris, 57
Grand Trianon (Versailles), 373–374

H

Hall of Mirrors (Versailles), 370–371
Hamlet (Le Hameau; Versailles), 373, 374
Hardouin-Mansart, Jules, 230, 232, 373–374
Harry's New York Bar, 363–364
Health concerns, 72
Hédiard, 333
Hemingway, 269
Hemingway, Ernest, 21
Hercules Salon (Versailles), 370
Hermès, 330
Hier, Aujourd'hui, et Demain, 313
Hiking, Fontainebleau, 392
Hippodrome d'Auteuil, 273, 280
Hippodrome de Longchamp, 273, 280
History museums, 254–256
History of Paris, 21–35
the 1920s, 32
beginnings, 24–25
books about, 42–43
contemporary Paris, 34–35
Louis XIV (the Sun King) and the French Revolution, 27–29
Middle Ages, 25–26
Napoleon, 29–30

postwar Paris, 33–34
the Renaissance and the
Reformation, 26–27
the Second Empire, 30–31
World War I, 31–32
World War II, 32–33
Holidays, 396
Home accessories, 334–335
Home Away, 104
Hometours International, 104
Horse racing, 280
Hospitals, 396
Hôtel Bethune-Sully, Gardens of
the, 311
Hôtel de Beauvais, 315
Hôtel de Bethune-Sully, 316
Hôtel de Clisson, 254–255
Hôtel de Crillon, 269
Hôtel de Lauzun, 284
Hôtel de Rohan, 255, 314
Hôtel des Ambassadeurs de
Hollande, 314
Hôtel de Sens, 315–316
Hôtel des Invalides/Napoléon's
Tomb, 232
Hôtel de Ville, 265, 281
Hôtel Dieu, 283
Hôtel du Vieux-Paris, 268
Hôtel Lambert, 284
Hôtel le Peletier de St-Fargeau,
244, 311
Hotels, 103–150. See also
Accommodations Index
1st Arrondissement (Louvre/
Les Halles), 110–113
2nd Arrondissement (La
Bourse), 113–114
3rd Arrondissement (Le
Marais), 114–115
4th Arrondissement (Ile de la
Cité/Ile St-Louis &
Beaubourg), 116–119
5th Arrondissement (Quartier
Latin), 133–138
6th Arrondissement (St-
Germain/ Luxembourg),
138–143
7th Arrondissement (Eiffel
Tower/Musée d'Orsay),
145–149
8th Arrondissement (Champs-
Elysées/Madeleine), 124–125,
128–130
9th Arrondissement (Opera
Garnier/Pigalle), 119–121
10th Arrondissement (Gare de
l'Est), 121
11th Arrondissement (Opera
Bastille), 121–122
12th Arrondissement (Bois de
Vincennes/Gare de Lyon),
122
13th Arrondissement (Gare
d'Austerlitz), 143–144

14th Arrondissement
(Montparnasse), 144
15th Arrondissement (Eiffel
Tower), 144–145
16th Arrondissement
(Trocadero/Bois de
Boulogne), 130–131
17th Arrondissement (Parc
Monceau/Place Clichy),
131–132
18th Arrondissement
(Montmartre), 123–124
alternatives to hotels,
106–107
bathrooms, 112
best, 5–9, 105–106
Chartres, 380
condos, villas, houses and
apartments, 103–105
Disneyland Paris, 387–388
family-friendly, 117
Fontainebleau, 393
Giverny, 383
hotel chains, 104
Left Bank, 104–105, 132–149
near the airports, 149–150
on the Right Bank, 104–105,
107–132
Hôtel Salé, 312
Hôtes Qualité Paris, 106
Hot lines, 396
Hugo, Victor, 227, 229, 278
Maison de, 311

I

Ice-skating, 281
Idyll Untours, 105
Ile de la Cité, 282–284
Ile St-Louis, 284–285
Institut de France, 265–266
Institut de Recherche et de
Coordination Acoustique-
Musique, 241
International Association for
Medical Assistance to
Travelers (IAMAT), 72
International Marathon of
Paris, 56
International Ready-to-Wear
Fashion Shows, 56, 58
Internet access, 80
Itineraries, suggested, 89–101
in 1 day, 89–93
in 2 days, 94–97
in 3 days, 97–101

J

J. C. Martinez, 322–323
Jacquemart-André, Musée,
246–247
Jadis et Gourmande, 333
Jardin d'Acclimatation, 273
for kids, 292

Jardin des Tuileries, 270–271
Jardin du Luxembourg,
271–272
Jardin du Palais Royal, 267
Jazz clubs, 351–353
Jean-Paul Gaultier, 329
Jean-Paul Hévin, 333–334
Jeu de Paume, 242
Jewelry, 335
Joan of Arc, 26
Joel Thiebault, 338
Jogging, 281
Jour de l'Armistice, 57
Journeywoman, 75

K

Keith Prowse, 345
Kiki de Montparnasse,
287–288
Kilomètre Zéro, 225
Kitchenware, 335

L

La Balajo, 354
La Belle Hortense, 360
La boutique de la CSAQ, 328
La Champmeslé, 362
La Chapelle des Lombards,
351–352
La Cité de l'Architecture et du
Patrimoine, 242–243
La Compagnie du Sénégal et de
l'Afrique de l'Ouest, 328
La Course des Garçons de
Café, 58
La Garerie 3A, 328
La Géode, 290
La Grande Arche de La Défense,
266
La Grande Cascade, 273
La Grande Mosquée de Paris,
259
La Java, 354
La Jokko, 328
Lalique, 326
La Loco, 354
La Madeleine, 260
La Maison Ivre, 325
La Maison Rouge, 323
L'Ane Rouge, 350
Language, 397
Language schools, 78
La Plaque Emaillées et Gravée
Jacquin, 341
La Quincaillerie, 334–335
La Tartine, 357
La Tuile à Loup, 340
La Vallée Village, 336
La Villette Jazz Festival, 58–59
Lavinia, 341
Layout of Paris, 65
Leather goods, 335–336
Le Bar de L'Hôtel, 360
Le Baron, 354–355

"Le Cabinet Fantastique," 291
Le Central, 362
Le China, 360
Le Cordon Bleu, 77
Le Depot, 363
Le Duc des Lombards, 352
Le Forum, 360
Left Bank
  accommodations, 132–149
  sights and attractions
    by arrondissement, 215
    highlights, 286–288
Le Fumoir, 360
Legal aid, 397
Le Gibus, 352
Le Hameau (Hamlet; Versailles),
  373, 374
Le Jockey, 287–288
Le Lèche-Vin, 361
Le Legende de Buffalo Bill
  (Disneyland Paris), 389
Le Louvre des Antiquaires, 321
Le Maison du Miel, 334
Le Musée du quai Branly,
  243–244
Leonardo da Vinci, 235, 236
  Mona Lisa, 237
Le Paradis Latin, 350
Le Petit Dakar, 328
Le Petit Journal, 352
Le Petit Journal Montparnasse,
  352
Le Piano Vache, 361
Le Porte Pot, 357
Le Queen, 363
Le Raidd, 363
Le Saint, 356
Le Salon Nautique de Paris, 59
Le Sancerre, 357
Les Bacchantes, 357–358
Les Bains Douches, 356
Les Catacombes, 278
Les Caves Taillevent, 341–342
Le Scopiton, 361–362
Les Coulisses, 356
Les Egouts, 278–279
Les Grandes Eaux Musicales
  (Versailles), 56–57
Les Halles, 285–286
Les Iles Grecques, 312
Les Mots à la Bouche, 74, 324
Le Soleil, 338
Les Taxis Bleus, 67
Les Trois Quartiers, 336
Le Sunset/Le Sunside, 352
Le Tango, 355
Le 3w Kafe, 363
Le Tropic Café, 362
LGBT travelers. See Gay and
  lesbian travelers
Librairie le Bail-Weissert, 324
Library (Versailles), 371
Lido de Paris, 350
Limoges-Unic/Madronet,
  325, 332
Lingerie, 336

Lingua Service Worldwide, 78
Literary landmarks, 268–270
Lost and found, 397
Louis², 361
Louis Vuitton, 331
Louis XIV, 27–28, 93, 230, 232,
  235, 254, 263, 267, 315,
  338, 370
Louis XVI, 28–30, 255, 259, 265,
  370, 371, 374
Louis XV Staircase
  (Fontainebleau), 391
Louvre, Musée du, 234–237

M
Mail, 397–398
Maison de Balzac, 269
Maison de la Truffe, 334
Maison de Radio-France, 56
Maison de Victor Hugo,
  269–270, 311
Makeup and beauty treatments,
  318
Maki, 340
Malls, 336–337
Manet, 233
Manet, Edouard, 37
Manufacture Nationale de
  Sèvres, 325
Manufacture Nationale des
  Gobelins, 253–254
Maps, 65
Marché aux Fleurs, 337
Marché aux Oiseaux (Bird
  Market), 337
Marché aux Puces de la Porte de
  Vanves, 337
Marché aux Puces St-Ouen de
  Clignancourt, 337
Marché Ave du Président Wilson,
  338
Marché Biologique, 333
Marché Buci, 333, 338
Matisse, Henri, 38
Meals and dining customs,
  50–51
Memorial Cloister, 258
Mémorial des Martyrs Français
  de la Déportation de 1945
  (Deportation Memorial),
  229–230
Mercure hotel chain, 104
Mercury Salon (Versailles), 370
Métro (subway), 65–66
Mobile phones, 79–80
Mojito Habana, 361
Mona Lisa (Leonardo da Vinci),
  237
Monet, Claude, 37, 247, 381
  Claude Monet Foundation
    (Giverny), 382–383
  Nymphéas, 244–245
Money and costs, 68–72
Montmartre walking tour,
  297–303

Montparnasse Shopping Centre,
  337
Montparnasse sights and
  attractions, 287–288
Morabito, 335–336
Mosquée de Paris, La Grande,
  259
Moulin de la Galette, 302
Moulin Rouge, 302, 350
Multicultural travelers, 75
Mur des Fédérés, 277
Musée Baccarat, 326
Musée Bourdelle, 250
Musée Carnavalet, 311
Musée Carnavalet-Histoire de
  Paris, 244, 283
Musée Cognacq-Jay, 250–251
Musée d'Art et Histoire du
  Judaisme, 254
Musée d'Art Moderne de la Ville
  de Paris, 251
Musée de Cluny (Musée National
  du Moyen Age/Thermes de
  Cluny), 248, 307
Musée de la Musique, 251
Musée de l'Armée, 230
Musée de l'Erotisme, 256–257
Musée de l'Histoire de France
  (Musée des Archives
  Nationales), 254–255
Musée de l'Institut du Monde
  Arabe, 257
Musée de l'Orangerie, 244–245
Musée des Arts Décoratifs,
  245–246
Musée des Beaux-Arts de
  Chartres, 380
Musée des Enfants, 251
Musée des Plans-Reliefs,
  231–232
Musée d'Orsay, 232–234
Musée du Louvre, 234–237
Musée du quai Branly,
  243–244
Musée du Vin, 257–258
Musée Edith Piaf, 251
Musée Grévin, 291
Musée Jacquemart-André,
  246–247
Musée Lambinet (Versailles),
  373
Musée Marmottan Monet,
  247–248
Musée Montmartre, 301
Musée National d'Art Moderne,
  241–242
Musée National des Arts
  Asiatiques-Guimet, 252
Musée National d'Histoire
  Naturelle (Museum of
  Natural History), 291
Musée National du Château de
  Fontainebleau, 390–392

Musée National du Moyen Age/
Thermes de Cluny (Musée
de Cluny), 248
Musée National Eugène
Delacroix, 249
Musée Nissim de Camondo, 252
Musée Picasso, 312
Musée Rodin, 249–250
Musée Zadkine, 253
Museum of Natural History
(Musée National d'Histoire
Naturelle), 291
Museums
art, 250–253
best, 15–17
craft and industry, 253–254
history, 254–256
Music, 47–49. *See also* Concerts
classical, 345–348
clubs, 348–356
Musée de la Musique, 251
tours, 78
Music stores, 338–339

N

Napoléon Bonaparte, 29–30,
216, 226, 376
Tomb, 232
National Museum of Modern Art,
241–242
Natural History, Museum of, 291
Neighborhoods
(arrondissements), 65
attractions by, 214–215
best, for getting lost, 17–19
brief descriptions of, 83–88
highlights, 282–288
shopping, 320–321
New Morning, 353
Newspapers and magazines, 80
New Year's Eve, 59
New York Habitat, 103
Nicolas, 342
Nightclubs and cabarets,
349–351
Nightlife, 344–364
bars, pubs and lounges,
356–364
gay and lesbian, 362–363
literary haunts, 363–364
club and music scene, 348–356
chansonniers, 348–349
dance clubs, 353
jazz, salsa, rock and more,
351–353
nightclubs and cabarets,
349–351
Disneyland Paris, 389
listings, 344
performing arts, 344–348
tickets, 344–345
Nikita, 336
North Rose Window, 229
Notre-Dame, Cathédrale de
(Paris), 225–230

Notre-Dame de Chartres,
Cathédrale de, 377–380
Nouveau Casino, 350–351
Now, Voyager, 74
Nuit Blanche, 347
Nymphéas (Monet), 244–245

O

Okawa, 362
Olivia, 74
Olympia, 348
Open Café/Café Cox, 363
Opéra Bastille, 56, 345–346
Opéra Comique, 346
Opéra Garnier, 56, 346
Opéra (Versailles), 371
Organized tours, 292–295
Orly Airport, 62–63
accommodations near,
149–150
Orsay Museum, 232–234

P

Package tours, 78
Palais Abbatial, 262
Palais Bourbon/Assemblée
Nationale, 266–267
Palais des Mirages, 291
Palais des Tuileries, 270–271
Palais de Tokyo, 253
Palais du Luxembourg, 271
Palais Royal, 267
P&O Ferries, 64
Panthéon, 267–268, 307
Parc de Bagatelle, 273–274
Parc de La Villette, 290
Parfums Caron, 339
Paris Airport Shuttle, 63
Paris Air Show, 57
Paris Art Market, 323
Paris Attitude, 107
Paris Auto Show, 59
Paris Canal, 295
Parisian Home, 107
Paris Museum Pass, 241
Paris Pass, 67
Paris Quartier d'Eté, 58
Paris Roller Rando, 294
Paris-Story, 255–256
Park Monceau, 274
Parks and gardens, 270–274
Parthenon frieze, 237
Passage de Retz, 313
Passports, 60, 397–398
Pastry, 206–207
Performing arts, 344–348
Perfumes, 318, 339
Petits Appartements
(Versailles), 371
Petit Trianon (Versailles), 374
Piaf, Edith, Musée, 251
Picasso, Pablo, 38
Musée Picasso, 312
Picnics, 170
Pierre Hermé, 207

Pietrement-Lambret, 334
Place de la Bastille, 308
Place de l'Alma, 288
Place des Vosges, 310
Place du Calvaire, 299–300
Place du Tertre, 300
Place Pigalle, 303
Place St-Michel, 303
Planning your trip, 55–81
calendar of events, 56–59
crime and safety, 72–74
entry requirements, 60–62
getting around, 65–68
health concerns, 72
money and costs, 68–72
special-interest trips, 77–79
specialized travel resources,
74–76
staying connected, 79–81
traveling to Paris, 62–64
when to go, 55–56
Plaza Athénée, 358
Poilâne, 334
Police, 398
Pont Neuf, 283
Portal of St. Anne, 228
Portal of St. Stephen, 228
Portal of the Cloisters, 228
Portal of the Last Judgment,
227–228
Portal of the Virgin, 227
Post offices, 397–398
Prix de l'Arc de Triomphe,
59, 280
Prix Diane-Hermès, 57
Prix du Jockey Club, 57
Promenade Plantée, 281
Proust, Marcel, 244, 274, 276,
356
Public Information Library, 241
Puppet shows, 289
Purple Roofs, 74

R

Rail Europe, 64
Rainfall, average, 55
Rambouillet forests, 375–377
Réciproque, 332
Release of the Beaujolais
Nouveau, 59
Renoir, Pierre-Auguste, 37, 233,
234, 302
RER trains, 66
Responsible tourism, 76–77
Restaurants, 49–50, 152–212. *See
also* Restaurants Index
1st Arrondissement (Louvre/
Les Halles), 158–165
2nd Arrondissement (La
Bourse), 166
3rd Arrondissement (Le
Marais), 166–168
4th Arrondissement (Ile De La
Cité/Ile St-Louis &
Beaubourg), 168–170

5th Arrondissement (Quartier Latin), 190–195
6th Arrondissement (St-Germain/Luxemburg), 195
7th Arrondissement (Eiffel Tower/Musée d'Orsay), 202–208
8th Arrondissement (Champs-Elysées/Madeleine), 176–185
9th Arrondissement (Opera Garnier/Pigalle), 170–172
10th Arrondissement (Gare de l'Est), 172–173
11th Arrondissement (Opéra Bastille), 173–175
12th Arrondissement (Bois de Vincennes/Gare de Lyon), 175–176
13th Arrondissement (Gare d'Austerlitz), 200–201
14th Arrondissement (Montparnasse), 201–202
15th Arrondissement (Eiffel Tower), 208–209
16th Arrondissement (Trocadero/Bois de Boulogne), 185–187
17th Arrondissement (Parc Monceau/Place Clichy), 187–190
18th Arrondissement (Montmartre), 176
best, 9–11, 152–153
cafes, 209–212
Chartres, 380–381
Chinatown, 201
by cuisine, 156–158
Disneyland Paris, 388–389
family-friendly, 186
Fontainebleau, 393–394
Giverny, 383–384
Left Bank, 190–212
Rambouillet, 377
range of, 154, 156
Right Bank, 158–190
Versailles, 374–375
Rex Club, 356
Richelieu wing, 237
Right Bank
accommodations, 107–132
sights and attractions
by arrondissement, 214–215
highlights, 285–286
Ritz, 358
Ritz-Escoffier Ecole de Gastronomie Française, 77
Rochers et Etang d'Angennes, 377
Rodin, Auguste, 38
Musée Rodin, 249–250
Roissybus, 62
Roissy (Charles de Gaulle Airport), 62
Roissy rail station, 62
Roman baths, 248–249

Romans (ruins and antiquities), architecture, 38–39
Rosebud, 364
Royal Chapel (Versailles), 371
Royal Portal (Chartres), 378
Rue de la Huchette, 304–305
Rue des Rosiers, 314
Rue du Chat-qui-Pêche, 305–306
Rue du Faubourg St-Honoré, 329
Rue Montorgueil market, 333
Rue Mouffetard market, 333

S

Sabbia Rosa, 336
Sacré-Coeur, 217, 301
Sadaharu Aoki, 207
Safety concerns, 72–74
St-Denis, Basilique, 258–259
Sainte-Chapelle, 237–239
St-Etienne-du-Mont, 260–261
St-Eustache, 261, 346
St-Germain-des-Prés (church), 261, 286
St-Germain-des-Prés (neighborhood)
attractions, 286–287
dance clubs, 353
St-Germain l'Auxerrois, 262
St-Julien-le-Pauvre, 306
St-Louis-en-l'Ile, 285
St-Pierre, 301
St-Séverin, 306
St-Sulpice, 262–263
Salle Cortot, 56
Salle des Gardes, 264
Salle des Gens d'Armes, 264
Salle Pleyel, 347
Salon de la Princesse, 255
Salon des Singes, 314
Salons du Palais Royal Shiseido, 339
Sanz-Sans, 355
Seasons, 55–56
Seine et le Canal St-Martin tour, 295
Senior travel, 75–76
Sèvres, Manufacture Nationale de, 325
Shakespeare and Company, 324
Shopping, 318–342
best buys, 318
etiquette, 319
hours, 319–320
neighborhoods, 320–321
Sights and attractions, 214–295.
See also Museums; Walking tours, self-guided
architectural and historic highlights, 263–268
by arrondissement, 214–215
cemeteries, 274–278
churches, 258–263

free or almost-free activities, 12–15
for kids, 289–292
literary landmarks, 268–270
museum discount card, 241
neighborhood highlights, 282–288
offbeat, 256–258
parks and gardens, 270–274
sports and recreation, 279–282
top attractions, 216–217, 225–240
underground, 278–279
Smoking, 398
Sorbonne, 307
S.O.S. Racisme, 74
Souleiado, 327–328
Sous-Bock Tavern, 355
Square du Vert Galant, 284
Stationery, 340–341
Stein, Gertrude, 251, 271, 287
Stravinsky fountain, 242
Sunday shopping, 319
Sustainable tourism, 76–77
Swimming pools, 281–282

T

Tableware, 341
Talmaris, 327
Taschen, 324
Tauck World Discovery, 79
Taxes, 398
Taxi G7, 67
Taxis, 67
Charles de Gaulle Airport (Roissy), 62
Orly, 63
Taxis Bleus, 67
Tea & Tattered Pages, 324
Telephones, 80–81
Temperatures, average daytime, 55
Tennis
French Open Tennis Championship, 57
tours, 78
Theater, 345
Théâtre des Champs-Elysées, 56, 347–348
Théâtre des Deux Anes, 348–349
Théâtre National de Chaillot, 348
The Different Company, 339
The Lady and the Unicorn tapestries, 248, 307
The Marais, walking tour, 308–316
The Moose, 361
The Quiet Man, 361
The Trianons (Versailles), 373
Thiebault, Joel, 338
Time zone, 398

Tipping, 398
Toilets, 399
Toulouse-Lautrec, Henri de, 38
Tour d'Argent, 264
Tour de César, 264
Tour de France, 58
Tour Eiffel, 239–240
Tour Montparnasse, 288
Tours
  escorted, 79
  general-interest, 78
  sightseeing, 292–295
Toys, 325
Trafalgar, 79
Train travel, 63–64
Transportation, 65–68
Traveler's checks, 71
Travel in France, 78

V

Val-de-Grâce, 263
Value-added tax (VAT-TVA in
  French), 398
  refunds of, 318–319
Van Cleef & Arpels, 335
Van Gogh, Vincent, 38
VE Day, 57
Versailles, 366–375
  daytime spectacles, 368, 370
  evening spectacles, 368, 370
  restaurants, 374–375
  traveling to, 366–368
  visitor information, 368
Versant Vins, 358
Viaduc des Arts, 323
Villa Calte, 251
Village St-Paul, 322
Village Voice Bookshop, 325
Virgin Megastore, 320, 338–339
Volunteer programs, 76–77

W

W. H. Smith France, 325
Walking, 68
Walking tours, self-guided,
  297–316
  Latin Quarter, 303–307
  The Marais, 308–316
  Montmartre, 297–303
Walt Disney Studios, 386
Water, drinking, 399
West Rose Window, 228
Wheelchair accessibility, 74–75
Whistler, James McNeill,
  234, 268
Wi-Fi access, 80
Willi's Wine Bar, 358
Wine bars, 356–358
Wines, 51–53, 341–342
Women travelers, 75
Wright, Richard, 268

Y

Yves Saint Laurent, 331
Yvon Lambert, 312

Accommodations

Air Plus, 149–150
Apollon Montparnasse, 144
Au Palais de Chaillot Hôtel,
  130–131
Best Western Regent's Garden,
  131
Bourgogne & Montana, 145
Castex Hotel, 118
Derby Eiffel, 146
Disneyland Hotel (Disneyland
  Paris), 387–388
Eiffel Seine, 144–145
Familia-Hôtel, 137
The Five Hotel, 133
Fouquet's Barrière, 124
Four Seasons Hotel George V,
  124
Gabriel Paris Marais, 121
Golden Tulip Opéra de Noailles,
  113
Grand Hôtel de l'Aigle-Noir
  (Fontainebleau), 393
Grand Hôtel des Balcons, 143
Grand Hôtel Doré, 122
Grand Hôtel Saint-Michel, 133
Grand Monarque Best Western
  (Chartres), 380
Hilton Paris Orly, 149
Hôtel Agora St-Germain, 133
Hôtel à l'Eiffel Rive Gauche, 148
Hotel All Seasons Paris Gare de
  l'Est Magenta, 121
Hotel Amour, 119
Hôtel Balzac, 128
Hotel Banke, 119
Hotel Bel-Ami, 138
Hôtel Bellevue & du Chariot
  d'Or, 115
Hôtel Britannique, 111–112
Hôtel Campanile de Roissy, 150
Hôtel Caron de Beaumarchais,
  117
Hotel Cheyenne/Hotel Santa Fe
  (Disneyland Paris), 388
Hôtel Chopin, 120–121
Hôtel d'Aubusson, 138
Hôtel de Crillon, 124–125
Hôtel de Fleurie, 139
Hôtel de l'Abbaye Saint-
  Germain, 139–140
Hôtel de l'Académie, 146
Hôtel de la Place des Vosges, 118
Hôtel de la Tour d'Auvergne,
  119–120
Hôtel Delavigne, 143
Hôtel de Londres Eiffel, 146, 148
Hôtel de l'Université, 146
Hôtel de Lutèce, 117
Hôtel de Nevers, 148–149
Hôtel de Palma, 132
Hôtel des Arts, 123
Hôtel des Chevaliers, 115
Hôtel des Deux Continents,
  141

Hôtel des Deux-Iles, 117–118
Hôtel des Grandes Ecoles,
  137
Hôtel des Jardins du
  Luxembourg, 133, 136
Hôtel des Marronniers,
  141–142
Hôtel de Vendôme, 110
Hôtel du Bourg Tibourg, 116
Hôtel du Jeu de Paume, 116
Hôtel du Louvre, 110
Hôtel du Ministère, 129
Hôtel Duo, 116
Hôtel du Palais Bourbon, 149
Hôtel du Parc-Montsouris, 144
Hôtel du Pas-de-Calais, 142
Hôtel du Petit Moulin, 114–115
Hôtel du Quai Voltaire, 148
Hôtel du 7e Art, 118
Hôtel du Vert Galant, 144
Hôtel Eldorado, 132
Hôtel Ermitage, 123–124
Hôtel Flaubert, 132
Hôtel Galileo, 129
Hotel Horset Opéra, 114
Hôtel La Manufacture,
  143–144
Hôtel Langlois, 120
Hôtel La Trémoille, 128
Hôtel Le A, 128–129
Hôtel Le Bellechasse, 145
Hôtel le Bristol, 125
Hôtel Le Clément, 143
Hôtel Le Sainte-Beuve, 142
Hôtel Le Six, 140
Hôtel Le Tourville, 146
Hôtel Lindbergh, 149
Hôtel Louis II, 142
Hôtel Luxembourg Parc, 140
Hôtel Meurice, 110
Hôtel Moderne Saint-Germain,
  137
Hôtel Montalembert, 145
Hôtel Particulier, 123
Hôtel Pavillon Bastille, 122
Hôtel Pershing Hall, 125
Hôtel Quartier Latin, 136
Hôtel Queen Mary, 129–130
Hôtel Radisson Blu Trocadéro
  Dokhan's, 130
Hôtel Regina, 110–111
Hôtel-Résidence Saint-
  Christophe, 137
Hôtel Ritz, 111
Hôtel Saint-Dominique, 149
Hôtel St-Jacques, 136
Hôtel Saint-Louis, 118
Hôtel Saint-Merry, 119
Hôtel Saintonge, 115
Hôtel Sully Saint-Germain, 136
Hôtel Thérèse, 112
Hôtel Verneuil, 148
Hôtel Victoires Opéra, 113
Hyatt Regency Paris-Charles de
  Gaulle, 150

Hyatt Regency Paris-Madeleine, 129
Kube Rooms & Bars, 123
Kyriad Hotel (Disneyland Paris), 388
La Musardiere (Giverny), 383
L'Apostrophe, 140
La Tour Notre-Dame, 136–137
La Villa, 141
Le Général Hotel, 121–122
Le Méridien Etoile, 131
Le Placide, 141
Le Relais du Louvre, 112
L'Hôtel, 138–139
Libertel Croix de Malte, 122
Minerve Hôtel, 138
Murano Urban Resort, 114
Newport Bay Club (Disneyland Paris), 388
Odéon Hôtel, 141
Park Hyatt Vendôme, 113
Pavillon de la Reine, 114
Plaza Athénée, 125, 128
Prince de Condé, 142
Pullman Paris Aéroport CDG, 150
Relais Christine, 139
Relais Monceau, 130
Relais St-Germain, 139
Renaissance Paris Arc de Triomphe, 131–132
Résidence Alhambra, 122
Résidence Lord Byron, 130
Timhôtel Le Louvre, 112–113
Timhôtel Palais-Royal, 113
Villa Madame, 142–143
Villa Royale, 120
Westin Paris, 111

Restaurants

Afaria, 208–209
Alcazar Restaurant, 197
Al Dar, 190
Allard, 197
Angélina, 165
Au Bascou, 167
Auberge Etchegorry, 200
Au Petit Monsieur, 173
Au Petit Riche, 170
Au Pied de Cochon, 162
Au Pied de Fouet, 207–208
Au Trou Gascon, 175
Aux Charpentiers, 199
Aux Lyonnais, 166
Bar des Théâtres, 184
Baudy (Giverny), 383–384
Benoit, 168–169
Blue Elephant, 173
Bofinger, 169
Brasserie Balzar, 190–191
Brasserie Flo, 172
Breakfast in America, 195
Cabaret, 163
Café Beaubourg, 210
Café-Brasserie St-Regis, 355

Café de Flore, 209
Café de la Musique, 210
Café des Deux Moulins, 212
Café Hugo, 311
Café le Départ St-Michel, 304
Café Panique, 173
California Grill (Disneyland Paris), 388–389
Carré des Feuillants, 158–159
Casa Olympe, 171
Chartier, 171–172
Chez André, 182–183
Chez Georges, 166, 188–189
Chez Gladines, 201
Chez Gramond, 197
Chez Janou, 167
Chez Jean, 171
Chez Jenny, 167–168
Chez l'Ami Jean, 208
Chez Michel, 172
Chez Ramulaud, 173–174
Chez Savy, 184–185
Chez Vong, 159, 162
Citrus Etoile, 183
Closerie des Lilas, 196
Coco de Mer, 195
Crémerie-Restaurant Polidor, 199, 269
Cristal Room, 185
Dalloyau, 207
Eric Kayser, 202, 204
Fouquet's, 210
Gordon Ramsay au Trianon (Versailles), 374
Goumard, 162
Guy Savoy, 187–188
Hard Rock Cafe, 170
Hiramatsu, 185
Inventions (Disneyland Paris), 389
Itineraire, 191
Jacques Cagna, 195
Jadis, 208
Joe Allen, 163
Juveniles, 165
Kambodgia, 187
Kim Anh, 208
La Bastide Odéon, 199
La Belle Hortense, 210–211
La Braisière, 189
L'Absinthe, 163
La Butte Chaillot, 187
La Cagouille, 201–202
La Cigale Récamier, 205
La Coupole, 211
La Crémaillère 1900, 300
La Crèmerie, 199–200
Ladurée, 183
Ladurée Royale, 206–207
La Famille, 176
La Fontaine de Mars, 204
La Grille, 172
La Maison Blanche, 180
L'Ambassade d'Auvergne, 168
L'Ambroisie, 168
L'Ami Louis, 166–167

L'Angle du Faubourg, 180–181
La Palette, 211
La Petite Chaise, 205
La Poste (Rambouillet), 377
La Poule au Pot, 163–164
La Régalade, 202
La Rôtisserie d'en Face, 198
La Rotonde, 211
L'Arpège, 204
L'Assaggio, 164
Lasserre, 176–177
L'Assiette, 202
L'Astrance, 185–186
La Tour d'Argent, 190
L'Avant Comptoir, 200
La Vieille Maison (Chartres), 380–381
La Vinoteca, 181
L'Ebauchoir, 175–176
Le Béarn, 165
Le Caveau des Ducs (Fontainebleau), 393
Le Chateaubriand, 174
Le Cinq, 177
Le Dalí, 162
Le François-1er (Chez Bernard), 394
Le Fumoir, 164
Le Georges, 169–170
Le Geôrges (Chartres), 381
Le Grain de Folie, 176
Le Grand Véfour, 159
Le Hide, 189
Le Jules Verne, 240
Le Louis II, 181
Le Manguier, 174
Le Mer de Chine, 201
Le Pamphlet, 167
Le Petit Marguery, 200–201
Le Petit Pontoise, 191
Le Potager du Roy (Versailles), 375
Le Pré Verre, 191, 194
Le Procope, 211–212
Le Pure Café, 174–175
Le Relais du Parc, 186–187
Le Resto du Roy (Versailles), 375
Le Rouquet, 212
Les Deux Magots, 212
Le Severo, 202
Les Gourmets des Ternes, 183
Les Ombres, 204–205
Les Papilles, 194
Le Timbre, 198
Le Vaudeville, 166
Le Violon d'Ingres, 205
Ma Bourgogne, 311
Mansouria, 174
Market, 183–184
Marty, 194
Mélac, 175
Michel Rostang, 188
Pierre Gagnaire, 177
Pinxo, 164
Pré Catelan, 273

Publicis Drugstore, 184
Quartier Chinois, 201
Rech, 188
Restaurant Caïus, 189–190
Restaurant de l'Astor, 181–182
Restaurant d'Hélène/Salon d'Hélène, 196
Restaurant du Musée d'Orsay, 205–206

Restaurant Les Fleurs (Giverny), 384
Restaurant Plaza Athénée (Alain Ducasse), 177, 180
Ribouldingue, 194–195
Sensing, 196–197
1728, 182
Spoon, Food & Wine, 182

Stohrer, 206
Taillevent, 180
Tang Frères, 201
Tokyo Eat, 187
Wally Le Saharien, 171
Yam' 'Tcha, 164–165
Yugaraj, 198
Ze Kitchen Galerie, 198–199

PHOTO CREDITS